8bar Bikes (page 16)

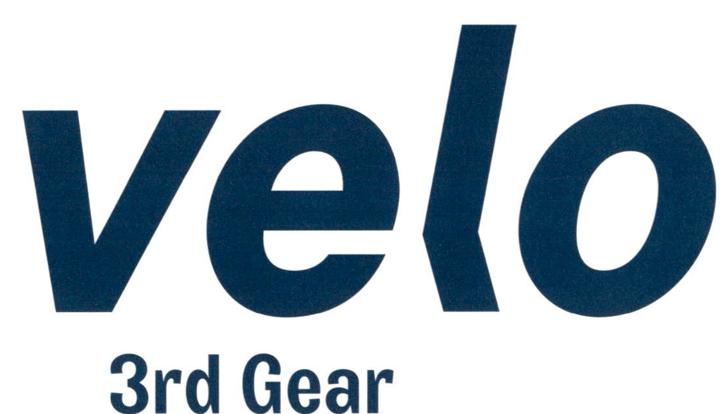

# 3rd Gear

## Bicycle Culture and Stories

gestalten

# Bicycle Culture and Stories

*Cycling is all about smelling the flowers and hearing the birds and feeling the wind in your hair. We're here to fight for the wind in people's hair.*

Cycling Without Age
(page 166)

# Preface

Text: **SHONQUIS MORENO**

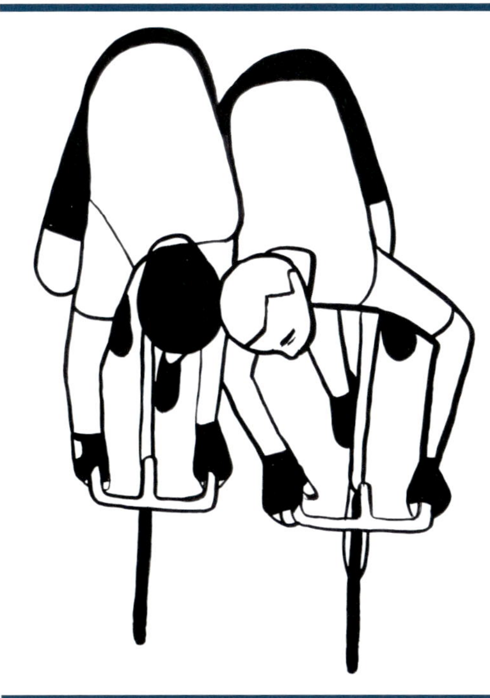

**Illustrations:** Created by Geoff McFetridge as a series of 40 original paintings on paper, these illustrations were then turned into limited edition shoes produced by Nike. Only 24 unique pairs were made of each sneaker in sizes 9, 10, and 11. On May 26, 2011, they were auctioned with a starting price of one-hundred dollars, with the proceeds donated to the MOCA Foundation.

His main bike is an orange Fuji Feather fixie named Gina. Gina replaced Petra, who was bought with high school graduation money and was with him until someone stole her in broad daylight off a street in Manhattan. Ralph Brescia has been biking around New York City for 16 years but, in the past five, he has become a daily rider. He rides to work, rides to run errands and, on weekends and summer evenings, he rides to explore. He has pedaled the length of Long Island in stages and finished the Tour de Queens once and the Five Boro Bike Tour twice. Recently he rescued a 1976 Raleigh Twenty three-speed folding bike from the curb where she was awaiting a garbage truck. Brescia had to give "Viv" a good scrubbing and replace her tires, cables, grips, and brake pads; later he will buy her a Brooks saddle, lighter-weight alloy wheels, a front rack to carry packages, and maybe a bell. He has done most of the work himself, but her forks were bent, so he took her to his local bike shop in Bay Ridge—where the motto is "Shut up and buy a bike"—to straighten them out. "Cycling in the city has changed in that it has become a thing," he says. "Bikes are now an accessory to substantiate one's cultural identity: there are the goal-oriented spandex sportos with carbon fiber frames that cost as much as a used car, the hipsters with vintage Schwinns and fixies and, for style-conscious couples, matchie-matchie Linuses and Shinolas, and then there are the folding bike people."

Tribes. While biking booms, it diversifies. In Pamplona, Spain, Eneko Astigarraga is the founder of Oraintxe, a bike messenger service and advocacy focused on urban biking and education. He is also a blogger posing questions about cycling culture today. "People of different profiles have begun to incorporate themselves into the urban cycling universe, adding diversity to it and showing that biking is, more than a trend, a personal choice about how to move around in cities," he says. "Hipsters and BMXers talk about cycling tribes, but both are marginal. Most of the people riding bikes are regular commuters, leisure cyclists, and more women of all ages, and this is changing the way we talk about cycling."

Perhaps the biggest signal of biking culture's spread is rather prosaic: in 2008, the U.S. Department of Transportation announced that commuter cycling had more than doubled since 2000 in the United States—a country famous for its lack of bike fluency. The cost of a car—in time, money, and health—has become prohibitive. But in Prague and Paris, even the metro rolls to a halt at midnight. New York's Roosevelt Island Tramway hangs dead in the air from 2 a.m. to 6 a.m. And in London, when the lift breaks down under Covent Garden station, passengers walk up 193 spiraling steps to reach the light of day. City dwellers are looking for ways to maintain their quality of life without moving out to the suburbs to, say, start a family. So bicycles, including non-traditional bikes like cargo bikes, increasingly sophisticated e-bikes and pedelecs (pedal electric cycles), smartphone and Bluetooth-connected bikes, and even bikes that fold at a touch, can help tilt the balance in favor of mobility, convenience, health, fashionability—and the city.

Twenty-five years ago in Baton Rouge, Louisiana, Mark Martin sold his car and began to travel locally only by bike. Ten years ago, he founded the city's first bicycling and walking advocacy. "After nearly 10 years of effort, we have begun to see a change in attitude in city government, along with tremendous increases in ridership, including commuters, and community involvement," says Martin, who rode a little over 8,500 kilometers last year. "Now there are two new groups started by women."

Strengthening its mainstream potential, biking has found strong proponents in the design world. Rob Forbes, founder of the furniture brand Design Within Reach, also launched Public Bikes in 2010, overseeing design and art direction. Forbes founded Public with sustainability in mind, but also because he was "seeing youth non-car culture emerge in the U.S." Forbes, who takes 30- to 50-kilometer weekend trips on a road bike, rides daily around San Francisco and stays in hotels that rent bikes when he travels in other cities—and writes a design-oriented blog based on his adventures. Forbes has seen more and more amateurs mounting bikes and certainly, as we are changing our relationship to bicycling, bicycling is changing our cities. In Berlin, the Radbahn project will create the first (mostly) covered 9-kilometer bike path through the city, and although Detroit has lost its automaking industry, it has gained 270 kilometers of bike routes. Other cities have also launched major efforts to turn derelict infrastructure like rail lines over to bicyclists. Ever since Brooklyn established the first American bikeways in 1894, New York City has anticipated cycling trends in the United States, but the city did not get a bike share program until 2013. It launched, however, with an impressive 4,300 share bikes and is expected to grow rapidly. In fall 2015 the city added its 1,000th mile of bike path, a number that doubled over the last eight years. It is not only New York: San Francisco can boast that it has the largest bike coalition in the United States. "Bikes are now commonly seen by all and respected by most," Forbes says. "It's no longer 'us against them."

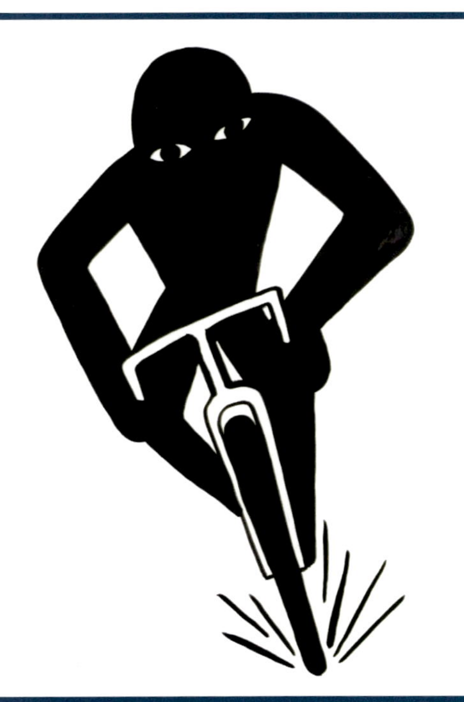

This is a trend that has been ratified by visionary brands that invite employees to use company-provided bikes on corporate campuses, like Google, Facebook, Twitter, and Apple—which uses Forbes's Public Bikes. If there is one thing that these brands do, it is proliferate self-expression, if only in 140-character bundles. They understand that the people, city, and planet-friendly values that define biking culture reach into every niche and tribe. These universal values are something that Milan-based new media publisher (and Tweetbook creator) Michele Aquila is seeing couched in ever-greater variety. Long involved with mountain biking and road cycling, he has co-founded a cycling repair workshop called Brugola Rossa (Red Hex Key) in Florence and a cycling team called Cicloidi that organized a 100-kilometer "non-competitive" ride over the toughest hills around Florence. "There is an incredible variety of cycling clubs and groups growing up here in northern Italy," he says, listing small communities like the Cani Sciolti Valtellina, a team that mashes up cycling and mountaineering; the Spokes & Nipples bloggers, who organize night rides and night climbs even in winter; and Track Bike Total War (TBTW), "the neglected children of the fixed gear world," as Aquile calls them. His 2016 calendar is already full of grassroots events: cyclocross, gravel or vintage bikes, bike polo, track cycling, randonnée, alleycats, killer climb races, and so on. "On the one hand, everything is fragmented," he says. "On the other, variety is to me the most entertaining attitude in cycling. And all of this is fuelled by social networks—Instagram, Strava, Facebook..."

As biking draws in a much more diverse range of devotees, self-expression and individual style are at a greater premium. In Moscow, photographer Alena Chendler publishes a blog called CyclesLady, posting portraits of stylish professional women—DJs, models, young mothers—who have begun to populate the city's streets with both bicycles and fashion. She started the project because she noticed an increasing number of women riding around wearing high fashion—trendy trainers, or skirts and dresses by the likes of Margiela, Prada, and Pugh. "The bicycle is the perfect transportation for the city," she writes, "and it is beautiful."

Giro senior brand manager Eric Richter suggests that some bike shops are taking a new approach to retail that more closely resembles a concept shop from the realm of fashion. Their goal is not simply to sell anything to everybody. Instead, they curate their shops' contents to reflect a point of view, seeing urban bicycling not just as a utility market, but also as one component of a lifestyle—a cultural component. By the same token, an industry has been

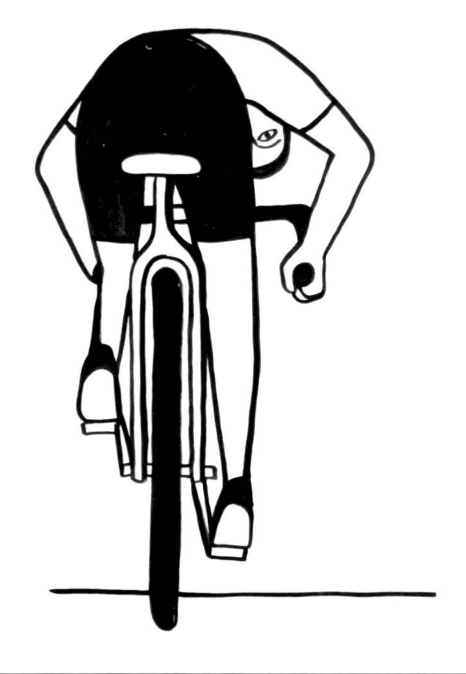

Narusk, creator and co-owner of Tallin-based Velonia Bicycles, designed his VIKS series without a seat tube and with a double-frame and flat narrow bars that give it a low-slung dynamism reminiscent of motorcycles. Since 2012, Narusk has seen the number of daily riders rise and with it the demand for unique bikes: people want to ride something that sets them apart them. Other builders, like Prague's Festka, are making made-to-measure bikes (bespoke fashion for the bicycling world) by using geometry and engineering to fabricate precision performance bikes for professionals and even amateurs who may not be able to feel the difference, but who know that Festka's team—a group of pros and national champions themselves—can build it.

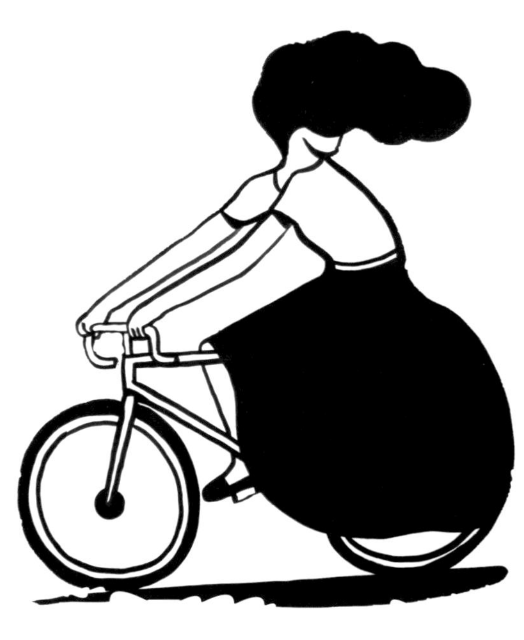

flourishing around cycling apparel and accessories—from jerseys, bags, helmets, and integrated or smart lights to mobile applications. And cycling apparel does not always look like cycling apparel: Quoc Pham shoes go from bike to business lunch. And even when the garments are more sporty or technical, they are materially inventive and graphical: one of Rapha's jersey patterns is based on time trial data while Segrasegra trousers look like casual streetwear but are made from bicycle inner tubes.

For now, there are relatively few extreme frame builders to serve the burgeoning demand for customization, but some are working with great originality. The materials my not be so different: titanium, carbon, chromium molybdenum, bamboo—add to that list wood, a film that turns the entire frame into a bike reflector, and materials that can be 3D-printed—but the parts, details, functionality, decoration, color schemes, and shapes are new. Some geometers and engineer-makers are deconstructing the frame and reforming or deforming it: the mechanical engineer Indrek

The premium placed on originality and uniqueness has also drawn artists into the crafting of bicycles: Death Spray Custom has designed forks based on the Seven Deadly Sins, Festka's Art Edition series includes a frame on which dense scribbling encodes the lyrics of two songs, and the wings on the Alerion's top tube were sculpted by the French artist Charles Boulnois.

Before art, after transportation, and always in a little competition with teamwork, riding is about individualism. Bikes have become one of the great tools of the outdoor trend, with ATBs, mountain, touring, and cross-country bikes at the forefront. Inspired by pioneers of bike travel and, increasingly, by those who not only do it, but also blog about doing it—sharing the how-tos and don't-dos—more people are embarking on longer journeys. Ridehouse Martin leads trips into the lush New Zealand landscape and even tests Mission Workshop apparel and bags on punishing rides in any weather and over all terrain. Along with his remarkable cycling photography and portraiture, graphic designer, photographer, and bike-packer Logan Watts shares information about gear, mapping, packing, and even the inadvisability of asking your mother to mail prescription medication to you during a ride through Mexico. From behind his bars and lens, Watts's photos, taken in the High Atlas, Costa Rica, South Africa, and the Sahara, celebrate empty space and earth extending to the horizon; difference—the unknown and the universal; and the freedom to leave home on your own leg-power with not much more than a tent and a toothbrush.

As the proverb says: the heart wills not purity, but adventure. The bicycle is a tool of that timeless hankering to get lost, really lost—even after mapping your route carefully—and then prove to yourself that you can find your way home again—sweaty, thirsty, sore, and just a little more you than you were before you put your feet to the pedals.

# Drops & Hooks

Text: SHONQUIS MORENO

opposite page: Night Riders YVR by Stefan Feldmann

## *On fixed-gear style, extreme frames, custom paint jobs, and alternative apparel*

There are beautiful women in Moscow, and then there are beautiful women in Moscow who ride Pashleys wearing Prada. Cycling is not just fashionable, it's a fashion tribe. It's social and self-expression: let-me-introduce-myself and who-are-you? It's reflective polka-dot socks and high-performance pants made from inner tubes. Or Kenzo and capes. In the morning, we clip in wearing a pair of leather trainers that we won't change out of all day, from bike to business lunch to dinner party to dancing. Repeat. Sure, you can get a frame that functions—or you can get a frame that cantilevers, takes wing, or has James Brown lyrics scribbled all over it. In code. Maybe it was painted by an artist—you'd recognize the name if we told you—or maybe we chose the design from 10,000 colors online. We supersize our own chainrings or buy forks custom-finished to represent the Seven Deadly Sins. We ride tandems with lovers and three-seaters with friends. And we think the pennyfarthing never went out of fashion.

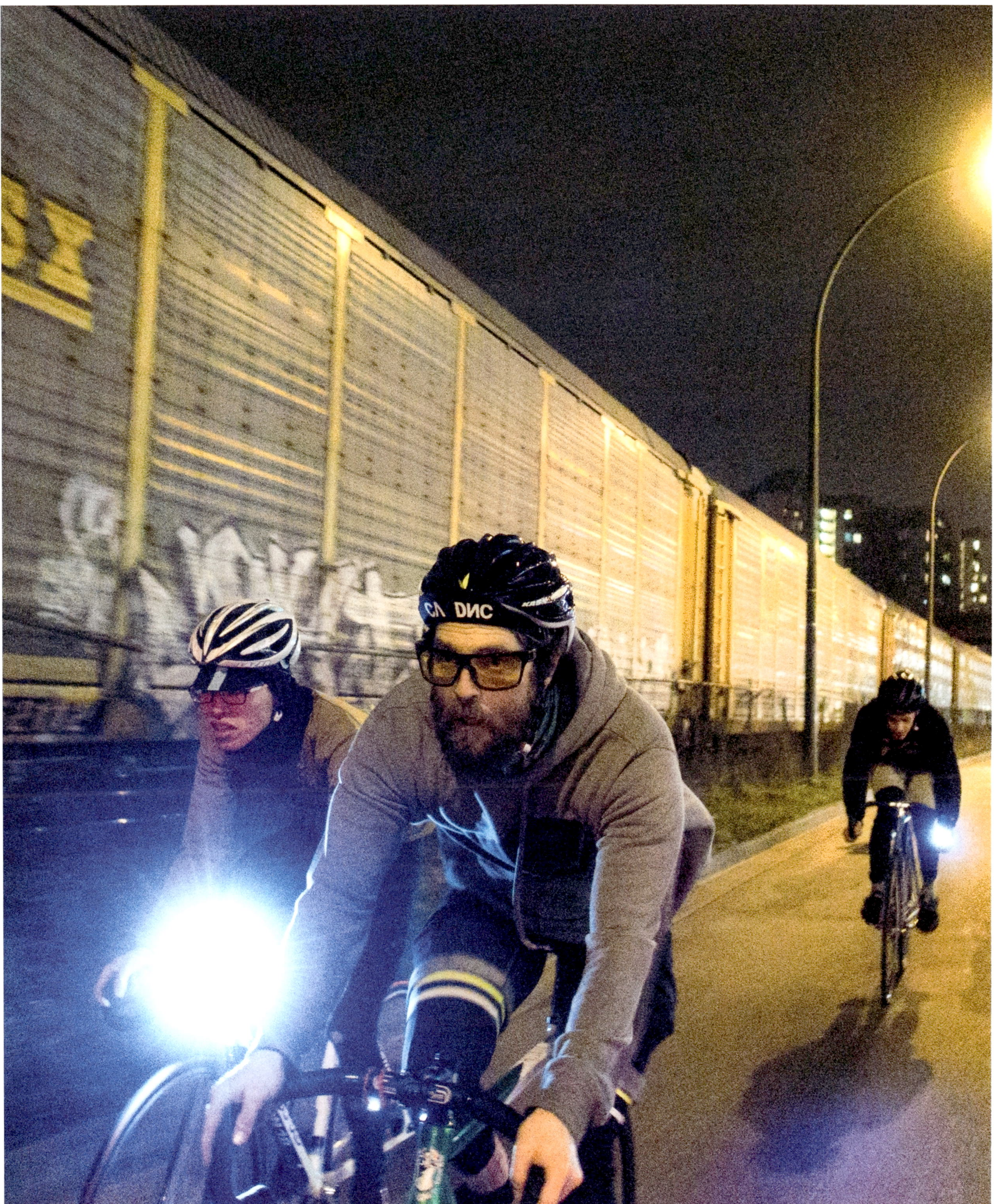

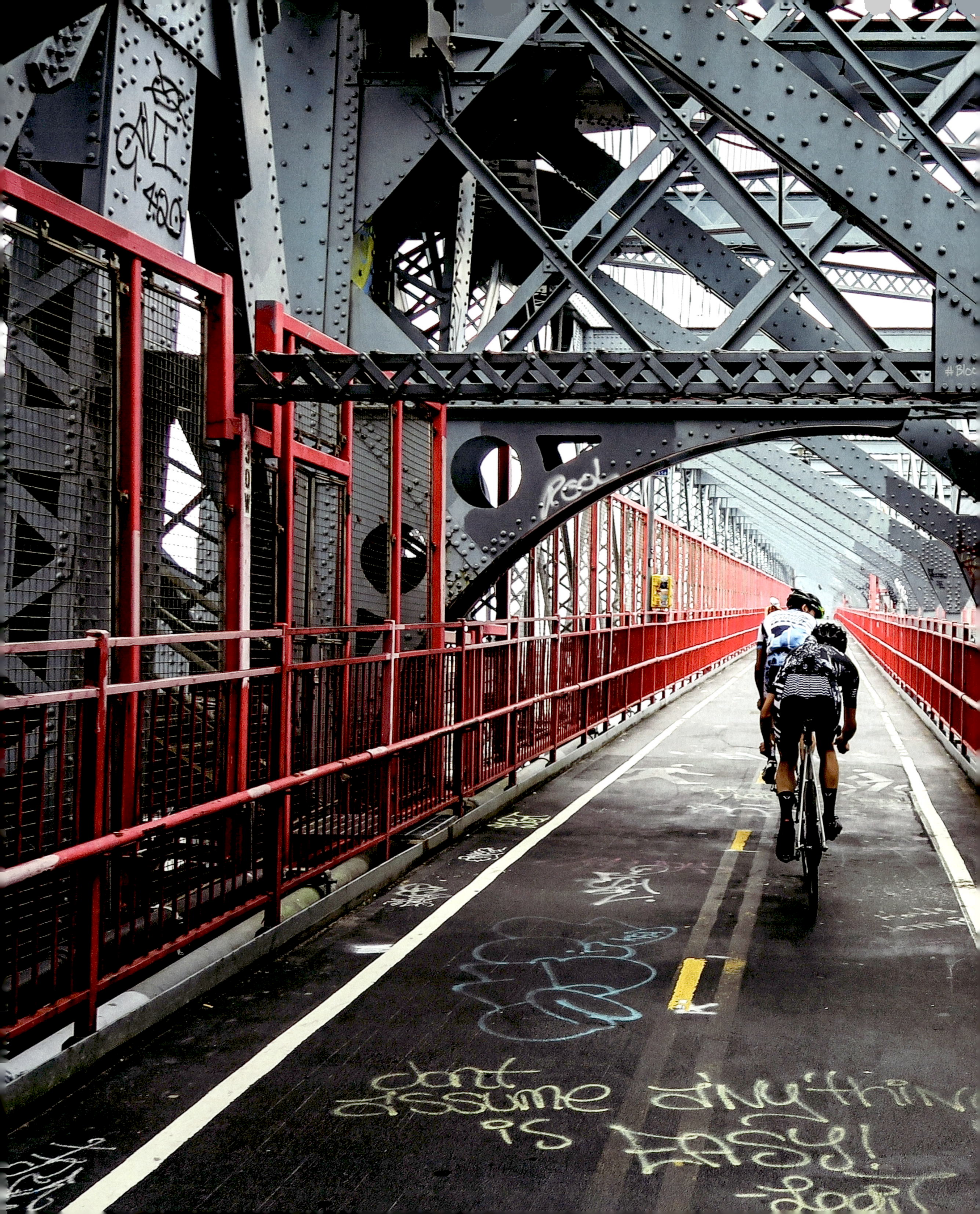
dont
assume
is
EASY!

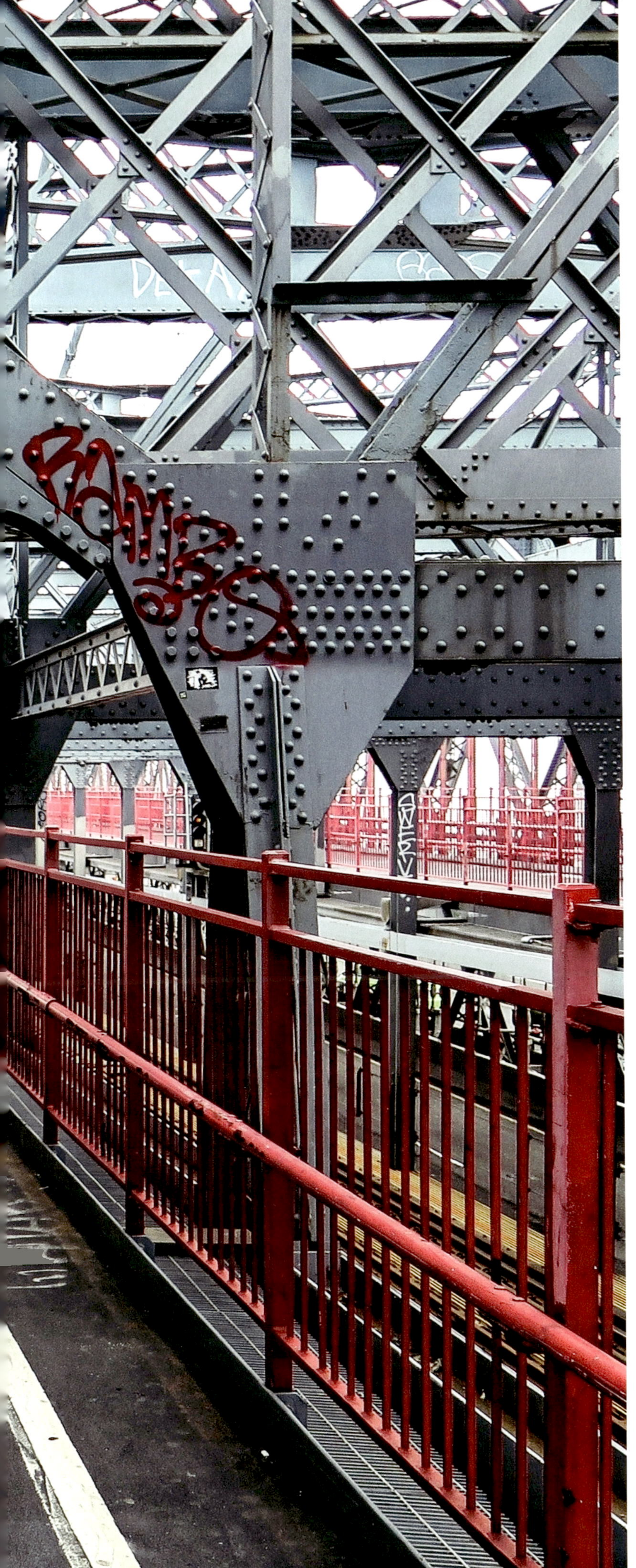

# *Bicycling through New York City*

ROMAN SIROMAKHA

The Redhook Crit race sends more than 300 cyclists from 29 countries careening down Brooklyn's streets on bikes without brakes—at night.

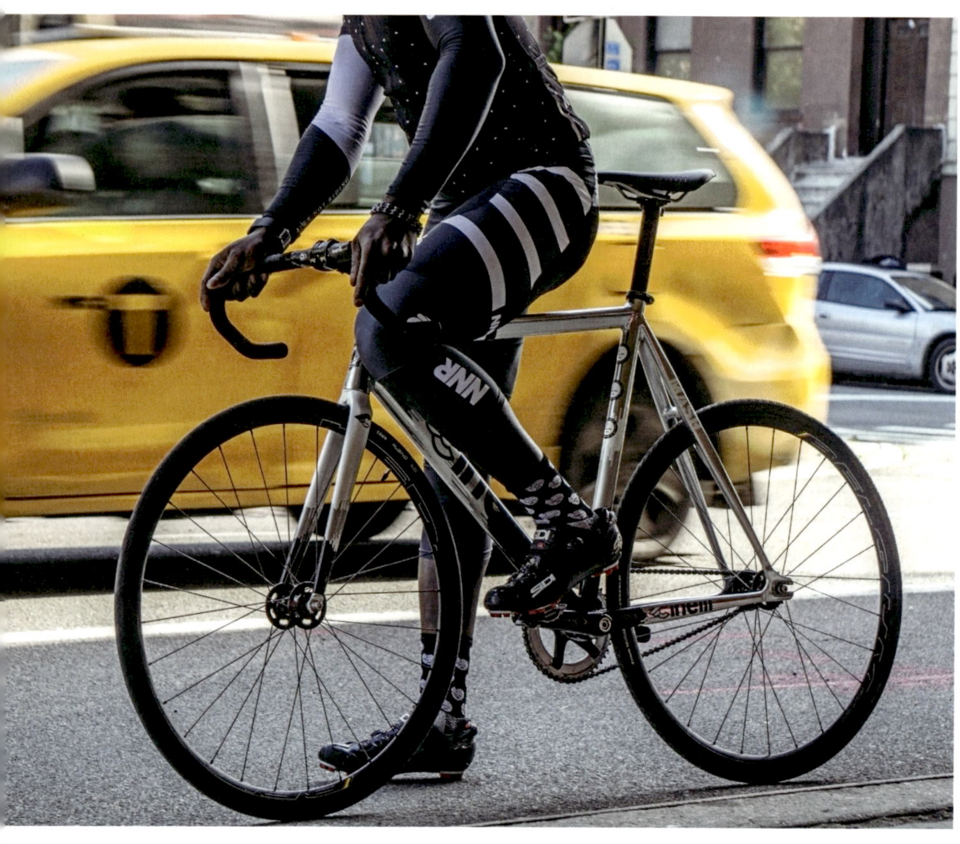
NNR

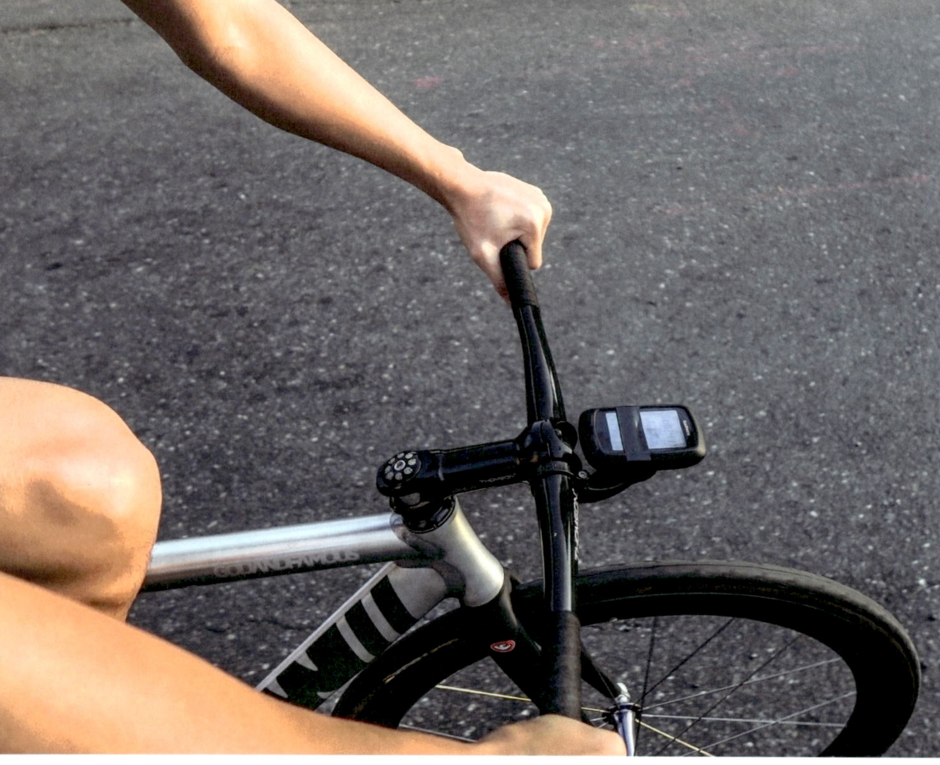

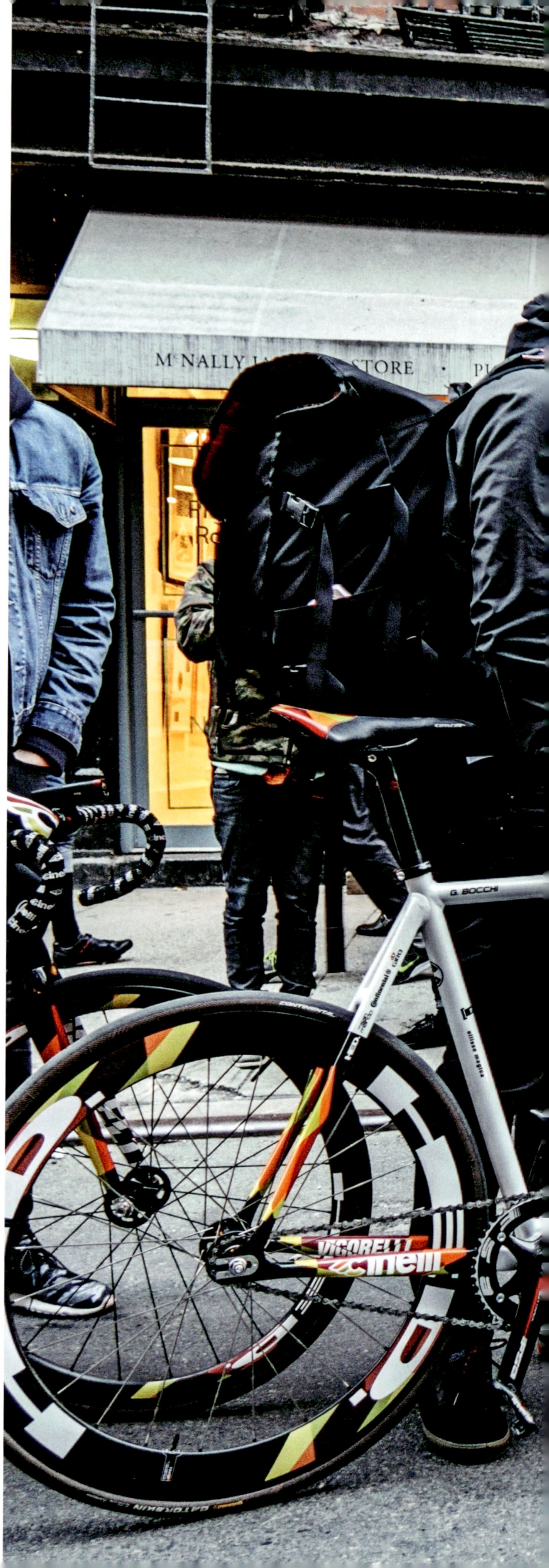

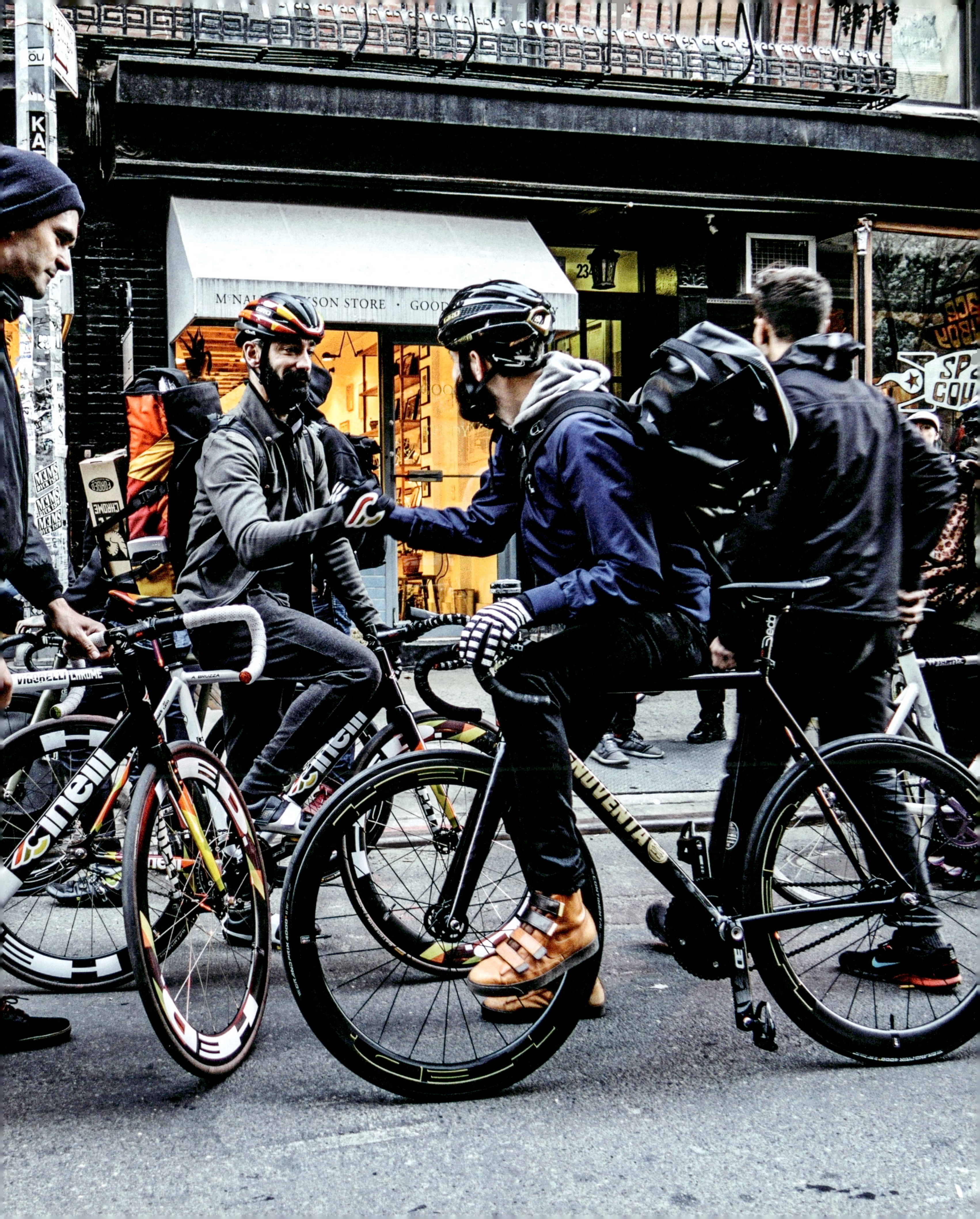
VIGORELLI CHROME
NOVENTA

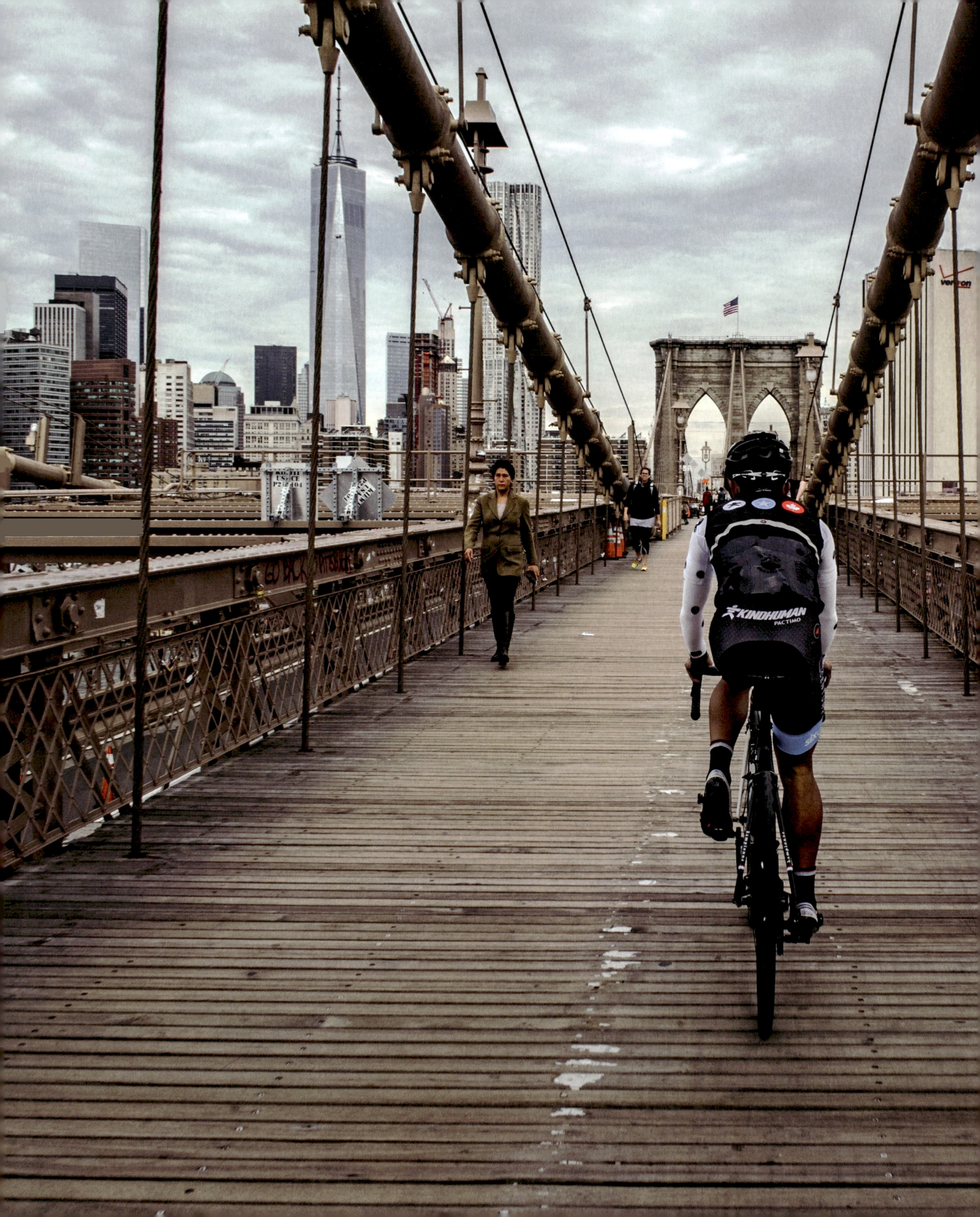
KINDHUMAN
PACTIMO

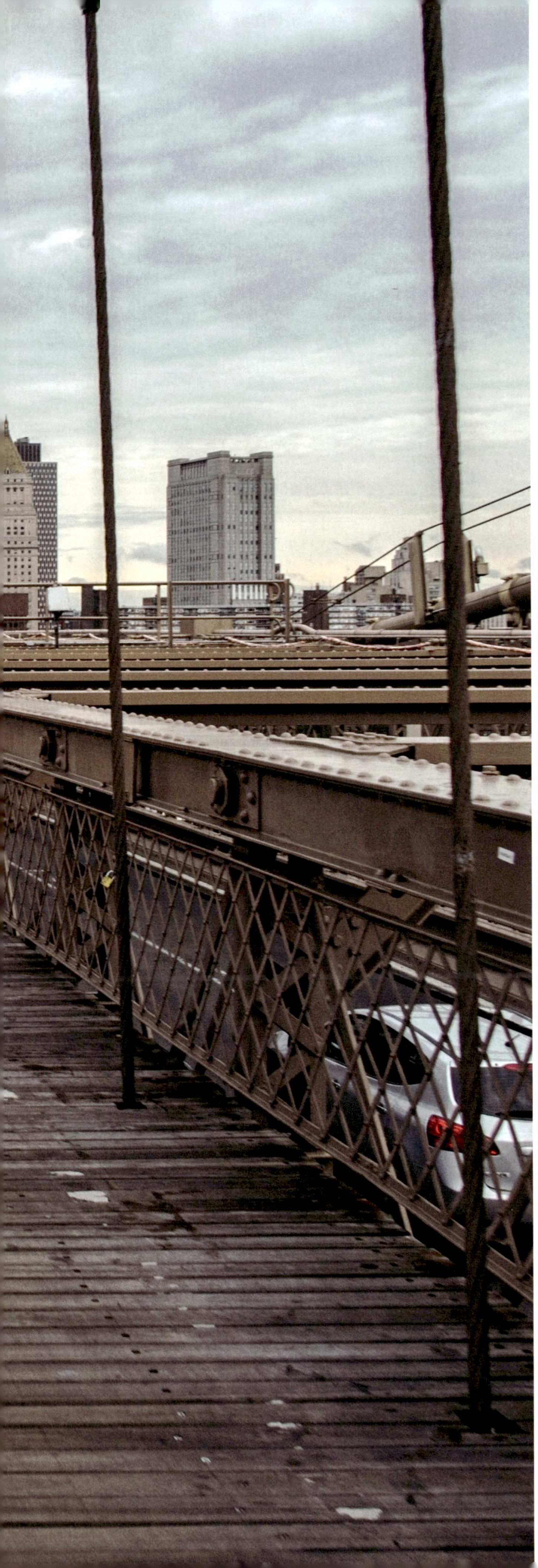

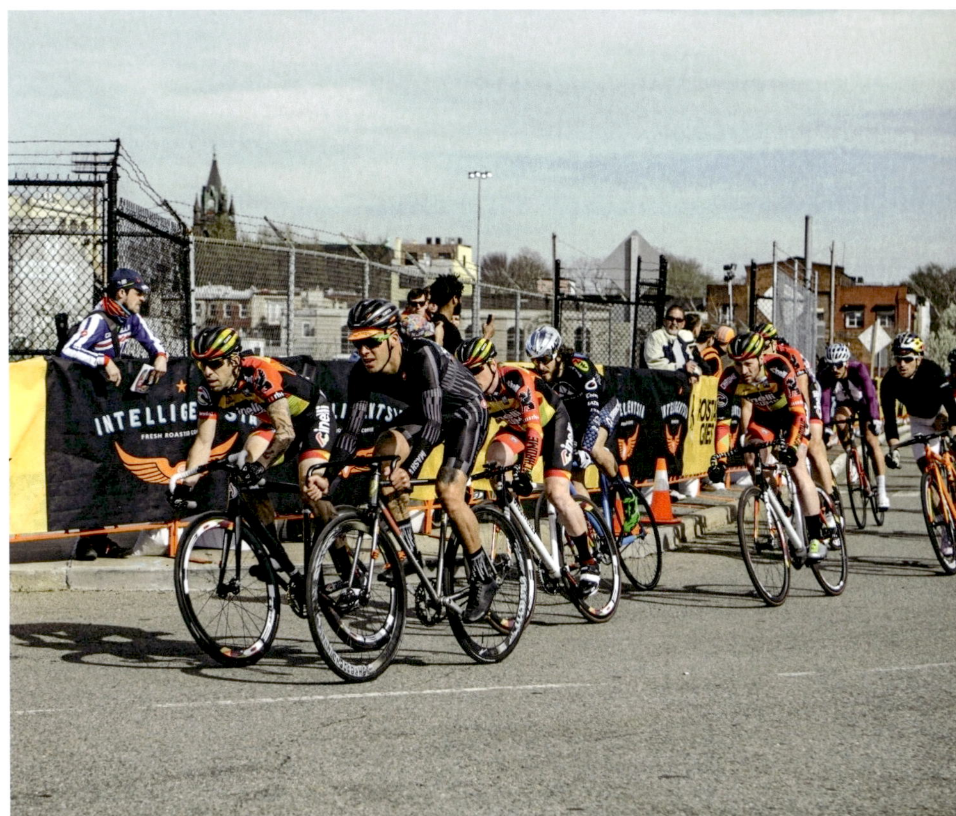

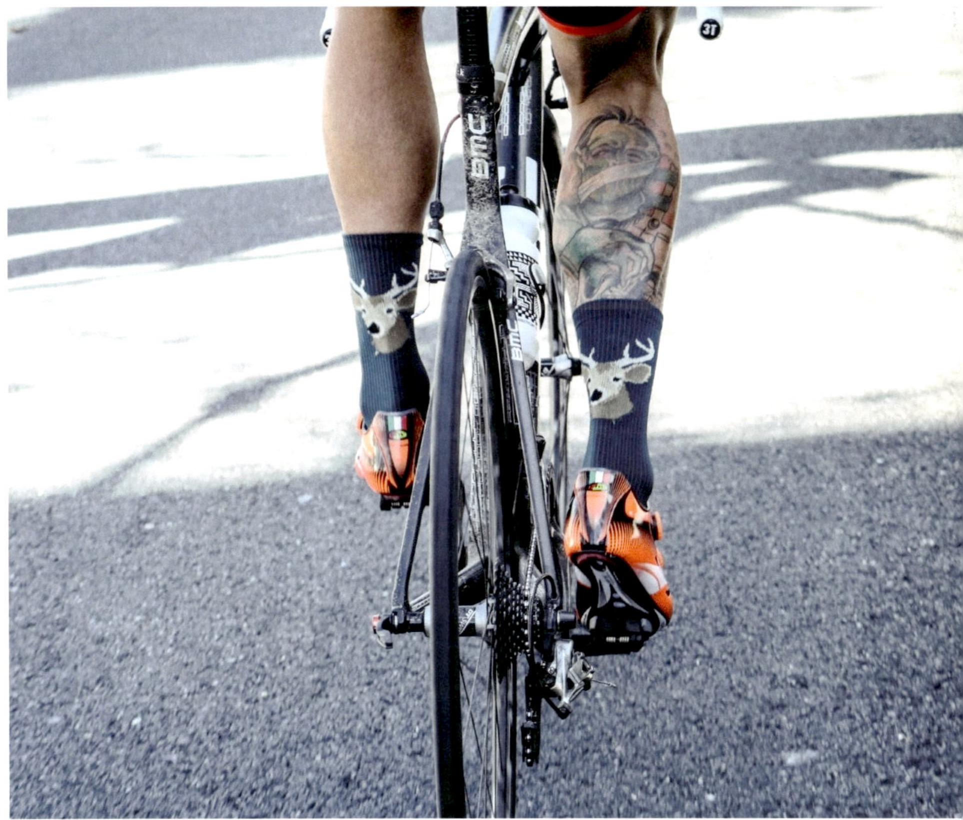

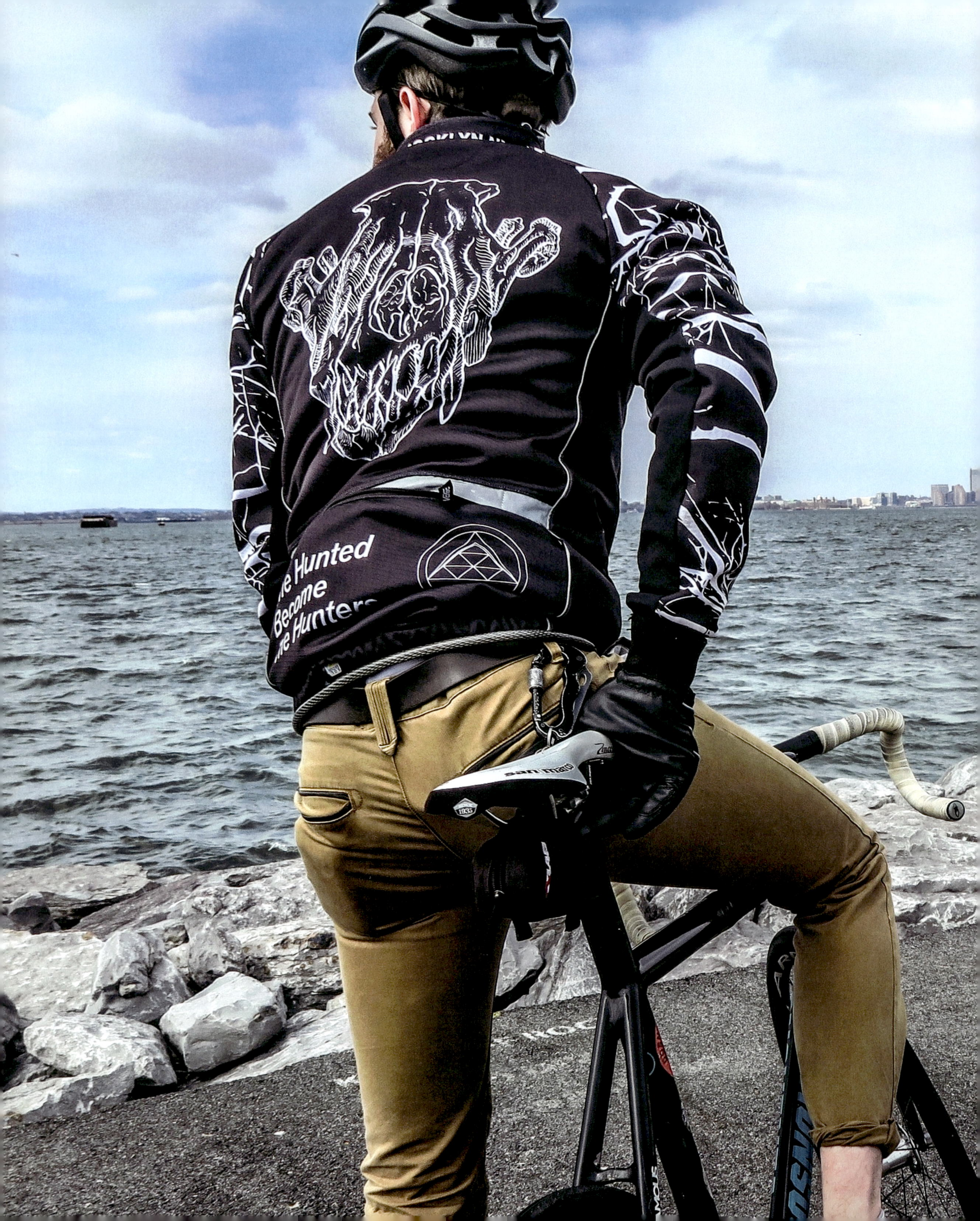
Hunted
Become
san marco
1935

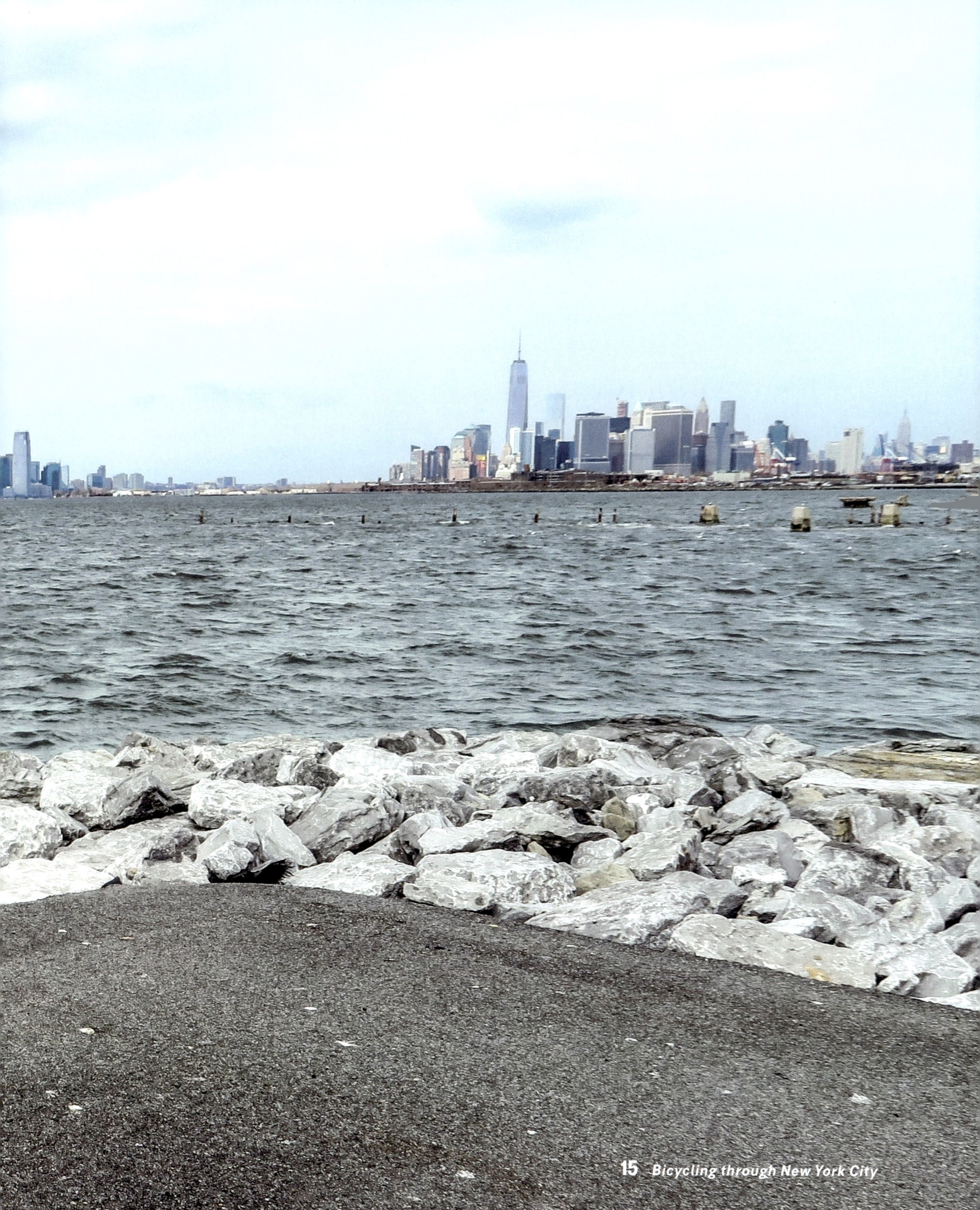

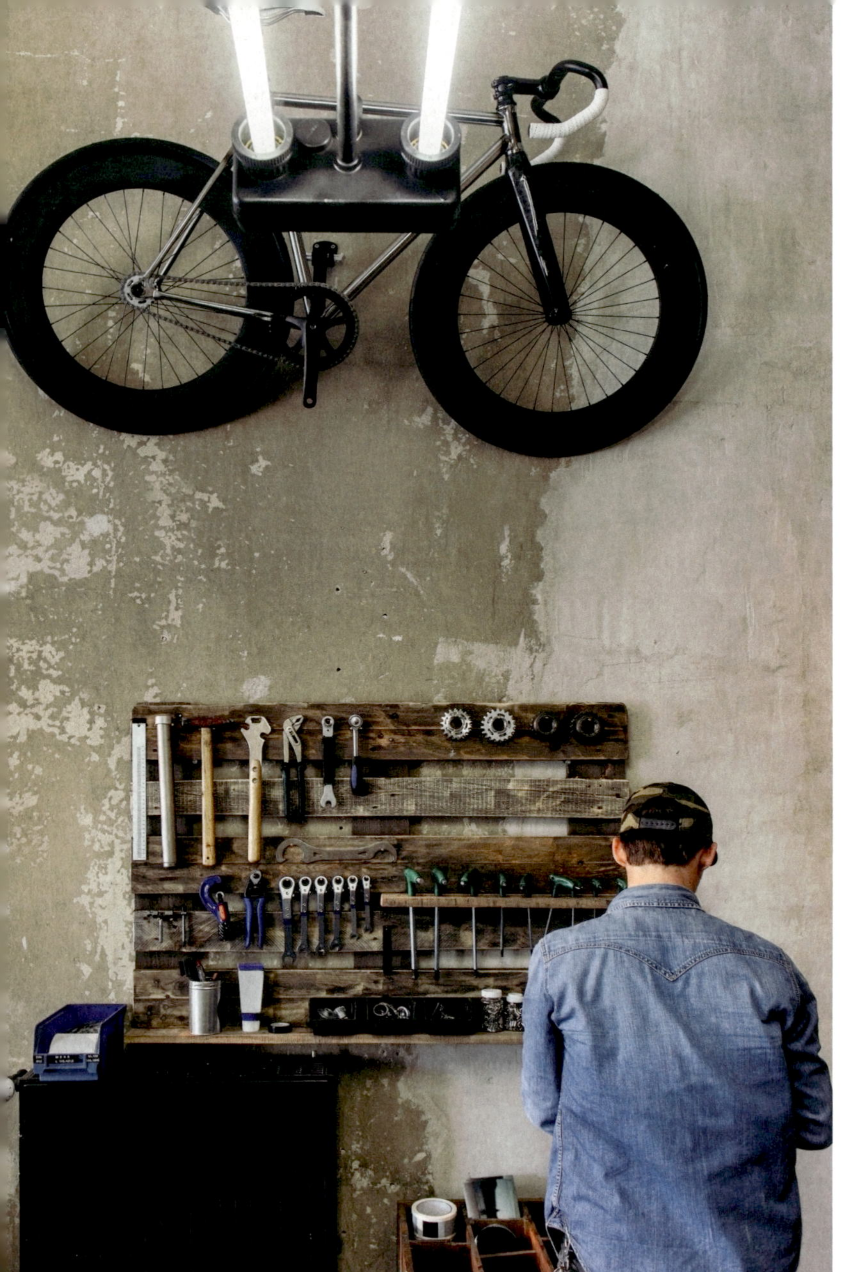

# 8bar Bikes

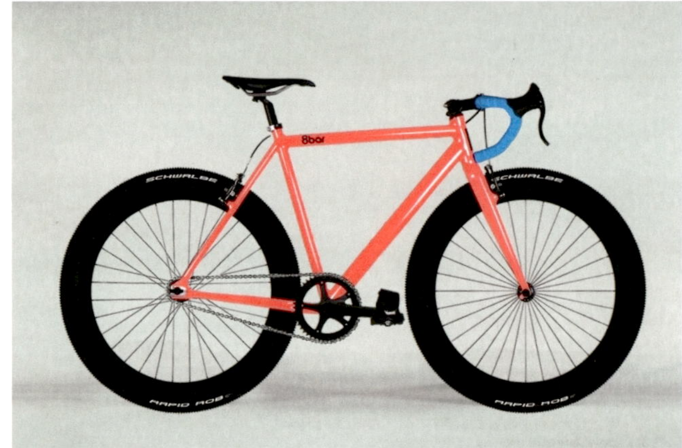


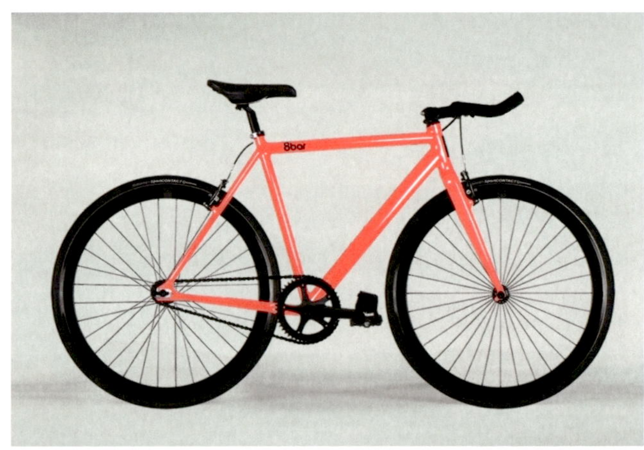


Based in the most dynamic district of Berlin, Kreuzberg, 8bar is not interested in being a run-of-the-mill bicycle brand. Instead, its business revolves around personalization, which has been taking the industry by storm. 8bar's urban bikes are never prefabricated and never identical; rather, each represents a unique artifact co-created by 8bar artisans and the future rider. 8bar provides high-quality components in a heady spectrum of colors and asks the client to become its collaborator, with total creative control over the look and feel of the final product. The idea is to mix colors and parts by using the intuitive 8bar Design-Your-Ride online configurator. Then, 8bar builds each design from scratch with the kind of obsessive attention to detail that drives the finest craftsmen in the industry. Instead of signing their creations with loud logos and branding, however, they humbly put the spotlight on the individuals who will one day ride them.

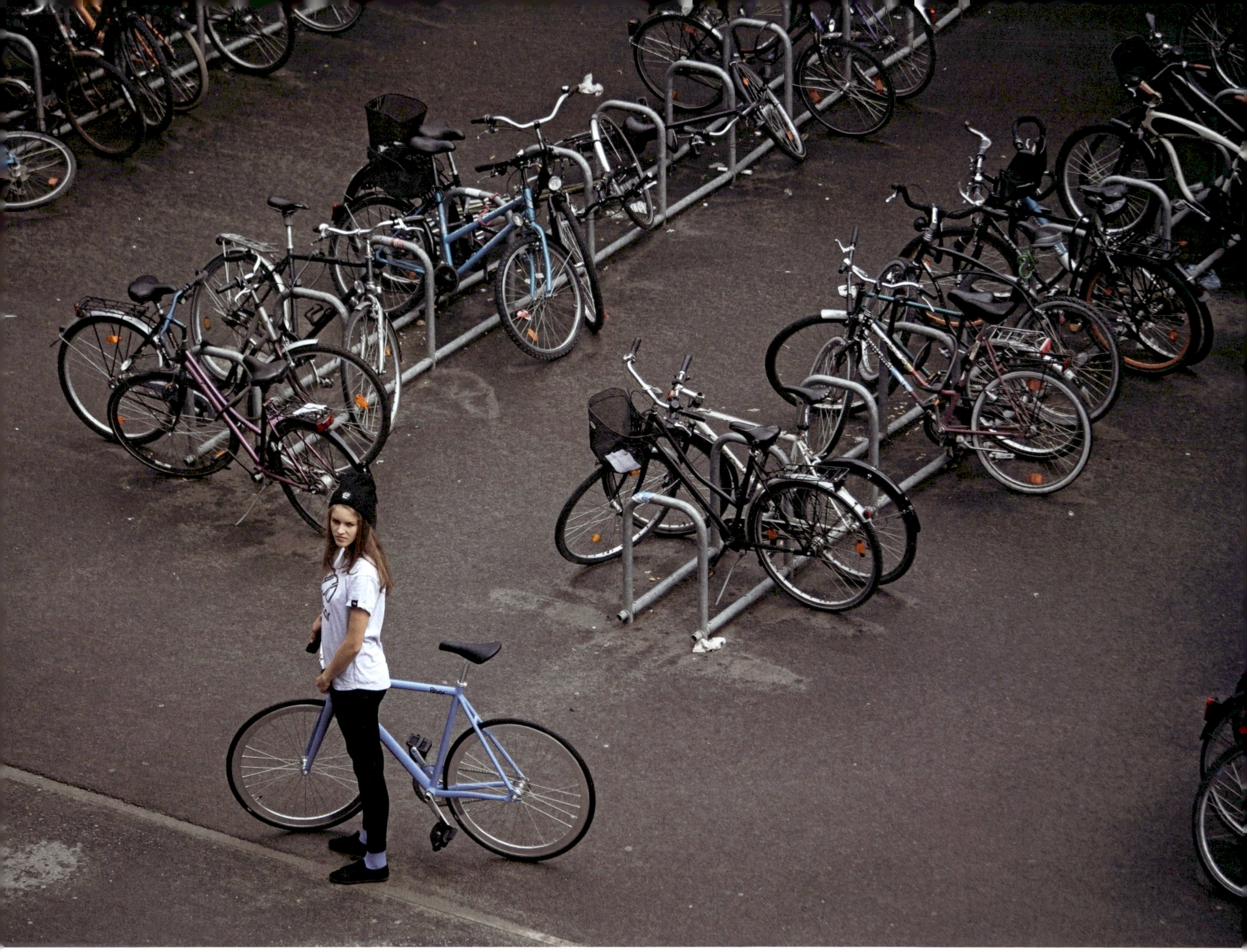

*8bar builds each design from scratch with the kind of attention to detail that drives the finest craftsmen in the industry.*

Stefan Schott, founder of 8bar Bikes

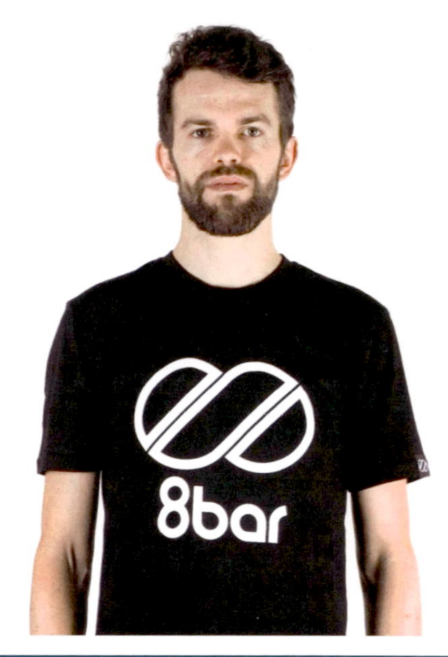

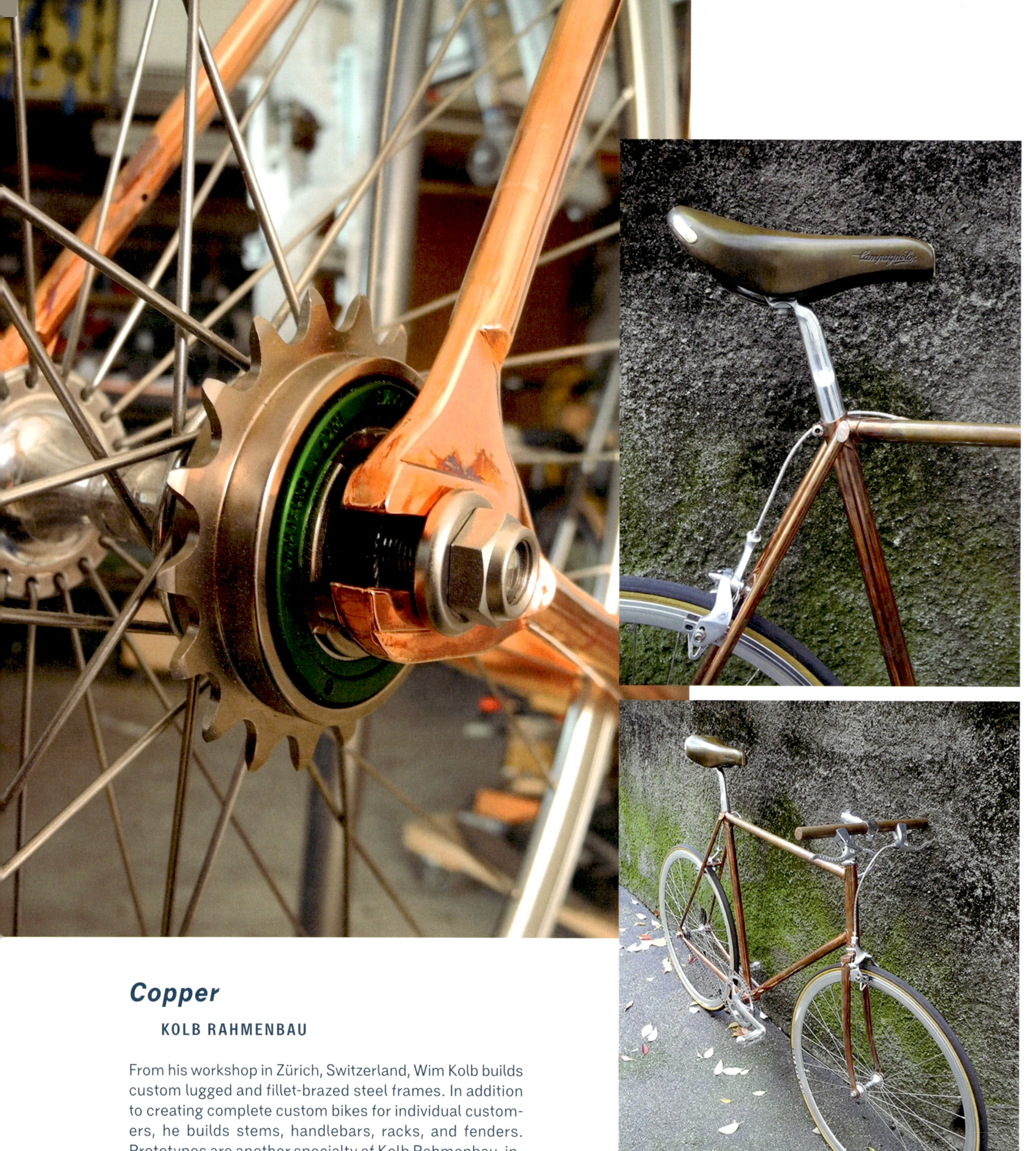

## *Copper*

**KOLB RAHMENBAU**

From his workshop in Zürich, Switzerland, Wim Kolb builds custom lugged and fillet-brazed steel frames. In addition to creating complete custom bikes for individual customers, he builds stems, handlebars, racks, and fenders. Prototypes are another specialty of Kolb Rahmenbau, including bike-related projects like a custom single-speed, silver-brazed and copper-plated bike with Ishiwata tubes and lugs.

**this page top:** Megatubes 2

**this page bottom:** Gold Track Bike

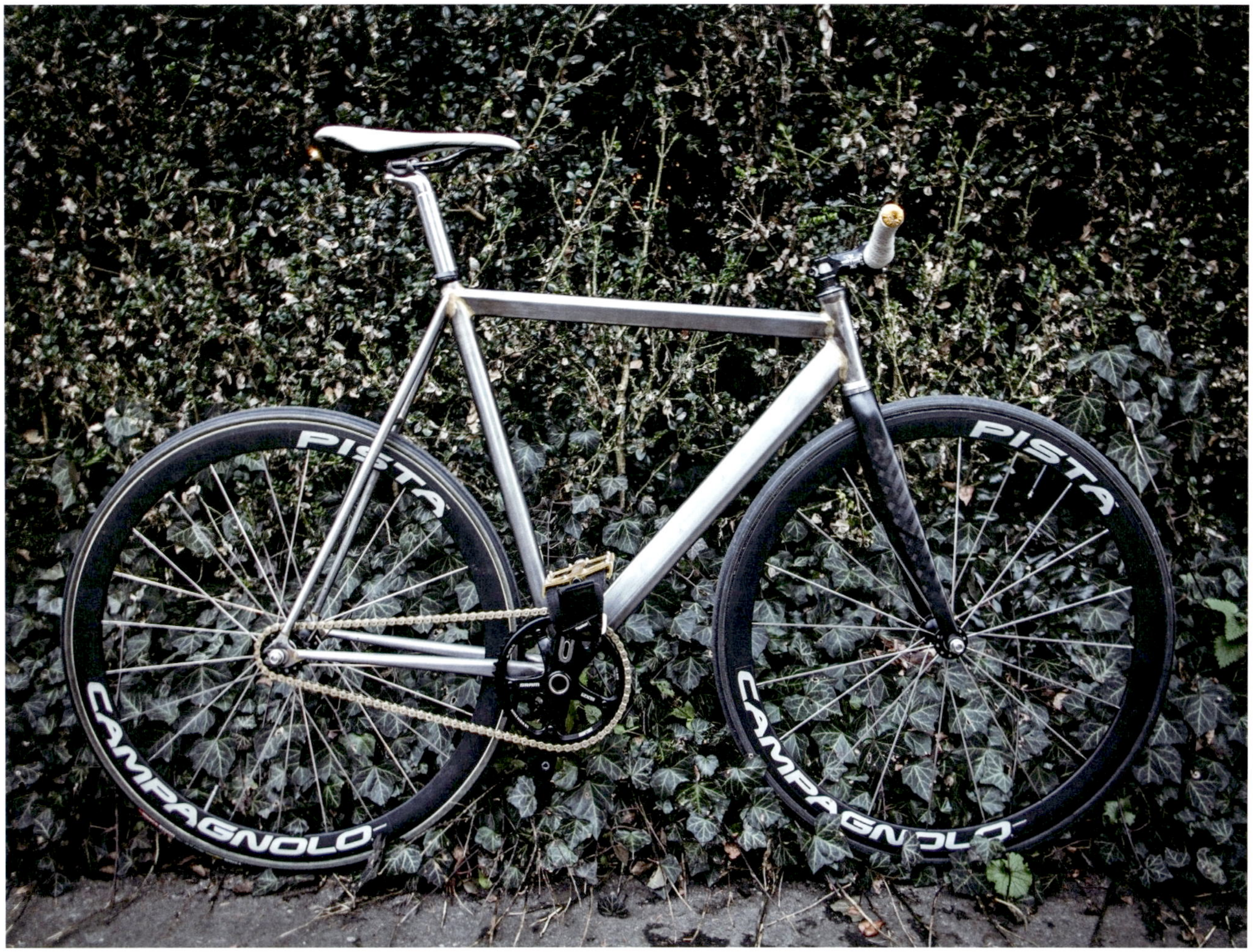

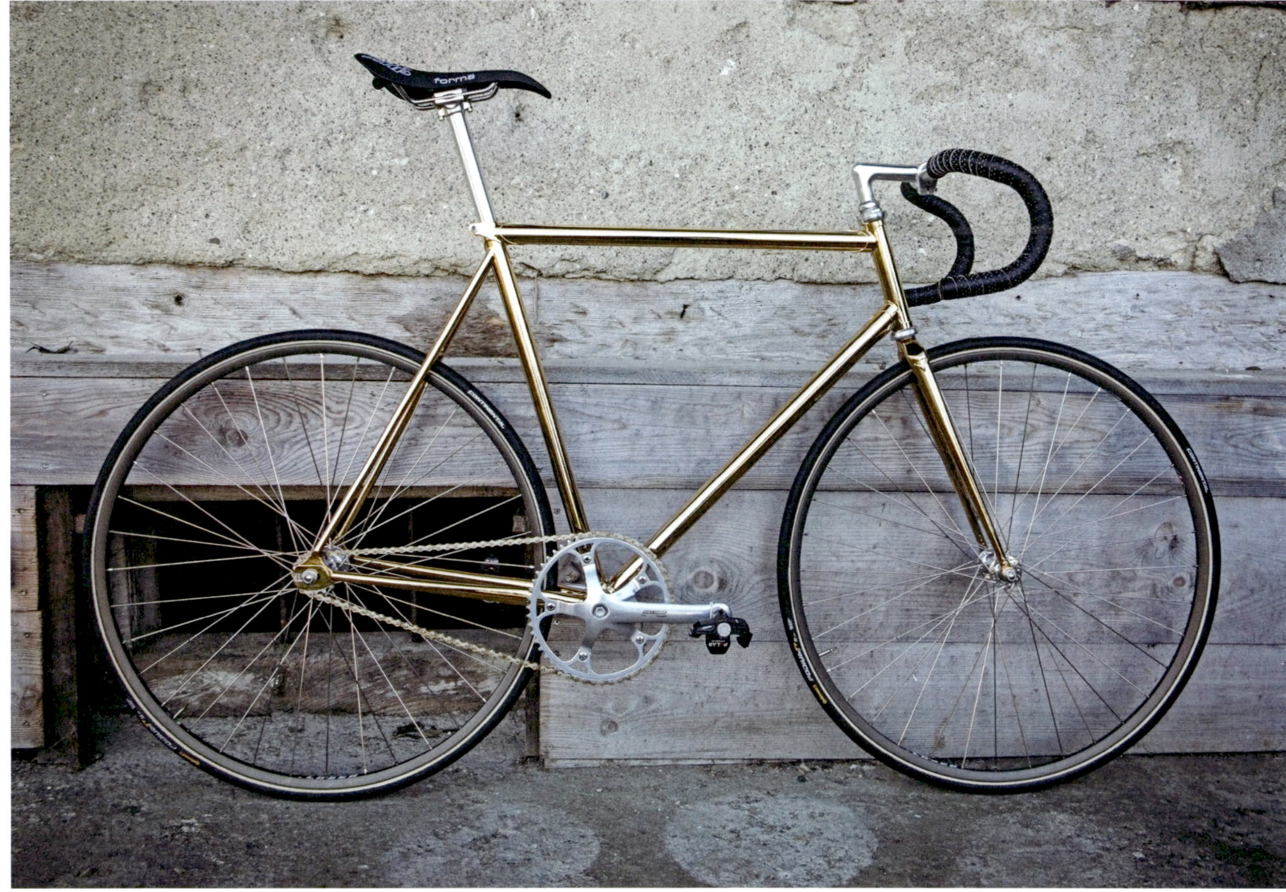

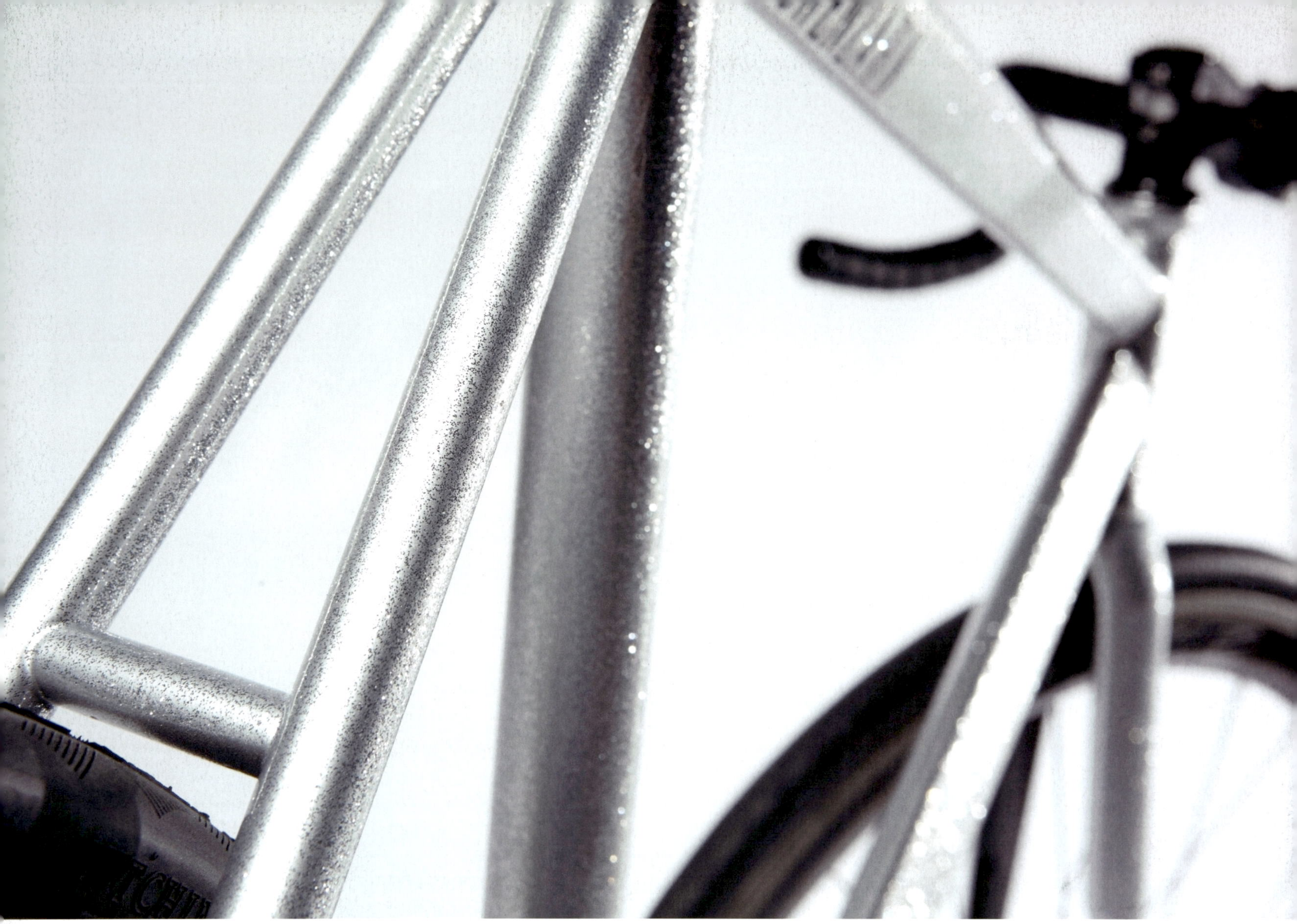

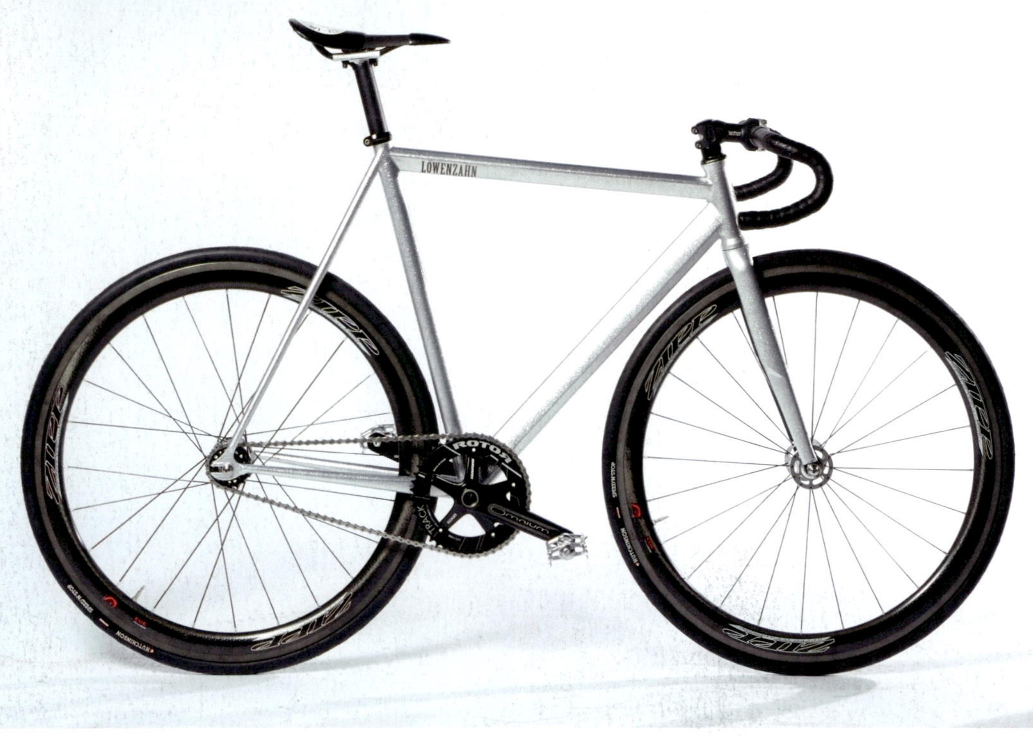

## *Megatubes*

**KOLB RAHMENBAU**

Kolb Rahmenbau produced this small series of fillet-brazed track bikes with Columbus Zona Megatubes for bike shop Löwenzahn in Basel, Switzerland.

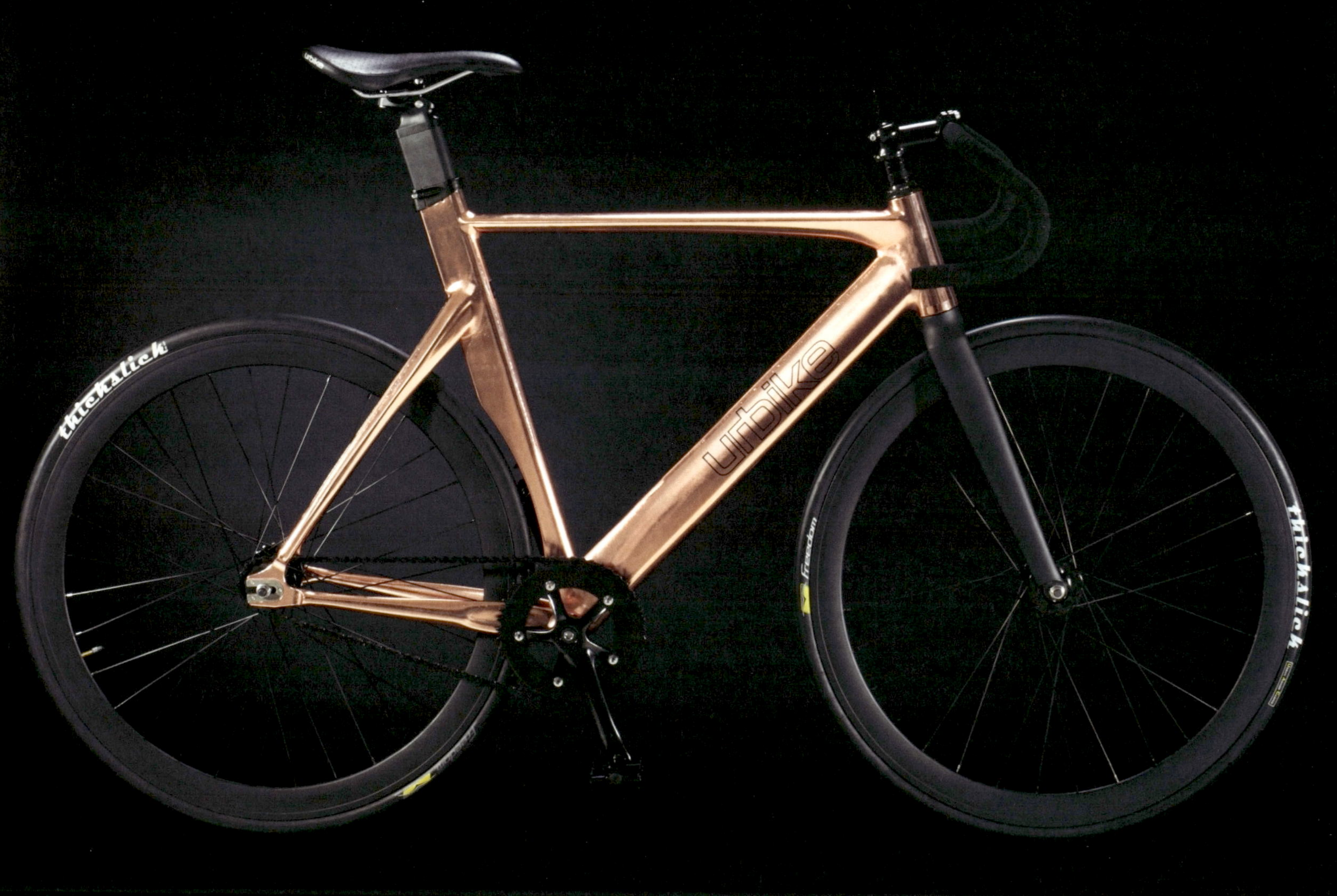


## *Aero*

**URBIKE**

Streamlined and aerodynamic, the Aero by urbike is as nimble and responsive as any modern racing bike. Inspired by high-quality triathlon bikes, the seat tube has a curved recess that creates a shorter wheelbase, resulting in a more reactive ride and a sporty, clean look. Its sturdy frame is reinforced with steel dropouts for extra rigidity and robustness. The hydro-formed AL6061 aluminum frame tubes, which come together in seamless, hand-sanded welds, create the illusion of a single piece of material. In keeping with its sleek design, the tapered head is smooth thanks to the seamless connection to the frame. Meanwhile, the high-quality aluminum fork is specially designed to house the internal headset and follow the bike's clean lines.

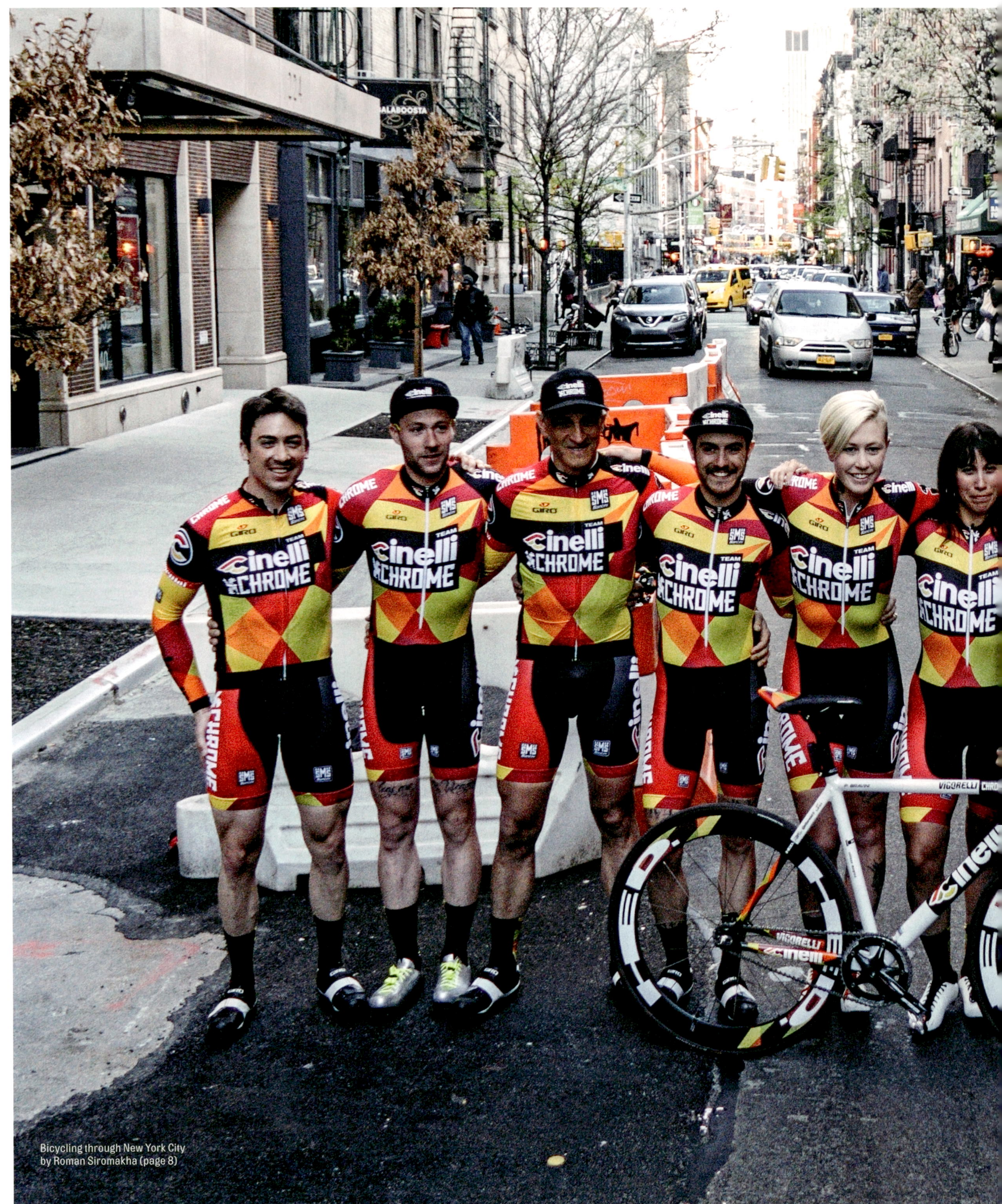


Bicycling through New York City
by Roman Siromakha (page 8)

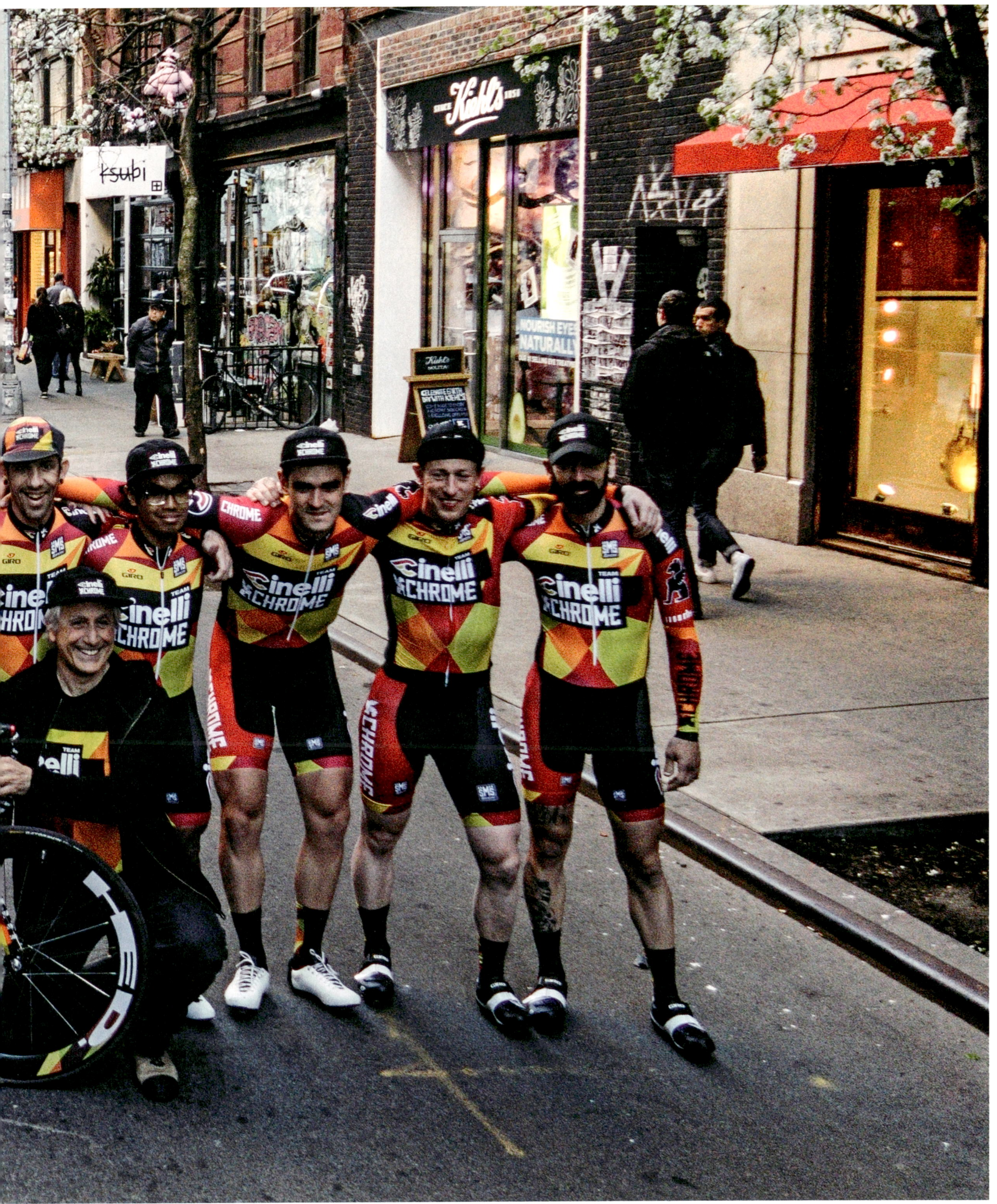
ksubi
Kiehl's
NOURISH EYES
NATURALLY
cinelli
CHROME
GIRO

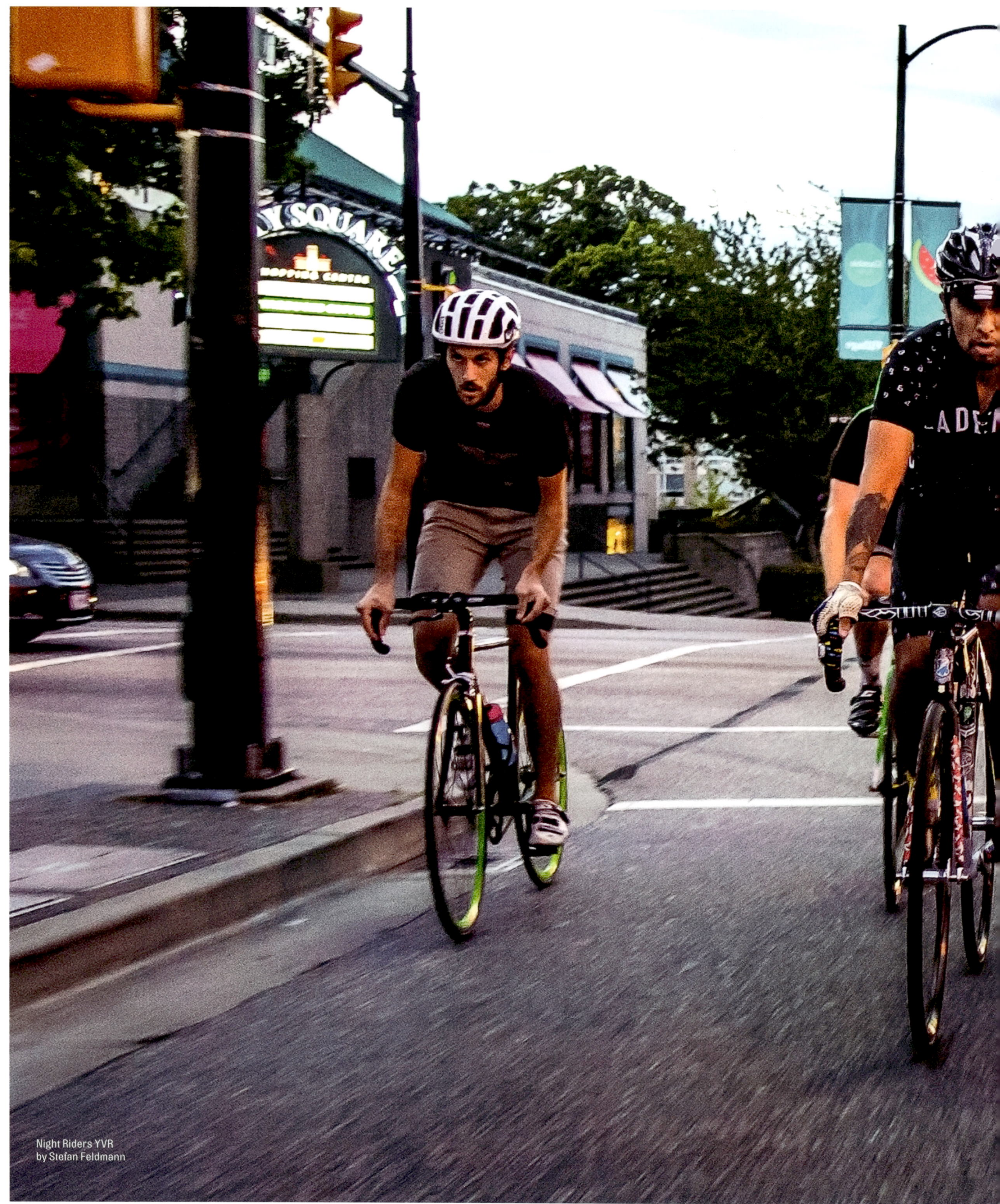


Night Riders YVR
by Stefan Feldmann

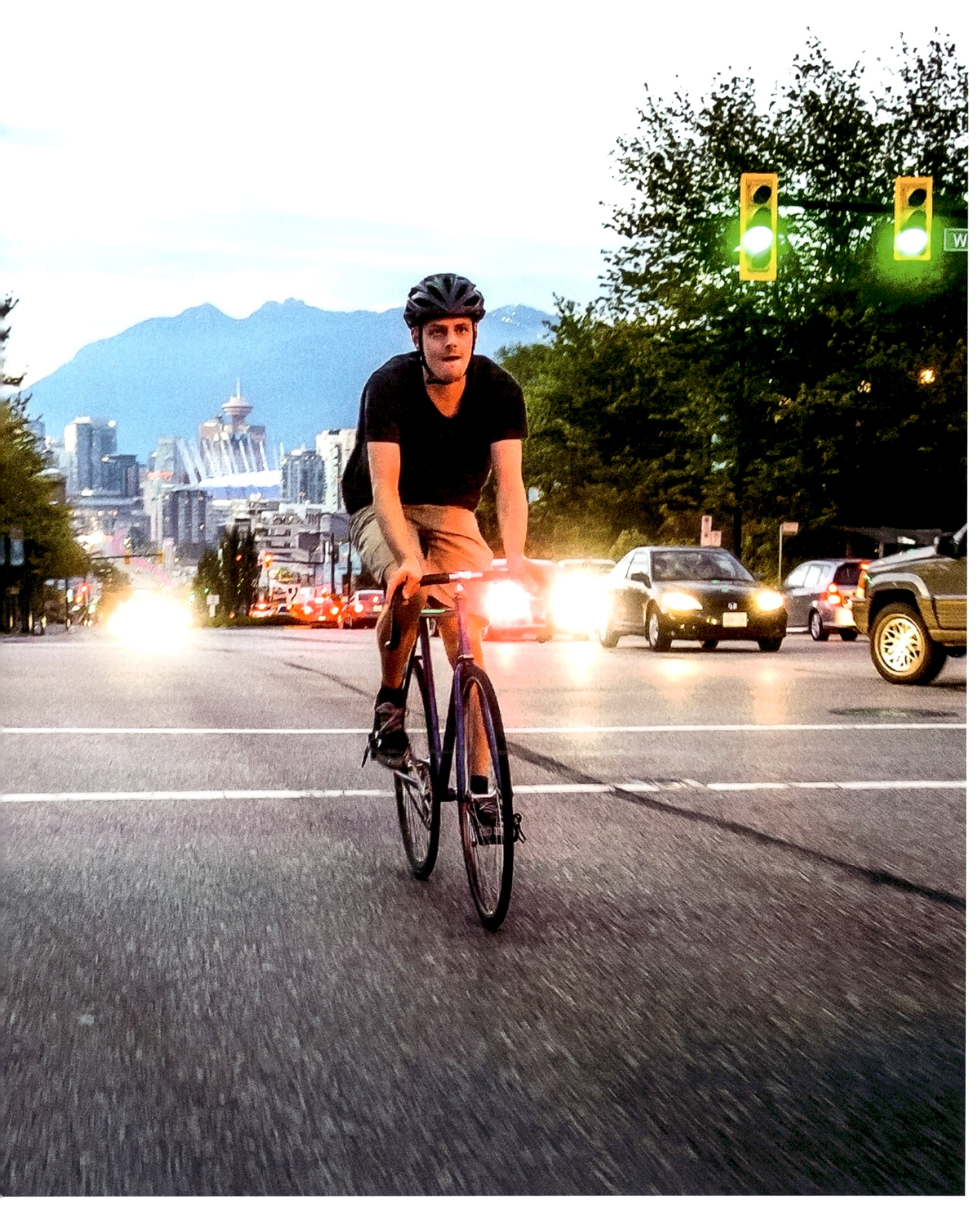

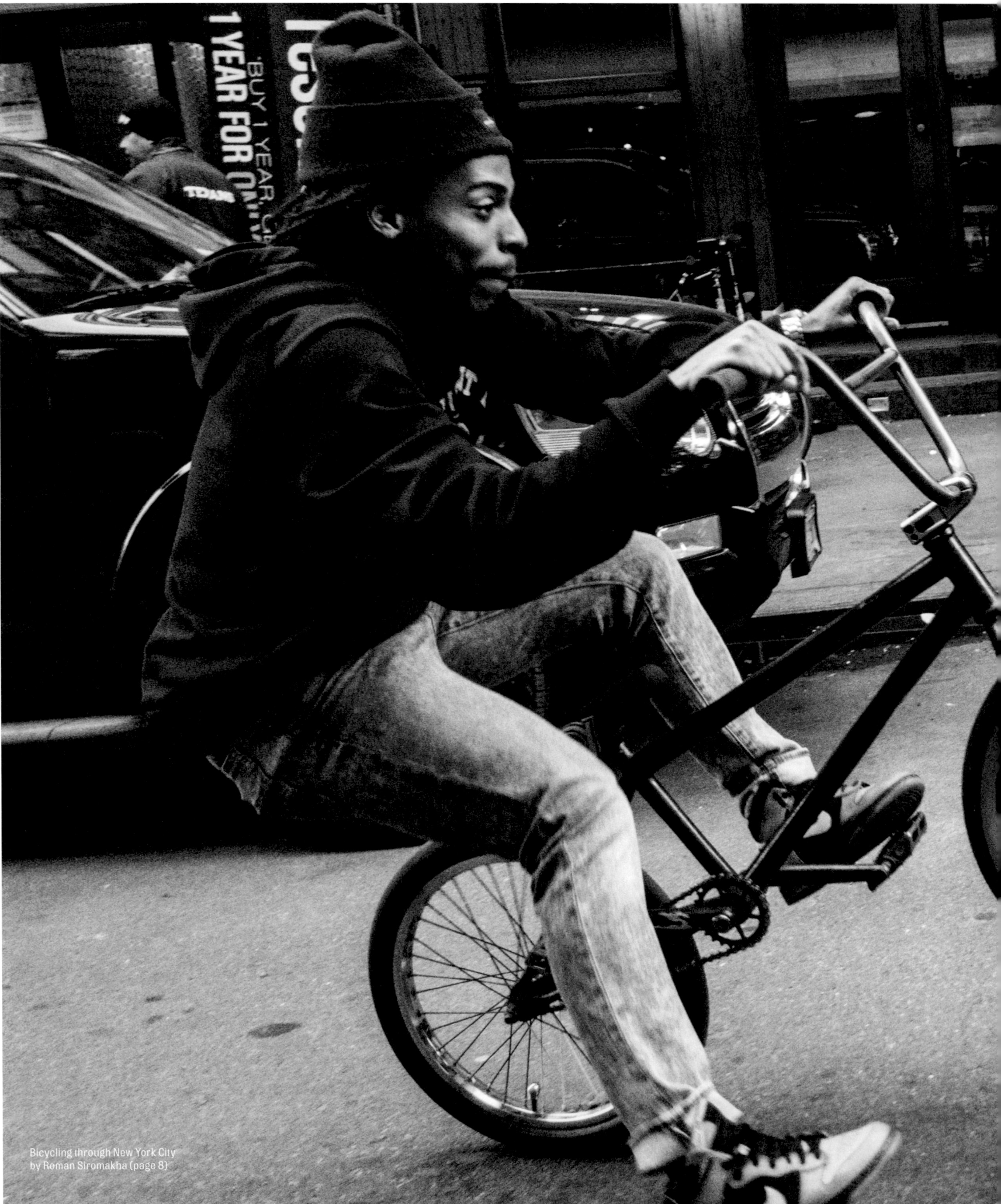


Bicycling through New York City
by Roman Siromakha (page 8)

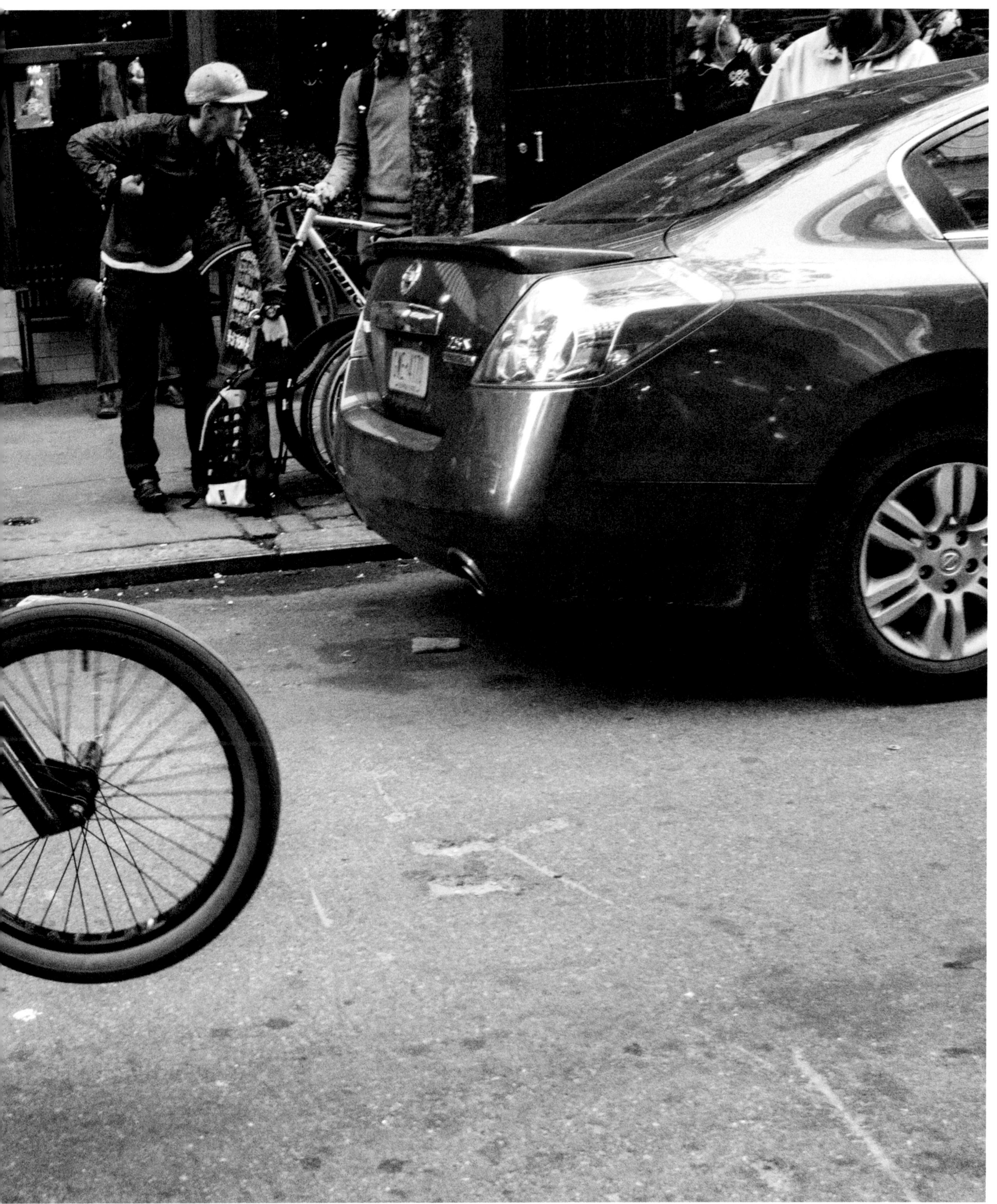

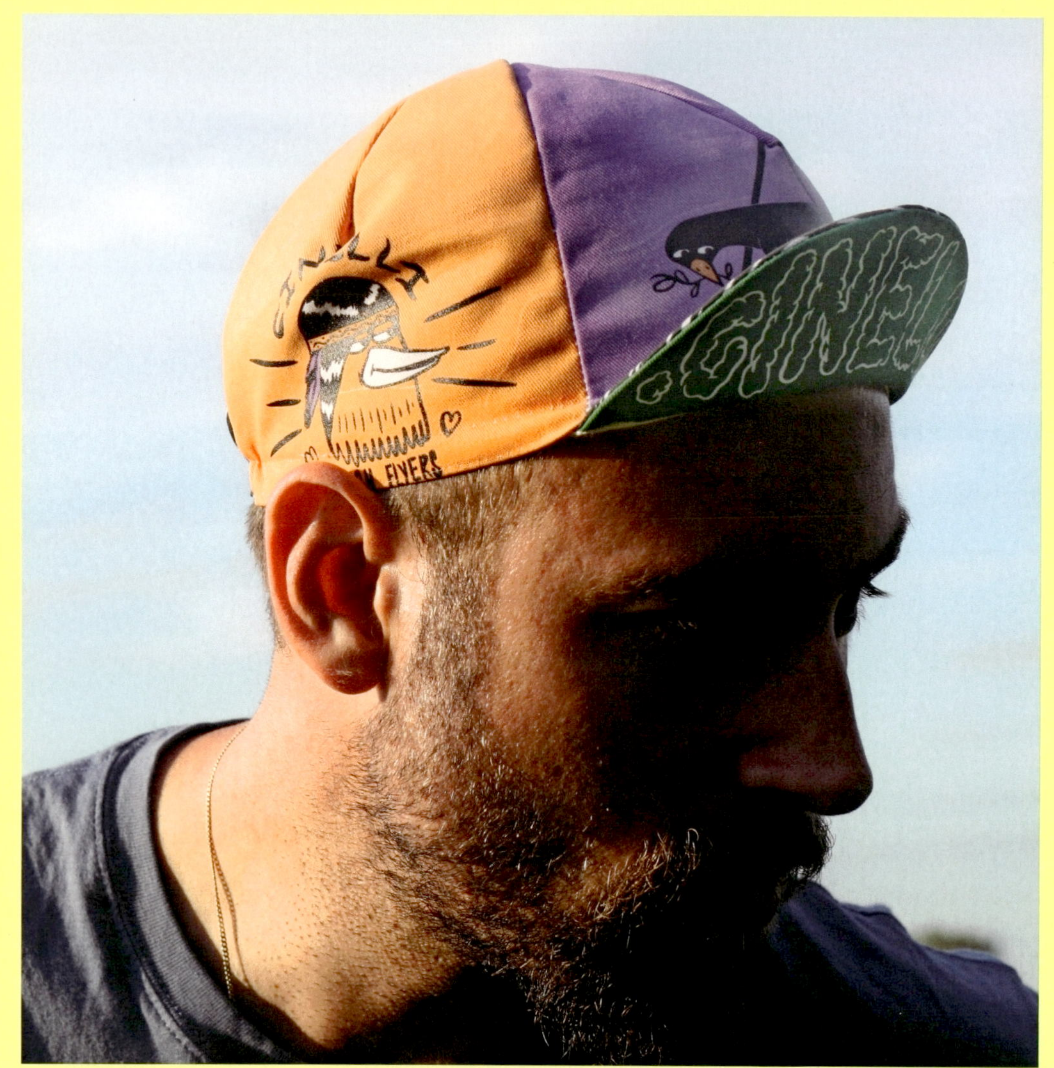


# Stevie Gee × Cinelli

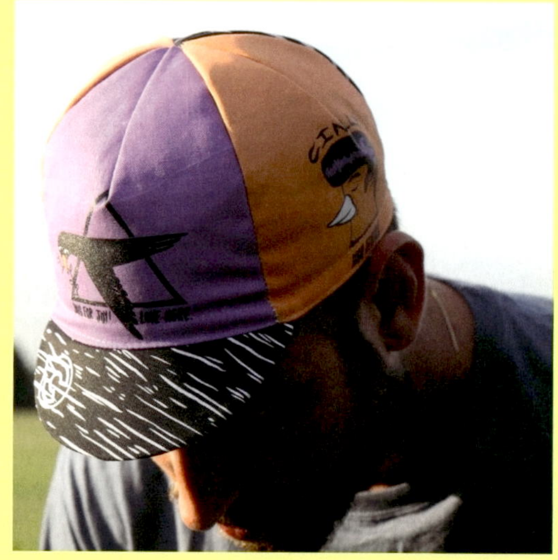

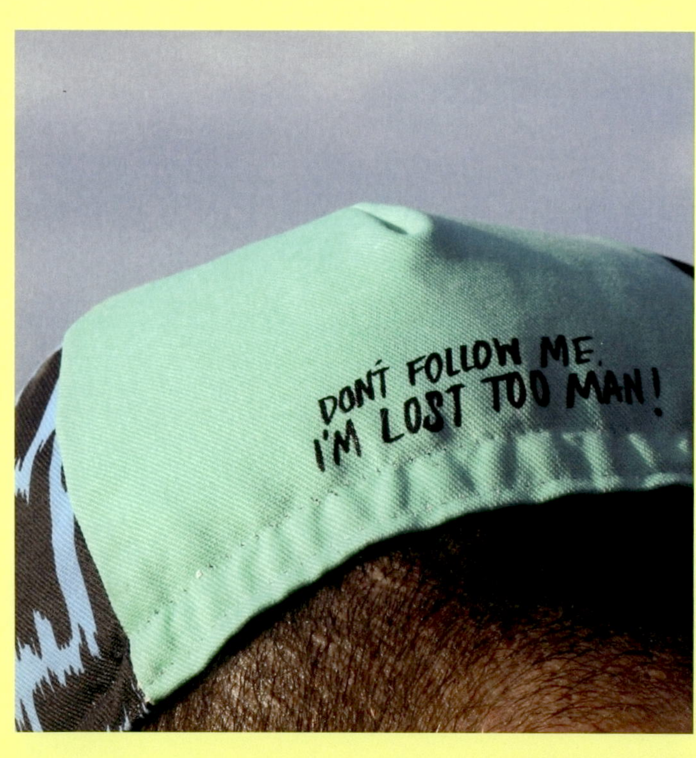


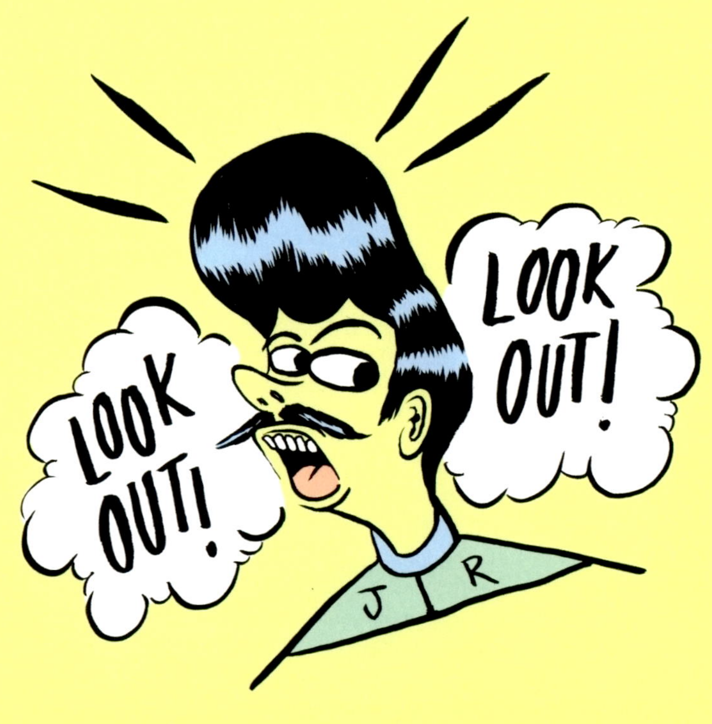

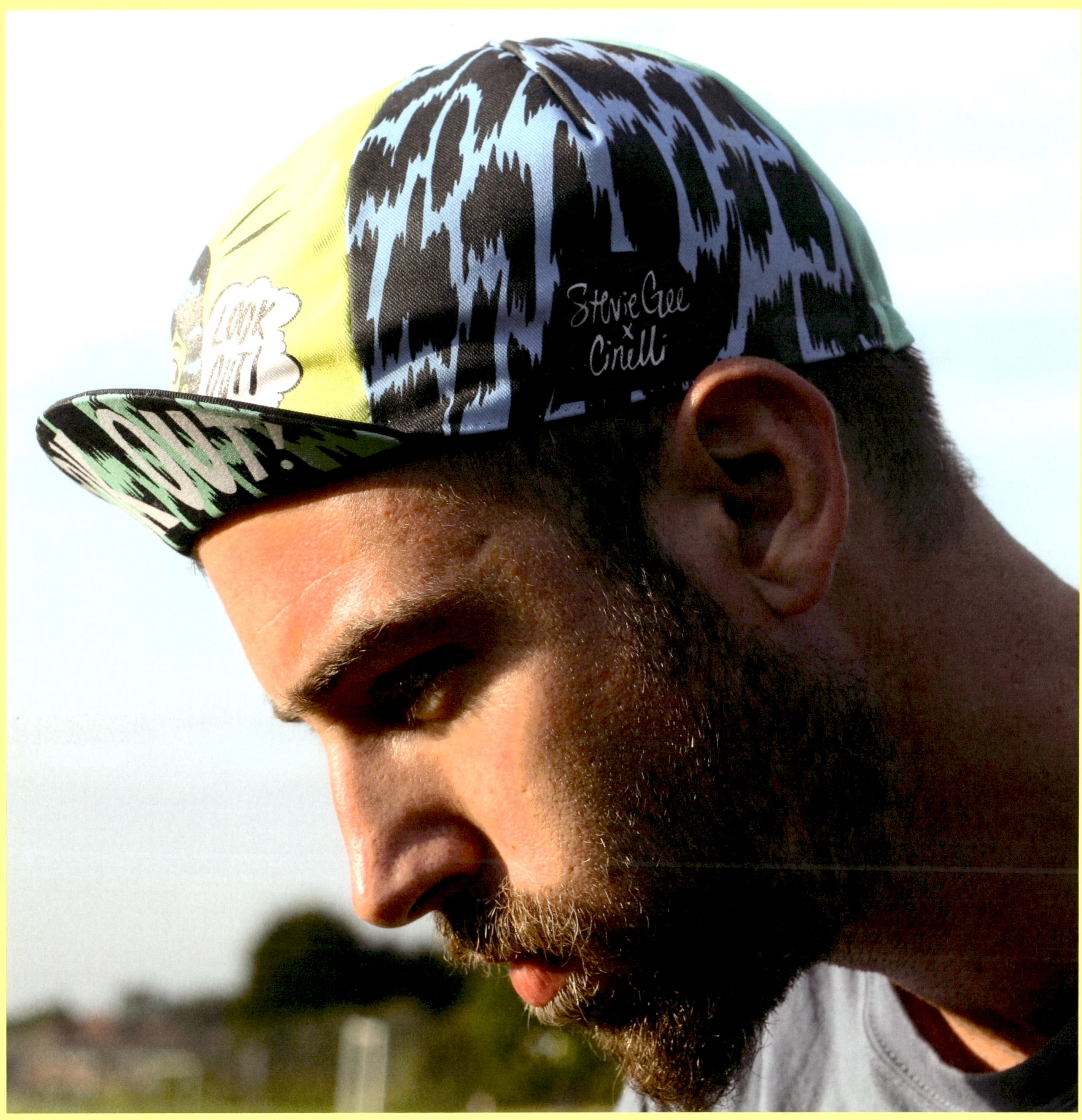


Legendary bicycle manufacturer Cinelli—which gave modern cyclists their first aluminum handlebars, plastic-core seats, and quick-release pedals—also began to bring art into the realm of riding with commissions like Keith Haring's Laser art bike. More recently, Cinelli president Antonio Colombo invited Stevie Gee, a graphic artist and illustrator who has left his mark on everything from snowboards, motorcycles, and motorcycle helmets to sculptures and album covers, to hand-paint a Vigorelli frame and forks for his Milan gallery. A second collaboration resulted in cycling caps illustrated with comic-book-like images and colors. Gee borrowed from his daily rides around London to create the graphical Look Out cap, inspired by the tangle of taxis, buses, car doors, and pedestrians that serve as obstacles to be gleefully dodged. His High Flyers cap, on the other hand, celebrates speed in the abstract and the "feeling of freedom you get when you fly through the city."

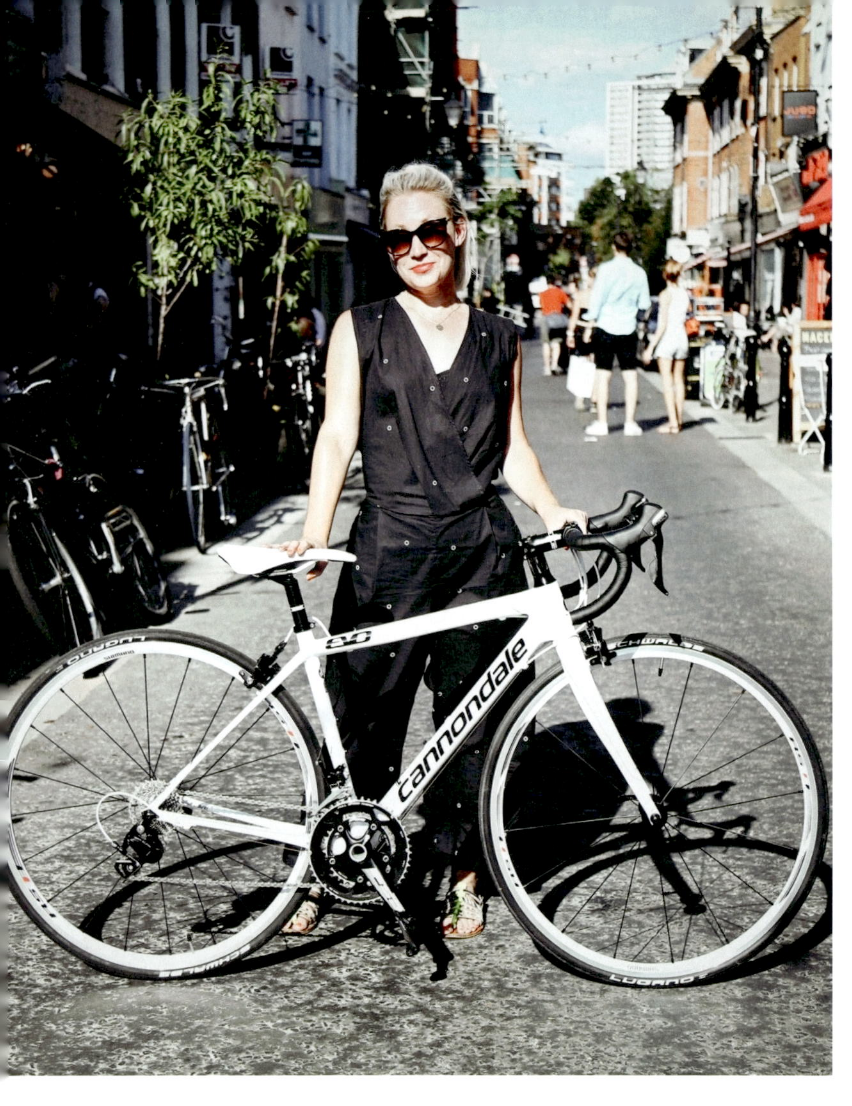


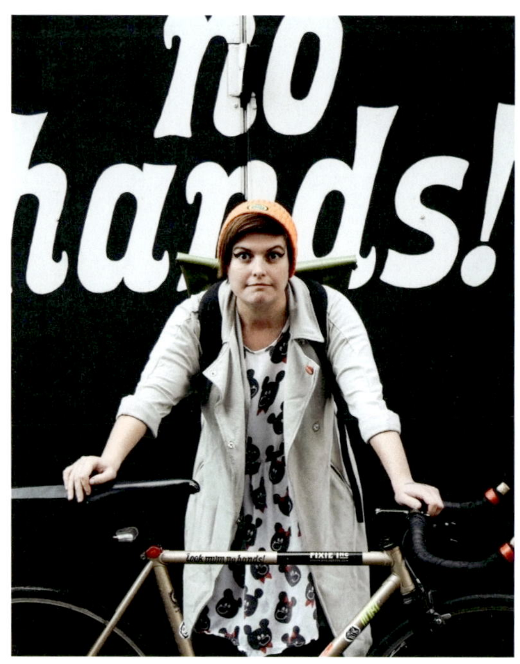


# Little Profiles

## LITTLE WHEELS

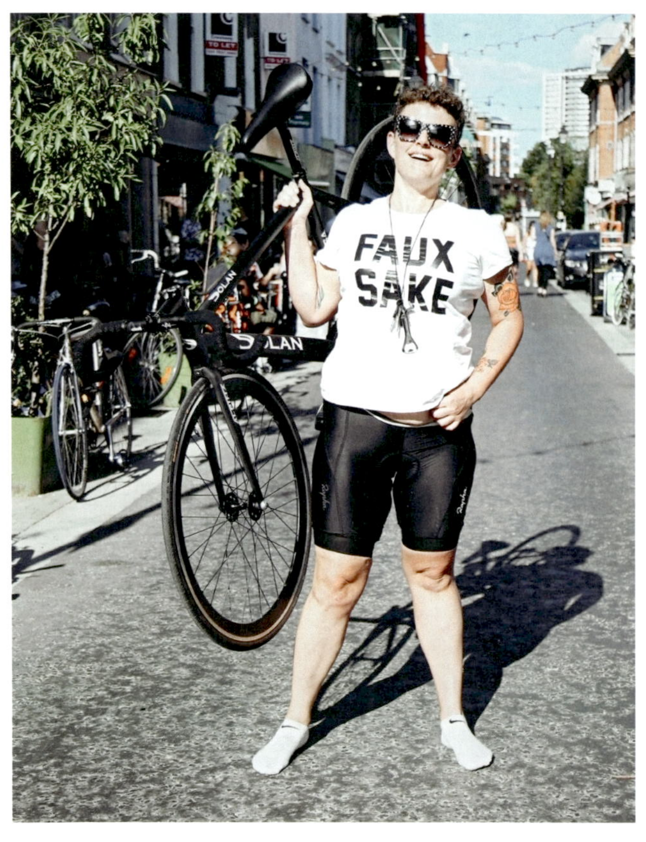


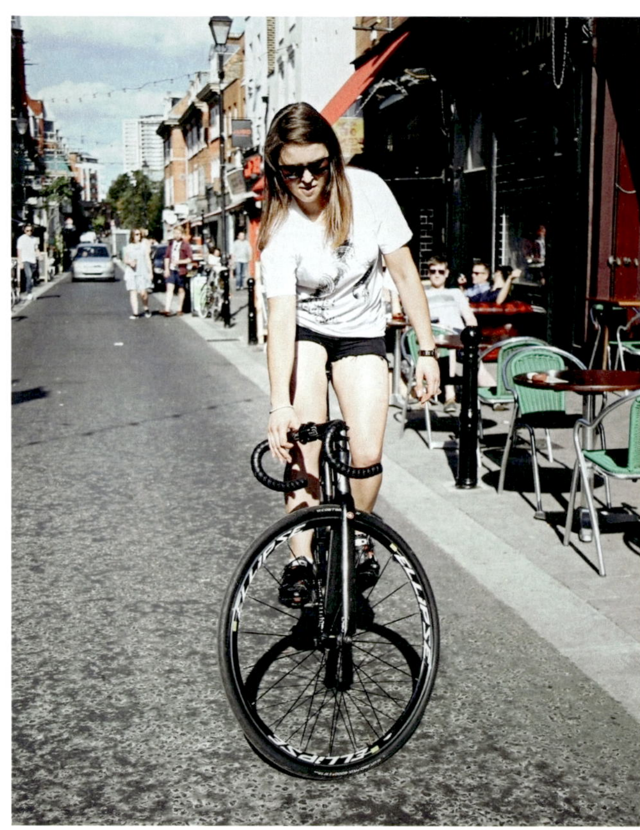

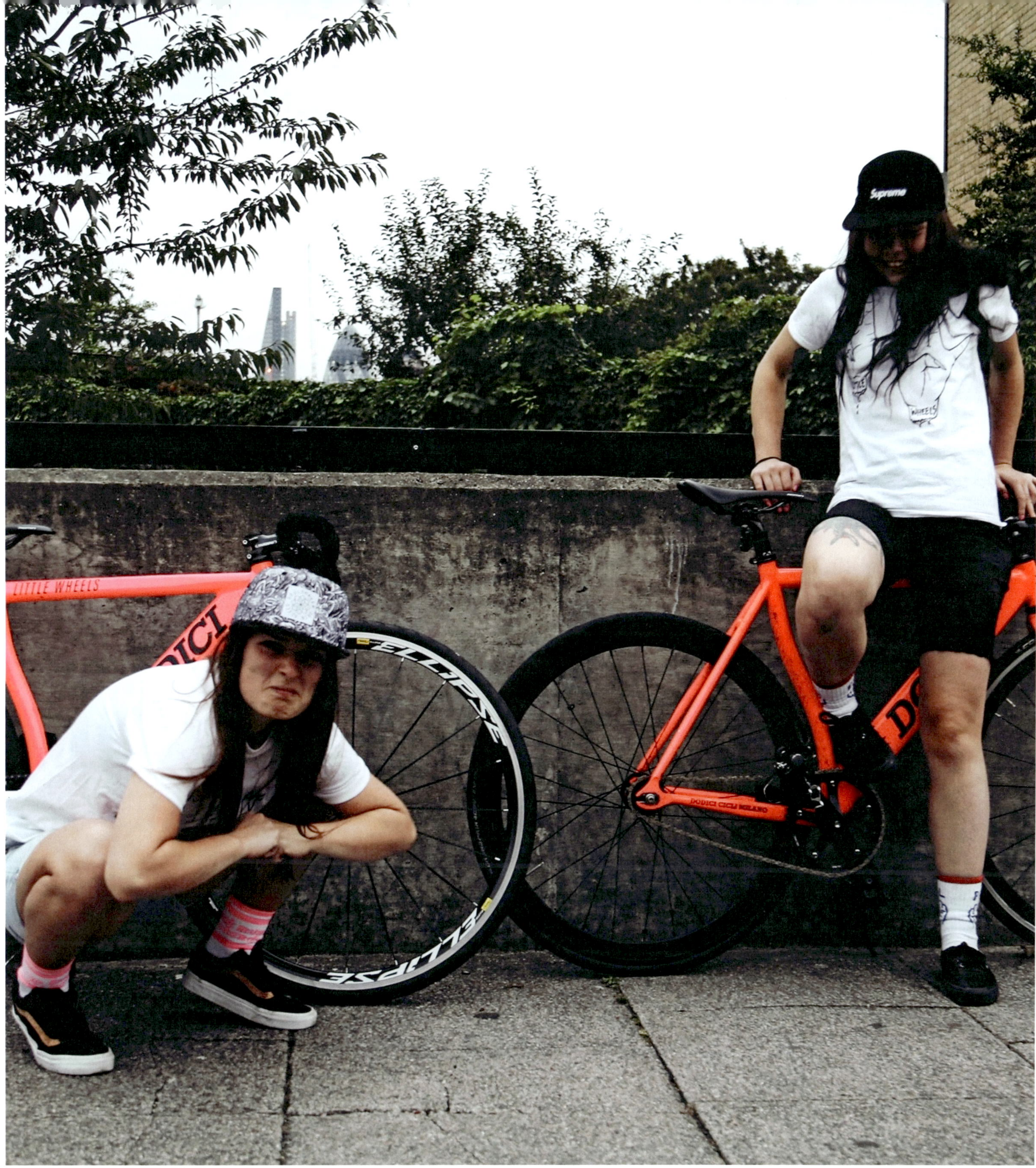


London is a crazy, hectic, and exciting place to live and also to ride. When two northern lasses met at the Herne Hill Velodrome, they discovered a common interest in fixed-gear bikes, fun, fitness, and racing. Looking for a place to share their stories, photos, and reviews, they launched the Little Wheels blog to promote all facets of women's cycling. Through a series of portraits that document the diversity of ladies who ride in London—from the casual commuter to the serious racer and everyone in between, Little Wheels paints an interesting portrait of who they are and why they ride, giving the reader an insight into the women who navigate the metropolis on a daily basis.

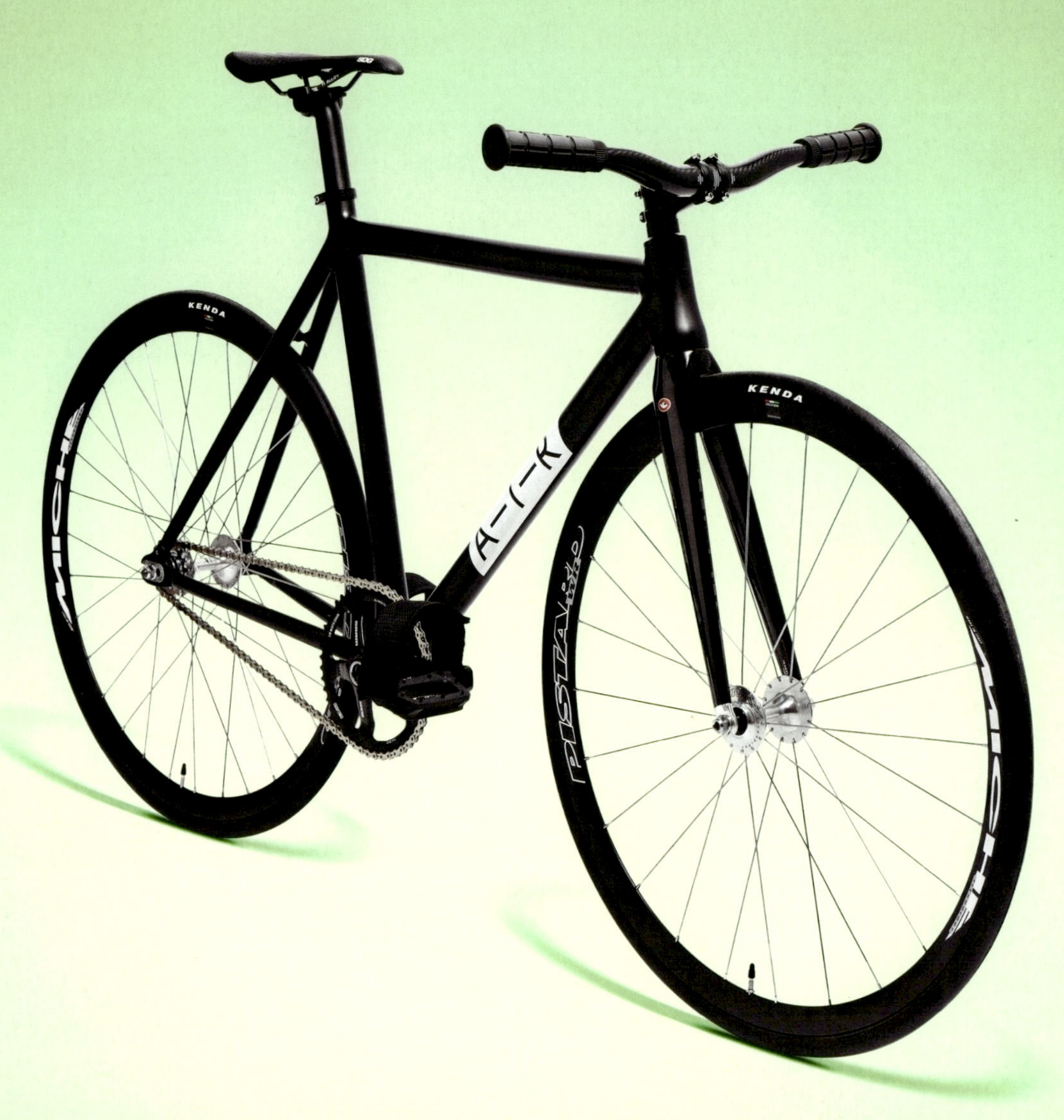


## And The Revolution (A-T-R)

In a neighborhood of Stockholm, Sweden, there exists a shop that is its own little universe, a place where its people evangelize the culture of cycling full time. And The Revolution is a small part of something much greater—a cycling revolution. There, visitors can forget everything they know about how a bike should be sold or purchased, because all bikes are designed, developed, and built in-house at And The Revolution. This system allows riders to add personal details to their bikes and guarantees a consistently high build quality. In the end, each customer's bike is functional and attractive, built to inspire, to last for years, and to withstand hills, wind, sun, and rain.

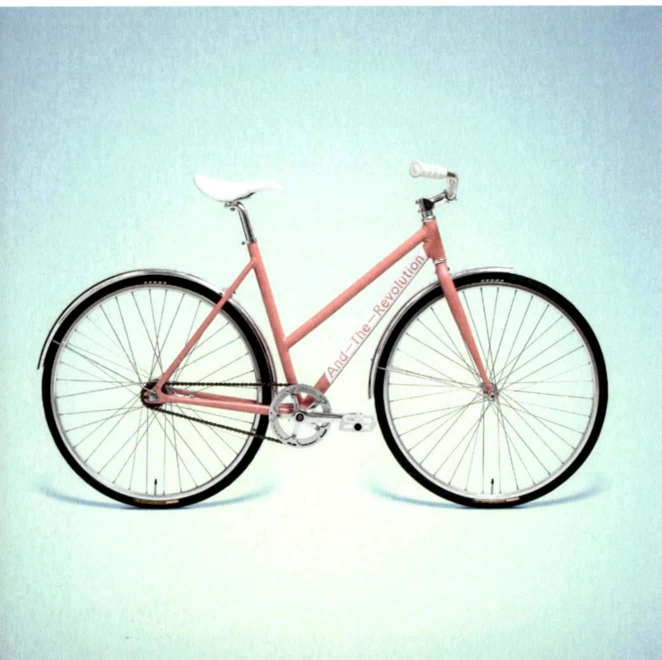


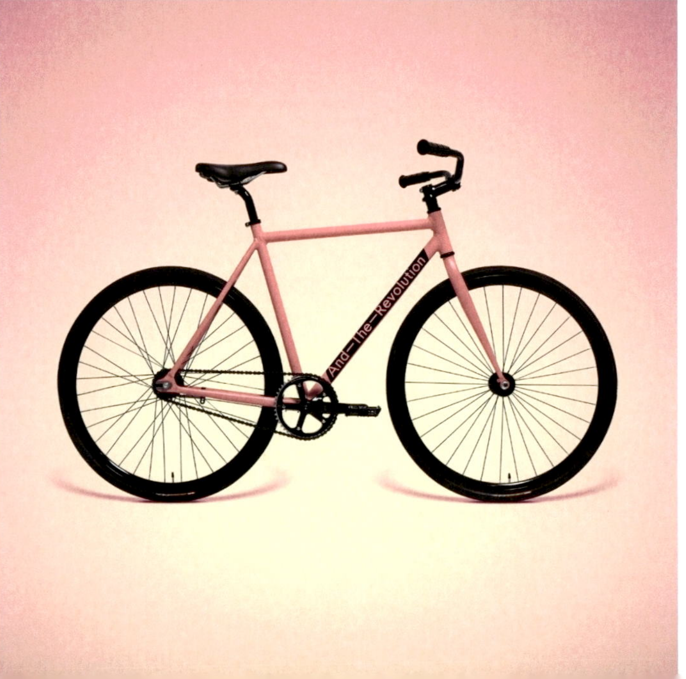

## *Gramercy*

### MARTONE CYCLING COMPANY

The goal at Martone Cycling is simple: bring design, style, and beauty to the cycling world with bikes that are attractive, practical, and easy to use. More than just a means of transportation, Martone bikes are works of art that are as beautiful riding down the street as they are stored in the home. Inspired by the landscape of California, their unusual and daring color palette is unique in the world of biking; the Gramercy is a perfect red.

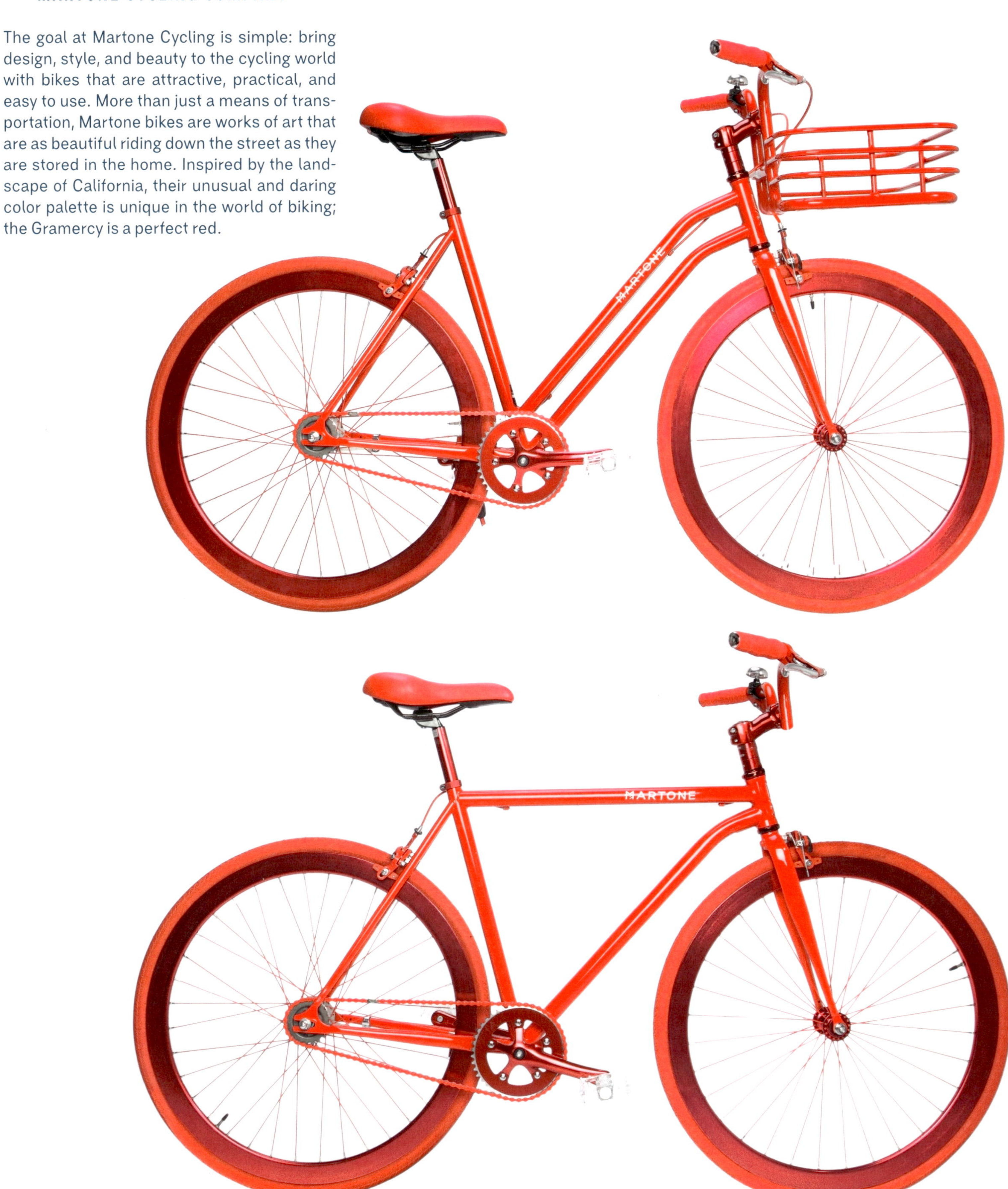

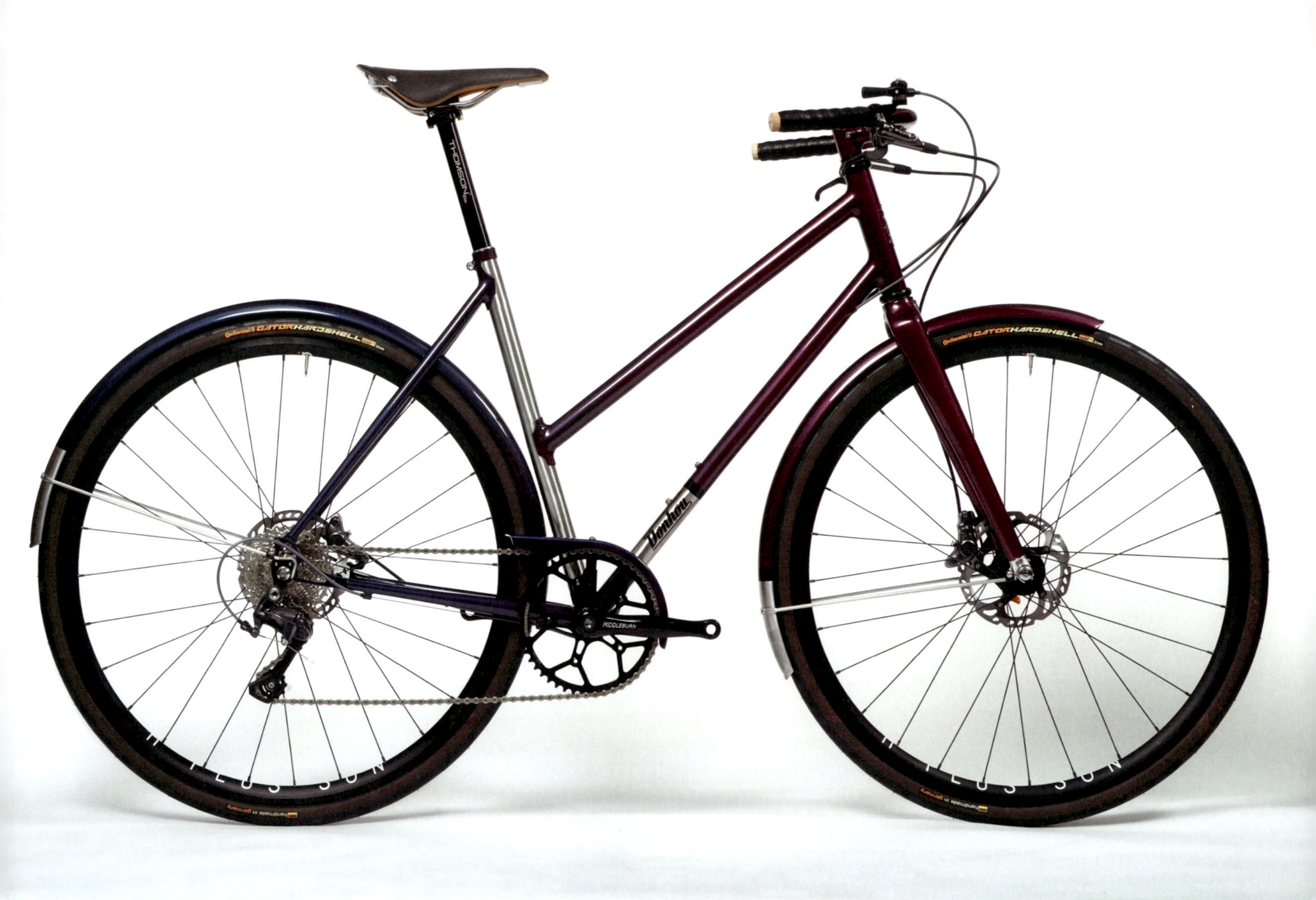

## *Burgeon*

**DONHOU BICYCLES**

The client came to us saying she wanted "a fast town bike that would make guys jealous," says frame builder Thomas Donhou. The Burgeon may have a step-through "girl's" frame and a custom swept-back bar-and-stem construction, but Donhou did his math, or rather, his geometry. Burgeon's frame features top-tube and seat-tube support, employing Reynolds 953 stainless-steel tubing with a hand-carved bi-laminated seat cluster. He compensated for lost stiffness by using oversized tubing, making the bike "as lively and responsive as it looks." And to turn the guys racing green with envy? A Brooks Cambium saddle and bar tape, exposed British-made stainless-steel Middleburn cranks with Shimano Ultegra shifters, and XTR hydraulic braking. "And," Donhou crows, "she can still wear a skirt while riding."

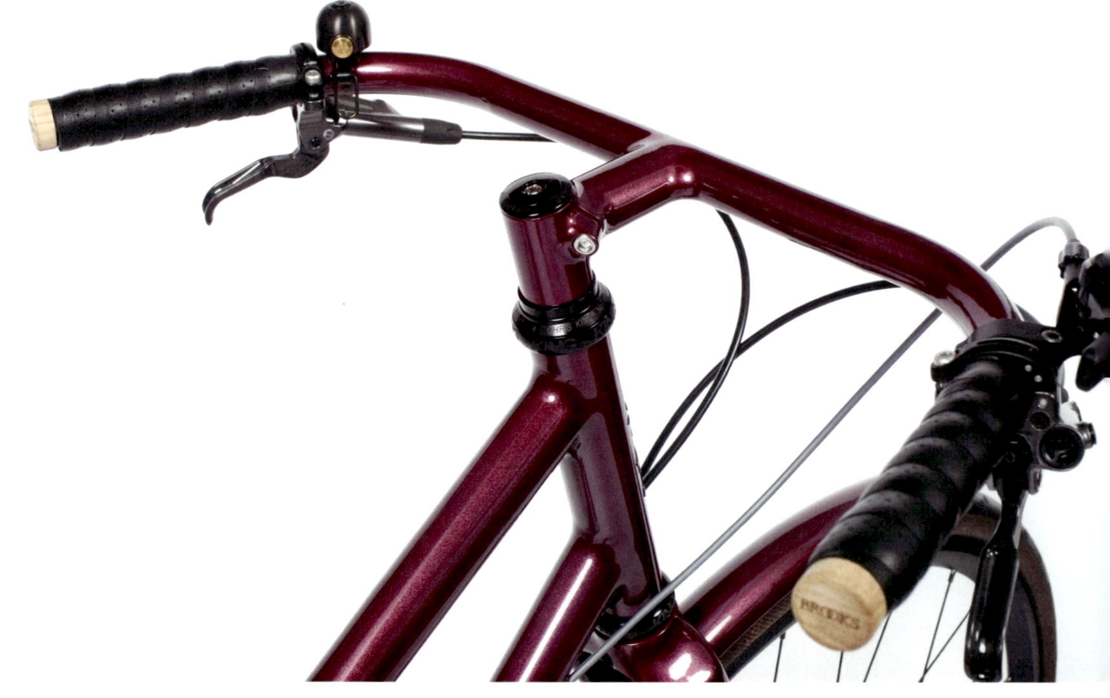

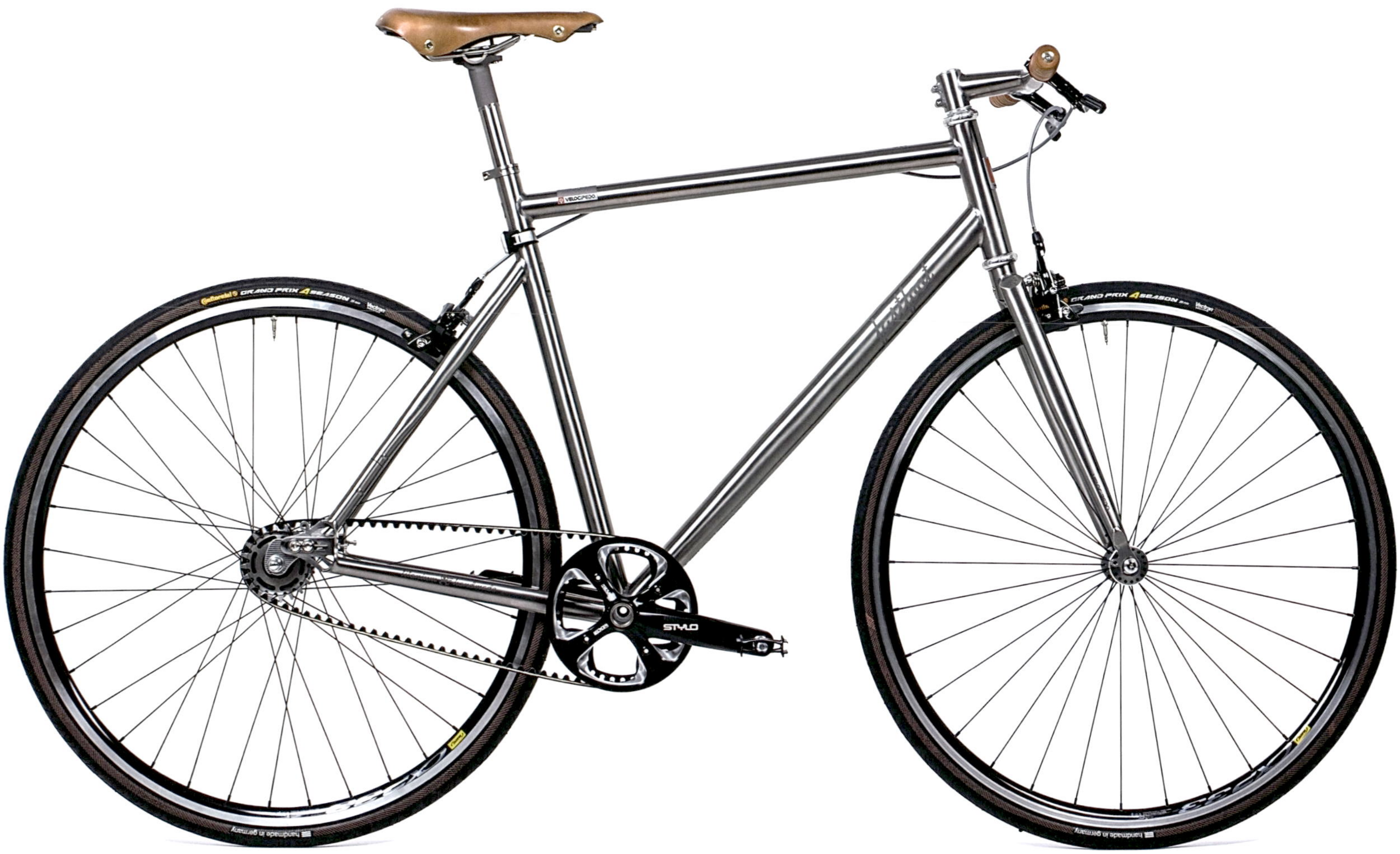

## *FastFoot*

**VELOCIPEDO.**

In a sense, bicyclists are fleet of foot even if they are not technically on foot. The Latin word from which this manufacturer takes its name was one of the earliest names for the bicycle: velocipede, from velox (fast) and pede (foot). VELOCiPEDO.'s obsession with pre-mass-production quality, design, engineering, and craftsmanship is old-school. The brand—launched in 2014 by Matthias Jeschke, a German car mechanic and design-school graduate—labors over every detail to create its "extremely limited" series and 25-year warranties. The nine-kilogram brushed and waxed titanium FastFoot—manufactured in a limited edition of just 25—is Jeschke's city speedster.

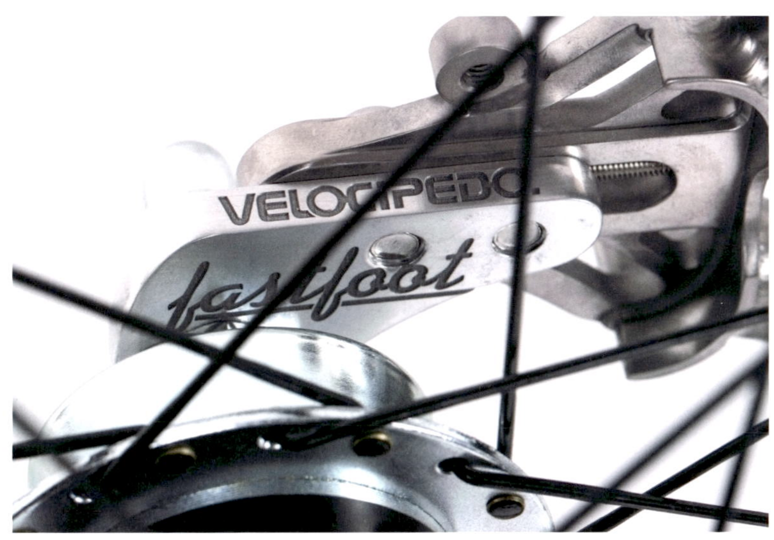


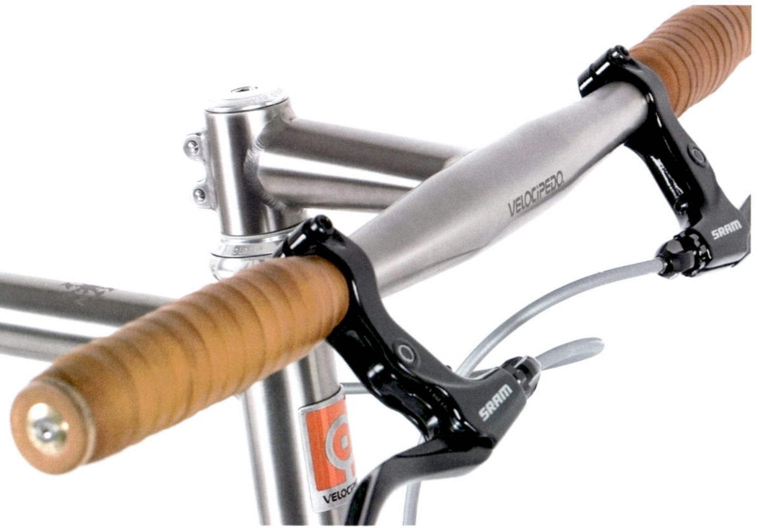

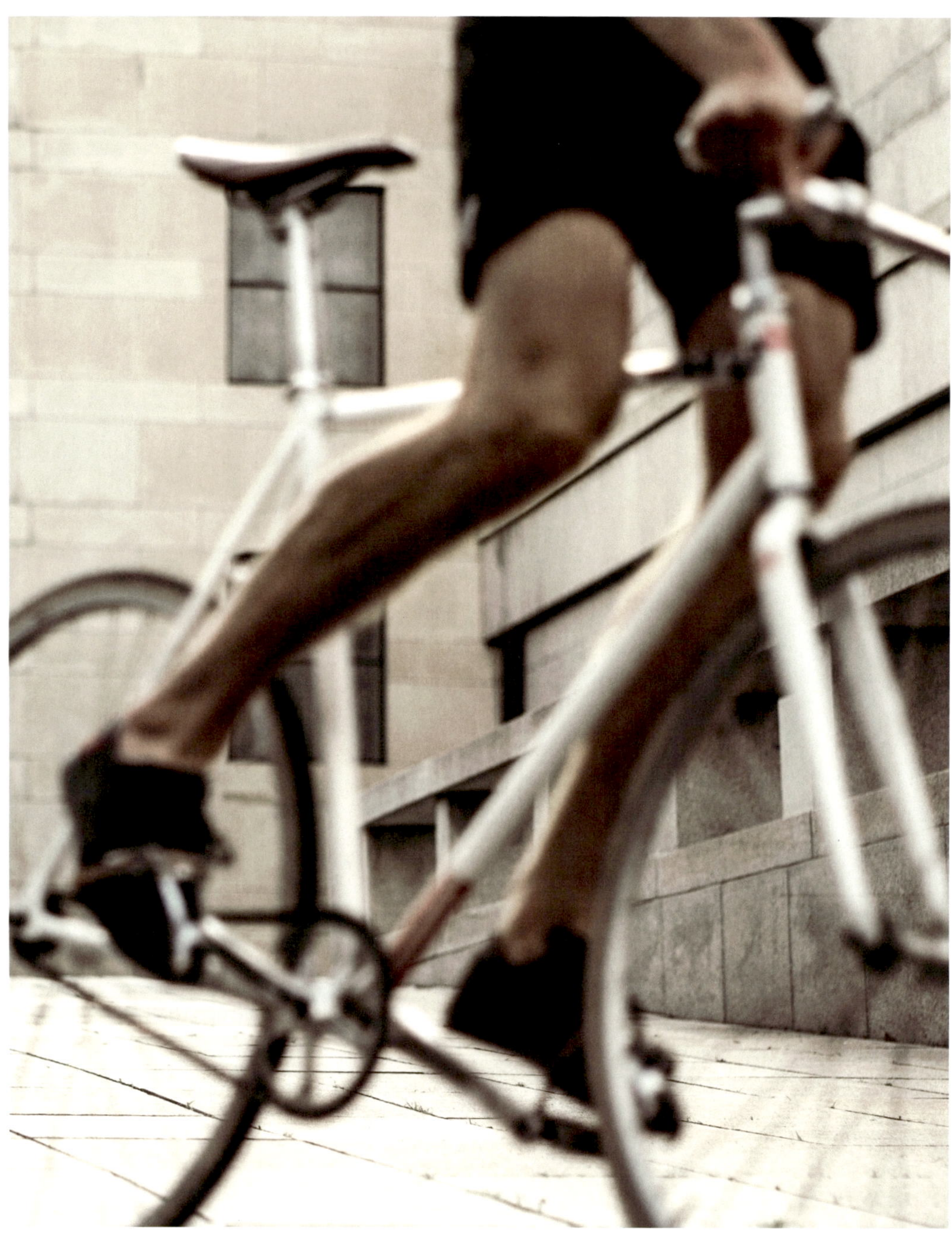

# Segrasegra

Prague-based Segrasegra, which translates to Sister Sister, was founded by two sisters, fashion designers Eliška and Dagmar Mertová. The two began to make high-performance clothes for contemporary cyclists by upcycling unusual materials—bicycle-tire inner tubes or weatherproofing fabrics—that had already experienced previous lives as high-performance cycling products. The women wanted to liberate cyclists from overdesigned, under-sophisticated, and onerously multihued sportswear. Their own garments now draw cycling apparel closer to urban street fashion, especially because the boutique line serves the needs of commuters with ready-to-wear bicycle-to-office wearables. Their goal is to synthesize avant-garde design elements with inventive organic materials that preserve the functionality needed for biking while embodying a spirit of elegance and chicness.

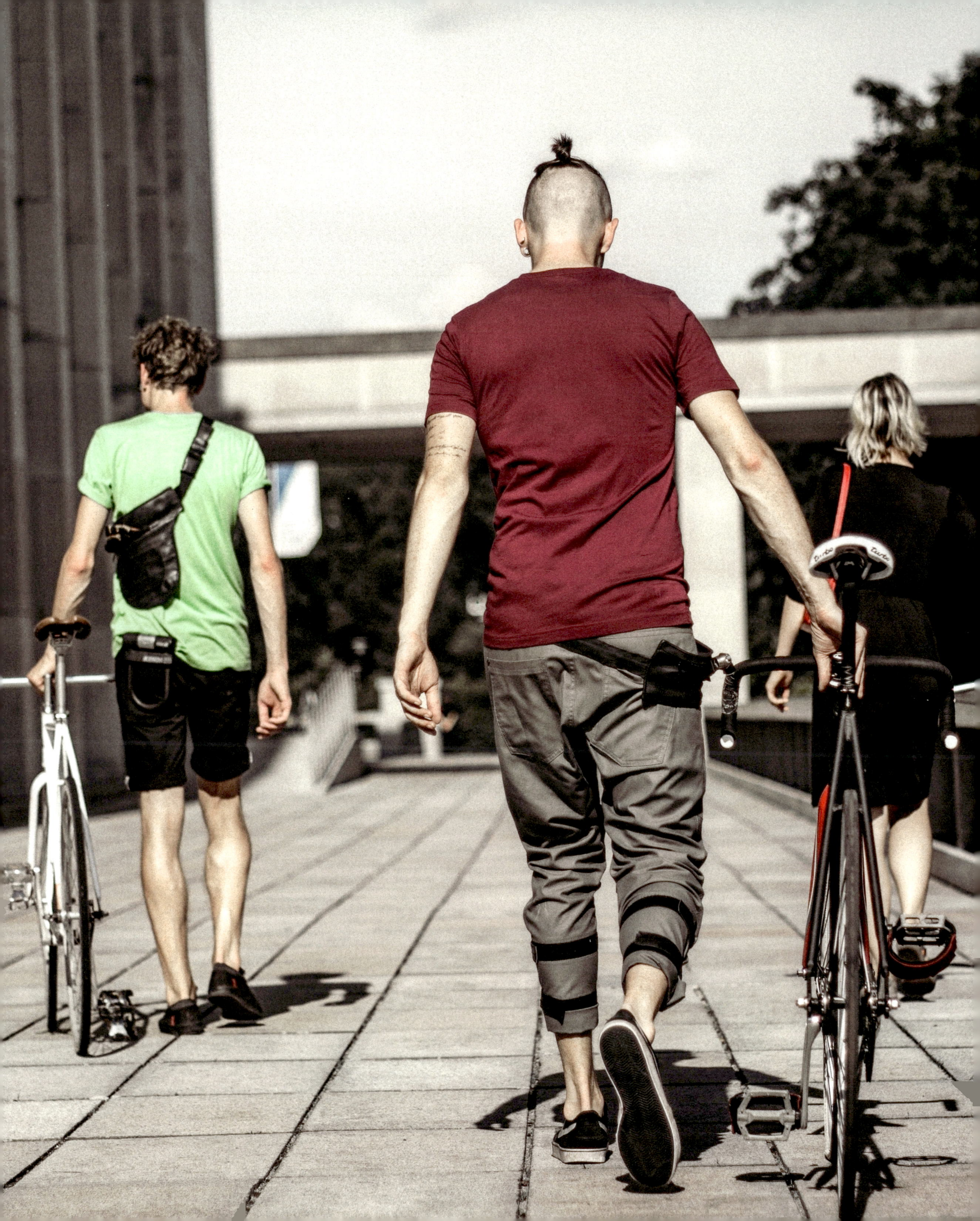

# Parts & tools

Components and parts are being redeemed, reformed, and deformed by the most forward-thinking builders today. Tools have become everything from art pieces on display in white-box galleries to toys rolled up in tooled leather that are so refined and handsome that it's almost—but not quite—a shame to get them dirty. You may start wanting to fix your bike as much as ride it.

## Nutter Cycle Multi Tool

**FULL WINDSOR**

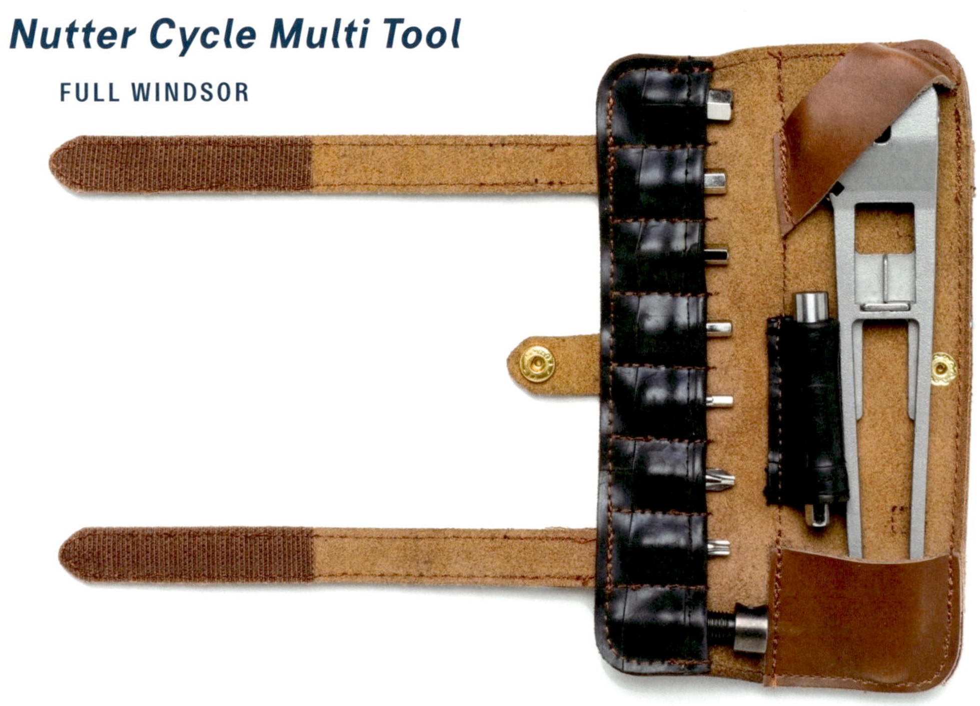

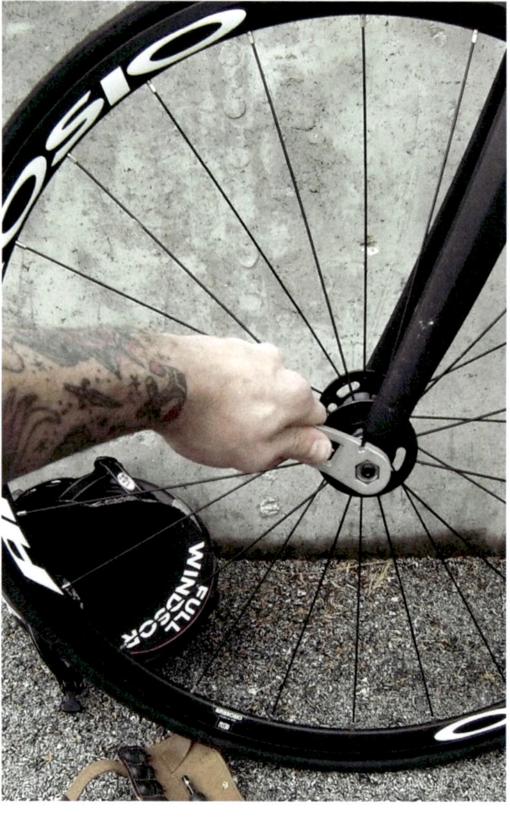


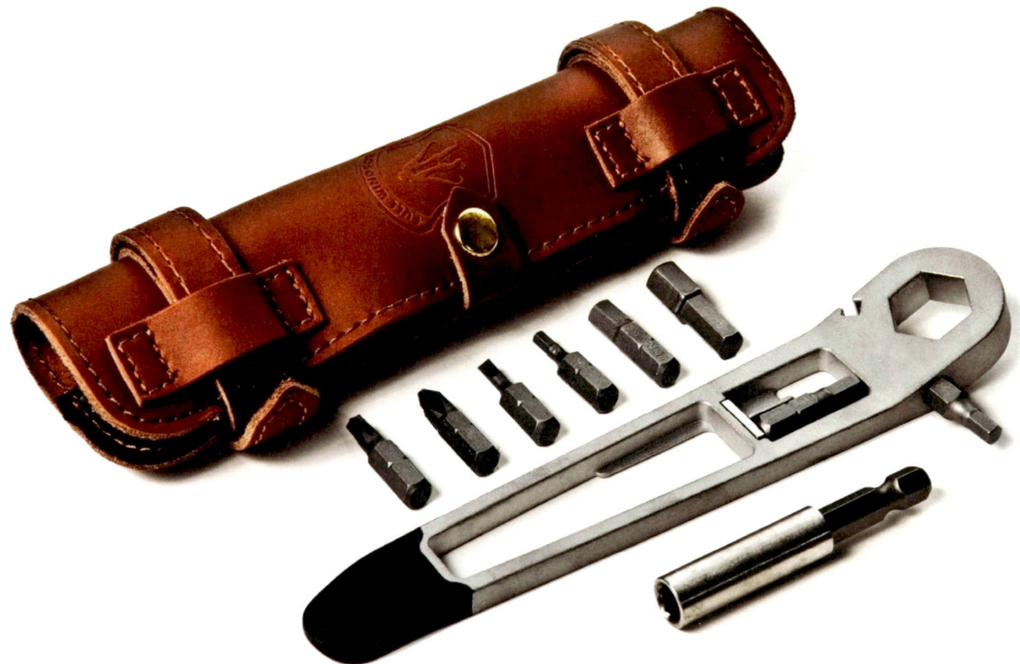

You might say everyone at Full Windsor is a bike nut. This cycle-accessory design company is passionate about riding bikes, designing innovative bike products, riding more bikes, and ensuring that every customer is fully satisfied. It is their innovation, hard work, and mucking around on bikes that lead to the invention of the Nutter, an all-in-one tool that can fix most common bike headaches. It was designed to combine all the tools needed when out on a ride, and its unique handle gives it more leverage than other multi tools. Weighing just 3.9 ounces (110 grams), the Nutter features a nylon tire lever, 15-millimeter box-head spanner, spoke key, multiple hex tool bits, Phillips- and flat-head screwdrivers, a T25 torx bit, a magnetic tool-bit extender, and a bottle opener.

## Seegras Steering Bar

SEEGRAS

Handlebars with no grips, no tape, no knobs? Seegras has made them a reality by completely reinventing the handlebar. Their whole new take on this basic component includes the introduction of 814 small holes on each bar end for a perfect grip and continuous airflow. Made of anodized aluminum, each Seegras handlebar is unique—with a serial number to prove it—and available only in select shops.

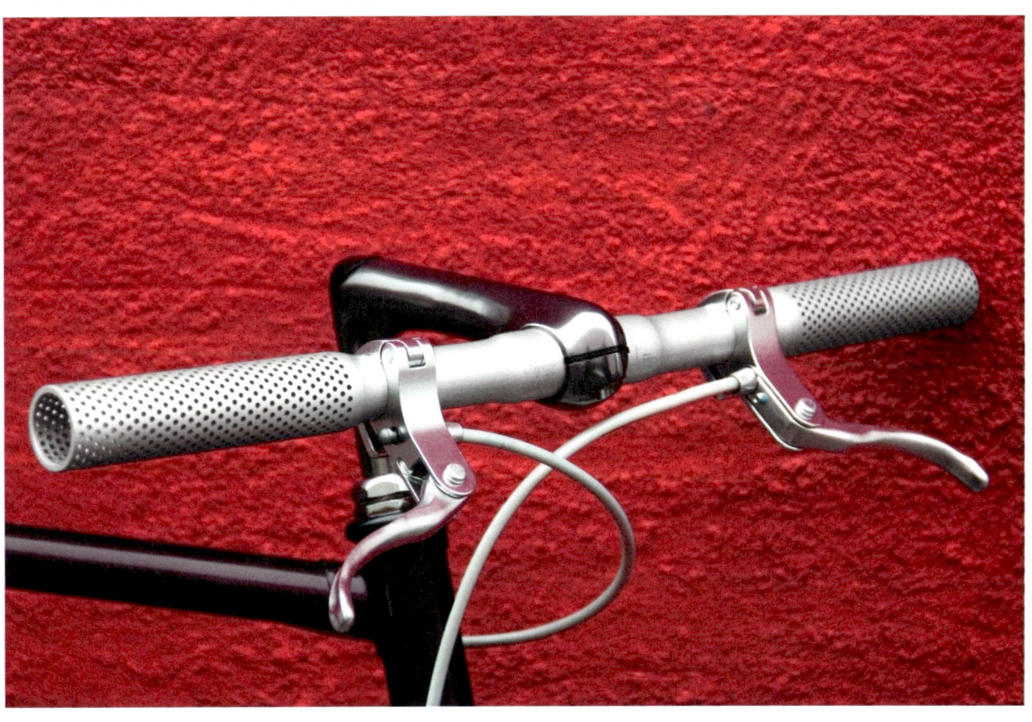

## Blockhead Stem IB

CW&T

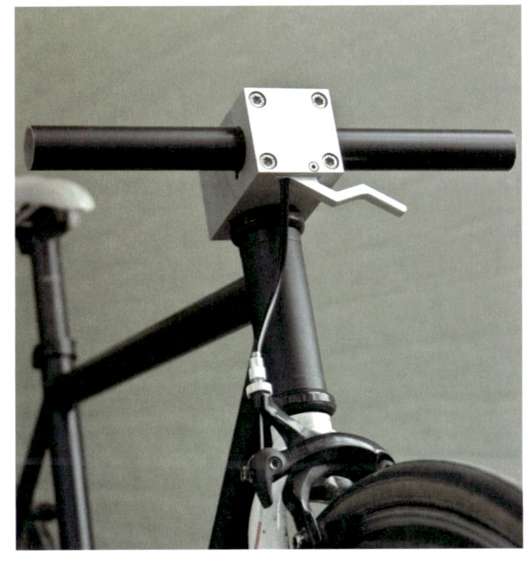

Sometimes it's nice to ride a fixie with a front brake. But brake levers tend to be massive, take up a lot of handlebar space, and have levers that are much longer than necessary. CW&T found a solution to the problem: make the lever part of the stem. For those riders who despise ugly, massive brake levers, this may be the answer. The Blockhead Stem IB, a blockhead stem with an integrated brake lever, tucks the lever neatly into the stem and is just long enough for two fingers. Designed to be used with a front brake so that the cable can be cut short and straight, the Blockhead Stem IB eliminates friction within the brake-cable housing. The stem's design is licensed under a Creative Commons Attribution-Non-Commercial-ShareAlike 3.0 license.

## Love Lever

PAUL

Based out of an old Texaco warehouse in Chico, California, Paul Component Engineering has been a staple of the bicycle community for over 25 years, working hard to produce the best parts available, one at a time. Their Love Lever is a lightweight, long-pull brake lever designed for two- or three-finger operation and easy adjustment, balancing comfort and weight without feeling flimsy. Compatible with all long-pull cable-operated brakes, these levers are recommended for use with their Motolite brakes, but they will work well paired with any v-brake or mechanical disc brake, such as the Klamper. These levers are machined in-house to exacting specifications. The pivots feature a lightweight hollow pin made of stainless steel and a large bearing surface; precise machining reduces play and allows the lever to swing smoothly. Love Levers are perennial bestsellers because of their action and ergonomics.

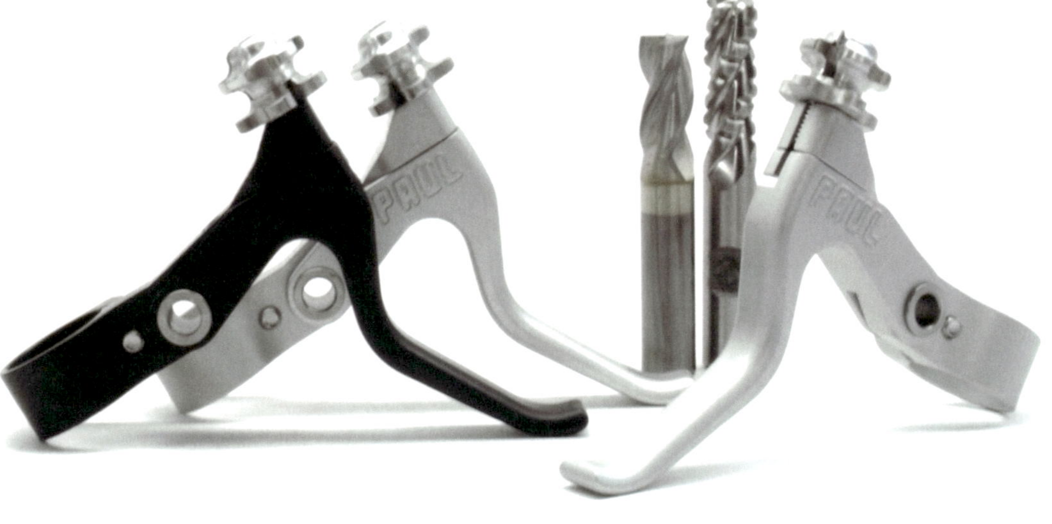

# Custom paint

Today, there are bikes painted by graffiti artists and bikes carved by sculptors. Even the most tech-oriented workshops are playing with art finishes, scribbling the lyrics of obscure songs by famous people about bikes on their frames, illustrating the surfaces of disc wheels, and mixing-and-matching thousands of colors. Online. Why not make your bike "bespoke"? It can speak for you, and of you.

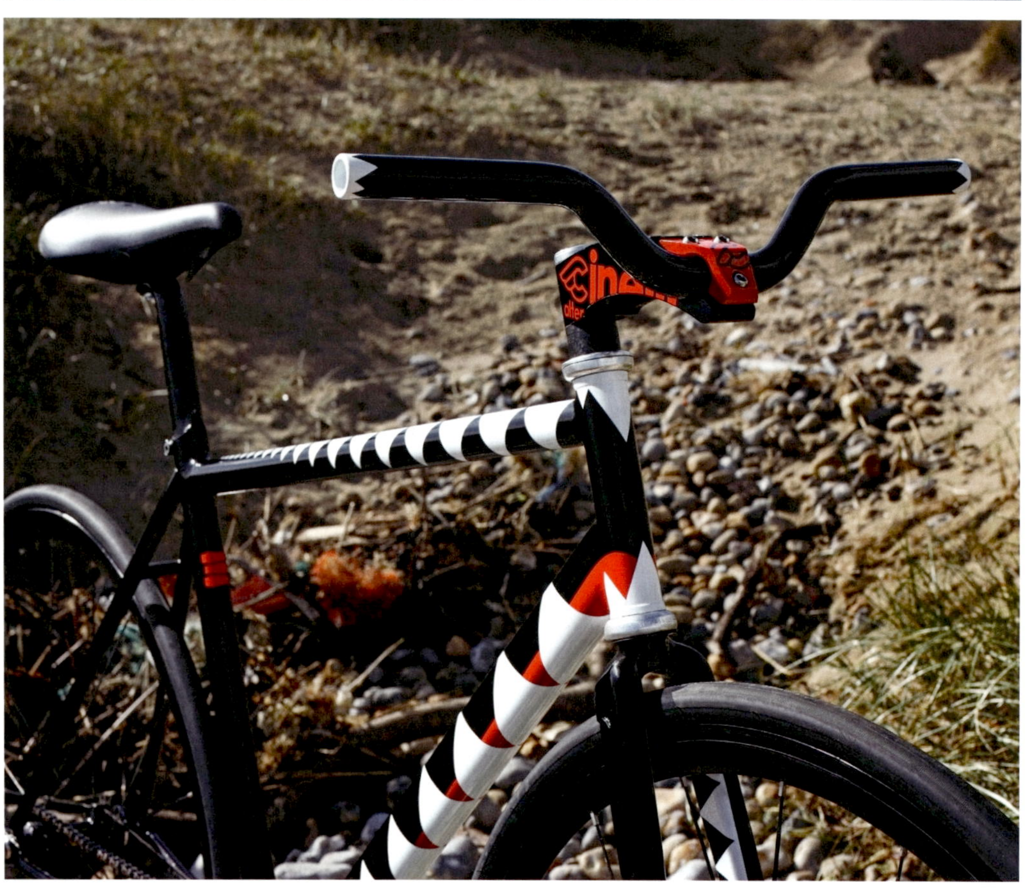

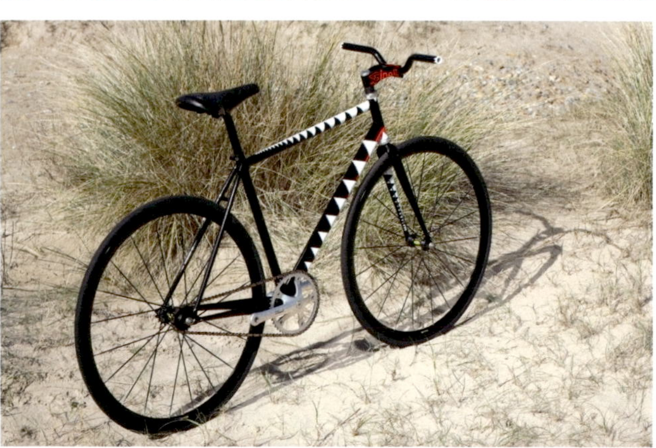

## Shark Bite

**DEATH SPRAY CUSTOM**

Inspired by the memorable shark-mouth nose art on old fighter planes, like those piloted by the Flying Tigers, the Bite project by London-based Death Spray Custom consists of three pieces, including a Racelite track bike.

## City CX Machine V2

**BEN FALCON PAINT**

With a keen eye for composition and texture, Ben Falcon strives to create a unique aesthetic for the beautiful objects we ride. As a professional painter, Falcon perfected his skills at Seven Cycles, the leading purveyors of customization. He went on to establish a state-of-the-art wet-paint department for Chris King, and currently devotes his talents to the Brooklyn-based Horse Cycles Paint Shop. Here the mission is to provide the cycling community with the utmost quality and precise finishes to adorn each customer's ride, be it a motorcycle, helmet, or custom frameset. When Cole Bennett approached Ben Falcon Paint, he wanted a high-concept paint job for his newly built CX frame to mark the launch of his new brand.

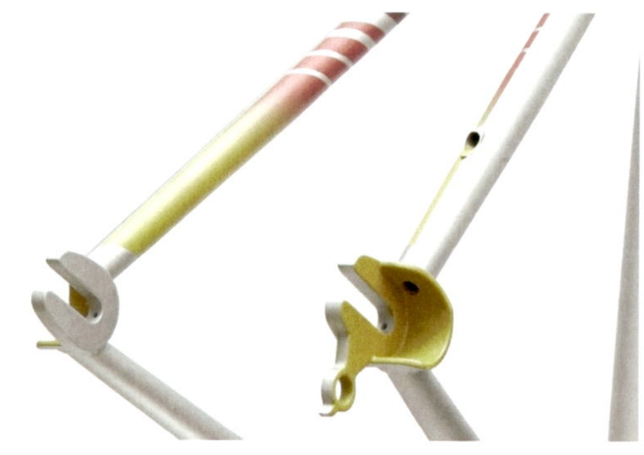

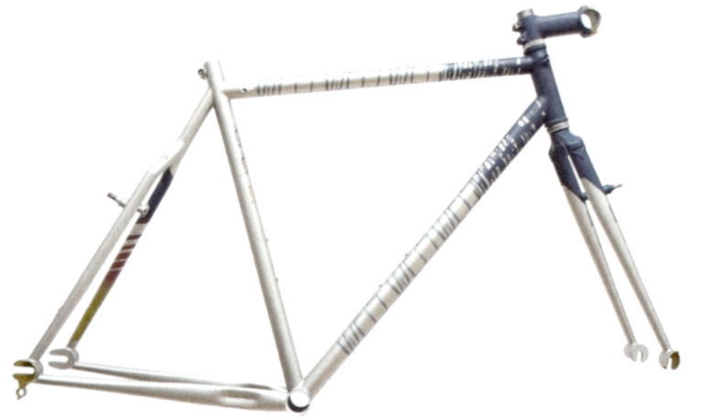

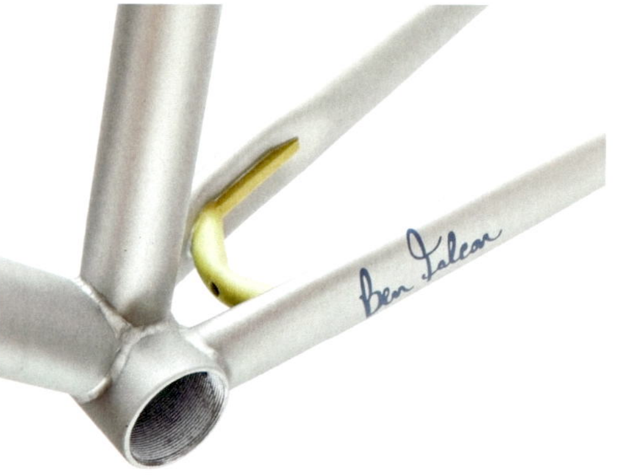

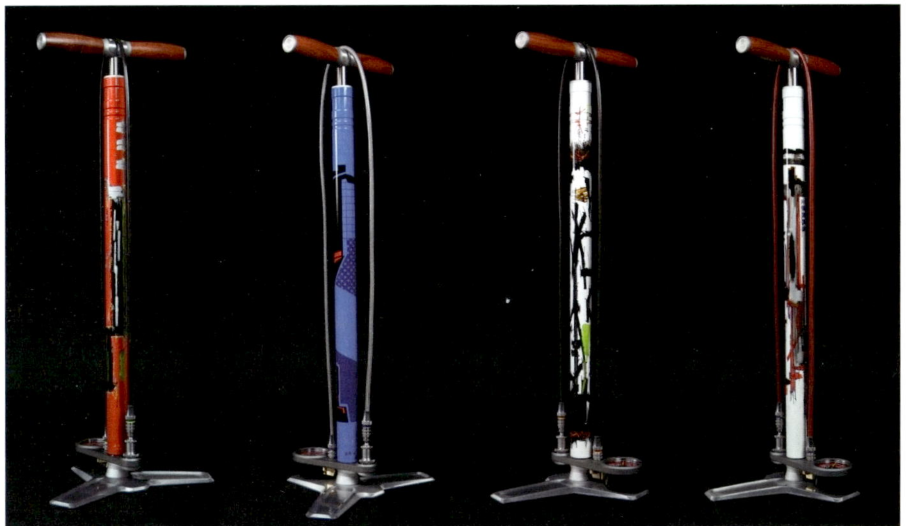

## Pegoretti Pumps

**SILCA**

Dario Pegoretti, one of the world's best-known builders, is also one of its most famous bicycle artists. For their first artist-edition pumps, SILCA asked Pegoretti to paint Ciavete artwork on their handmade SuperPista Ultimate pump. Each pump painted by Pegoretti is created completely by hand; no two are exactly alike. Some correspond to current themes that Pegoretti is working on with his own bicycles and others are one-off concepts, created spontaneously as he paints. These one-off ideas, known as Ciavete, truly must be seen to be understood and appreciated.

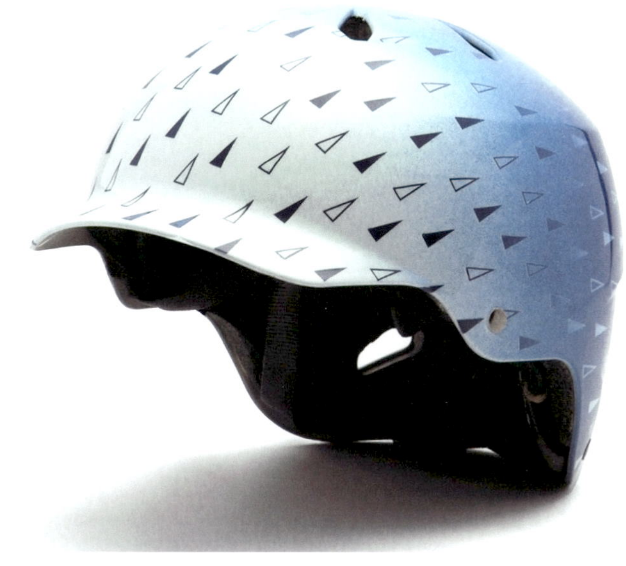

## Bern Bicycle Helmet

**BEN FALCON PAINT**

The Bern bicycle helmet was created as concept work by Ben Falcon Paint and Horse Cycles Paint for *Details*.

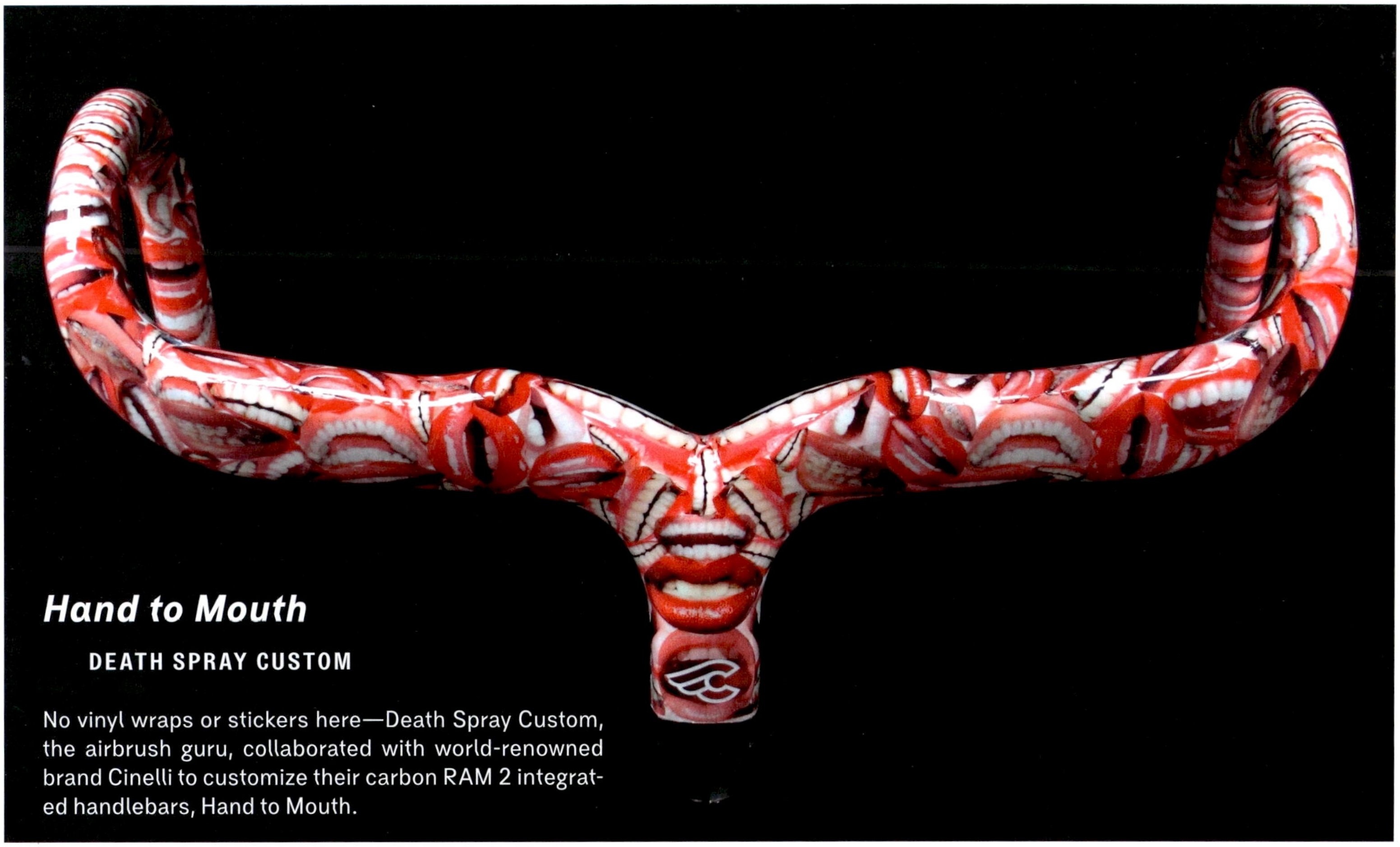

## Hand to Mouth

**DEATH SPRAY CUSTOM**

No vinyl wraps or stickers here—Death Spray Custom, the airbrush guru, collaborated with world-renowned brand Cinelli to customize their carbon RAM 2 integrated handlebars, Hand to Mouth.

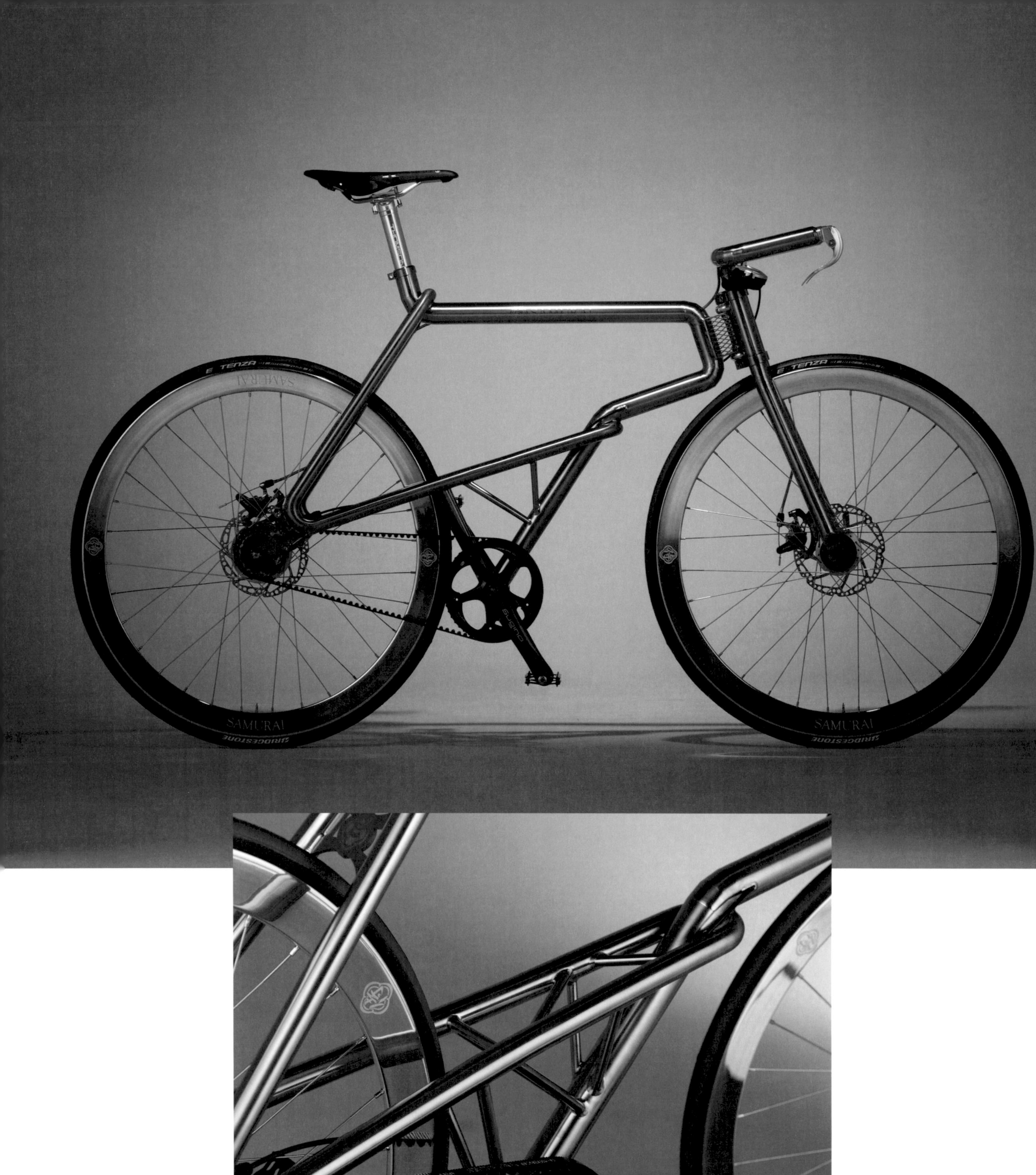

E TENZA
E TENZA
SAMURAI
SAMURAI

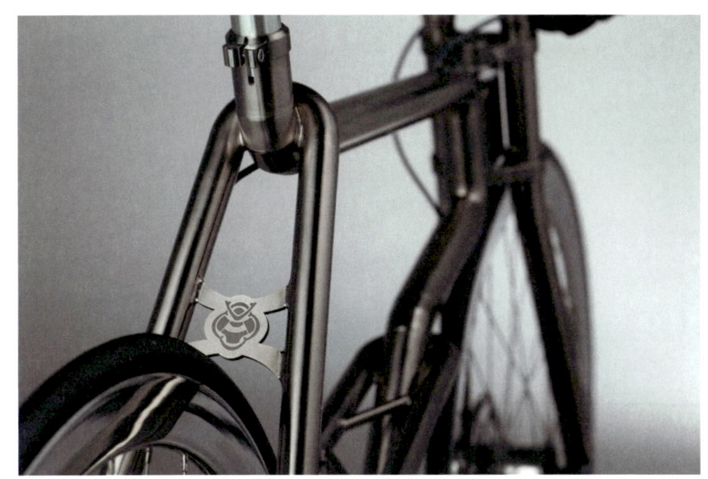

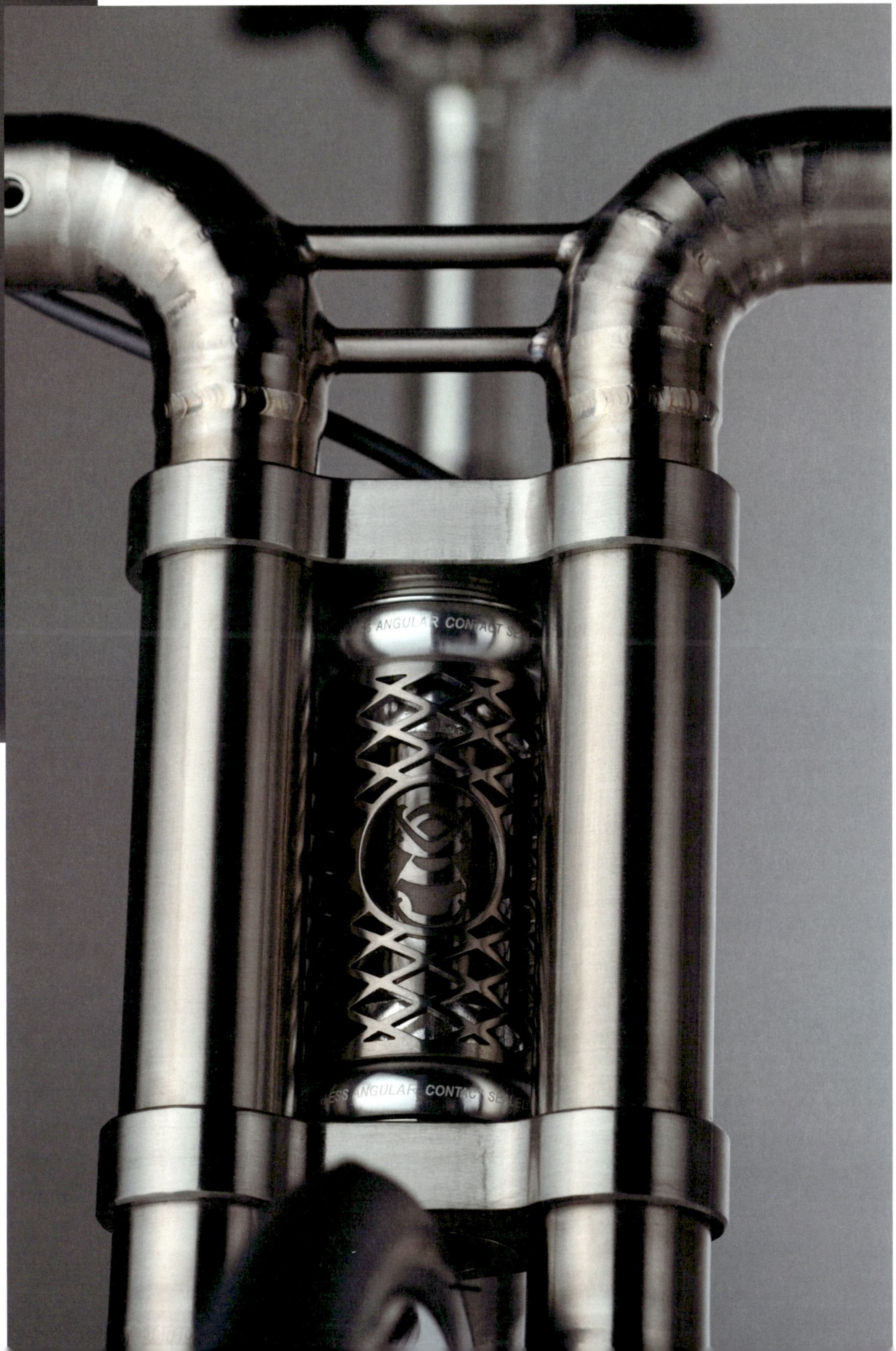

# Samurai

**KAZUSHIGE MIYAKE**

Ti-3A1-2.5V: that's the chemical make-up of the supple titanium alloy used to shape the frame of Kazushige Miyake's Kyoto-made Samurai. The bike is the product of embracing Japanese tradition, masterful craft skills, and devoted artisanry—and then fusing them with a material that combines durability, lightness, and pliability. Special titanium alloys were used to sculpt the frame, handlebars, front fork, and seatpost. Without the seat tube, the Samurai recalls the shape of the bows carried by the Japanese warriors who give the bike its name. The curved section of the frame also features a welded structure consisting of fan-shaped segments that reference sturdy but artful samurai armor.

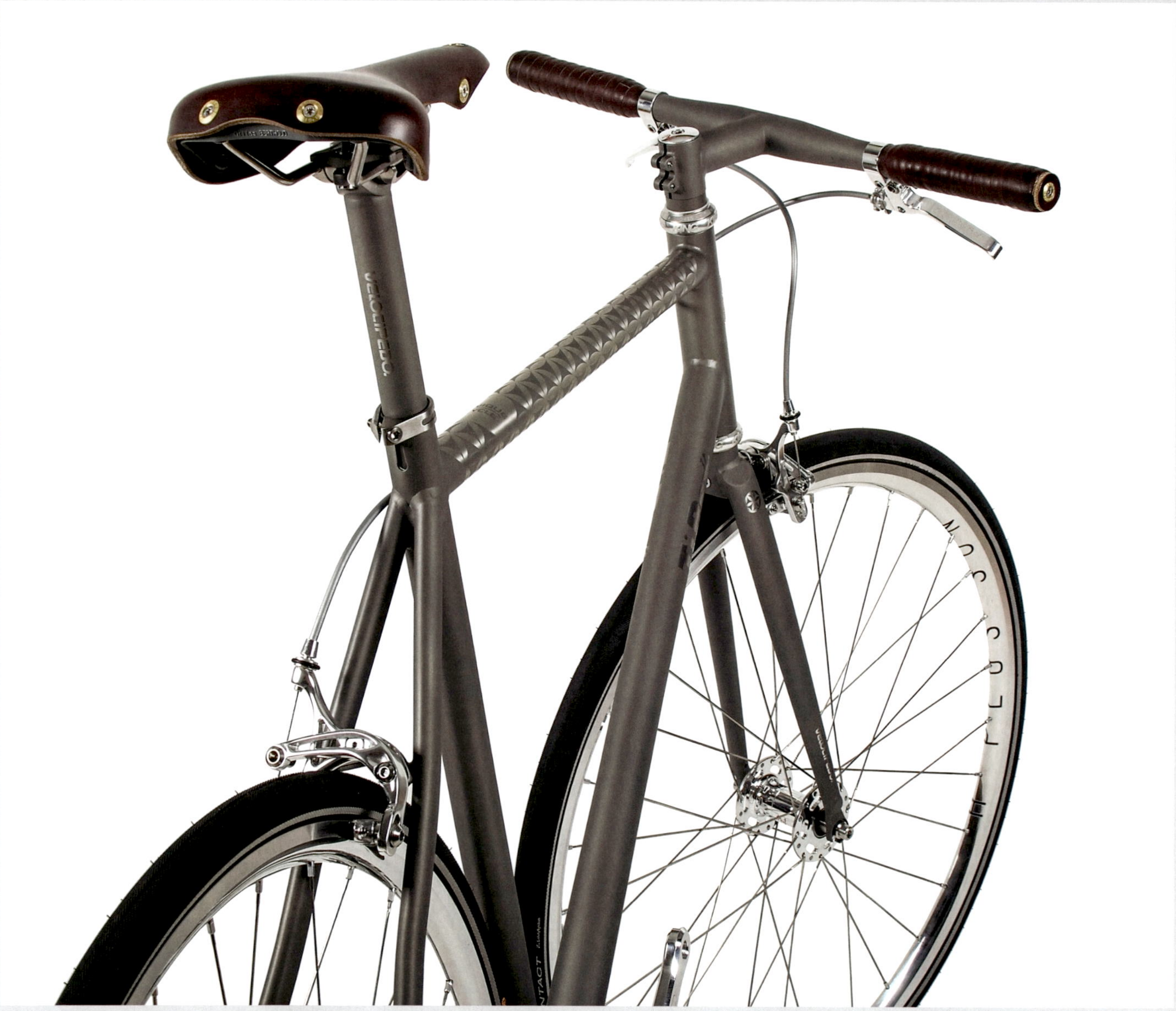

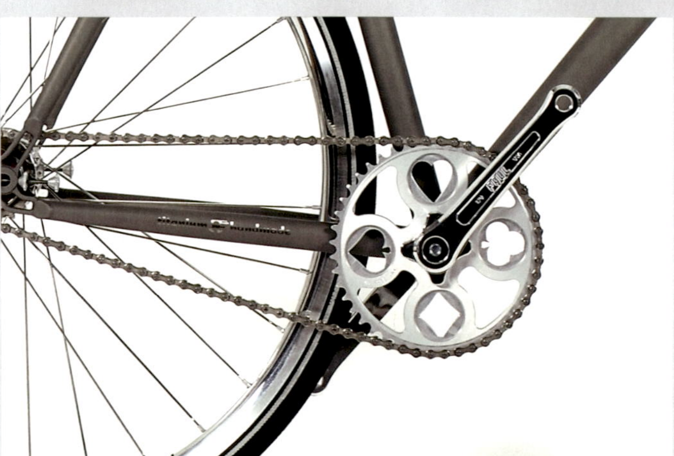

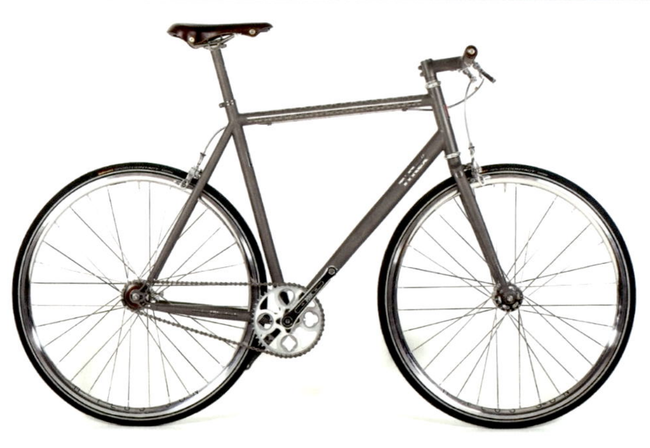

## *TiRex*

**VELOCIPEDO.**

The TiRex, a one-off bicycle and the king of the titanium dinosaurs, is designed to be both road royalty and as fierce as its namesake. The size-58 frame is sandblasted and sleek so that, after it eats up city streets, it will still look pretty enough for the living room. In spite of its asphalt appetites, the TiRex weighs in at a trim 7.5 kilograms and comes with wheels handmade by Komponentix in Berlin, reflective sidewall tires, and a Chris King headset. Although the logo is always discreet, it is obvious that designer Matthias Jeschke has a love of form and composition that drives him to spend hours designing patterns and typefaces.

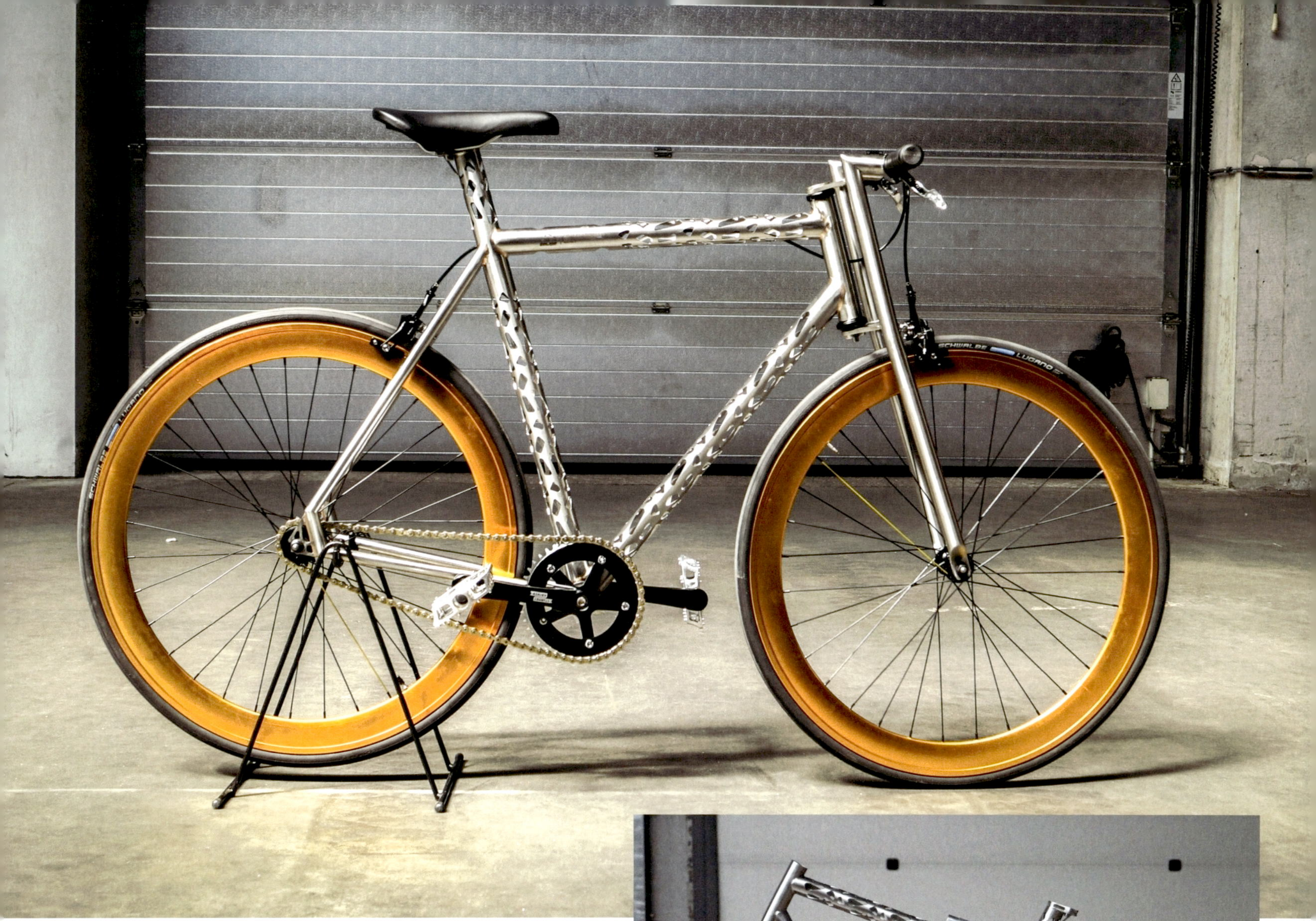

## *Erembald*

### ELEVENTWENTYSEVEN

Named for a distinguished family involved in the historical murder of an important Bruges leader, the aggressive-looking Erembald laser-cut bicycle represents a Belgian farewell to mass production and an effort to bring micro-manufacturing back to a high-wage country. Tobias Knockaert created the bicycle for ElevenTwenty-Seven using a laser tube-cutting machine during an internship for his master's thesis. He developed laser-cut snap connections and a parametric design to enhance flexibility and speed throughout the manufacturing process, making every bike bespoke without adding costs or requiring the reorganization of machinery. Each bicycle begins life as a jigsaw puzzle snapped together and welded so that the saddle and handlebars can be fixed according to a rider's personal measurements, eliminating the need for a stem and seatpost. With its over-dimensioned tubes, the Erembald is heavier (12 kilograms, or 26.5 pounds) than similar bikes, but it is also about ten times stiffer and five times stronger.

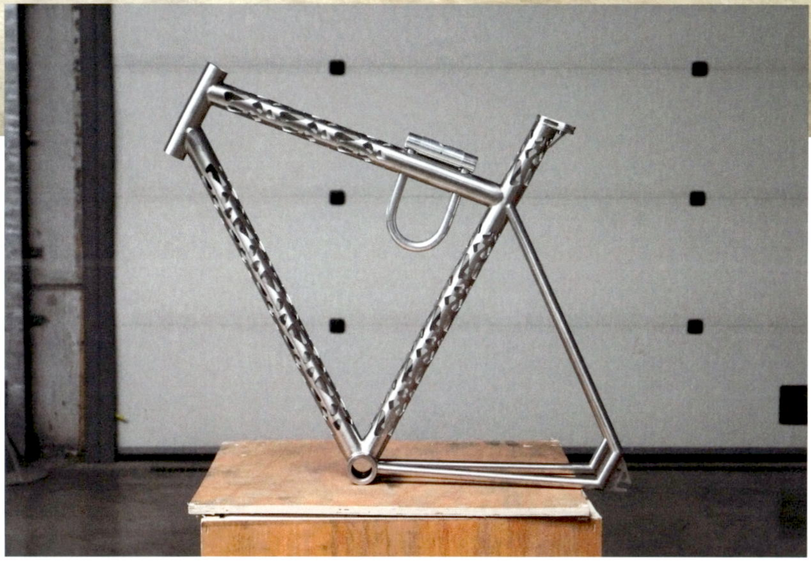

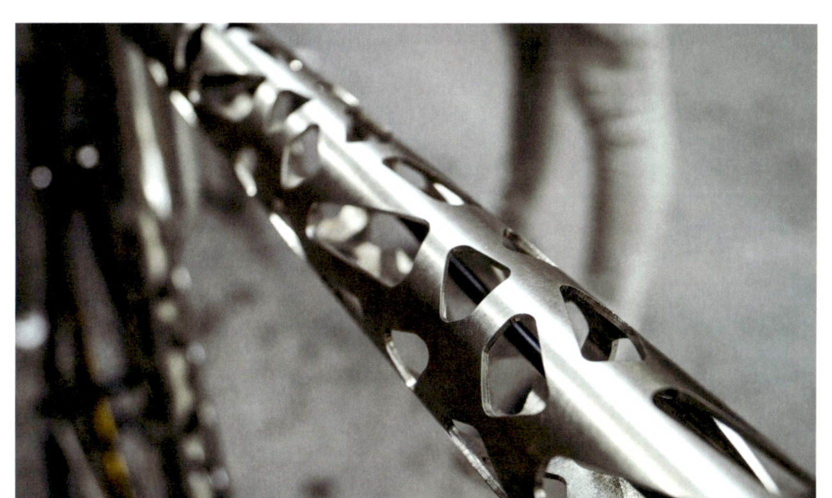

# Indrek Narusk & Velonia Bicycles' VIKS

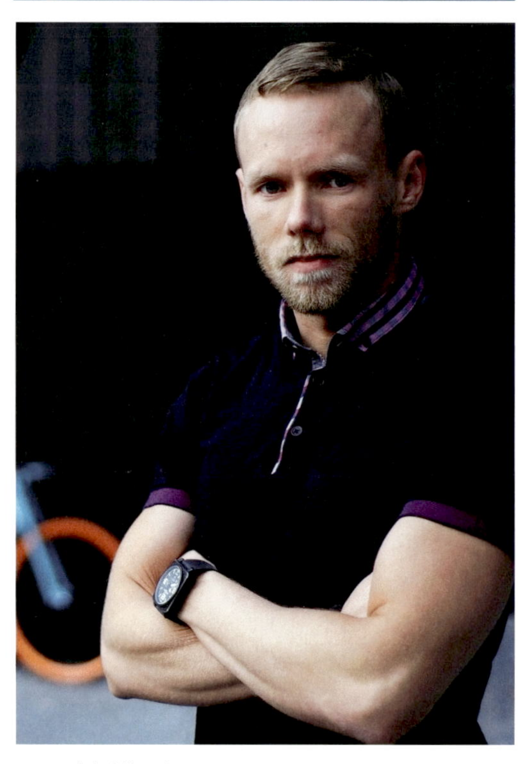

Indrek Narusk, creator, co-owner, designer, and engineer of Velonia Bicycles

When I was a kid, I used to pull everything apart to see what's inside.

Indrek Narusk, creator, co-owner, designer, and engineer of Tallinn-based Velonia Bicycles, recalls "I never wanted to be an astronaut or a movie star. From the time I got my first mountain bike, I just dreamed about working in the bicycle industry." Narusk wrote an undergraduate thesis about the full-suspension mountain-bike frame and launched GrabCAD, an engineering-services site that became the world's biggest, but by 2012, he had indeed begun working in the bicycle industry. And he started with Velonia and the VIKS.

For bikes with muscular bodies, it doesn't get much more barely-there than the VIKS. A showcase "100 percent urban" bike, it is both hard and curvaceous and distinct mostly for what it doesn't have: a seat tube. Its doubled-up frame—two radiused, parallel tubes paired with supernarrow, superflat handlebars—makes the VIKS the ultimate in "nothing more, nothing less" design. At the core of the bike, where the sense of connection, strength, and structure usually resides, the VIKS voluptuously frames an unusual amount of completely empty urban air.

If it looks as if this takes a certain sleight of hand, it's because it does. It takes two days to cut, bend, TIG weld, and sand the most basic VIKS frameset, which consists of 59 steel parts and requires the fabrication of custom jigs, and another full day to sandblast and finish it—about the same amount of time it takes to hand-build four standard-geometry frames.

That VIKS is special is evident in the number of collaborations it has sparked. Velonia has made a midnight-blue frame popping with scarlet rims for fashion designer Paul Smith. It partnered with Netherlands-based Velowland to create a solid-steel café racer that looks like bent wood thanks to a wood-grain veneering technique typical in the renovation of historical buildings. The VIKS Raw, built with London design collective Artisan Werks, goes in the absolute opposite direction, leaving the steel frame and its scorched weld seams pornographically naked.

While the commuter bike world has boomed, the unusual designs by Narusk, who teaches frame building at the Estonian Academy of Arts, remain thrillingly extreme. The bike world has long been one not just of athleticism, personal transportation, and adventure, but also of self-expression. Today, among a wildly diverse range of riders, self-expression, and therefore the VIKS, is at a premium. "There are not many companies making different things like we do, but there is a real market for something different out there," Narusk says. "People like to stand out. They want to ride something that not everyone else around them is riding."

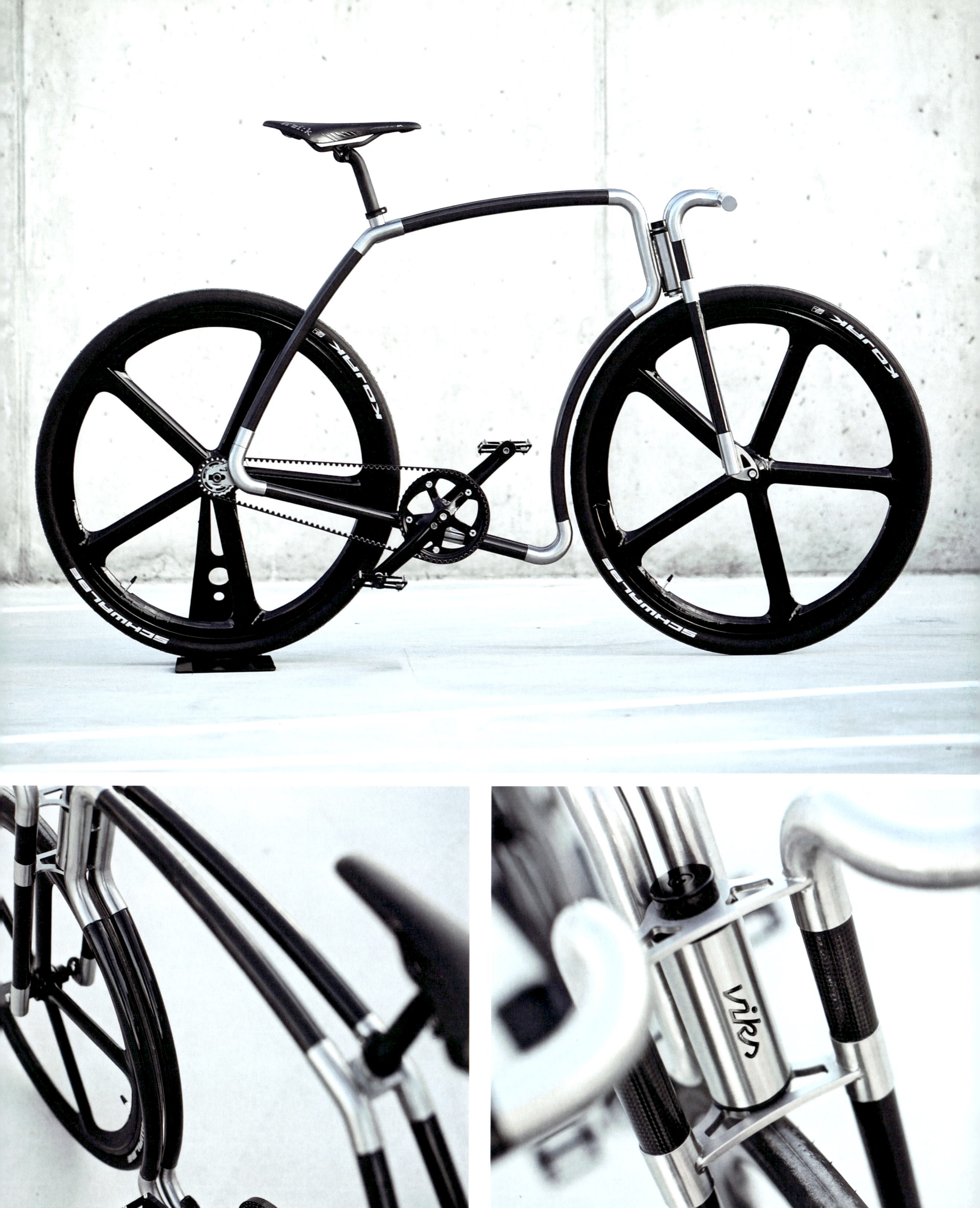
SCHWALBE
viks

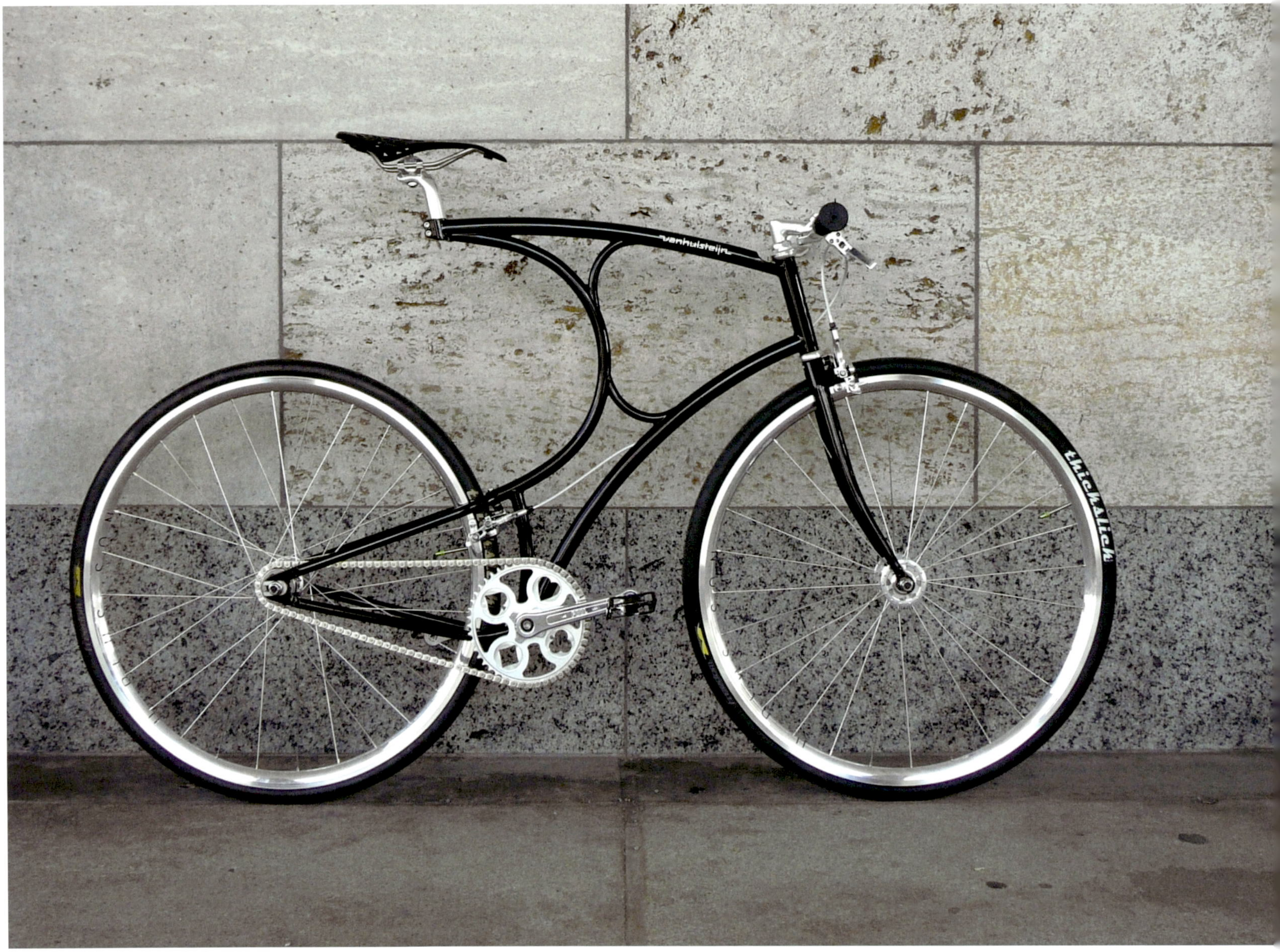

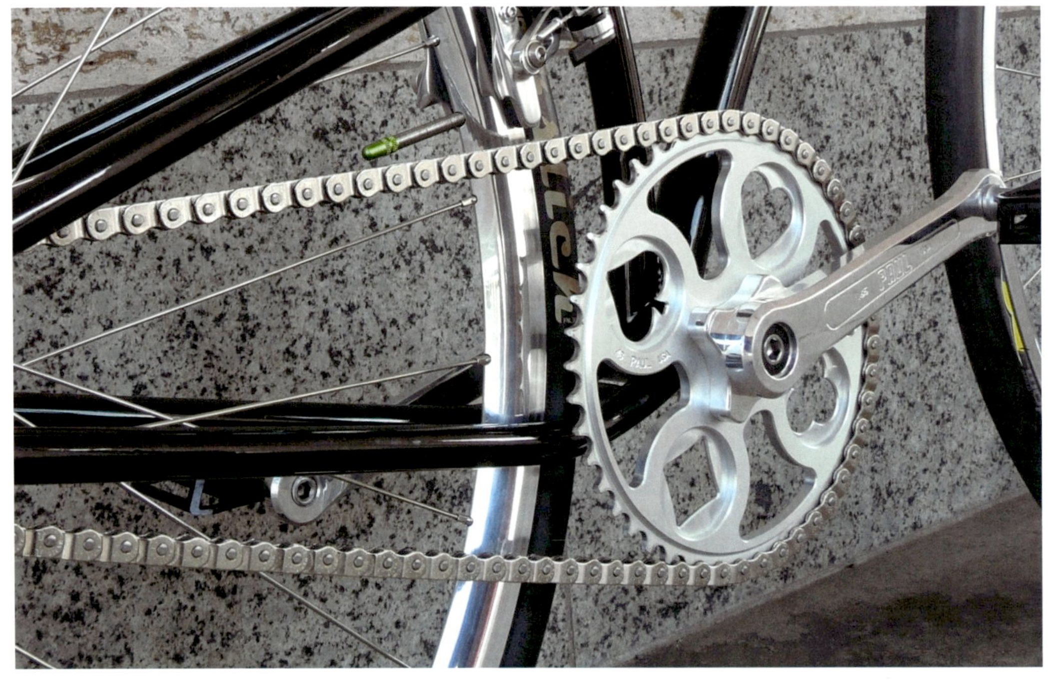

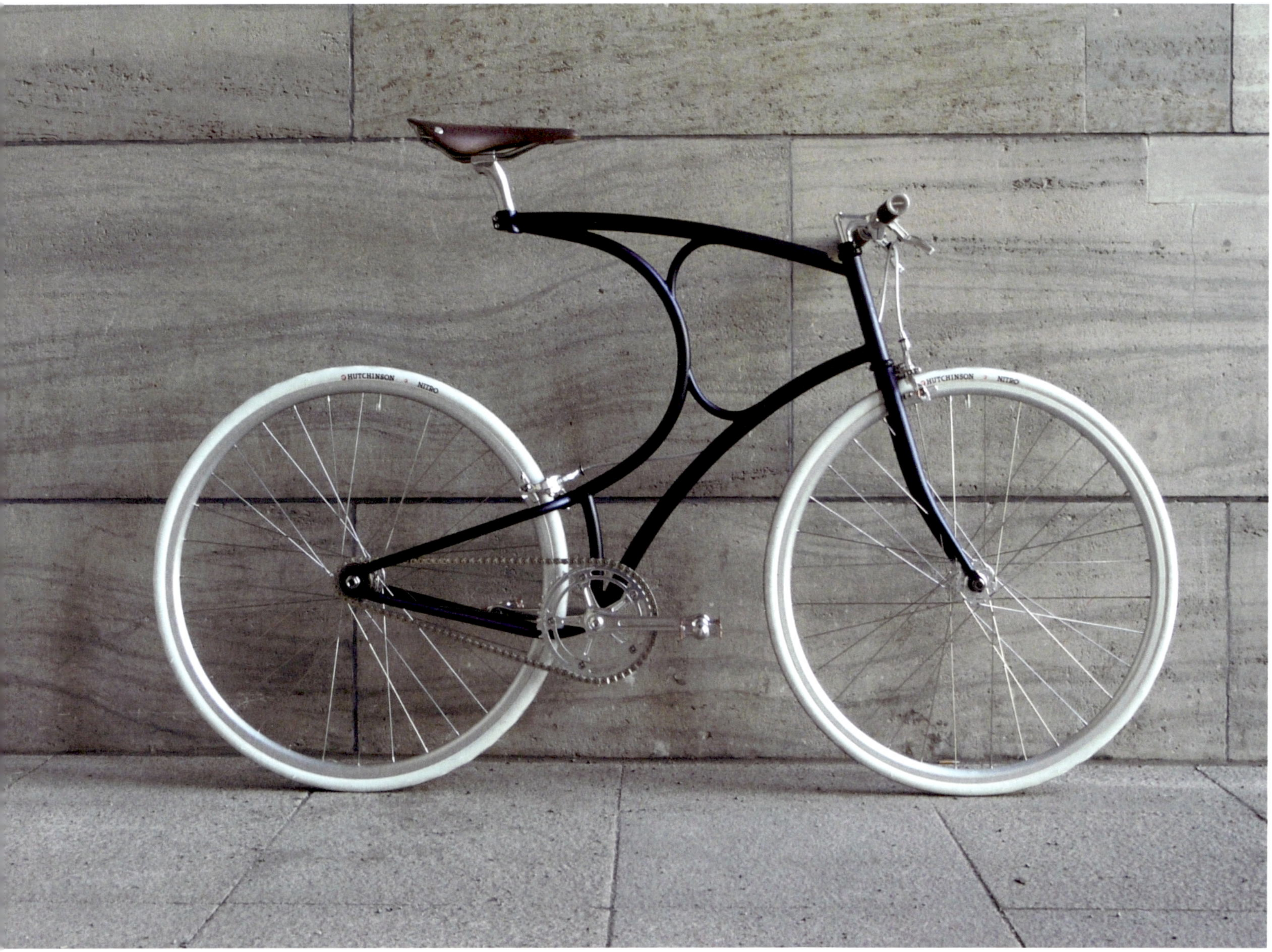

# Vanhulsteijn

### AUFTRAGSRAD

Auftragsrad's Vanhulsteijn takes its name from its designer, Herman Van Hulstein. The frame is handcrafted from stainless steel and TIG welded; the threaded one-inch fork is made of aluminum. All Auftragsrad frames are professionally powder coated, though uncoated frames and polished finishes are available as well.

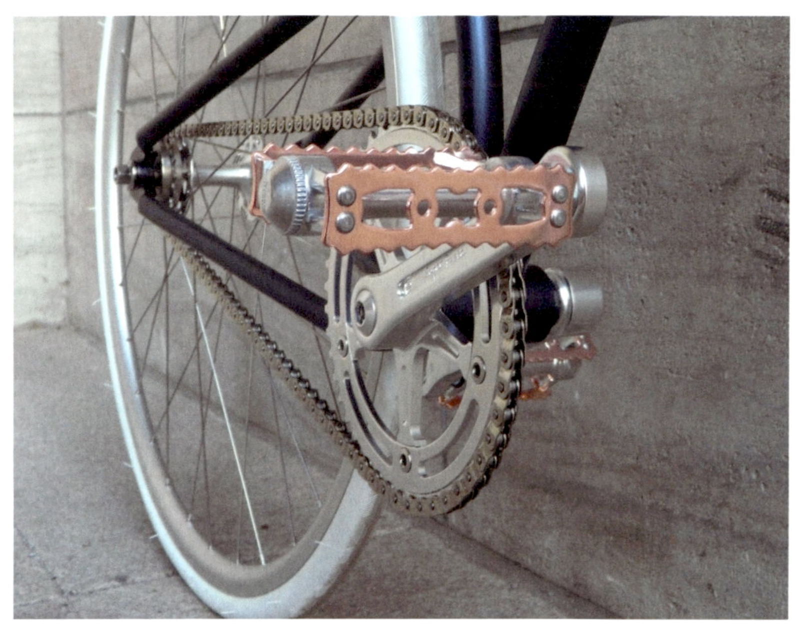

Reflective polka-dot socks and glow-in-the-dark striped shirts. Today there are inventive ways to make sure people know you're coming and to see where you're headed: USB-charged lights, lights integrated into your seatpost, and traffic signals projected onto your back. In fact, forget bike reflectors. You can turn your whole frame into a bike reflector.

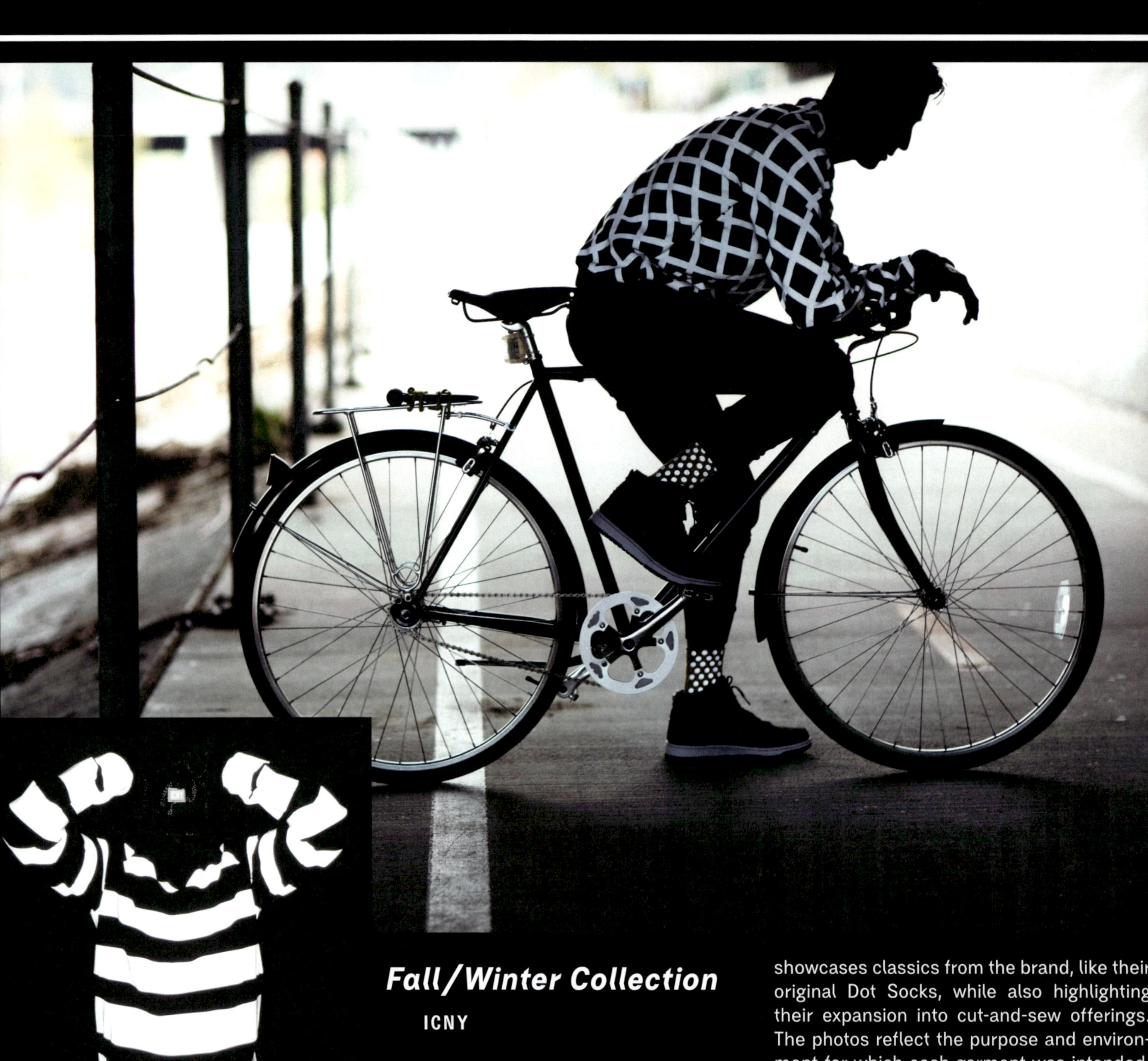

## *Fall/Winter Collection*

**ICNY**

Los Angeles-based photographer Ja Tecson managed to capture ICNY's Fall/Winter Collection in a new light. This series of images showcases classics from the brand, like their original Dot Socks, while also highlighting their expansion into cut-and-sew offerings. The photos reflect the purpose and environment for which each garment was intended. The ICNY Fall Winter Collection is available now on icnysport.com and at ICNY retailers worldwide.

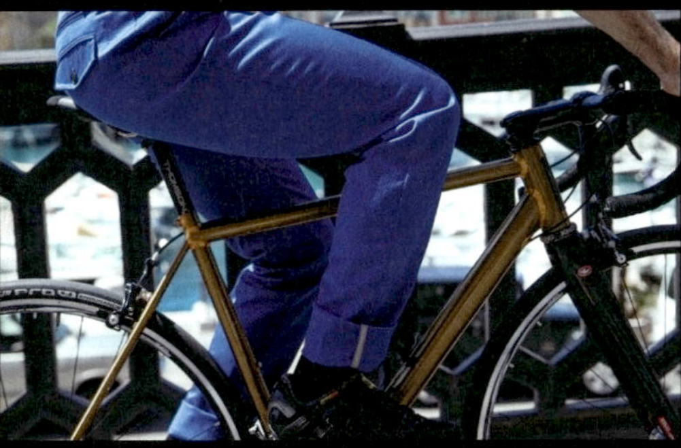

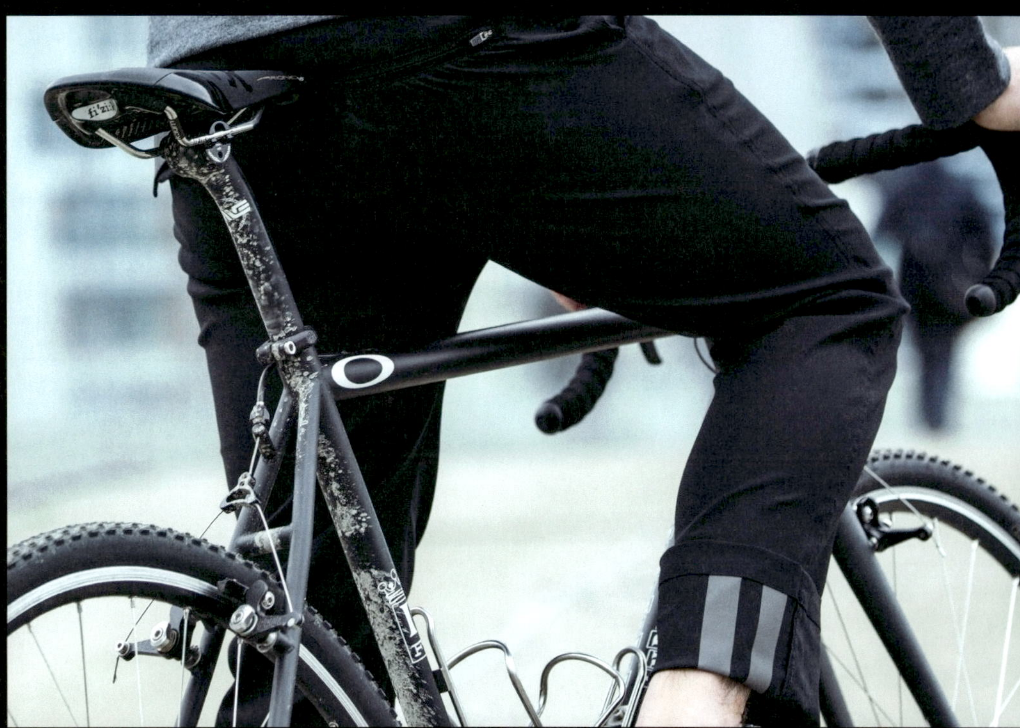

## Bernadette

**CAFÉ DU CYCLISTE**

Named for the French café that served as the founders' favorite mid-ride pit stop, biking-apparel label Café du Cycliste combines serious cycling with tailored tech and French chic. As one might expect from a French fashion house, premium fabrics inspire the designers during their daily rides around the Cote d'Azur, resulting in truly elegant cycling clothing for men and women. Bernadette combines comfort, performance, and style in a classic chino. Offset seams in the seat section prevent chafing and discomfort, while a selection of pockets accommodates all essentials. Other features include a premium fabric that is lightweight and fast-drying with enough stretch to allow for a full range of movement, belt loops, a timeless cut for off-the-road style, a removable reflective panel in the rear pocket, and reflective detailing on the interior of the leg for nighttime safety.

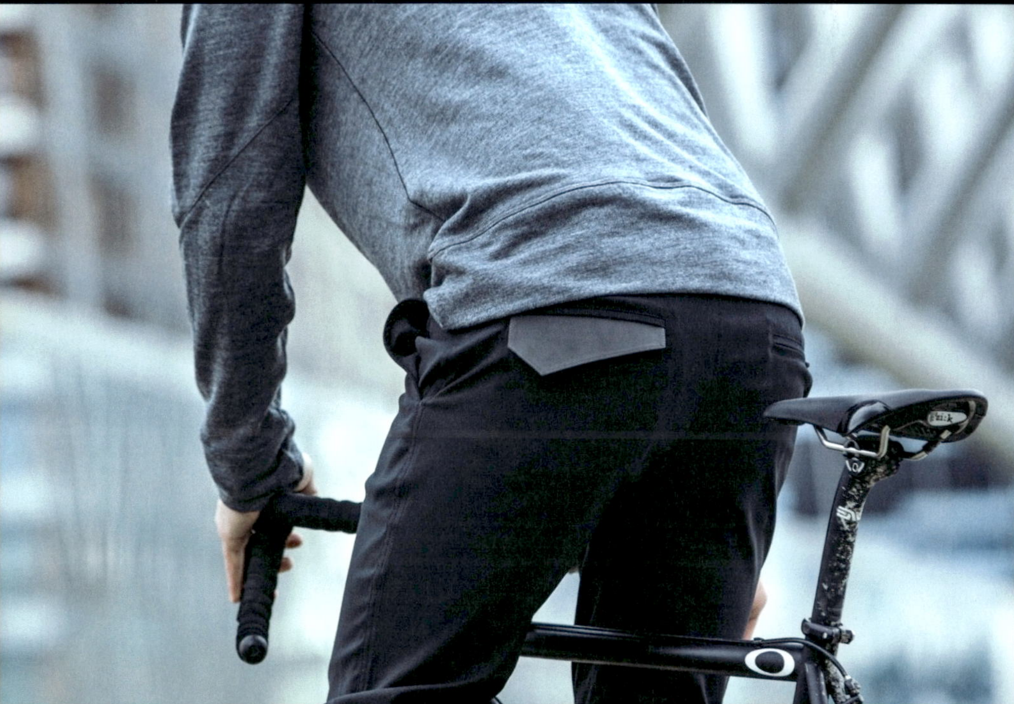

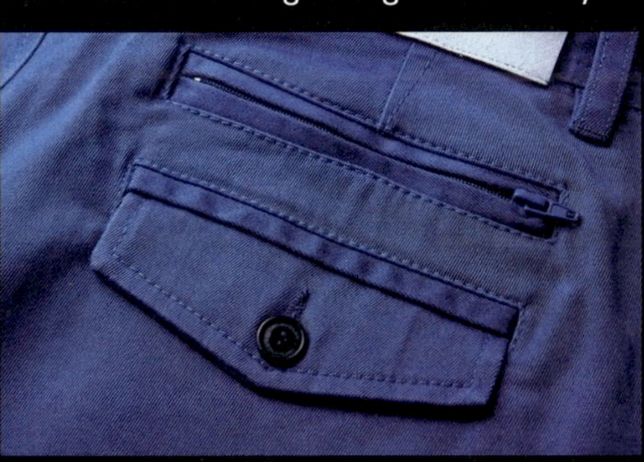

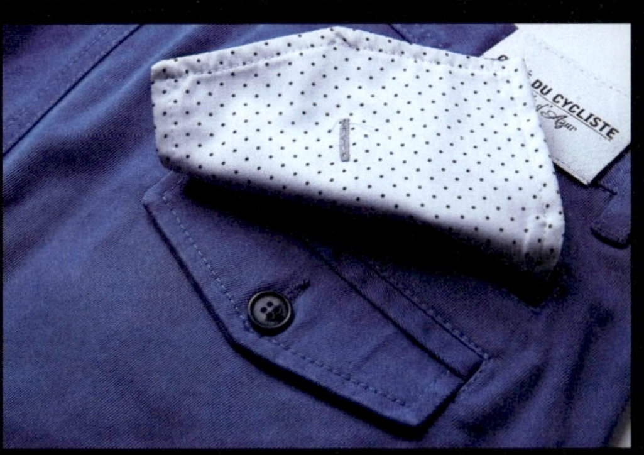


## Aether Bike Pant

**AETHER**

What is the ideal garb for the city commuter? Apparel that transitions easily from the road to the office by combining technical designs with clean aesthetics—and AETHER's Bike Pant has those requirements covered. Its highly breathable, water-repellent stretch-twill Schoeller fabric makes for a slim, modern fit that works in the office but is also comfortable enough for bike commuters. In addition to the streamlined aesthetics, subtle bike-friendly features abound throughout the design, including a reflective back-pocket flap that tucks in at work and 3XDRY wicking technology that quickly dries sweat. Reflective stripes on the interior of the bottom cuffs provide additional safety and visibility when the pant legs are cuffed.

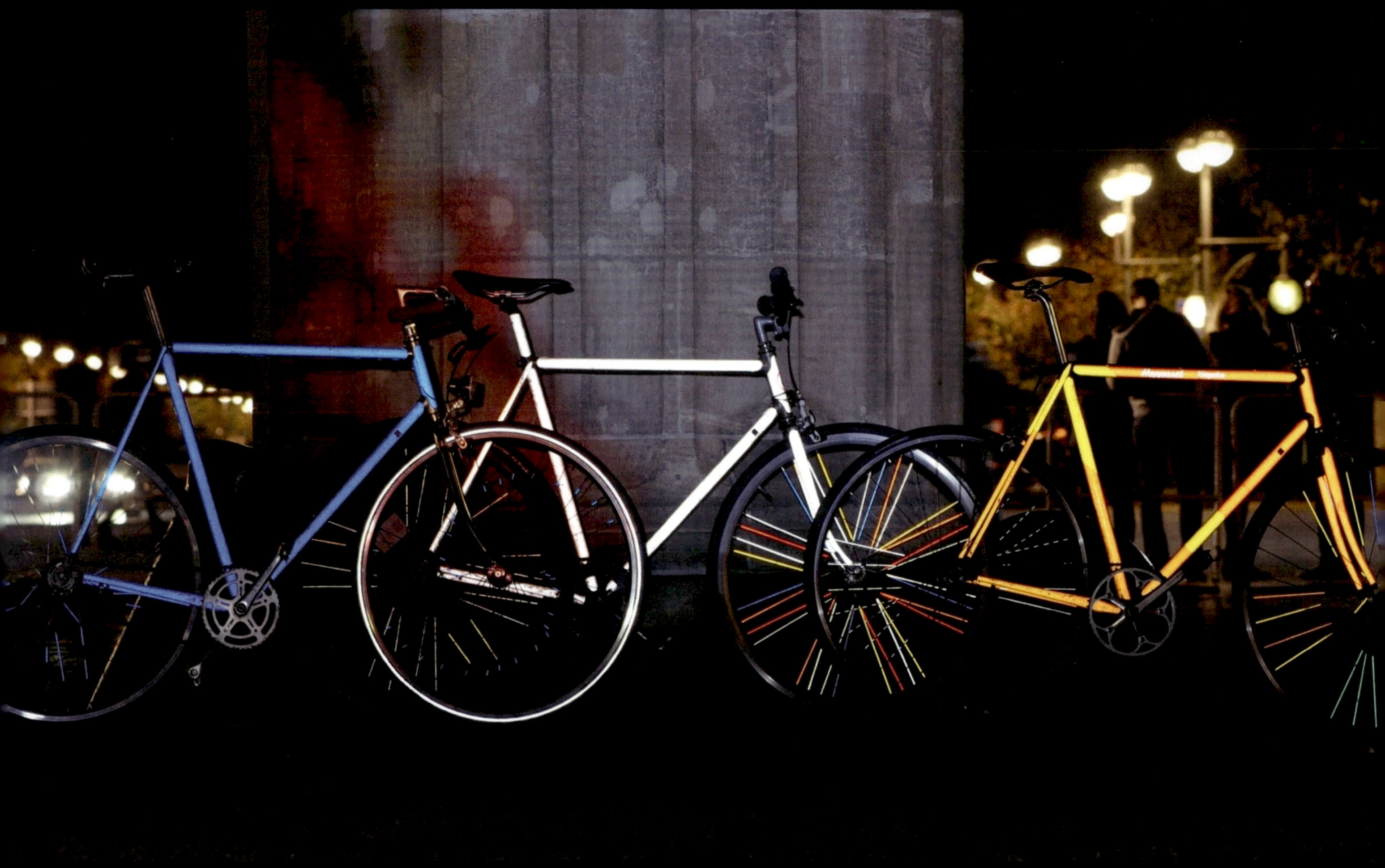

## The Reflective Bicycle

### HAPPAREL BICYCLES

Who needs bike reflectors when your entire bike is a bike reflector? This may be the world's first entirely reflective custom bicycle frame. Searching for a way to increase the visibility, and thereby the safety, of cyclists while improving rather than dampening the aesthetics of the bike, Happarel Bicycles began research and development in 2012, exploring the potential of reflective sprays, paints, and glass beads, among other materials. Ultimately, the team selected a film that is weather-, scratch-, and corrosion-resistant for up to seven years, workable with certain handcrafting techniques, and durable. Each bike's finish is created in collaboration with the client, with options to select colors, logos, text, and other elements.

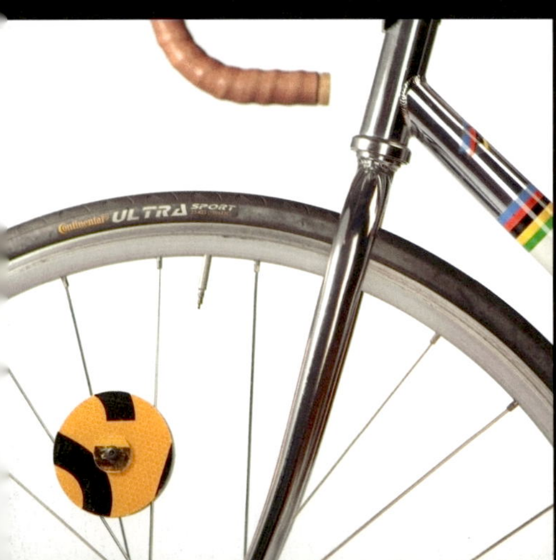


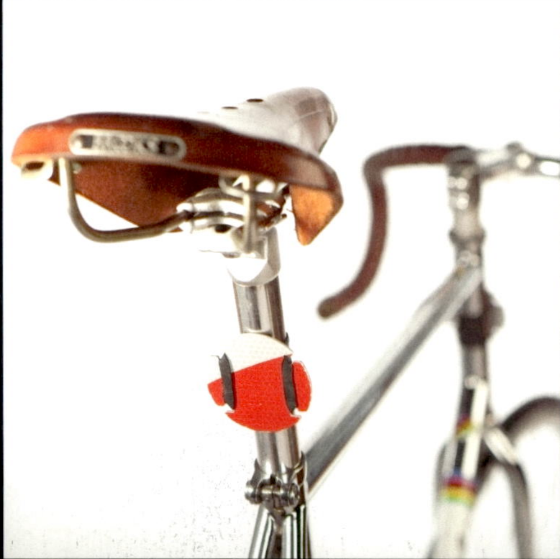

## Cyclesign

### TRENT JANSEN

Cyclesigns are unique bicycle reflectors made from used road signs, each with its own story of a previous life by the roadside. The Rear Reflector, with a strap cut from old bicycle tubes, simply wraps around the seatpost or front tube of a bicycle, while the Wheel Reflector fits easily around the spokes of a bicycle wheel. Both Cyclesign products stay true to the company's commitment to repurposing; the felt padding and fasteners are the only new materials used in the manufacture of these reflectors.

# Lucetta magnetic bike lights

**PALOMAR**

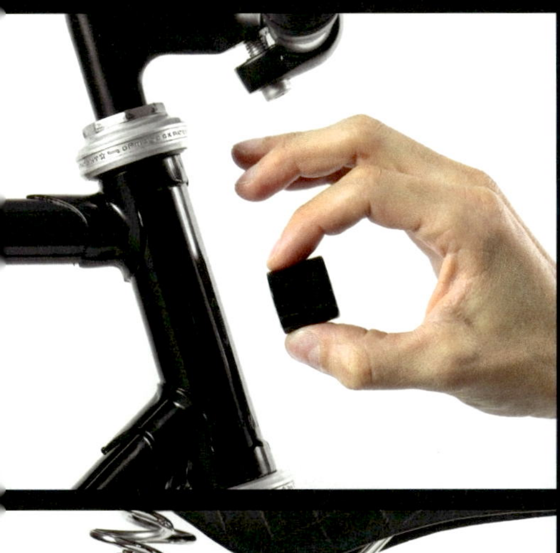

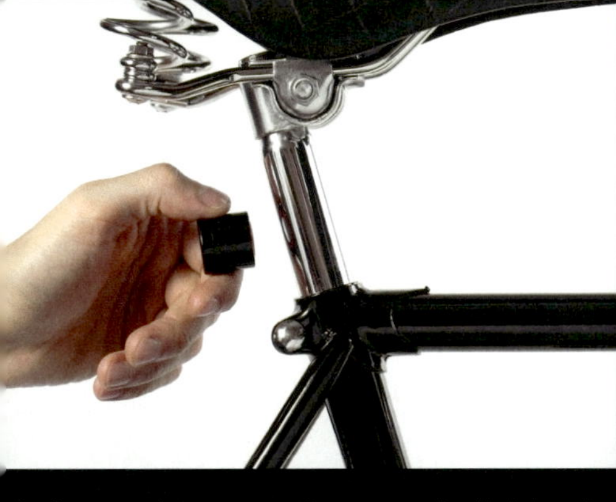

Made up of two small magnetic lights, the Lucetta is an innovative and essential bike light. Easy to attach to any bike, the two small lights—one red and one white—switch on with just a click and are guaranteed to stay securely in place even on the bumpiest streets. Select from a steady beam, a slow flashing light, or a fast one simply by clicking the light on the bike. The Lucetta is water-resistant and offers a super-wide angle of visibility, with a run-time of up to 40 hours. When you reach your destination, remove the lights, join them together and slip them into a pocket until your next outing.

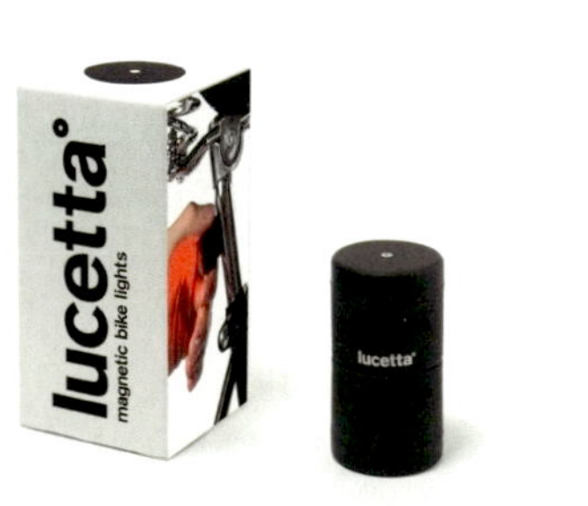


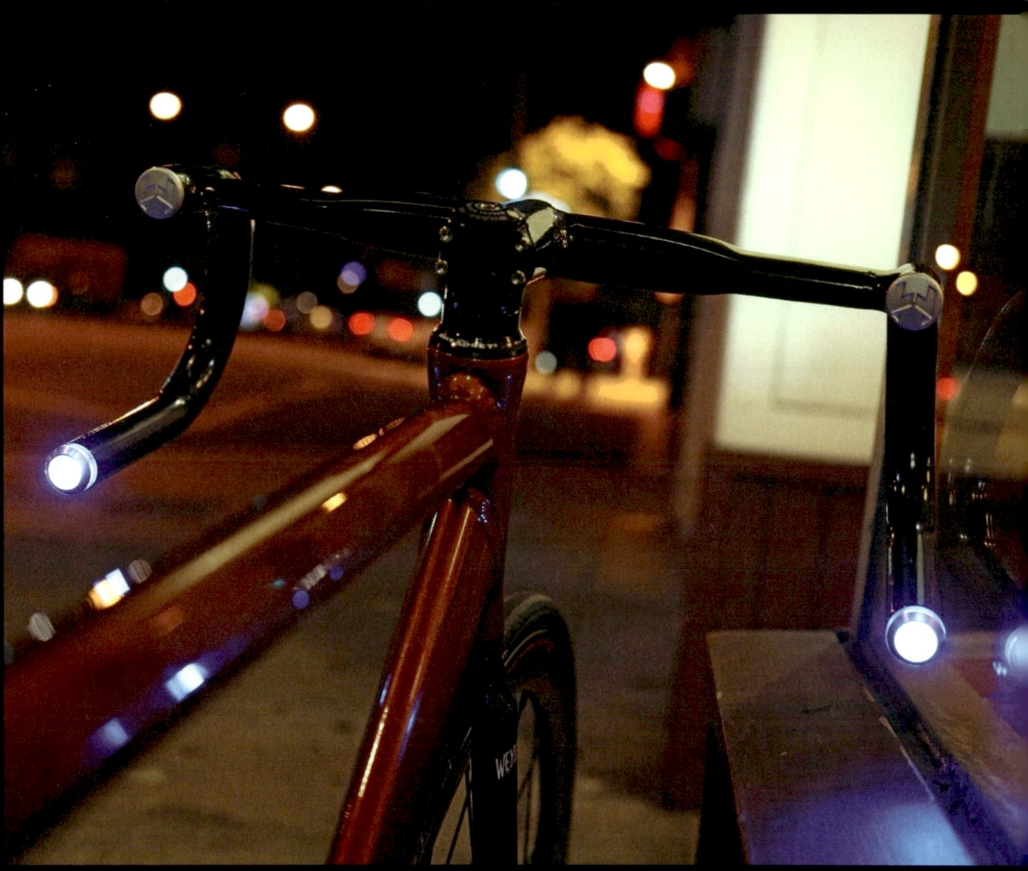

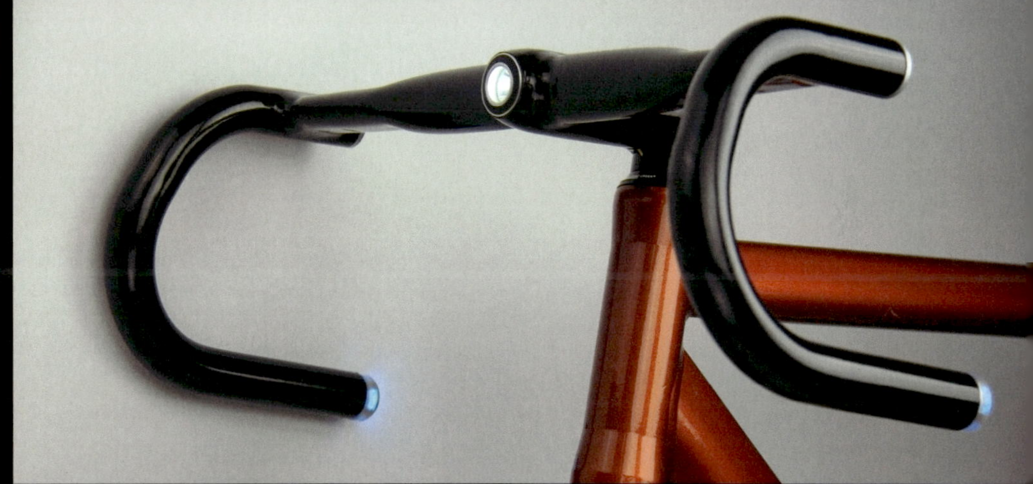

## Helios Bars

Helios Bars are an integrated handlebar, headlight, and blinker system for bicycles. Once the bars have been mounted—all it takes are four screws—the bike gets smart. Connecting the bars to an accompanying iOS app via Bluetooth Smart unlocks features like ambient lighting, iPod and music controls, turn-by-turn navigation, and a visual speedometer that shifts through different hues based on the speed of the bike. The handlebars have a robust CREE LED in front with an angle of illumination similar to that of a car headlight and rechargeable batteries that keep the brights on for nine hours at a time. The rear LEDs operate like a car's blinkers, allowing riders to press a button on either side of the stem to signal turns. A built-in GPS module also allows owners to track their bike's location from anywhere in the world via SMS—they can expect a Google Maps link within 30 seconds—in those rare moments when they are not riding it.

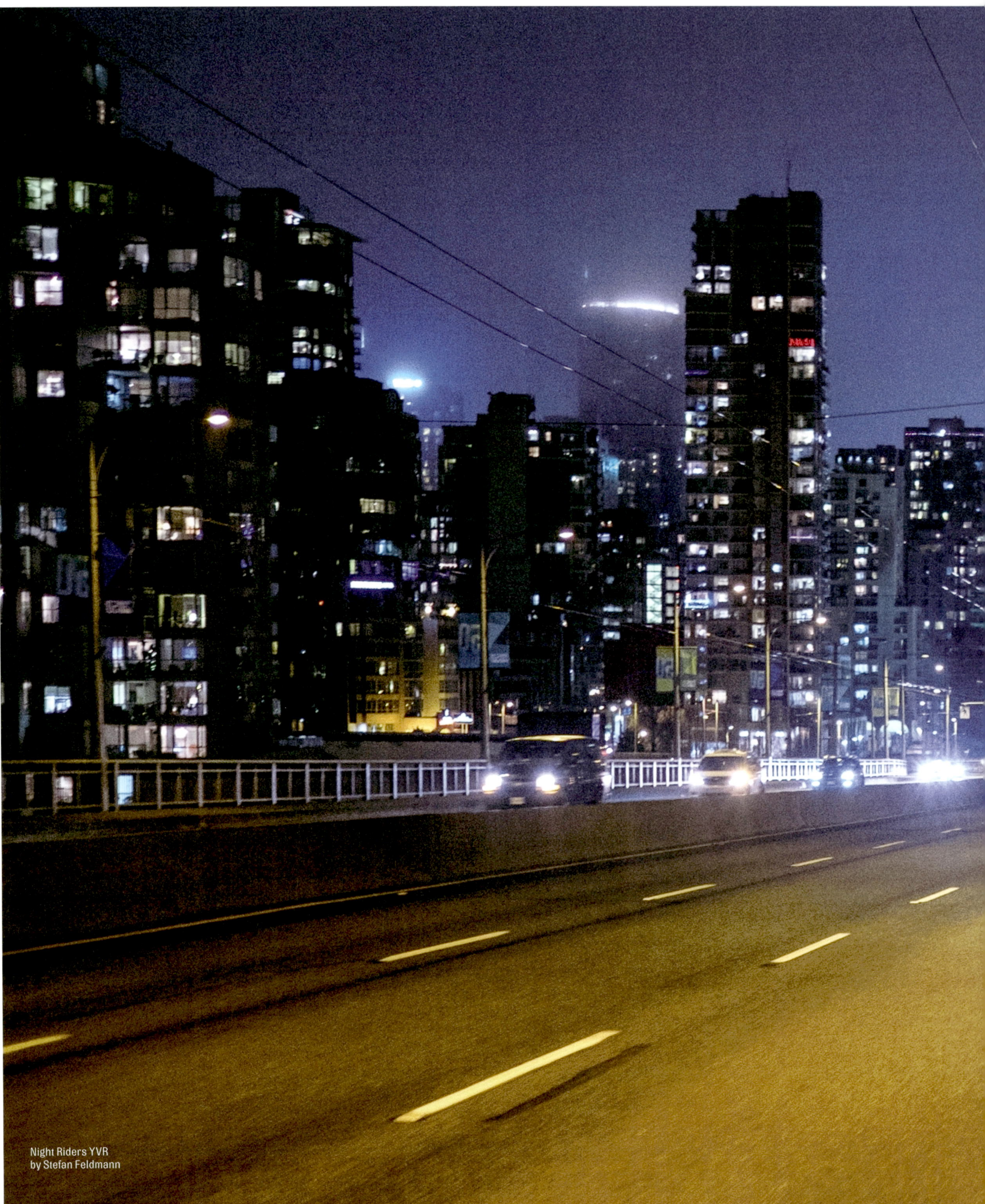

Night Riders YVR
by Stefan Feldmann

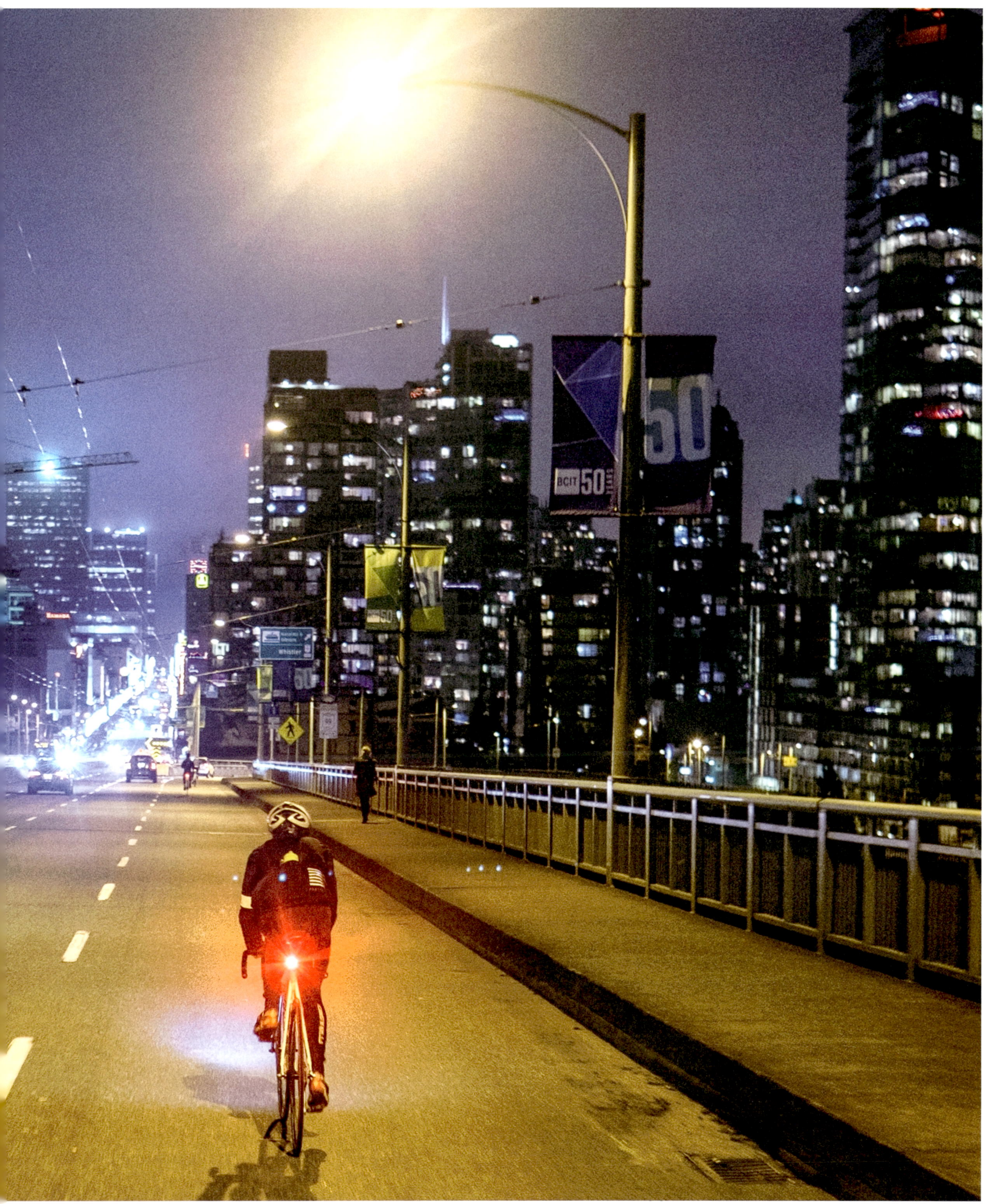
50
BCIT 50
Whistler

**oppiste page:** Ridehouse Martin (page 72)

# Grander Touring

Text: **SHONQUIS MORENO**

*On mountain bikes, cross-country, ATB, travel bikes, long tours, quick rides, downhill, and freedom*

We ride not to feel the wind in our hair, but because when we ride we feel like we are the wind. We pedal cross-country to get there on our own two feet. Sometimes we charter helicopters to the summit just to make the downhill longer. We've felt the damp in our bones while bothying in Scotland and had asthma attacks in the suburbs of Shanghai. We stay in hotels that have pedal-through check-in and wear clothes made of fabrics that your military hasn't even dreamed of yet. When we get lost, it's because we want to, in gnarly single track, Sequoias and silence, icy rivers and cols, panoramas and the impossible Pacific Coast Highway. We've got ATBs and fat wheels and snacks in our packs and they've always brought us home again, thirsty. We've changed more flats than we can count, almost rode into the Arctic Circle, flipped over our handlebars and landed on our feet. Twice. We've been rained on. We've been curious. We've been very, very cold. We ride because bicycling is a free country. And on the way, we've seen sunsets you'd never believe.

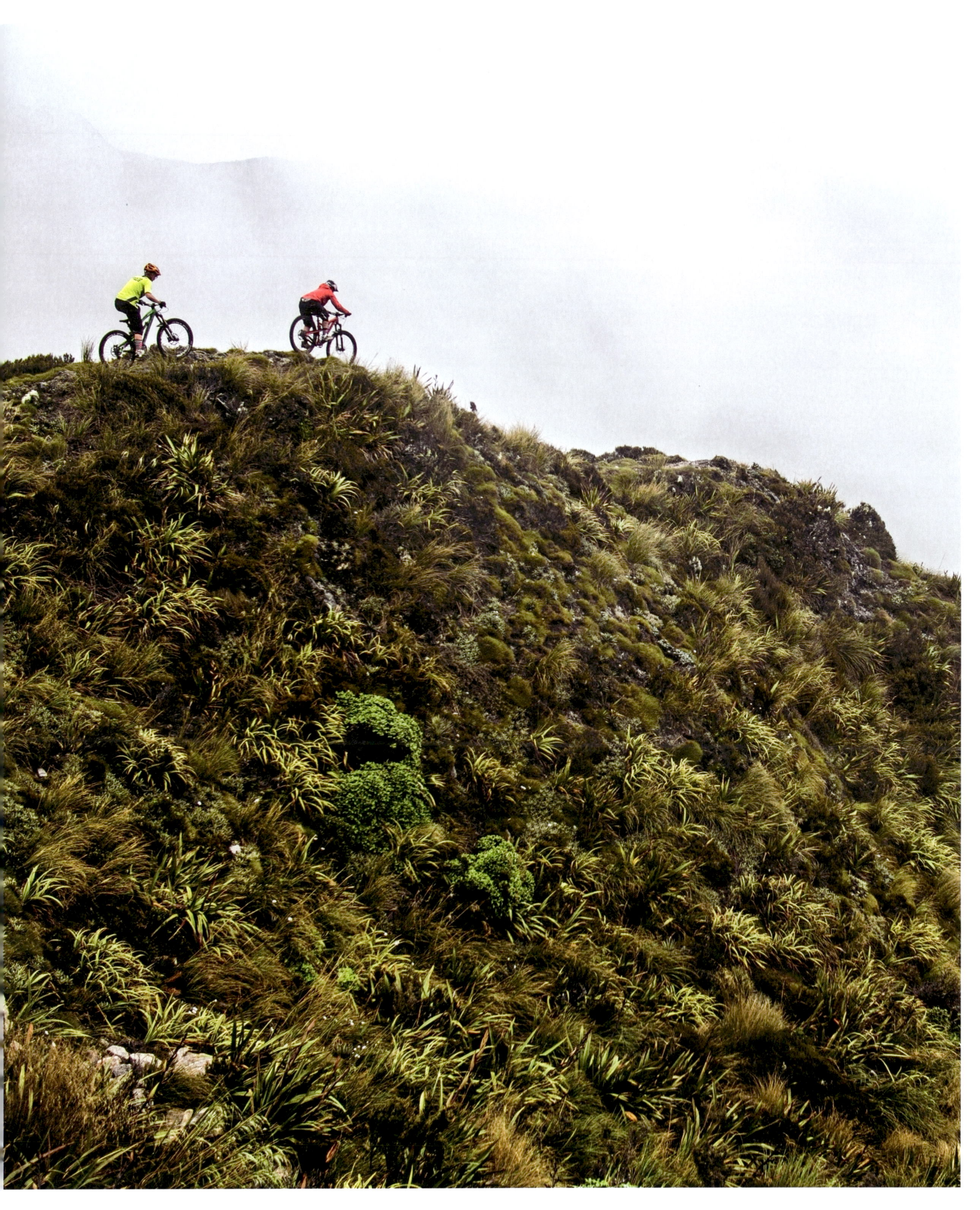

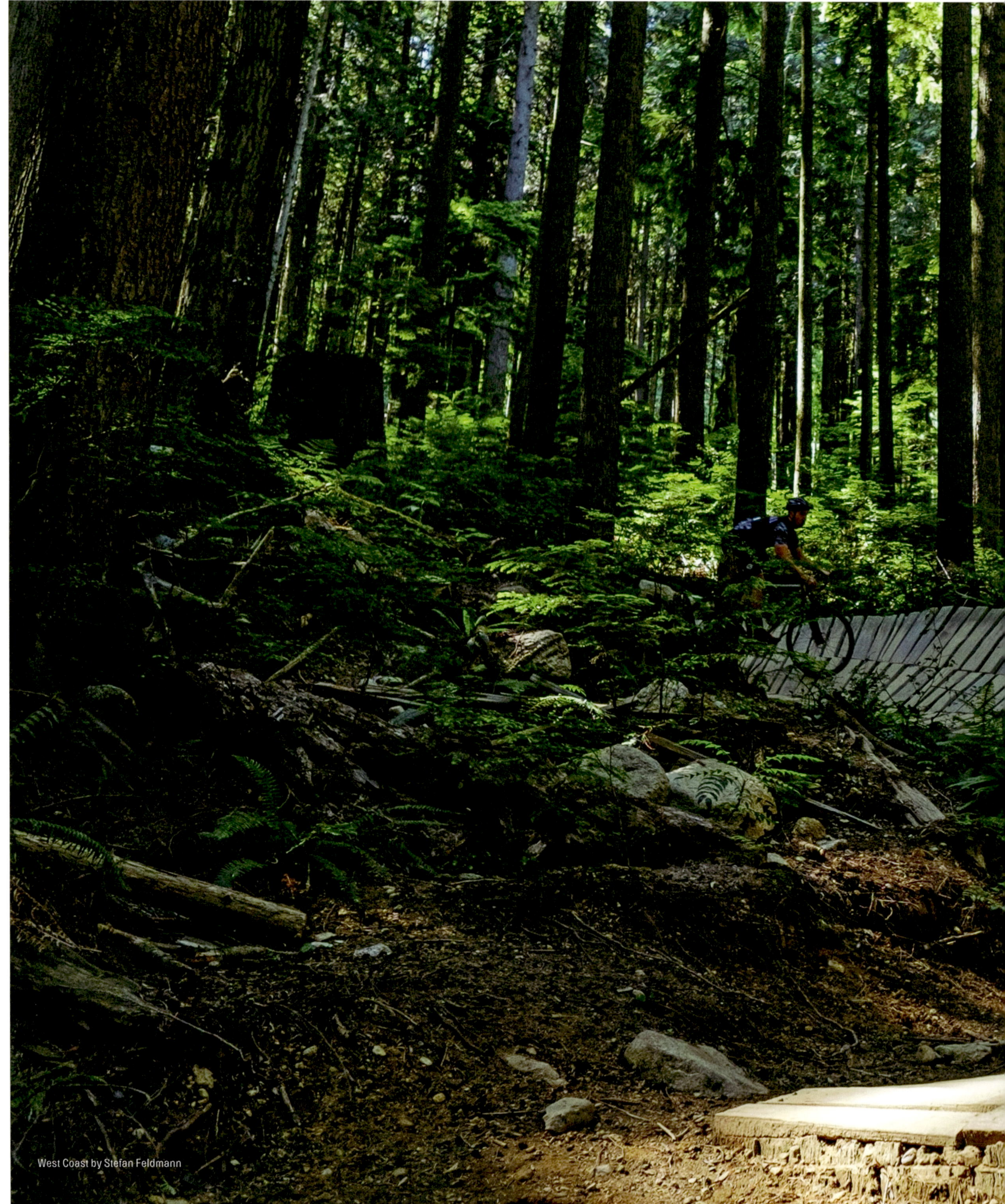
West Coast by Stefan Feldmann

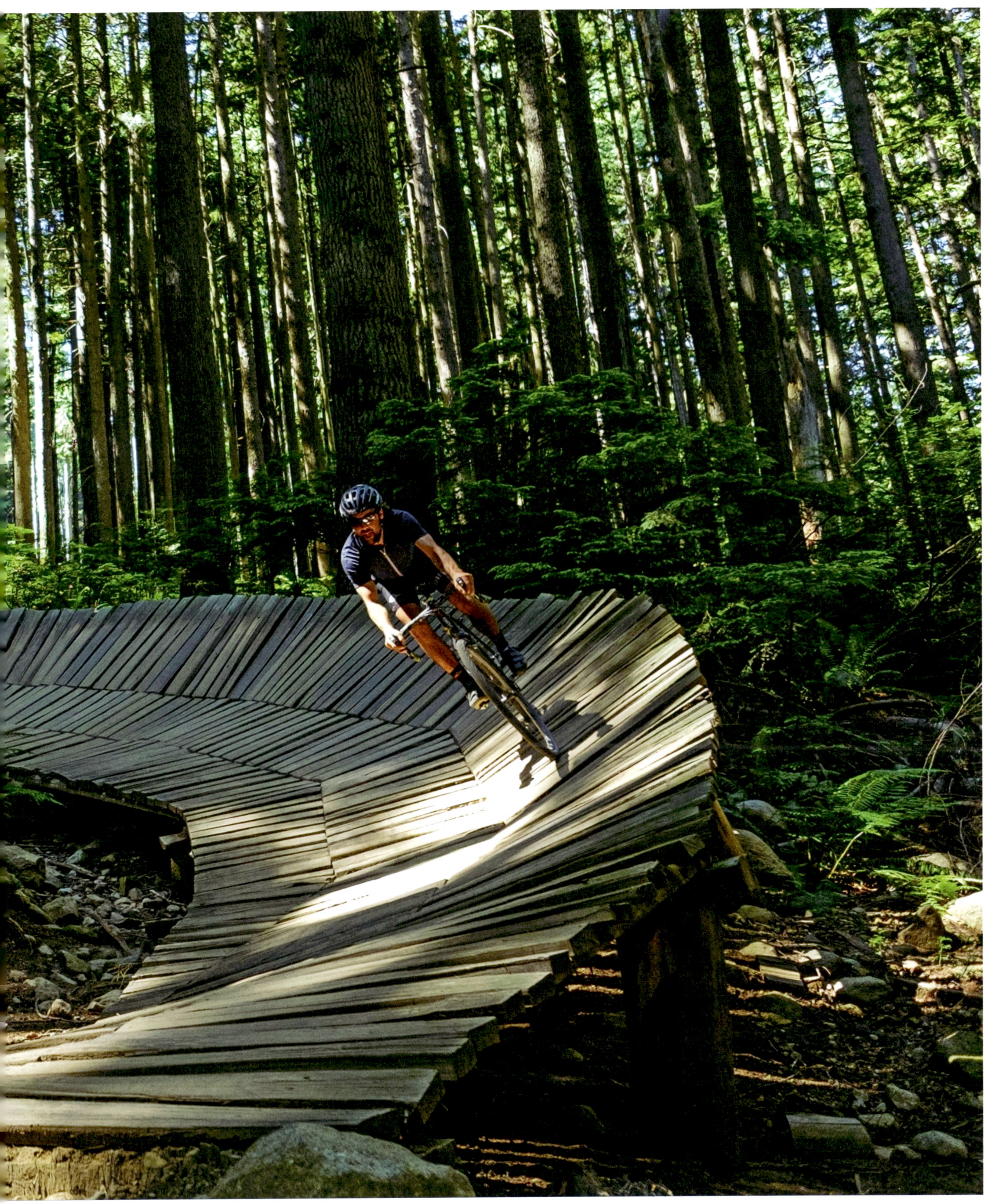

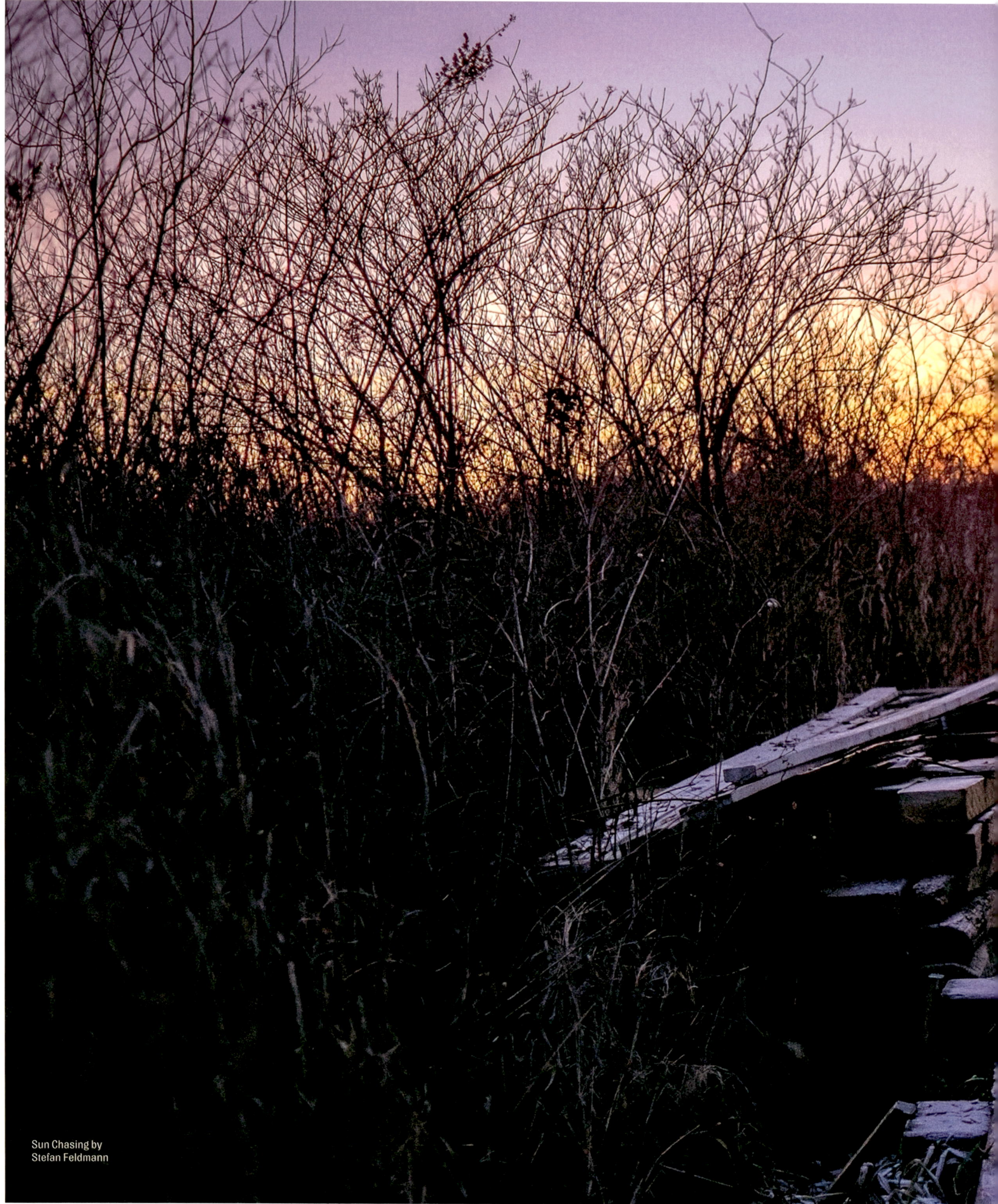

Sun Chasing by
Stefan Feldmann

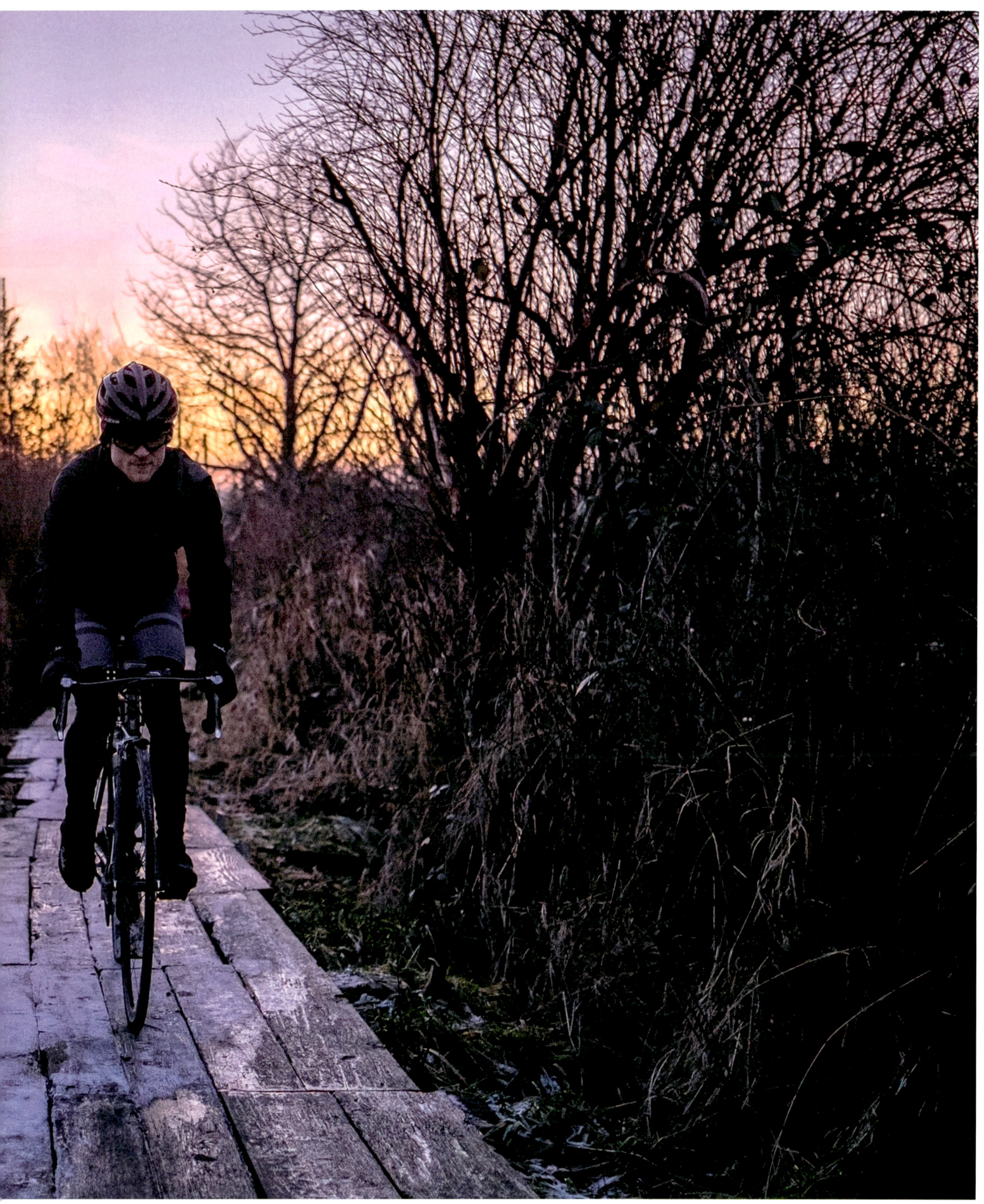

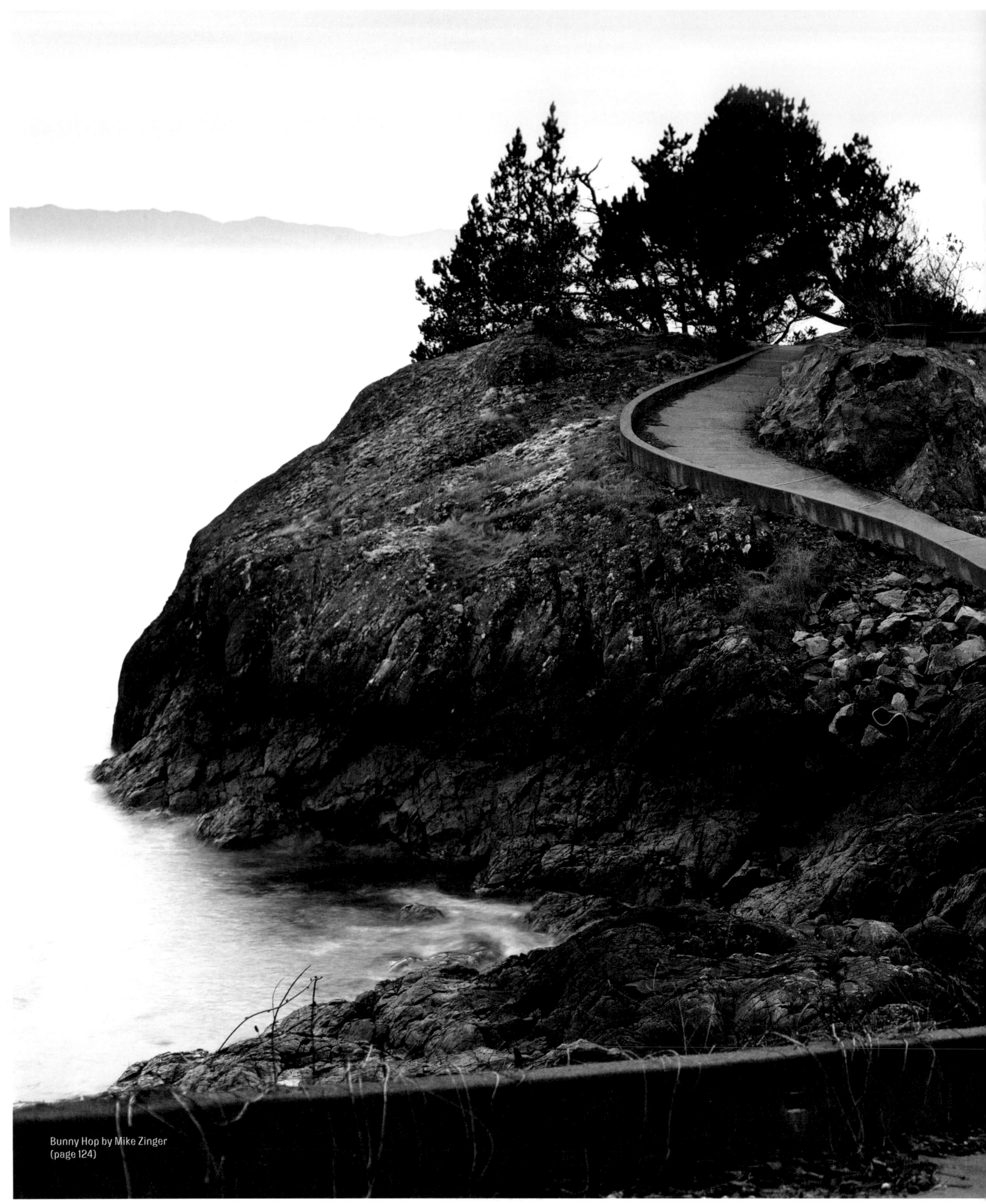

Bunny Hop by Mike Zinger
(page 124)

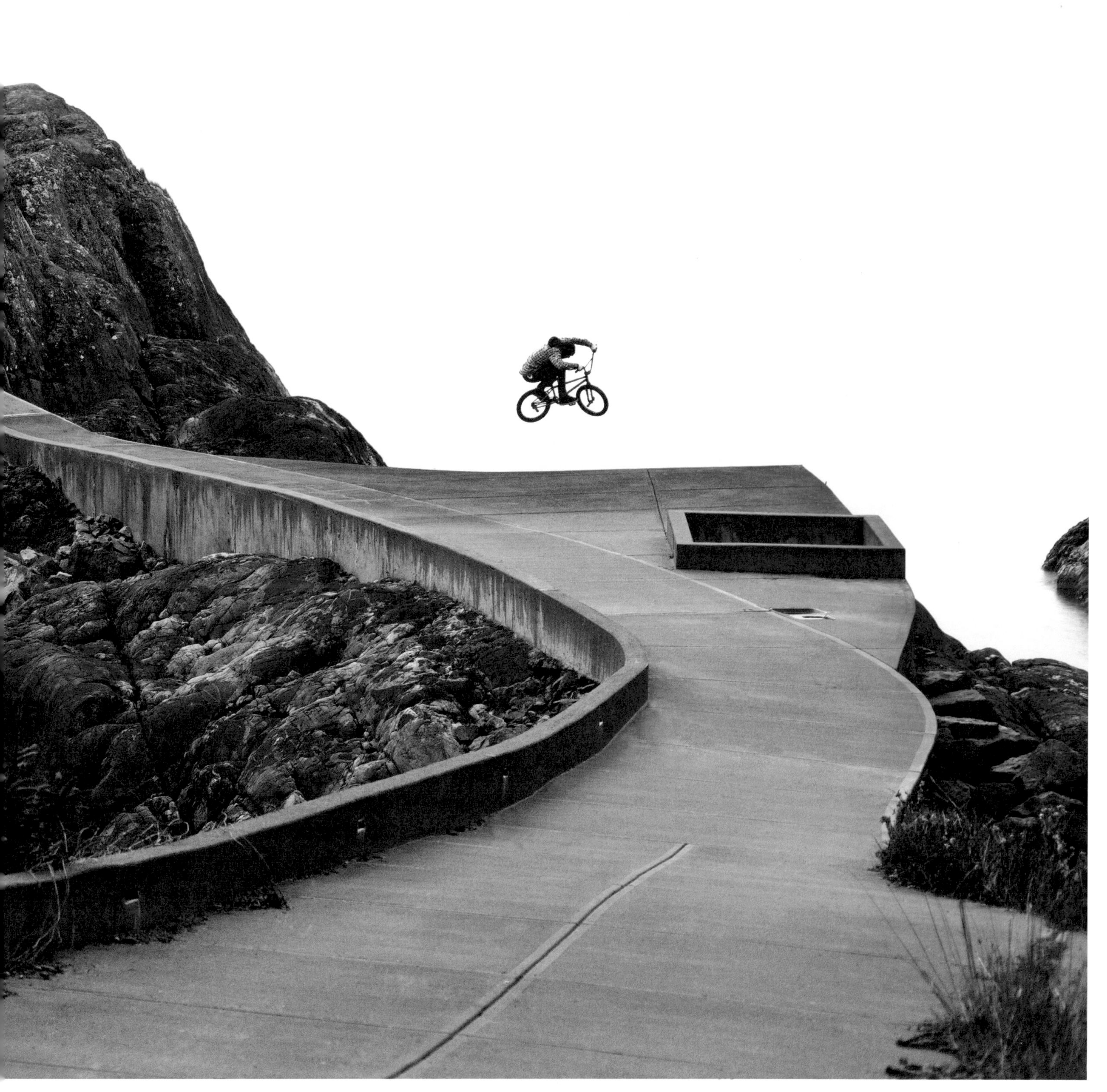

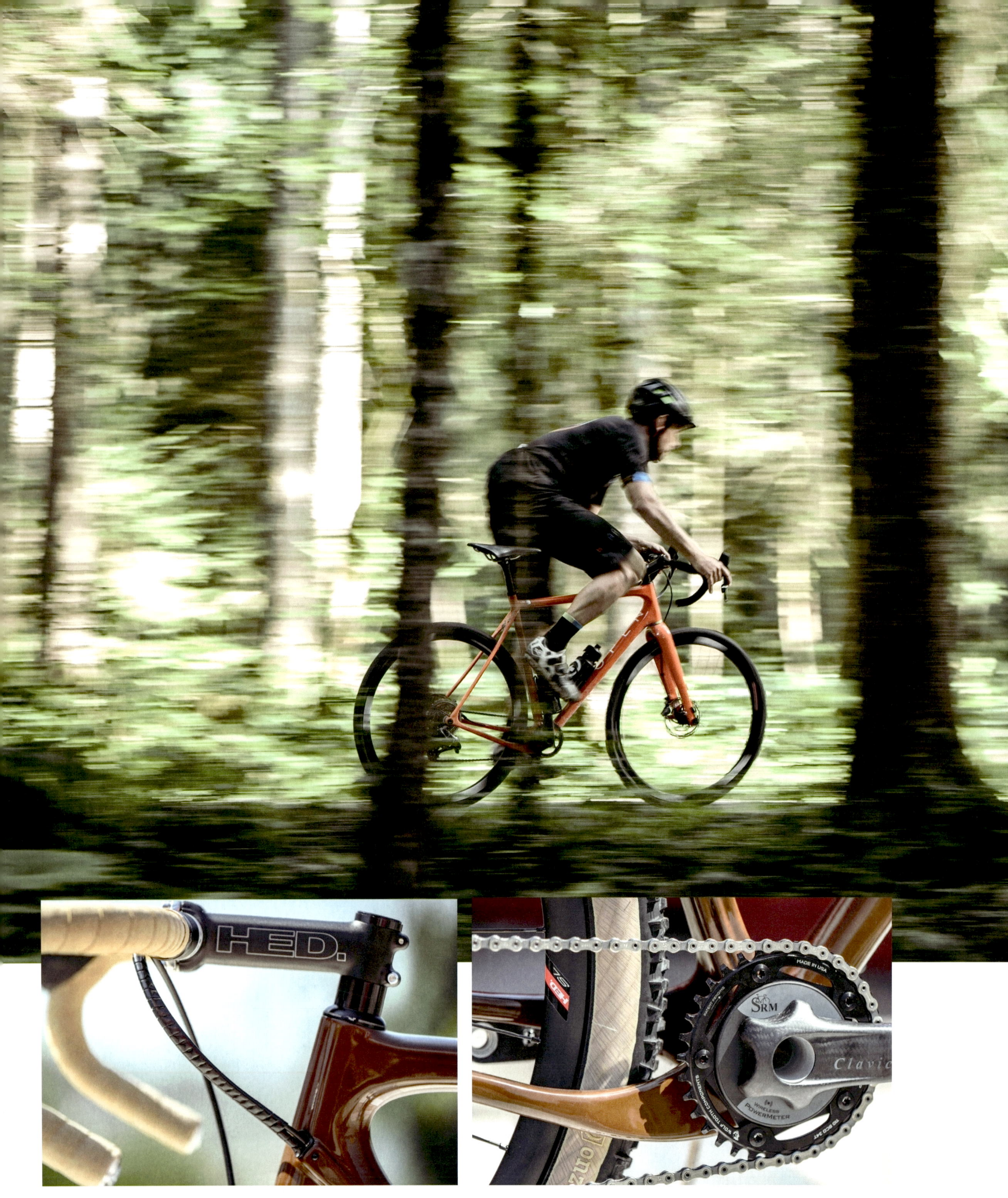
HED.
MADE IN USA
SRM
WIRELESS
POWERMETER

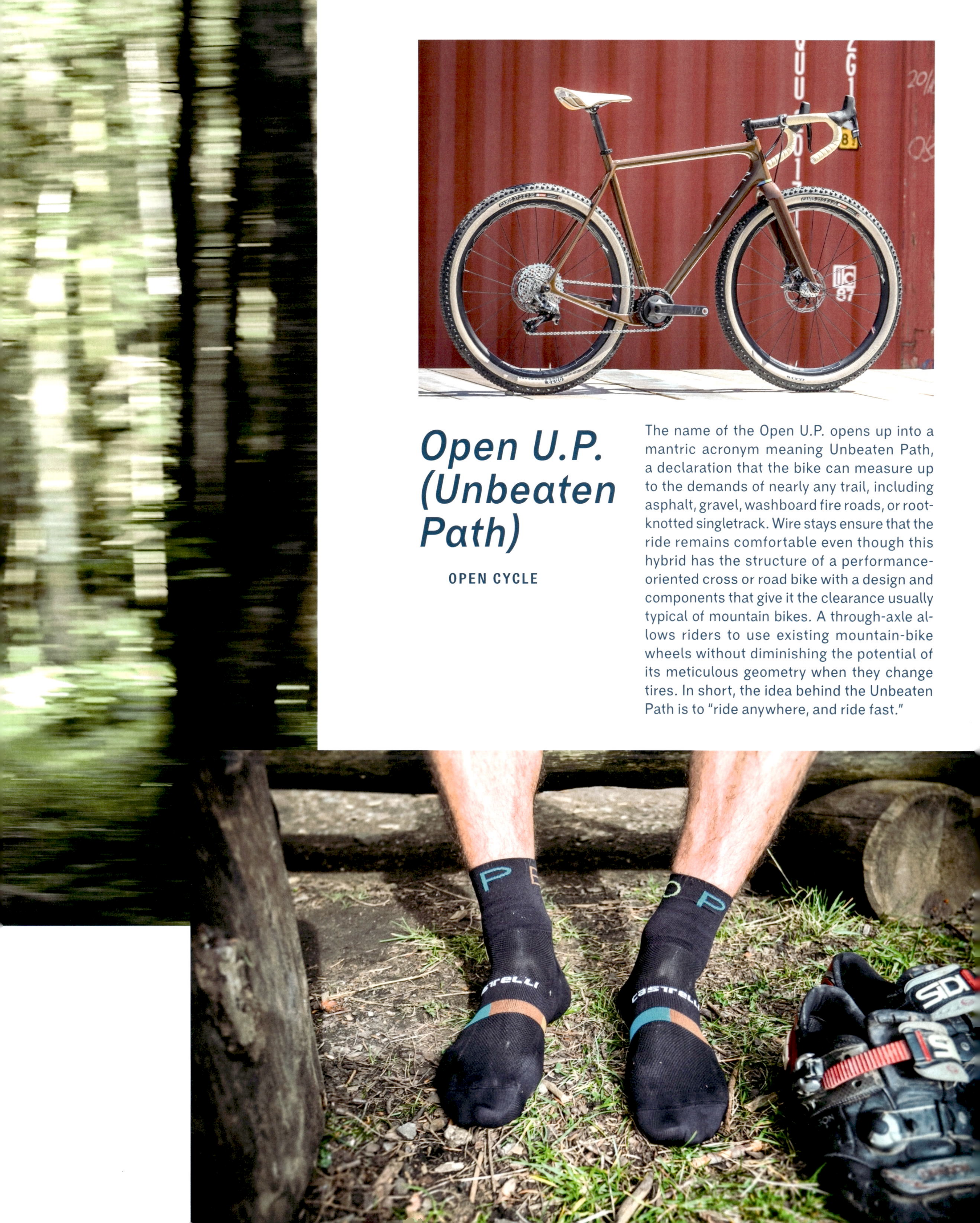

## Open U.P. (Unbeaten Path)

**OPEN CYCLE**

The name of the Open U.P. opens up into a mantric acronym meaning Unbeaten Path, a declaration that the bike can measure up to the demands of nearly any trail, including asphalt, gravel, washboard fire roads, or root-knotted singletrack. Wire stays ensure that the ride remains comfortable even though this hybrid has the structure of a performance-oriented cross or road bike with a design and components that give it the clearance usually typical of mountain bikes. A through-axle allows riders to use existing mountain-bike wheels without diminishing the potential of its meticulous geometry when they change tires. In short, the idea behind the Unbeaten Path is to "ride anywhere, and ride fast."

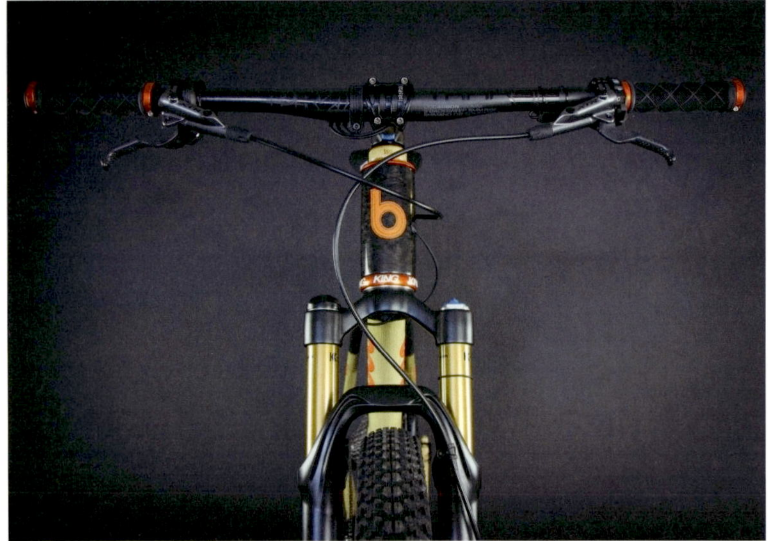

# Boo Bicycles

It might seem like an odd material for a bike, but bamboo is well-suited to bike building. As a natural composite, it offers stiffness similar to that of carbon fiber and it possesses phenomenal vibration-damping abilities. Colorado-based Boo Bicycles offers the best of all worlds: bamboo bikes that are stiff and durable, nimble and confident, lively and smooth. Boo handcrafts their bikes with Tam Vong bamboo—also known as "iron bamboo"—that is grown on their own plantation in Vietnam. Chosen for its superior quality, Tam Vong bamboo is stronger by weight than steel and used to build everything from bridges to scaffolding.

**left:** Boo SL-M 29er mountain bike

**right:** Boo SL-G gravel race bike

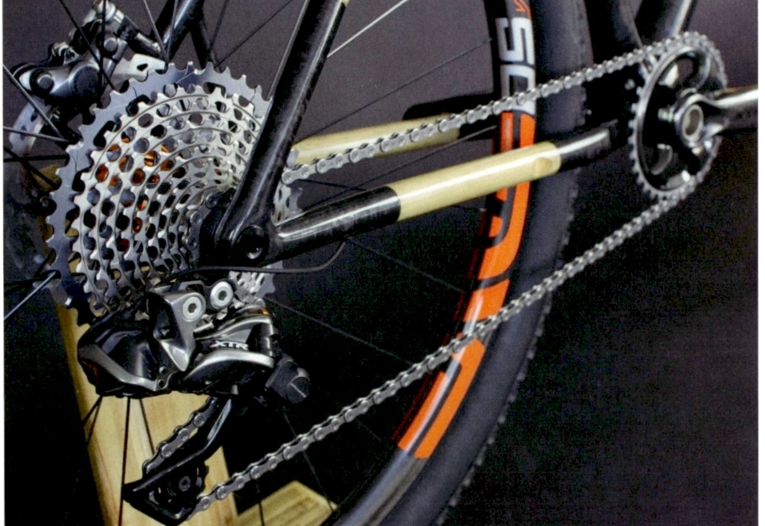

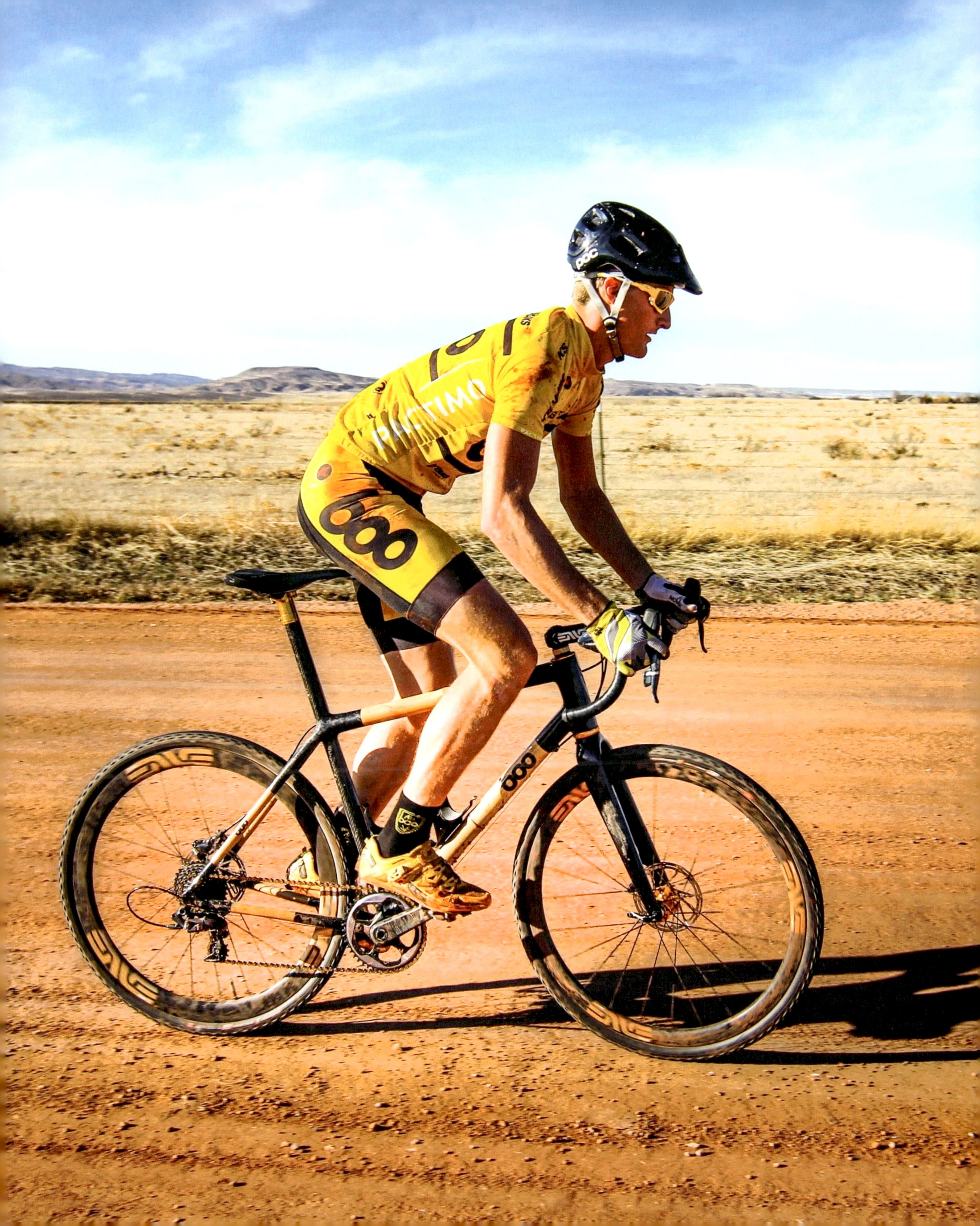
PACTIMO

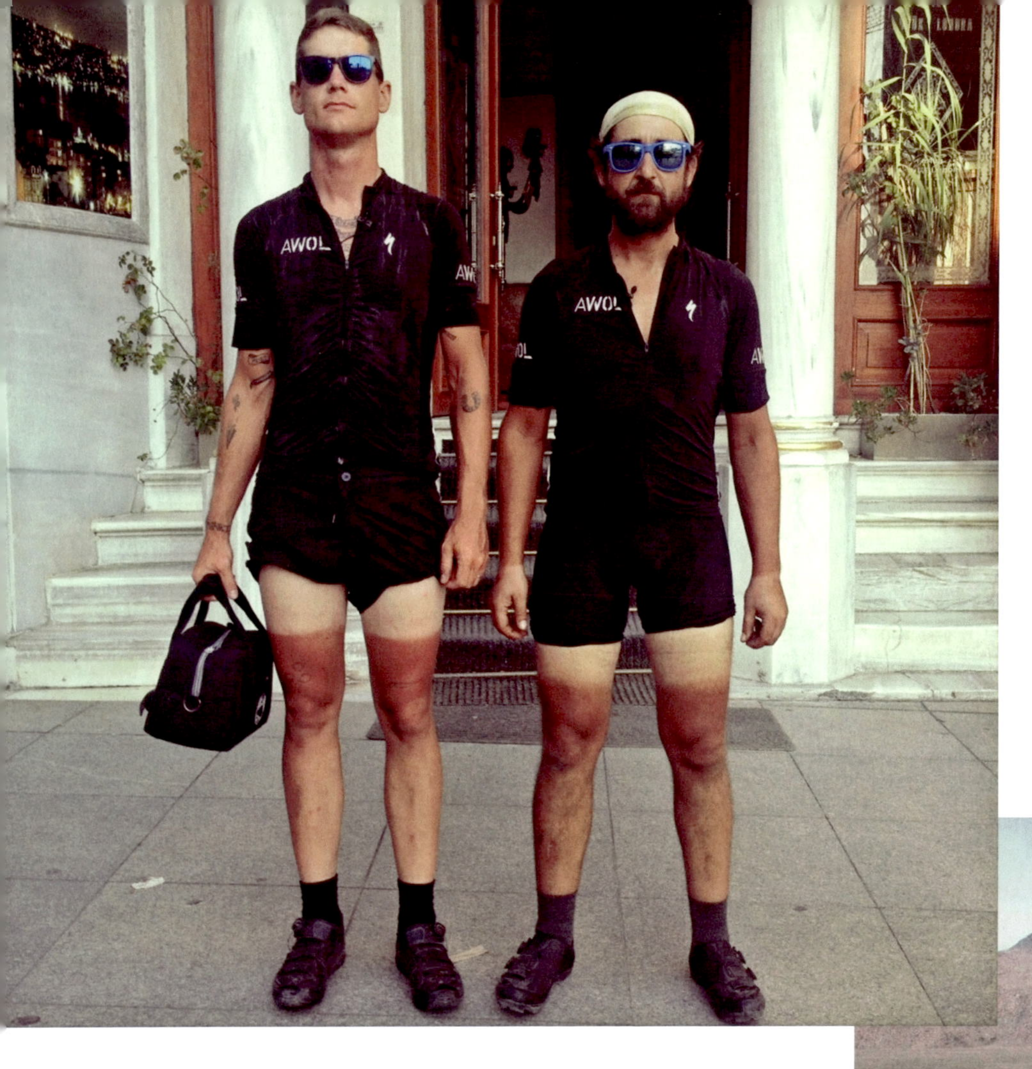
AWOL
AWOL

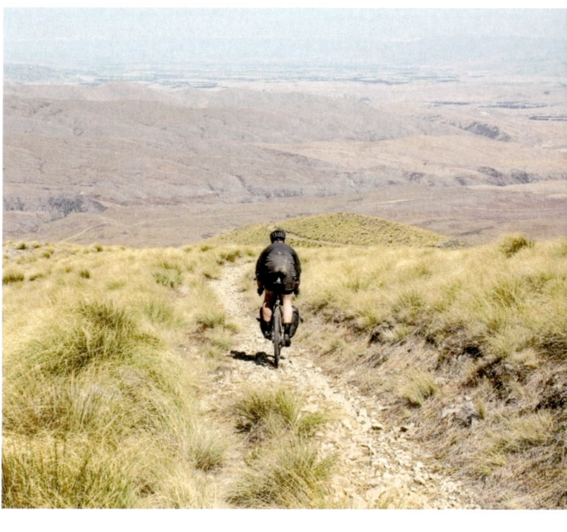

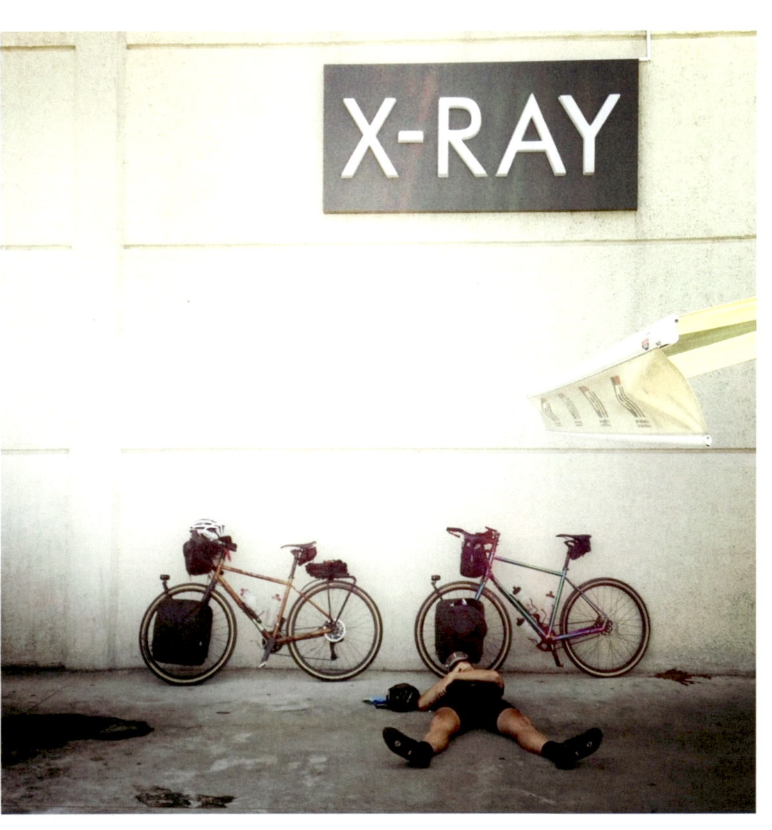
X-RAY

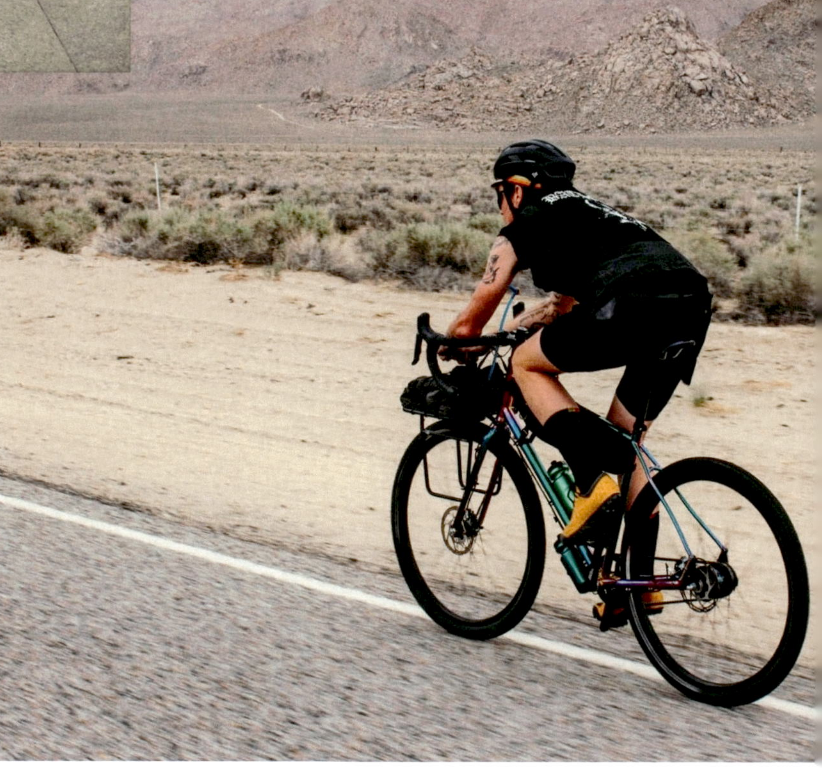

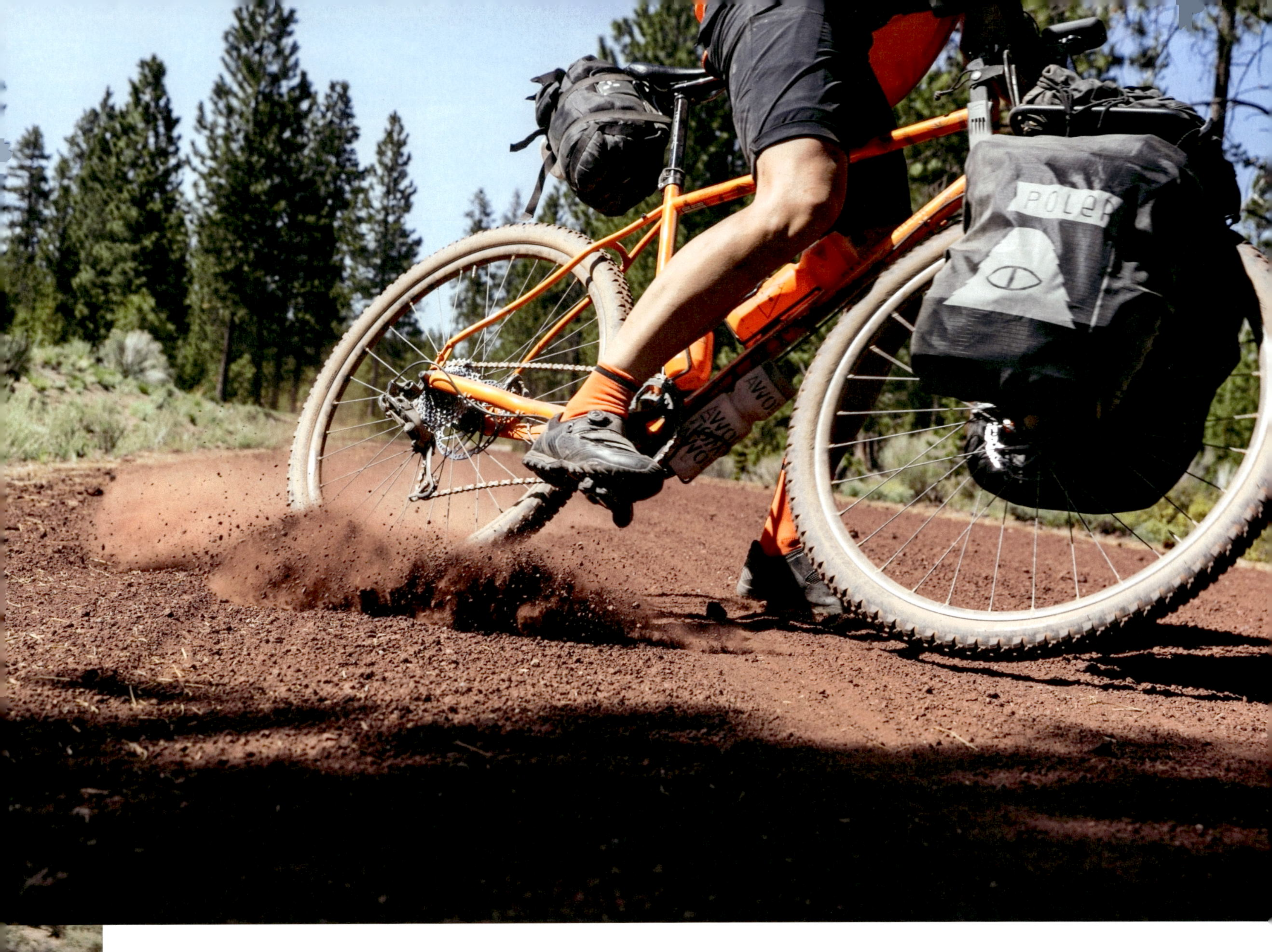


# AWOL

**ERIK NOHLIN**

The AWOL is an adventurous soul wrapped in a heavy duty, do-anything body, on or off the road. Erik Nohlin has been with it since day one, as a designer, rider, and ambassador. He rode his AWOL on the first ever Transcontinental Race—3,200 kilometers from London to Istanbul—and since then the two of them have crossed the New Zealand Alps from east to west, overlanded the Sierra Nevada with the bike on his back, ridden across Oregon, and made more epic skids than man can count. It's nothing less than a man-and-bike love affair.

# Stinner Frameworks

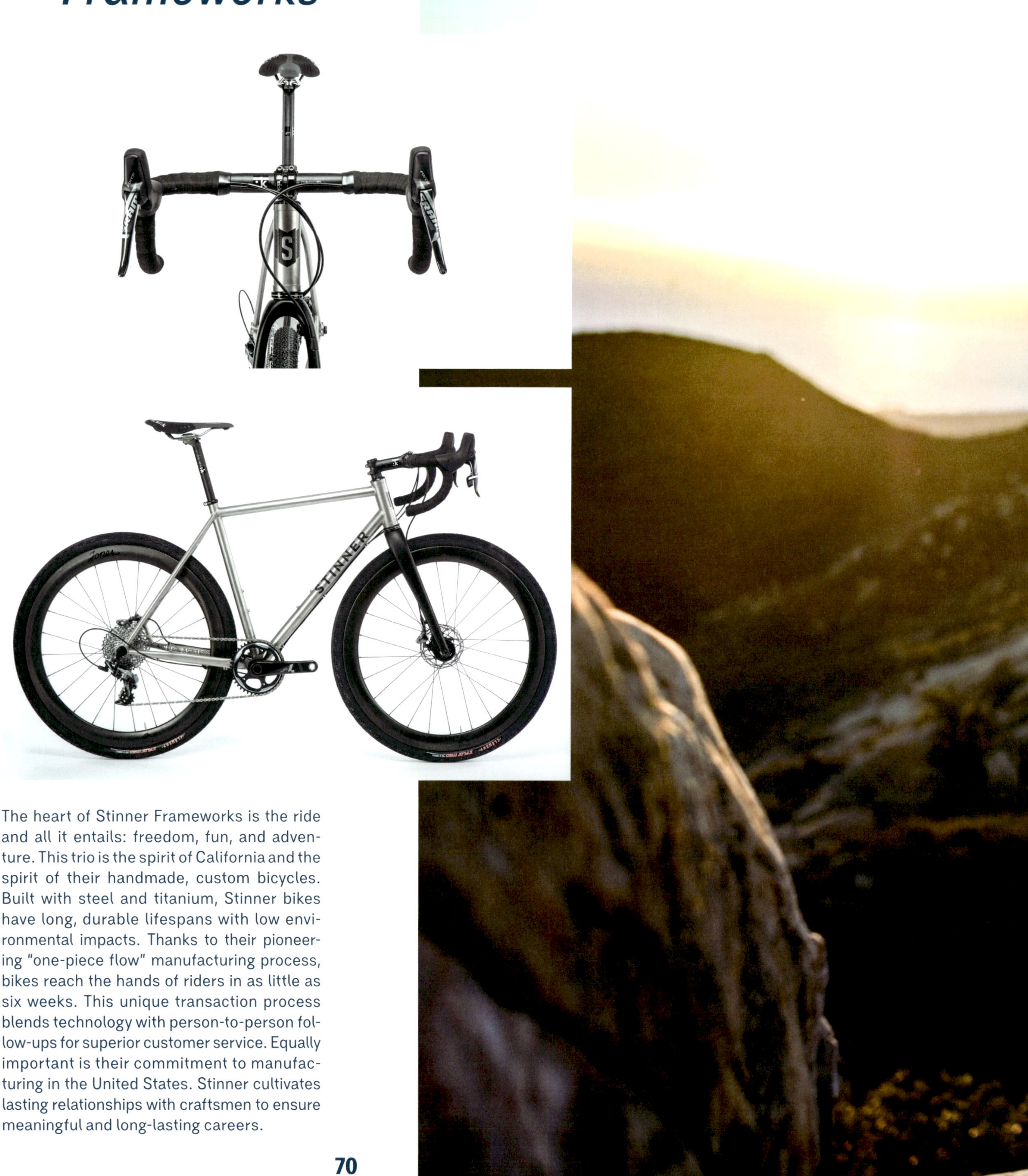


The heart of Stinner Frameworks is the ride and all it entails: freedom, fun, and adventure. This trio is the spirit of California and the spirit of their handmade, custom bicycles. Built with steel and titanium, Stinner bikes have long, durable lifespans with low environmental impacts. Thanks to their pioneering "one-piece flow" manufacturing process, bikes reach the hands of riders in as little as six weeks. This unique transaction process blends technology with person-to-person follow-ups for superior customer service. Equally important is their commitment to manufacturing in the United States. Stinner cultivates lasting relationships with craftsmen to ensure meaningful and long-lasting careers.

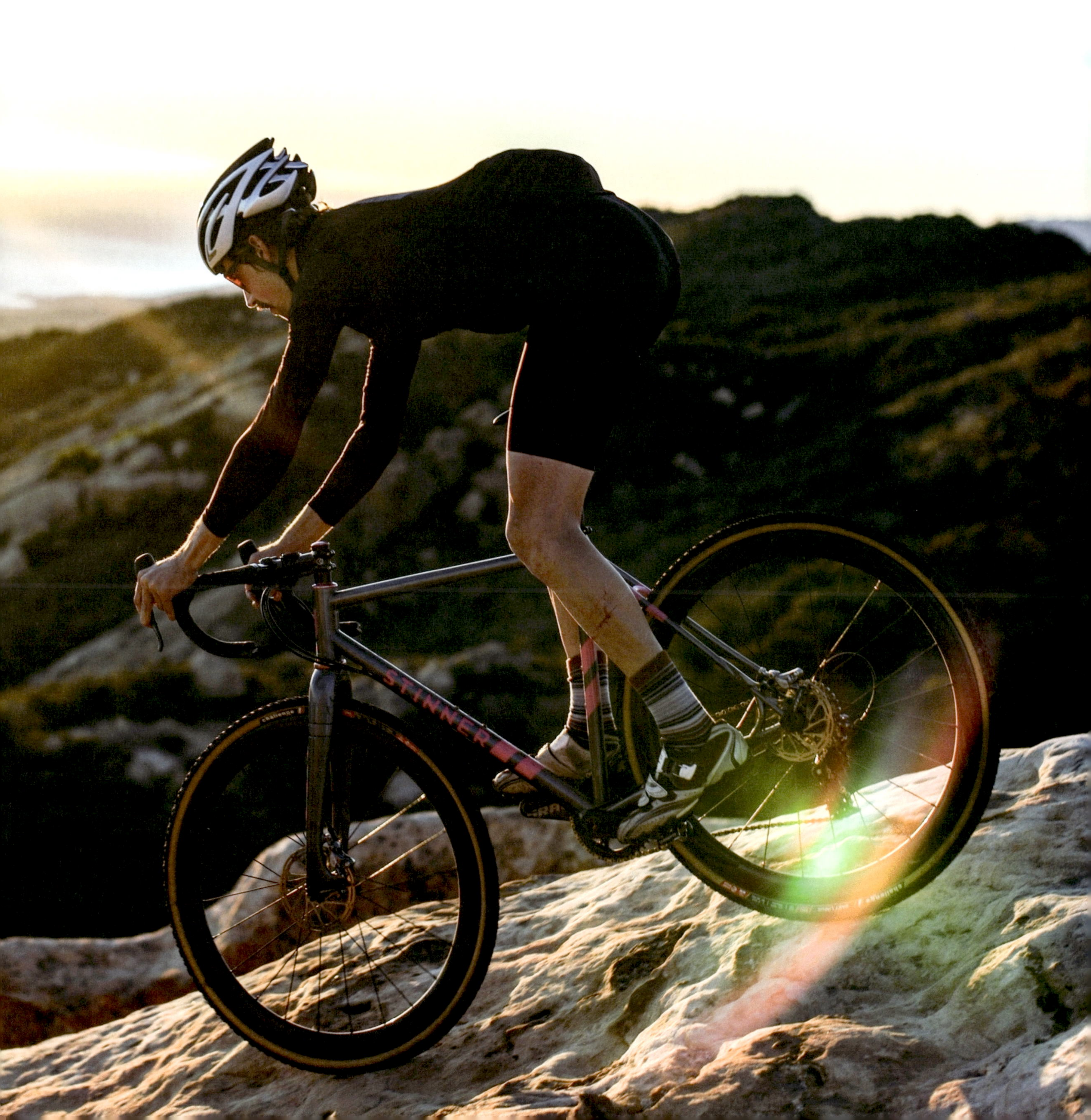
STINNER

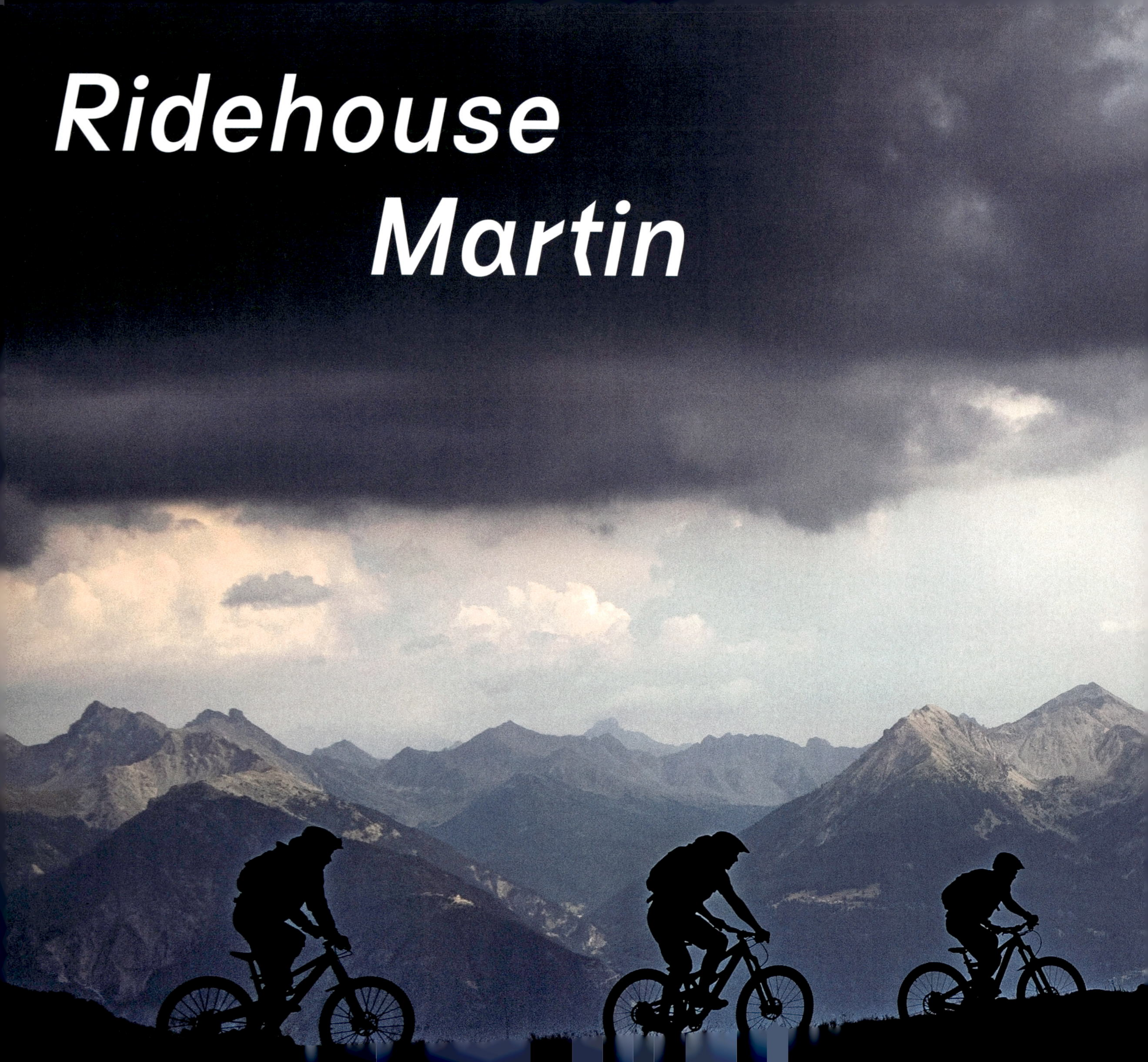
Ridehouse
Martin

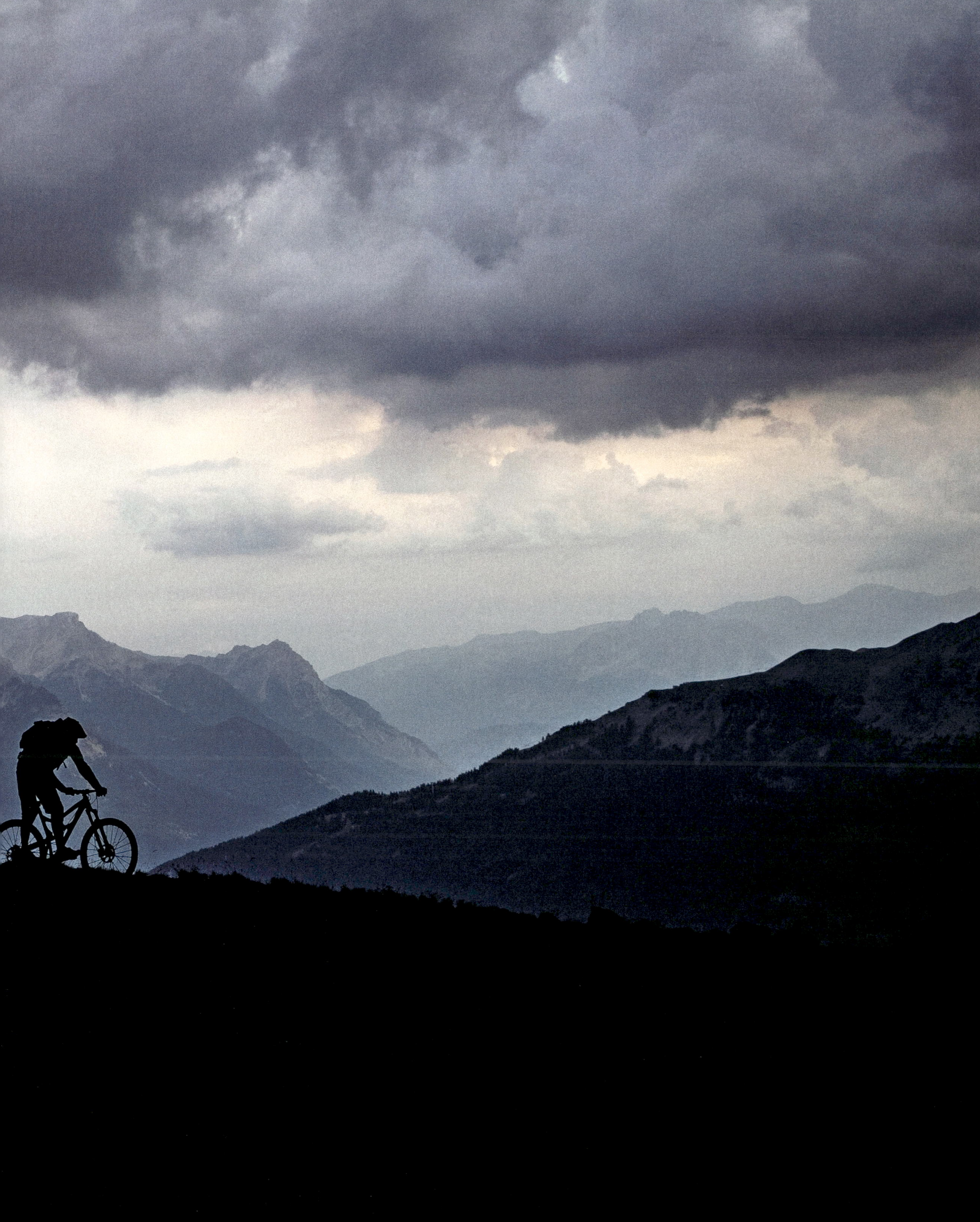

We know that mountain biking in New Zealand is some of the best in the world—perhaps the very best—because Anka and Sven Martin say it is.

These two outdoor adventurers conducted extensive, bicep-, ab-, glute- and semitendinosus-punishing "trail research" around the entire globe, and then decided to settle down in Nelson and call it home—so they should know. Since 2011, after 11 years riding and racing around the world in Norbas and World Cups, the Martins now guide boutique mountain-bike adventures in their "off seasons" on multiday heli-drops with backcountry overnighters, and full- or half-day "samplers" from Nelson, the "sunniest town in New Zealand," which sits at the tip of the South Island, overlooking the Tasmanian Sea. Lush New Zealand boasts a wealth of ecosystems, biodiversity, and geography; the two owners of Ridehouse Martin describe riding there as "otherworldly" and, in Sven's photographs, it is: In the Land of the Long White Cloud, the wilderness feels impossibly alive, the sea views are

***Ridehouse Martin***

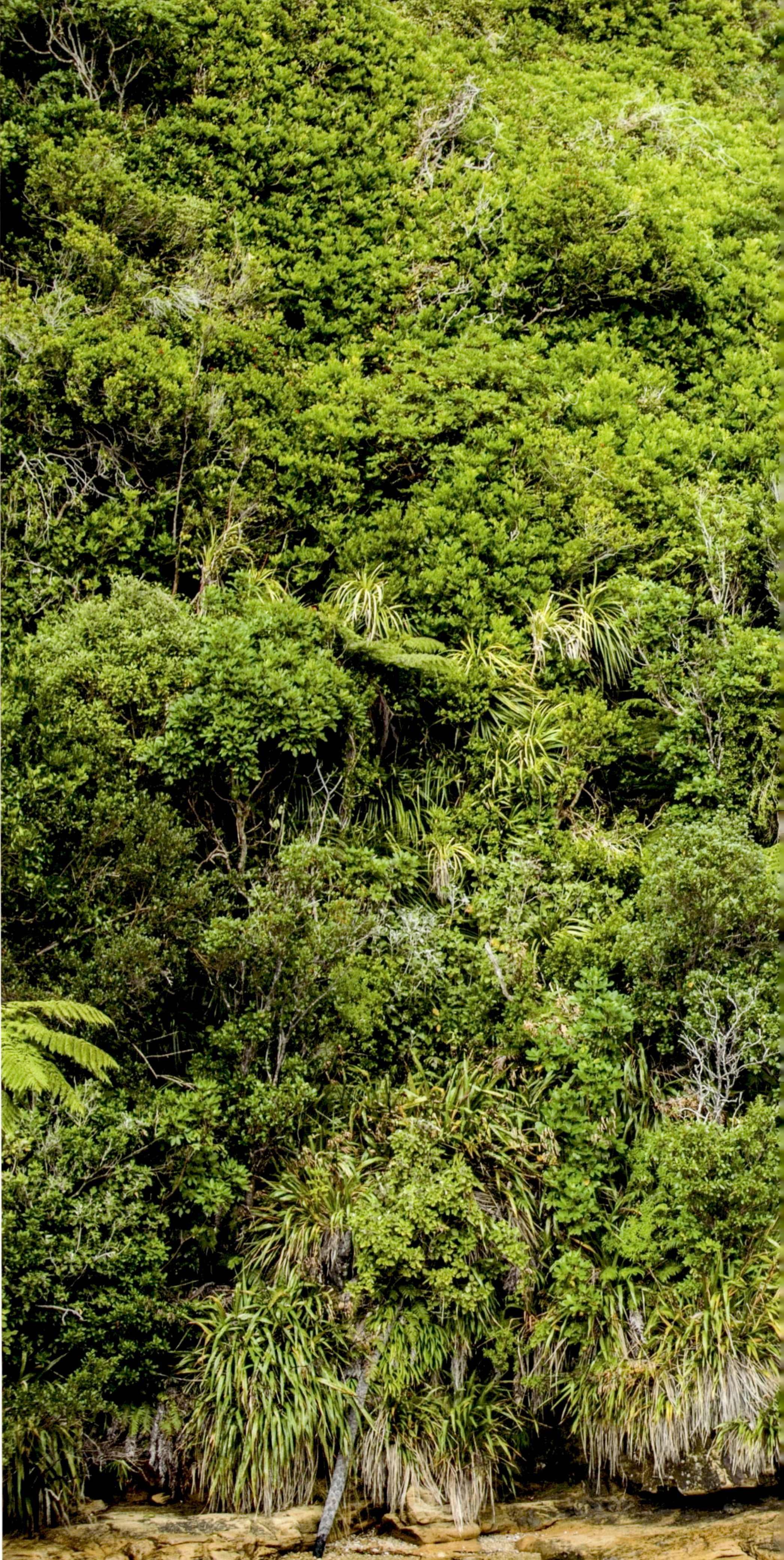

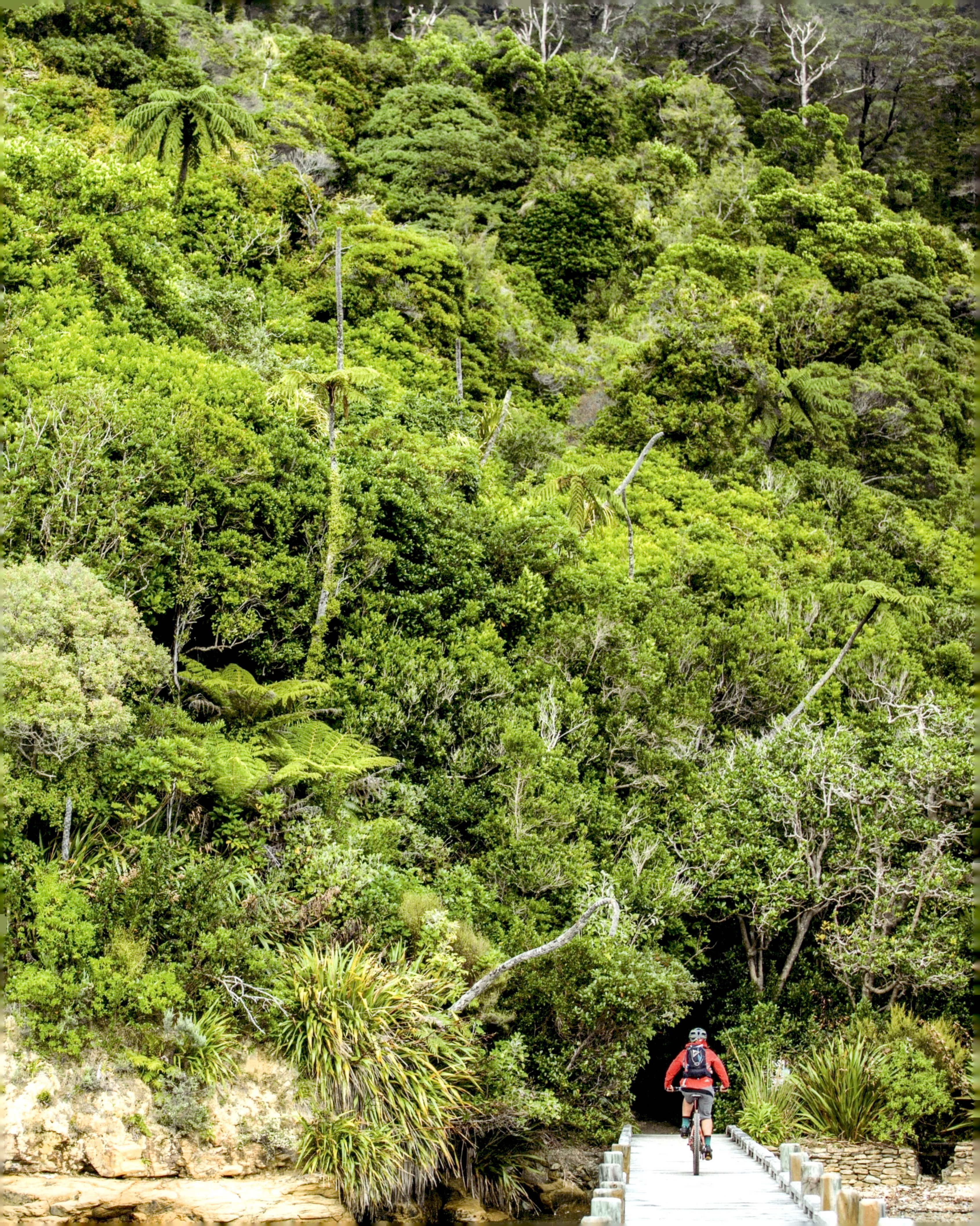

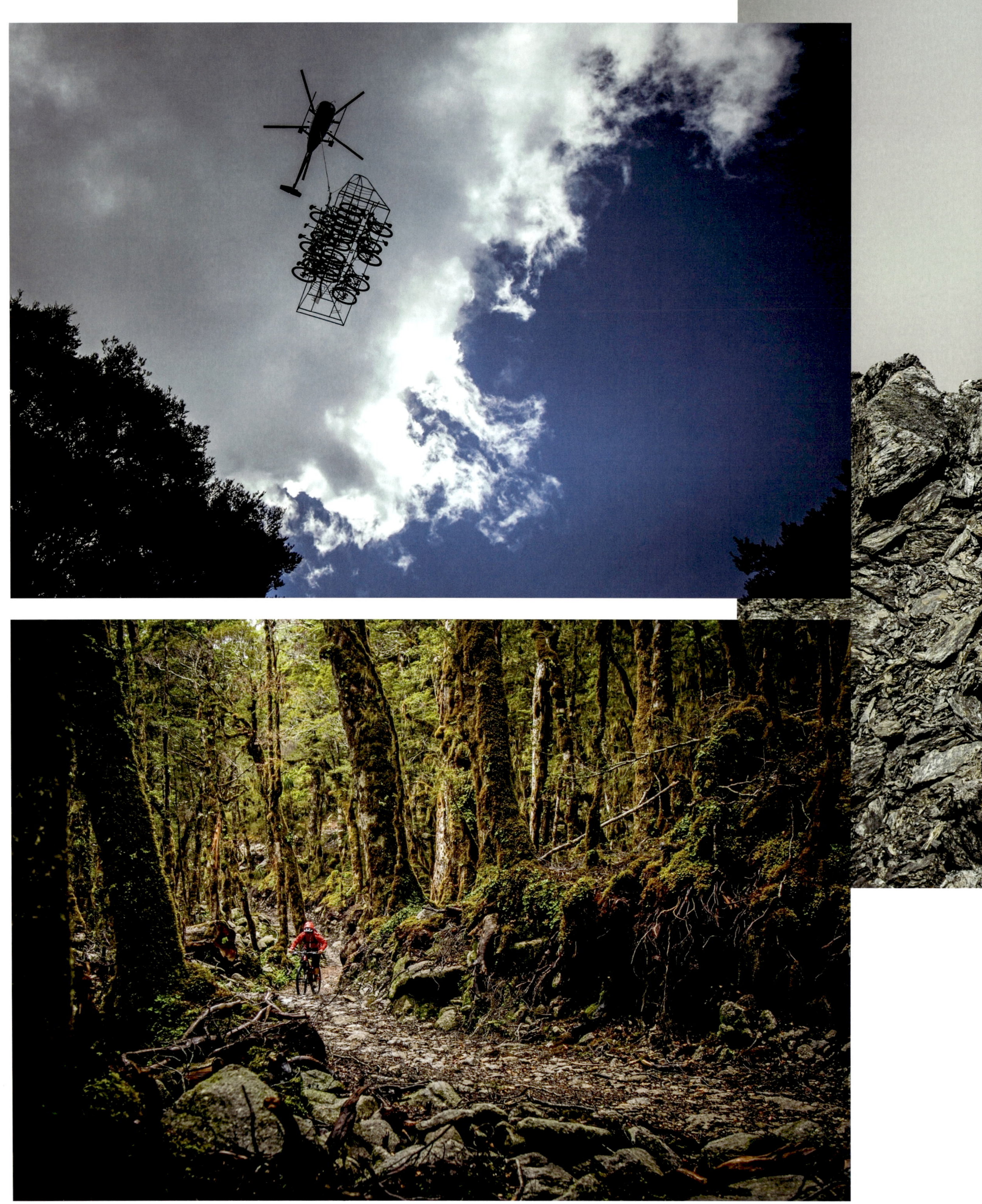

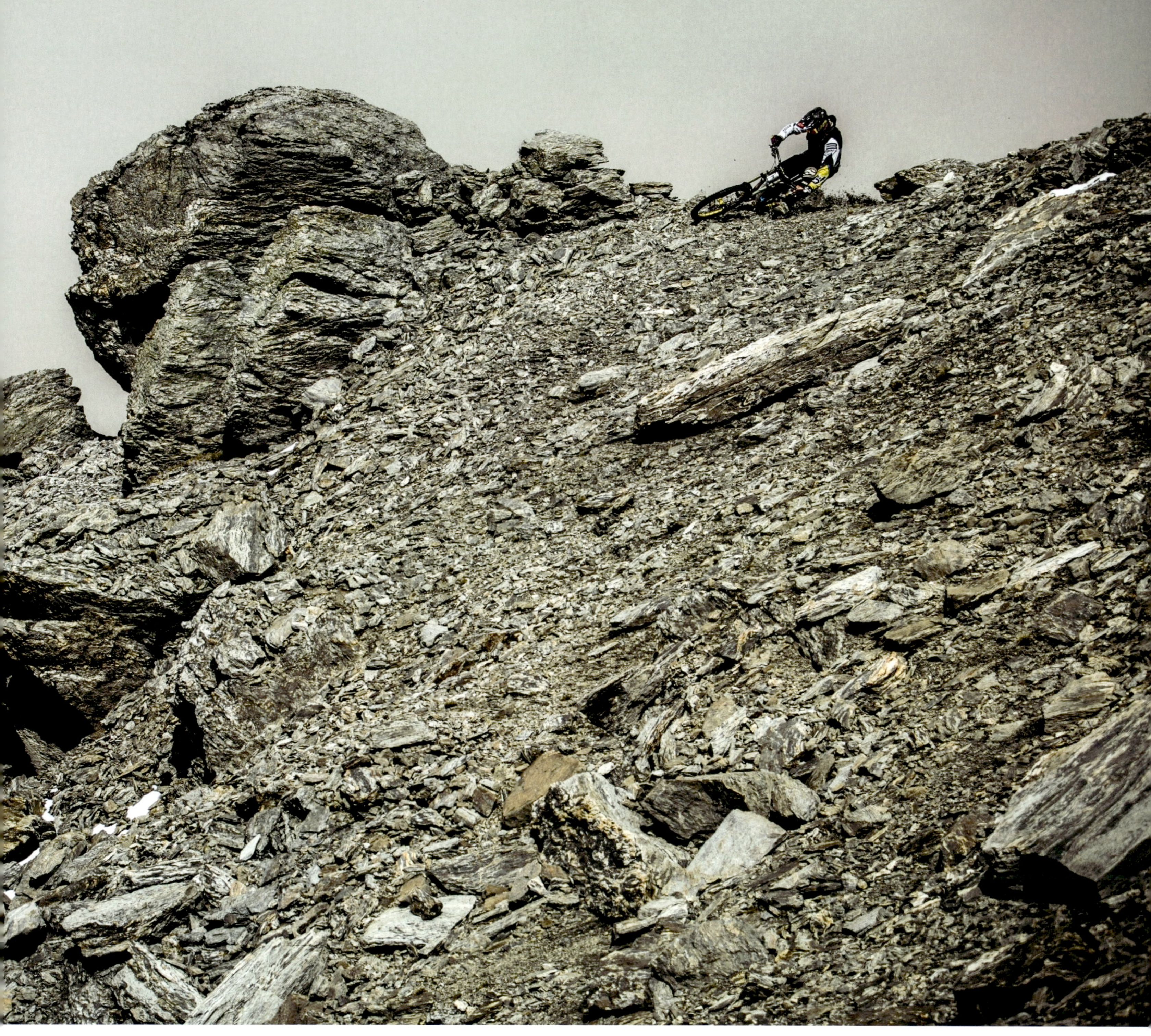

dizzying, the ferns are prehistoric in size, and so are the tree roots, the hairpin turns, and the morning mists, which flow over the ridges like an inland sea. There are moss-cushioned trees, chestnut-winged birds, and boulders colored by lichens. Little bays glow with emerald waters and offer wooden piers off of which to do backflips before lunch. Ending a day of flying and twisting down gnarly track, you may find a sea lion on the sand with his whiskers raised to the setting sun. Because the husband-and-wife team prefer to take the road, path, or track less traveled, the rides they choreograph involve climbing, hike-a-biking, and a few shuttles by land, helicopter, and boat before reaching those supernaturally beautiful, euphoric downhills. (Anka, who teaches Vinyasa yoga, calls them "flowy.") When it's winter in New Zealand, the couple migrate like birds to an old van parked somewhere in Europe, Canada, or the United States, following the course of Anka's Enduro races, professional riding, and trips she leads through the Provencal mountains, as well as the World Cup mountain-biking circuit, which Sven photographs professionally. The wealth of biking and outdoor experience the two have

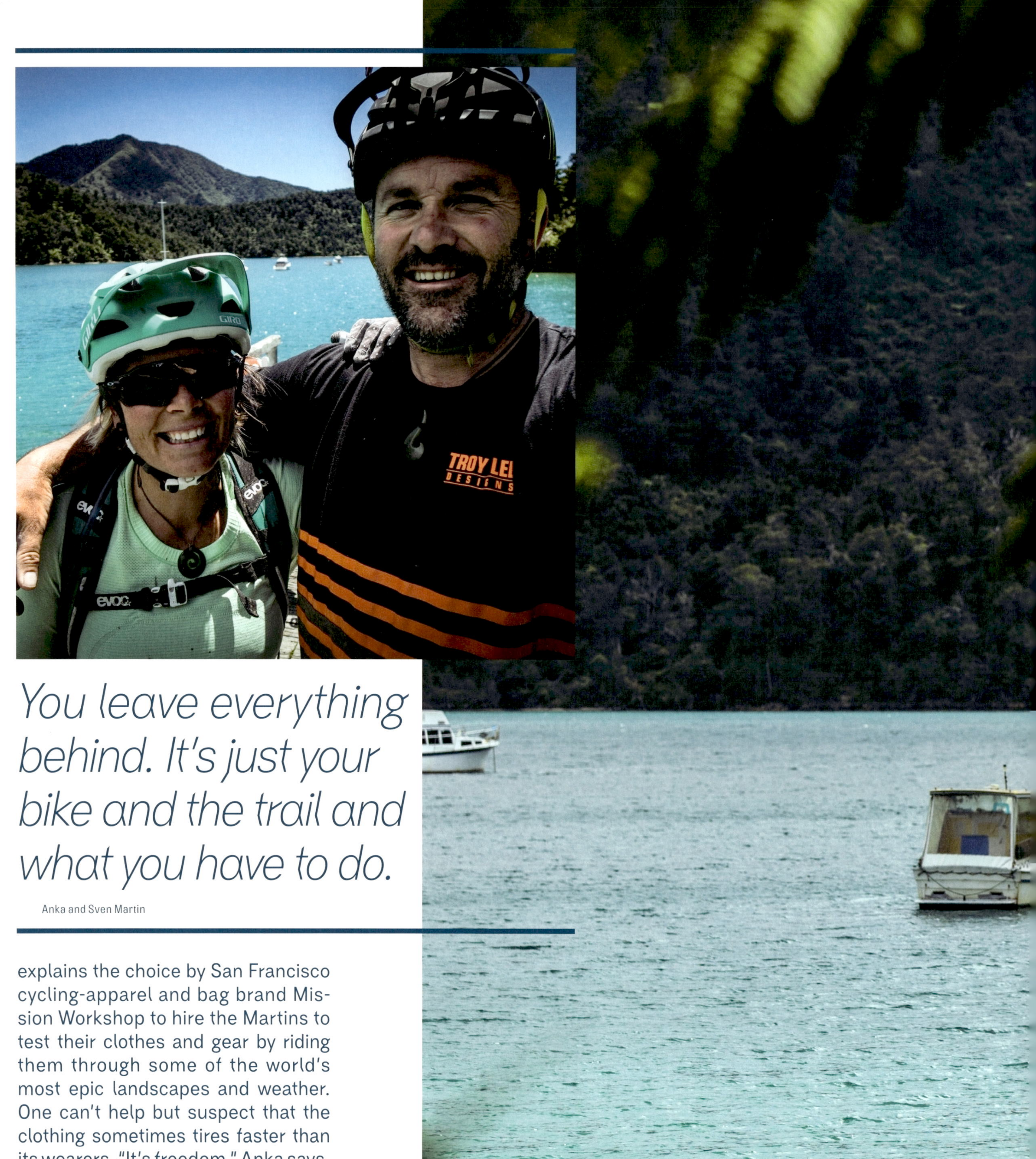


*You leave everything behind. It's just your bike and the trail and what you have to do.*

Anka and Sven Martin

explains the choice by San Francisco cycling-apparel and bag brand Mission Workshop to hire the Martins to test their clothes and gear by riding them through some of the world's most epic landscapes and weather. One can't help but suspect that the clothing sometimes tires faster than its wearers. "It's freedom," Anka says. "You leave everything behind. It's just your bike and the trail and what you have to do."

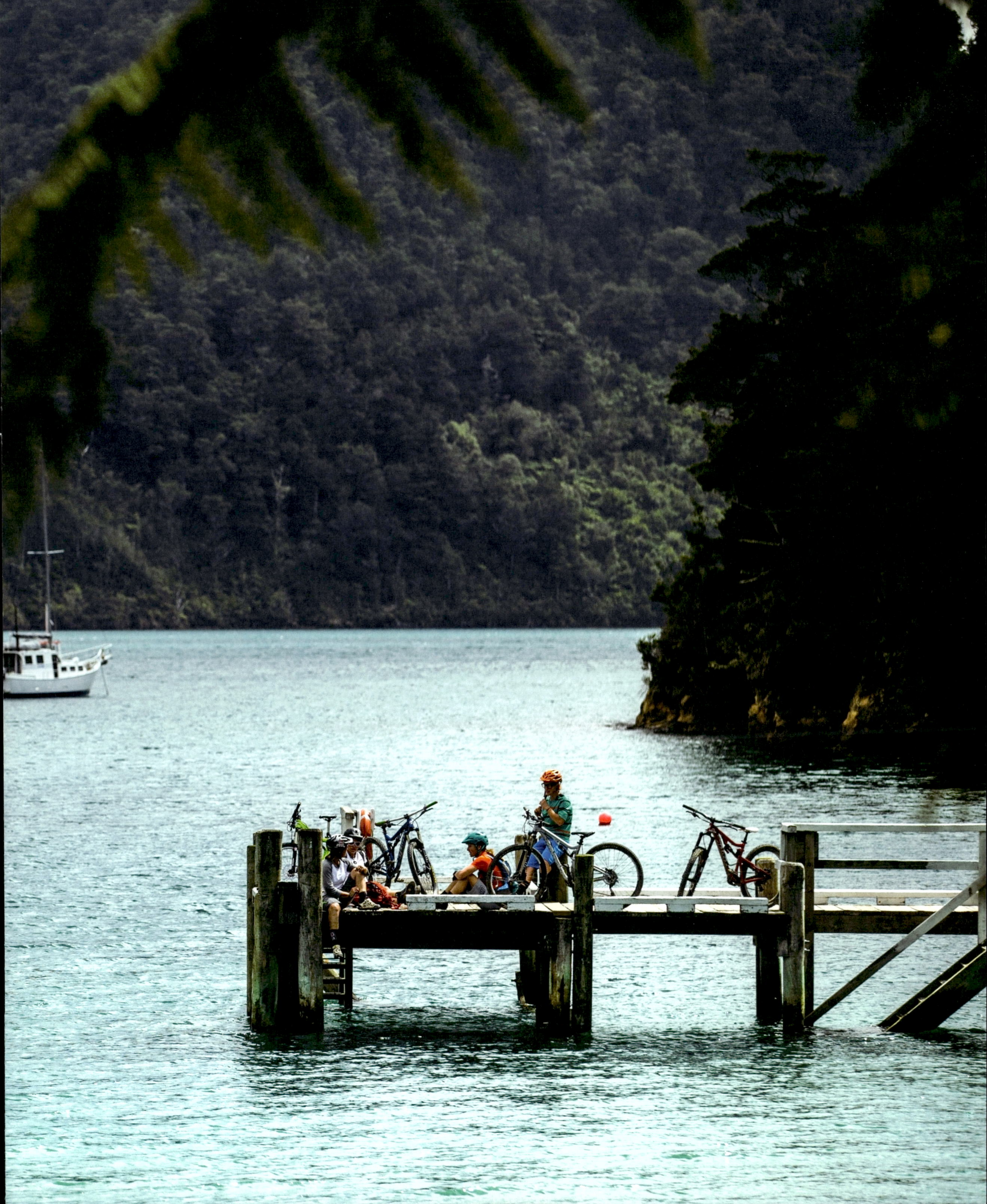

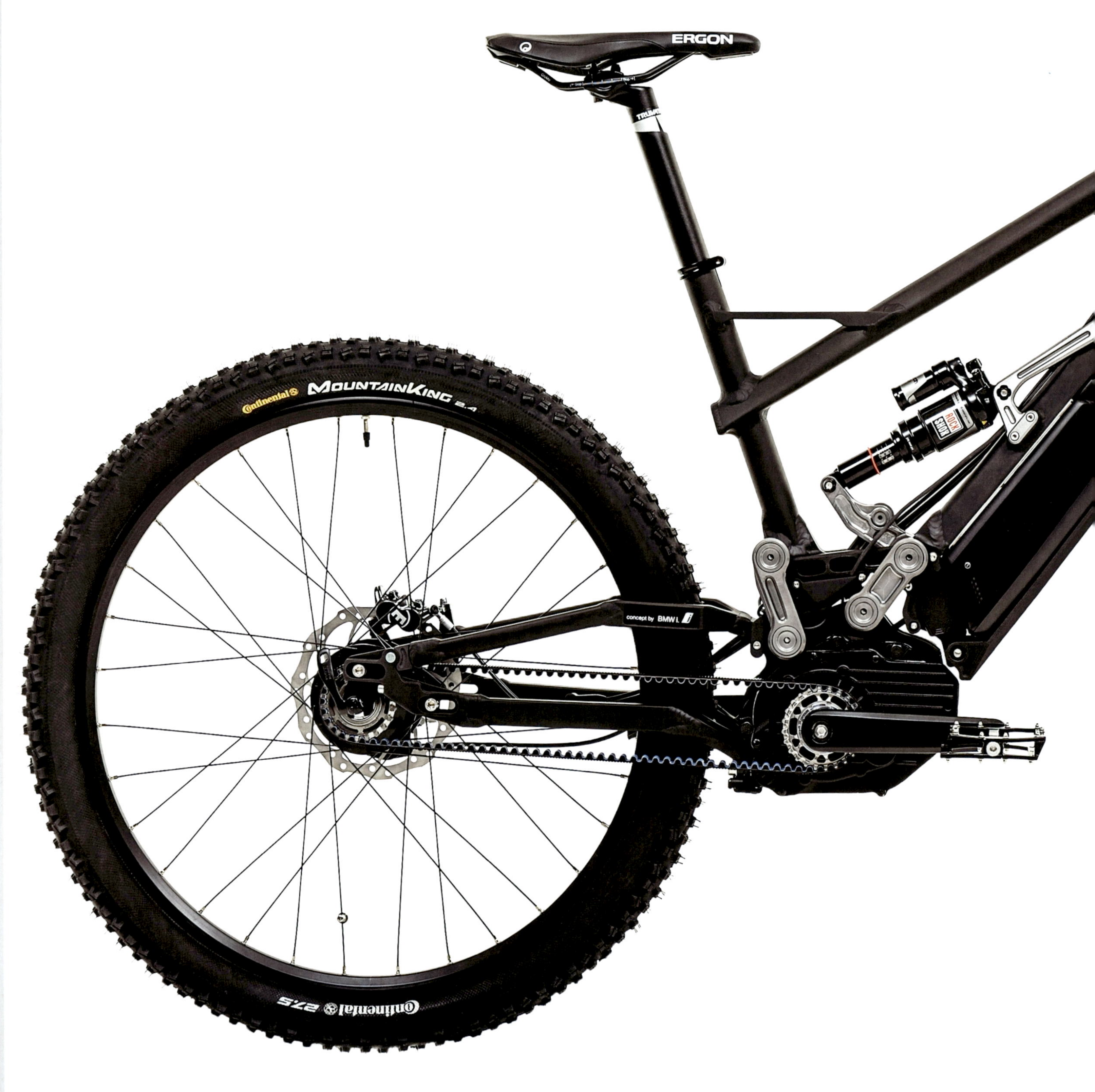
ERGON
Continental
MountainKing 2.4
ROCK SHOX
concept by BMW

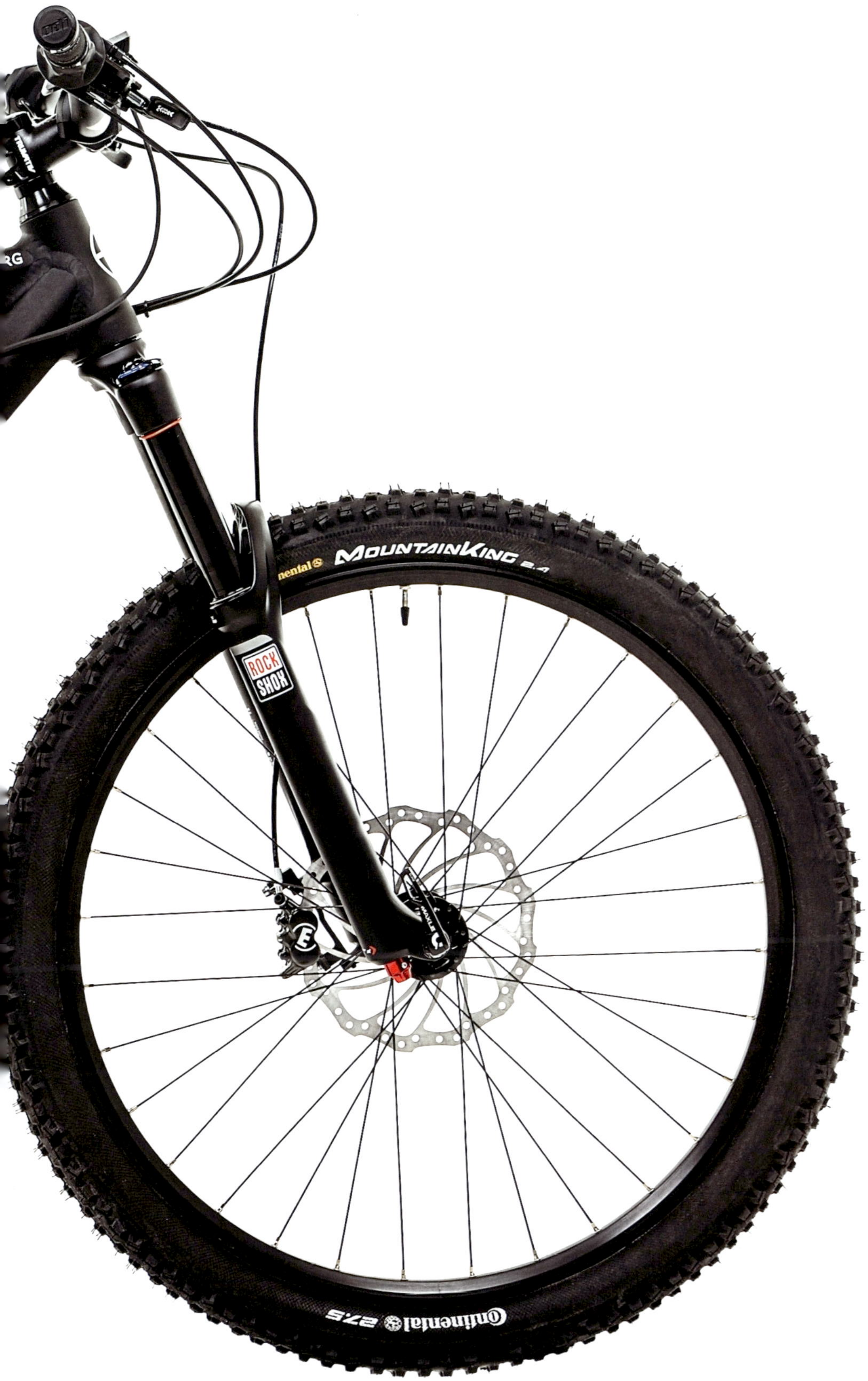

# HNF Heisenberg

This might be the BMW of bicycles. HNF Heisenberg has licensed an innovative suspension technology from the automaker, which makes climbing and descending downhill or alpine terrain a thrill instead of a strain. In the XF1 model, BMW's i-division technology enables HNF to combine a back-wheel suspension with a durable, maintenance-free Gates Carbon Drive belt system that has 150 millimeters of travel, which allows it to unleash its inner tiger. The builders mounted its robust Bosch engine flexibly, which gives it the freedom to vibrate. Even when it it's maxed out eating up gnarled trail and putting the shock absorbers through their paces, the length of the belt remains constant. It is, as its designers say, "an endurance machine."

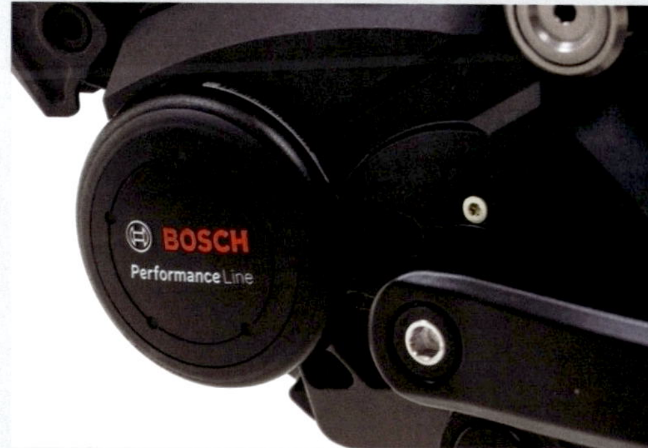


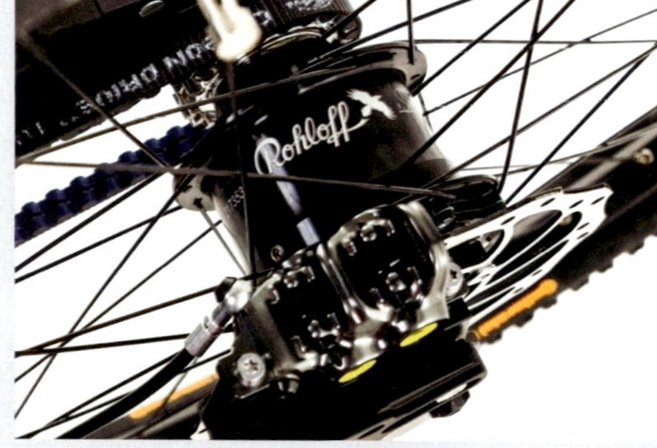

# Rennstahl 853 Pinion Reiserad

FALKENJAGD

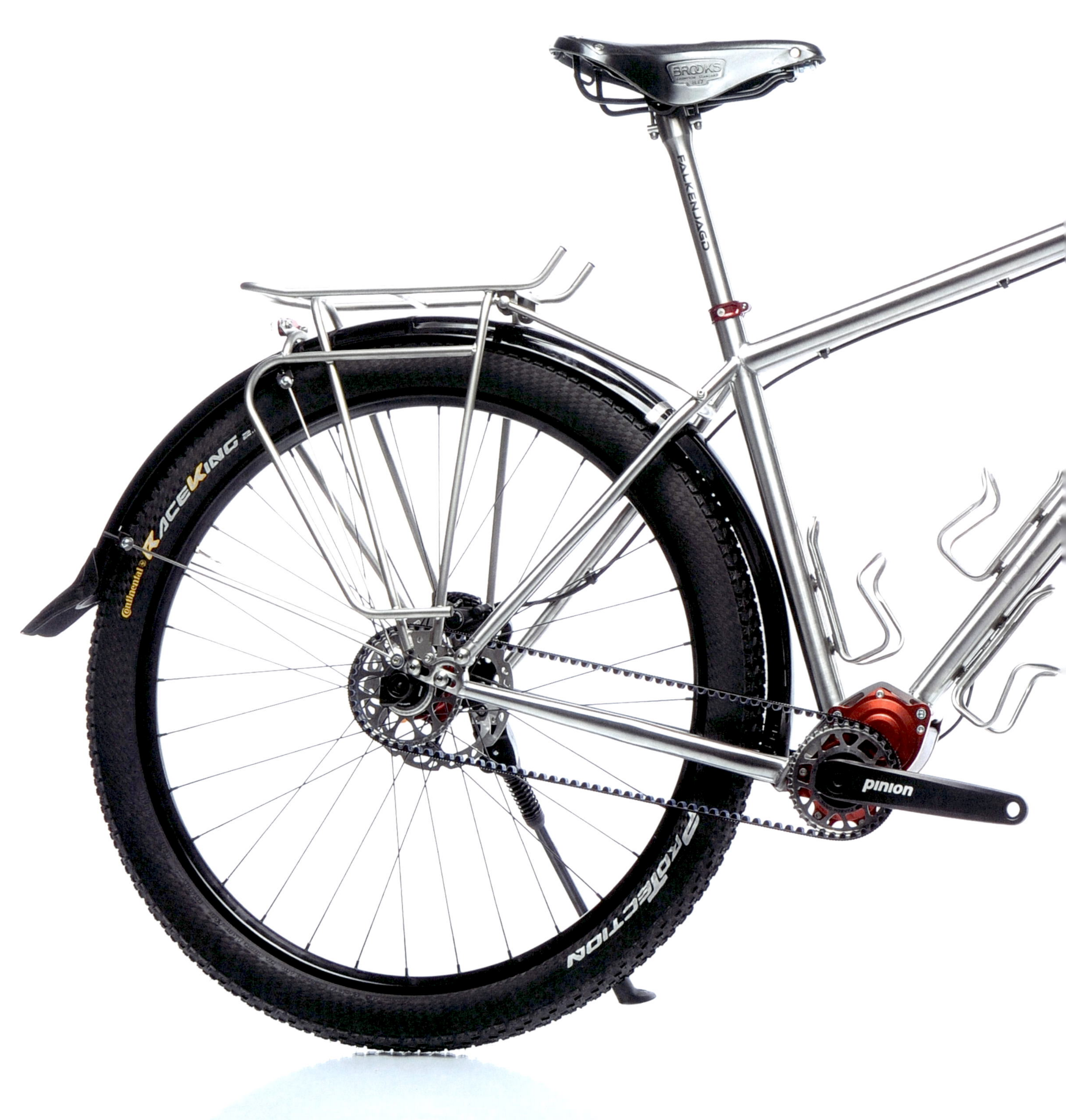

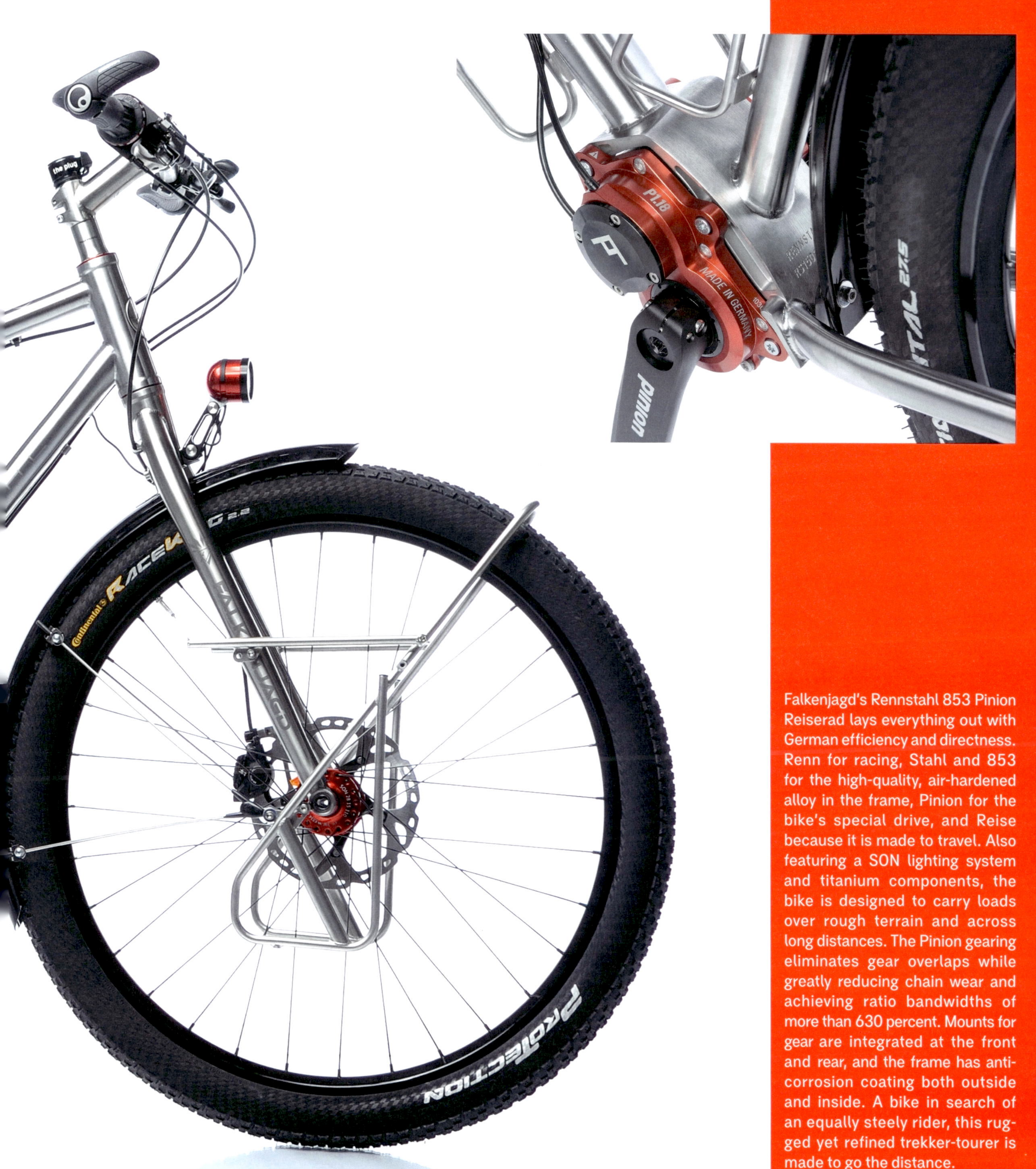


Falkenjagd's Rennstahl 853 Pinion Reiserad lays everything out with German efficiency and directness. Renn for racing, Stahl and 853 for the high-quality, air-hardened alloy in the frame, Pinion for the bike's special drive, and Reise because it is made to travel. Also featuring a SON lighting system and titanium components, the bike is designed to carry loads over rough terrain and across long distances. The Pinion gearing eliminates gear overlaps while greatly reducing chain wear and achieving ratio bandwidths of more than 630 percent. Mounts for gear are integrated at the front and rear, and the frame has anti-corrosion coating both outside and inside. A bike in search of an equally steely rider, this rugged yet refined trekker-tourer is made to go the distance.

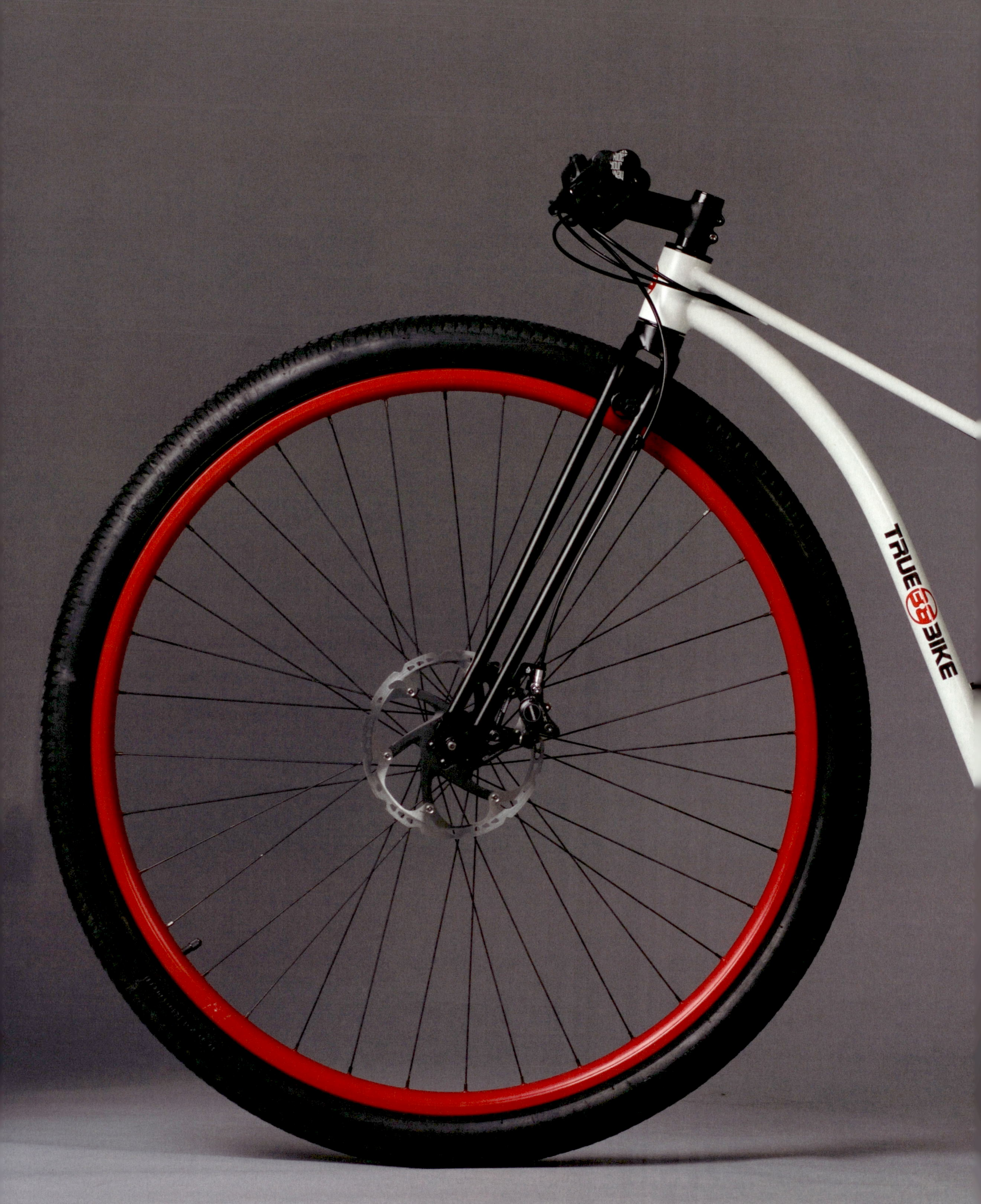
TRUE 36 BIKE

# TrueBikes

Relative to the potently linear lines of some of the bikes out there, the frame and fork of Bratislava-based designer Robert Dilik's TrueBike boast a refreshingly hand-drawn look, which makes the ease with which it can roll over rocks, roots, curbs, and stairs that much more delightful. The TrueBike is truly big: the handcrafted steel frame features oversize—even dominating—36-inch wheels. Dilik's design lets riders attain higher speeds while covering a longer distance with each revolution of the pedal. The higher air volume in each tire lends a pair of cushions to the ride while the rider's lower center of gravity relative to the high wheel axle gives them greater traction. Dilik also custom-designs his TrueBikes to make each one suitable to the future owner's particular style of riding, from mountain biking, bikepacking, or commuting to darting down the middle lane through rush-hour traffic to deliver that last package.

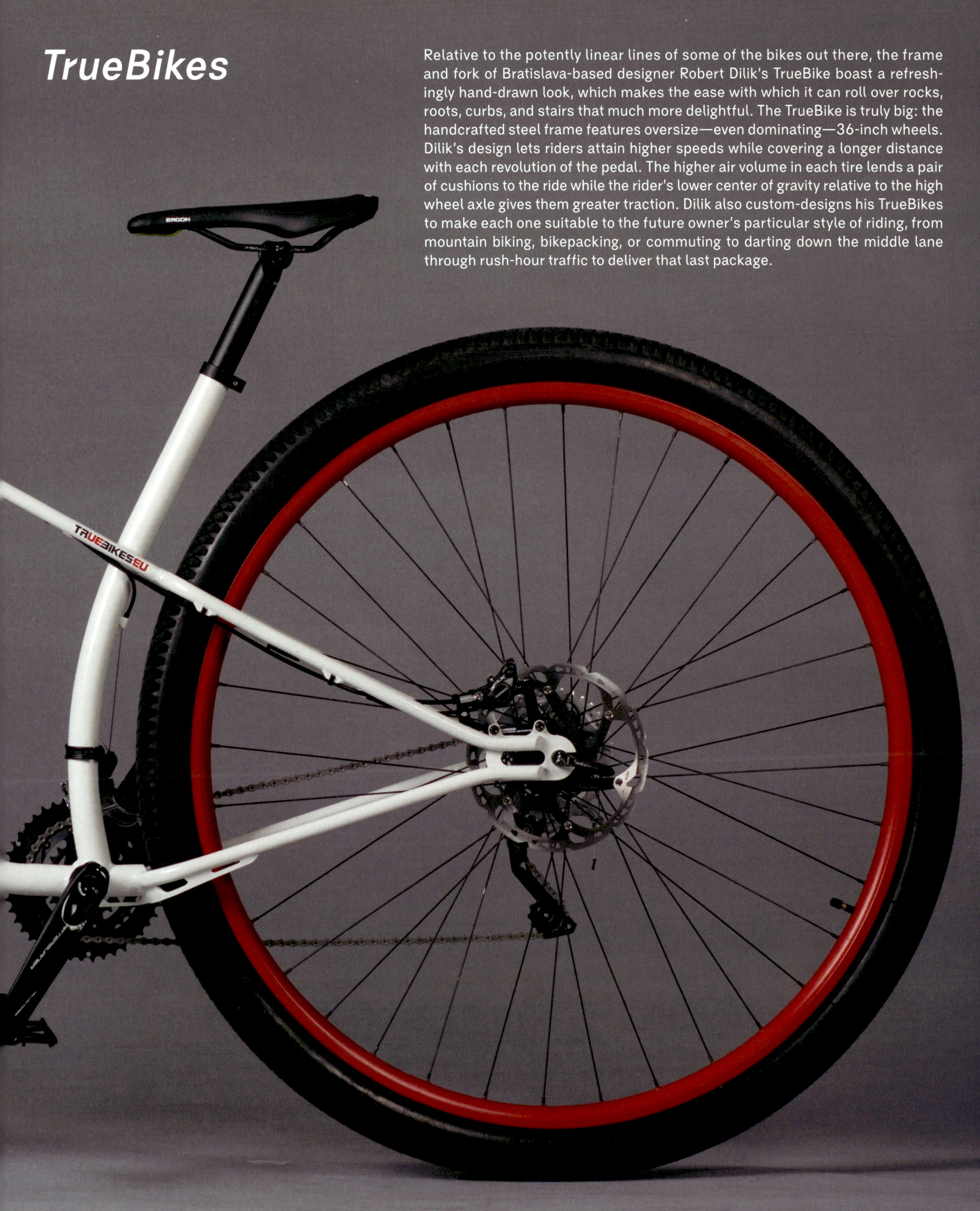

## *Snakedriver*

### 44 BIKES

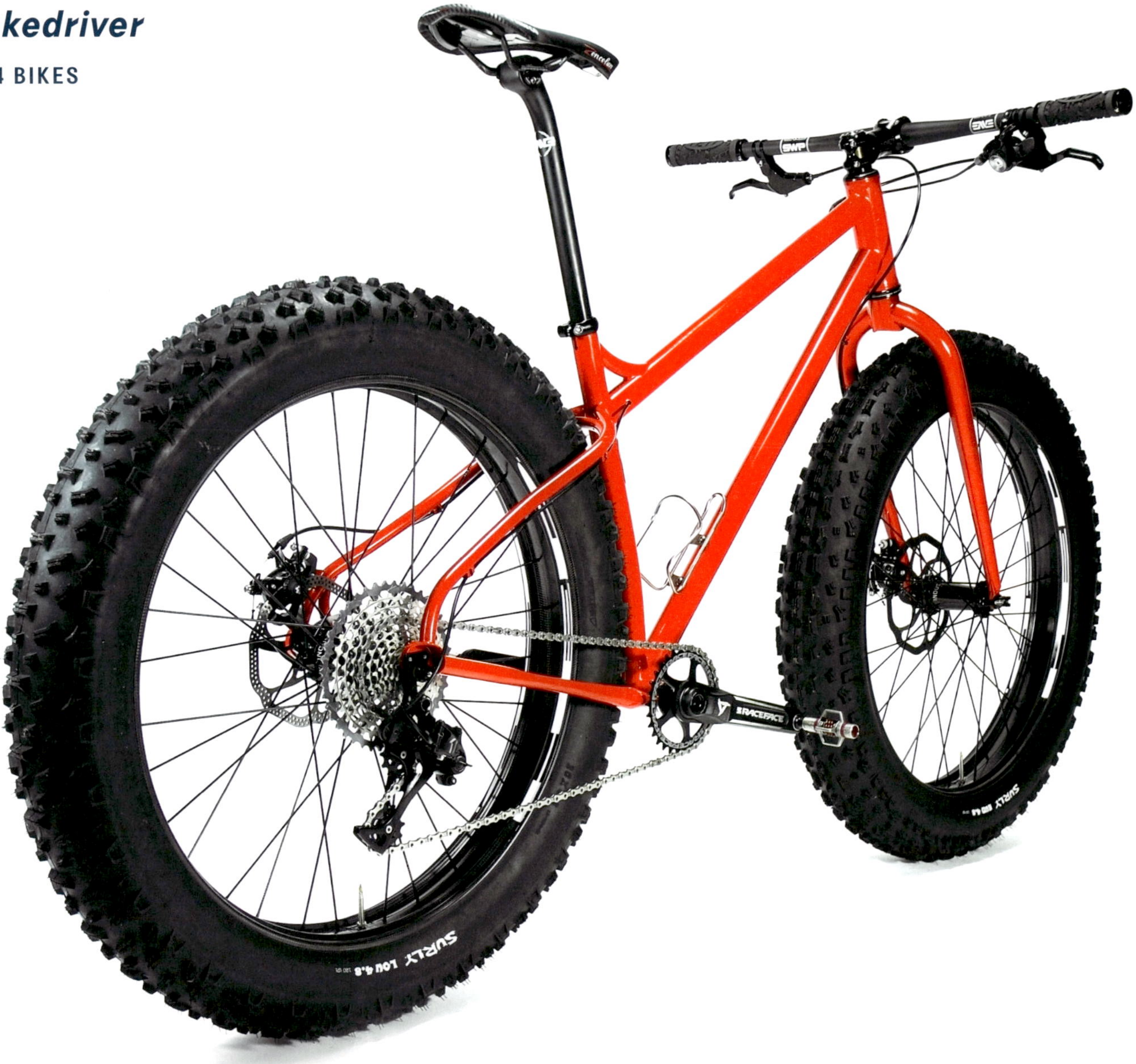

This is the kind of bike that can get you out there—way out there. And then get you back again. The Snakedriver is designed for riders looking for serendipity and people who like to get lost before they find their way again. Kristofer Henry's version of a fat bike, with all its "low-slung swoopy sweetness," is the result of many joyful rides in directions unknown. Henry, who originally trained as an industrial designer and is acutely process- and methodology-driven, has taken this big-wheeled beauty through multiple rigorous design iterations and four prototypes in order to hone its cute yet tough geometry and setup. Now the Snakedriver is capable of weathering the bitterest New England winters and the heavy snowfall for which New Hampshire remains infamous. Each season of riding—whether under clear skies or through the mud while "picking bugs from between your teeth"—provides Henry with fresh on-trail feedback that is then applied to the design tweaks that follow.

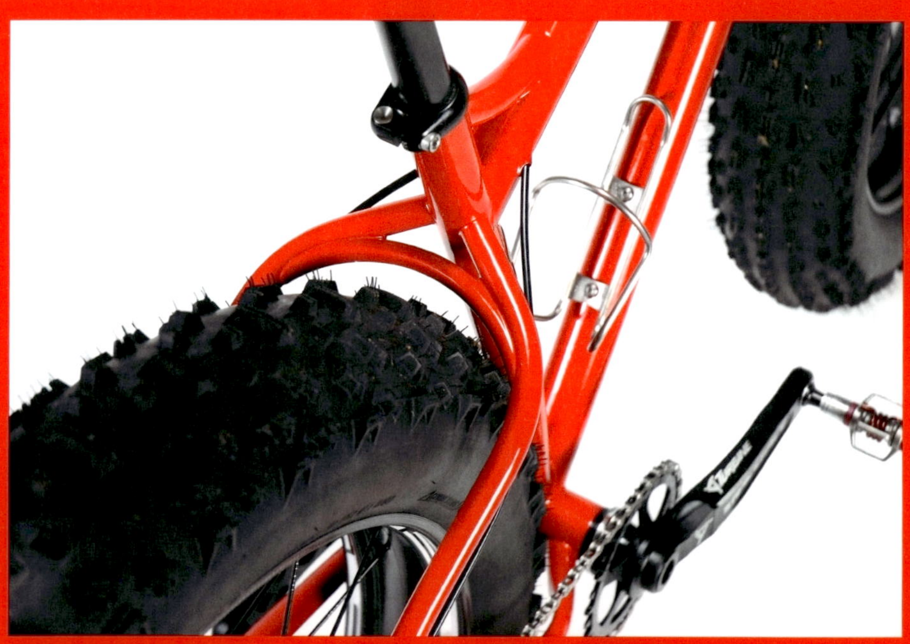

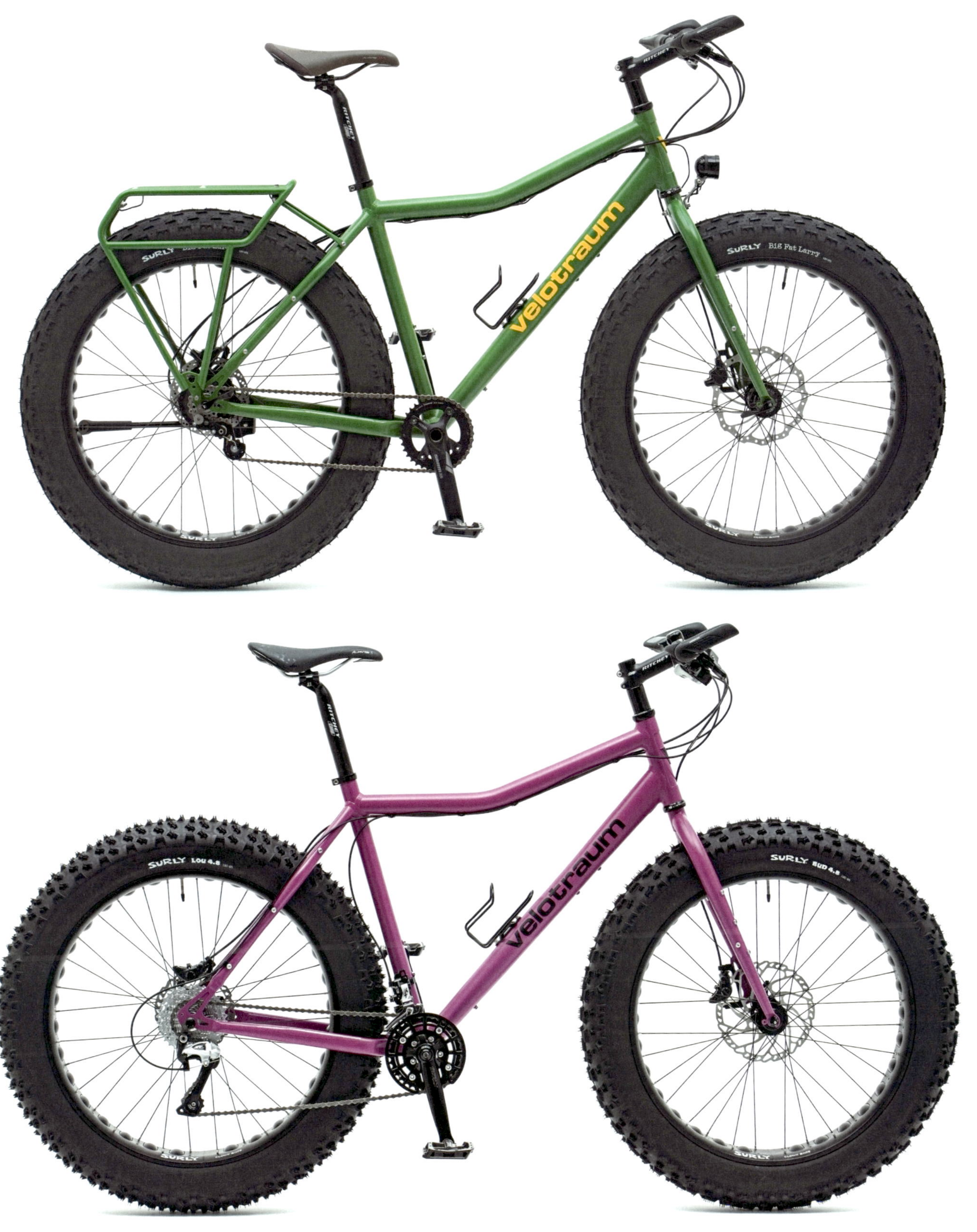


## *Pilgrim*

**VELOTRAUM**

Velotraum's Pilgrim bike combines a mountain bike with a touring bike for a whole new riding experience that opens up new paths and horizons. Whether it be gravel, sand, mud, or snow, the Pilgrim's XXL tires traverse rough ground with a balance of ease, perfect control, and comfort. Its outstanding off-road technology opens up snowy winter climates to touring cyclists and mountain bikers alike, providing safety and comfort on the same two wheels—all without complicated or maintenance-intensive components. The Pilgrim is definitely prepared for all situations and challenges.

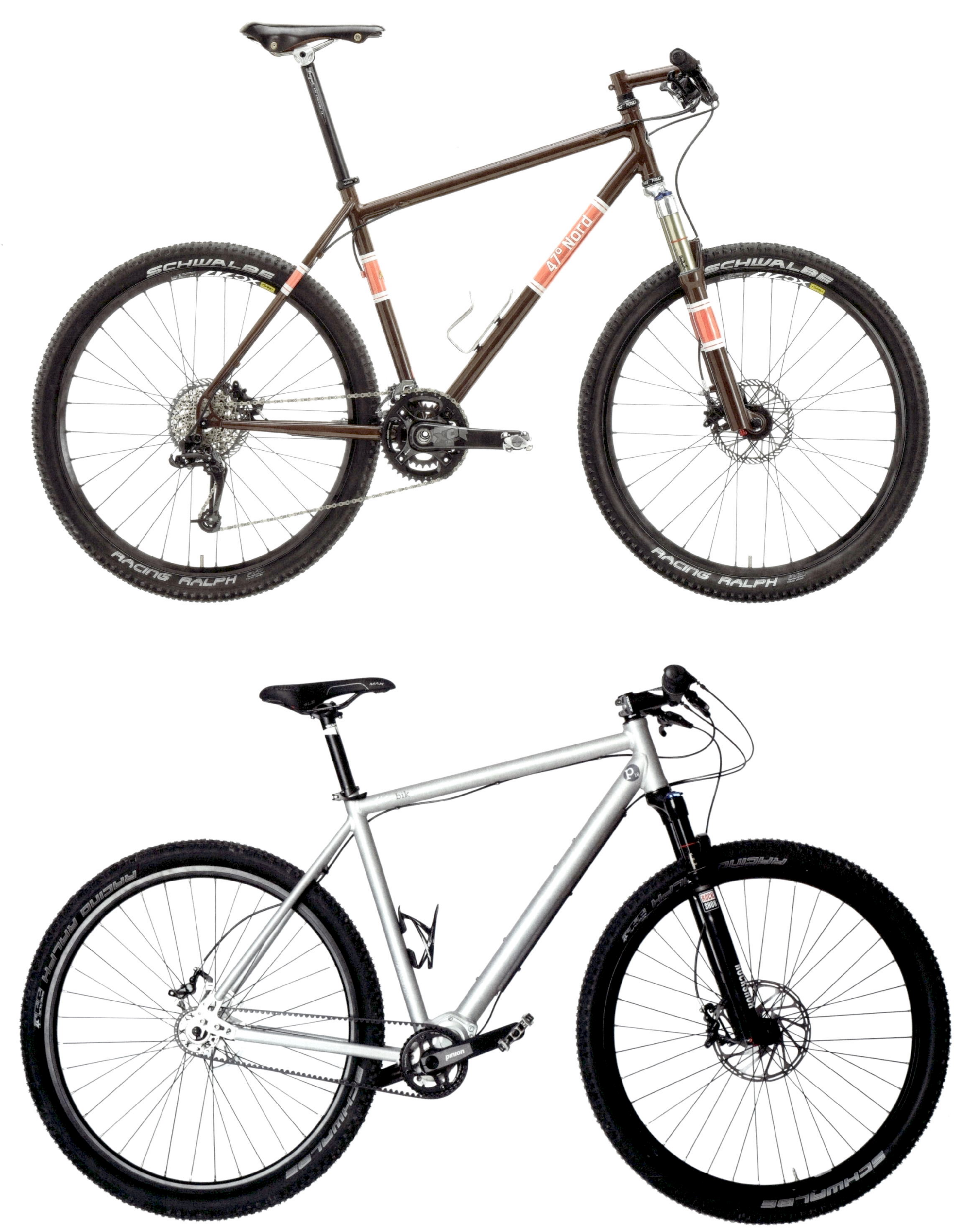
SCHWALBE
47° Nord
RACING RALPH
pinion

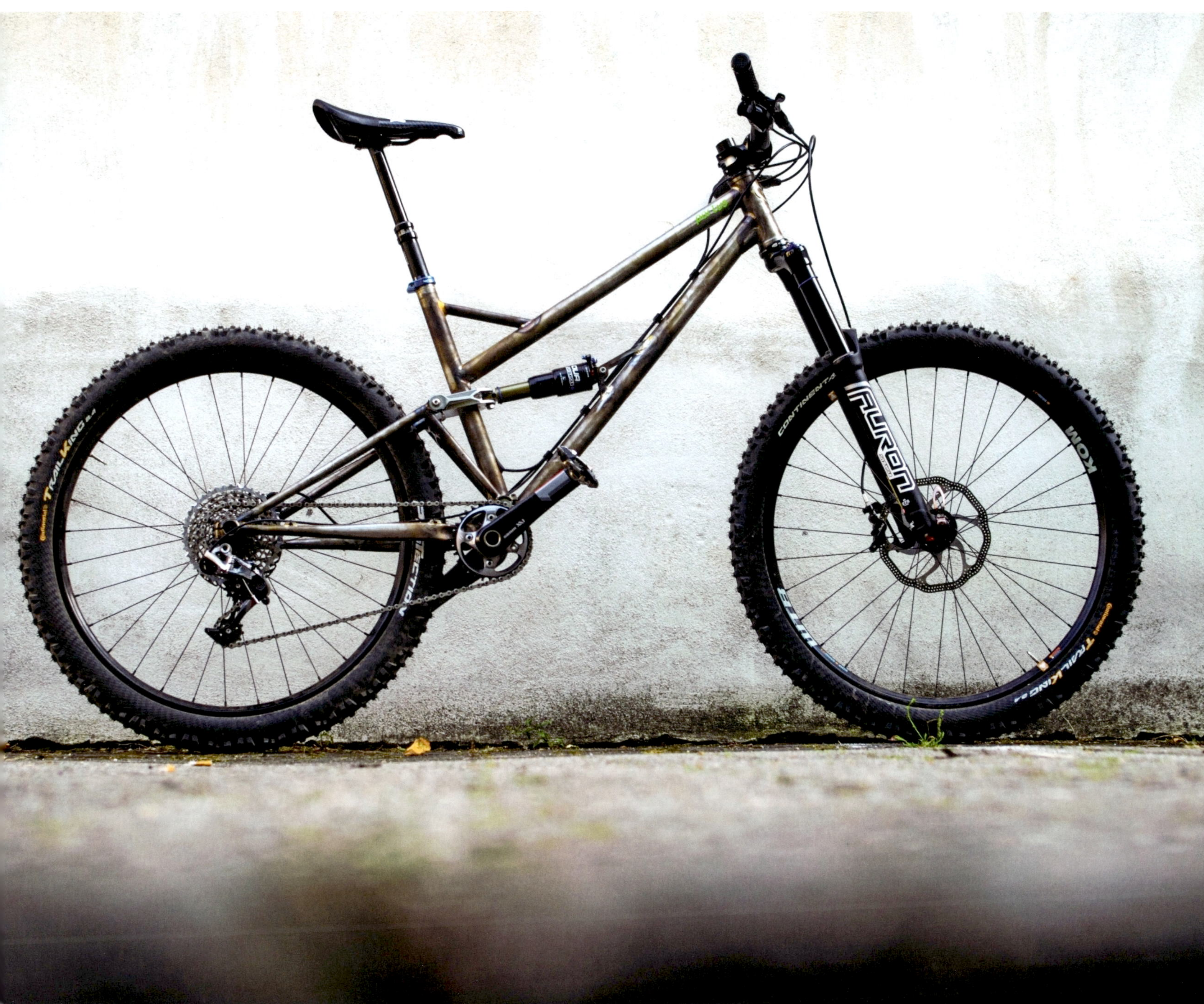


opposite page, top:

***Freyr***

**47° NORD**

Freyr, one of the most important gods of the Norse religion, was associated with sacral kingship, virility, prosperity, sunshine, and fair weather, and was pictured as a phallic fertility god. Freyr bestowed peace and pleasure on mortals and chose the shining, dwarf-made boar Gullinbursti as his mount. With the Freyr, 47° Nord seeks to harness the god's epic reputation in a bespoke hardtail mountain bike made with a CrMo steel frame, a custom-painted frame and fork, and cable routing threaded inside the top and down tubes.

opposite page, bottom:

***P29***

**FLITZ**

Flitzes often come in dual models: one version with a motor, the other without. So too with the P29, which is sleek while retaining the sturdy good looks of a mountain bike. Weighing in at a couple kilos less than the other models, it is built for "sport driving" over a variety of terrain and comes equipped with a RockShox fork, Selle Italia seat, Gates Carbon Drive power transmission, and a GO SwissDrive EVO, which makes it, for those not riding to escape it all, "smartphone ready."

this page: ***ICB2.0 steel***

When the top German mountain-biking news site mtb-news.de challenged its community to crowdsource a bike design, the response was overwhelming. Together with Alutech Cycles and engineer Stefan Stark, they developed a full-suspension trail bike that met the needs and wishes of the project's participants. What might be the first ever internet community bike has a single-pivot linkage system and is set for production in Taiwan in the near future. Because of their customization expertise, Portus Cycles was asked to join the project as a partner. Almost every dimension, like the wheelbase, stack, reach, and steering angle, can be tweaked in their workshop in Pforzheim, Germany, where they use quality tubes from Reynolds, Columbus, True Temper, and Dedacciai.

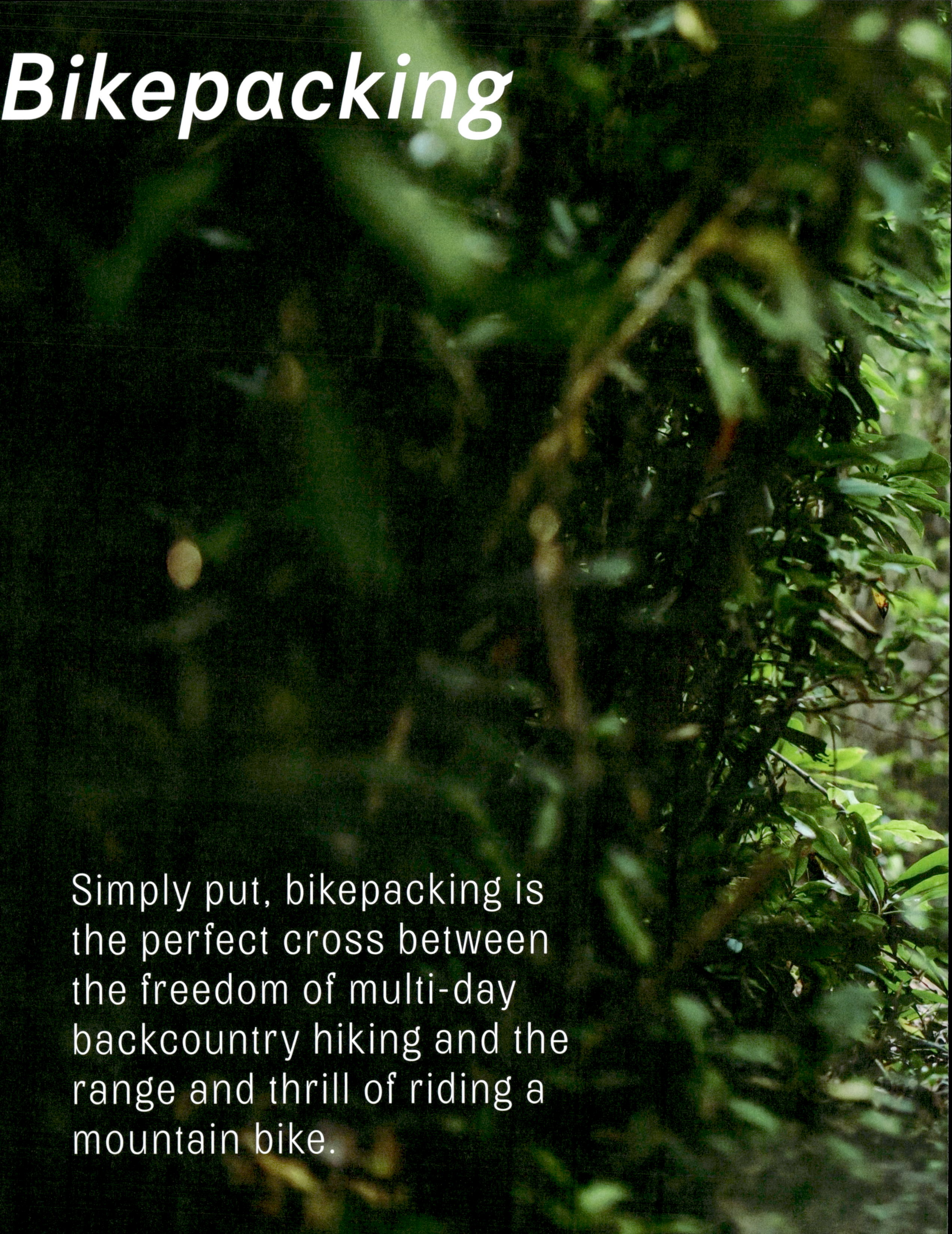

# Bikepacking

Simply put, bikepacking is the perfect cross between the freedom of multi-day backcountry hiking and the range and thrill of riding a mountain bike.

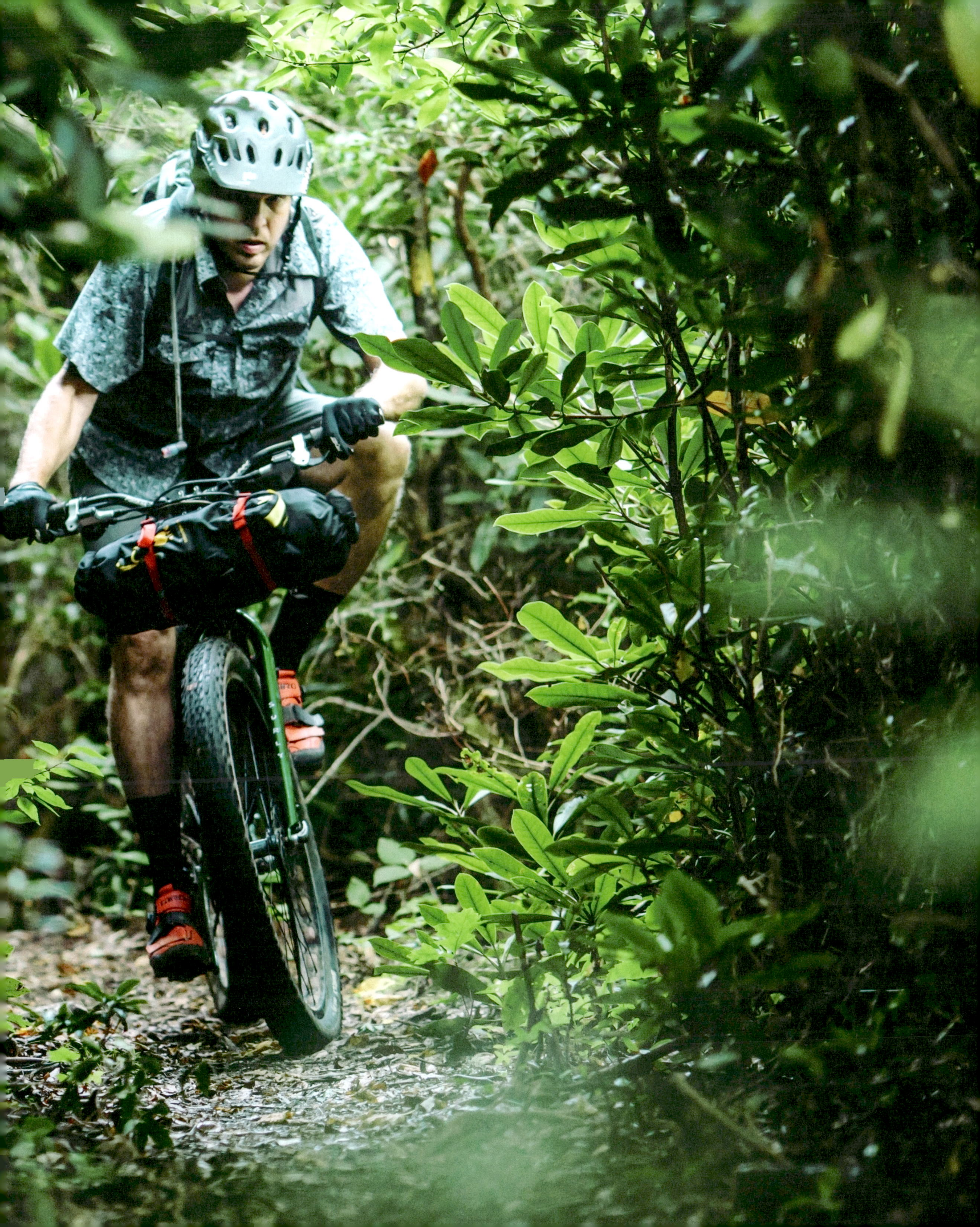

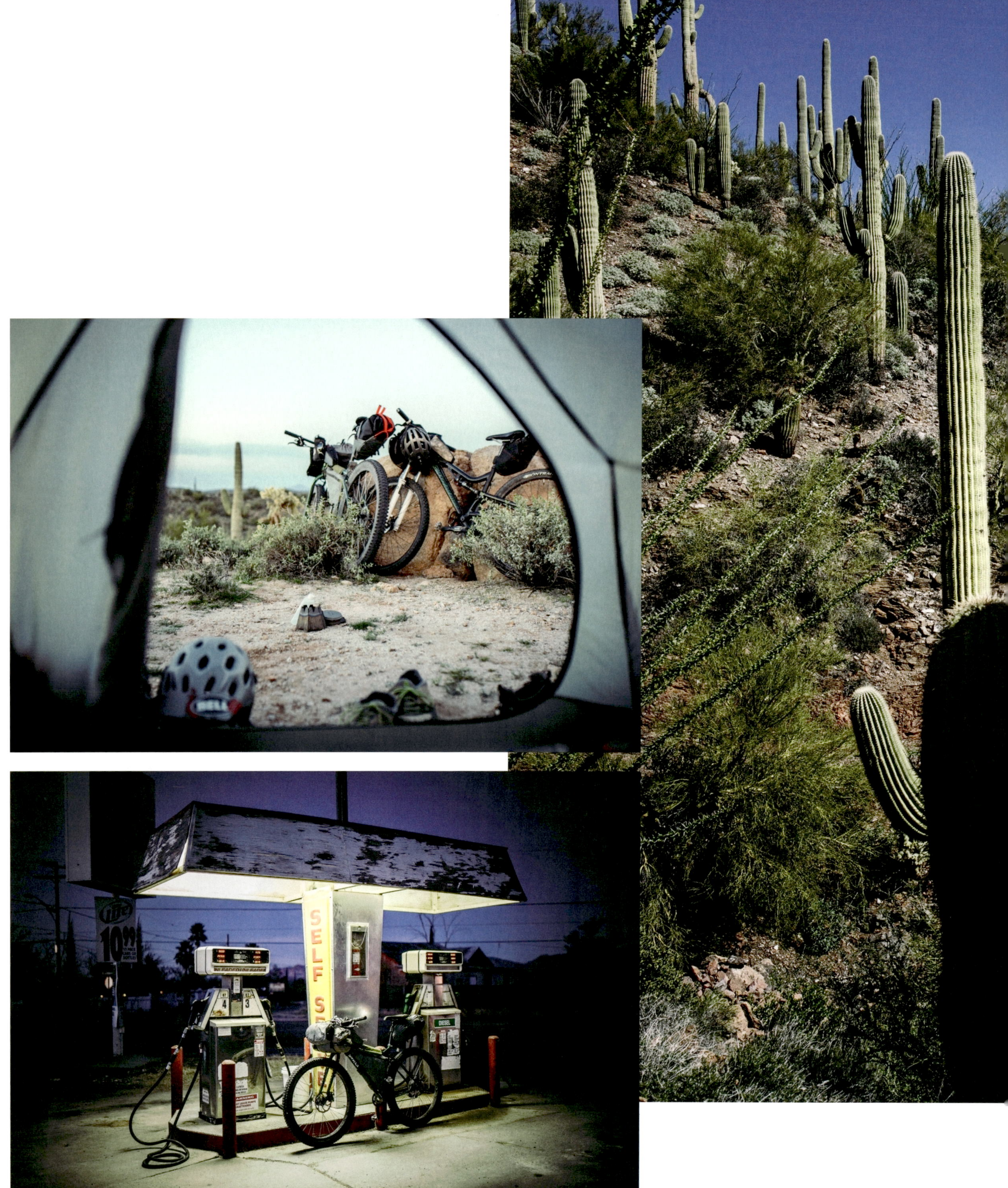
SELF

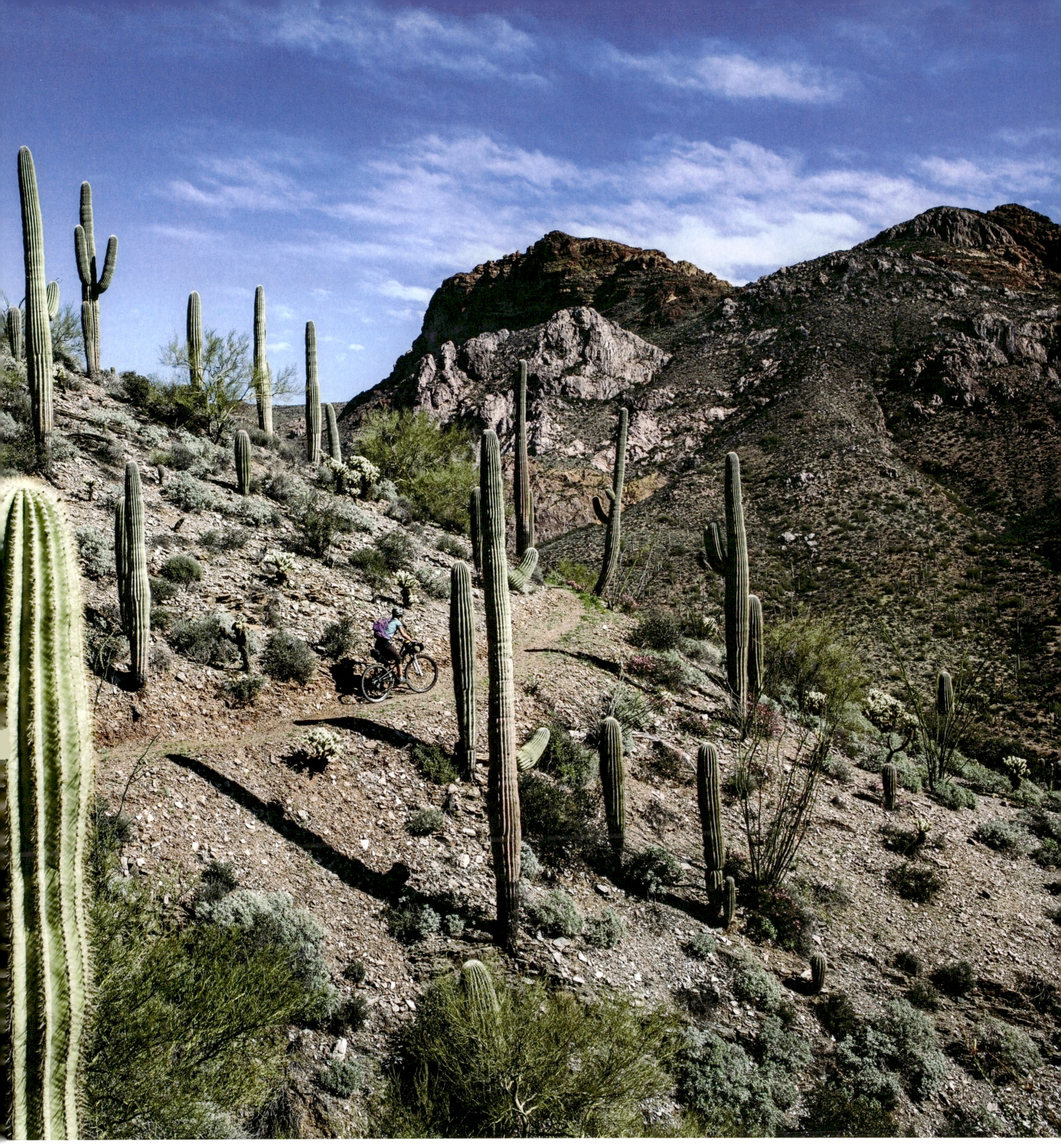

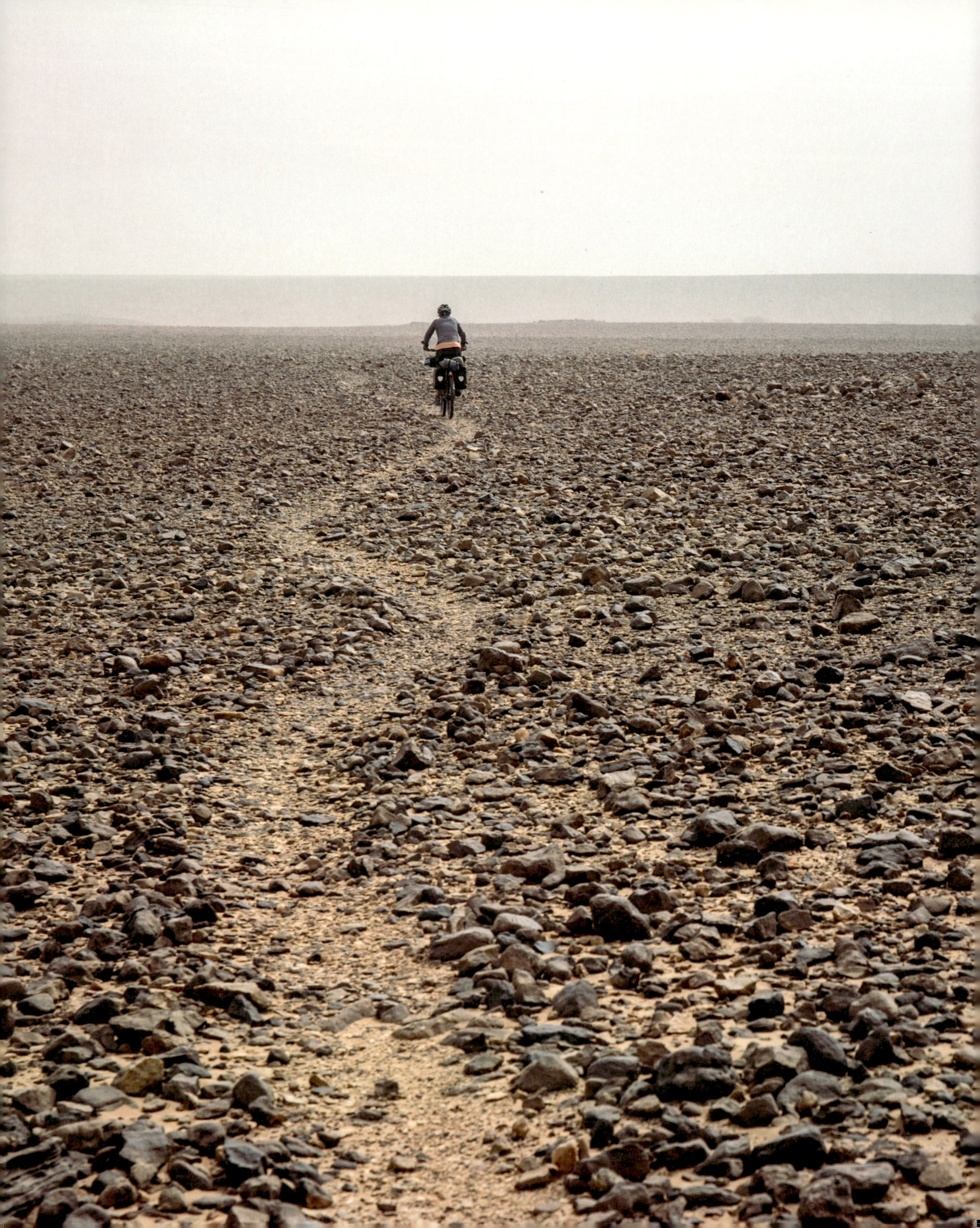

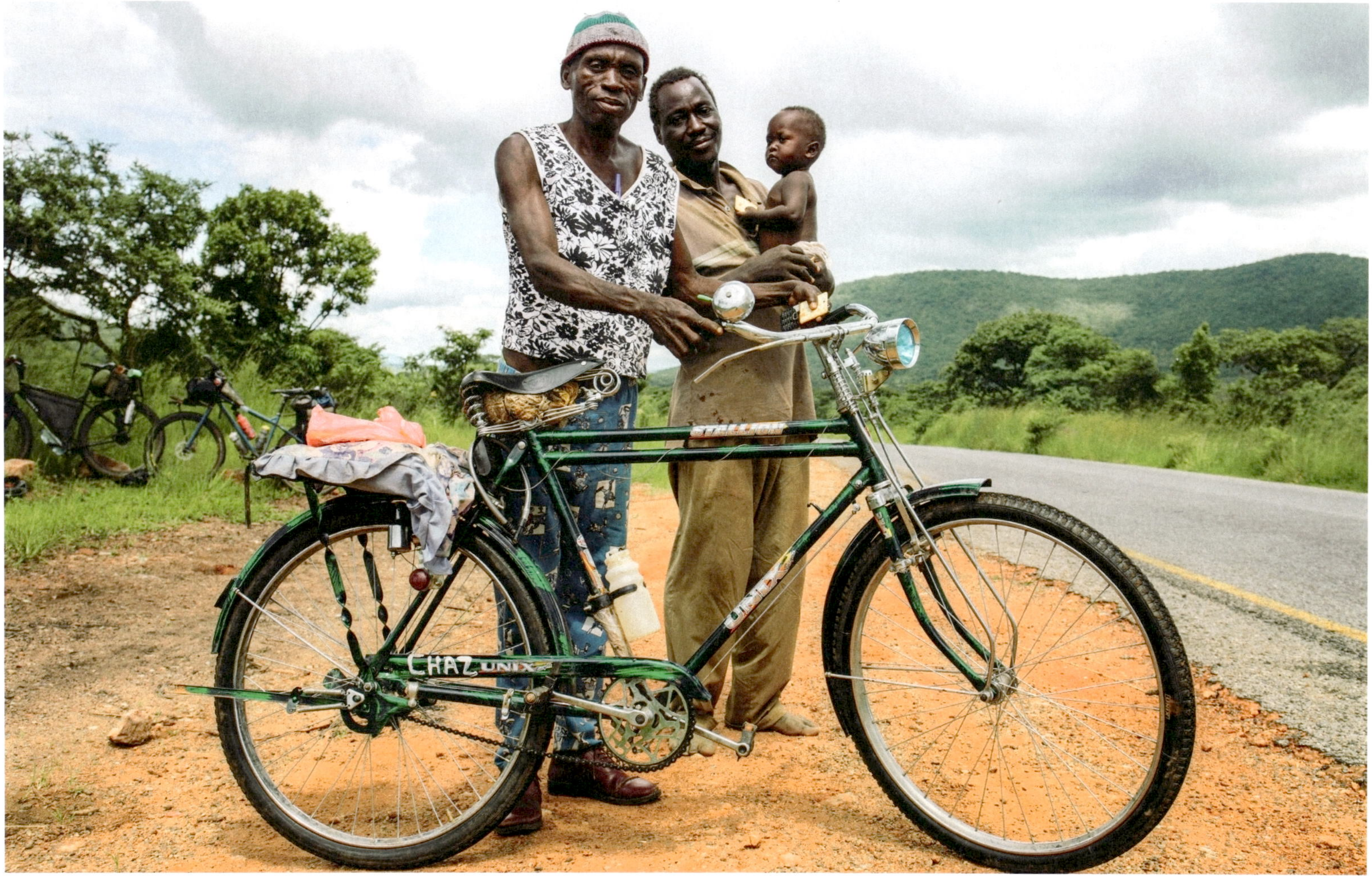

It's about exploring little-traveled places via single-track trails, gravel, and abandoned dirt roads. Multi-day mountain biking is at the heart of bikepacking—carrying only the bare necessities on a lightweight bike, with routes ranging anywhere from 40 miles to several hundred, jaunts that span weeks. Almost all reliable mountain bikes can be made into capable bikepacking rigs. Choosing the right route is the key to enjoyment, whether it involves forging a new path or following an existing one. *The Bike Book* is a compilation of stories and advice from bikepacking.com, including useful tools to help bikepackers make informed decisions about planning a ride, packing, and dealing with varying terrain and weather conditions.

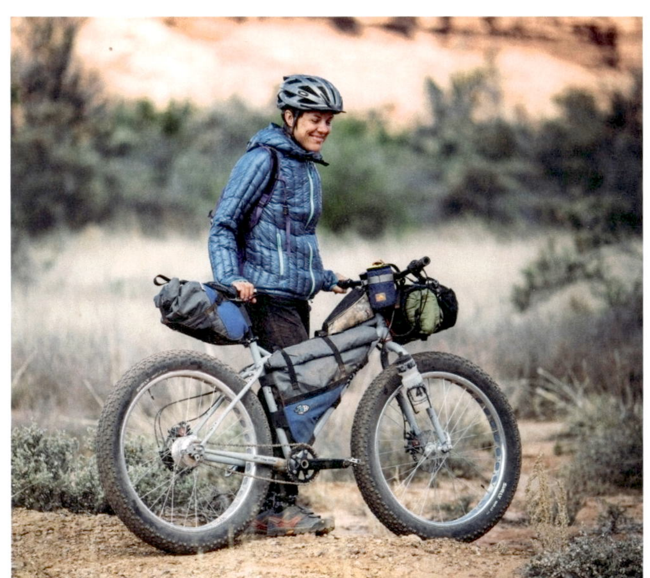

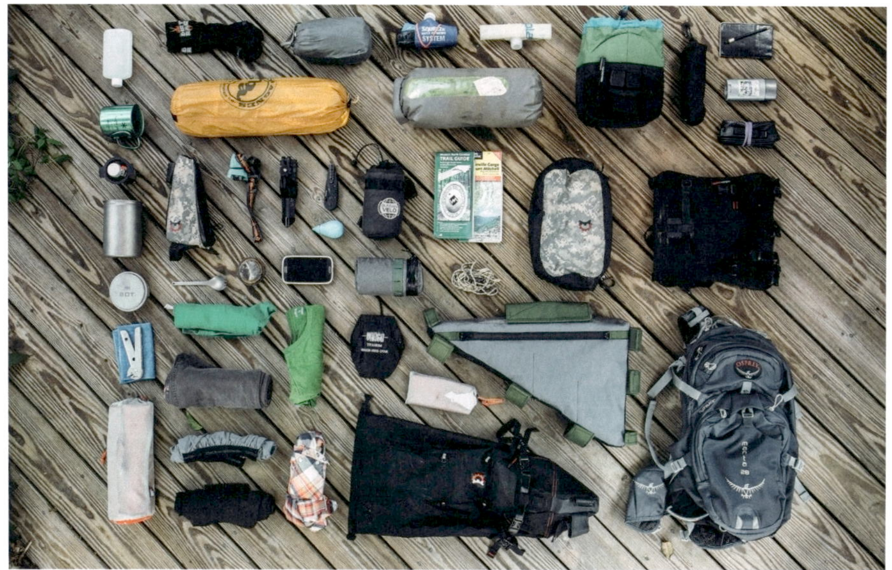

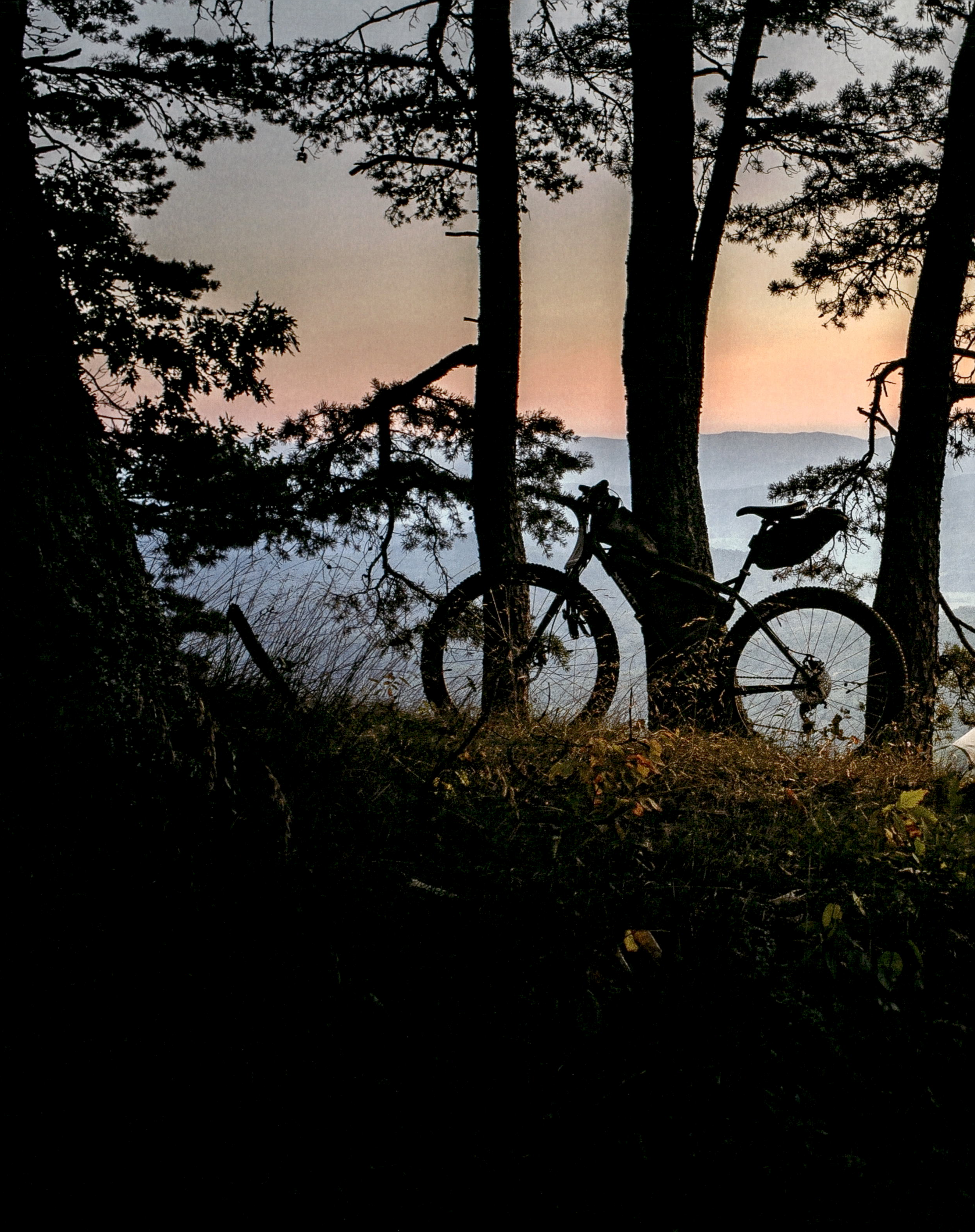

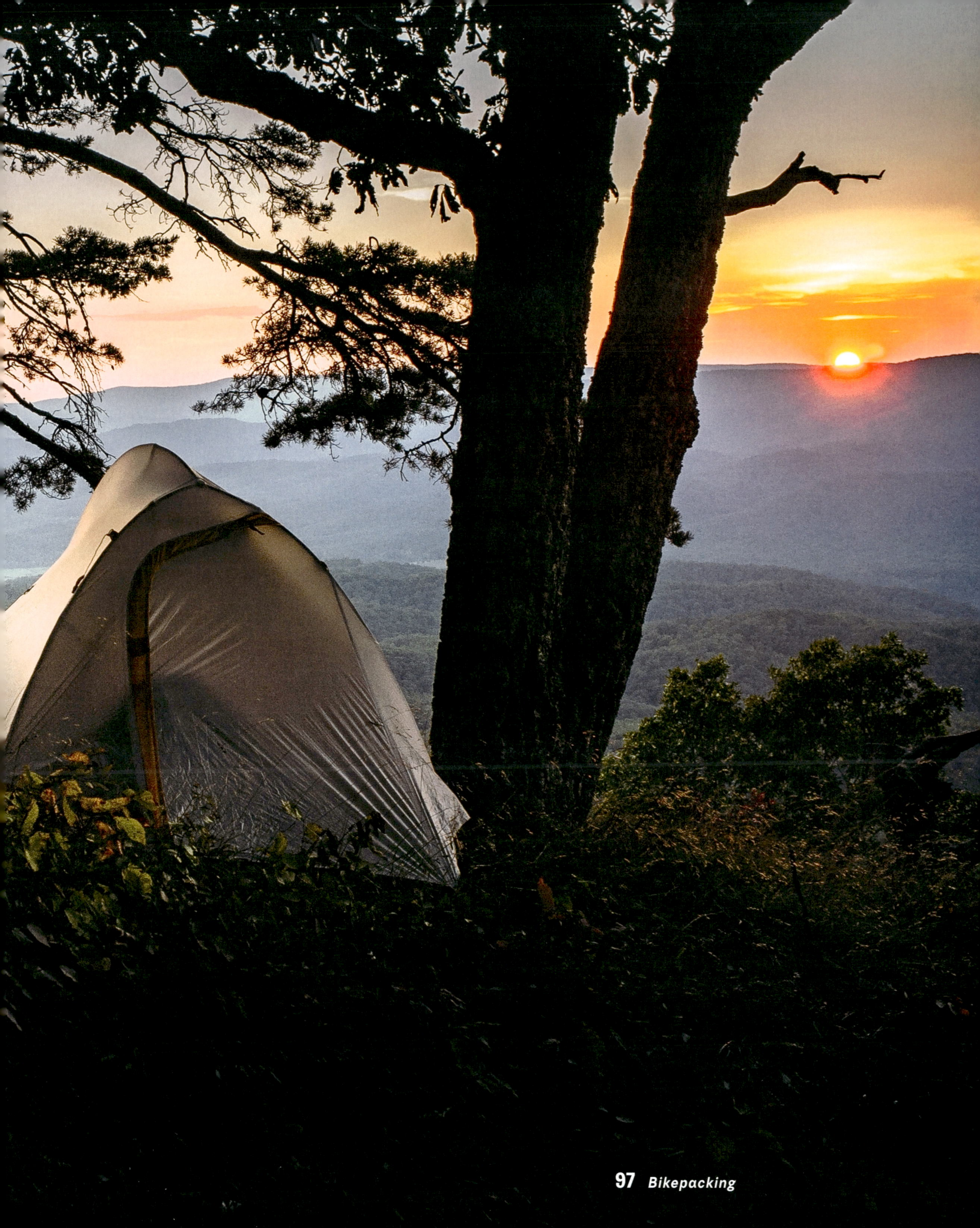

# Travel Oregon

Travel Oregon's Seven Wonders campaign highlights the state's diverse natural beauty.
To celebrate it, they asked seven Oregonian bicycle builders to create one-of-a-kind bicycles inspired by each location.

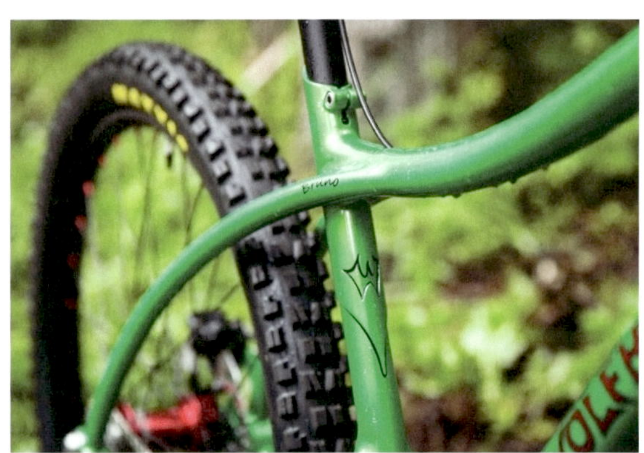

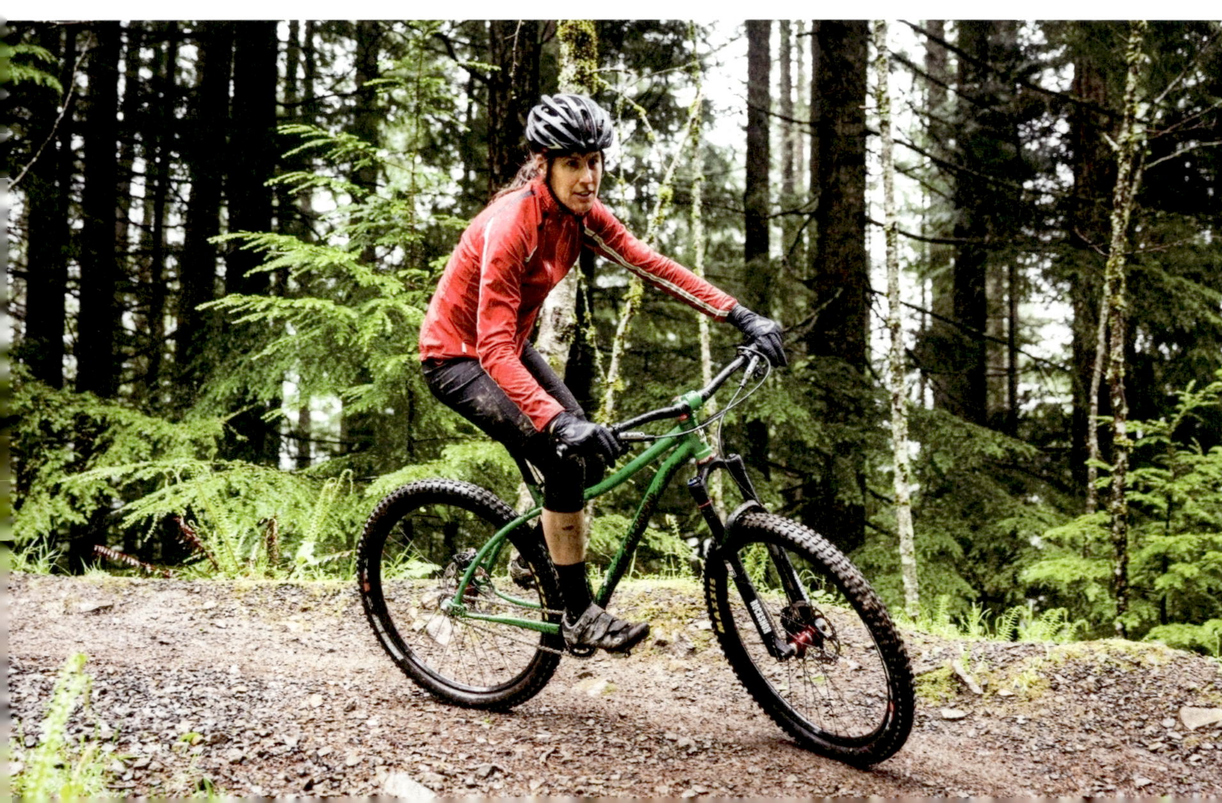

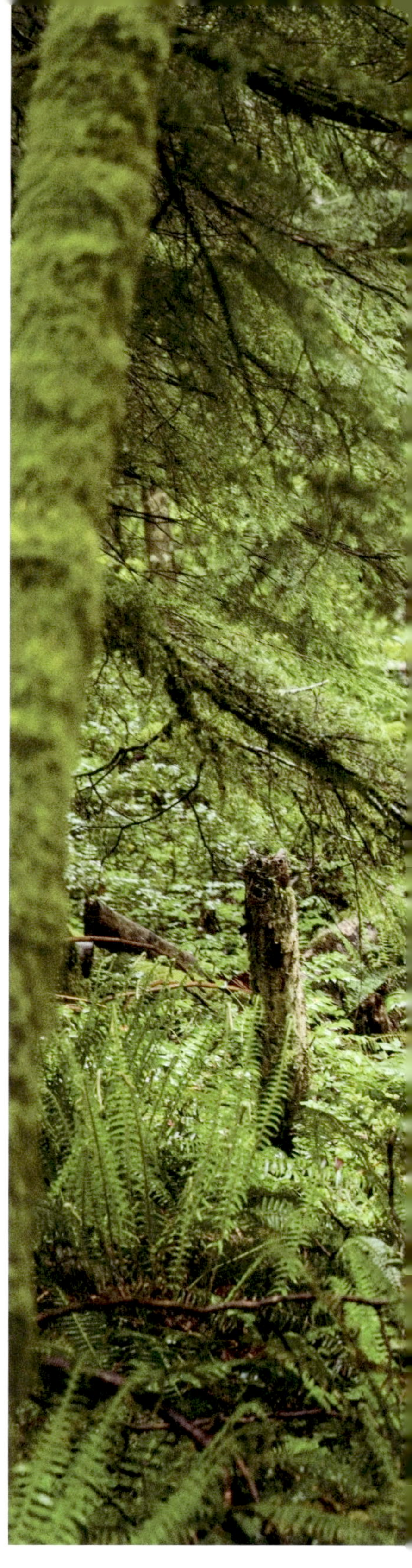

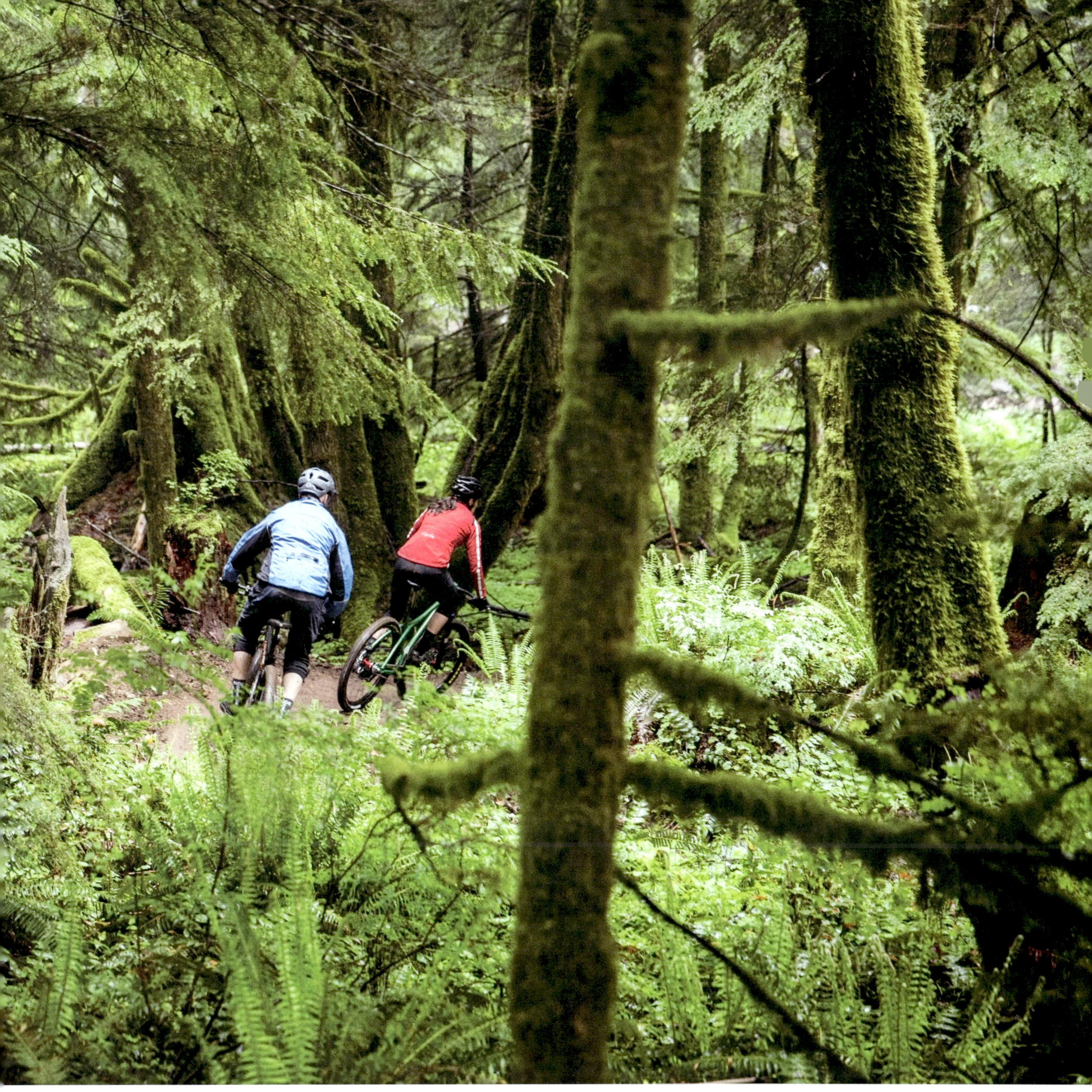

# Mt. Hood Bike

When Travel Oregon asked the state's best bicycle builders to design one-of-a-kind bicycles for its premier natural attractions, Fred Cuthbert was tasked with creating the Mt. Hood bike. Mt. Hood serves as Portland's backyard and is a biking destination for residents and visitors alike. Knowing the bike needed to be able to handle anything, including lift-assist, free rides, full downhill, and all-day, single-track rides through the wilderness, he set out to make something that could do anything and everything—and that's exactly what he's done. His single-speed mountain bike incorporates plenty of features and still comes in at an astonishingly light 28 pounds (12.7 kilograms). There are beefy 2.5-inch tires, a suspension front fork with five to six inches (13-15 centimeters) of play, and an adjustable-height seatpost for riding in a bike park or on other extreme terrain.

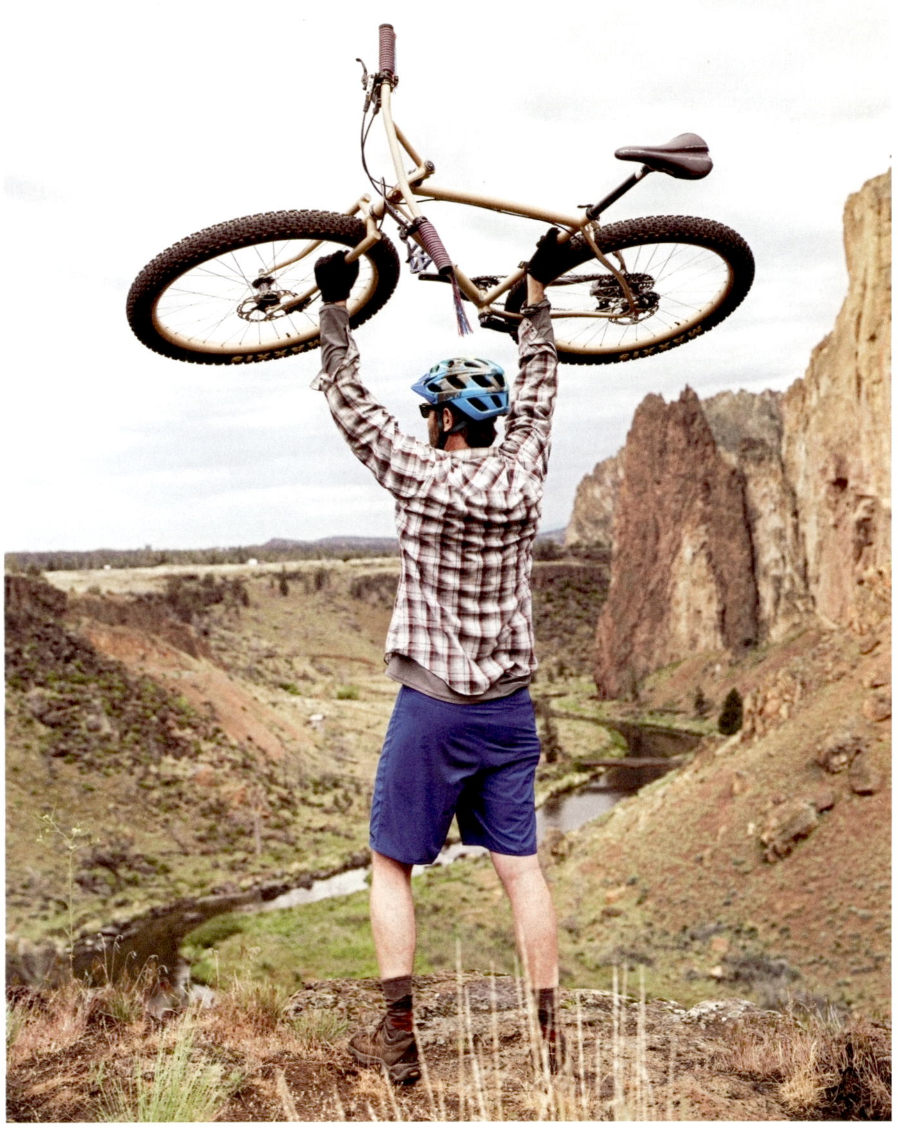

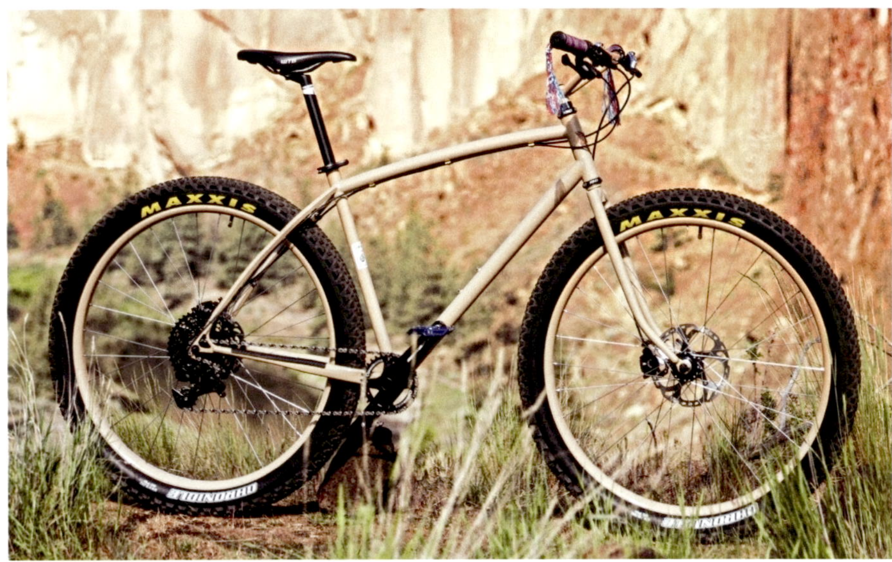


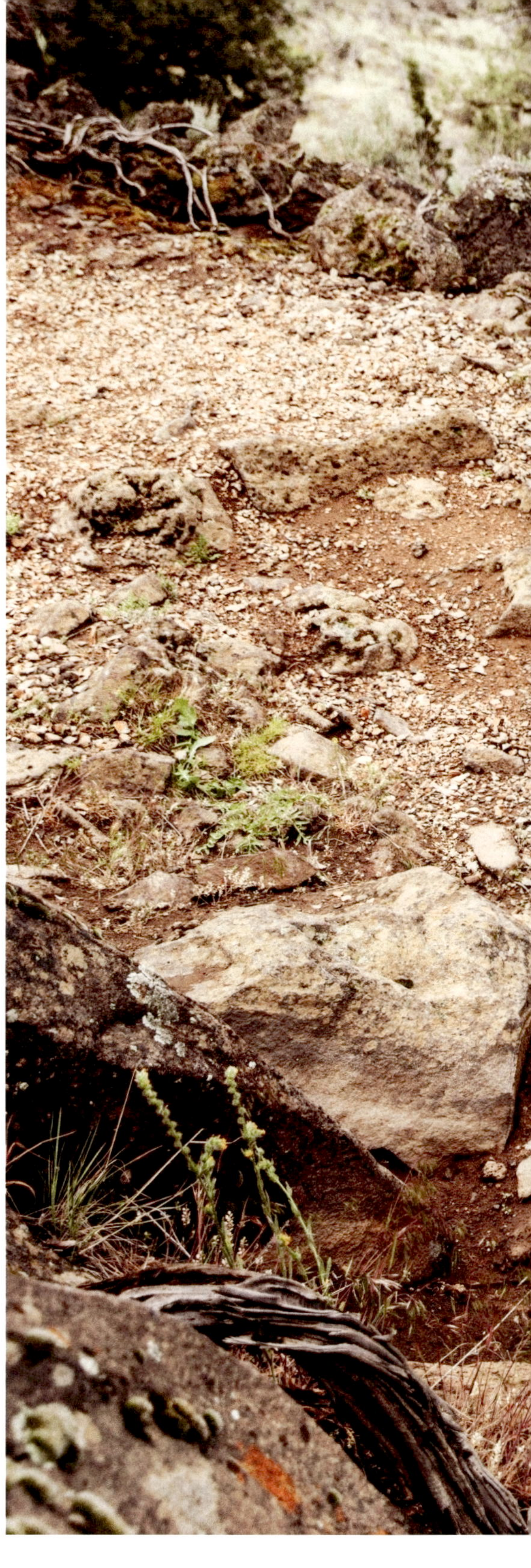

# Smith Rock Bike

Smith Rock, one of Oregon's most breath-taking natural monuments, offers a myriad of recreational possibilities. Its sheer walls, unique structure, and pristine setting make it a favorite for rock climbers from around the world. Travel Oregon asked designer Wade Beauchamp to build a bike that reflected the area's unique features. Beauchamp knew that the trickiest thing about riding at Smith Rock is the amazing scenery—which makes it hard to focus on the trail—so his custom mountain bike has 29-inch wheels, the proper gearing for climbing steep roads, and disc brakes for

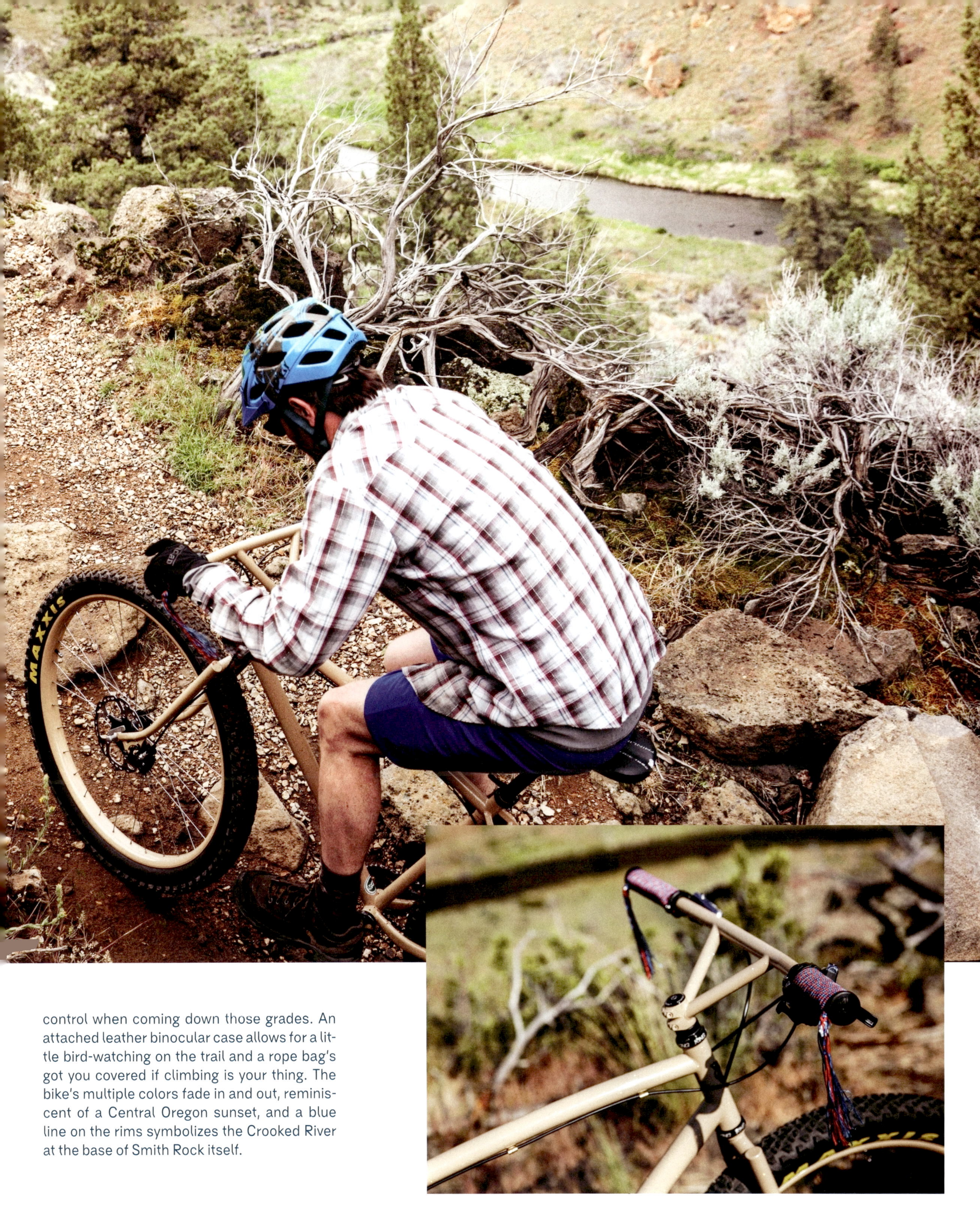


control when coming down those grades. An attached leather binocular case allows for a little bird-watching on the trail and a rope bag's got you covered if climbing is your thing. The bike's multiple colors fade in and out, reminiscent of a Central Oregon sunset, and a blue line on the rims symbolizes the Crooked River at the base of Smith Rock itself.

# Oregon Coast Bike

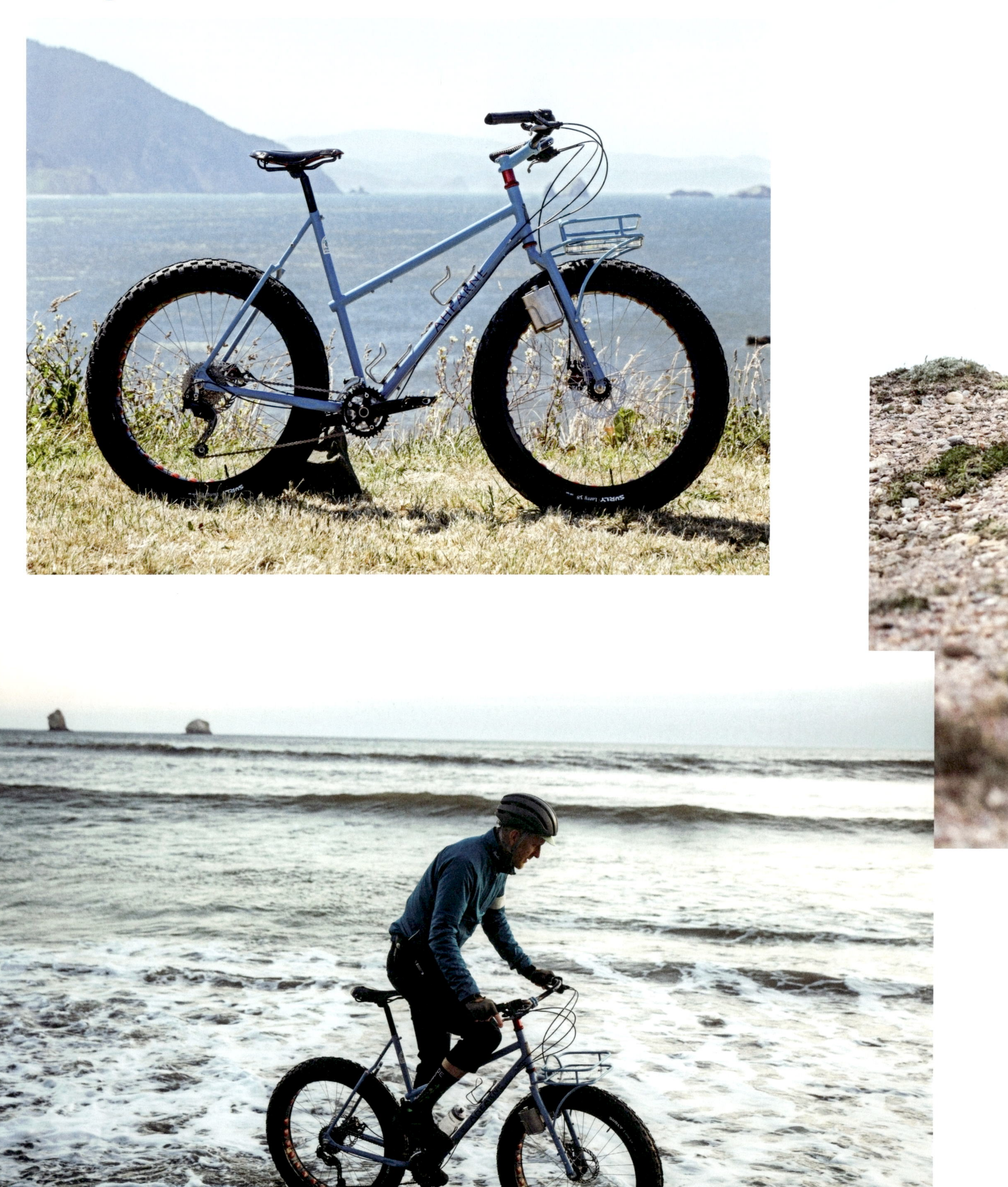

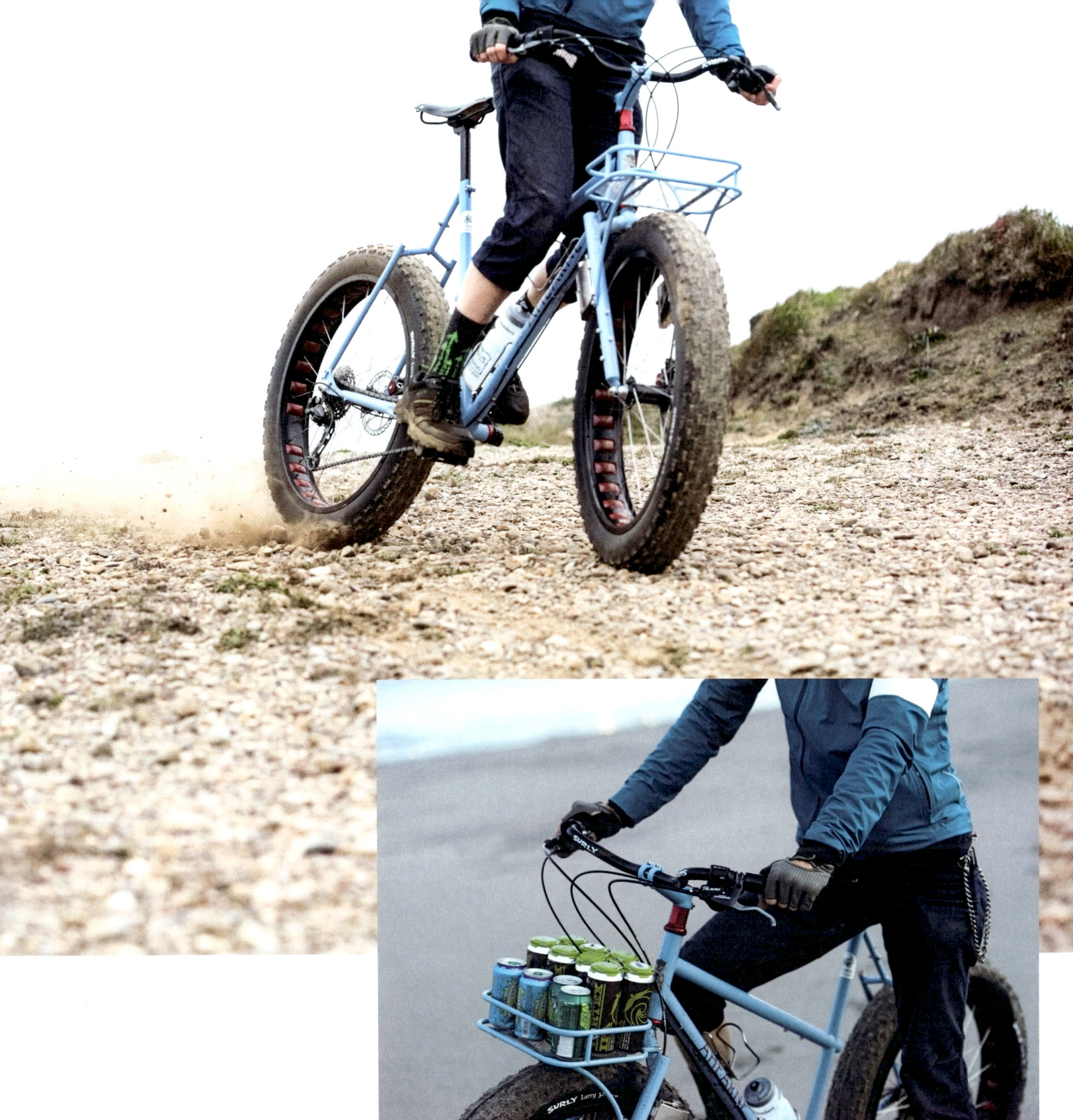


In some places, riding is as much a state of mind as it is a physical activity. When asked by Travel Oregon to design a bike to represent the state's iconic coastline, Joseph Ahearne set out to capture the experience of riding through a unique environment where beauty is everywhere. His fat-tire beach cruiser has the giant four-inch tires of an all-terrain vehicle, enabling it to ride on any surface, including a sandy beach. Low gearing allows the rider to spin through loose sand or dirt, and the frame's semi-step-through top tube slants severely downward for easy jump-offs in tight spots. No beach bike would be complete without a nod to laid-back beach culture, so the bike's front rack can carry two six-packs to a beach party and includes a flask carrier for sunset drinks on the sand.

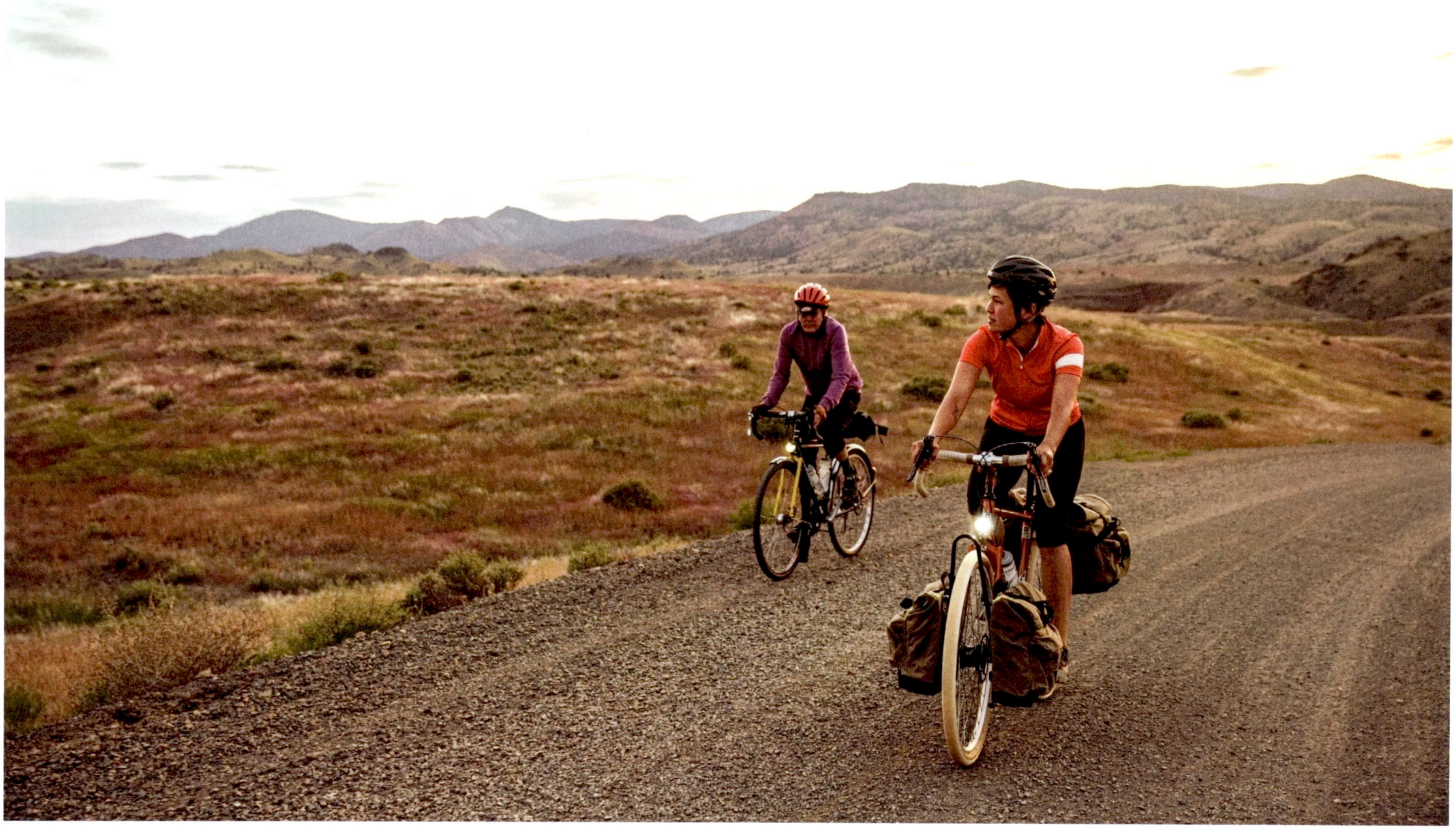

# Painted Hills Bike

Building a bike that reflects the rugged beauty of Oregon's Painted Hills is a difficult task. When Portland-based builder Christopher Igleheart accepted the commission from Travel Oregon to do just that, he knew he could draw on both his degree in geology and his many years as a cyclist. Due to the state's diversity of terrain, Igleheart designed a versatile, straightforward touring bike with tons of details intended to make it able to go anywhere. Its steel frame is strong, light, and stable; disc brakes provide added stopping power on any surface in any condition. Wider tires and a set of fenders keep things comfortable and clean, and expedition-quality storage bags from Portland's Black Star can carry enough supplies for days. If you need extra sustenance, however, dinner is often swimming nearby in this part of Oregon, so there's a case below the top tube for a fly rod.

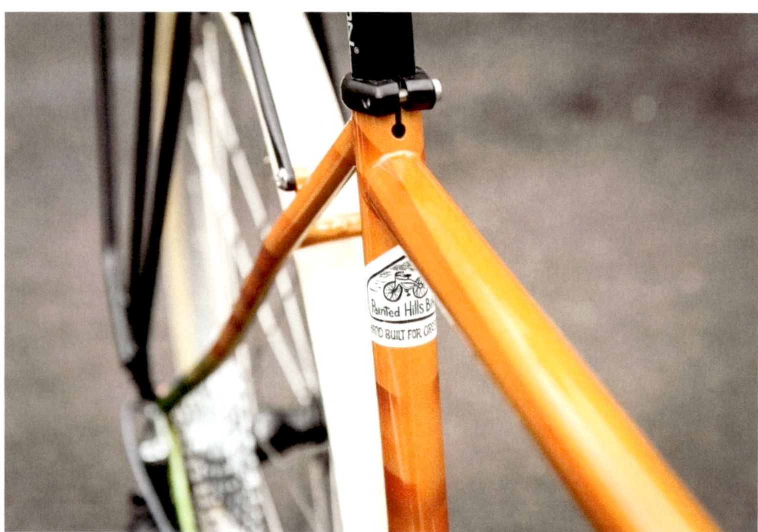

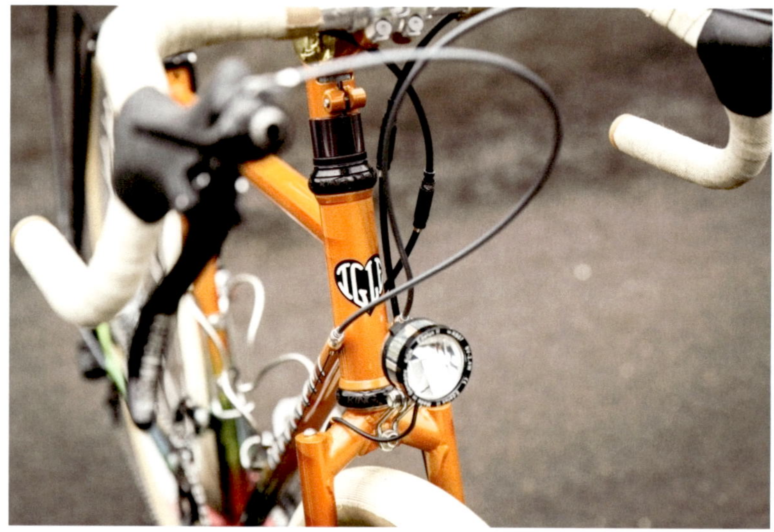

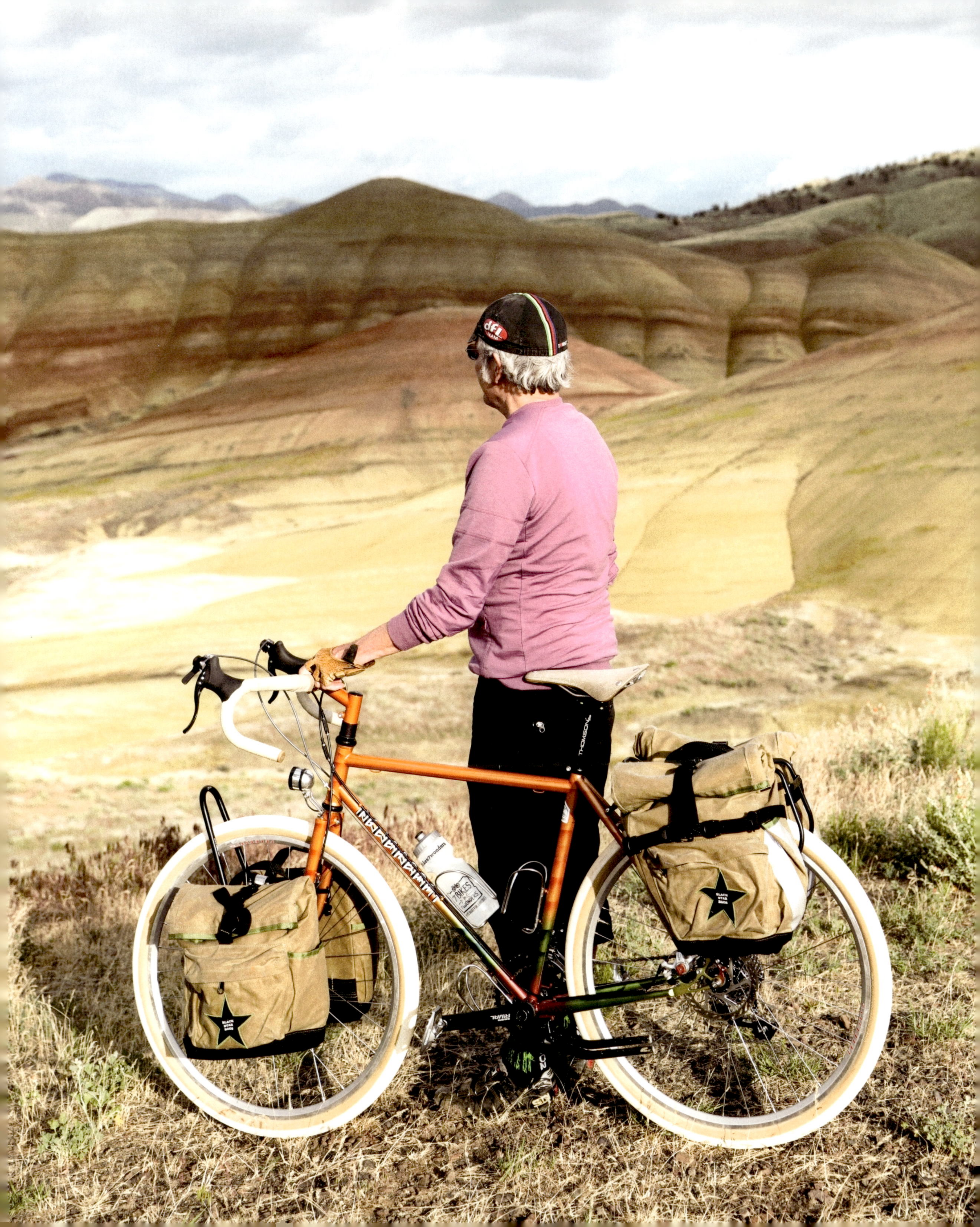
THOMSON

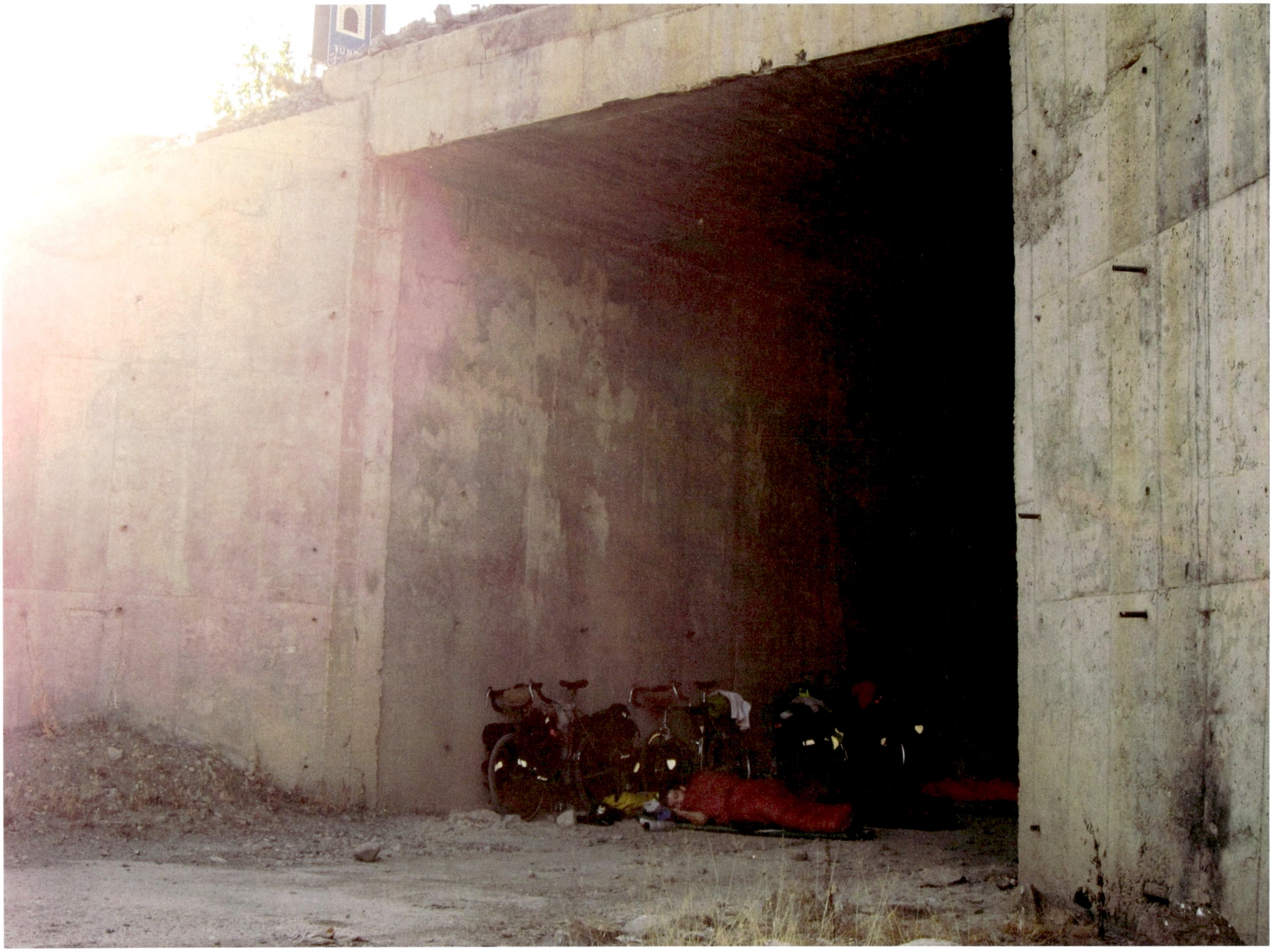

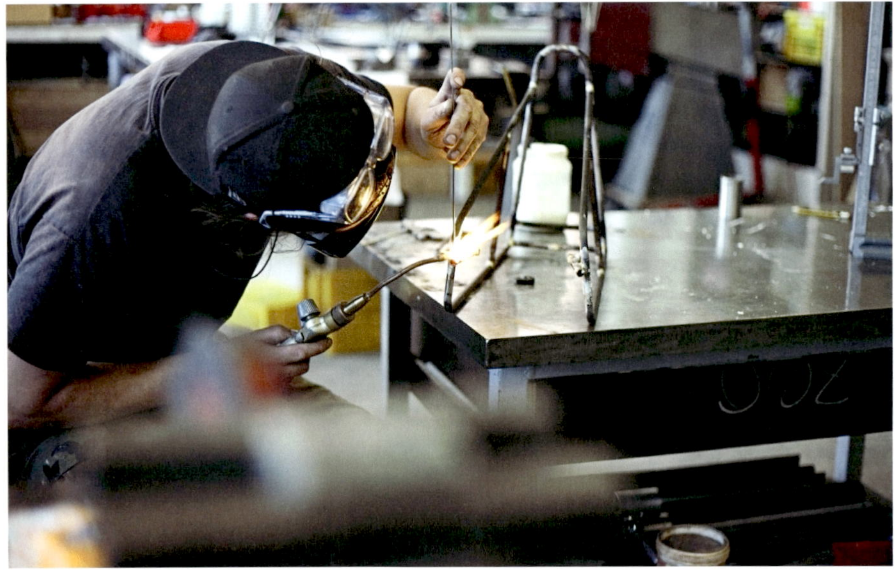

# Chacha

FERN
FAHRRÄDER

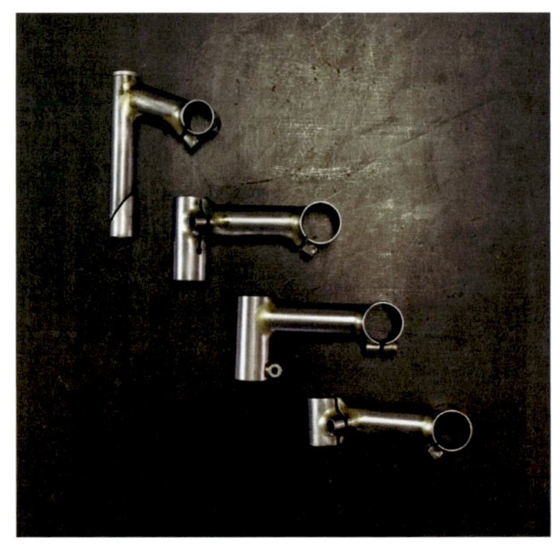

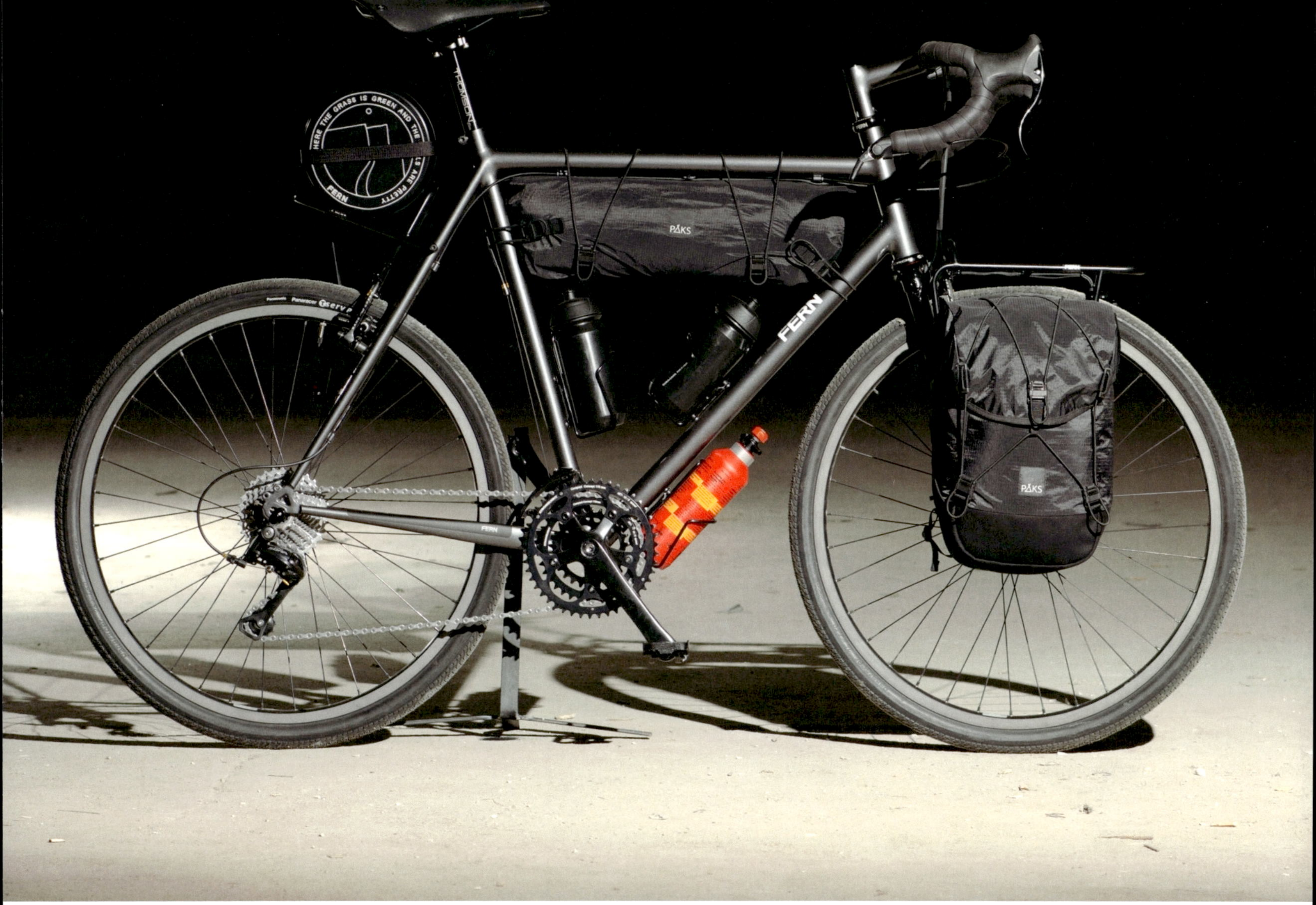

If touring isn't about curiosity and freedom, what is? "Curiouser and curiouser" is, in fact, a good description of Berlin-based designers Florian Haeussler and Phillip Zwanzig of Fern Fahrräder. Haeussler started his life on the road in 2006, pedaling the 2,700 kilometers from Budapest to Istanbul on an ancient mountain bike, with only one working brake and eight (sometimes) working gears. Schoolmate Zwanzig had just returned from a 3,700-kilometer trip from Malaga to Berlin. Their dissatisfaction with most production frames led Haeussler to trade in his designer's pencil for a welding torch and file to create what would become the Chacha (named for a Georgian brandy). Fern's bicycles mix the genius of historical French frame builders like Rene Herse and Alex Singer with modern improvements. And of course, they field-tested the Chacha themselves around the Black Sea. On their return to Istanbul, they found that they had traveled full circle—on their own hand-built frames—in only six years.

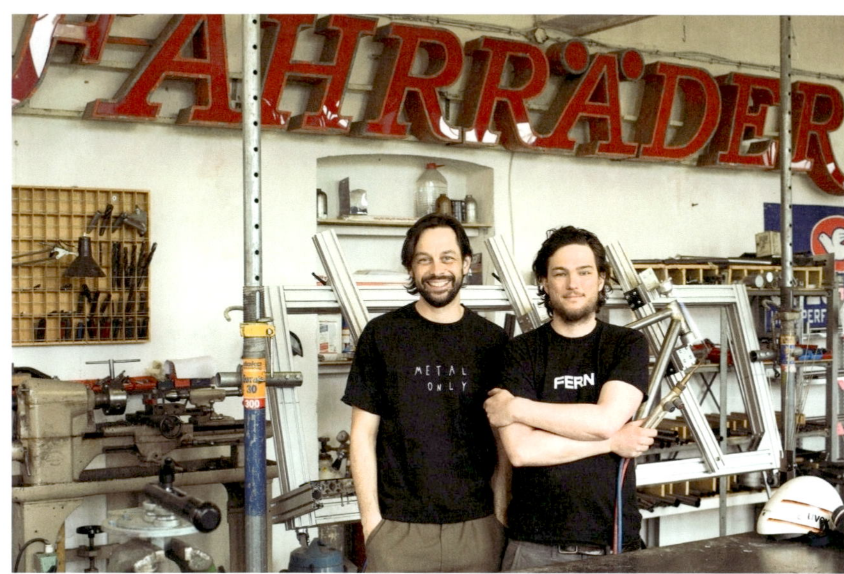

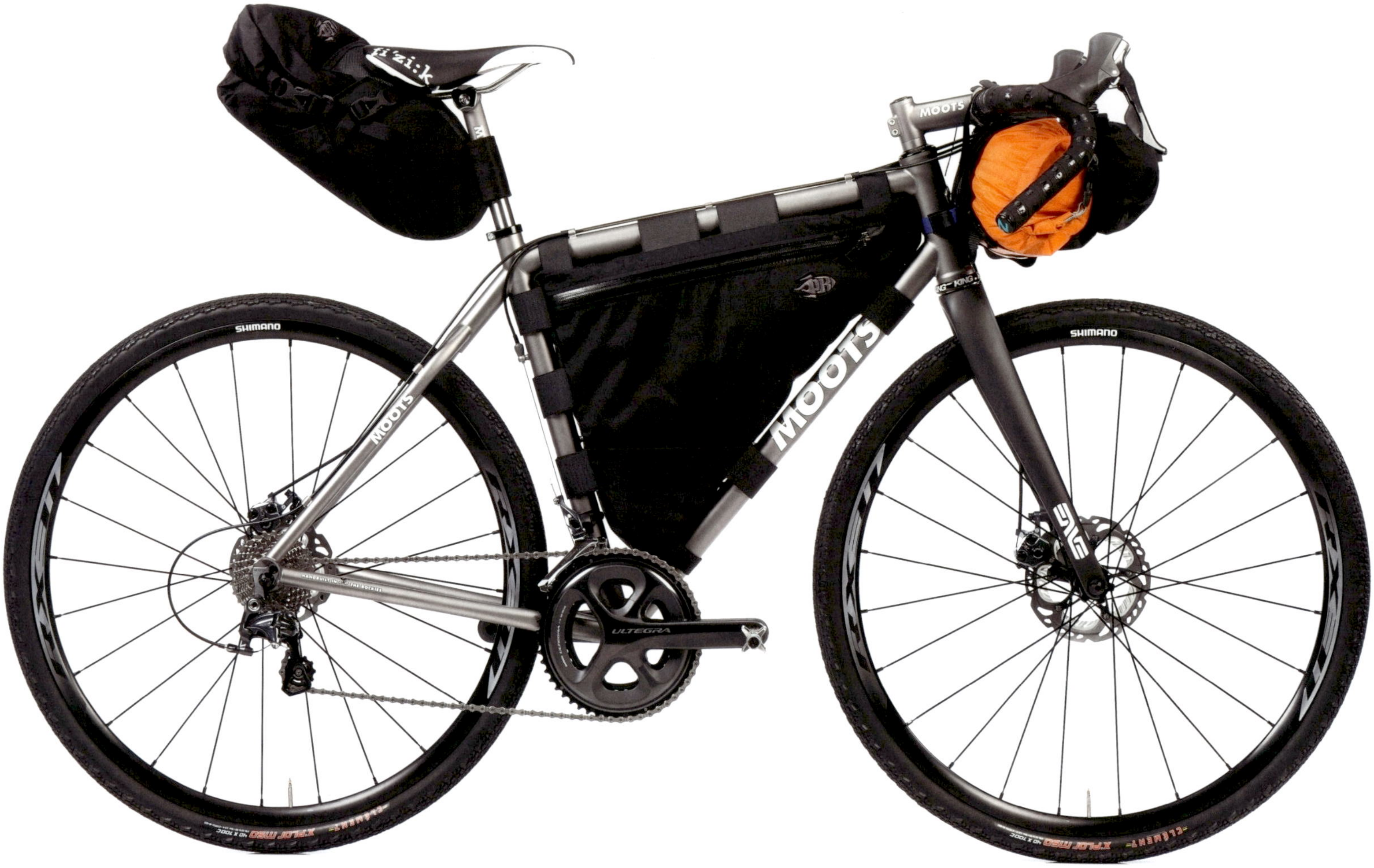

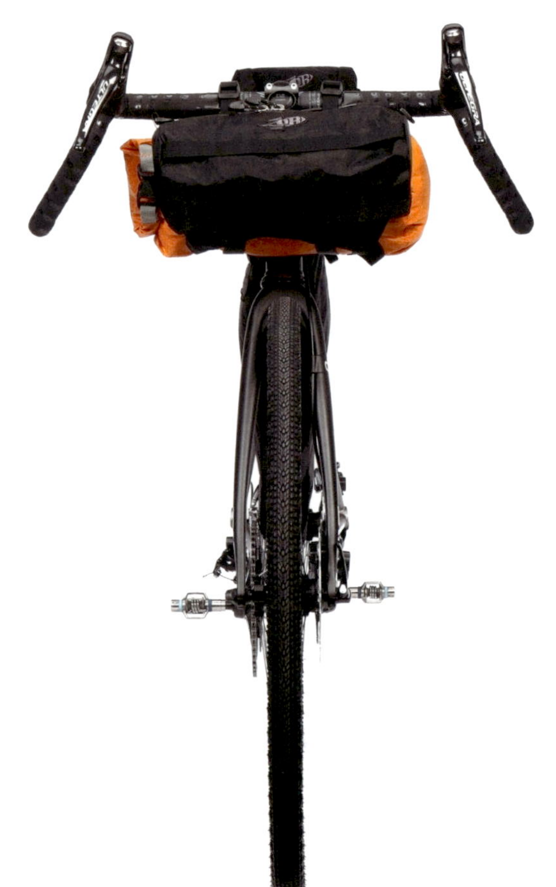

## *Routt 45*

**MOOTS**

Maneuverability and durability are two essentials on any cycling adventure. Moots designed and built the Routt 45 to handle any journey through mixed terrain. The bike tackles conditions from paved roads to rugged two-tracks by accommodating a range of tires from 23-millimeter skinnies to 45-millimeter knobbies. Designed in Steamboat Springs, Colorado, the Routt 45 is hand-built from 3/2.5 Pi Tech titanium tubing. Its 45-centimeter chain stays add tire clearance and a more stable platform, a lower English-threaded bracket ensures a better road feel, and a 44-millimeter head tube produces a tapered fork. The list of high-end features goes on, but the most impressive, if intangible, is Moots' lifetime warranty on craftsmanship and materials.

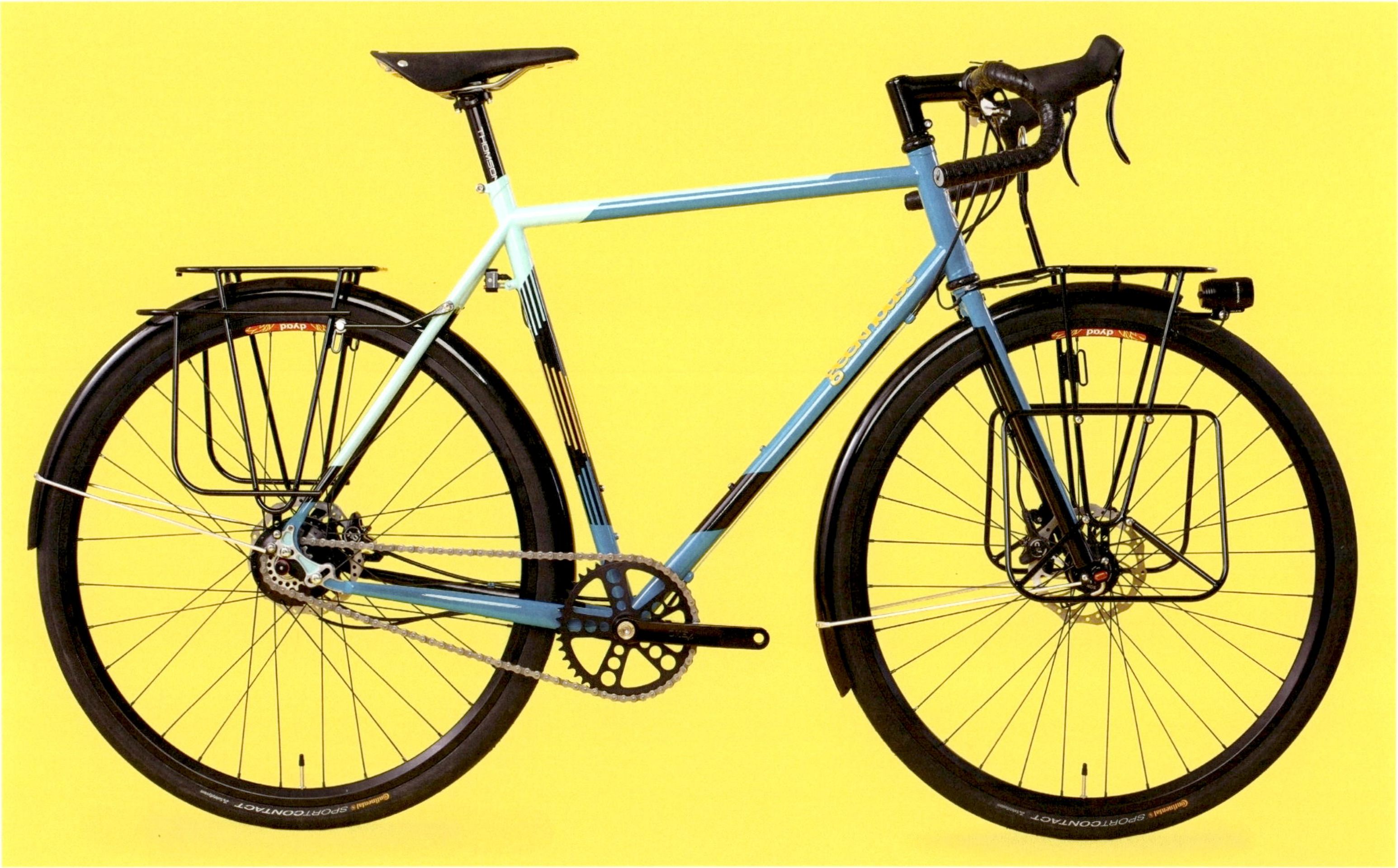

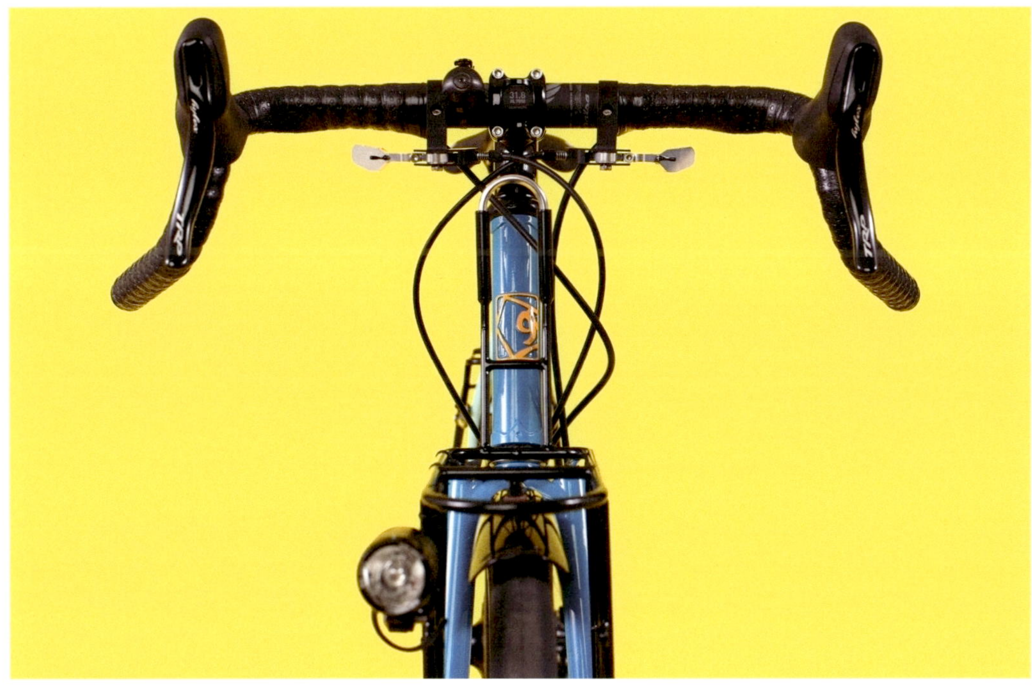

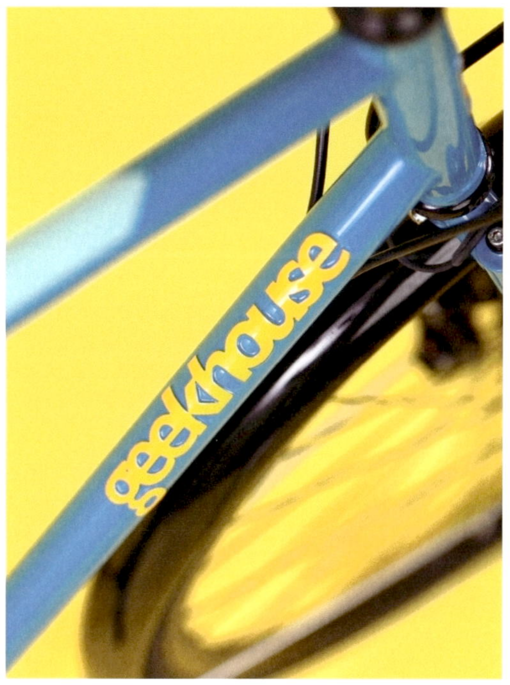


## *Woodville Tourer*

**GEEKHOUSE BIKES**

When new client Deb F. asked Boston-based Geekhouse Bikes to design and build a custom bike for her, the brief was simple: she wanted the works. By the time the bike was delivered to her in Los Angeles, it was one of the most complicated bikes the company had ever made. Christened the Woodville Tourer, it is the ultimate city/touring bike and it makes no compromises. The project was a team effort: constructed by Golden Saddle, its parts include customized front and rear Velo Orange racks and a Rolloff 14-speed internal rear hub. Adria Klora designed the paint scheme and Rudi Jung of Black Magic Paint brought it to life.

# Top & bottom

Ever think you'd live to see the day when that clumsy Styrofoam eyesore that matted your hair into helmet-head was turned into something swank? Or when your bike shoes would stop making you look like an injured elf? Well, you made it. There's something for everyone in the new shapes, hues, and materials of cycling headgear and footwear. Safety may prove a boon to your social life.

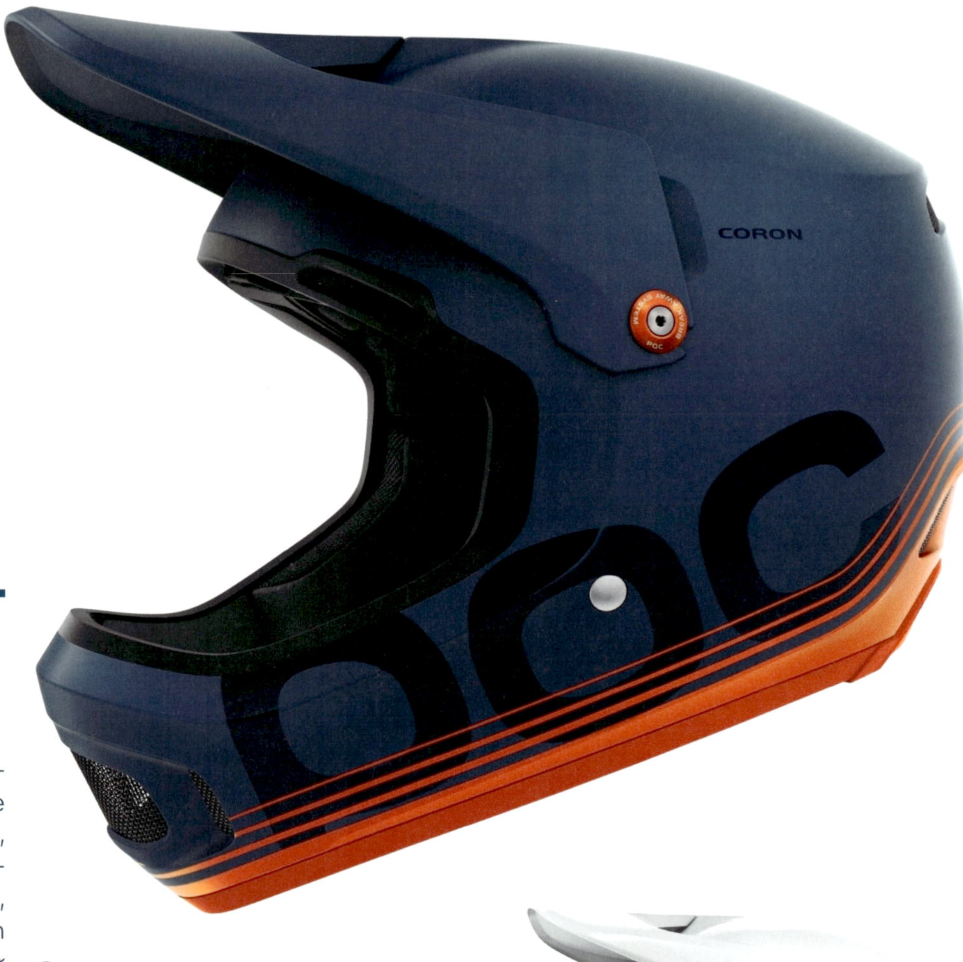


## Cipher

**GIRO**

With a fiberglass shell, plush interior padding, and vented brow ports for comfort, the Cipher™ is built around the ASTM F1952 Standard, meeting the demands of freeride, downhill, and enduro. Vinyl Nitrile padding along the jawline enhances impact management in this critical area, while the integrated POV-camera mount and built-in speaker pockets dial in sounds and images—altogether it's a new level of performance for a new era of riding.

Giro comes from Santa Cruz, California, a unique location where the surf meets the mountains. It attracts people of an independent mindset—people who love the outdoors, who set their own priorities, and who are inclined to put human values ahead of corporate interests.

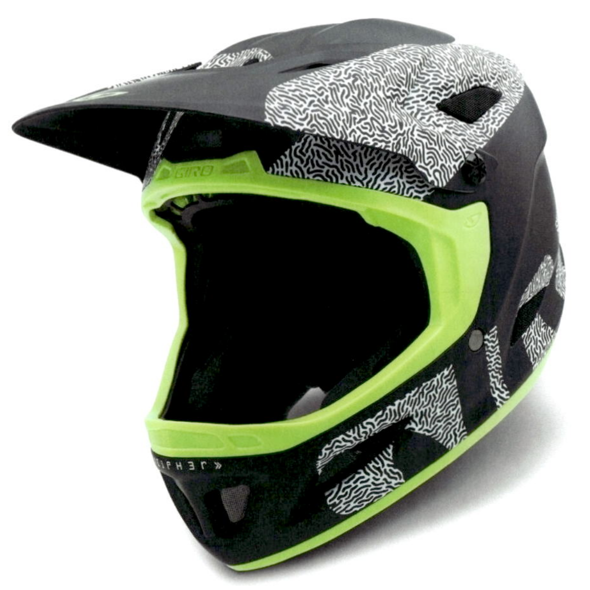

## Coron

**POC**

As developers and makers of revolutionary ski helmets, POC knew they could transfer their technological know-how to bike helmets. They were right on—now their helmets meet the demands of a wide range of bike users, from downhill, dirt, free-ride, and BMX to MTB and road bikes. The helmets' unique unibody construction and POC's new approach to the strategic use of EPS, ventilation, aerodynamics, and visibility provide improved protection with ultimate performance. Developed in collaboration with POC team athlete Martin Söderström, the Coron offers a high level of protection, ventilation, and comfort. It incorporates a new type of shell material called M-FORGE®, an advanced fiber material that outperforms older shell materials in terms of multi-impact performance, durability, and low weight.

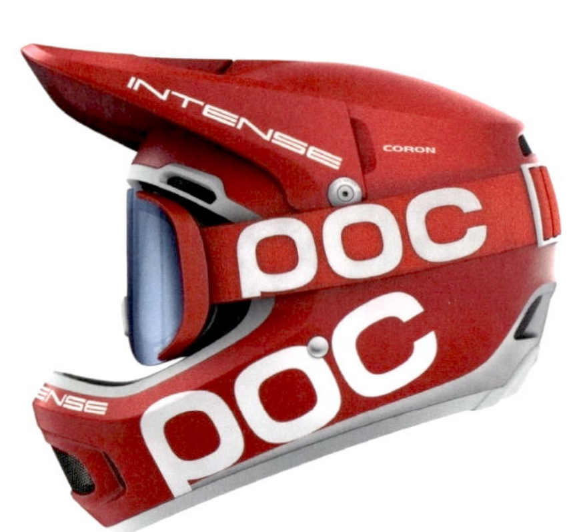

## Empire™ VR90

GIRO

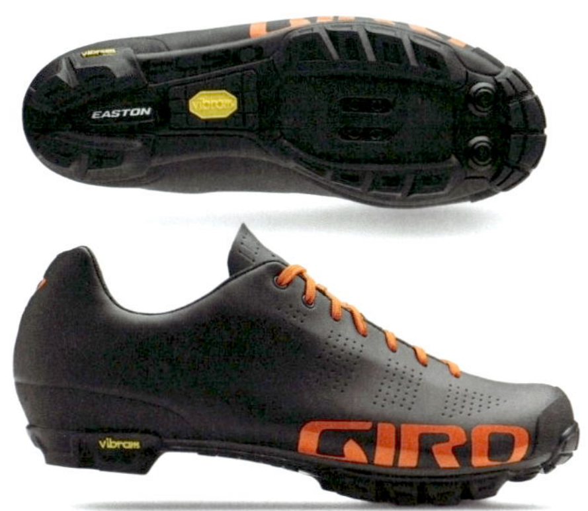


The Empire™ VR90 is a new direction in high-performance off-road shoes. The Special Reserve edition in anodized glowing red is already worn by the pros, and now it can be on your feet, too. Only available in limited quantities through select retailers, the Special Reserve products are an opportunity for Giro to test new concepts and ideas, like the lightweight one-piece upper for unrivaled comfort and an Easton® EC90 full carbon outsole with Vibram® Mont molded-rubber tread for relentless grip. The upper is made of a breathable Evofiber™ synthetic fabric from Teijin® for superb fit and support that won't stretch out with wear or weather. The adjustable SuperNatural Fit footbed lets you fine-tune the fit and arch support for maximum pedaling efficiency.

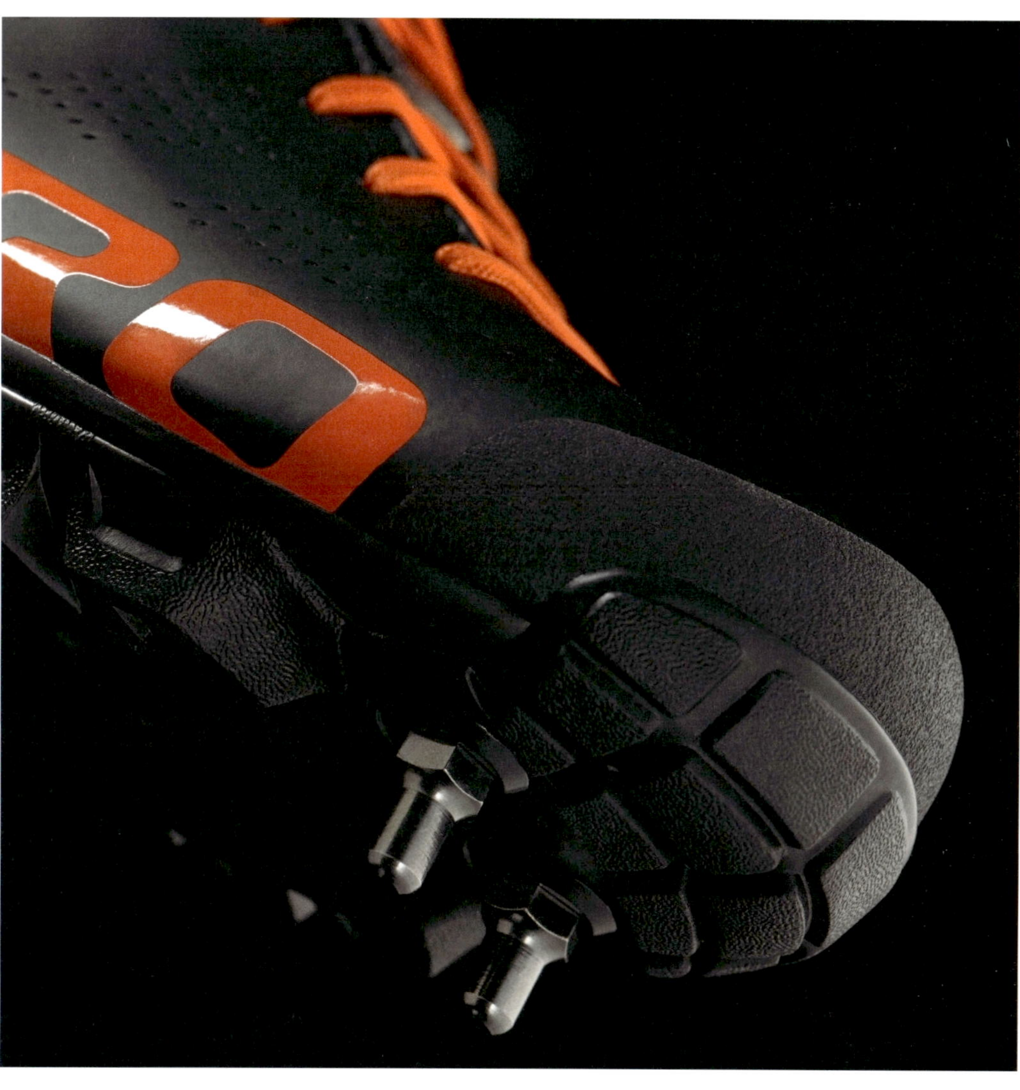

## Mido Riding Boots

PEDAL ED

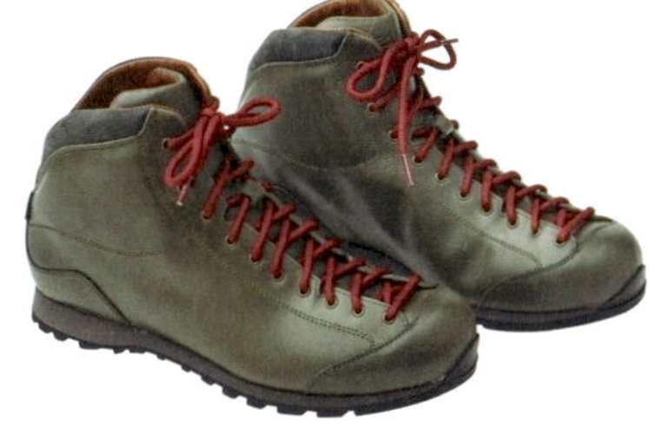

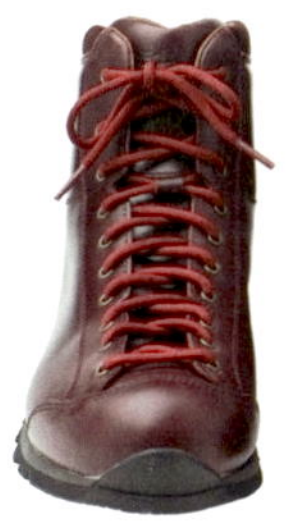

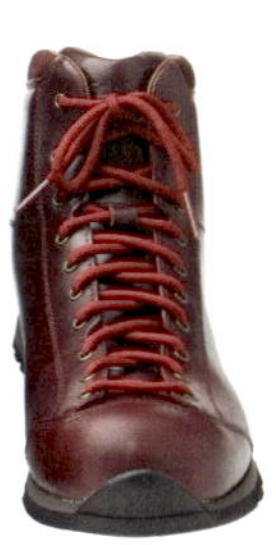

After 15 years working as a designer in the Japanese fashion industry, Hideto Suzuki discovered a love for cycling and began to create his own cycling apparel. Now PEdAL ED designs beautiful, functional, award-winning collections that complement the cycling lifestyle. Suzuki's belief that each feature of a garment can improve function and performance is the guiding philosophy of the company and their comfortable, long-lasting garments. Their Mido riding boots are classic hiking boots with an updated Vibram sole, for a thin profile that reduces bulk, and a toecap for use with pedals. A special low-cut ankle and reflective heel element complete these practical, everyday shoes.

## Tourer Boot

QUOC PHAM

The Tourer Boot is made-to-order—a beautifully styled and smartly designed solution for today's multifaceted cyclist. Combining all-natural leather uppers and a grippy rubber sole, the Tourer Boot integrates into a fully recessed MTB-compatible pedal system while achieving the ideal balance between a natural walking gait and the requisite stiffness of a clipless cycling shoe. For the cyclist, the result is a sumptuously comfortable piece of footwear that instills confidence both on and off the bicycle and one that looks at home in any setting. The Tourer Boot is available in tan and black.

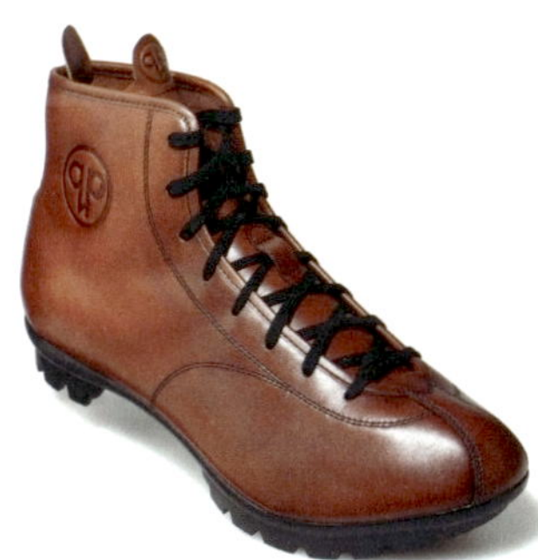

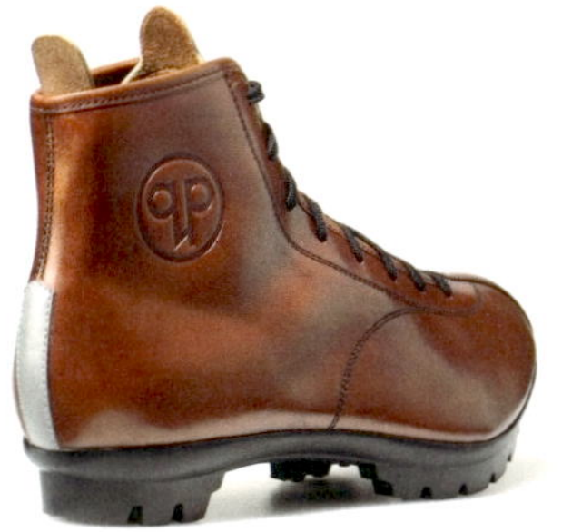

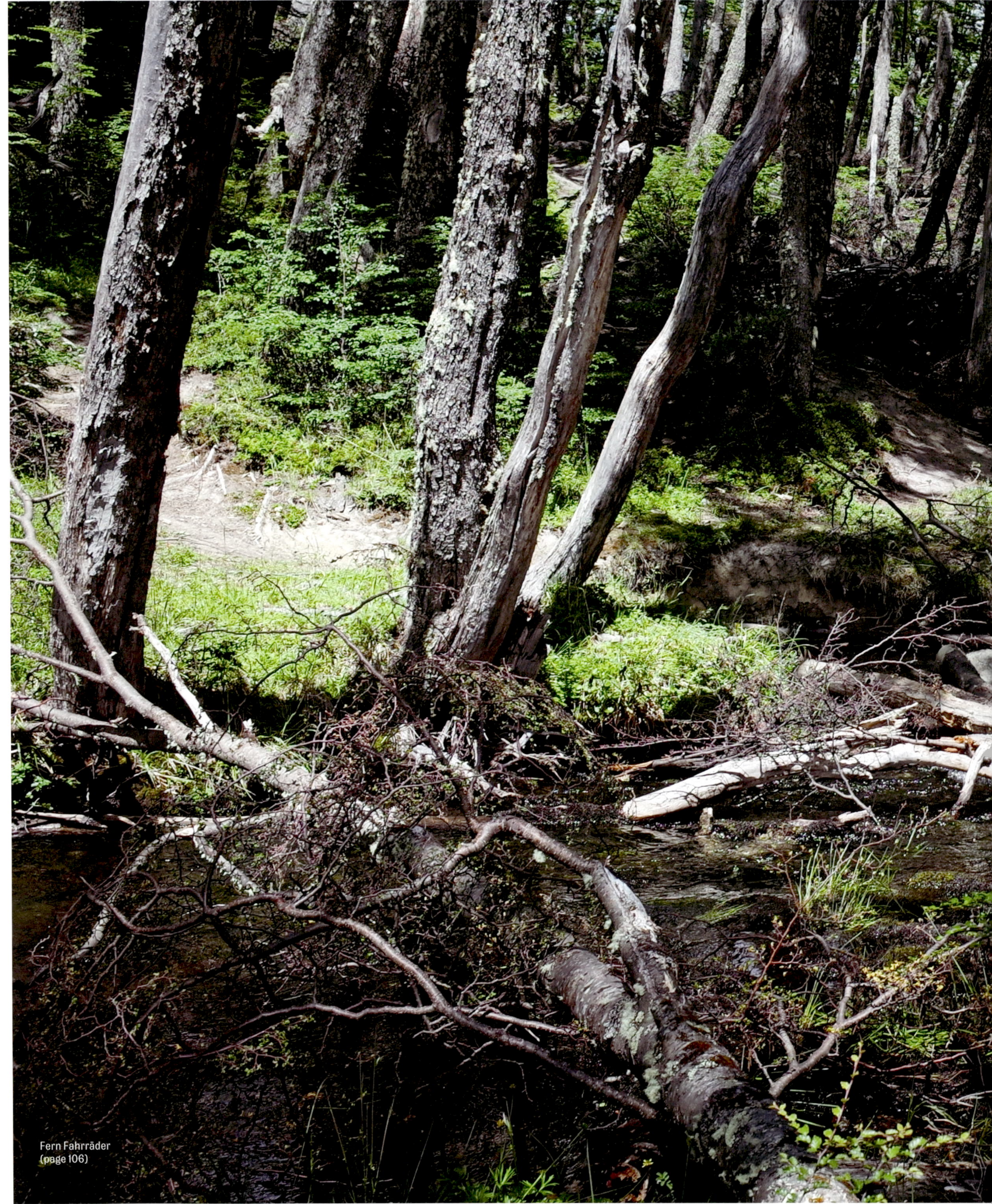

Fern Fahrräder
(page 106)

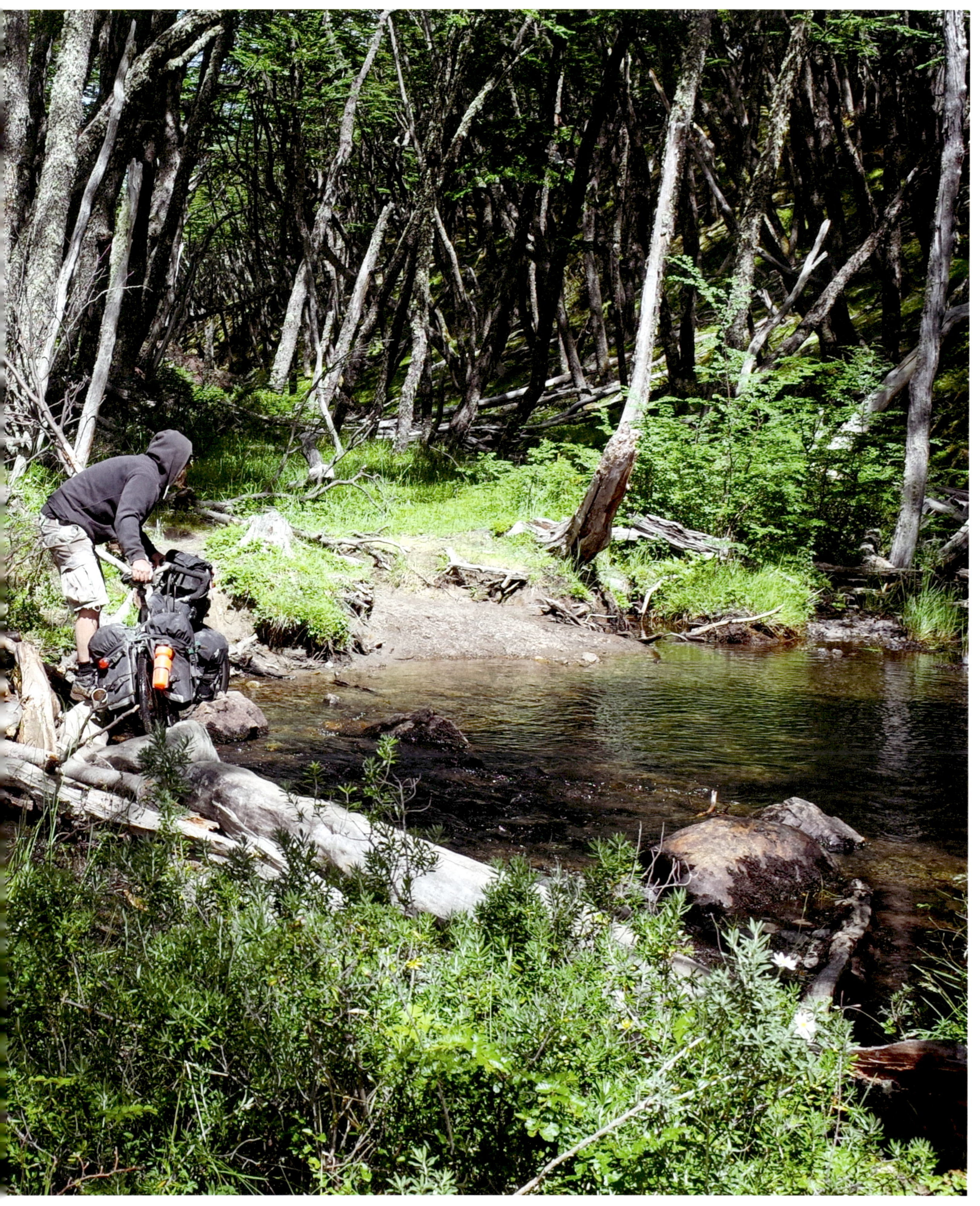

# Littleford Bicycles

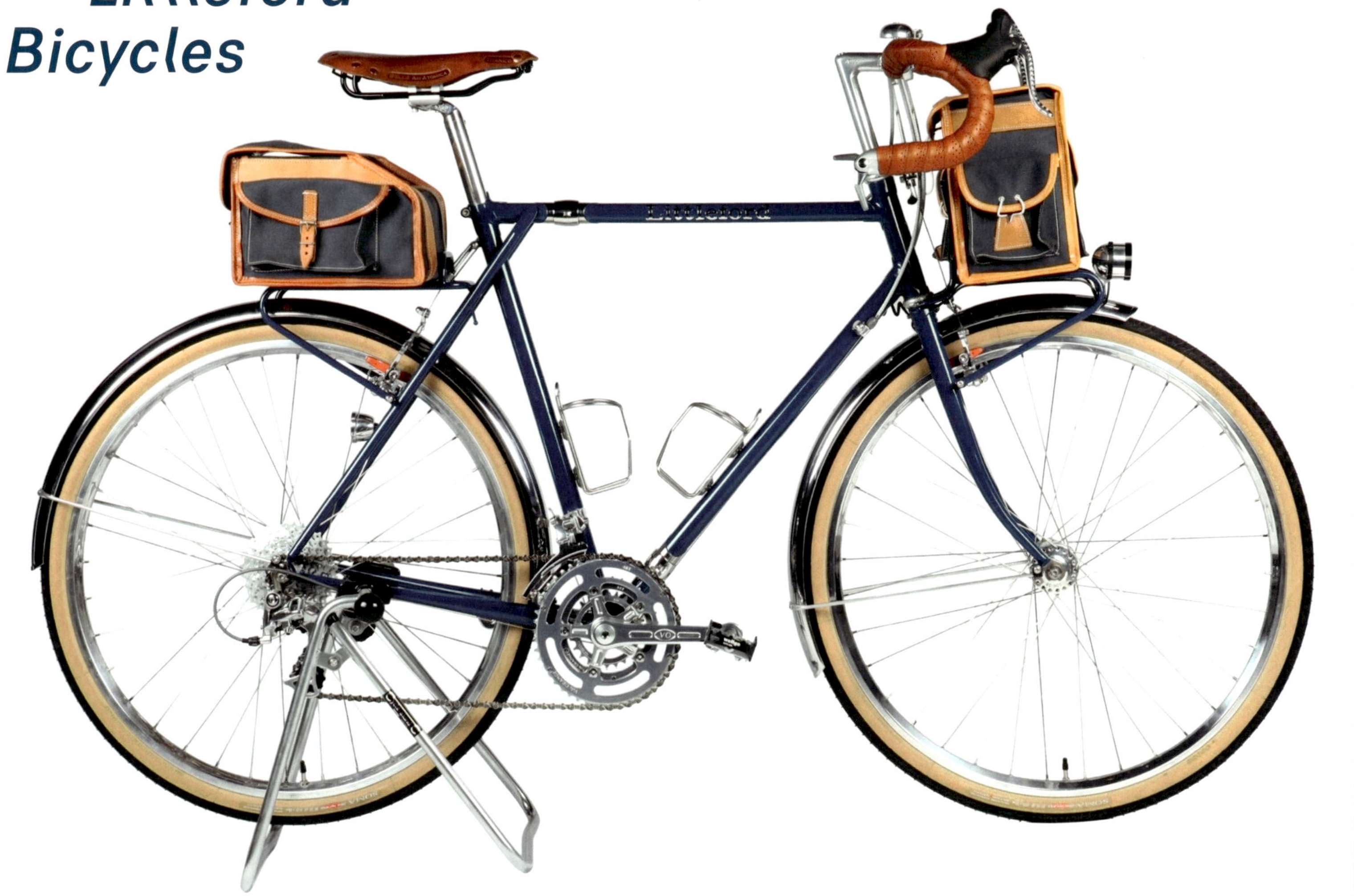

Jon Littleford of Littleford Bicycles has just one goal in mind and that is to keep his riders comfortable for life. Because every Littleford bike is custom-made in his shop in Portland, Oregon, there are no set models. However, handy options and personal touches abound, including easily detachable custom racks. The racks are the key components of any optimally built touring bike, and Littleford's custom racks are stronger, lighter, and more rigid than production racks because of their frame-specific designs. Each bike is designed and built with an emphasis on durability, usefulness, and the belief that the beauty of good design is enhanced by the inevitable signs of daily, practical use.

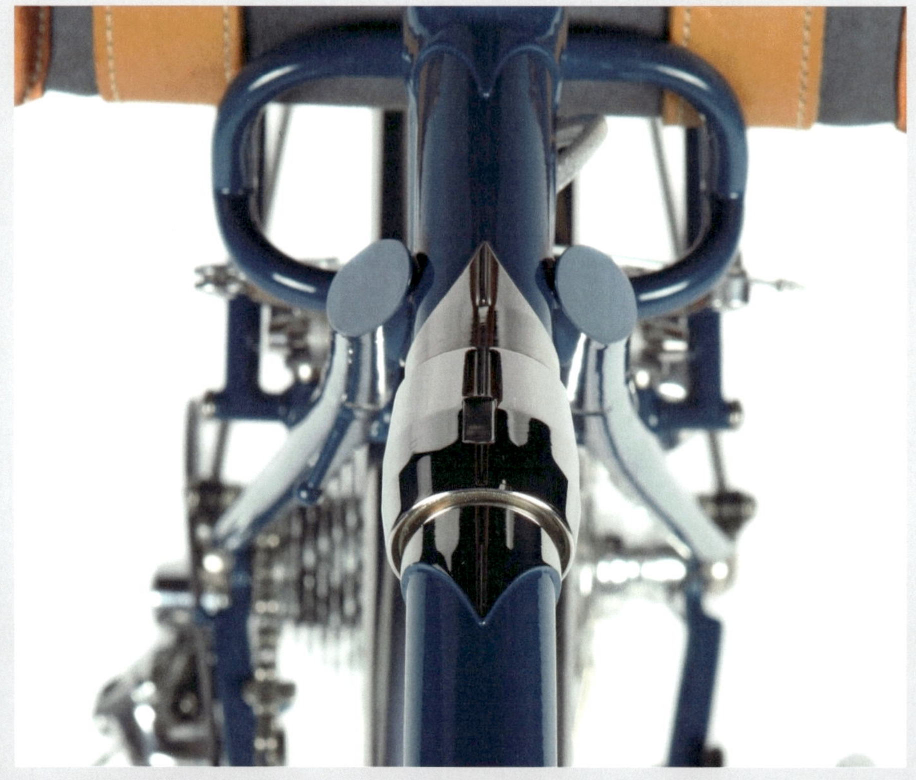

**opposite page:**
Ocean, collapsible rando,
front and rear

**this page:** Burgandy,
an "All-Roundonneur"

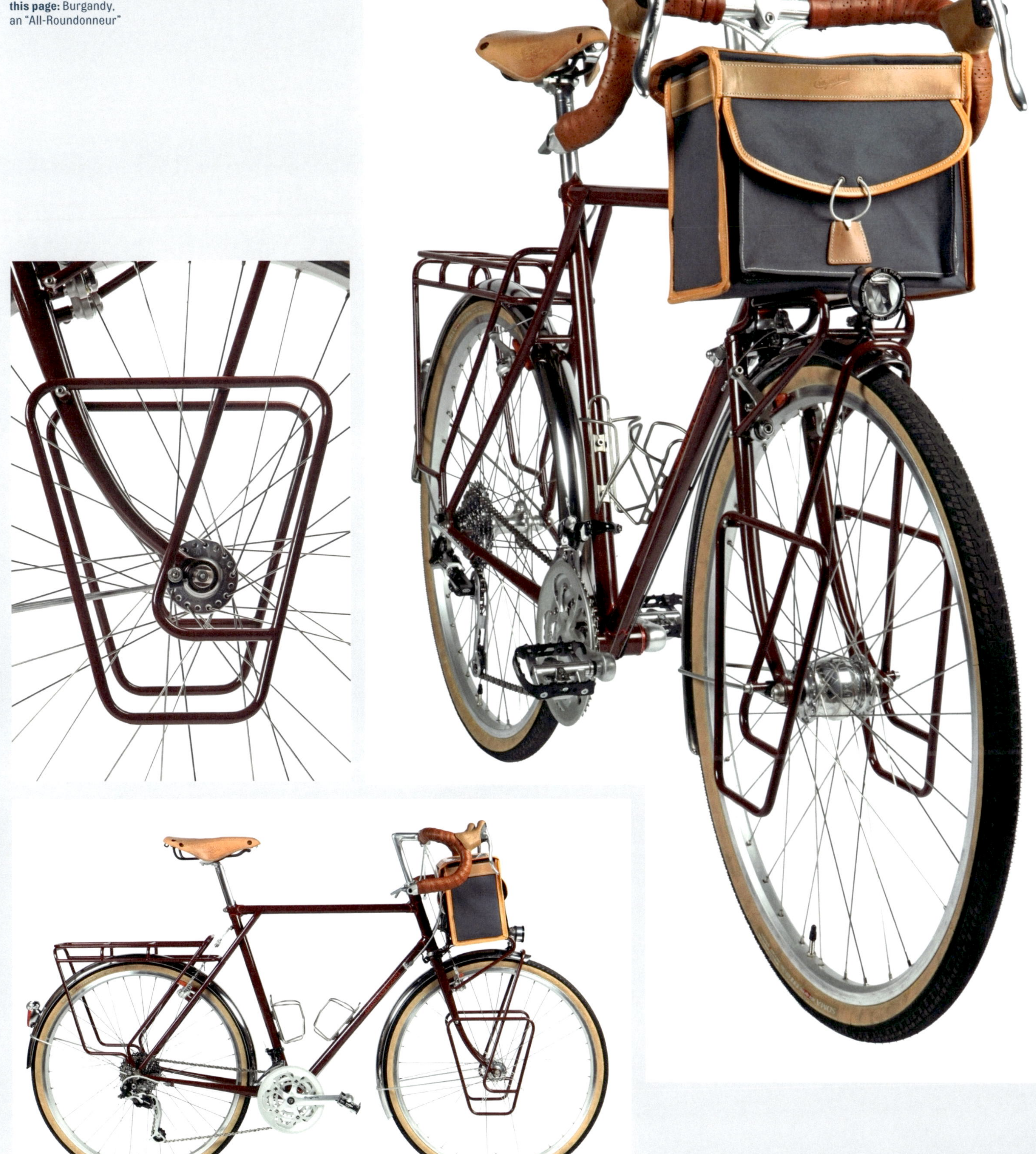

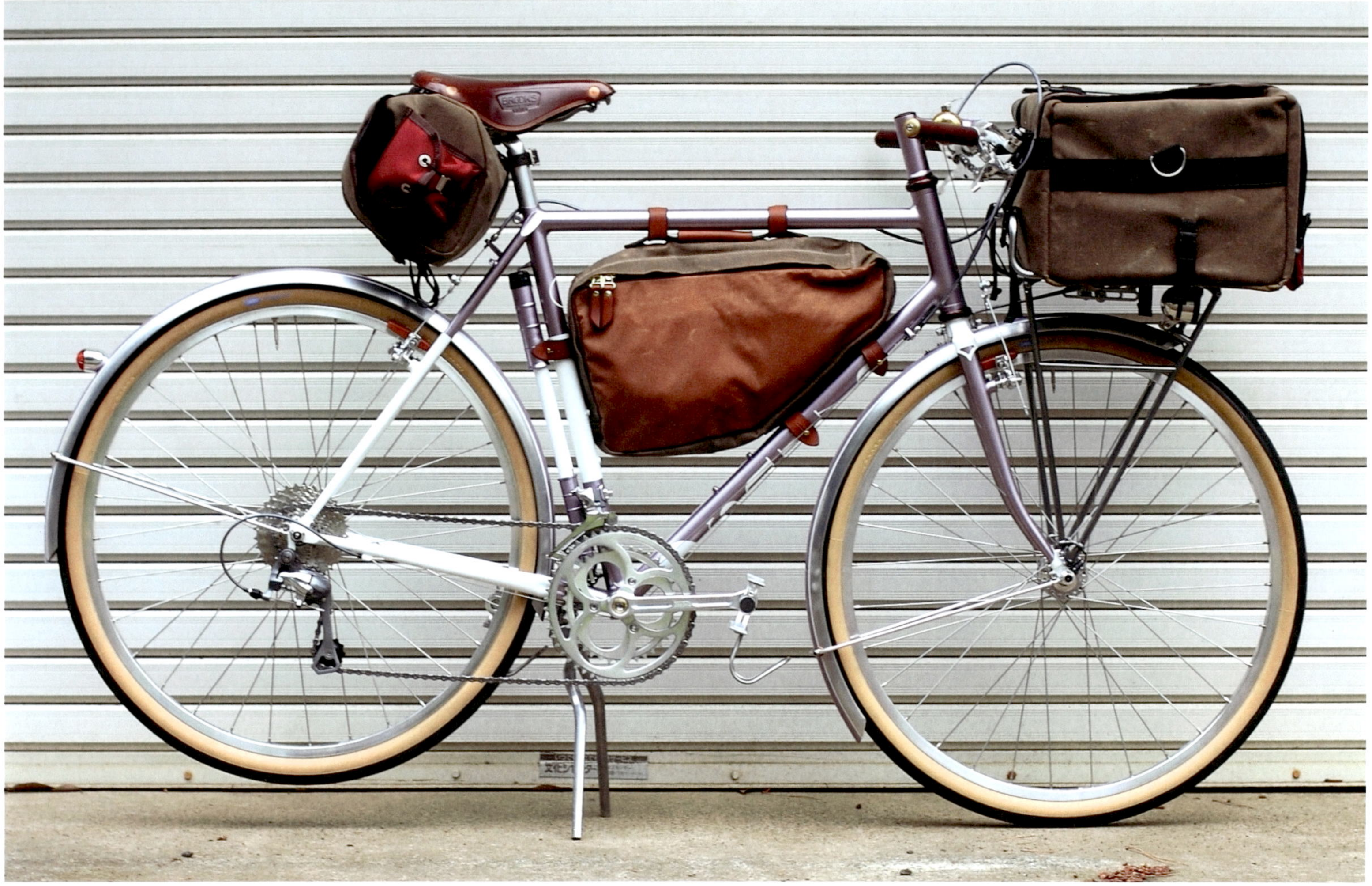

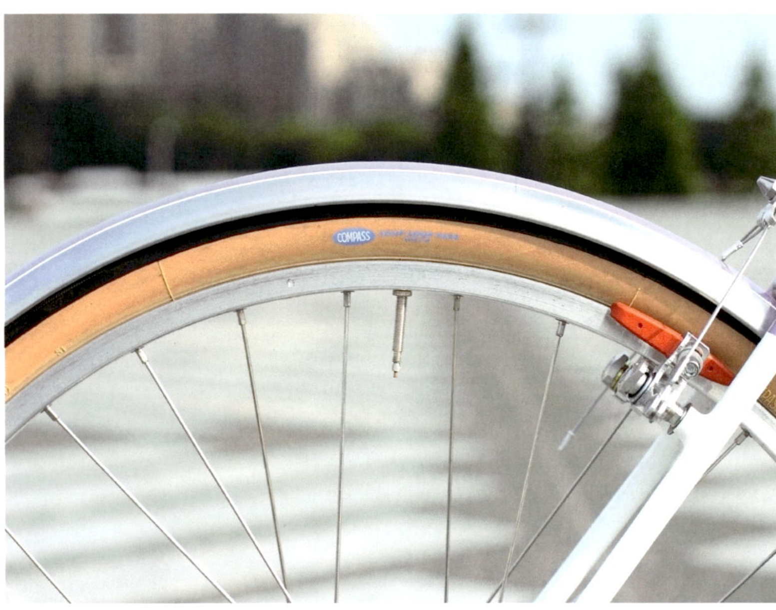


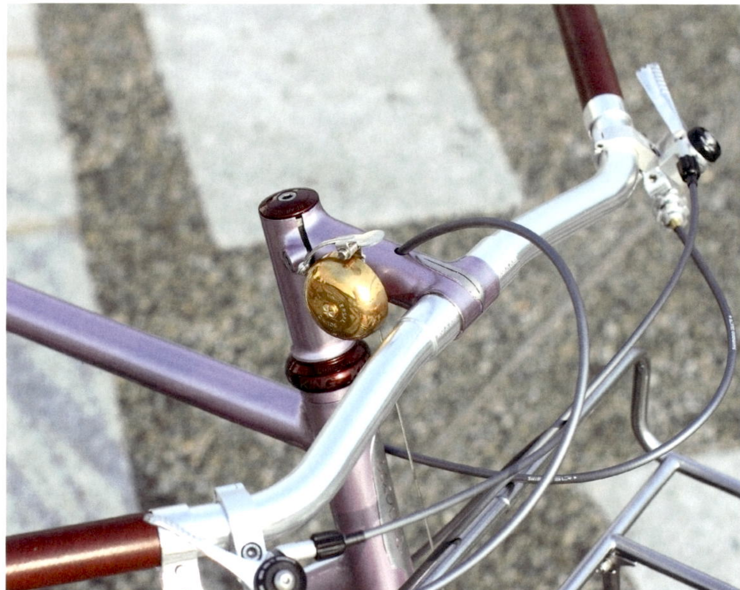

## *Commuterando!*

**ICARUS**

Many frame builders may groan when faced with making commuter frames, which require braze-ons and extras like racks, fenders, a pump, and a kickstand. And they are freighted with clearance issues particular to city streets. But not Icarus. The Commuterando!'s frame, fork, and stem sport fillet-brazed construction. The Japan-based client needed wheels that could weather the commute, but also port small loads for long-distance courses or audax cycling, also known as randonneuring. The frame has an unusual bottom-bracket cable routing and a custom stem featuring a bell mount and an internal brake hanger. Its round tubing and 650B 38-millimeter tires cushion urban scrapes and the inevitable bottoming-out, as well as the bumpage and lumpage that characterize any entertaining dirt trail.

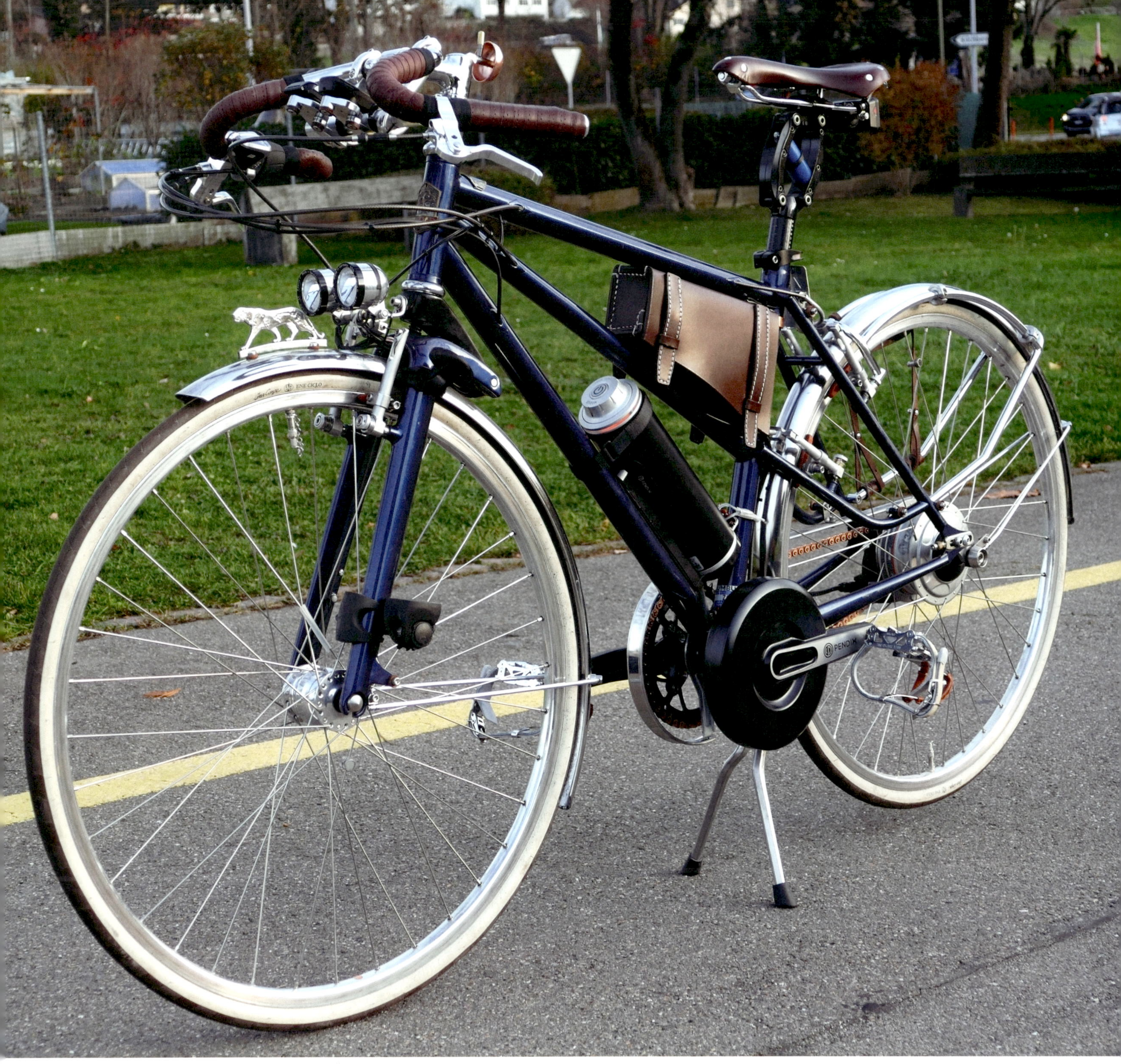

## *Blaha*

**KOLB RAHMENBAU**

Every feature of the Blaha was custom designed by Kolb Rahmenbau for the client, Mr. Blaha. After the final build was complete—it took two years—it included a Pendix e-motor, double rear brakes from Paul, double headlights, a Harmony electronic shifting system from NuVinci, a stainless custom rack, and many other details.

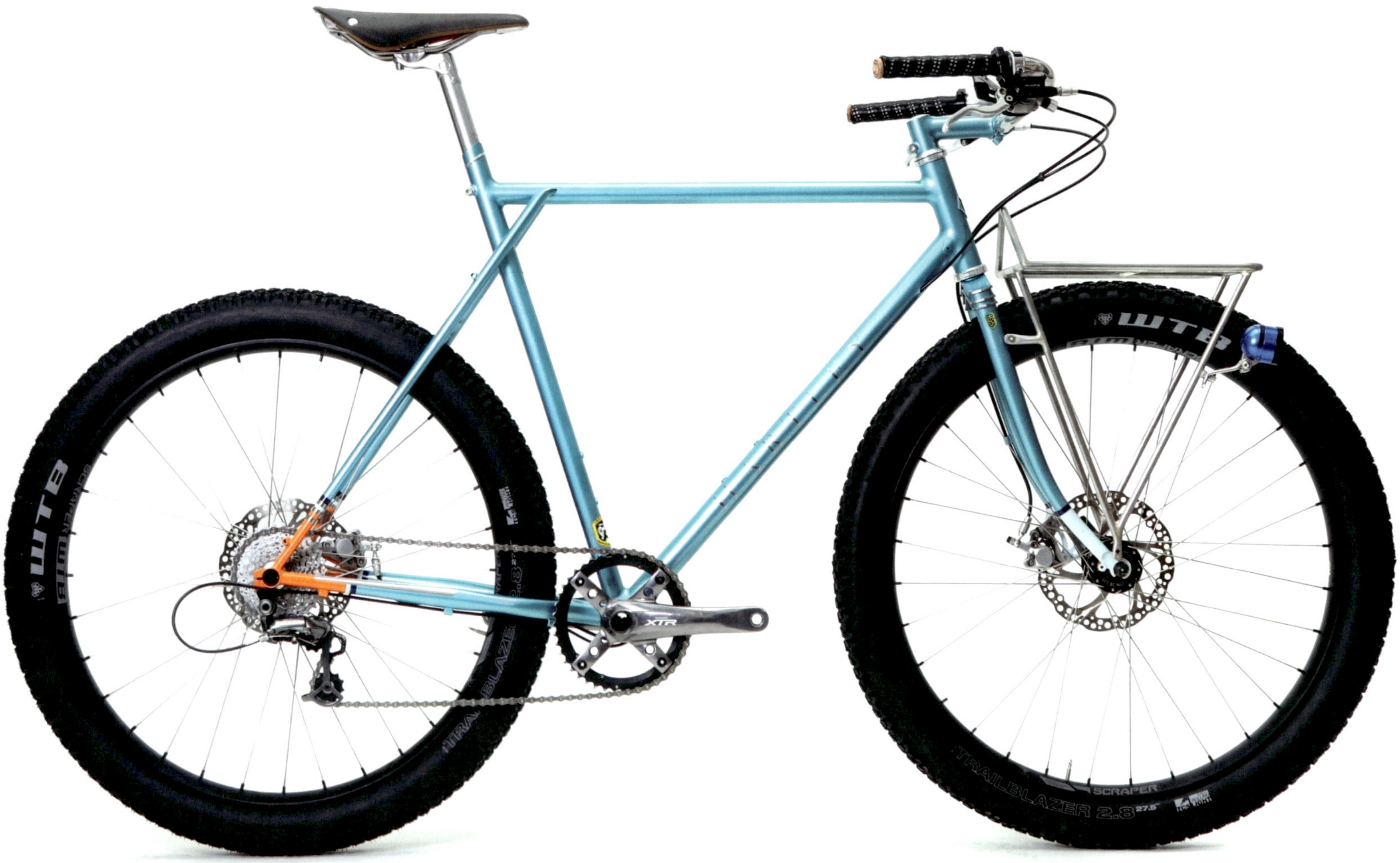

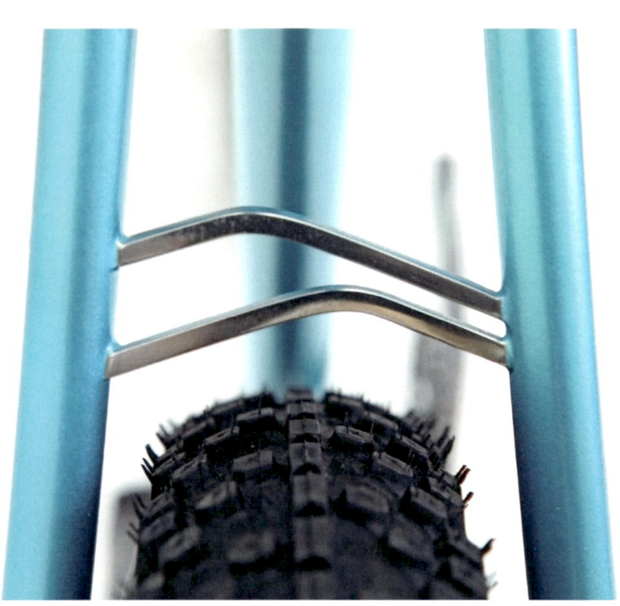

# Porkeur

## HARTLEY CYCLES

The saucily named Porkeur was built for a cycling photographer who shoots off-road in the Pyrenees with delicate equipment in tow. It had to dominate seasonal ground conditions while cushioning its cargo. "This bike needed to be FAT," Caren Hartley says, "or at least a little porky." But neither liked the fat bike look, so she made a hybrid: a semi-fat hauler with the chic lines of a midcentury French porteur. The Porkeur pairs a tough but slender Reynolds 931 stainless-steel tubeset with pillowy WTB semi-fat tires by drawing the seat stays forward into a triple triangle and using a Boost 148×12 through rear axle to accommodate the tires but keep the stays straight. Then Hartley added handmade asymmetric details that echo the topographical contours of the mountains over which the client rides.

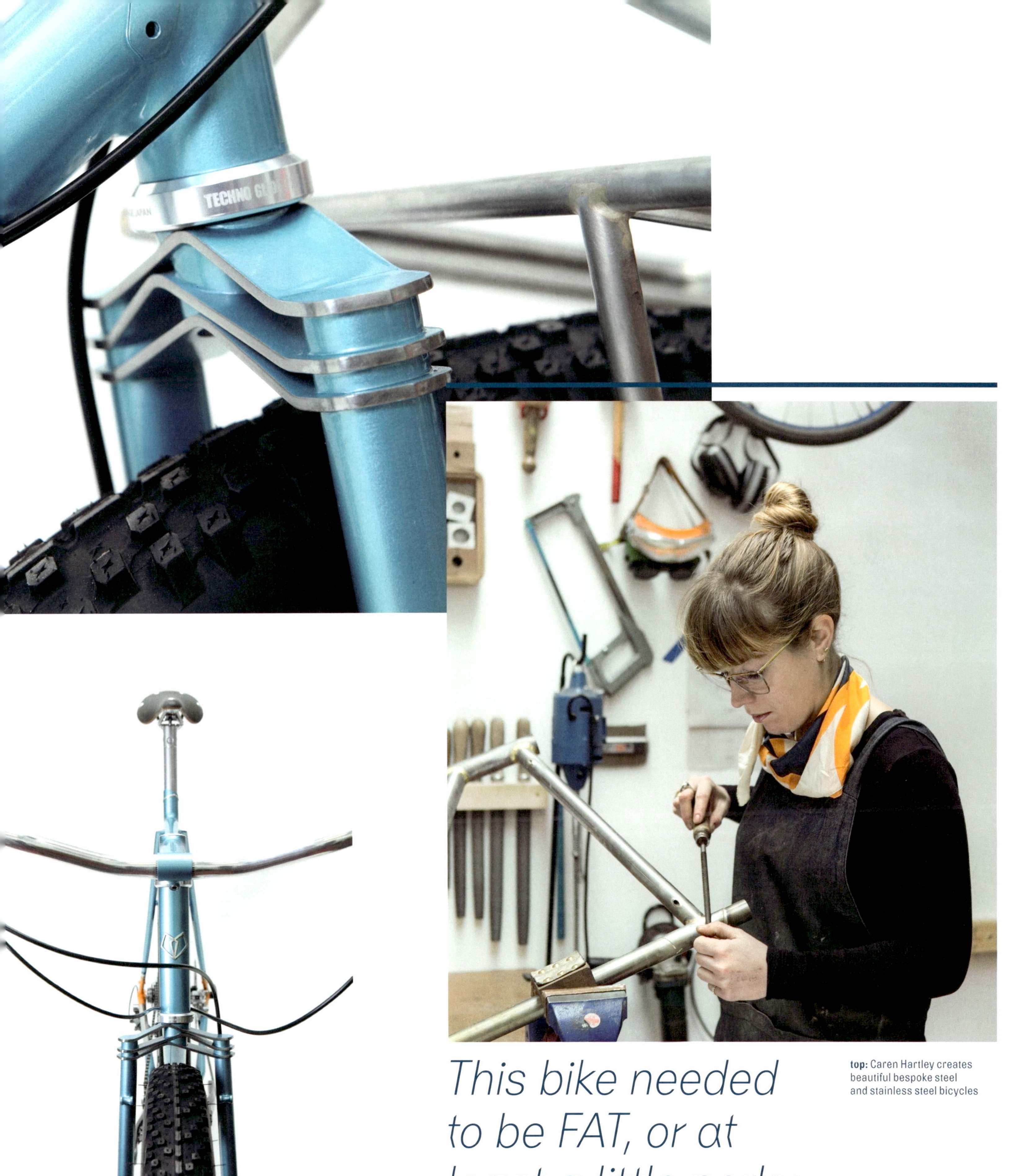

*This bike needed to be FAT, or at least a little porky.*

**top:** Caren Hartley creates beautiful bespoke steel and stainless steel bicycles

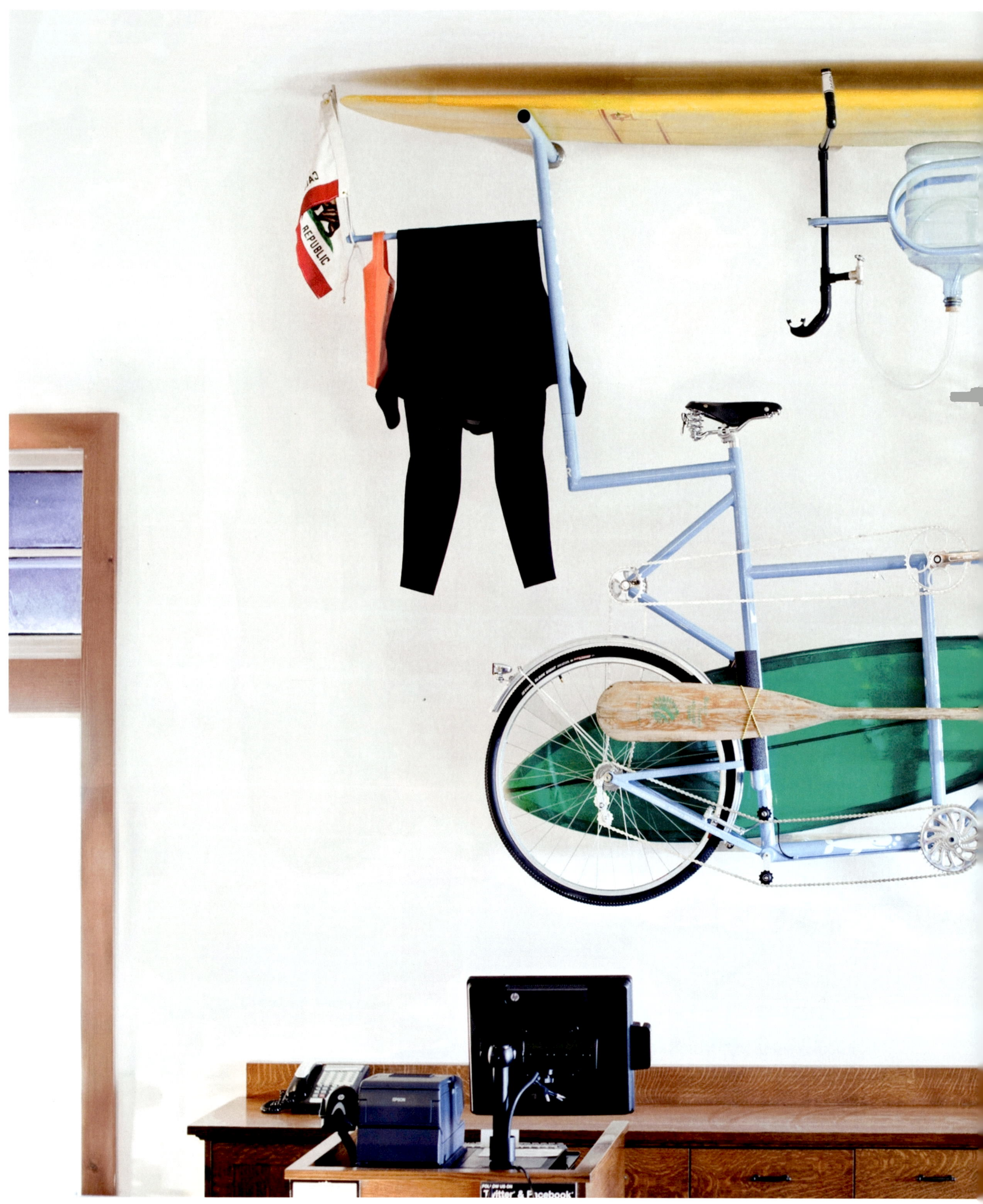
REPUBLIC
Twitter & Facebook

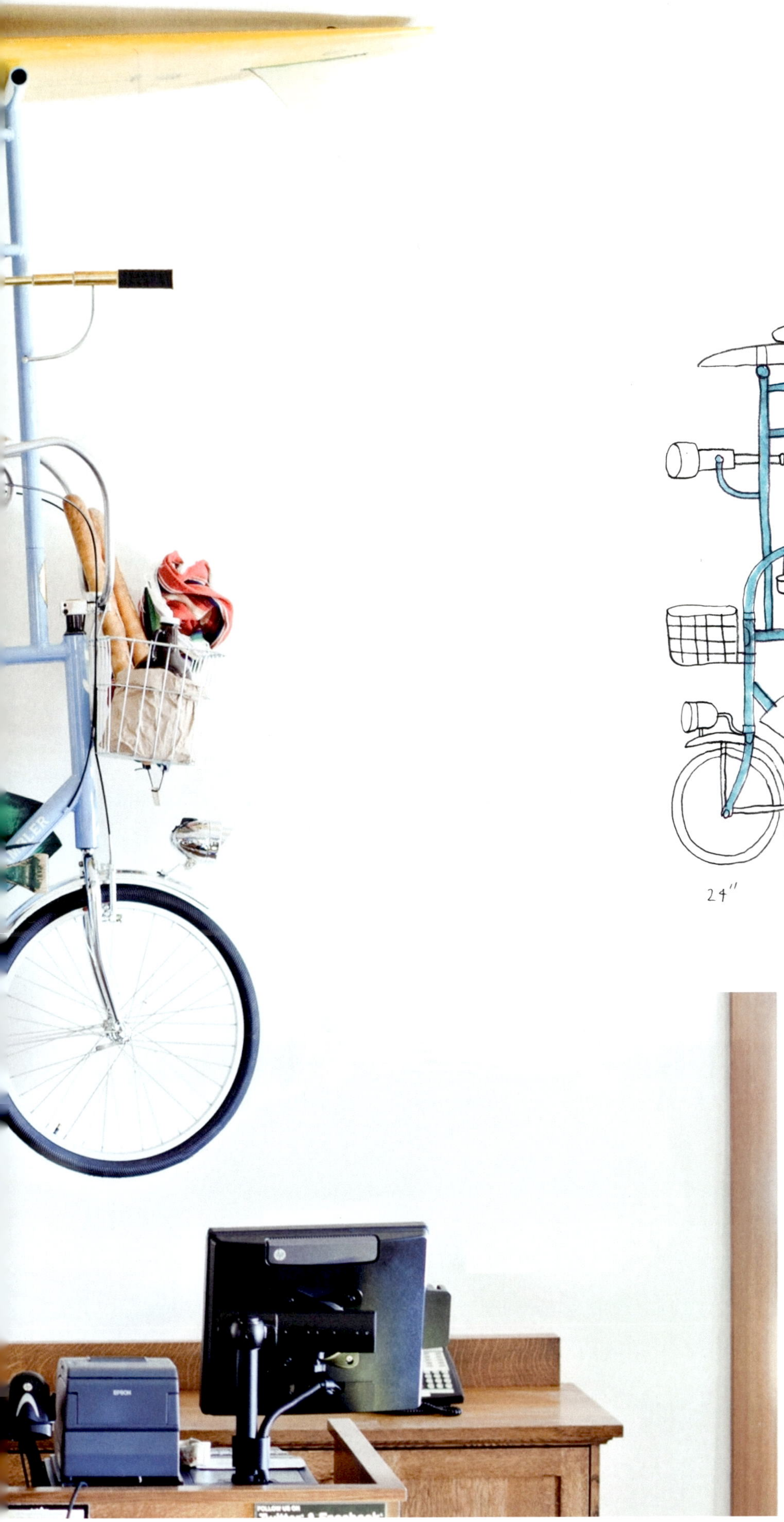

# Patagonia Sea Rambler

**GEOFF MCFETRIDGE**

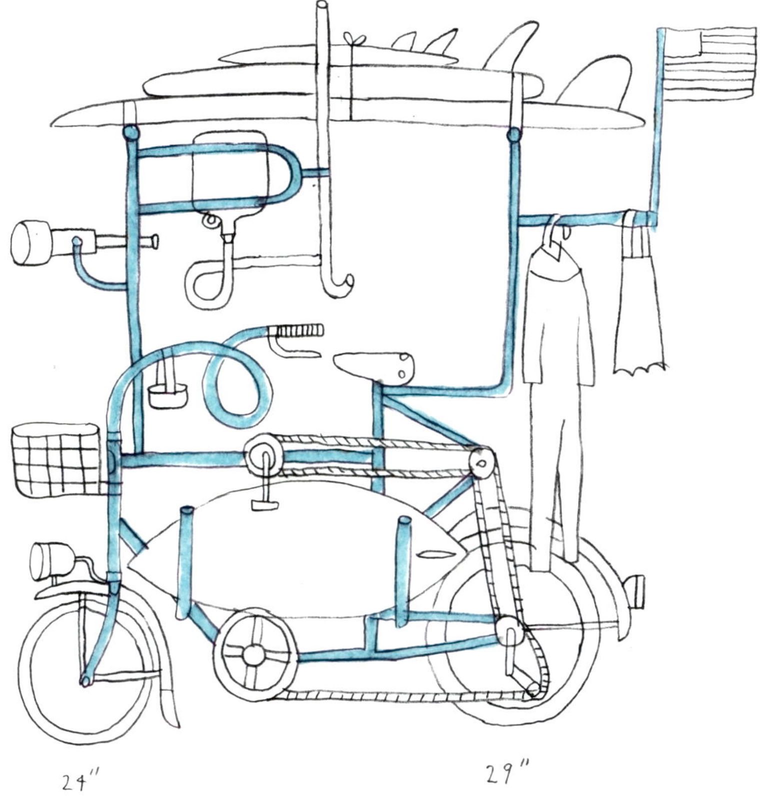


Painted the color of the sea and covered in intricate, hand-painted stencils, the Sea Rambler's frame is an unmistakable indication of the unique nature of the project. Its other unusual features include a telescope on the handlebars, a shortboard and paddle attached to the frame, and a wetsuit-drying rack. The bicycle, a collaboration between Los Angeles-based artist Geoff McFetridge, Patagonia, and Gold Coast Cycles MFG, is the kind of project invented in daydreams—but then actually produced as a one-off, fully functional bike designed and made in the United States. In the end, the Sea Rambler is a statement about machines and how they embody the complex relationship between concept and design.

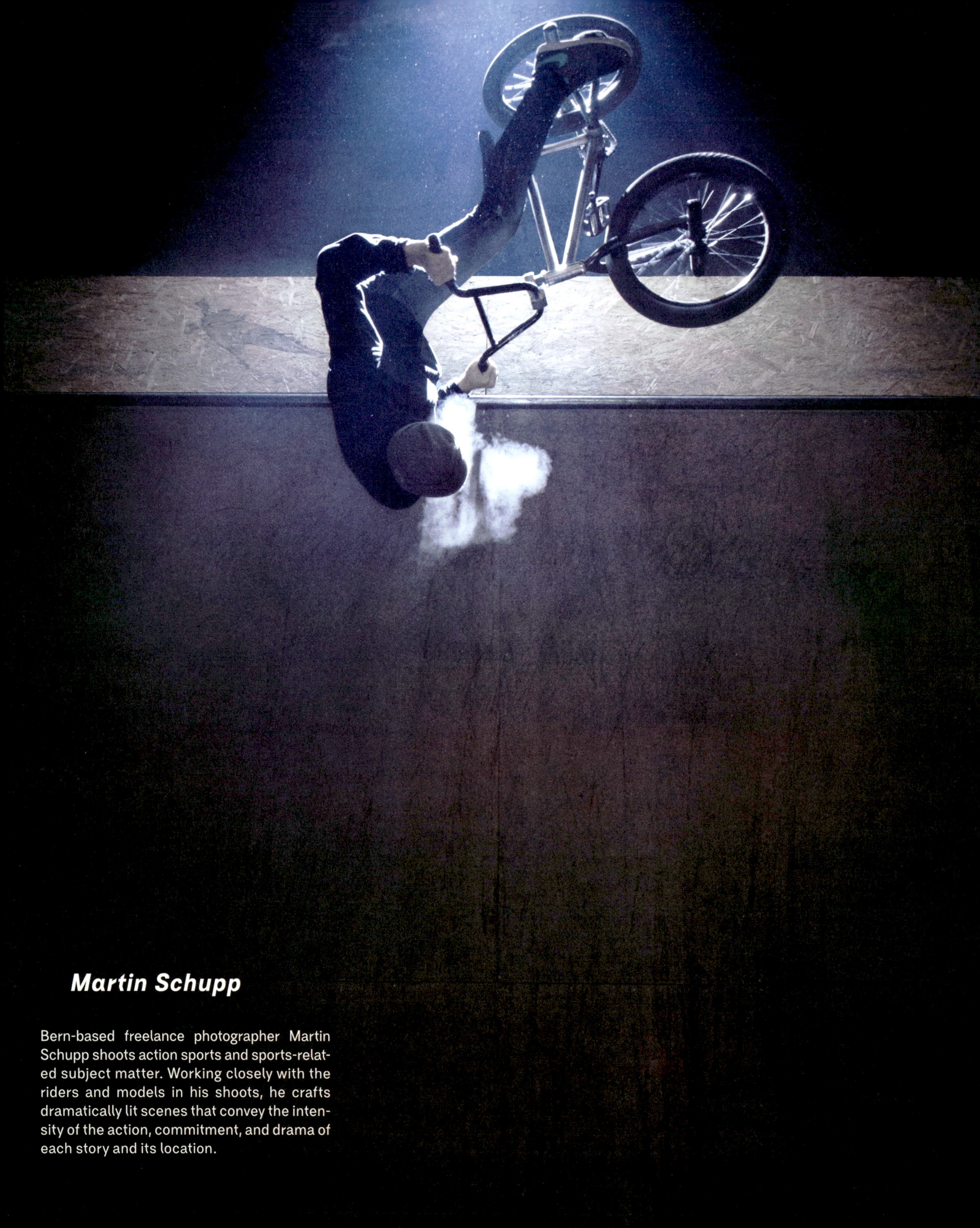

## *Martin Schupp*

Bern-based freelance photographer Martin Schupp shoots action sports and sports-related subject matter. Working closely with the riders and models in his shoots, he crafts dramatically lit scenes that convey the intensity of the action, commitment, and drama of each story and its location.

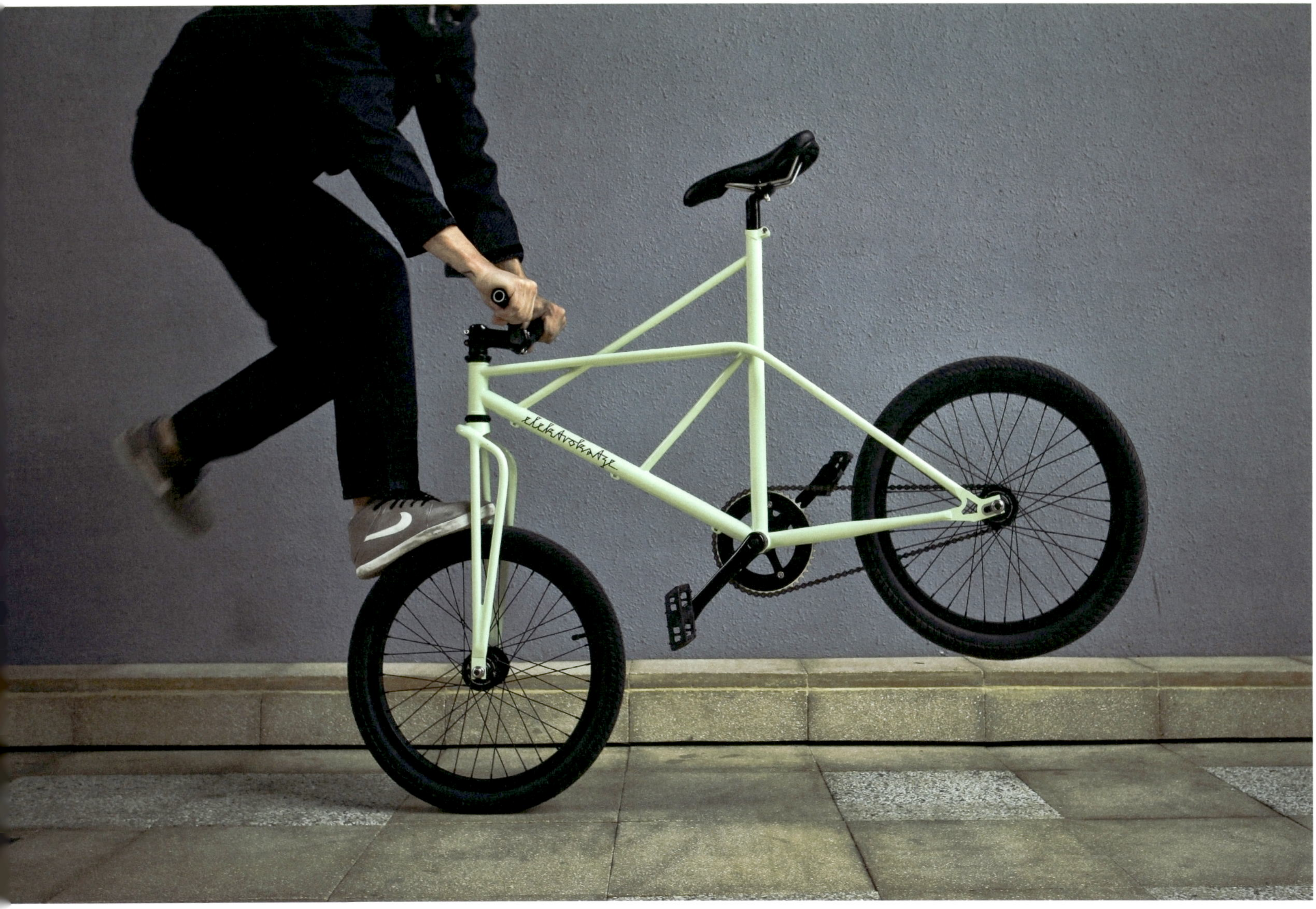

## *Elektrokatze from Katze Customs*

### CHOWPOURIANLAB

As a small business of doers and makers, Katze Customs takes pride in retaining the freedom to create what they love: everyday objects that will last a lifetime. Working with local suppliers and artists who share a commitment to and pride in craftsmanship, Katze Customs produces small batches of the objects they create with a strong focus on design. Their newest collaboration with ChowPourianLab, a handmade still-frame bike welded by Colossi Cycling, comes as a single-speed or fixed-gear with shortened handlebars and 20-inch wheels. The Elektrokatze is currently a working prototype in testing. Weighing in at 2.4 kilograms, this new street-style bike is light and compact, providing an agile riding experience on a full-size frame—perfect for tooling around the city.

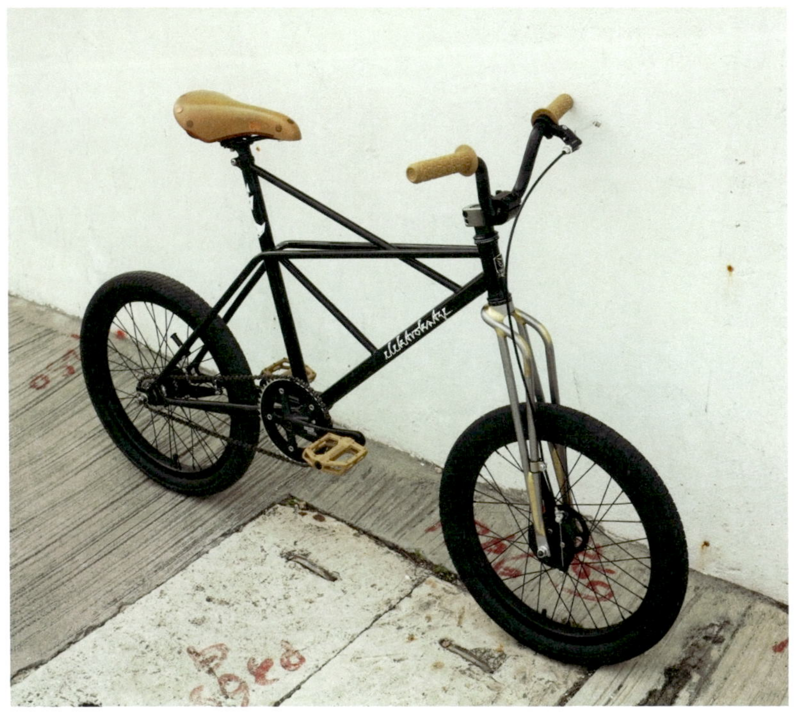

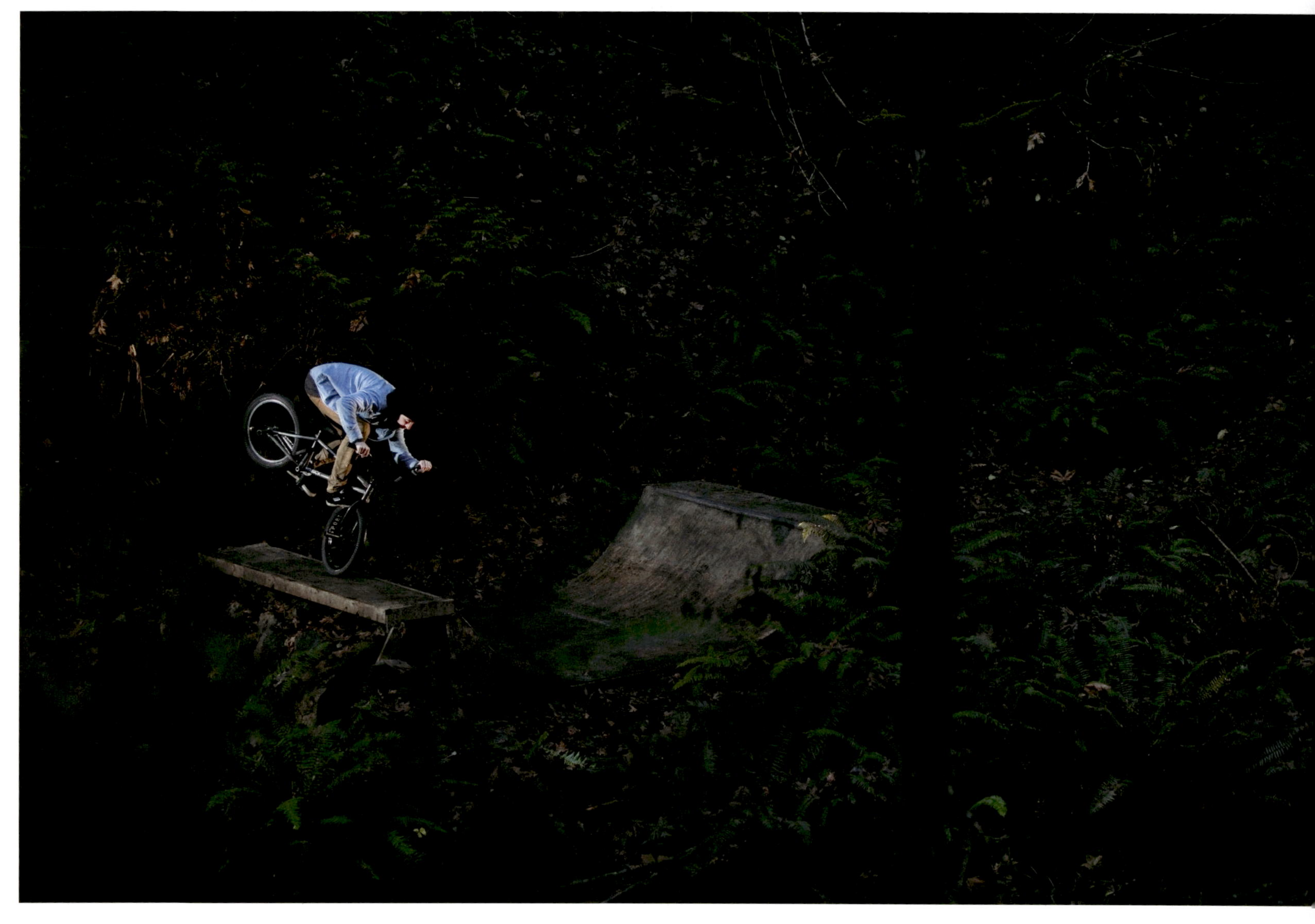

# *Mike Zinger*

Photographer Mike Zinger grew up riding BMX on his native Vancouver Island in British Columbia. He and his friends would shoot photos of each other for fun, but for him it eventually grew into a career. Over the years, Zinger's kit has included a 2MP compact digital camera with a super-slow shutter, a DSLR, and a medium-format film camera. No matter what his equipment, Zinger continues to ride BMX, something he sees as giving him a leg up on other photographers when it comes to understanding both the sport and the athletes.

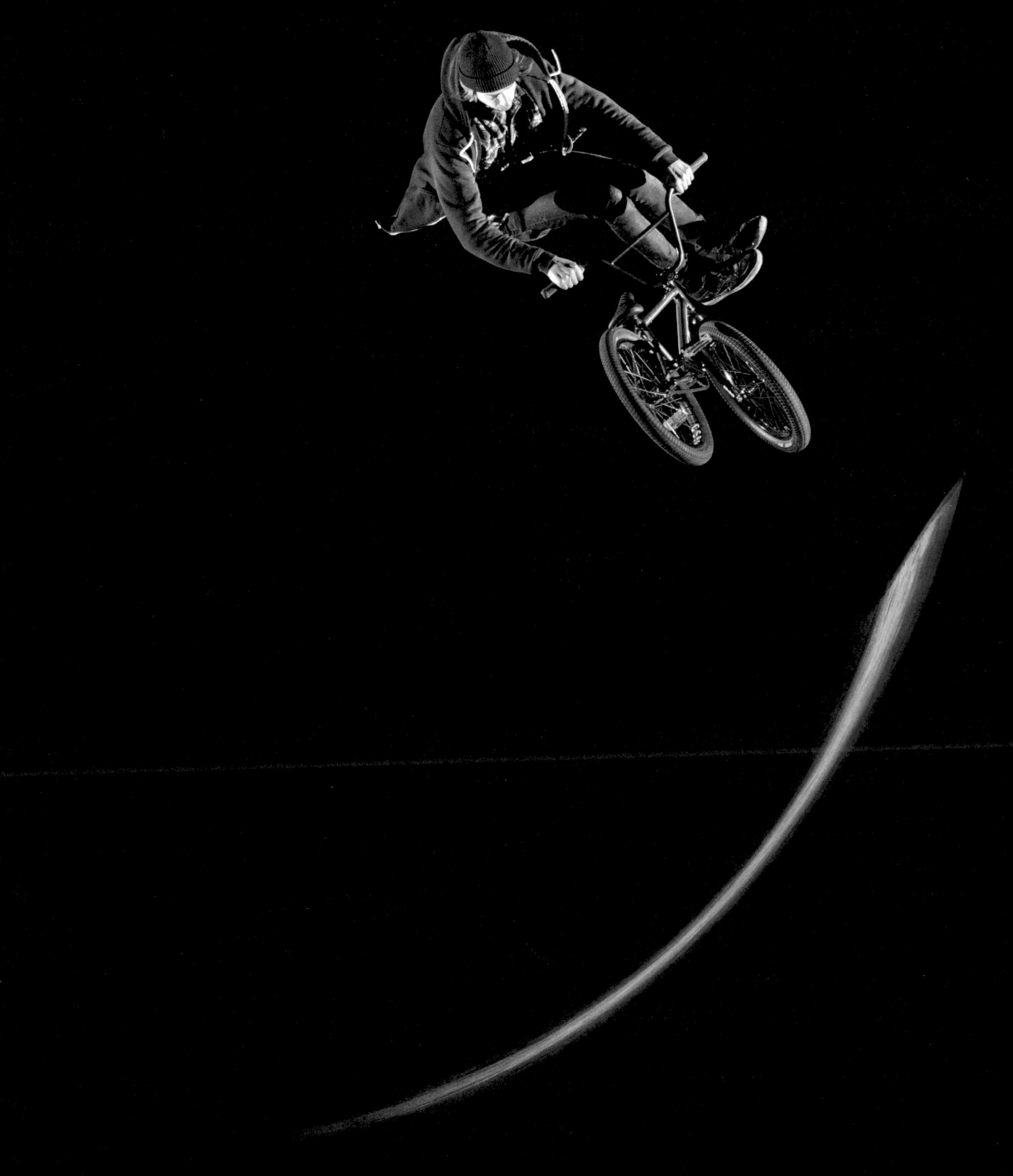

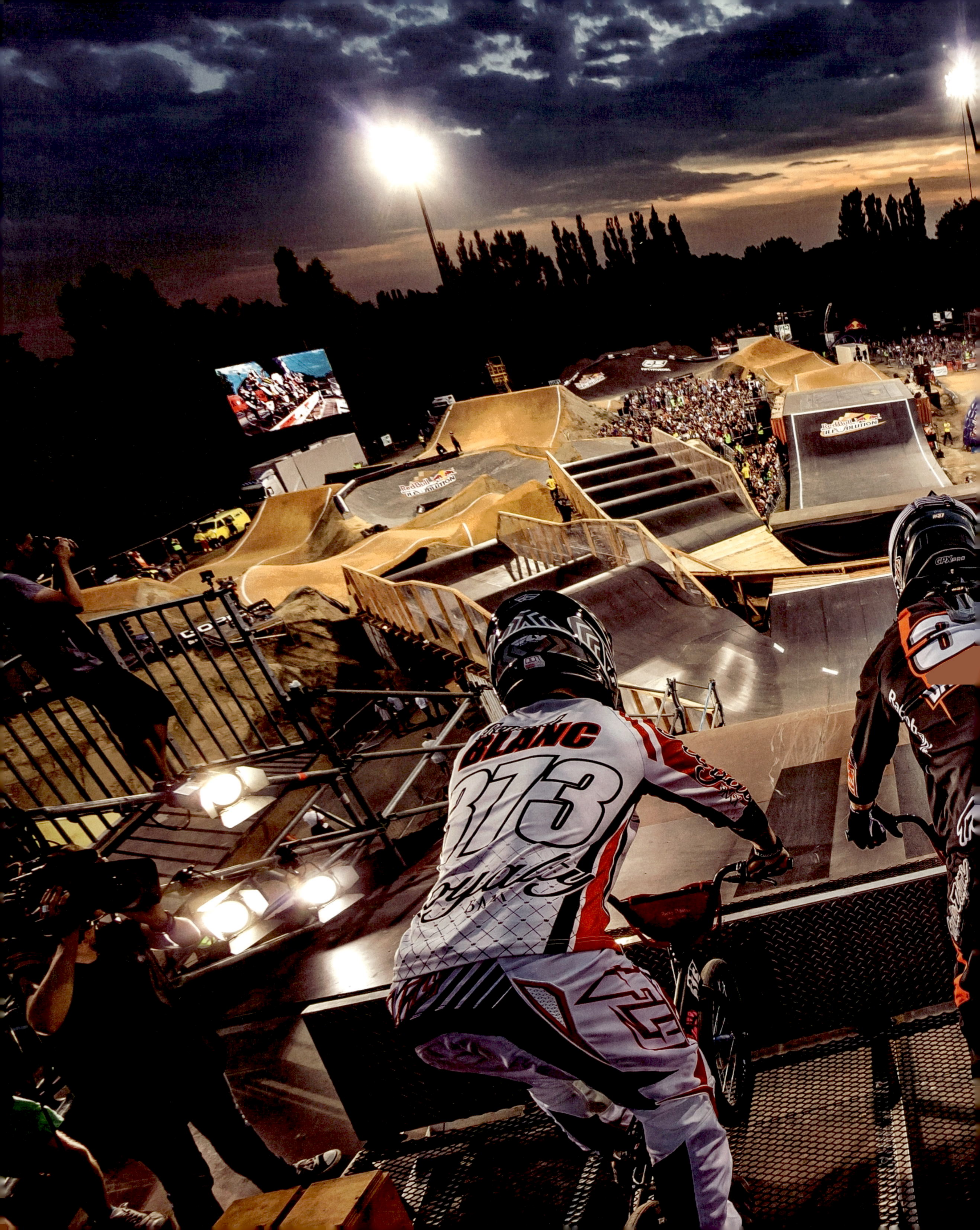
BLANC

# Mellowpark

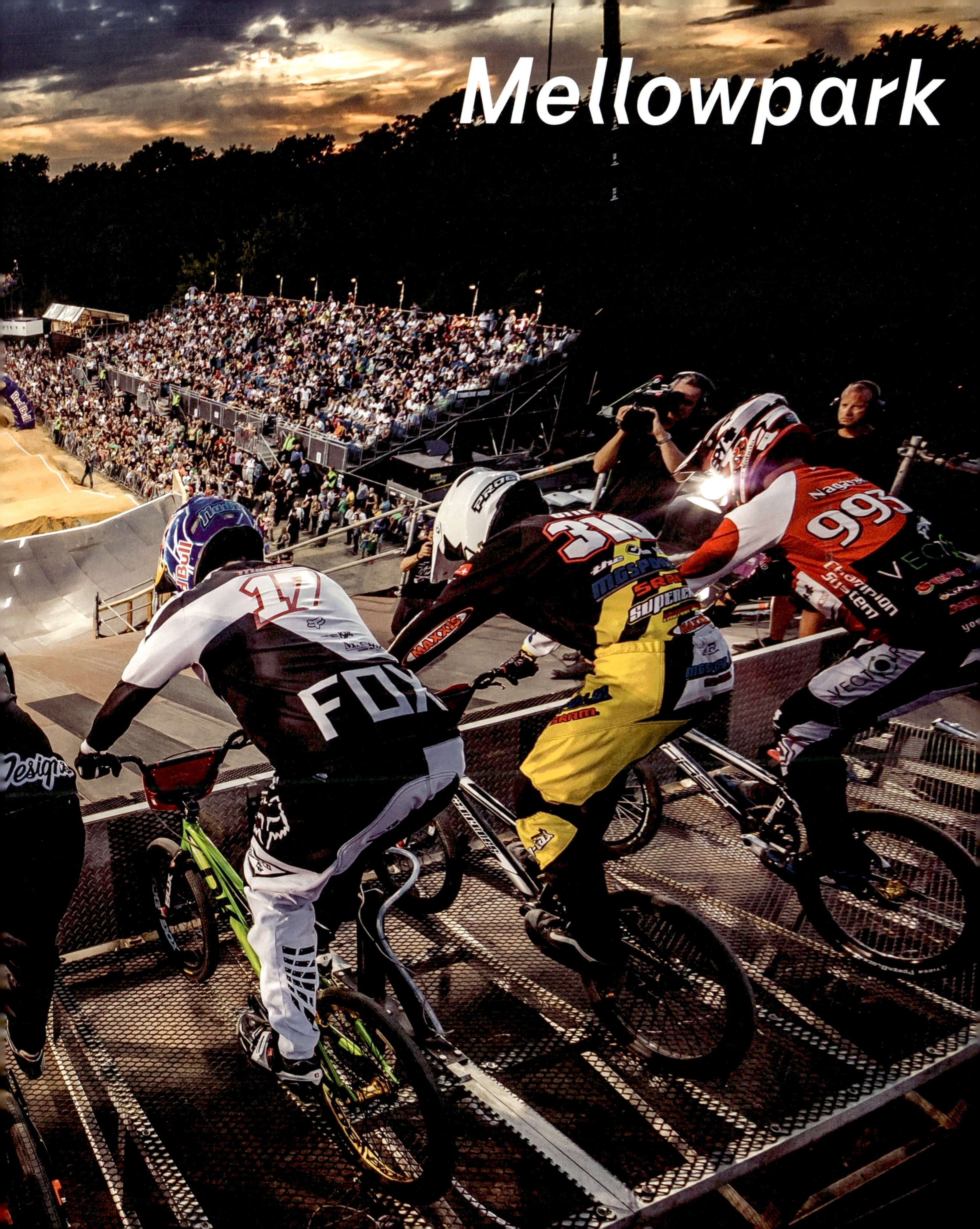

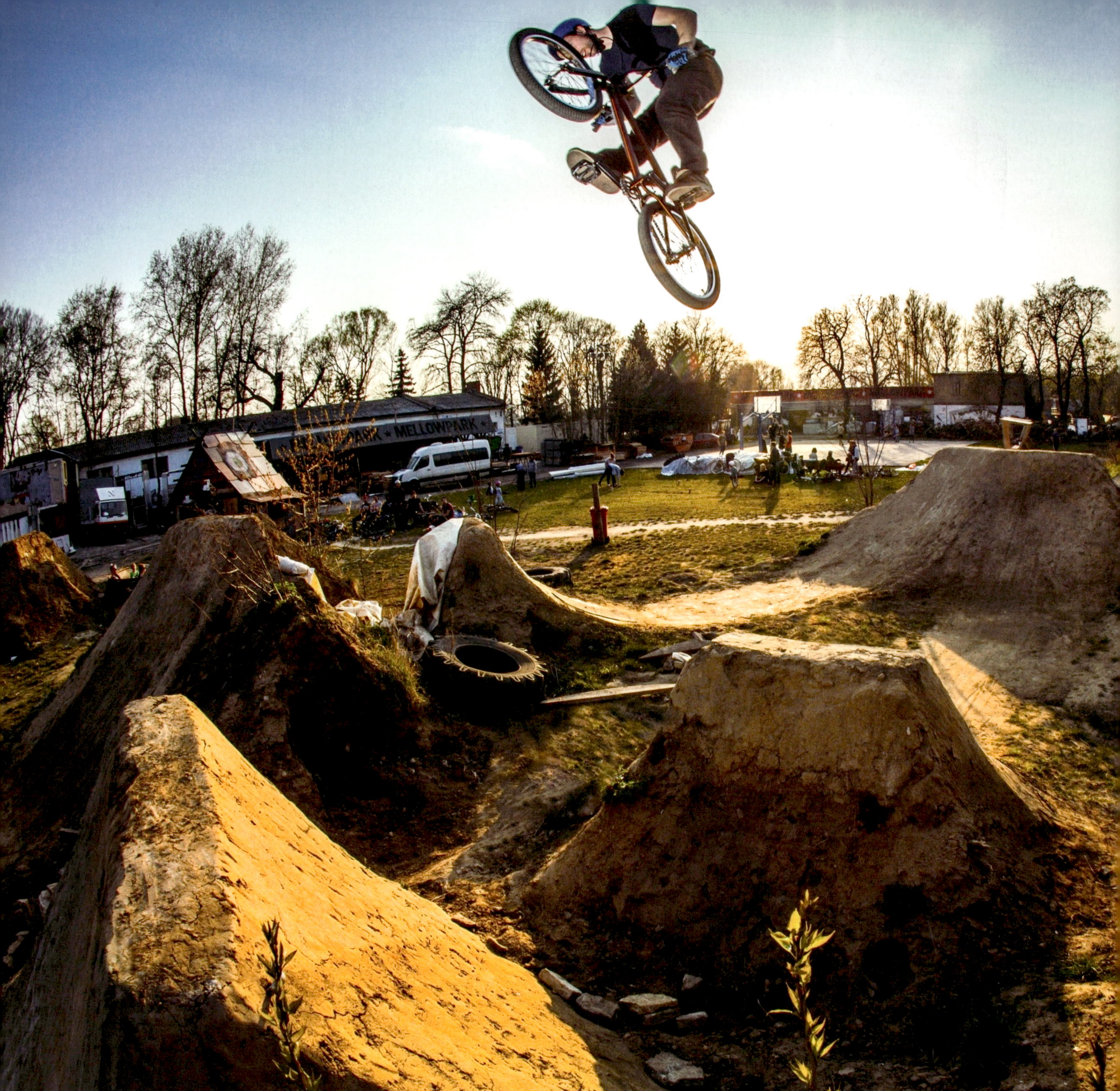


Mellowpark, a fixture of Berlin's BMX scene, was founded over twenty years ago by teenagers. It is known for its versatile ramp setups and numerous freestyle events that attract hundreds of thousands of BMX freestylers. Freestyle BMX is not bound to hard rules, allowing the freestyler to decide whether to jump over hills or ramps or to grind handrails. It is, ultimately, about individual creativity—and a lifestyle. During Mellowpark's lifespan, BMX has evolved from a subculture into a well-established Olympic sport whose lasting popularity means teenagers, kids, and parents all ride together.

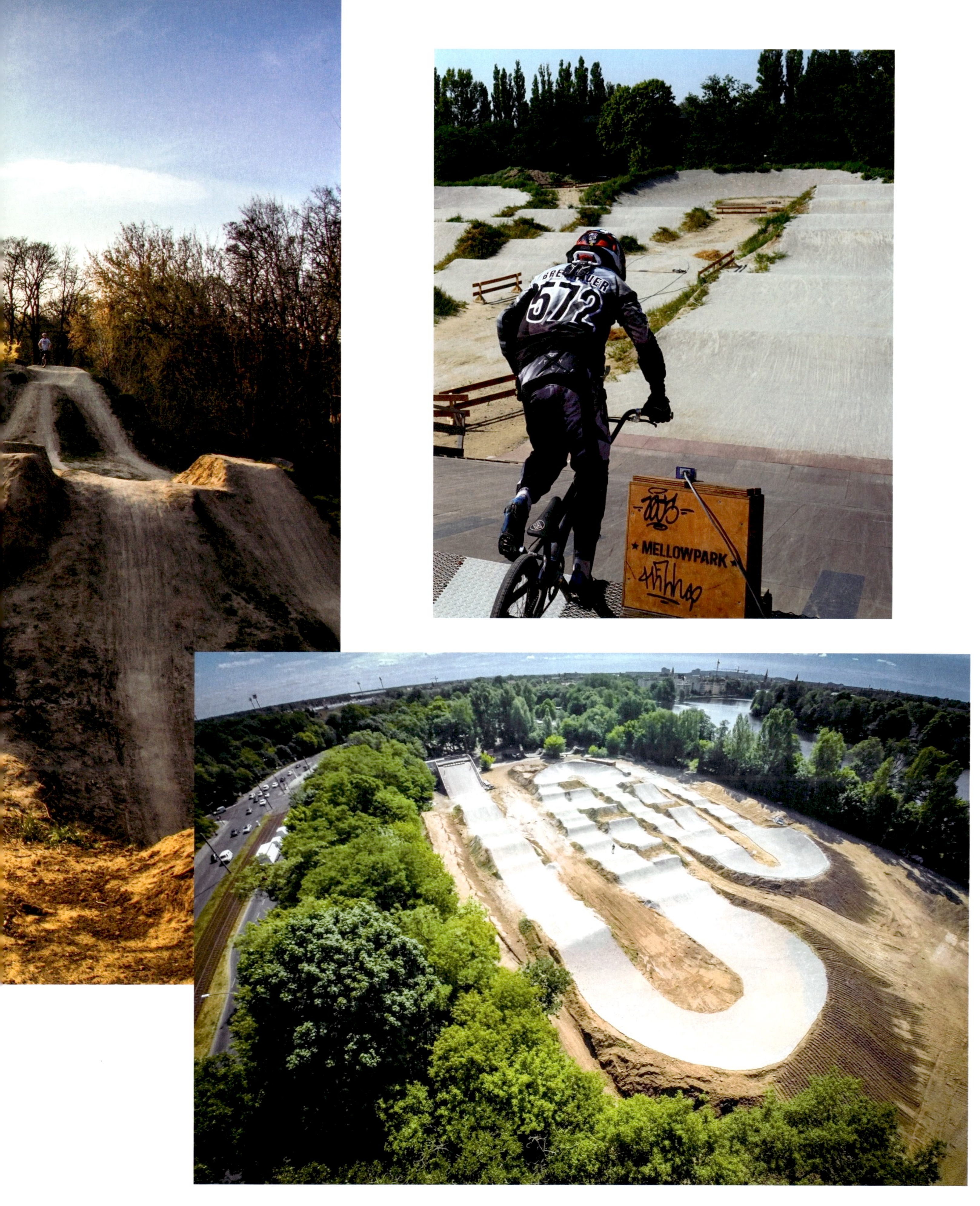
BRE
572
★ MELLOWPARK ★

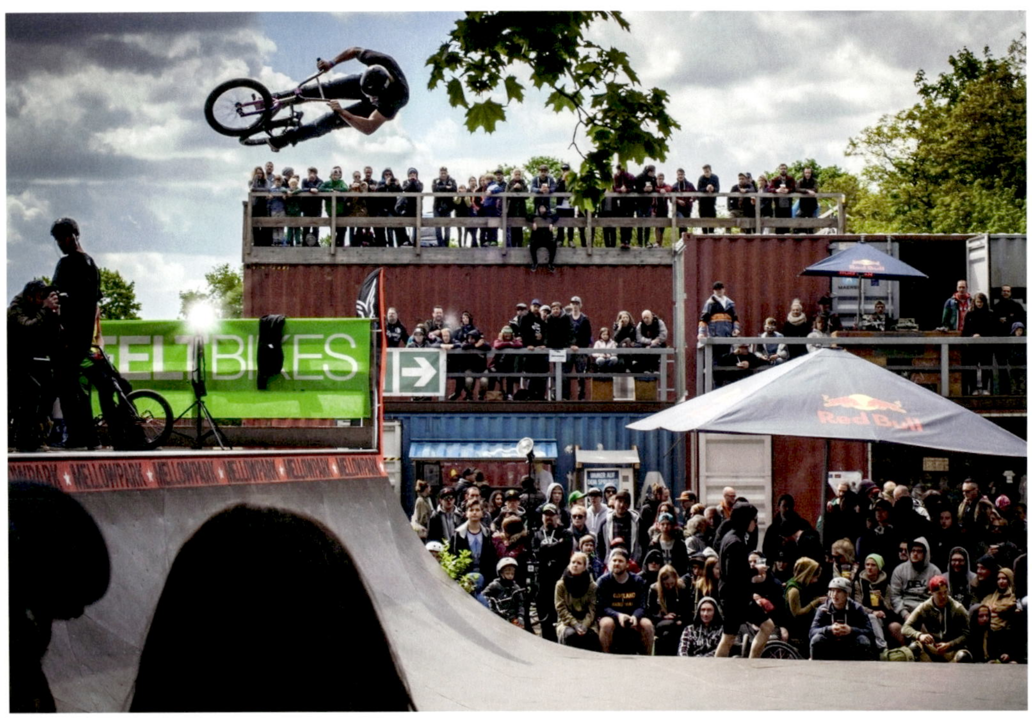


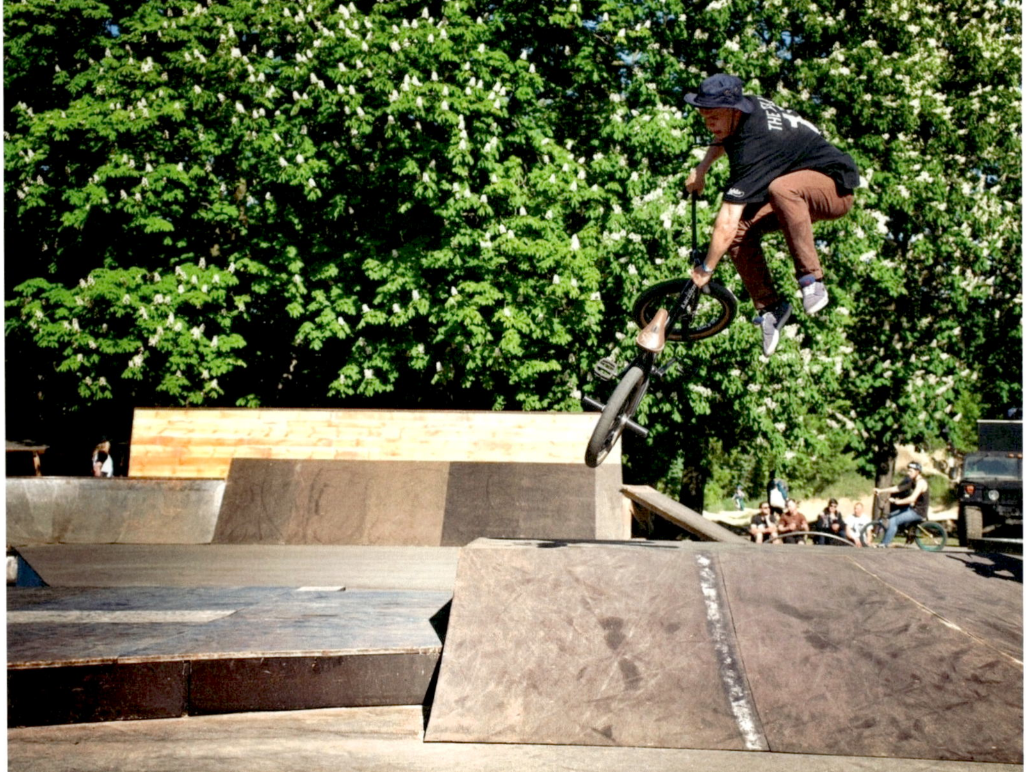

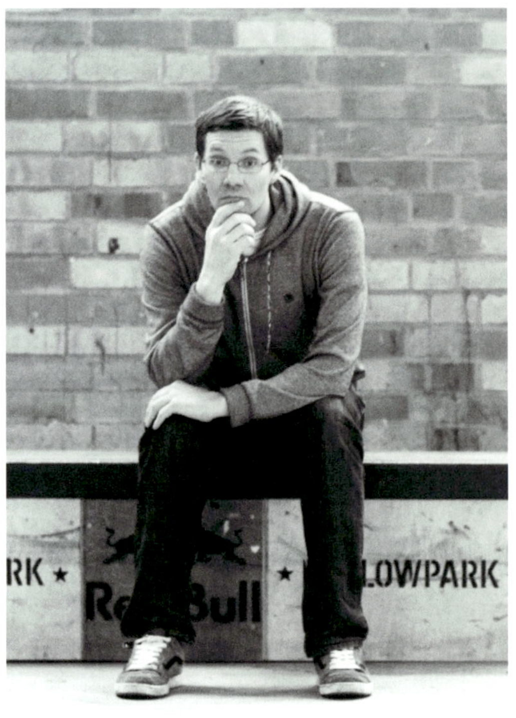


*Freestyle BMX is not bound to hard rules, allowing the freestyler to decide whether to jump over ramps or grind handrails.*

Jens Werner, chairman of Mellowpark

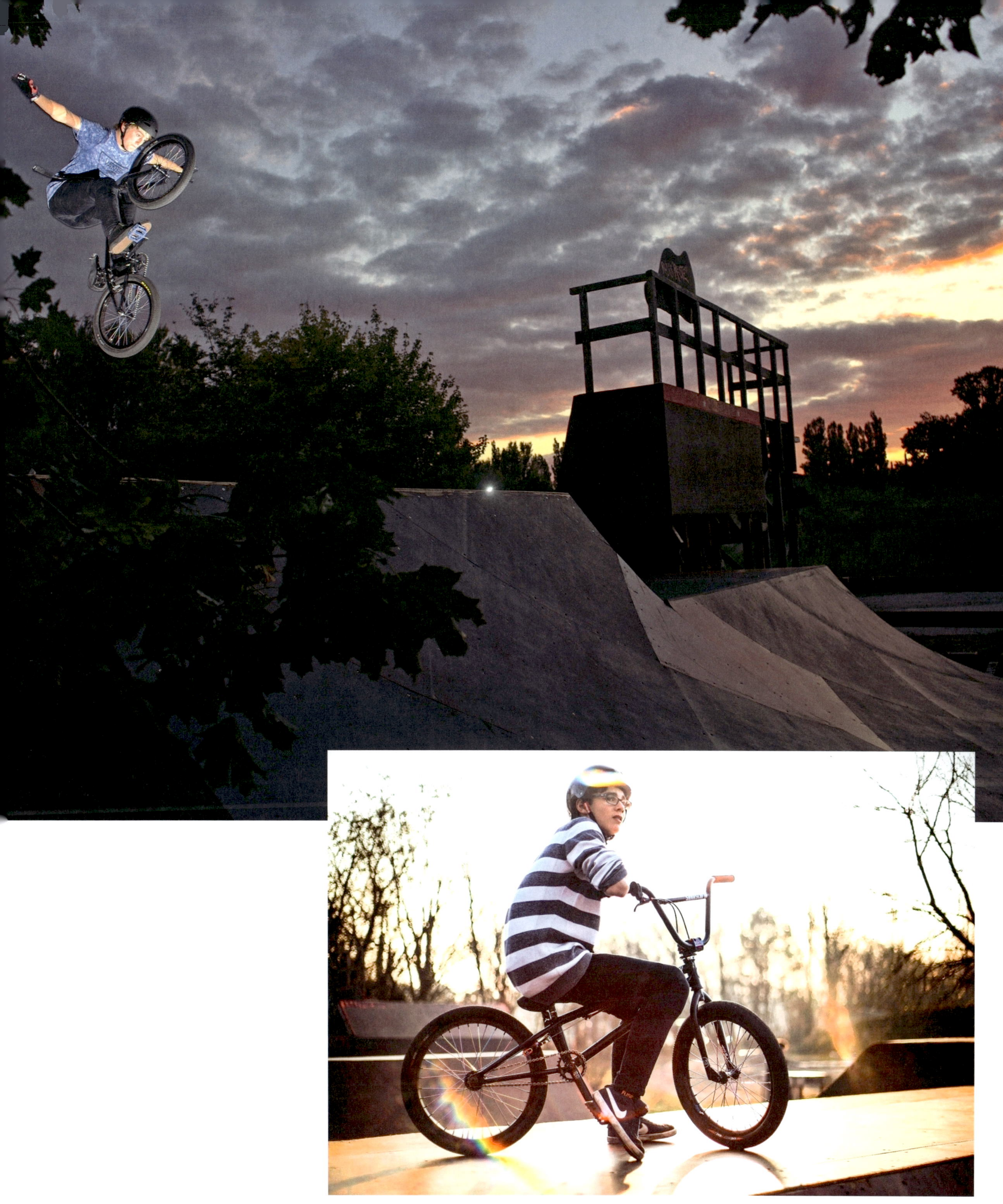

# Crosstown Cadences

oppiste page:
Boréal Bikes
(page 148)

Text: SHONQUIS MORENO

## *On cargo bikes, folding bikes, e-bikes, pedelecs, tech-connected bikes, and the new commute*

We're sick of the Metro closing at midnight, waiting for the lift at the Covent Garden station, and sweating on the L train in summer. We're sick of gas prices and car insurance and trying to find parking that isn't there. We even think that Kiss & Rides aren't very kissy. Policemen park in the bike lane to write us tickets for not riding in the bike lane. But that's okay. Who says quality of life in the city is low? We're not the young parents who moved to the suburbs. We carry our kids in cargo trikes and buy fresh tubes from a vending machine on the corner. Yeah, there are bike shops that sell bikes, but ours serve vegan brunch and host wine tastings; they're concept shops and clubhouses. We use our folding bikes to tow canoes and go from pedaling to paddling, from pedaling to pedelec. We bike to nightclubs and bars, on first dates and blind dates. Wearing our helmets. Sometimes. Our bikes navigate by Bluetooth and commute to work through snow and they look good enough to hang in the living room. My bike looks just the way I want it to. No one else has a bike like mine.

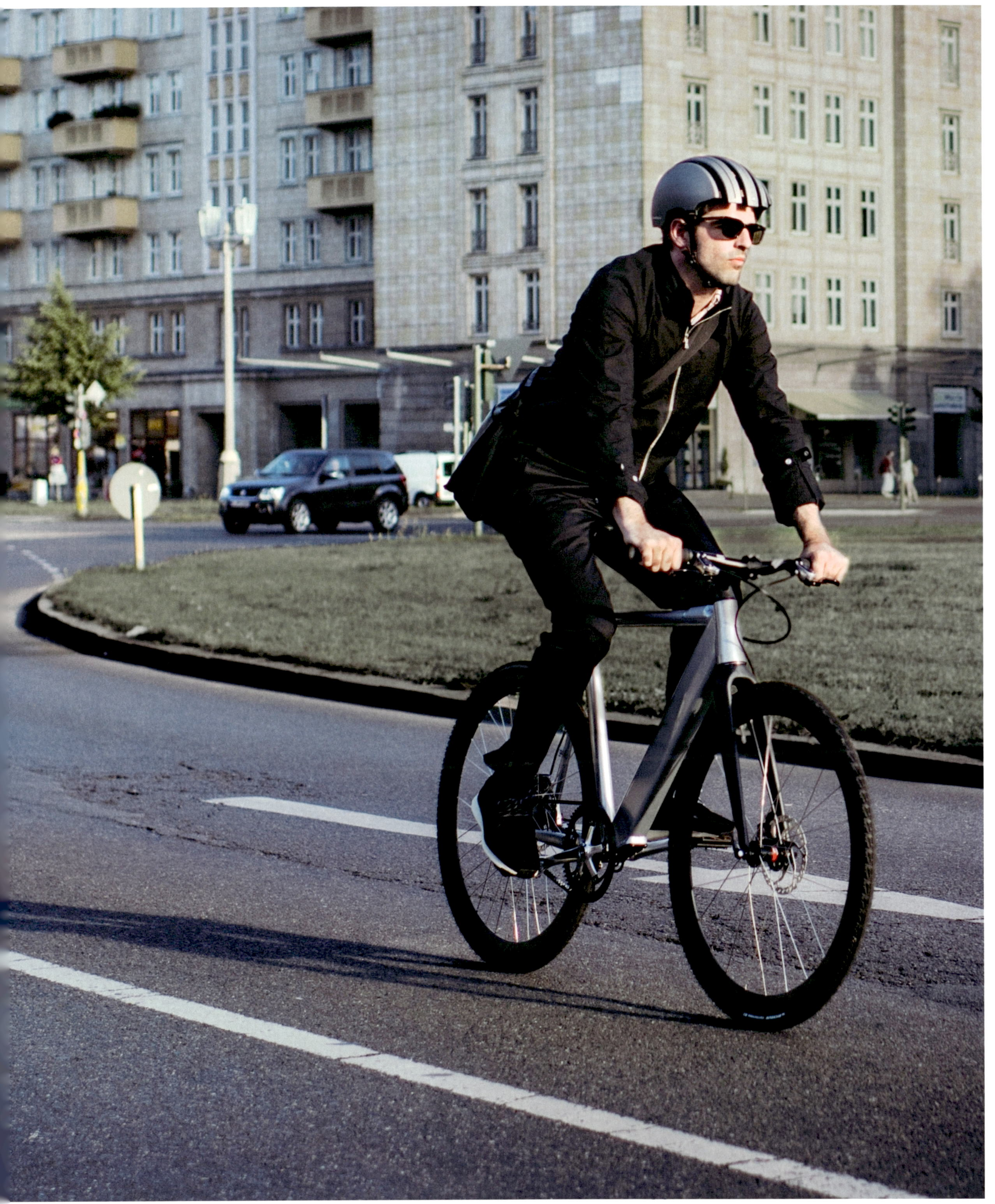

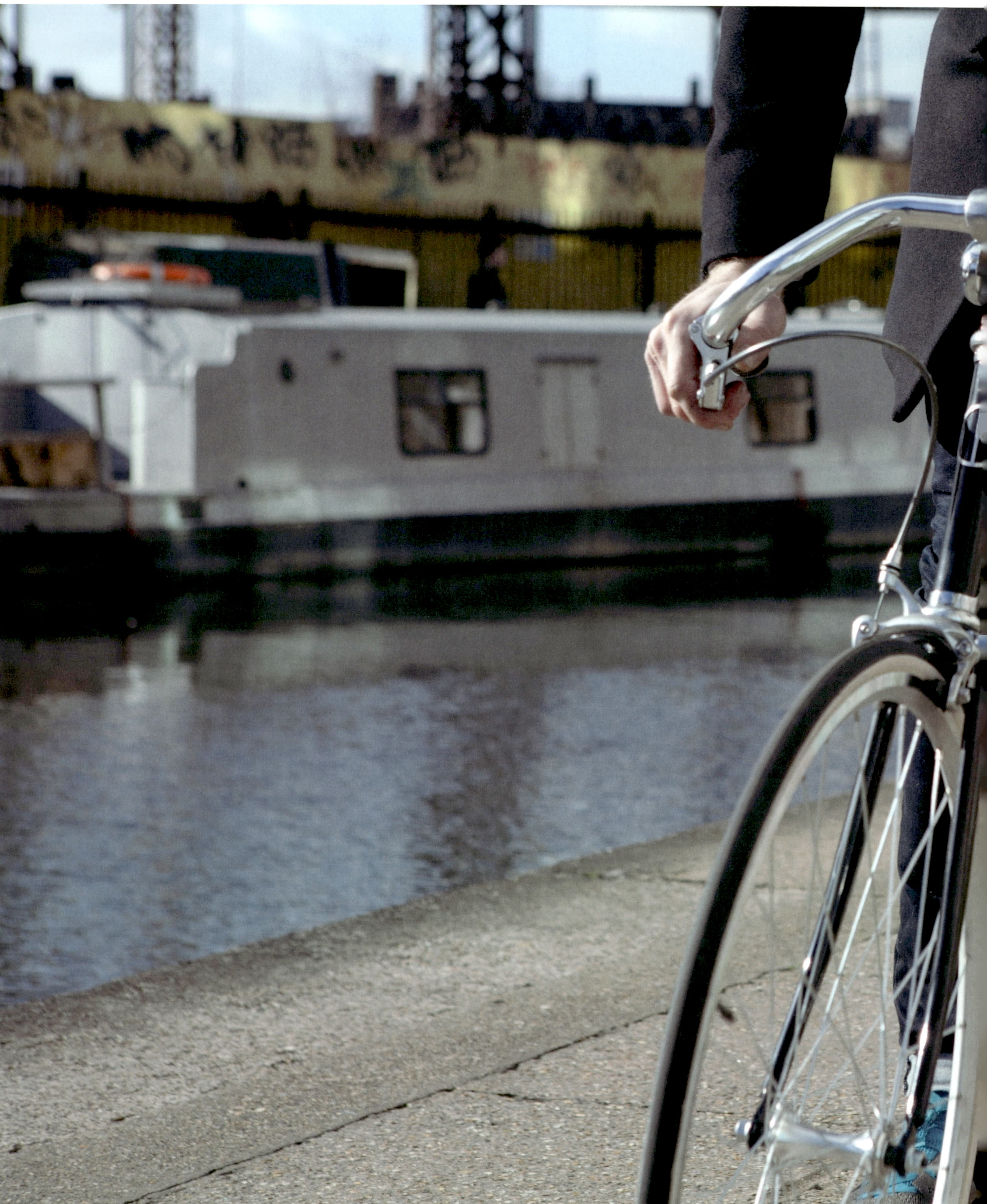

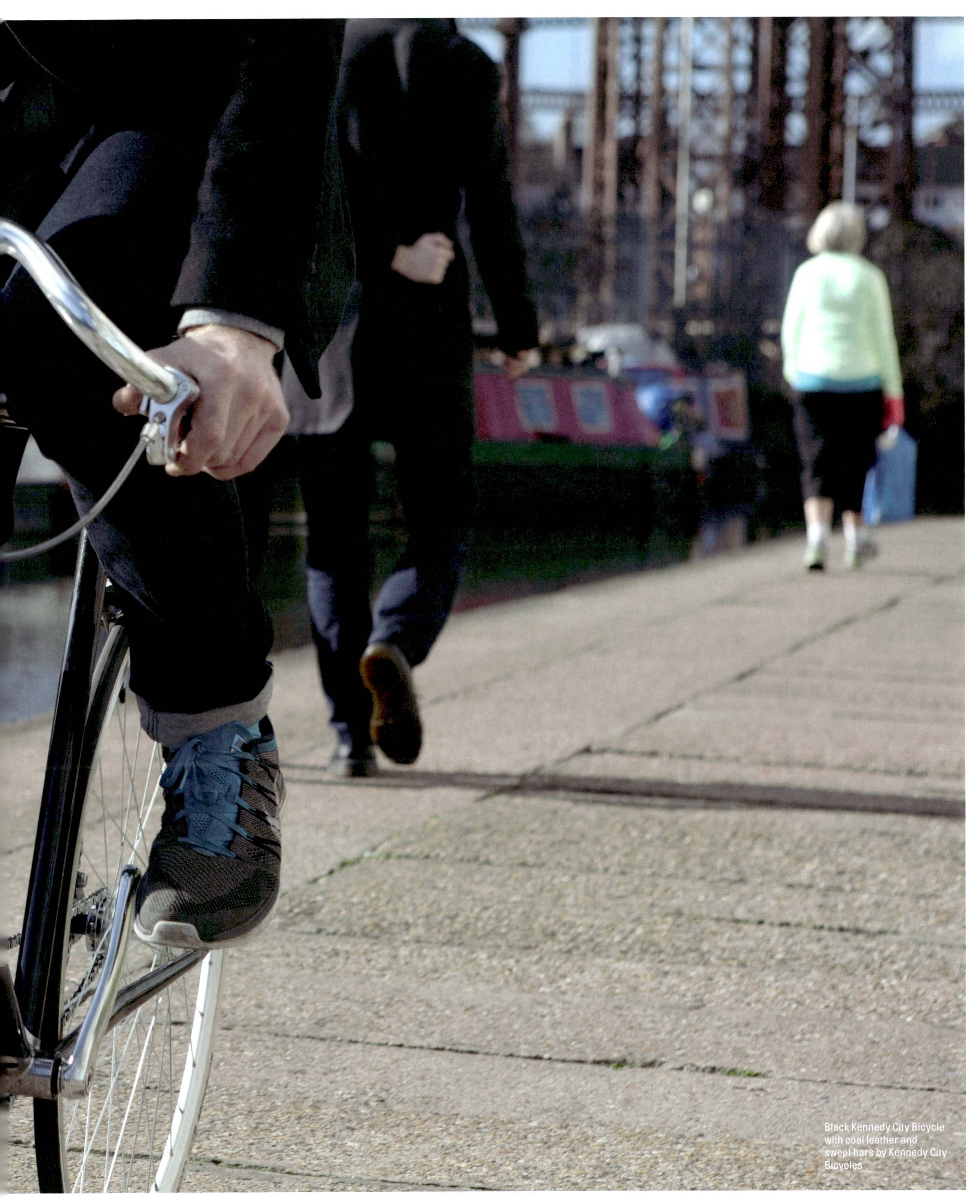

Black Kennedy City Bicycle with coal leather and swept bars by Kennedy City Bicycles

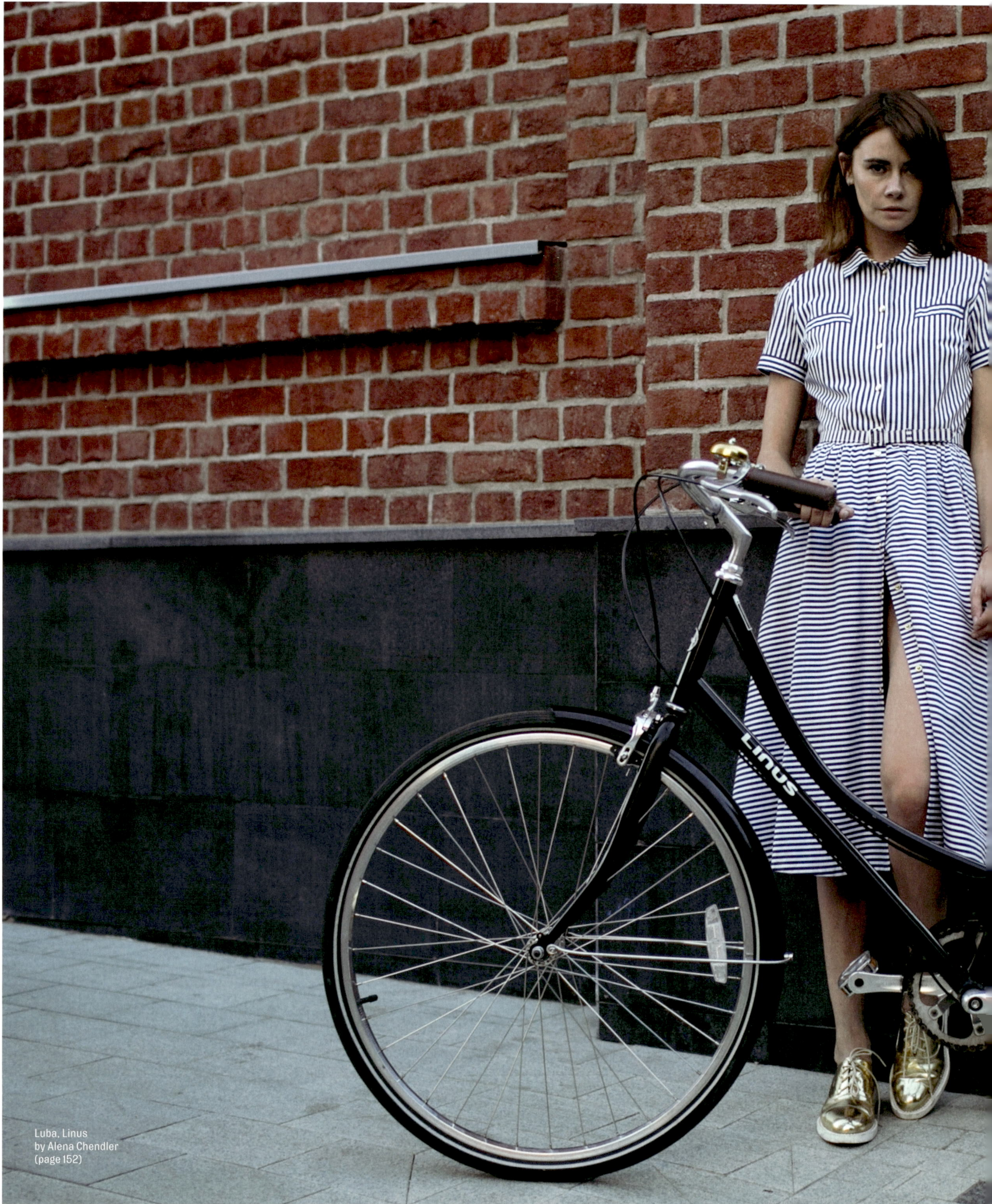


Luba, Linus
by Alena Chendler
(page 152)

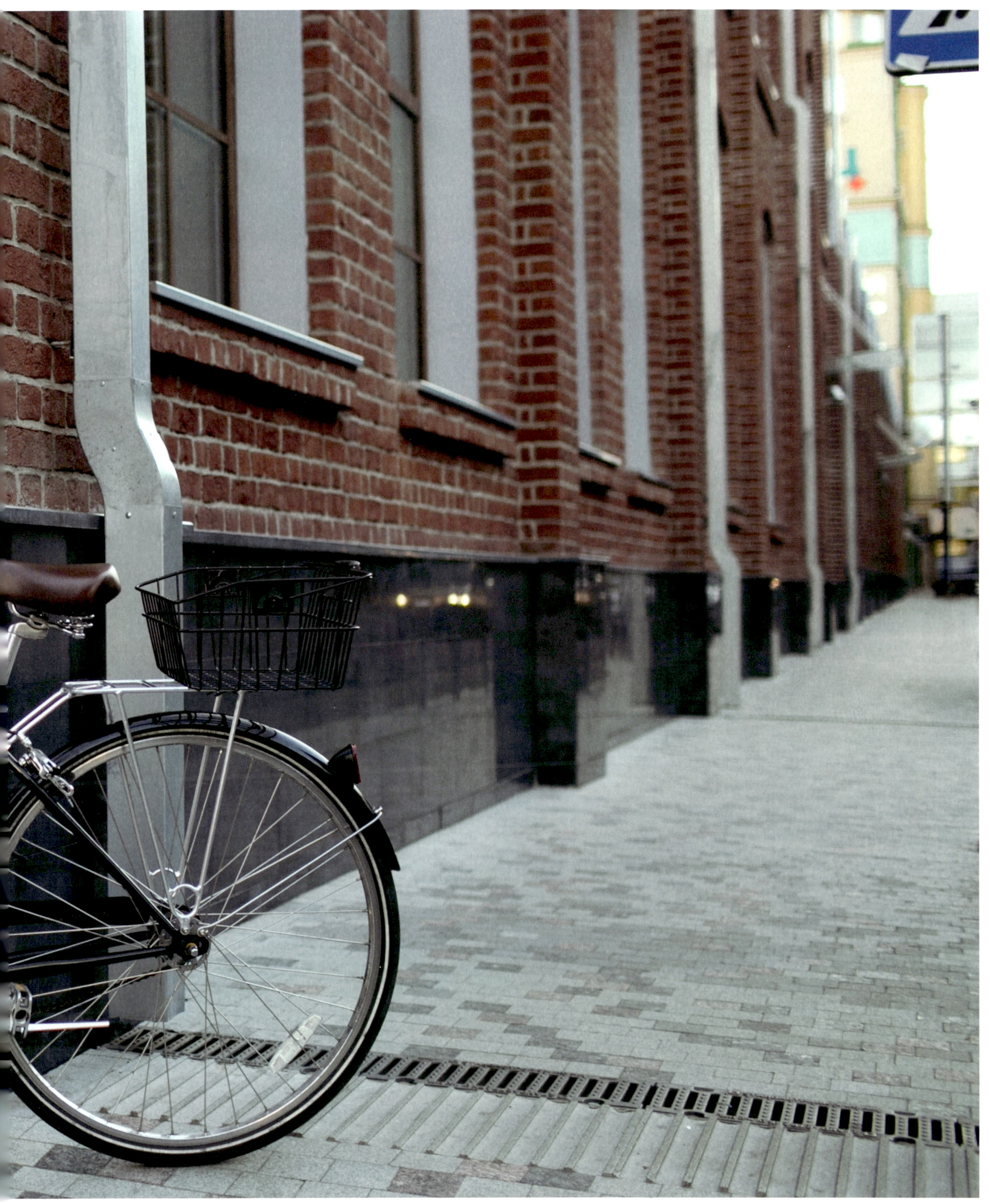

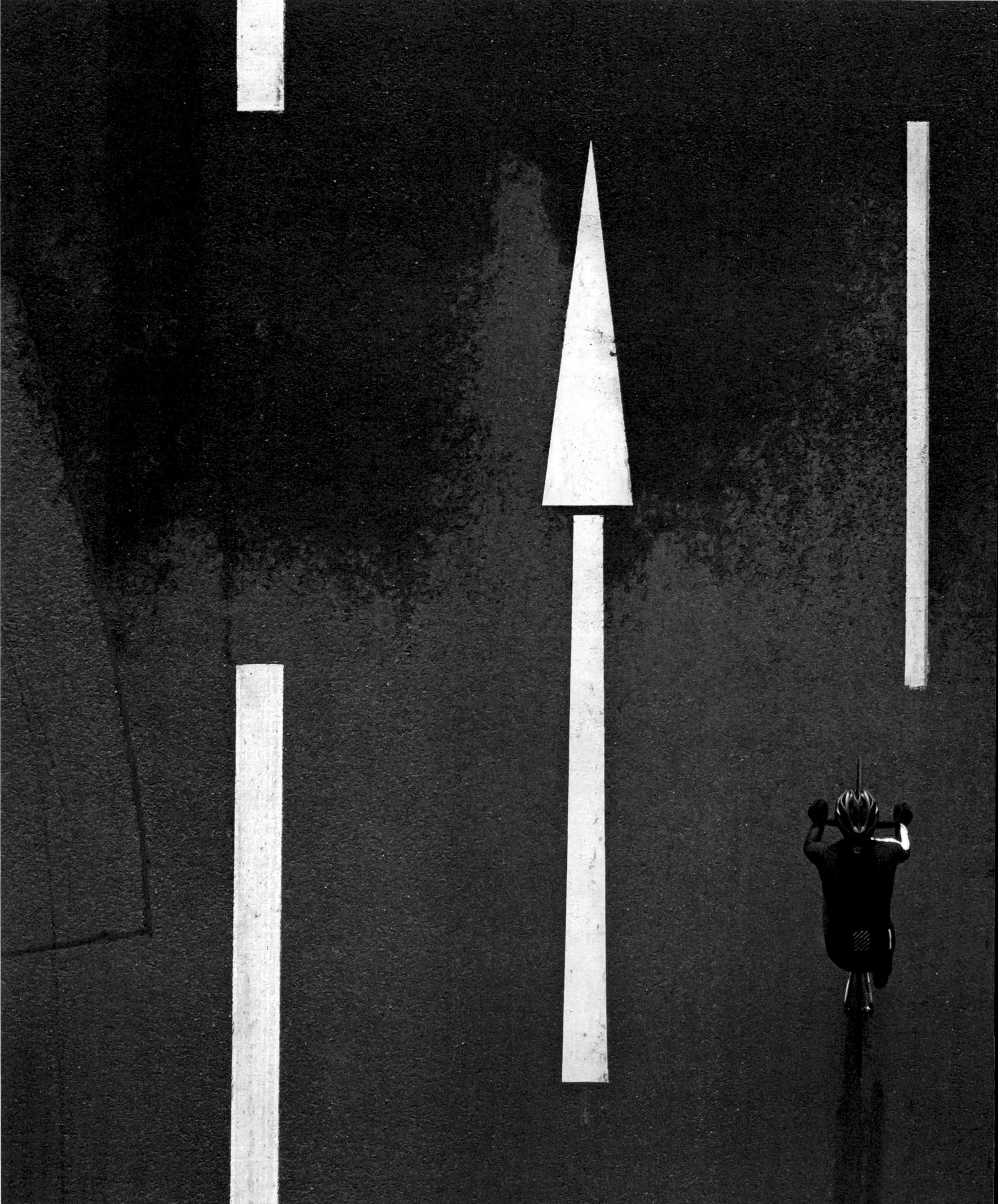

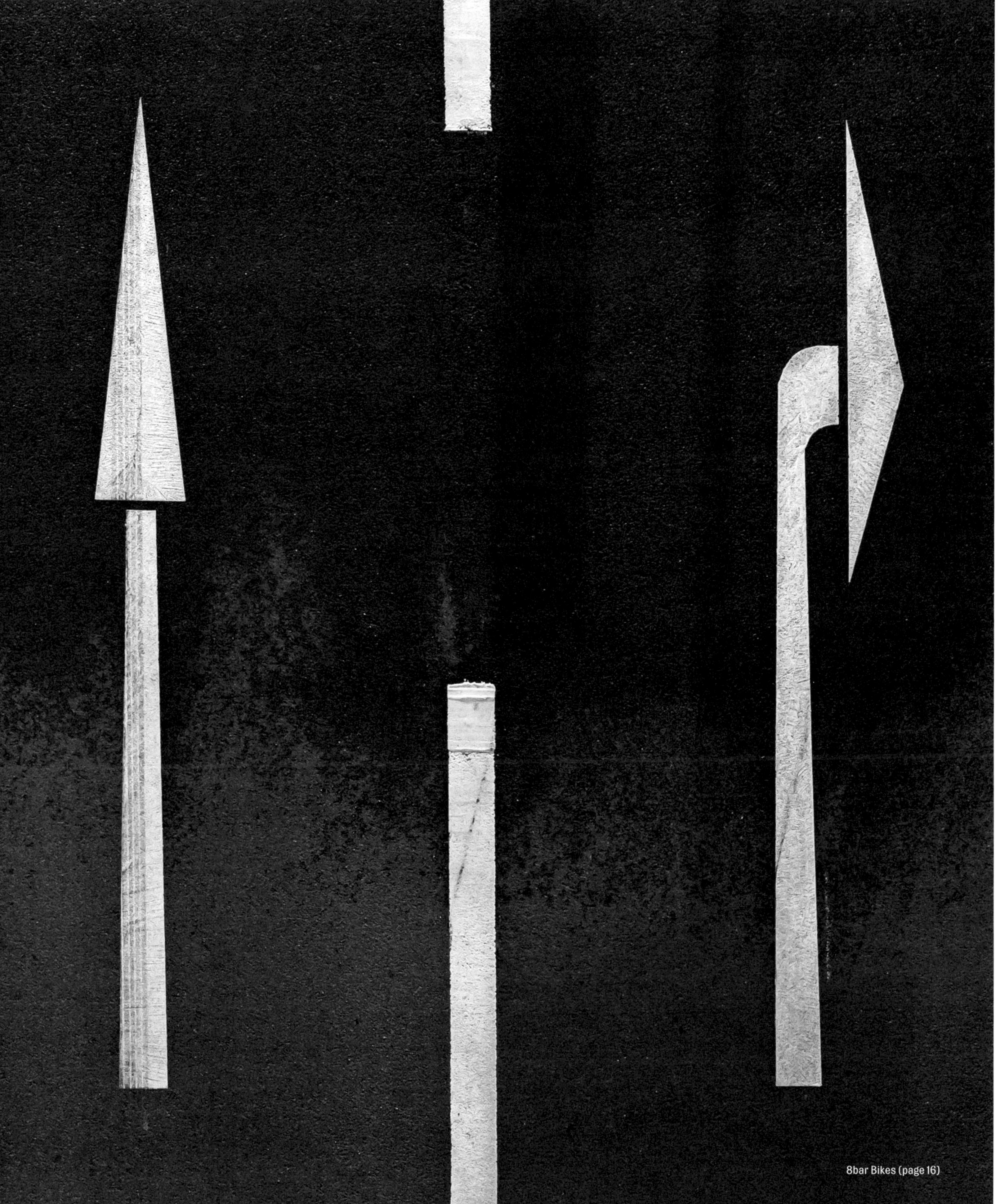

8bar Bikes (page 16)

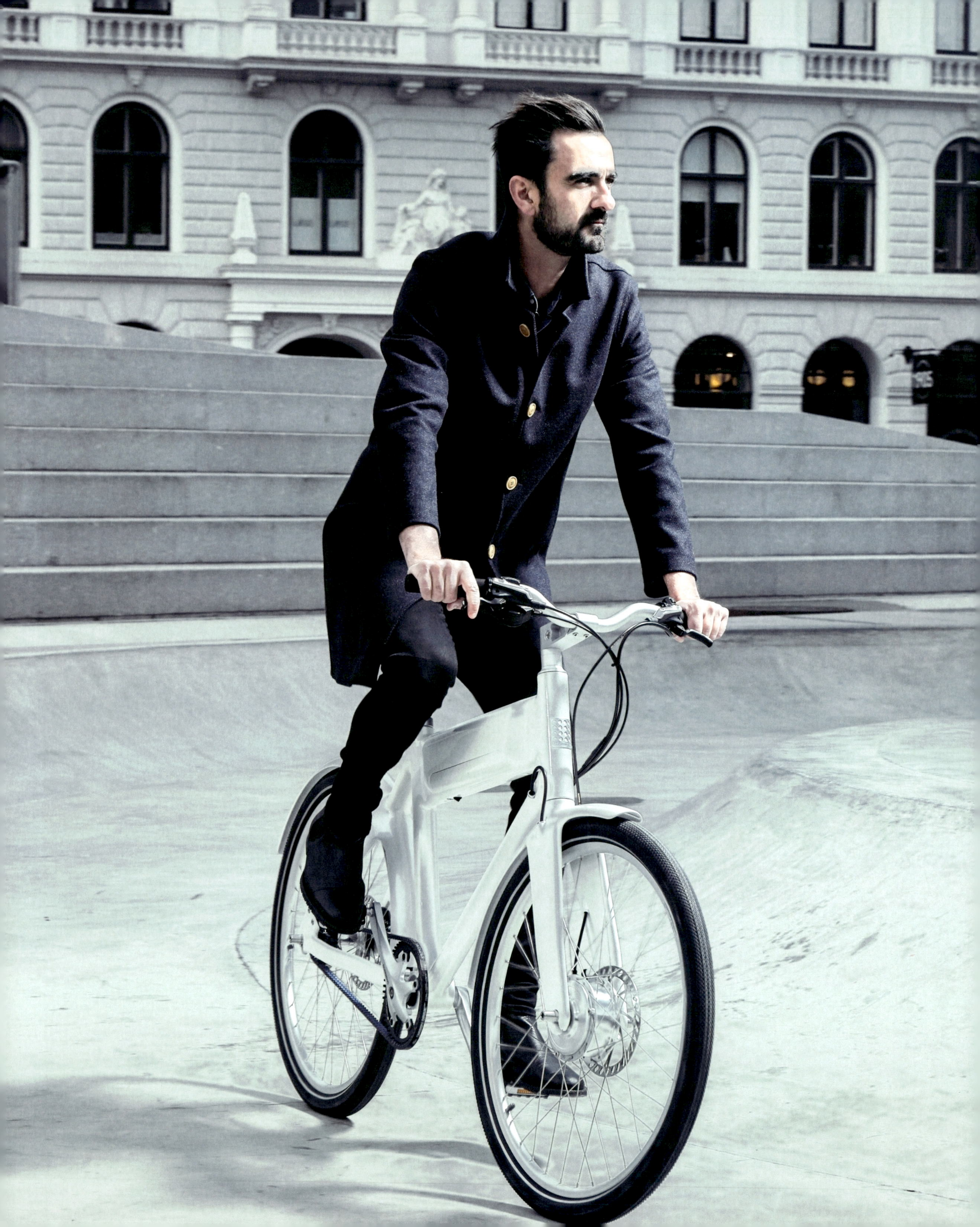

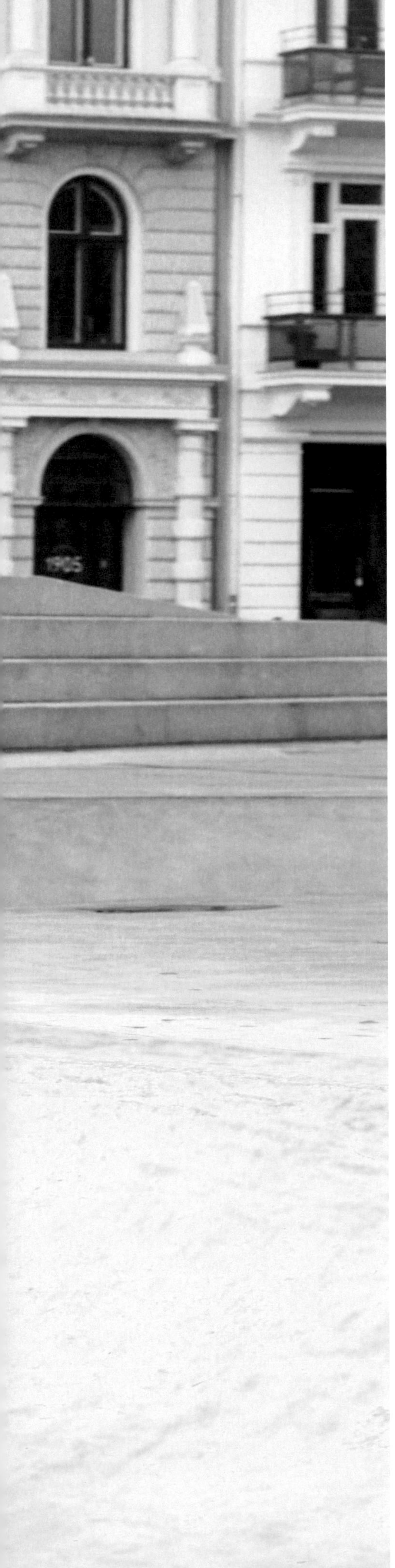

# OKO

## BIOMEGA

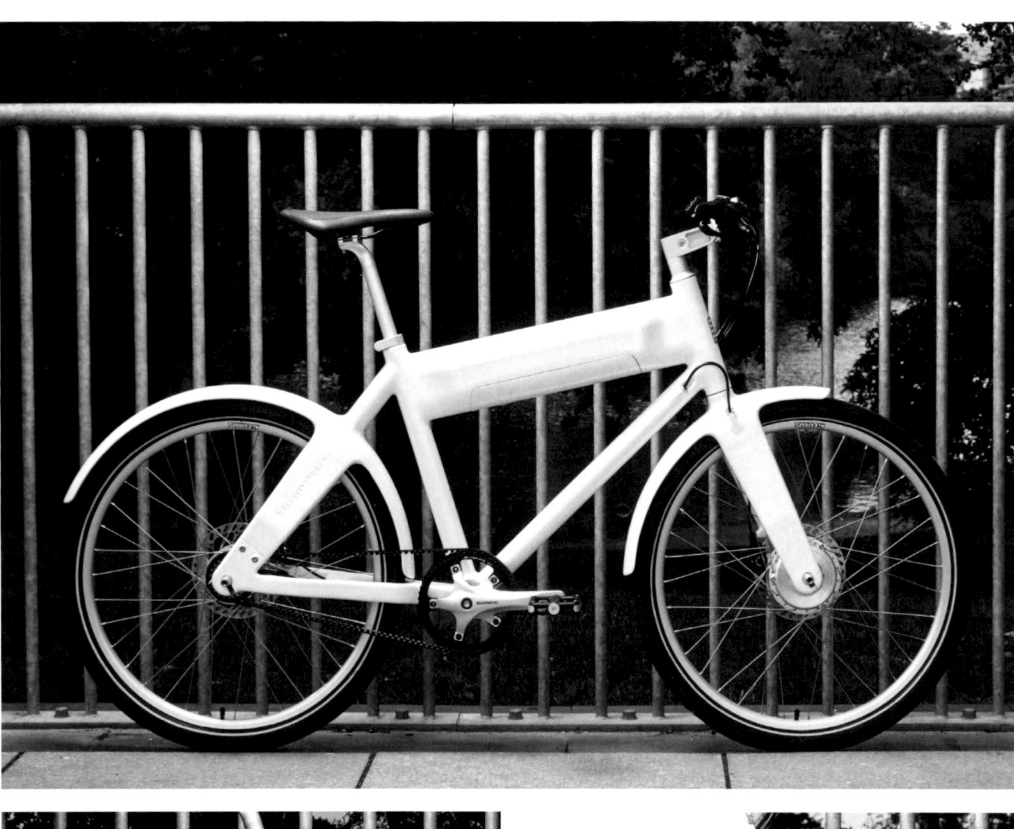

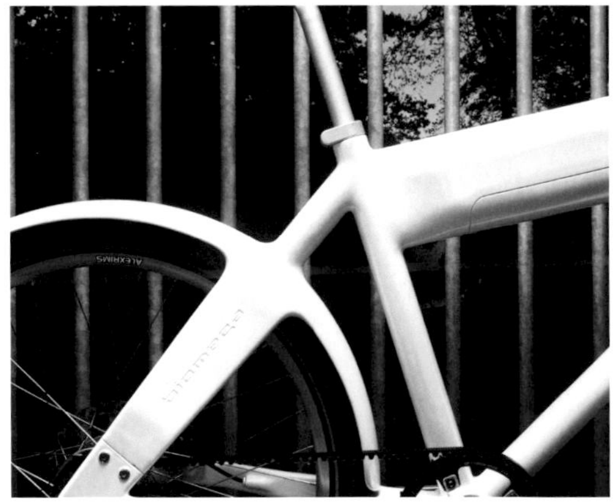

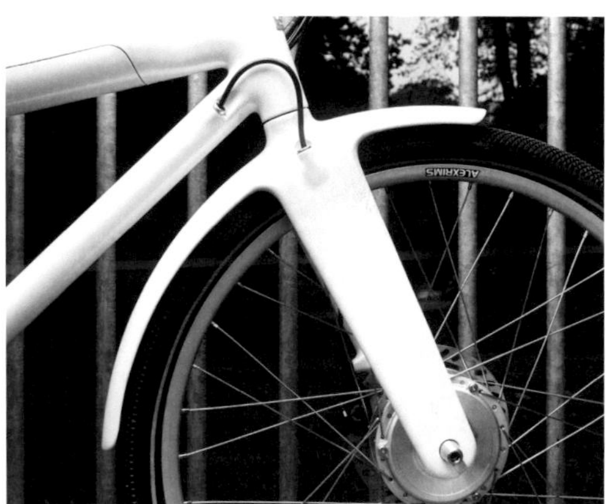

Bringing an efficient, state-of-the-art e-bike to the market is an international undertaking. To do so, collaborators Biomega and KiBiSi tapped talent from Denmark, France, South Korea, and China, ensuring that the OKO e-bike fits the needs of urban commuters, wherever their streets may be. Created for easy and stylish urban transportation, the OKO is an evolution in commuter bike design. At 20 kilograms including fenders, it is one of the lightest commuter e-bikes available and boasts perfect balance thanks to a center of gravity that is in the middle instead of the rear. This super strong, chainless carbon bike comes fitted with integrated front and rear mudguards and is equipped with an ingenious carbon belt drive.

## *Blackline*

**MNML × METHOD**

The designers at Minimal teamed up with the makers at Method to conceive and prototype the BLACKLINE—what they call "the ultimate urban utility bike"—for the Oregon Manifest Bike Design Challenge, an invite-only platform for innovation in bike design. The team's creation is universal in its appeal, yet imbued with Chicago's distinct character. In fact, they could not help but be influenced by the fact that they were designing through one of the harshest winters in a city of harsh winters. In the end, the BLACKLINE was dedicated to "the tough, all-weather warriors that commute year-round" in the lakeside Windy City. It is kitted out with an oversize steel tube frame with bubble tires, Helios smart handlebars, an LED headlight and side blinkers, and a maintenance-free foul-weather-busting drive train. Durable but refined, tough and cool-headed, tech-heavy but minimal, a little poetic and a lot street-savvy, the bicycle is a fitting tribute to Chicago's iconic elevated train lines.

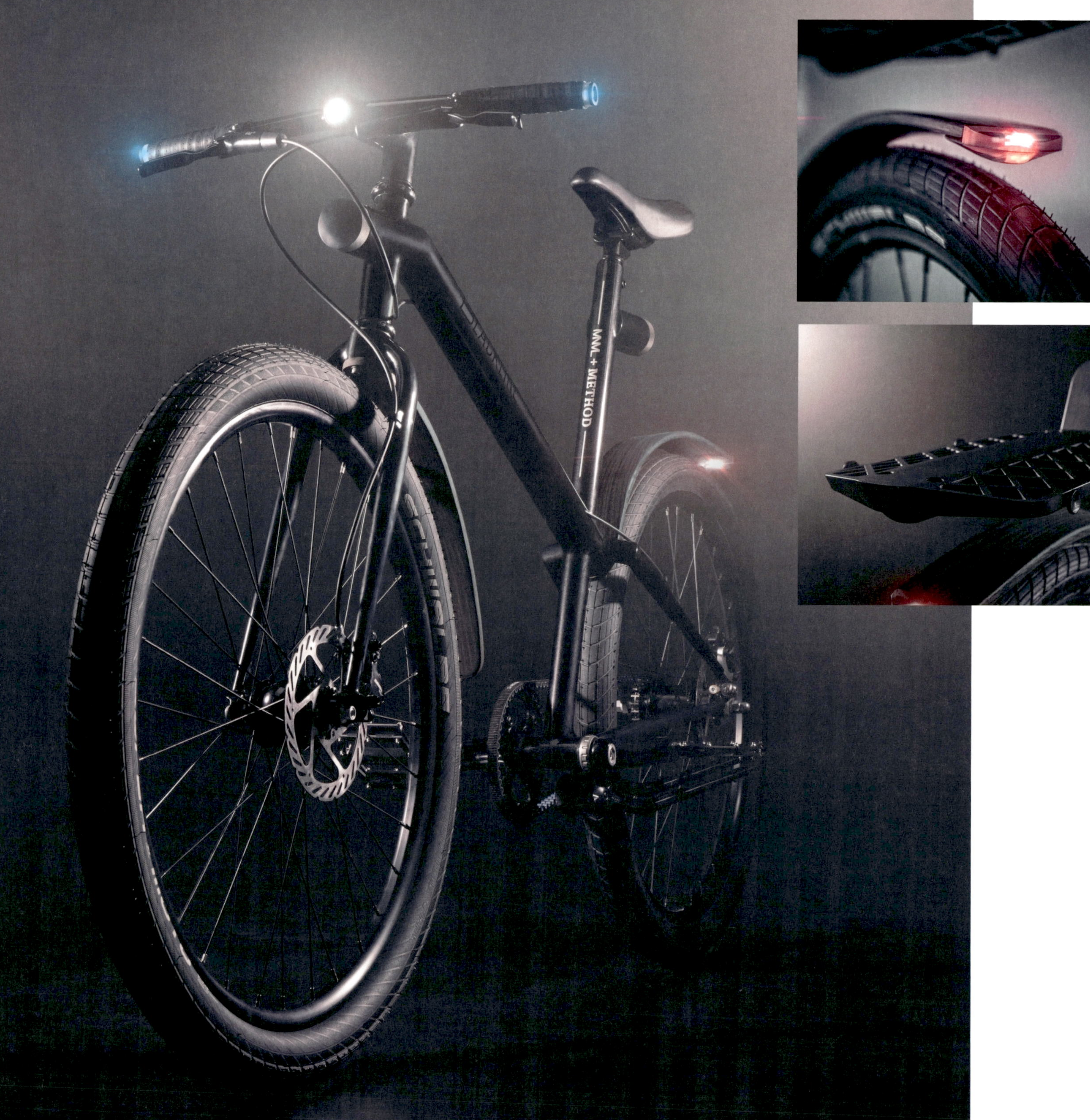

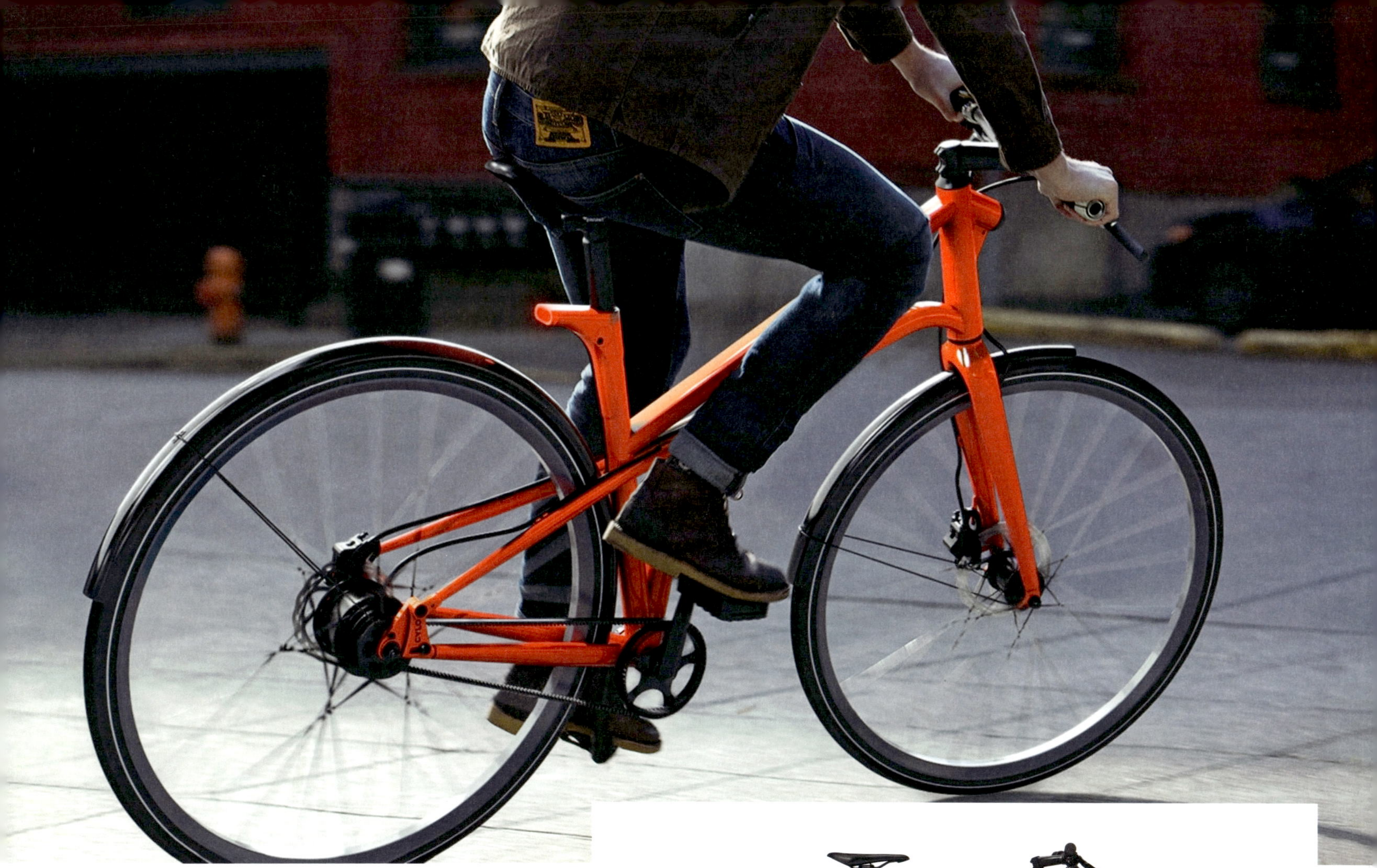

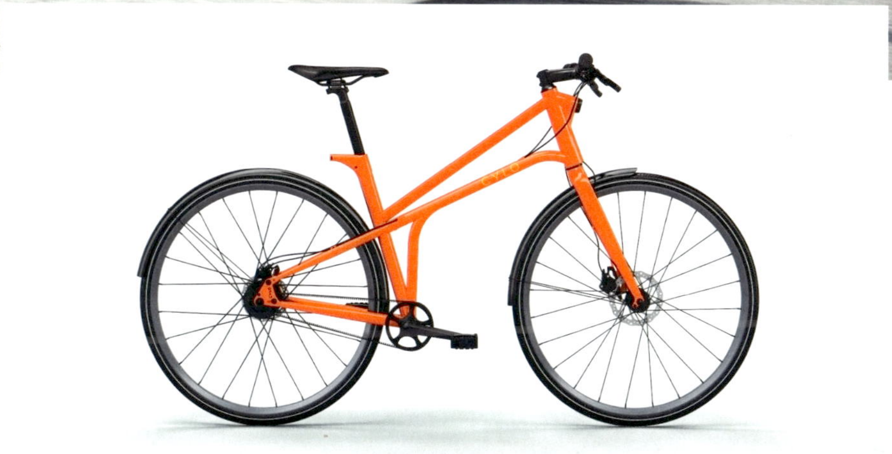

## *Cylo 1*

**CYLO**

Without built-in components, riders accrue add-on after add-on and end up with "a Mr. Potato Head bike," say the makers at Cylo, who looked to performance bicycles like the Flying Scotsman x-frame and Lotus track-racing bikes when they made this sleek city cycle. They built its "accessories" into the body, crafting integrated fenders and embedding dynamo-powered LEDs in the stem and post. Also kitted out with a Gates Carbon Drive belt, internal gears, disc brakes, and tough Shimano components, the CYLO 1 is produced locally in Portland, Oregon, which was crucial for the owners—a former Nike art director and a venture capitalist who has survived both the Ironman and winter commutes in Berlin. Owning a bike that you simply get on and ride is one of the best ways, they say, to "own your city."

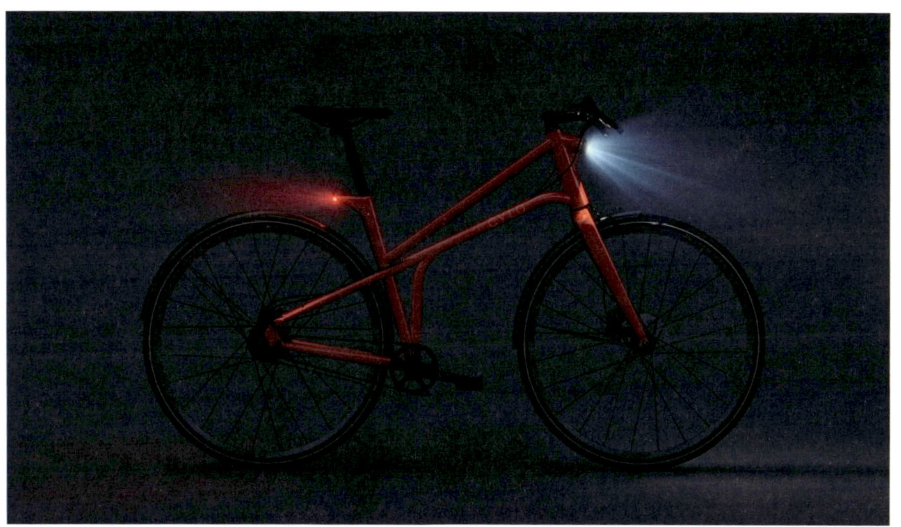

# *Footloose*

**MANDO**

Want to be footloose and fancy-free? Seoul-based international auto-parts brand Mando developed one of the world's first chainless bikes and then innovated the folding e-bike, a hybrid of automotive components and smart technologies that allows British designer Mark Sanders to hide the less-than-sleek bits inside a frame whose form is inspired by the wing bone of a seagull. The Footloose and Footloose IM are devoid of the chains that scream "bicycle" to many. Powered by Mando's Series Hybrid System and using software and a throttle or pedals, riding them is as effortless as driving a car, which opens cycling up to broader demographics. A display for the 36V lithium-ion battery shows the remaining charge and the riding speed (which maxes out at 25 kilometers per hour). Riders can shift manually, but they can also let the artificial intelligence kick in, automatically sensing road gradients and shifting gears with the same intensity as leg-powered pedaling.

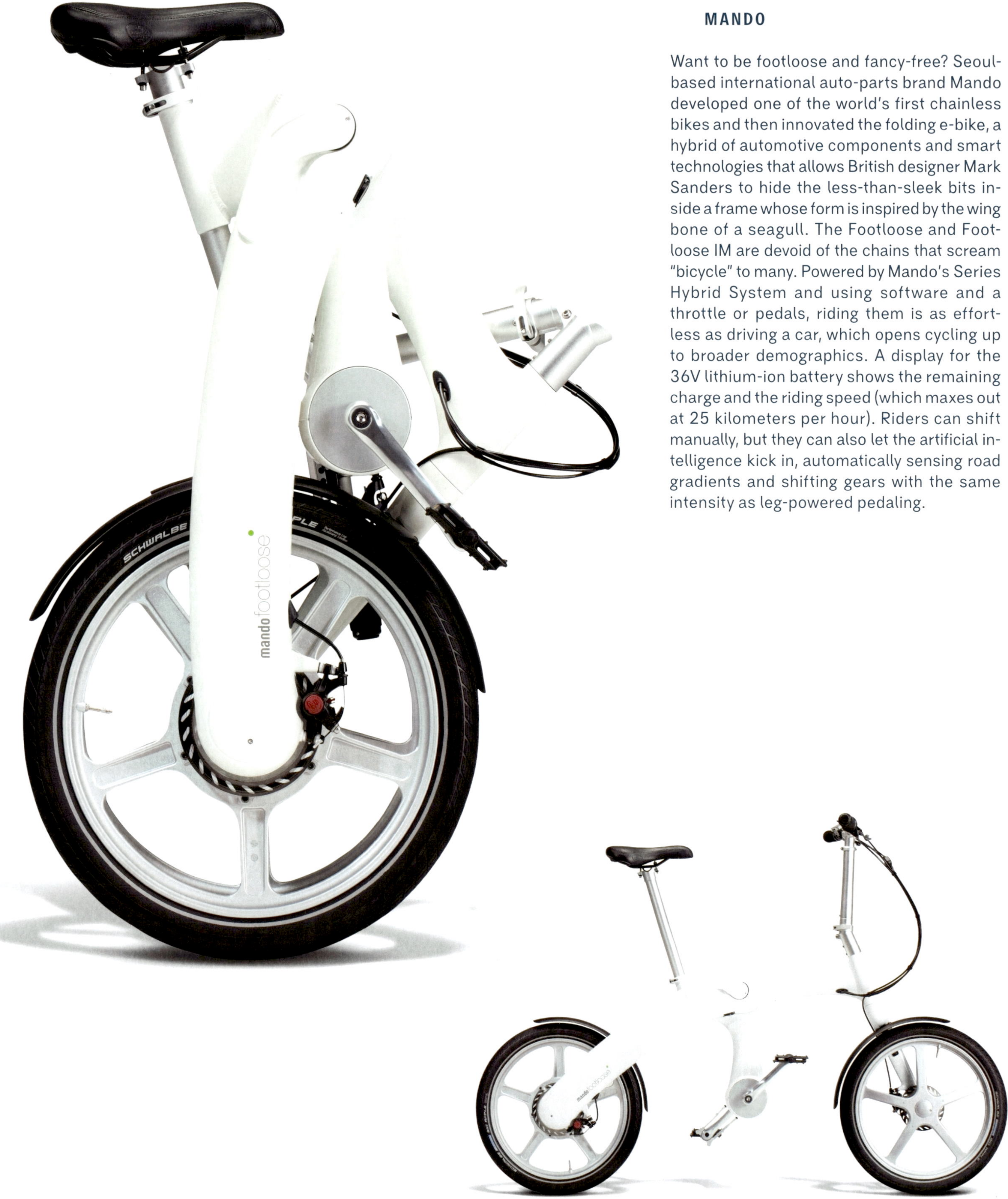

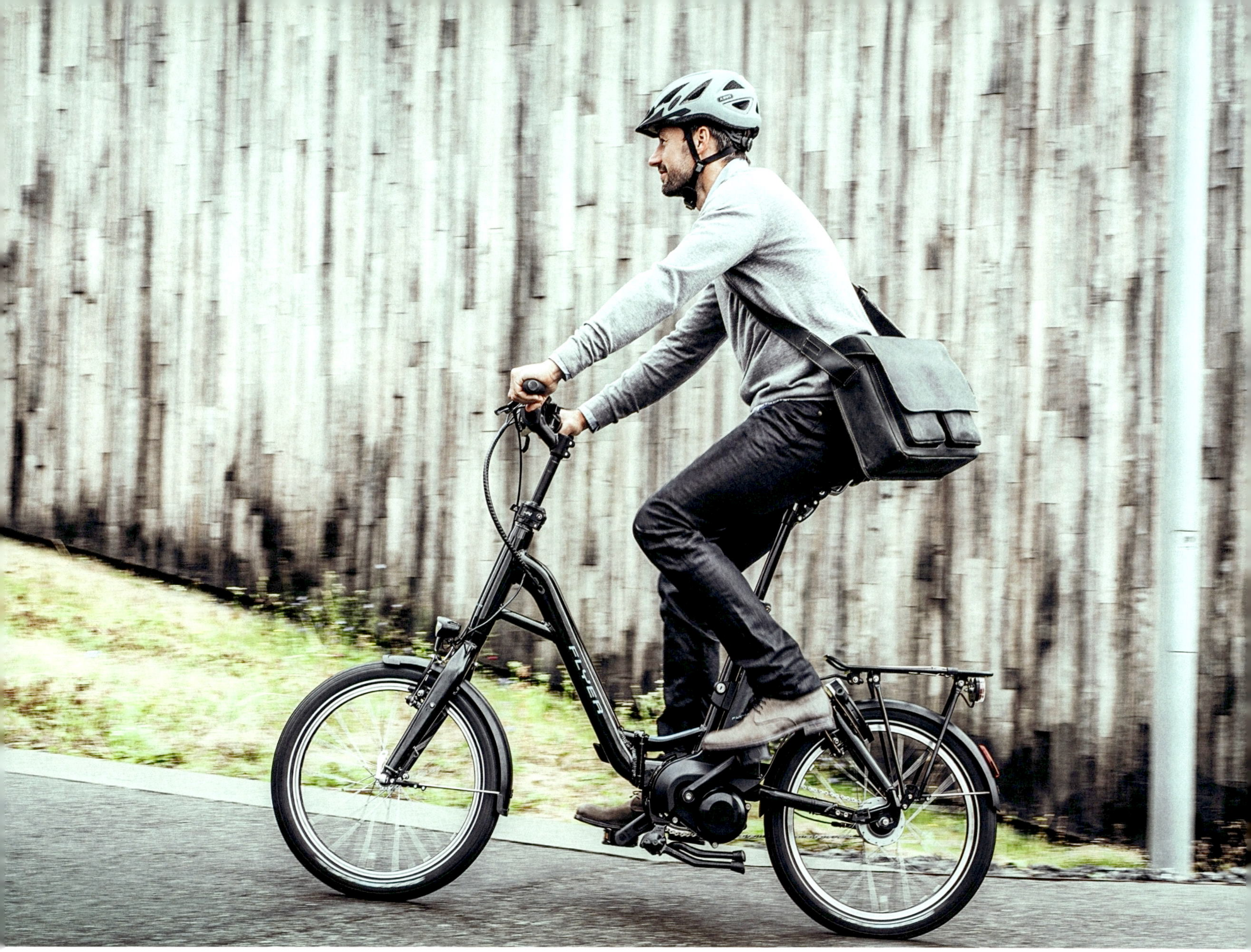

## *Pluto*

**FLYER**

FLYER saw an opportunity to combine the flexibility of a folding bike with the power of an e-bike. The result is the Pluto, an e-bike that is as easy to fold as it is to ride, making it the ideal mode of city transportation for commuters who also travel by car, train, or even boat. Folding down to the size of a piece of luggage while still retaining a step-through design and room for an LCD screen, the versatile bike is also easy and comfortable to ride in diverse urban situations. Equipped with high-quality components from Panasonic, Shimano, and Schwalbe, it is fast, safe, and fun.

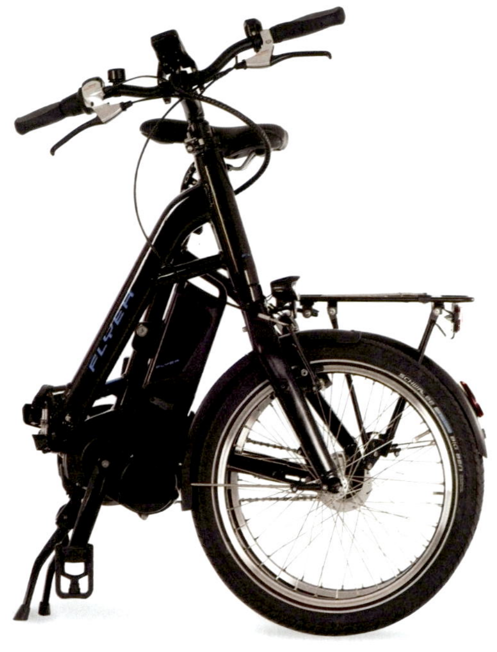

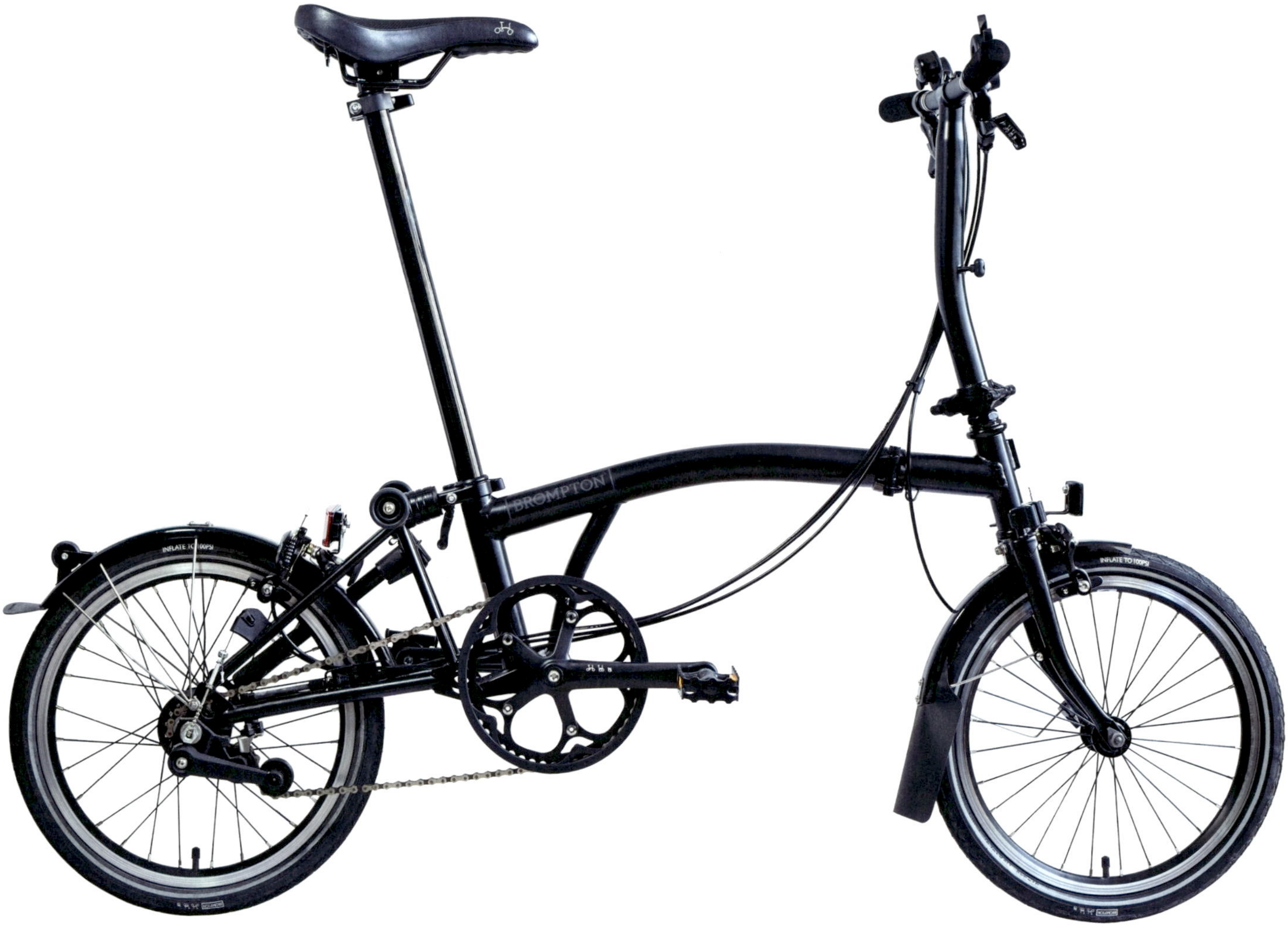

## Black Edition

**BROMPTON BICYCLE**

t takes only 20 seconds to fold and unfold a Brompton bike, which is exactly the kind of perfection that comes from refining a design over the course of 25 years. This ease of use makes Brompton bikes easy to take anywhere, whether on public transport or into the office, bar, or cafe. Its compact shape and small wheels improve performance by allowing great acceleration and maneuverability—traits ideal for city riding. Rough surfaces and longer distances are no problem thanks to the suspension system and long seatpost, which combine to ensure a comfortable ride. The all-new Black Edition s completely matte black, but made-to-order colored models are available as well.

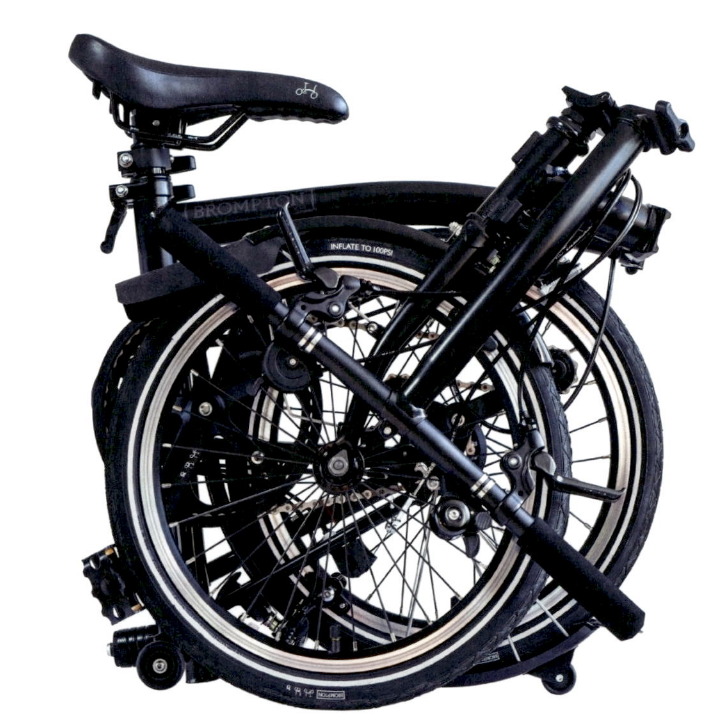

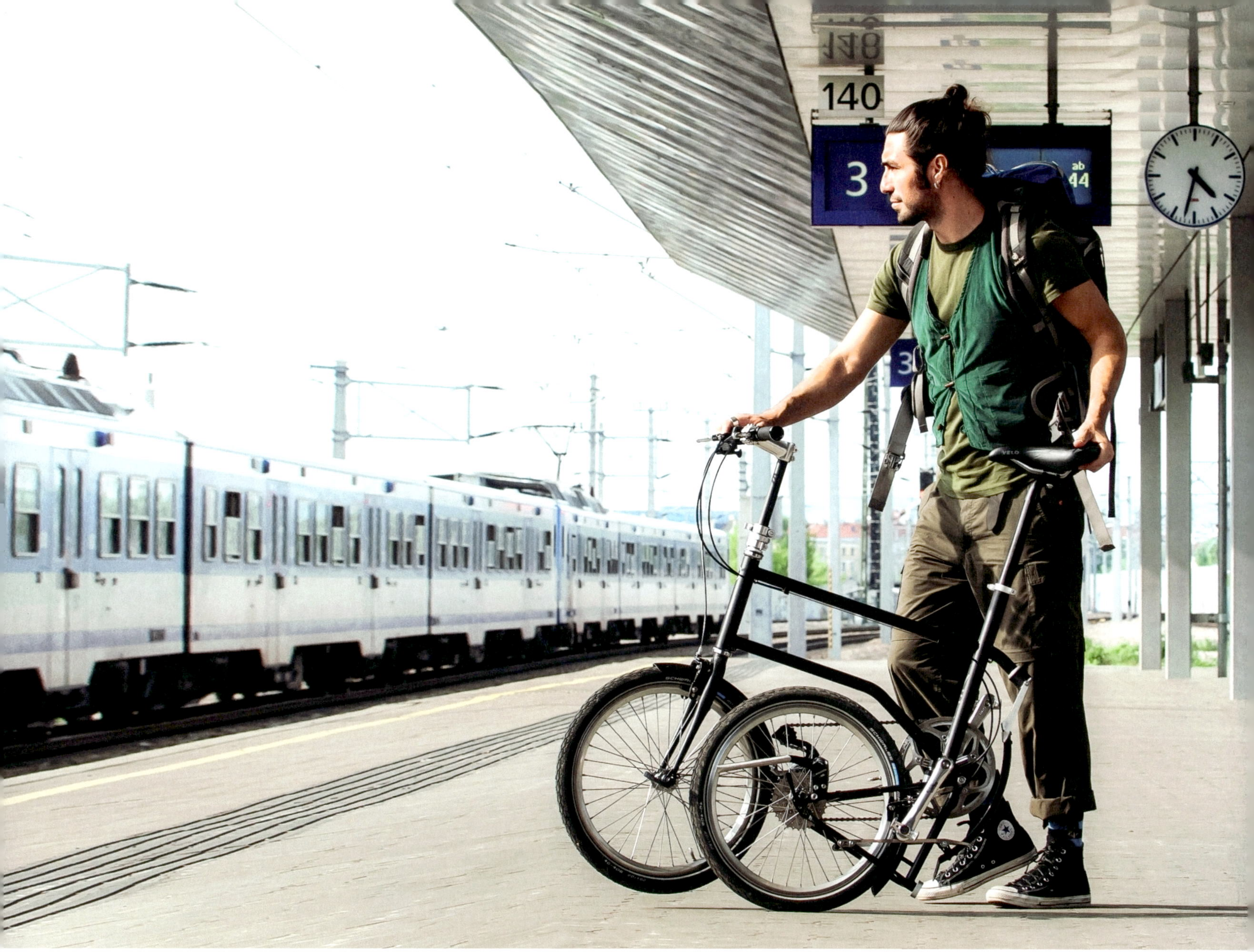

## *VELLO bike*

The handcrafted VELLO may be a compact folding bicycle, but it was designed with 20-inch wheels and easy maneuverability in mind, enabling it to dominate short or long distances and tackle stop-and-go street riding. Before you can say randonneuring, it can be folded to half its size using a unique mechanism and then wheeled along instead of lugged. This makes it ideal for making the transition from pedal power to public transportation or for slotting into crowded elevators. The VELLO has a chrome-molybdenum steel frame, a magnetic release, and a rear suspension system into which the folding mechanism is built. The suspension helps smooth out bumpy rides while the foldable fenders keep the rider spic-and-span.

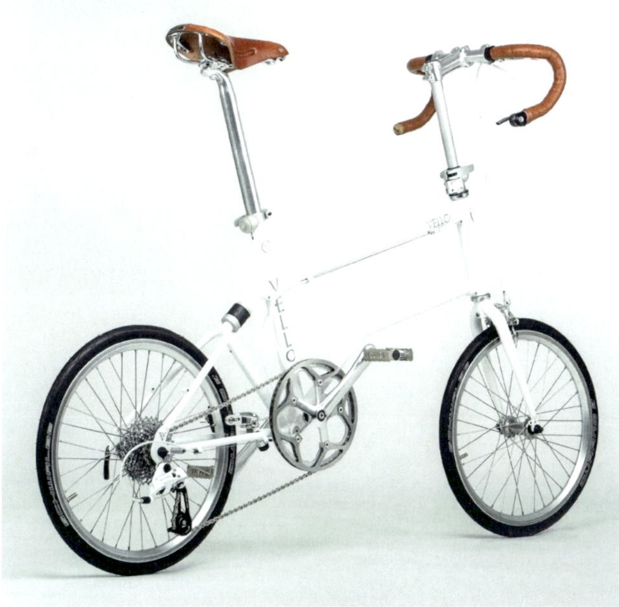

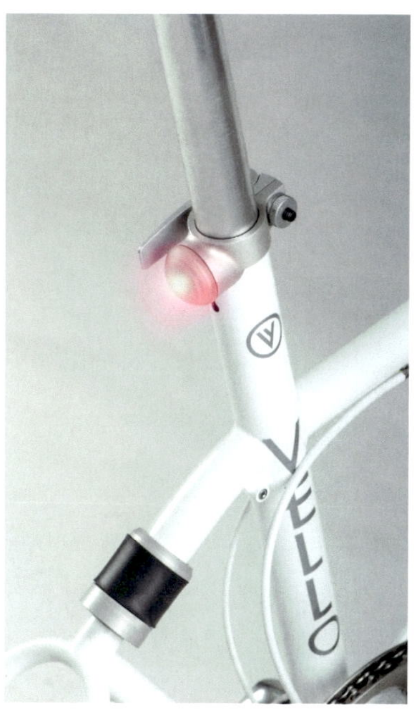

# *Holoscene LR with smrtGRiPS*

**BORÉAL BIKES**

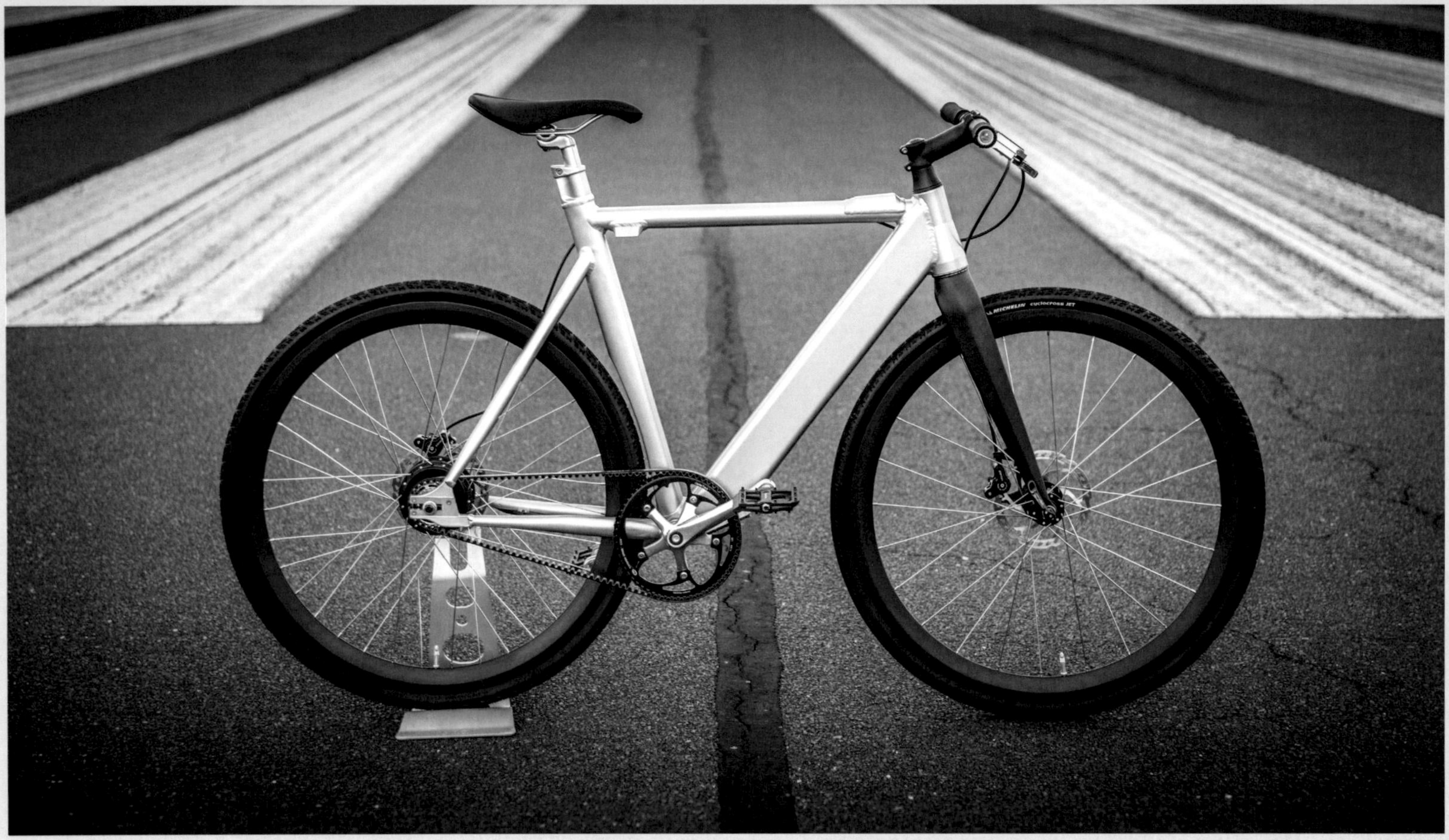

On first moving to Berlin, Montreal-born product designer Louis-P. Huard used his smartphone to navigate, but it proved difficult or distracting in bright light, rain, or busy situations. So Huard worked to create a transparent form of connected riding that would make riders safer and rides more fun. His solution, made from an impact-resistant polymer and aircraft-grade aluminum, is the Holoscene e-bike and smart handlebars called smrtGRiPS. They unite Bluetooth LE and GSM modules in order to adapt seamlessly to both on- and offline riding situations—for example, using sensory cues like haptic feedback via vibration of the handlebars to guide riders on their routes or to warn of approaching vehicles or traffic. The e-bike also tracks rider behavior to help cities get smarter about urban planning.

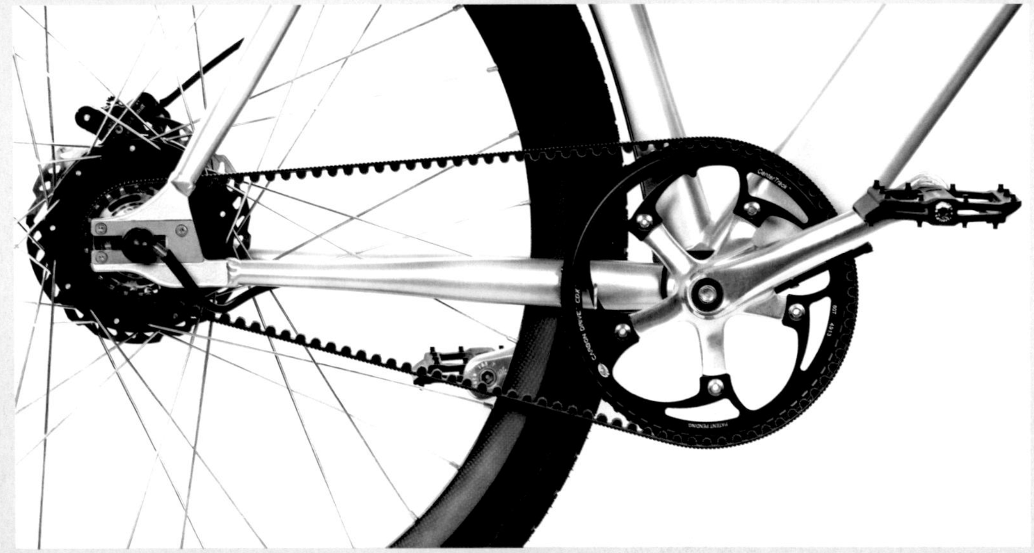

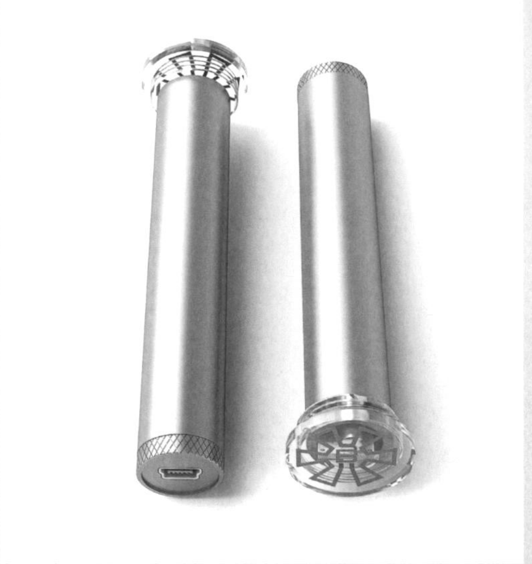

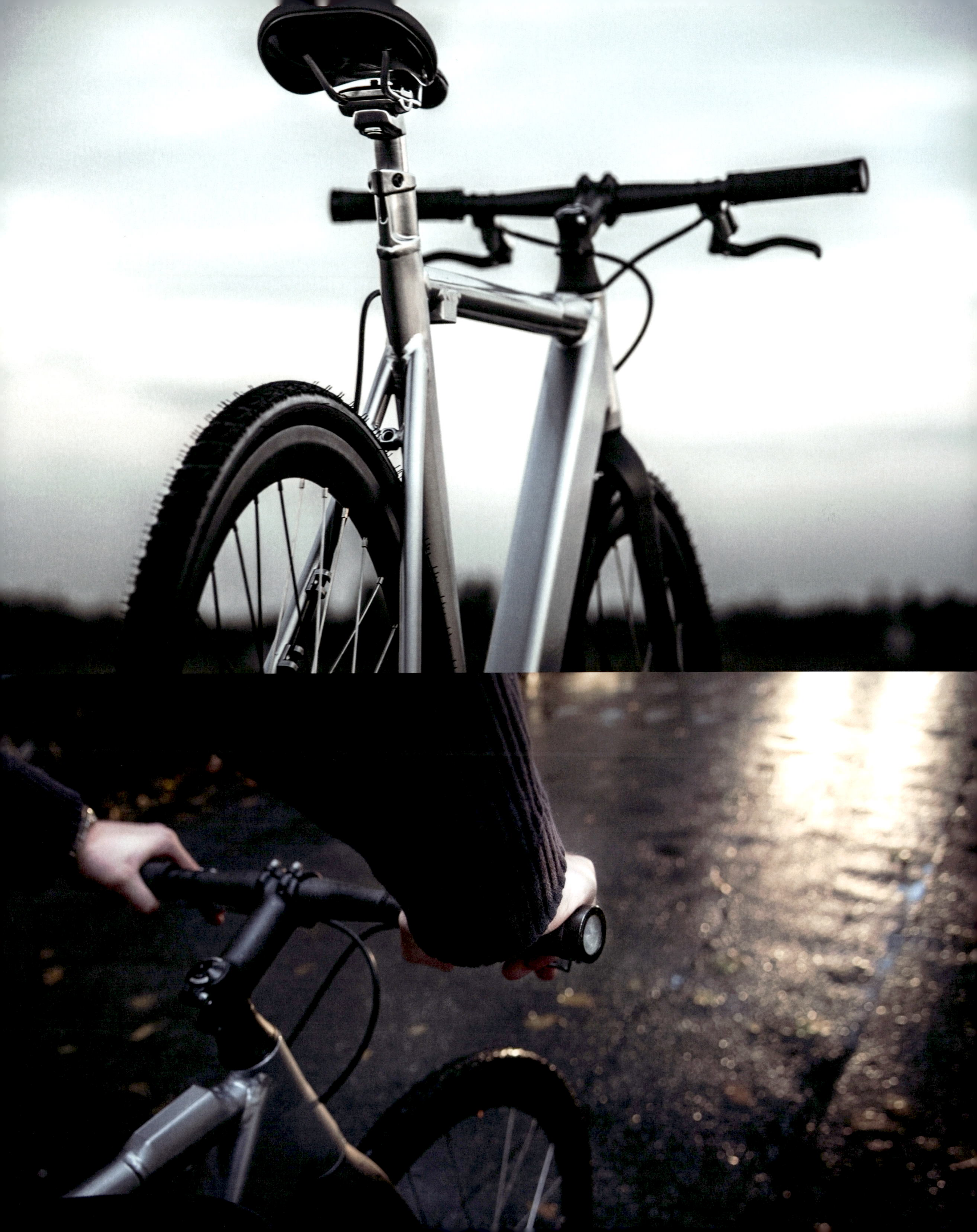

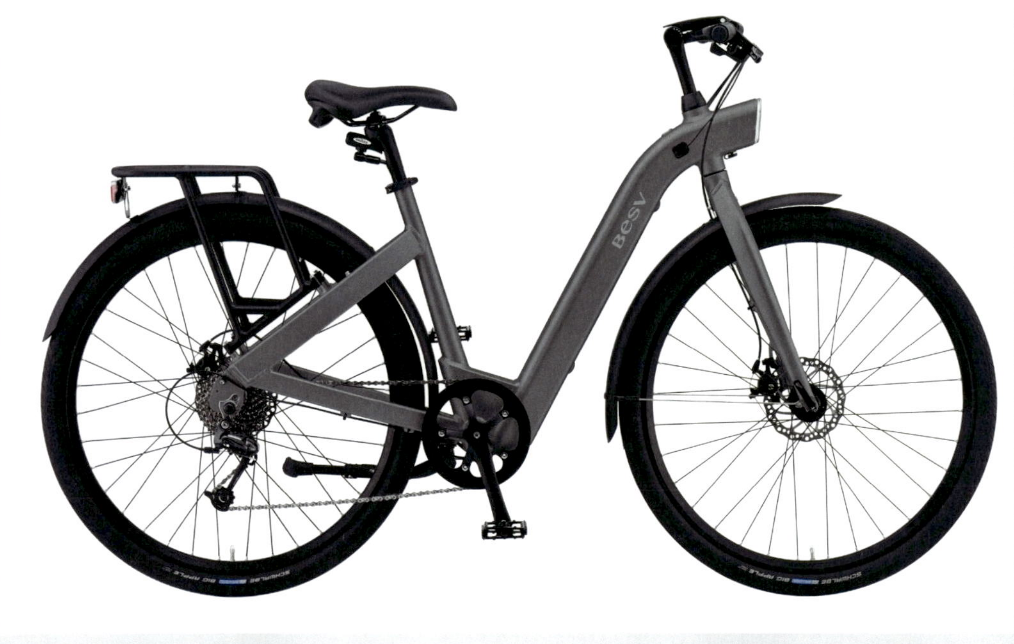


# CF1 + JS1 + LX1

## BESV

It could be said that BESV has achieved perfection with their three-model line of electric bicycles. Stylish and flexible, they also offer an assortment of clever features for different types of riders. A one-touch start button keeps things simple on the minimalist CF1 model. Its LED lighting elegantly communicates the state of the battery, and a switch on the handlebar controls power-assist levels. The JS1 pedal-assisted electric bicycle features a durable frame for long-lasting performance and is the ideal ride for trips both short and long. Equipped with BESV's advanced proprietary Algorithm power drive system, the LX1 is the company's premium model and boasts a stylish design available in white, orange, or gray, as well as a sturdy aluminum frame.

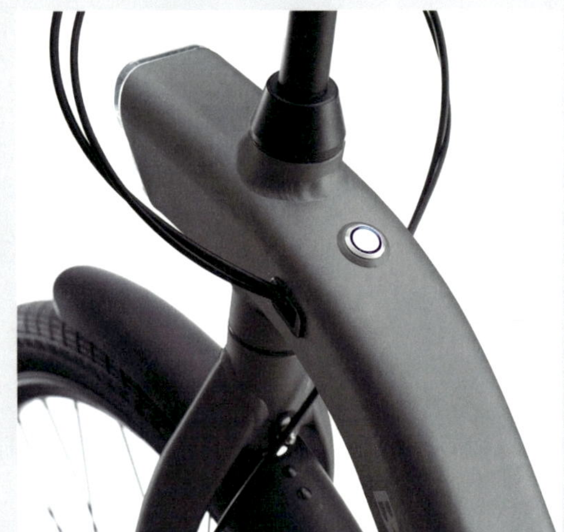

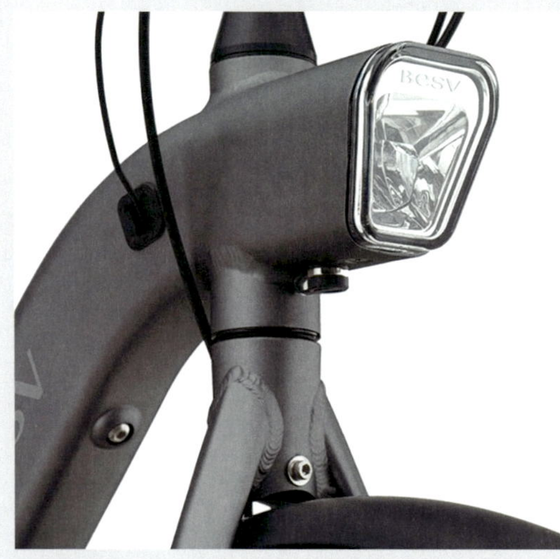


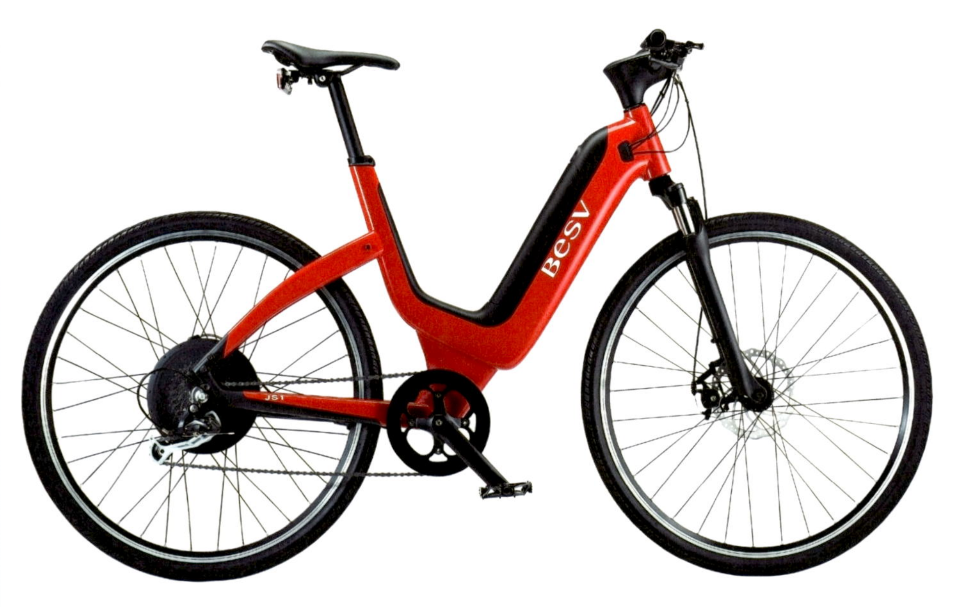


**top left:** CF1 electric bicycle with one-touch start button.

**bottom left:** JS1 pedal-assisted electric bicycle with integrated display.

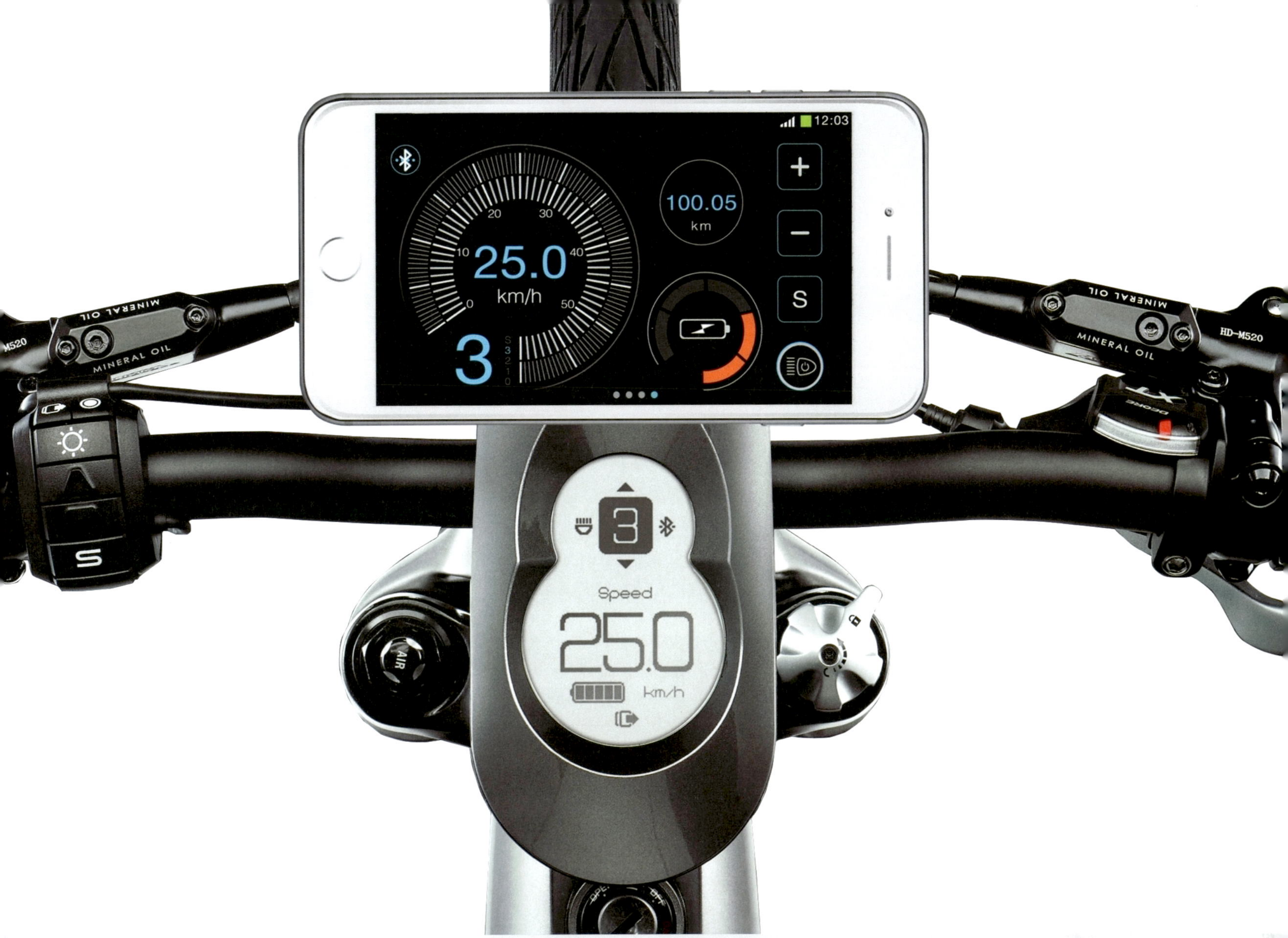

**right:** LX1 premium pedal-assisted electric bicycle. Contain your smartphone and use the BESV smart app.

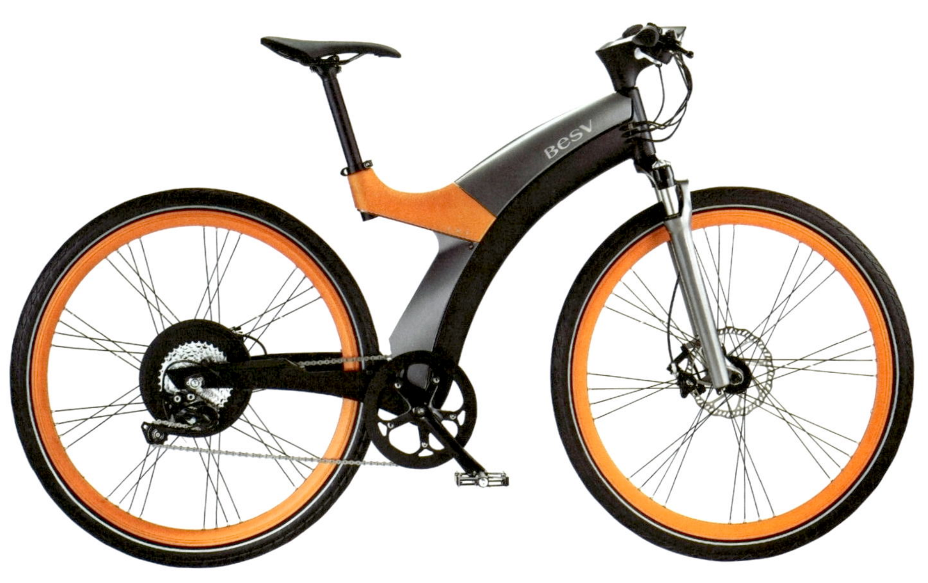

# Cycles Lady

## ALENA CHENDLER

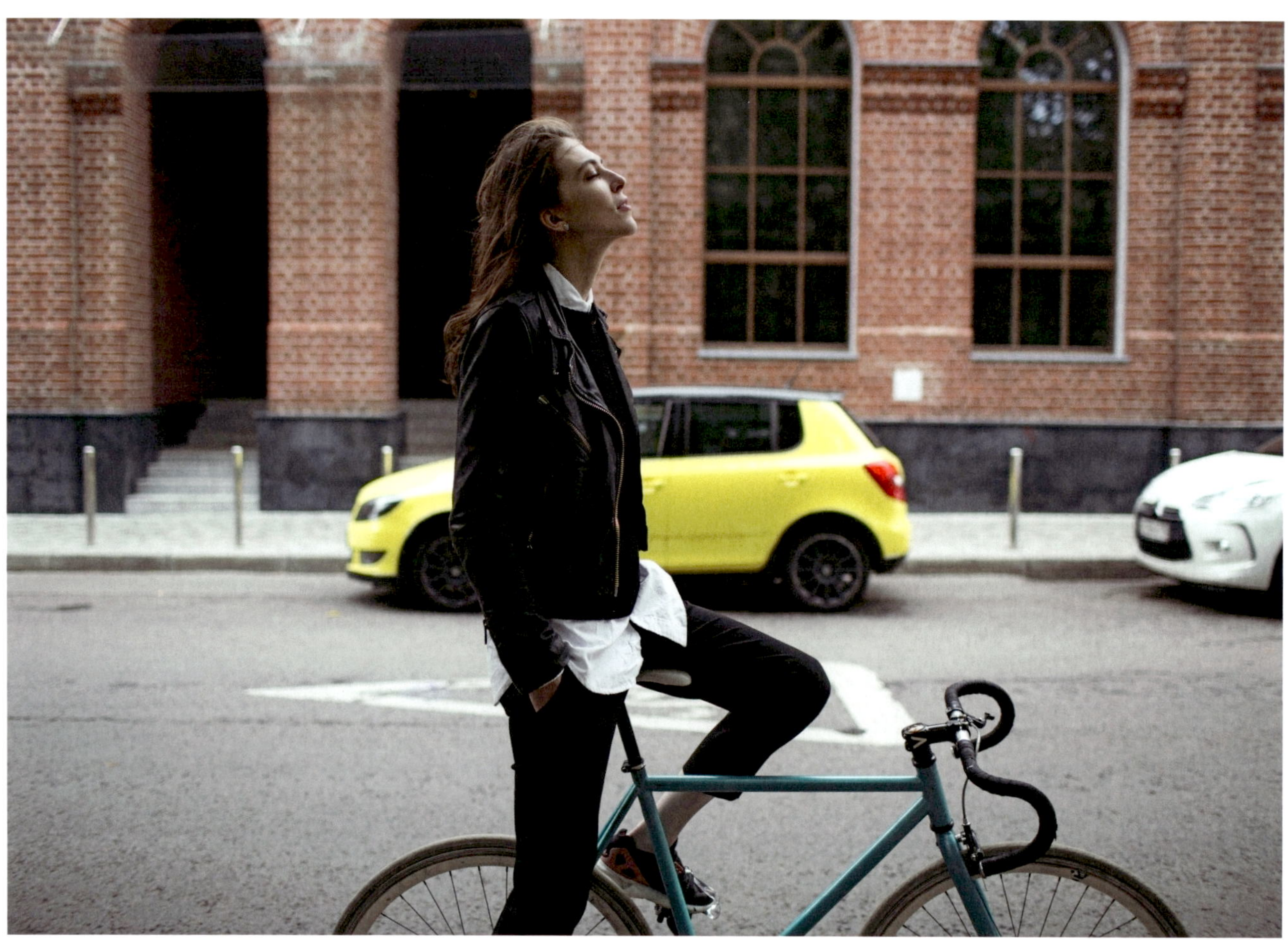

High heels, skirts, and dresses—this is the type of cycling gear worn by the women in fashion photographer Alena Chendler's photographs. As a believer in the bicycle as the perfect mode of transportation for the city, Alena Chandler launched her Cycles Lady blog in the summer of 2012 to showcase women on eye-catching vintage bikes. Based in Moscow, her work captures the beauty of the city's women and the personalities of the bikes on which they choose to cruise the town by highlighting the shape and materials of the baskets, cup holders, and leather seats.

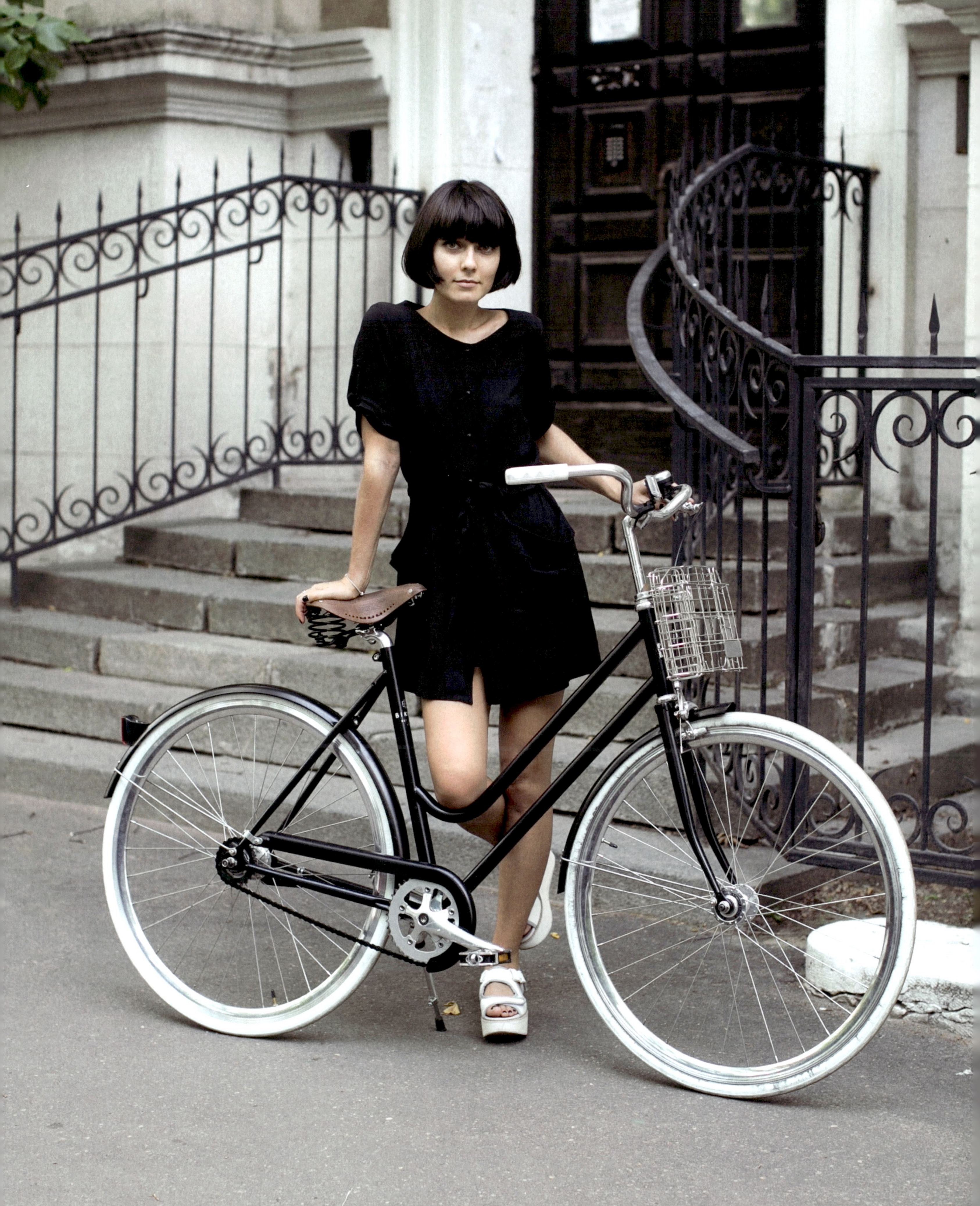

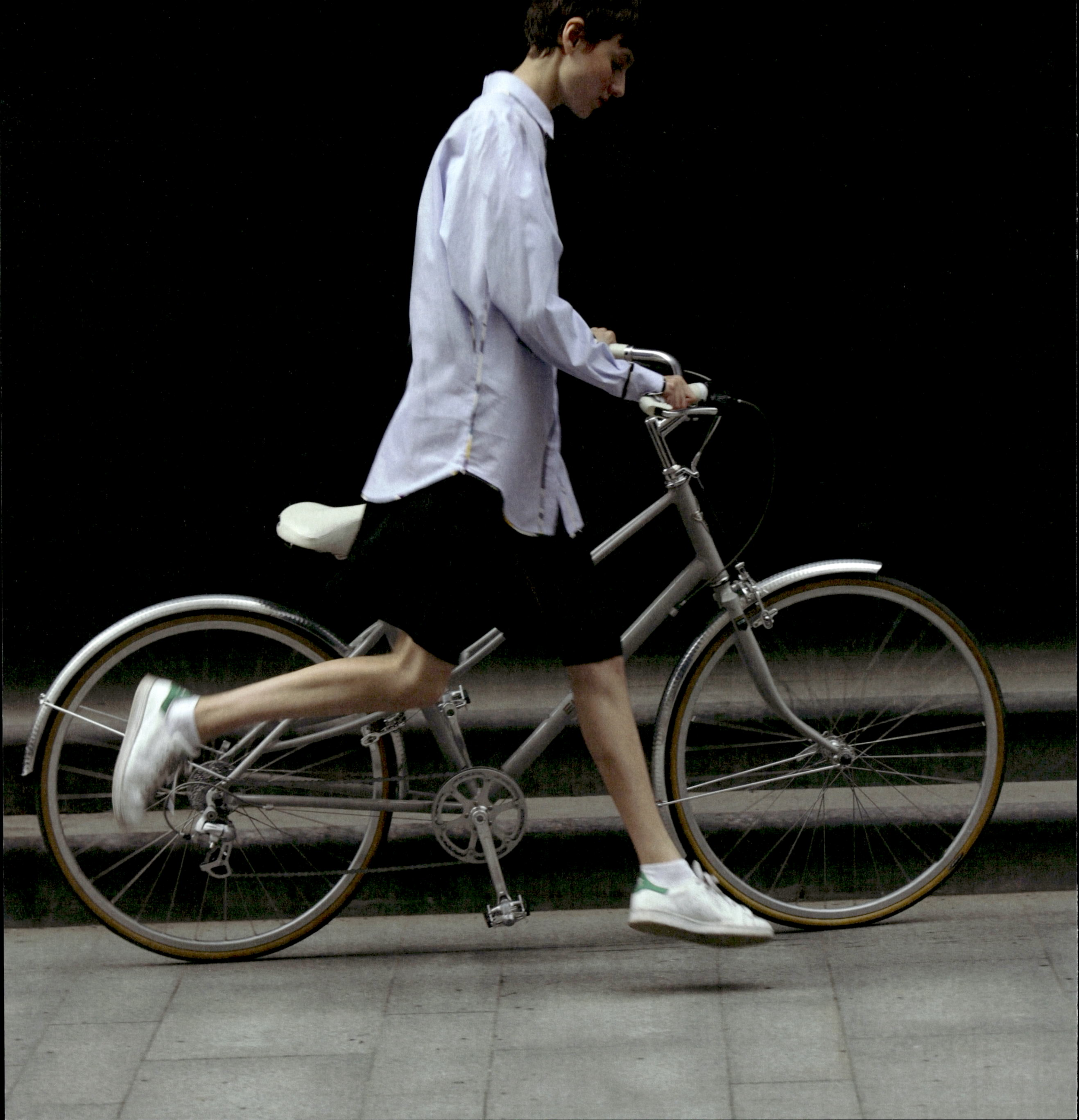

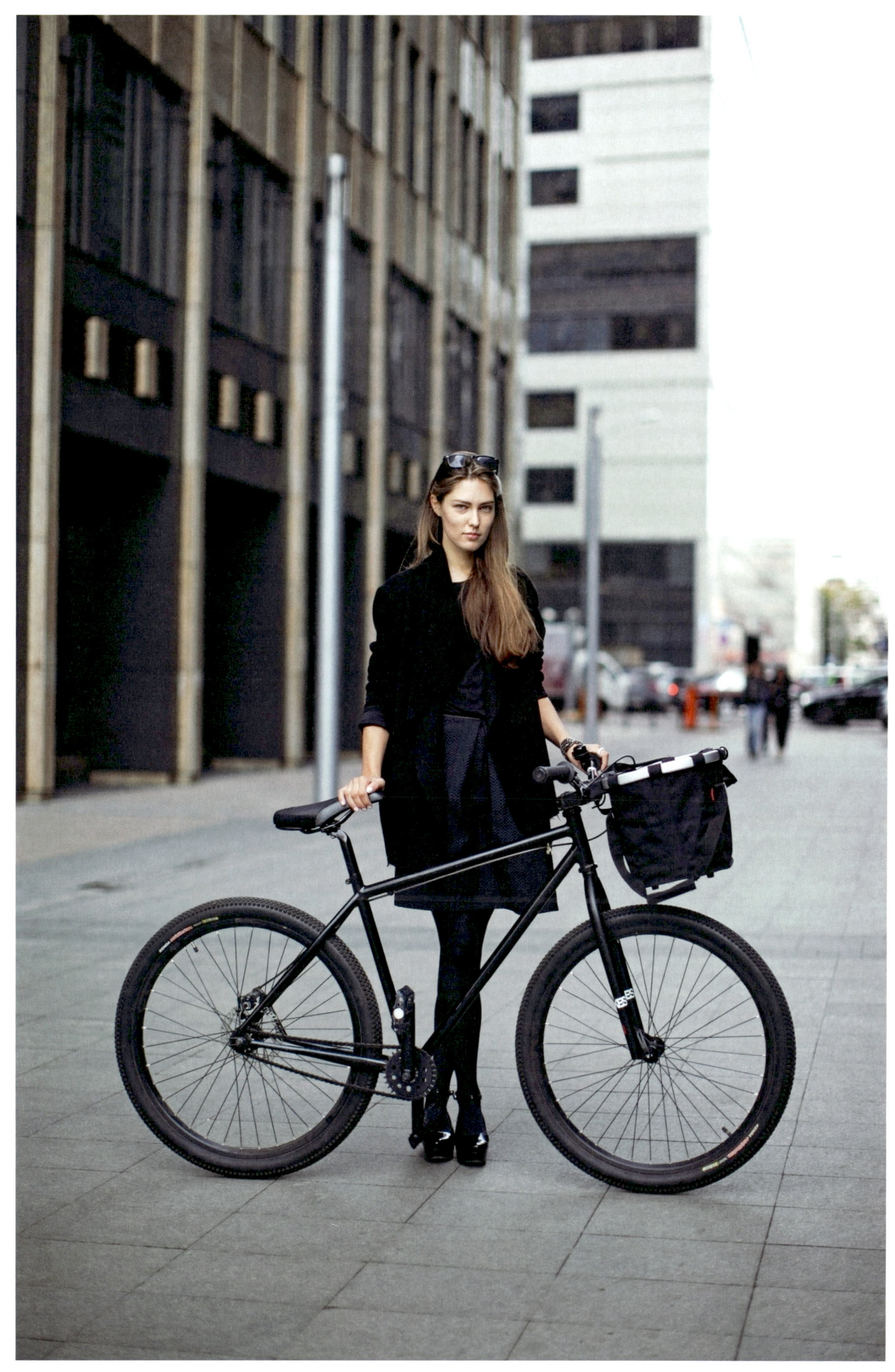

# Fashion

Think: color-block Marni trainers and breezy Chanel shirts and modish street clothes tough enough to be worn while cycling because they're made from upcycled inner tubes. Leather sneakers and classic British hunting shoes made for clipping in. Cycling apparel doesn't necessarily look like cycling apparel anymore. In fact, at this point you'd probably better stop lumping it in with "gear."

## Thousand Helmets

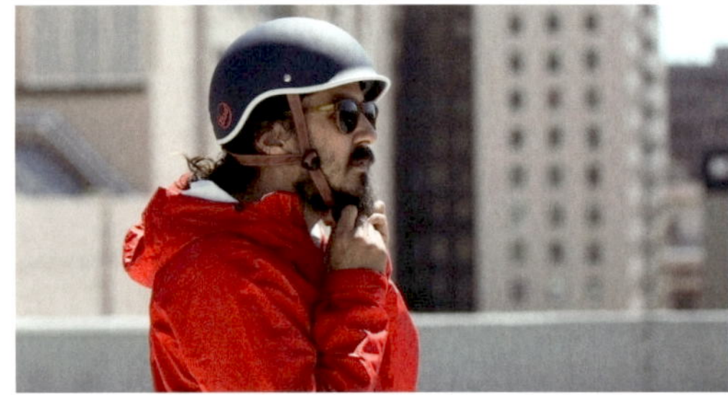

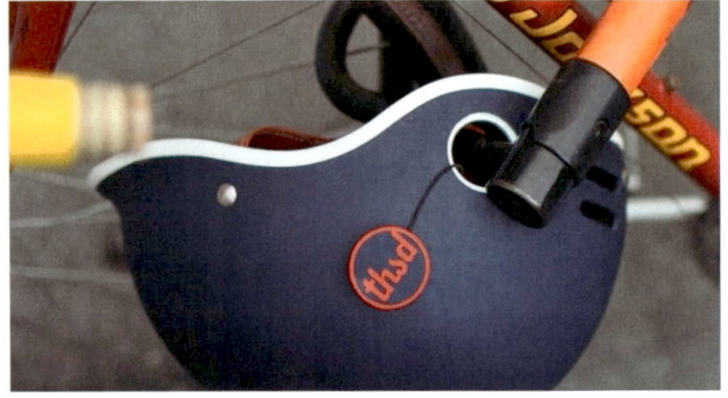

In 2012, Gloria Hwang lost a friend to a bicycling accident. Never a fan of bike helmets herself, she began to wonder how to change the stigma around wearing a helmet. The experience inspired her to start Thousand, a brand of ultra-protective yet stylish bicycle helmets that are fun to wear. Inspired by everything from vintage motorcycle helmets to Jack Kerouac's travels, Gloria and her team spent over a year thoughtfully designing a lifestyle-driven helmet with high-five-worthy features, including a secret, patent-pending PopLock—a secure and convenient way to leave a bike helmet behind. With its intuitive, clean design, the Thousand helmet is protective and made for the urban explorer.

## Quoc Pham

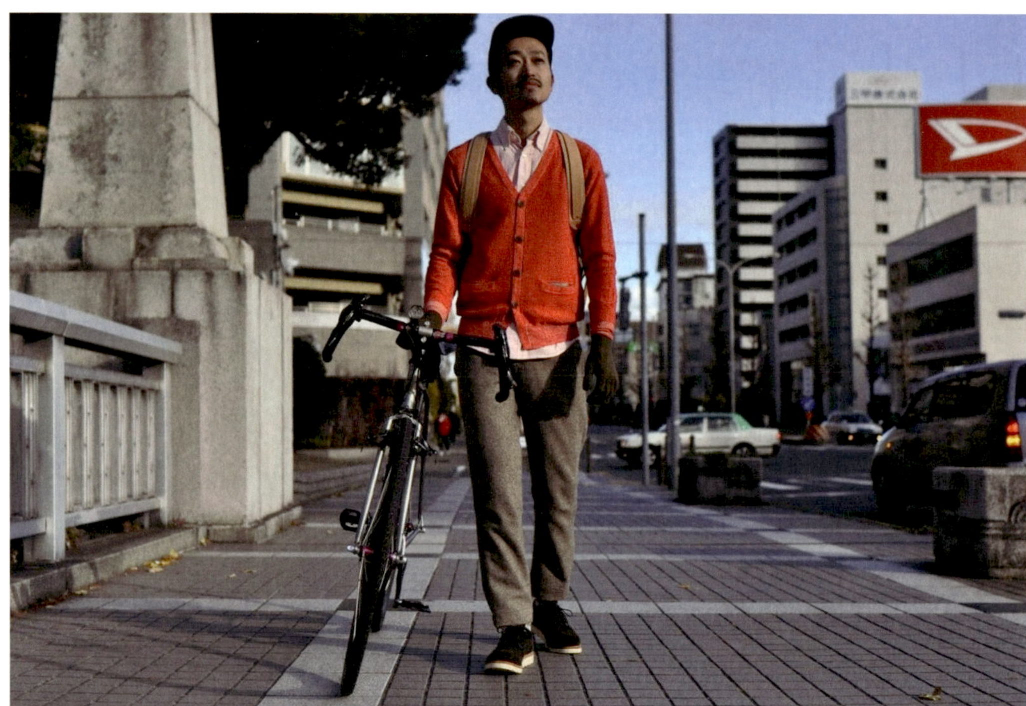

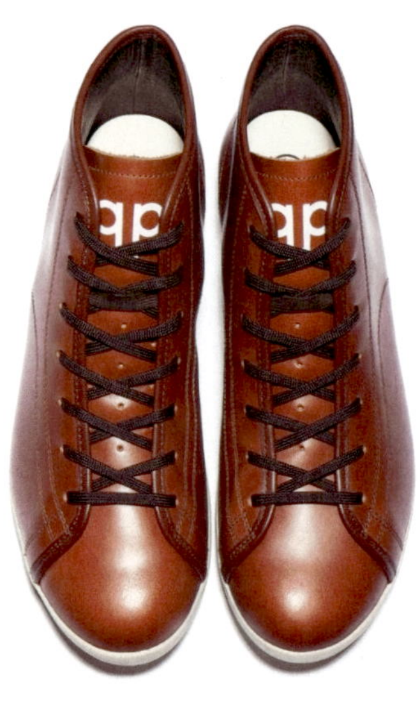

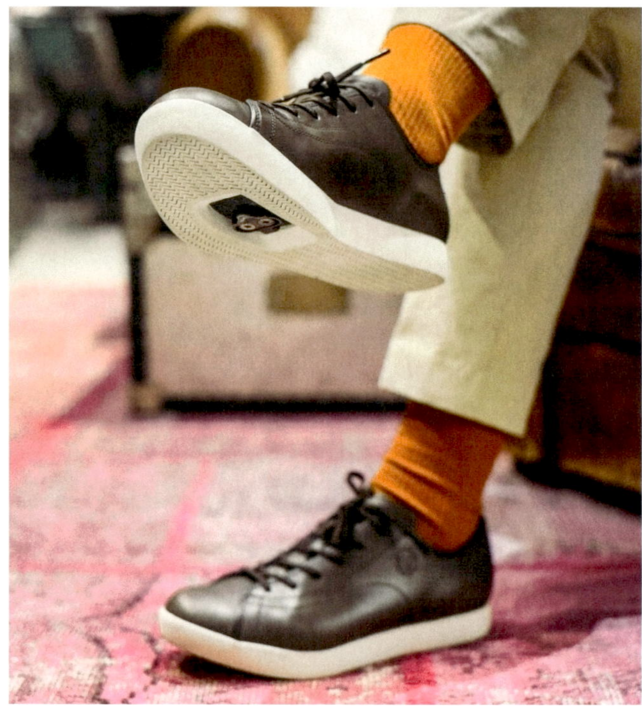

Urbane, which connotes big-city sophistication, is a good way to describe cycling footwear brand Quoc Pham. QP considers cycling to be as integral to daily life as going to work, so it makes sure that its customers can integrate their cycling shoes into every part of their daily lives. The Derby shoe, which contemporizes, citifies, and cyclifies a classic English hunting shoe, has a layered structure that makes it as comfortable off the bike as on. QP's Fixed is not a reference to a fixie, but with the brand's signature 3M reflective heel strip, natural leather, and rubber sole, it can be worn while riding one. By combining traditional leather shoemaking with contemporary sneaker construction, QP has also refined the trainer. QPs go "from cycle to sidewalk" to business lunch to dinner date.

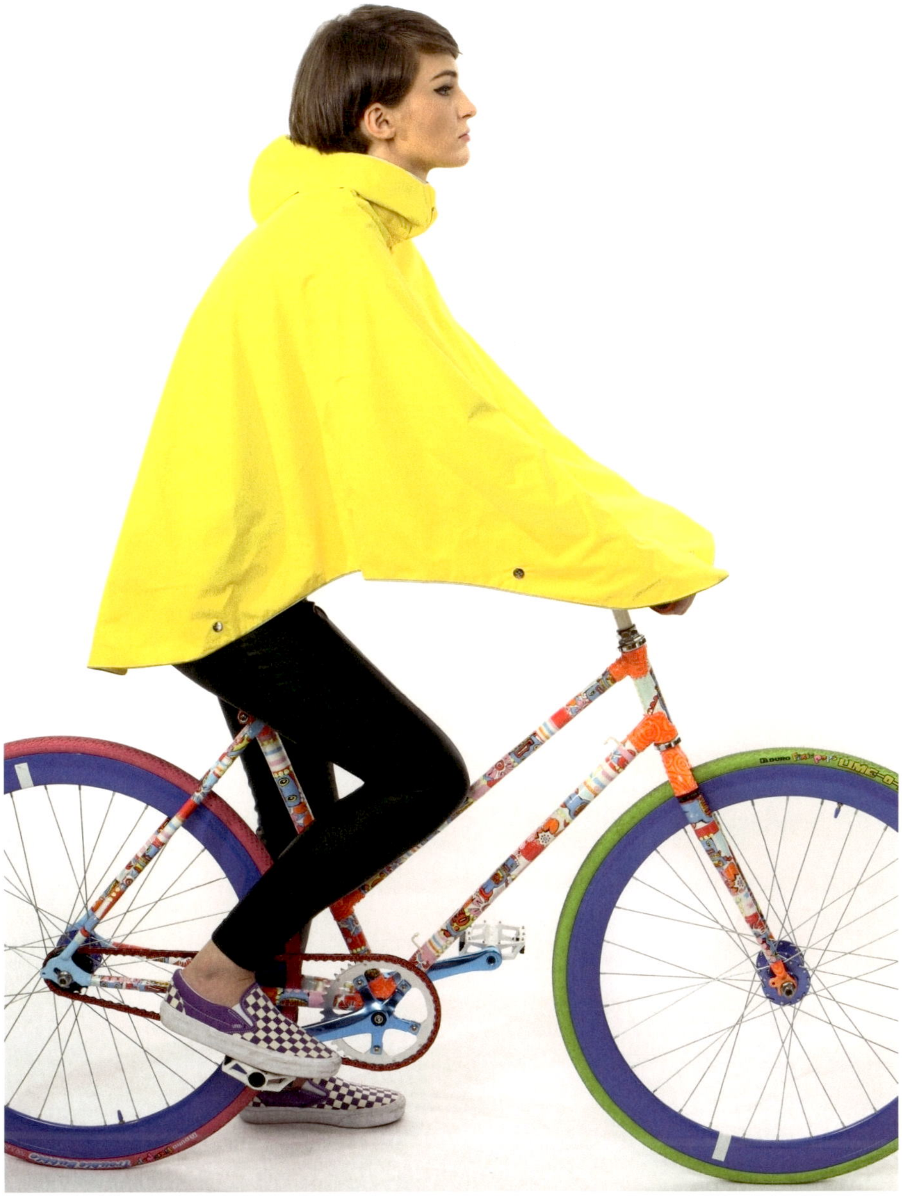

## *Urban Poncho*

**OTTO LONDON**

Is it pouring rain? Is the sun shining? For cyclists bundled up in Otto's Urban Poncho, the question is moot. This all-weather garment, designed with the urban cyclist in mind, features a waterproof Oxford nylon outer to ensure maximum dryness when the rain falls and handlebar straps that keep laps dry. For those who happen to find themselves out and about on a crisp, dry day, the Urban Poncho sports stud buttons that create a sleeve-like fit, turning the poncho into a casual jacket. The two-way waterproof zipper provides easy access to a secure inner pocket that keeps your phone and wallet safe and dry. For the night riders out there, the Urban Poncho's reflective piping ensures visibility even after the sun goes down.

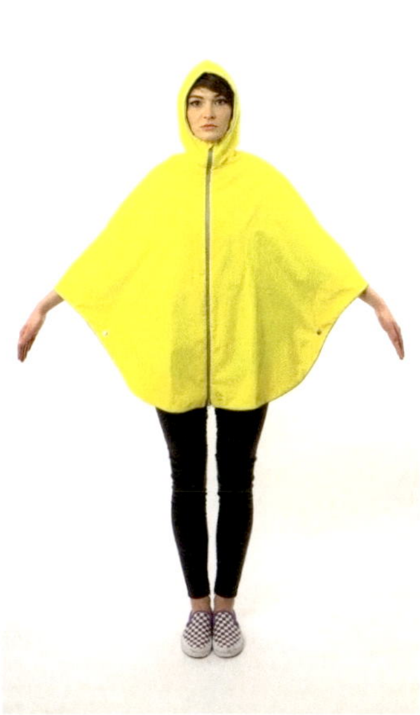

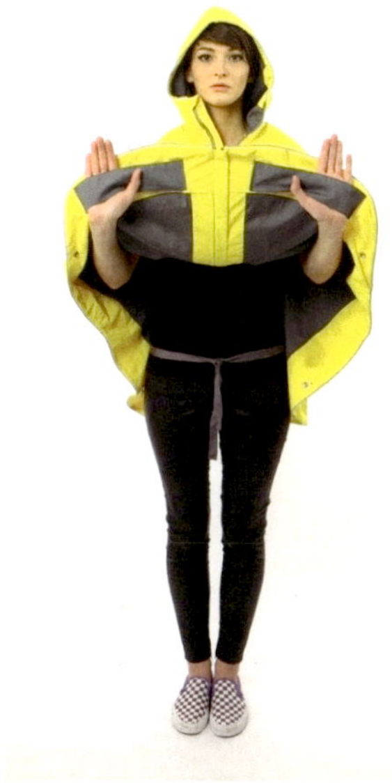

## *Radkappe*

Whether you're en route to the office, heading to the farmer's market, or off on an excursion to the lake, the first-edition Radkappe makes every bike ride a pleasure. When the weather doesn't cooperate, the visor on the front of the helmet provides protection from pouring rain and glaring sun. The cutout at the back ensures comfort with all sorts of hairstyles, including buns and ponytails. Made with EPS and PVC, the Radkappe is available in glossy Vanilla Beige, Mighty Blue matte, and Dark Grey matte. Like all Radkappe helmets, the first edition is not only super-stylish, but also provides maximum safety.

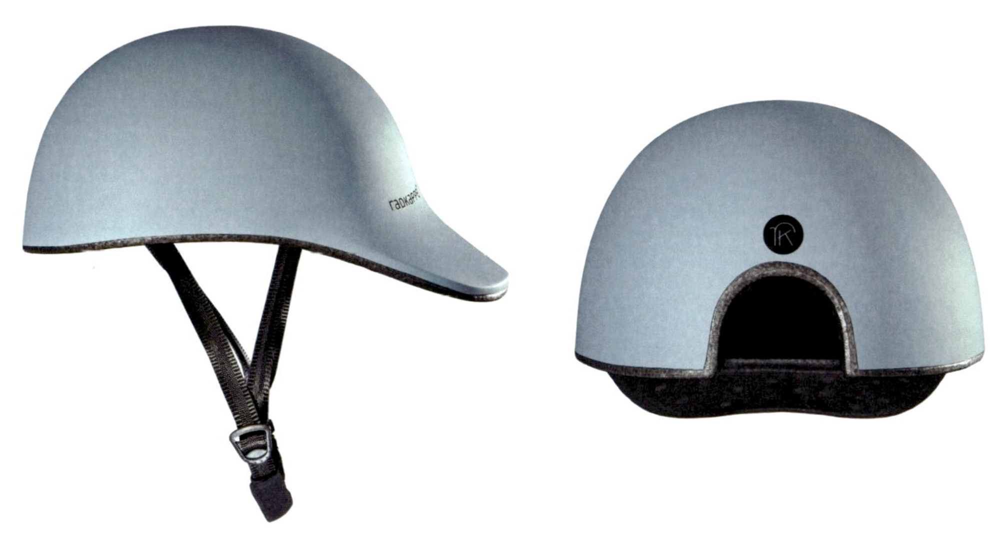

# Bags

Bags exemplify the synthesis of cycling life with real life, making it that much more real. Forget the messenger bag, if you want to. Even saddle bags pack up into Calvin Klein-ish minimalism, garment bags for clothes worthy of being called garments—because cyclists wear those too. Meanwhile, more graphical choices can, much like sneakers do, tell the world "I'm a maximalist and my bike is too."

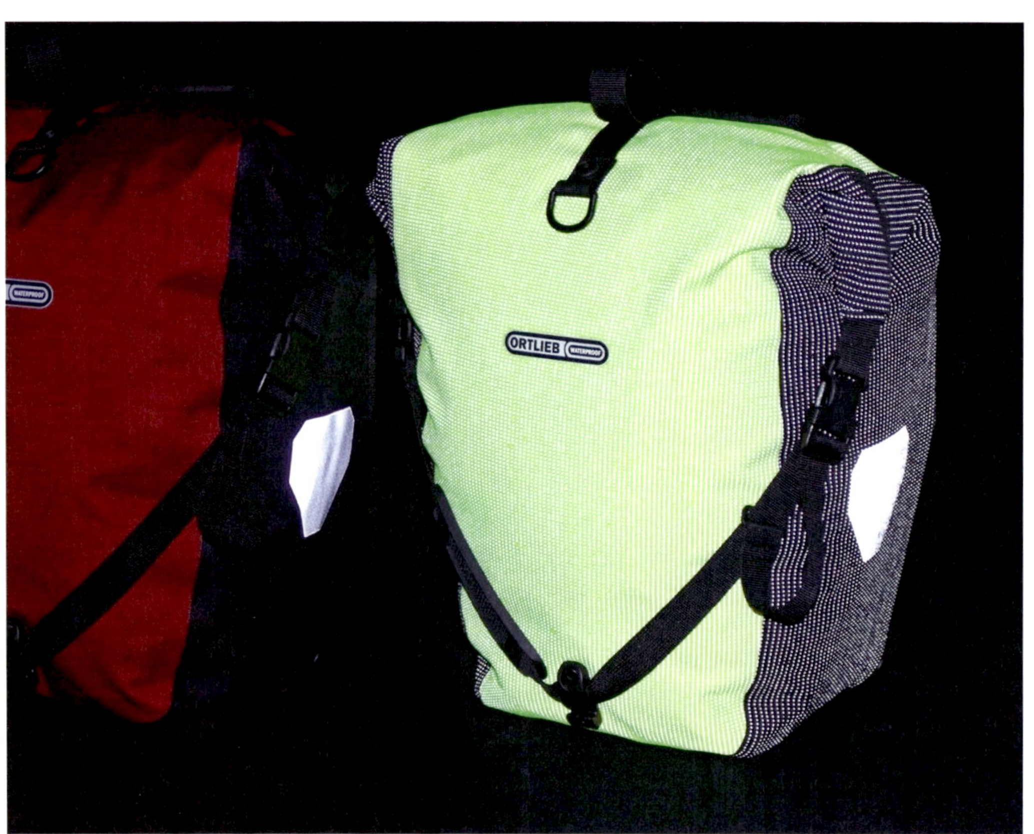


## Back-Roller High Visibility Panniers

**ORTLIEB**

Back-Roller High Visibility panniers are reflective and waterproof, providing superior visibility and performance in wet weather conditions. The spacious panniers have an inner pocket for organization, and their symmetrical shape allows heel clearance for comfortable cycling. Used as individual bags, the panniers can be mounted on the left or right side of the bike or carried like a shoulder bag with the supplied strap. The Ortlieb QL2.1 system allows fast and easy mounting and removal of the panniers with one hand. The QL2.1 hooks can be adapted to the rack without additional tools and are suitable for tube diameters from 8 to 20 millimeters. Optional accessories include the Ortlieb harness system, which converts the Back-Roller into a daypack, and an anti-theft device that can be integrated into the upper mounting rail.

## Commuter Daypack City

**ORTLIEB**

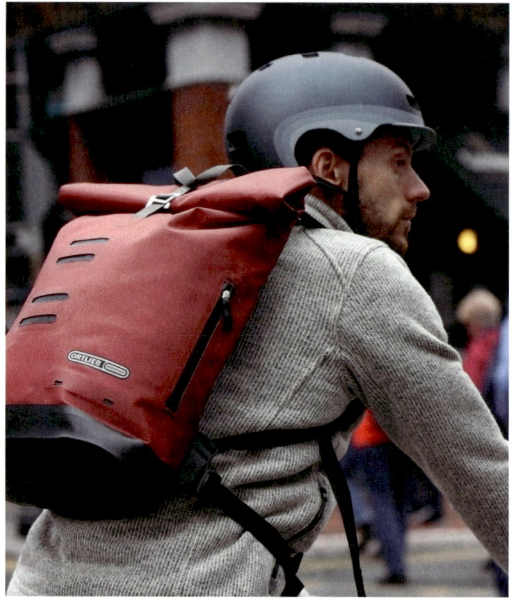

A clean design aesthetic is the calling card of Ortlieb's Commuter Daypack City, a waterproof backpack made for modern urban living. Even in heavy rain, belongings are sure to be protected by its abrasion-resistant PU-laminated nylon fabric and quick-access roll closure.

A large main compartment offers plenty of space; laptops and tablets are safely stored in a padded sleeve. Foam pads with ventilation channels and removable chest and shoulder straps ensure carrying comfort. Further features include a zippered outer pocket, an organizer with inner pockets, a fixing loop for U-lock and rear light, and a reflective logo.

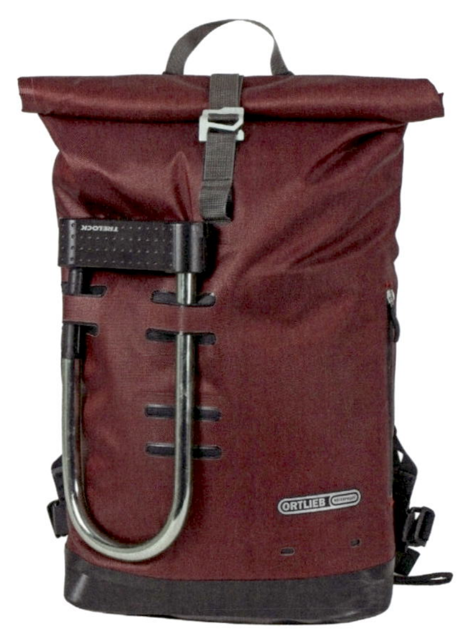

## The Classic 2.0 Garment Pannier

**TWO WHEEL GEAR**

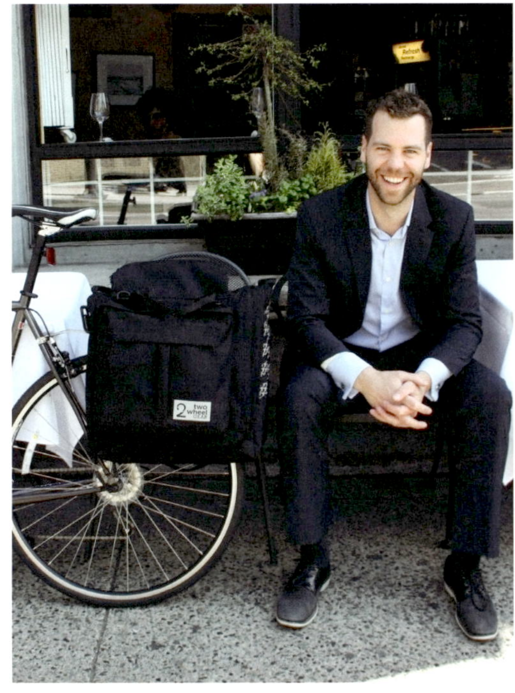

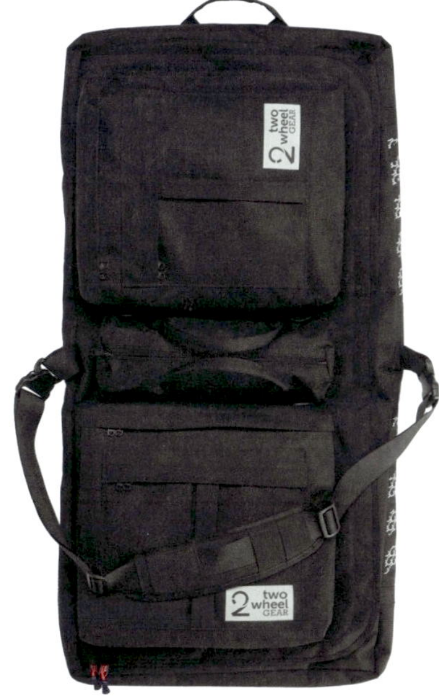


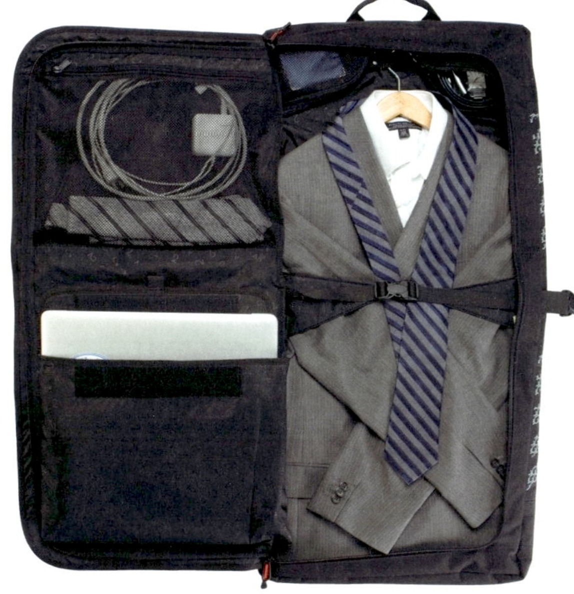

The scene: 1999 in Calgary, Alberta. Geophysicist Craig Coulombe is an early bike commuter frustrated by the few options he has to transport wrinkle-free suits to his office. In an inspired moment of can-do innovation, he borrows his mother-in-law's sewing machine and fashions the first pannier to transport clothes on hangers. Eventually, his small invention would become a big business and the Classic Suit Bag would go on to be Two Wheel Gear's signature product. Now called the Classic 2.0 Garment Pannier, the bag is a favorite of executive-types who cycle to the office but need to know that their suits will arrive crisp and dry when they get there. The bag has room for everything a commuter could need and sports tough, waterproof fabric for all-weather use.

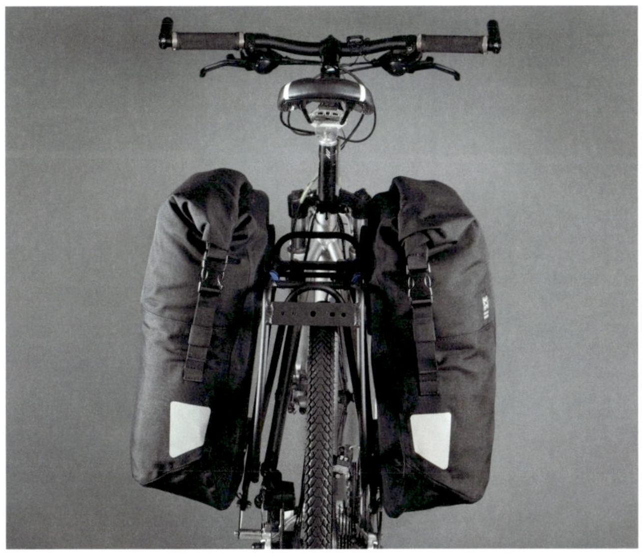

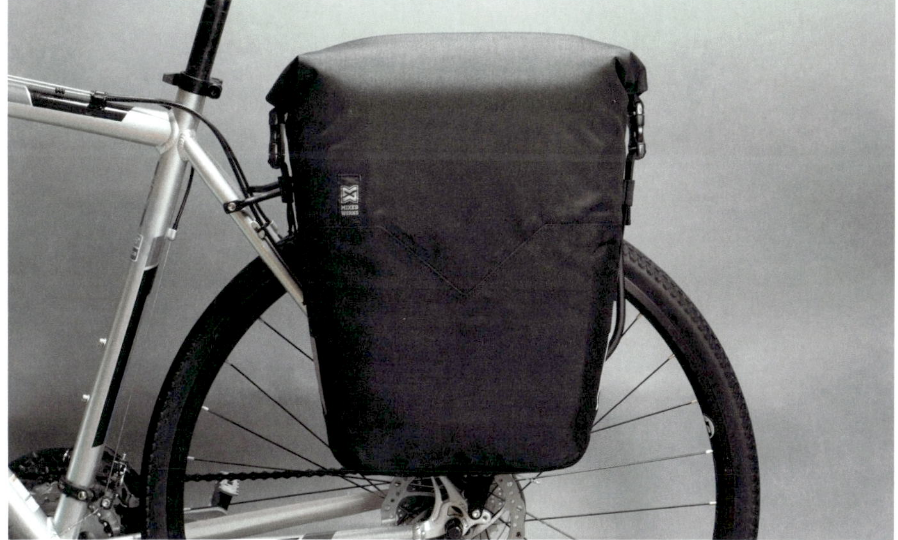

## Blackbird Panniers

**MIXED WORKS**

The assortment of necessities that a rider may need to carry across town or country is endless. As avid cyclists, the designers at Mixed Works know all about the value of flexible messenger bags, bike bags, and accessories that can durably transport anything that needs to come along for the ride. Blackbird Panniers are thoughtfully designed to accommodate any situation and can be used as a small rear pannier or as a large front pannier. Made from durable Cordura, Mixed Works products are designed and handcrafted in Poland in small collections that allow the makers to devote attention to the smallest details and exercise total control over the quality of each product.

# MK1 & MK1-E

**BUTCHERS & BICYCLES**

What happens when a bicyclist starts a family? Two wheels become three. The cargo trike—which can transport kids just as easily as groceries and new household appliances—is a practical item that has long made European cities like Copenhagen and Amsterdam family-friendly. Based in Copenhagen's historical Meatpacking District, Butchers & Bicycles set out to ensure that bicyclists do not have to compromise the joy of riding when they are toting freight on three wheels instead of riding fast and free on two. The three engineers behind Butchers & Bicycles hand-manufacture the MK1 and MK1-E, which are "built to tilt"—riders can lean into turns in the same unchecked manner as they would on their fixies or road bikes without the fear of clumsily tipping over. The trikes are available with or without an integrated electric motor and come with a range of conveniences—a locking "glove compartment," smartphone straps, and even a coffee cup holder.

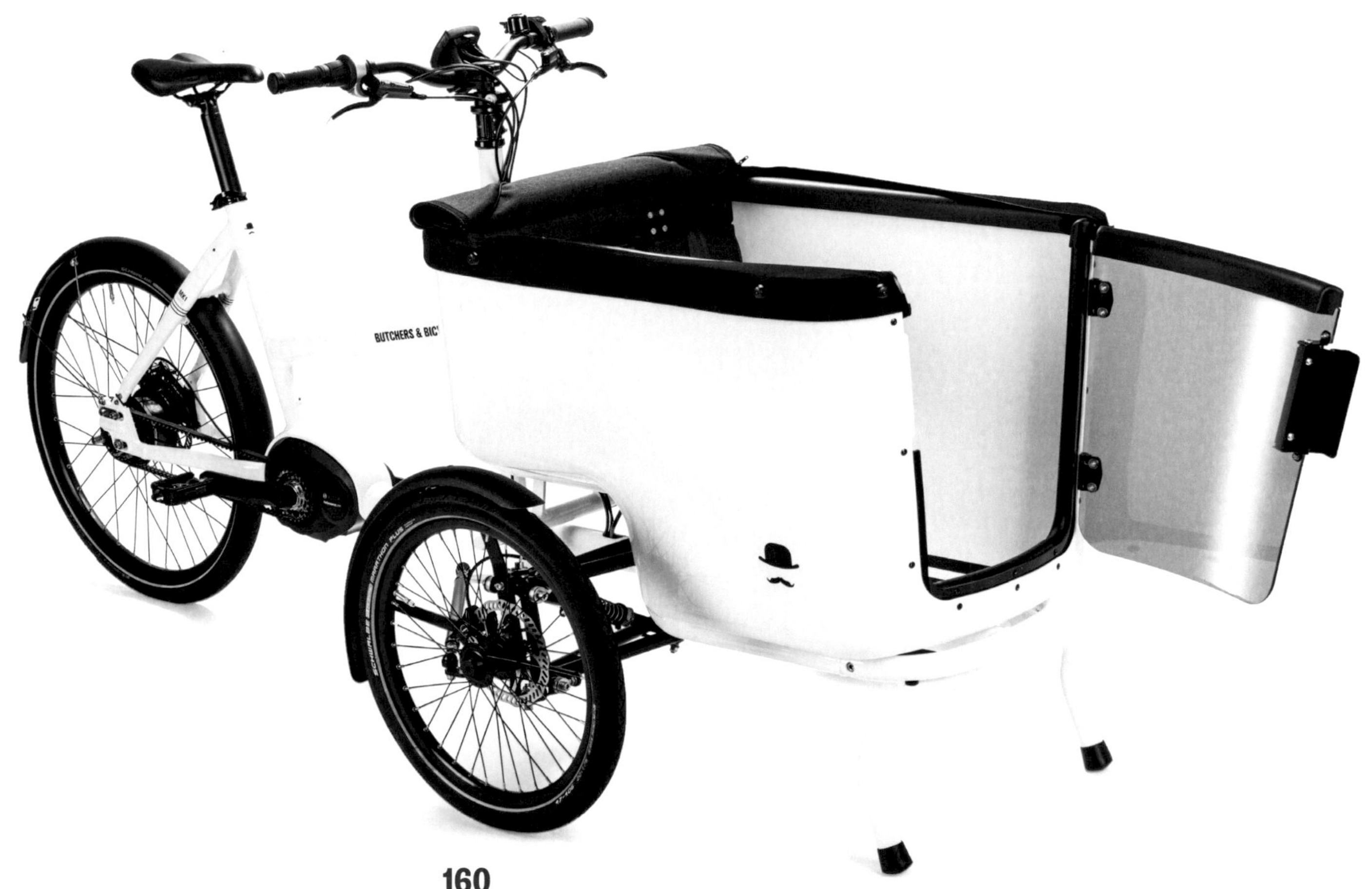

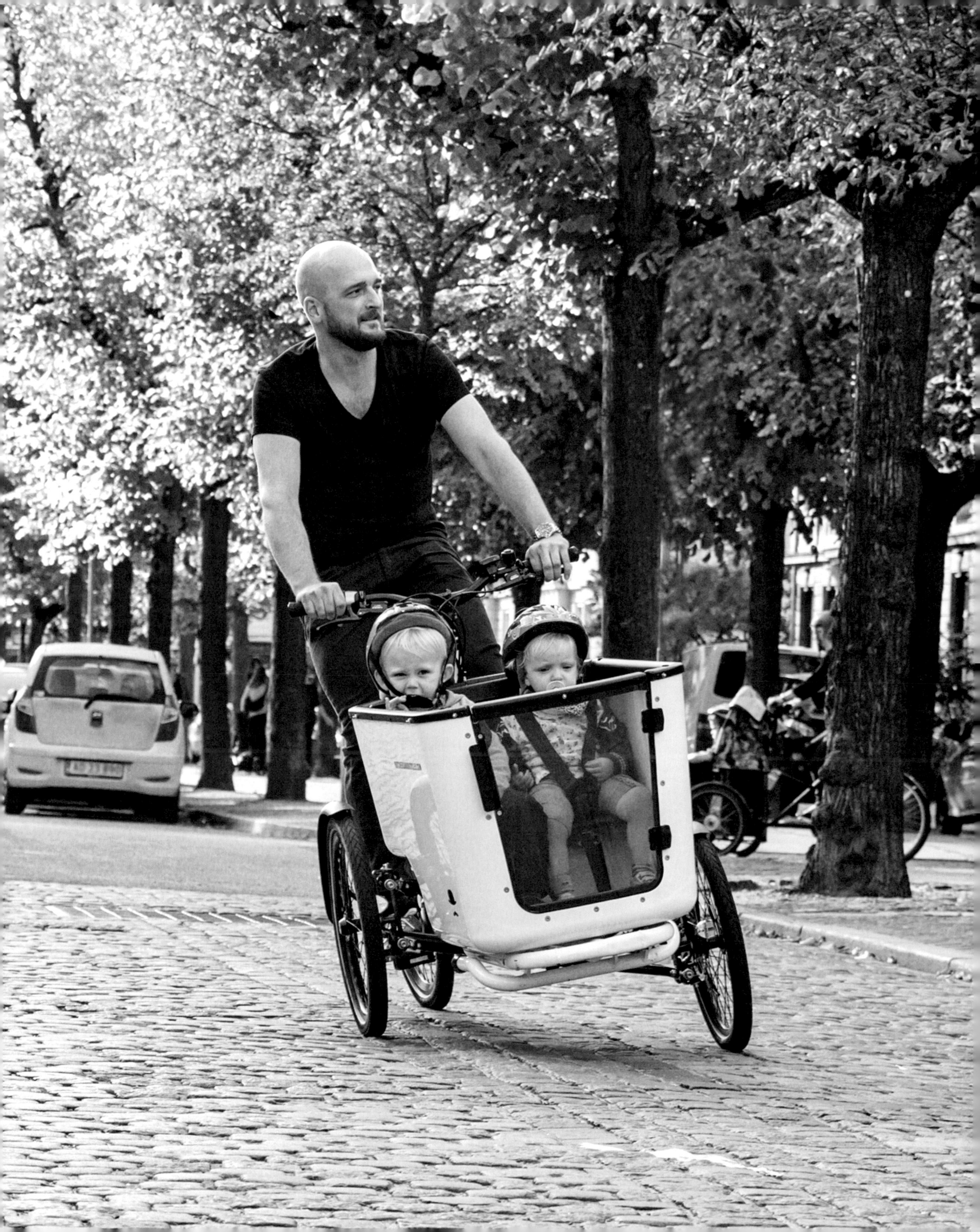

# STePS eBullitt

**LARRY VS HARRY**

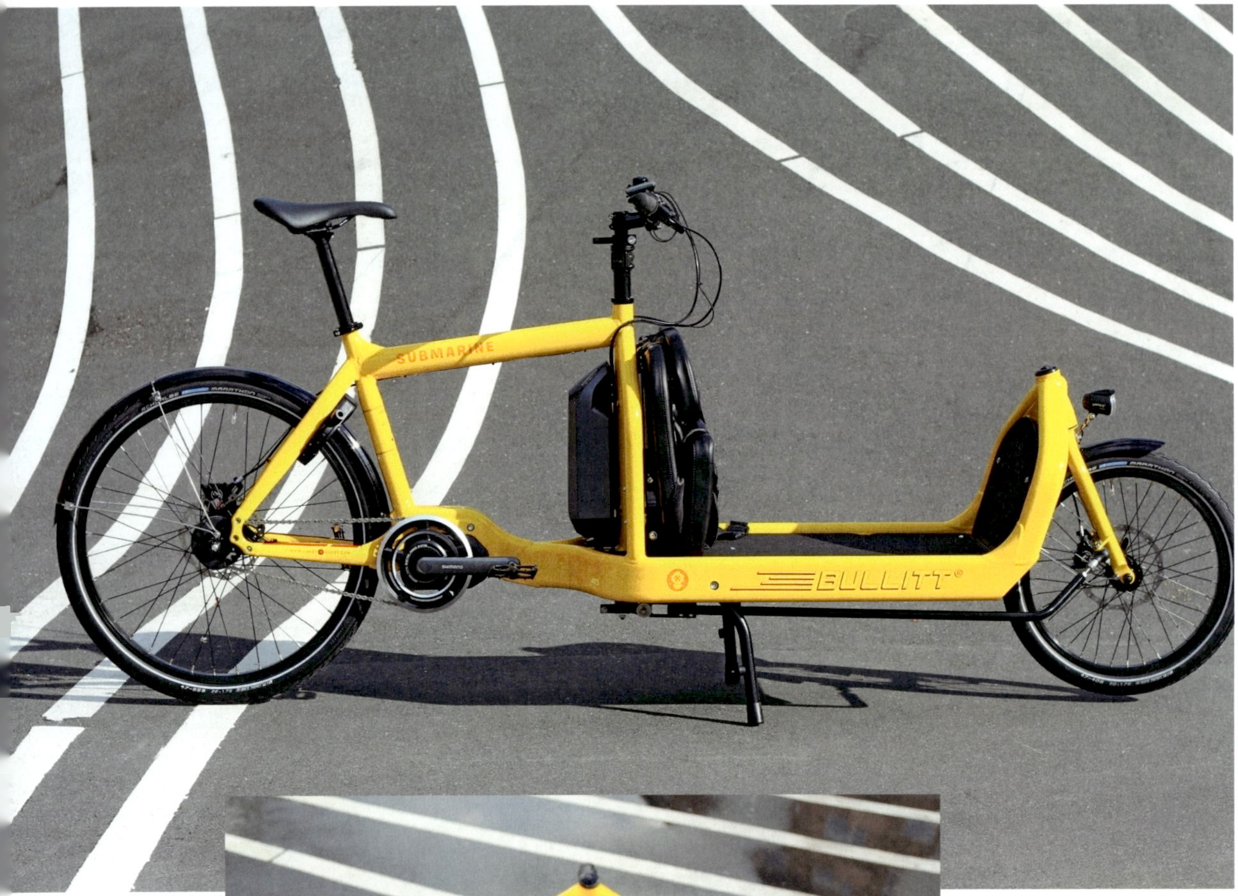

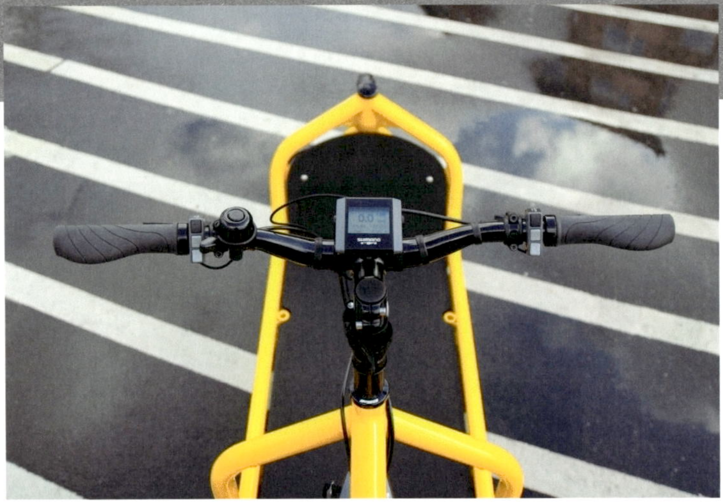

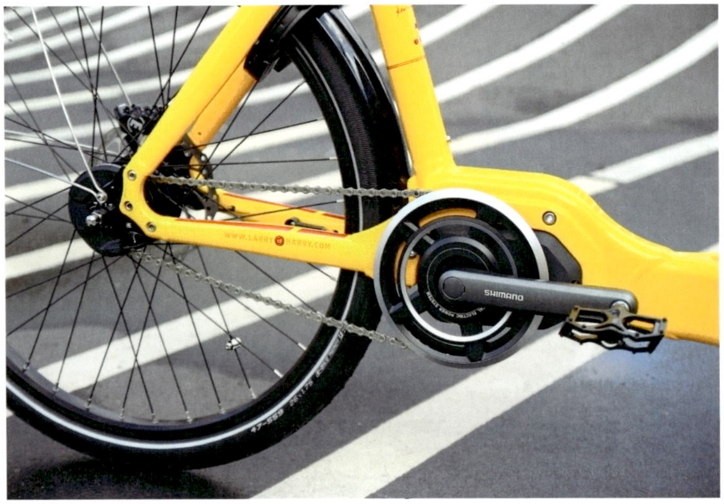

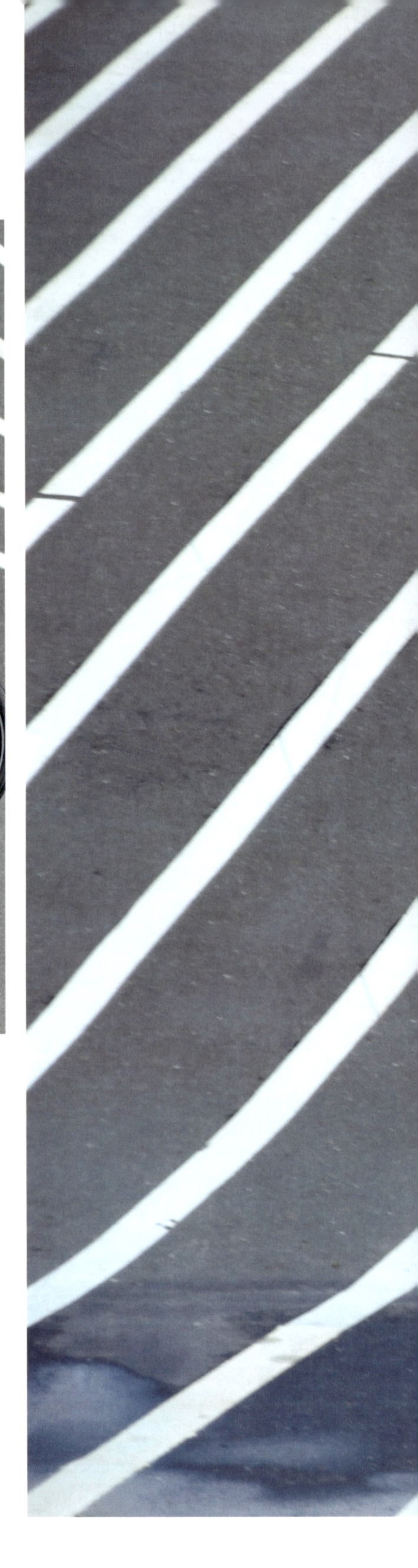

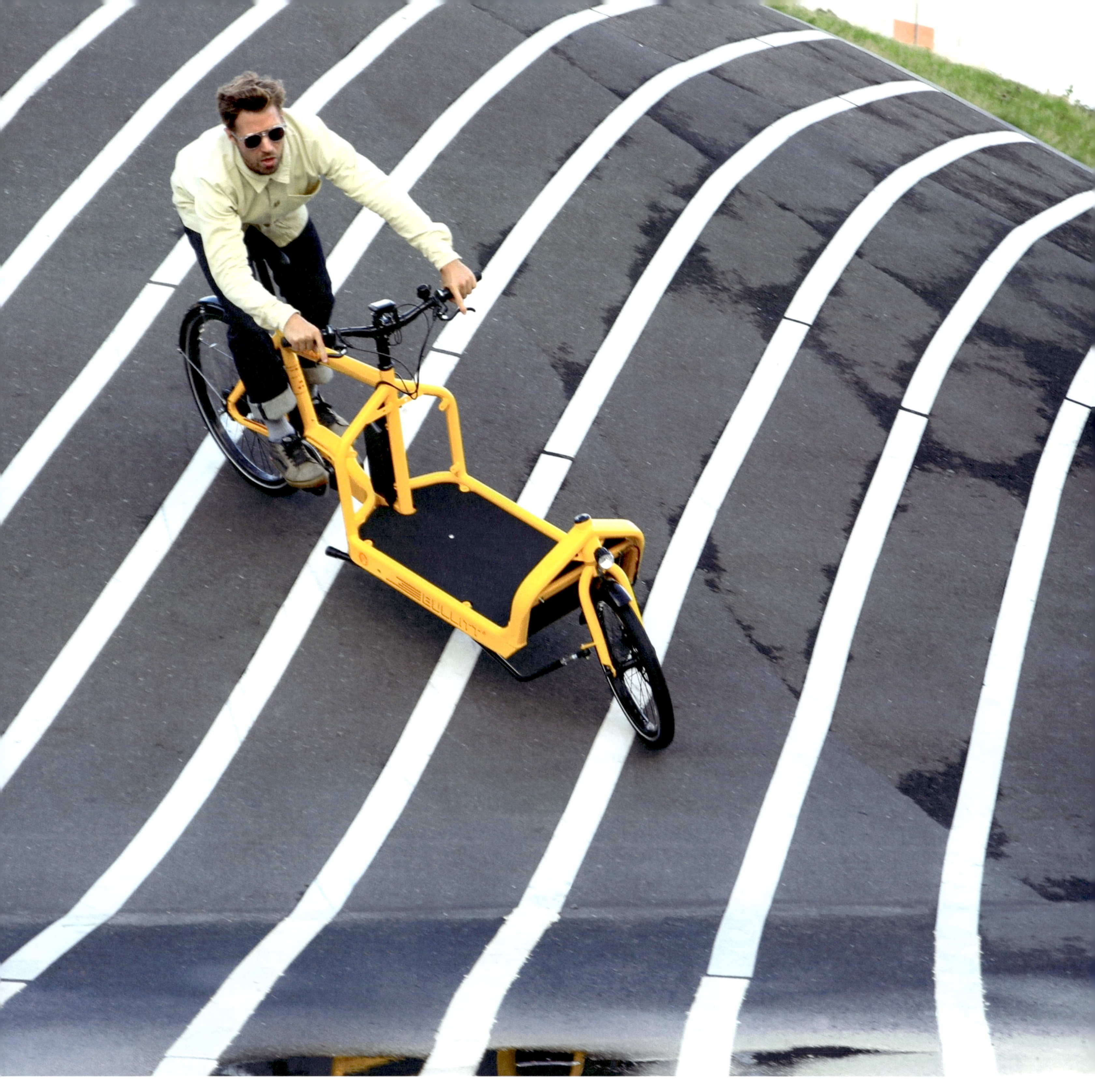

As Copenhageners, Larry and Harry have always biked as much as they could—not just because it's green, cool, and cheap, but because it's the most convenient way to get around town. For 20 years, Harry used a 60-year-old Danish Long John cargo bike to get from contracting job to contracting job. At the time, Larry worked for a manufacturer that made the best cargo bikes in the world—but Harry's vintage Long John was faster, lighter, and more maneuverable. So Larry and Harry decided to build the perfect cargo bike based on the Danish Long John. With a range of 125 kilometers, their Shimano STePS eBullitt is the best-integrated cargo bike on the market, making light work of the steepest hills and strongest headwinds. Shimano's Alfine hub provides smooth, reliable shifting, and at 3.2 kilograms, the motor is one of the lightest out there. Charging is convenient and quick at just four hours.

# *Load*

**RIESE & MÜLLER**

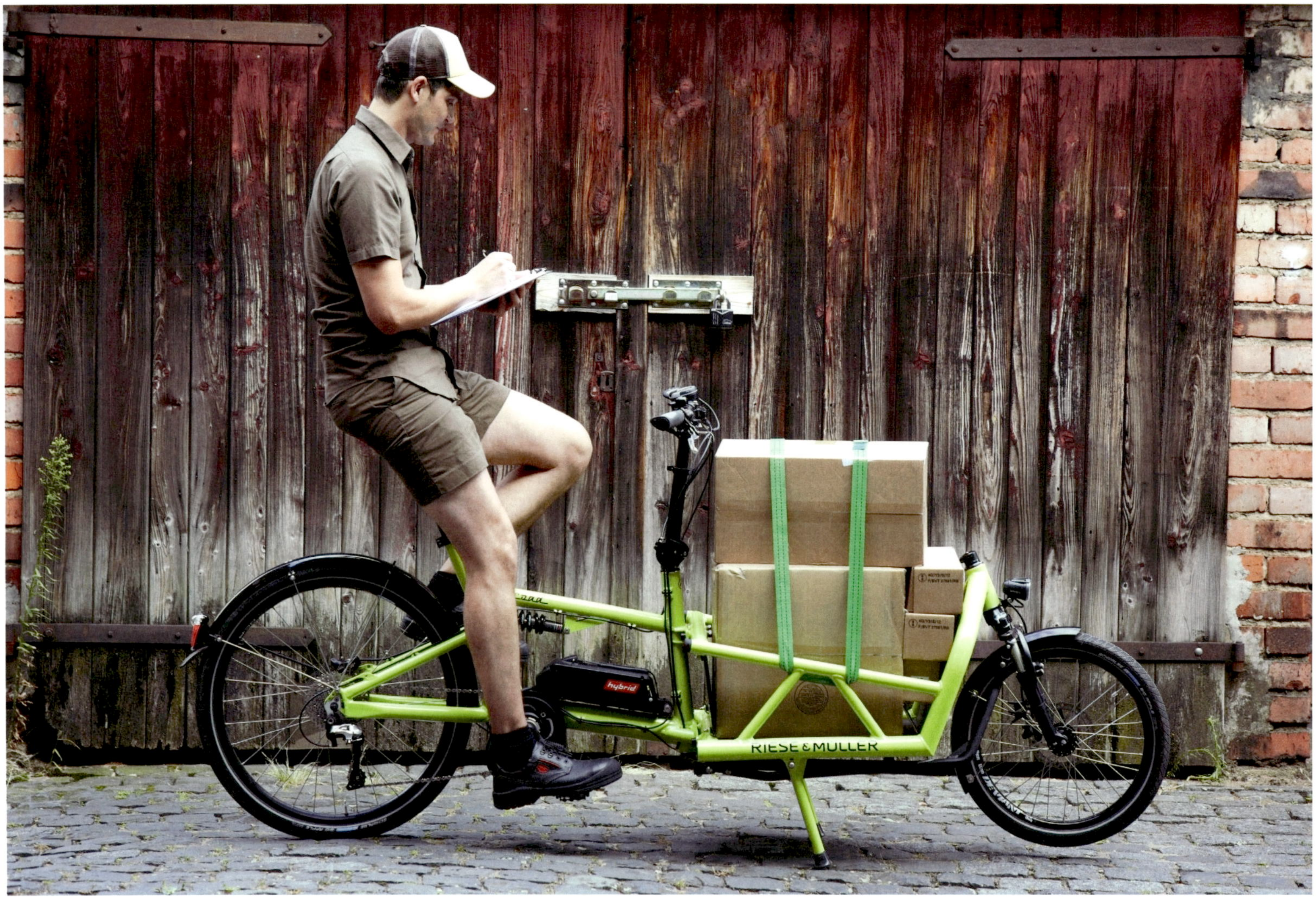

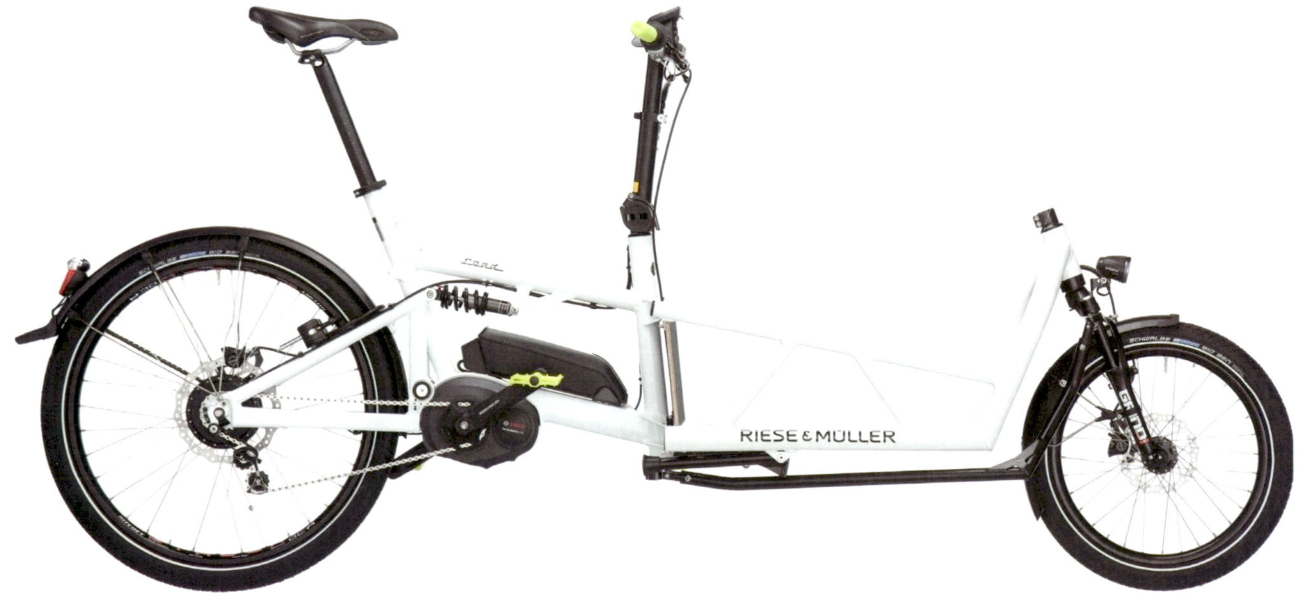

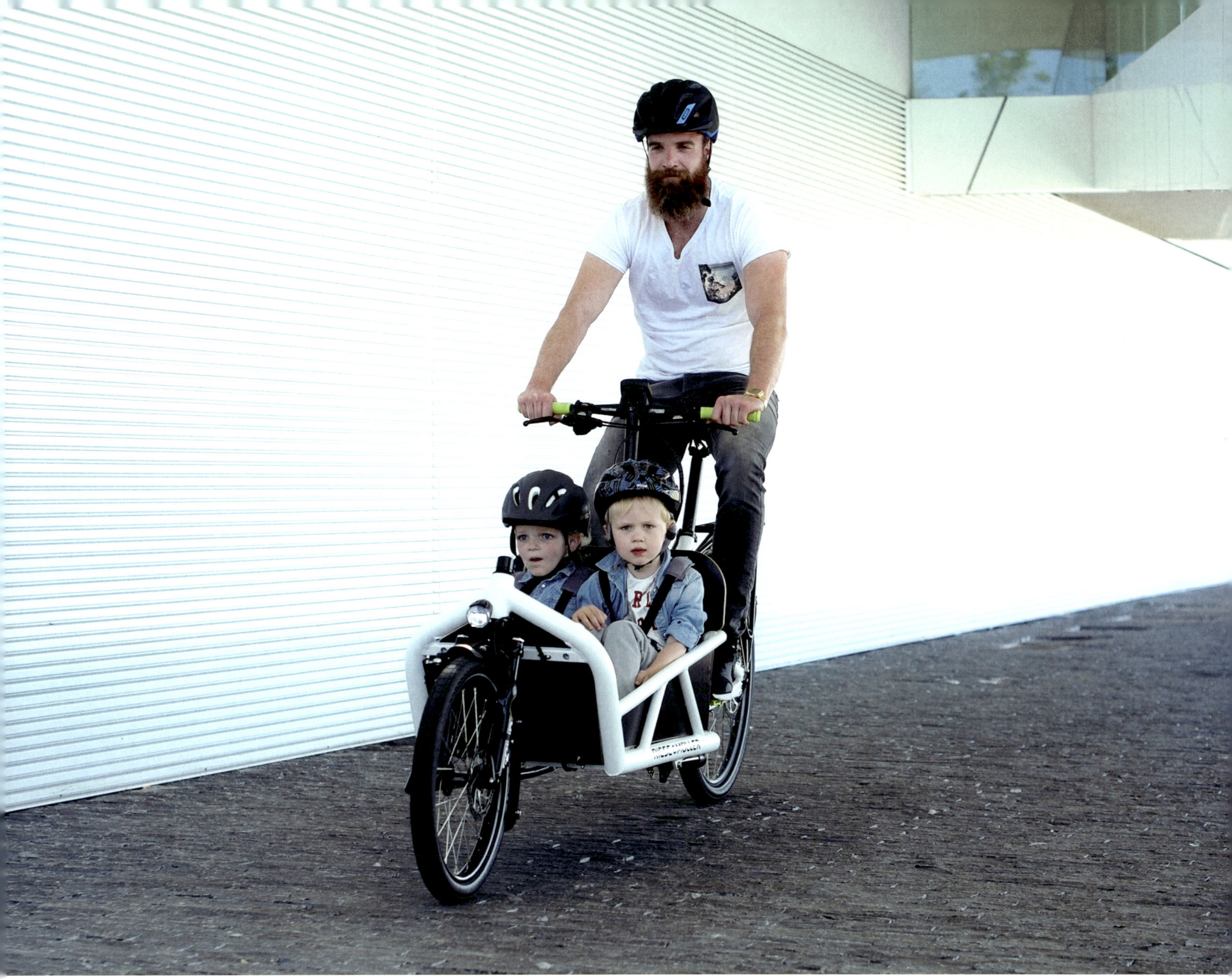

Cargo cyclists need to accomplish a wide range of tasks throughout the day, using their rigs to transport children, go shopping, deliver packages, or get away into the countryside. The new Load sport model from Riese & Müller is an e-cargo bike that can do it all, with wide black balloon tires, a minimalist aesthetic, and a discreet LED lamp on the back. It has a Bosch Performance Cruise drive unit and a 500-watt-hour Bosch battery to ensure it can go the distance. The efficient ten-speed Shimano derailleur provides pedaling power with optimum efficiency. Riese & Müller also offer an expanded line of accessories, including a folding box and seat with a seatbelt for two small children, a rain cover, and a waterproof, sealable GFR cargo box with a carrying capacity of up to 200 liters.

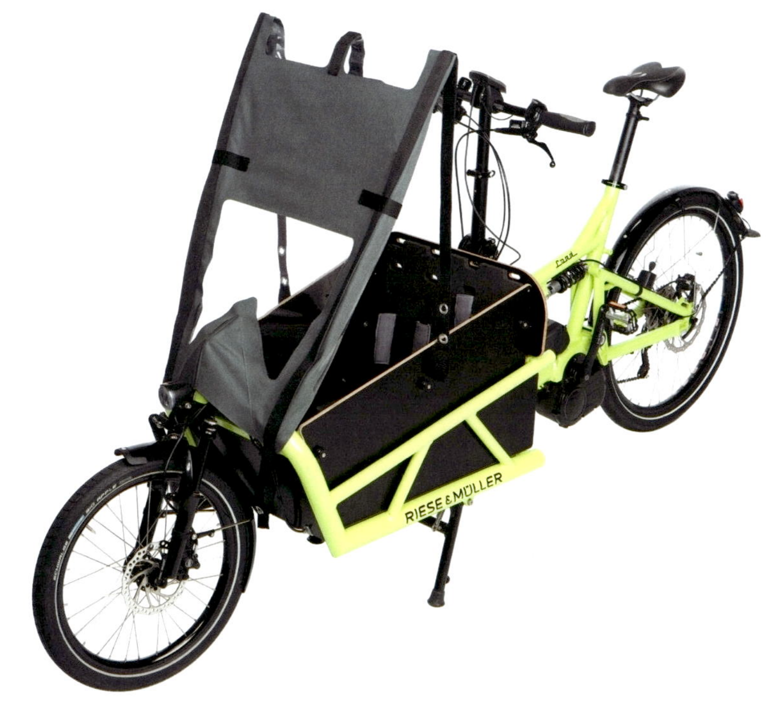

# Cycling Without Age

Cycling Without Age pairs volunteer cyclists with elderly passengers, allowing older generations a chance to get out and experience the city and the countryside from the bike path.

Ole Kassow bikes to work every morning because he loves cycling. If you ask him, Kassow will describe 1930s Copenhagen as "a jolly inferno of bicycles," mourn the midcentury displacement of bikes by cars, and tell you that the bicycle is not just the most convenient mode of transportation, "it also happens to be the happiest."

The idea for Cycling Without Age was also born on Kassow's daily commute. On his way to work he would bike past Torkil, a chatty 97-year-old walker-bound nursing-home resident who lived a life of limited physical mobility that was far outstripped by his active mind. Inspired, one day Kassow rented a rickshaw bicycle, took it to the nearest nursing home and offered to take anyone who wanted one for a ride. A woman named Gertrude took that first ride, an hour's tour along the Copenhagen waterfront, after which, Kassow recalls, "I left in a rare spirit." The next day, the director of the nursing home rang him up and asked him to continue the rides. Soon, the city bought him five rickshaws and then, suddenly, he had first 15 and then 30 volunteers to pedal them. Today, Cycling Without Age has spread to 100 nursing homes and a number of other cities in Denmark and has even made its way to Norway in spite of that country's extreme terrain.

"Cycling is all about smelling the flowers and hearing the birds and feeling the wind in your hair," Kassow says. "We're here to fight for the wind in people's hair." People who had not spoken in years started talking again. People suffering from dementia became less aggressive and began to lift the spirits of fellow residents when they returned. A doctor once even prescribed Cycling Without Age to an elderly patient. Kassow learned that simple bike rides could have a profound impact on quality of life, not just for elderly passengers, but also for the young pedalers. He even discovered that he was also benefitting from his public service: the rides gave him insights into his city that he had never had before. He made many unlikely friends, whose memories peopled the streets around them as they rode. Then, during a three-day, 300-kilometer rickshaw adventure ride to Hamburg, something funny happened. During the evenings and overnight, Kassow realized that his frail passengers were leaving something in the accompanying luggage bus that had seemed indispensable to them only hours before when the ride had begun: their walkers.

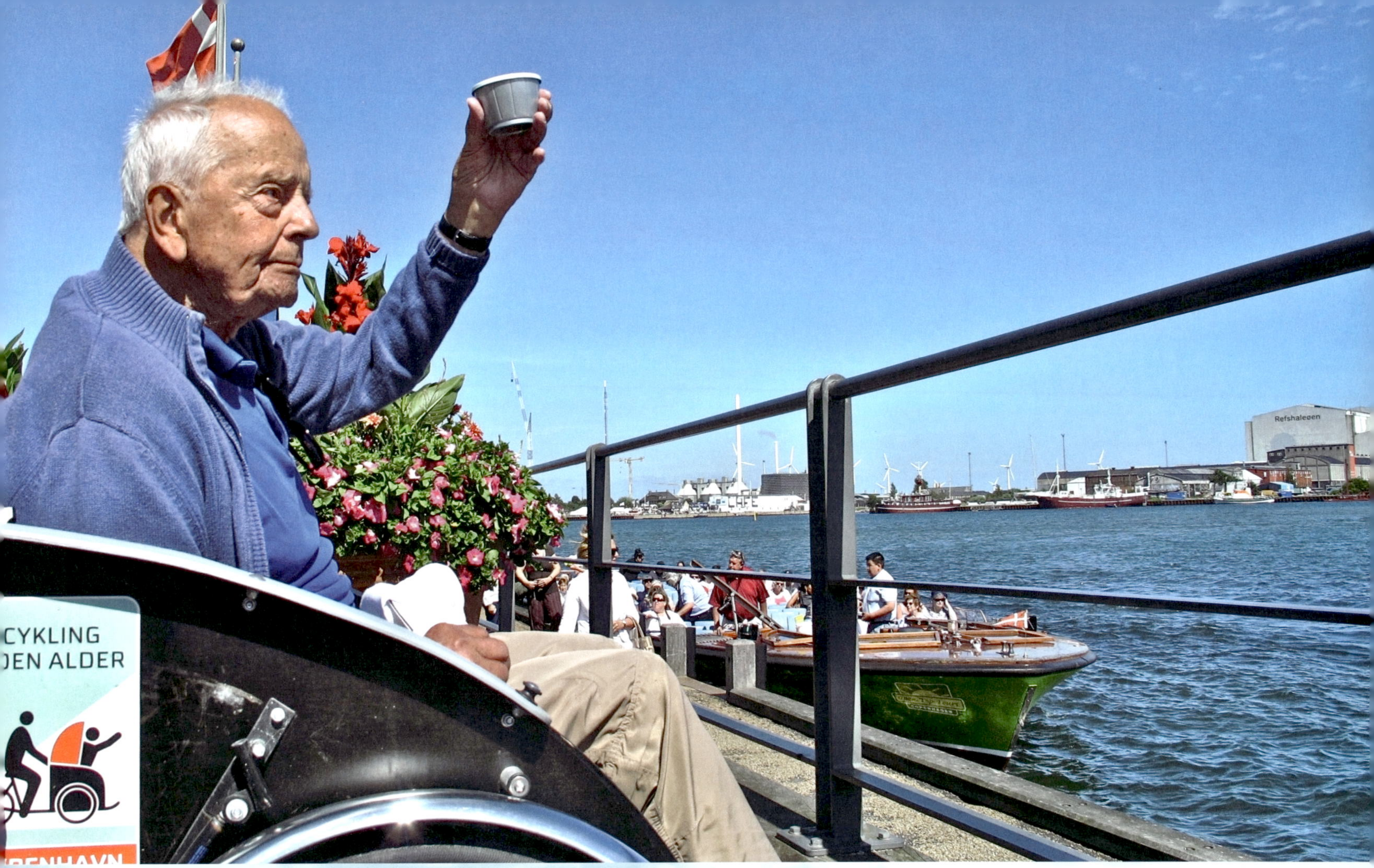

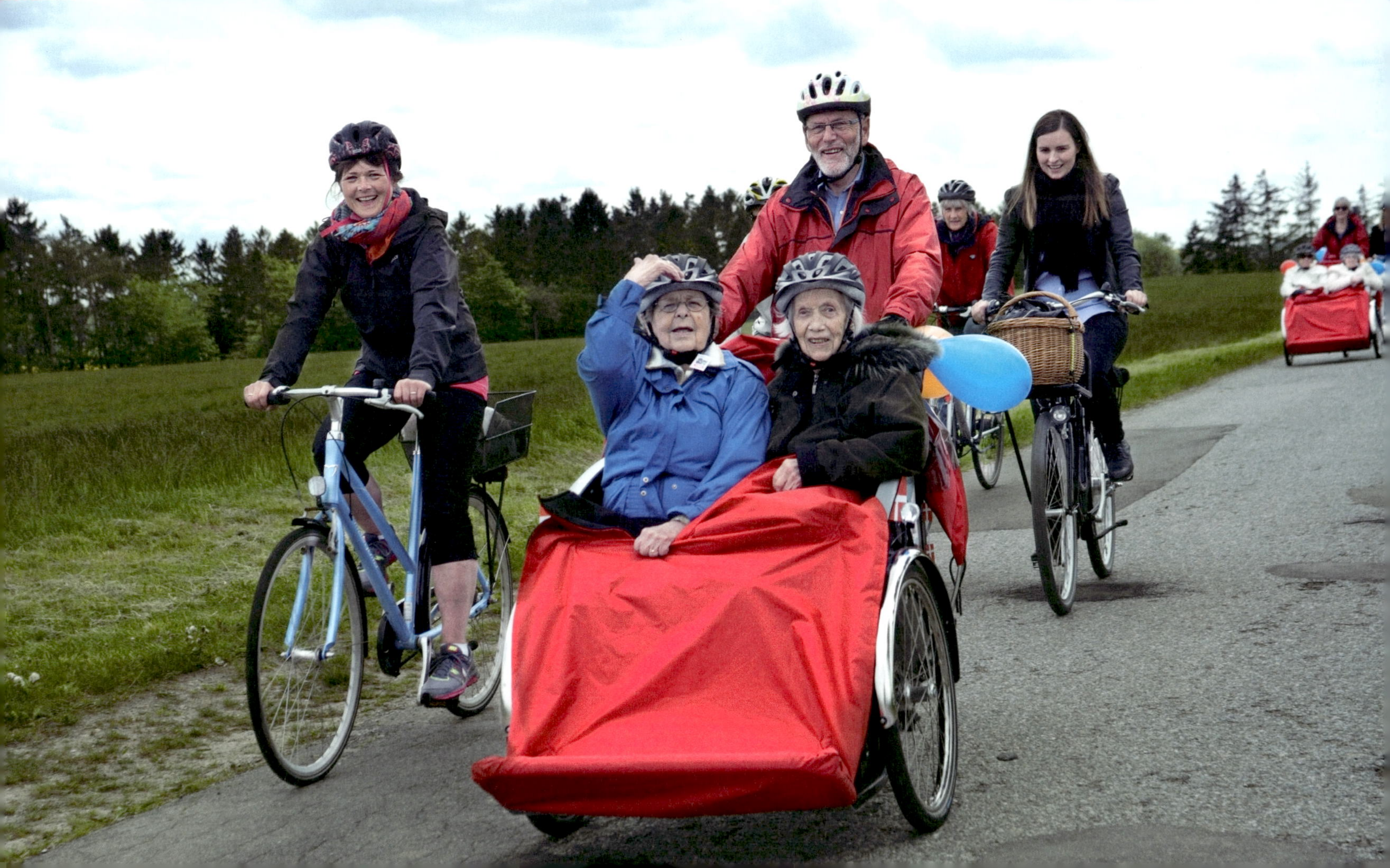

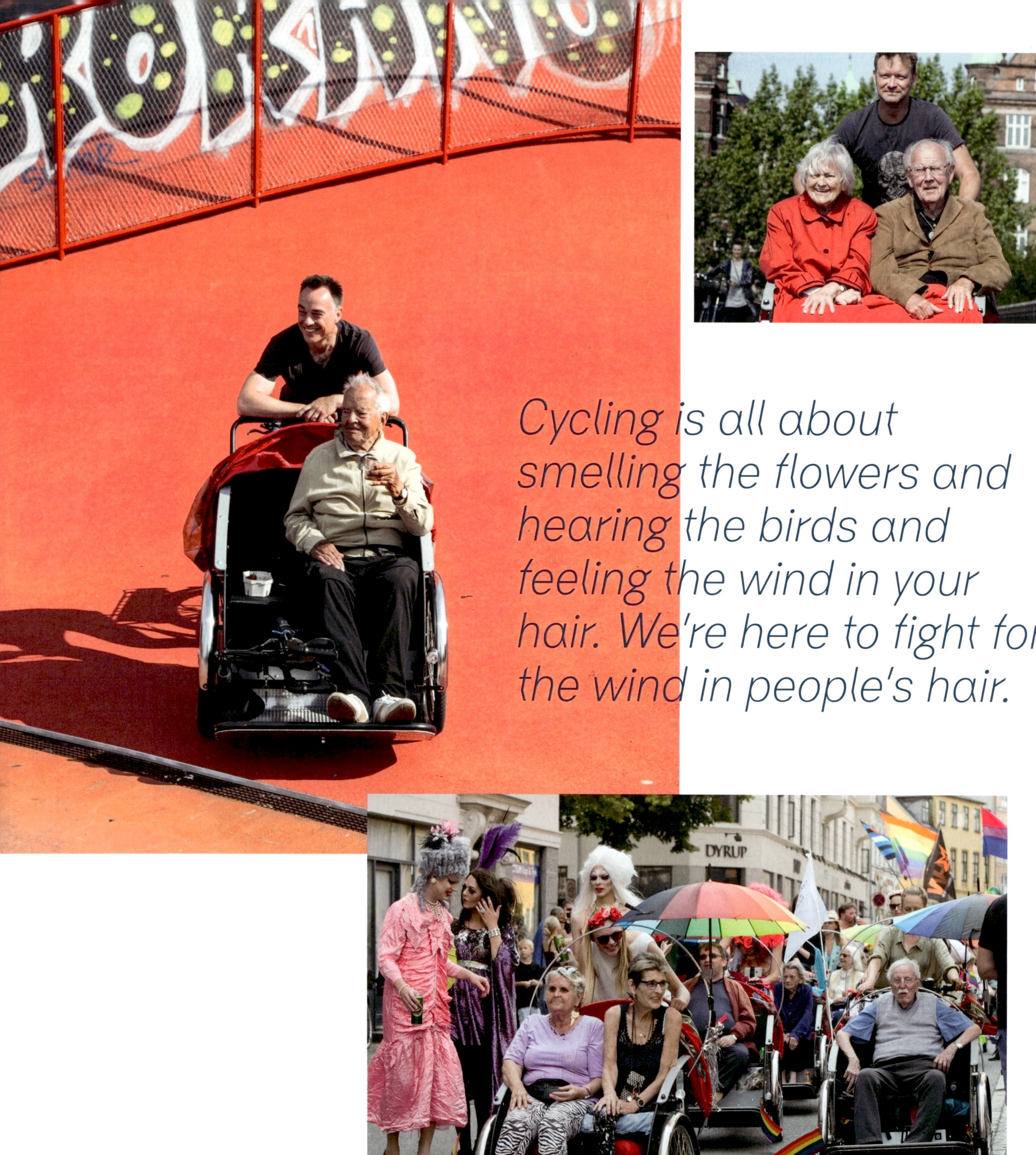


*Cycling is all about smelling the flowers and hearing the birds and feeling the wind in your hair. We're here to fight for the wind in people's hair.*

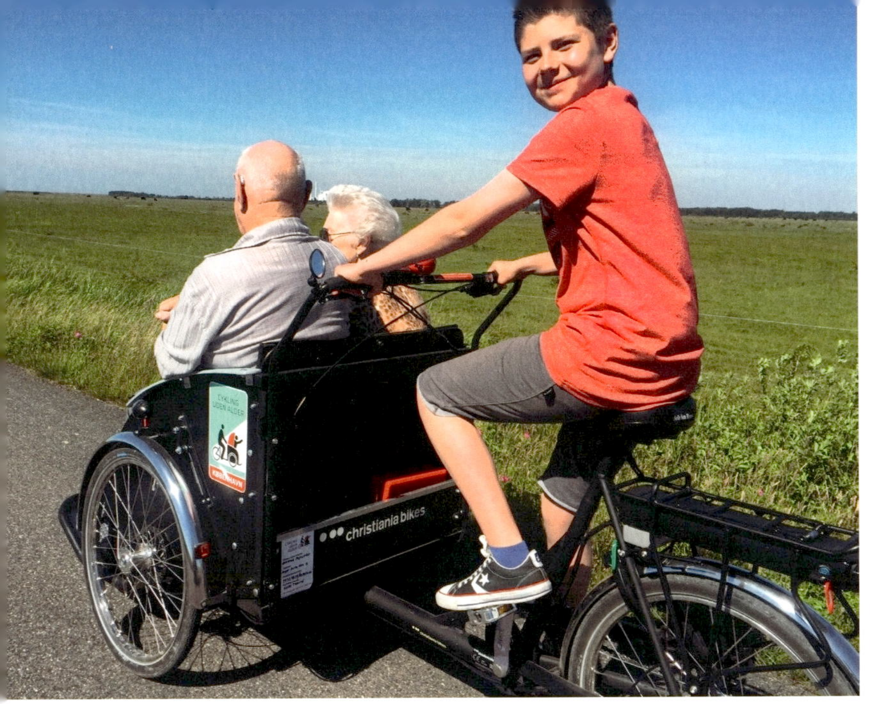
christiania bikes

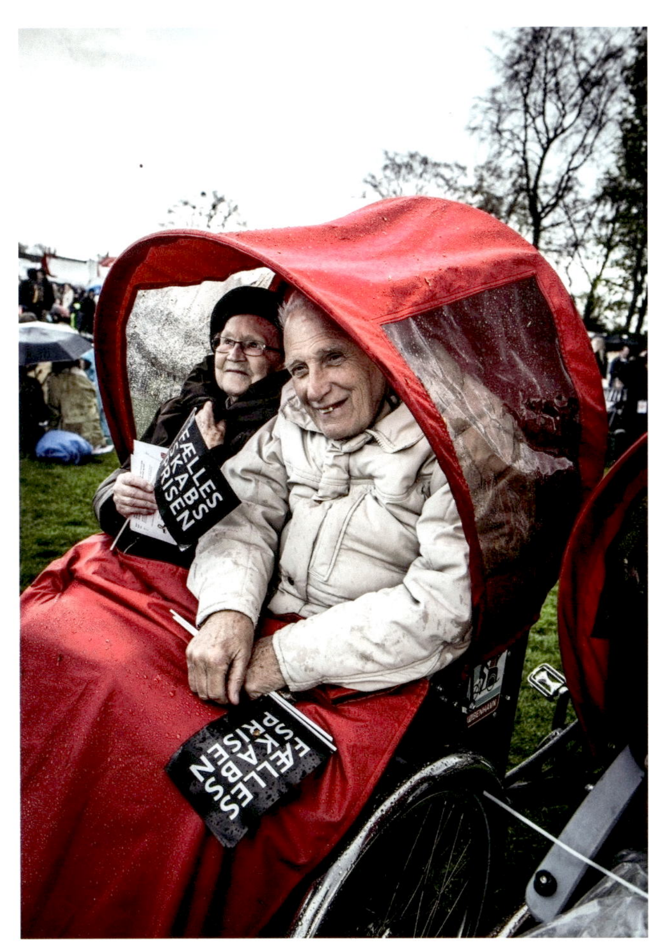

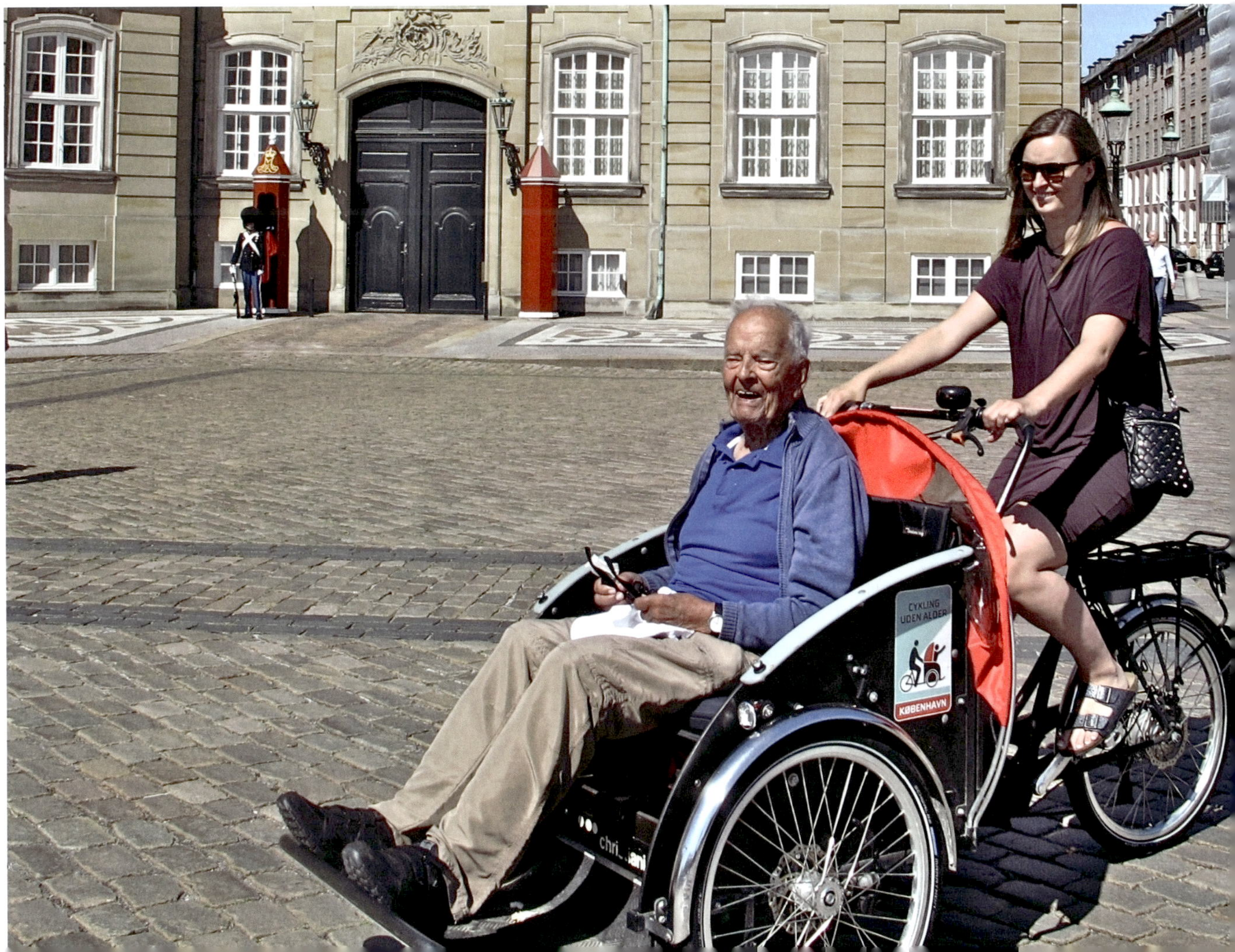

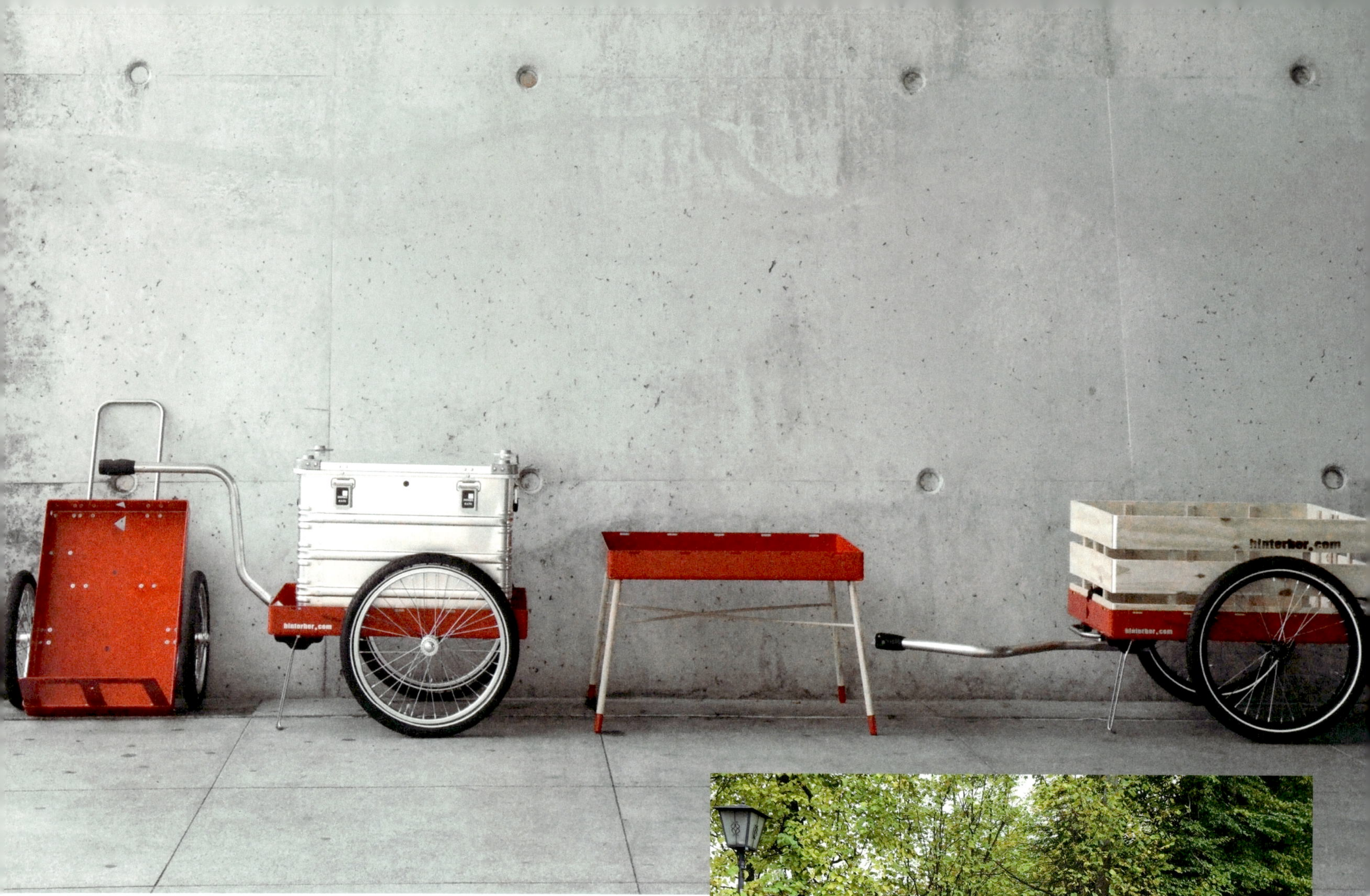

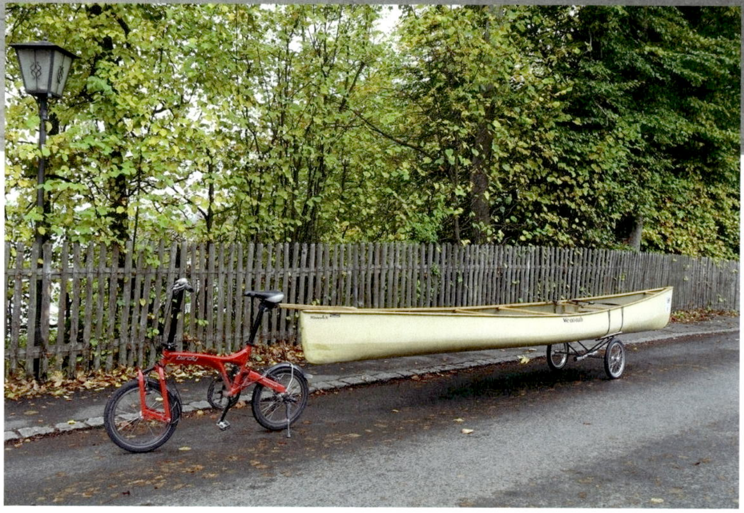

this page: **_Munich bike trailers_**

**HINTERHER**

With the Hinterher bike trailer, every bike can be transformed into a cargo bike. In only a few seconds and using just a single tool, it can be switched from a trailer to a dolly to a handcart to a backpack trailer or even a shopping cart. When not needed, the Hinterher folds down for easy storage. Perfect for families or professionals, its aluminum chassis is durable and completely recyclable—a contribution to the movement for sustainable transportation. Made with high-quality materials, it is produced regionally and with a completely modular concept.

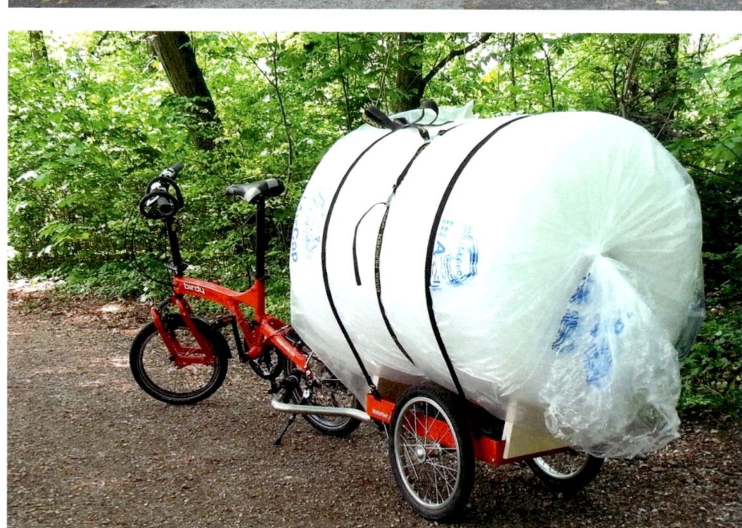

opposite page: **_Lastenrad_**

**KOLB RAHMENBAU**

Kolb Rahmenbau's custom-made cargo bike features a space-saving, foldable front rack and a double front-wheel stand.

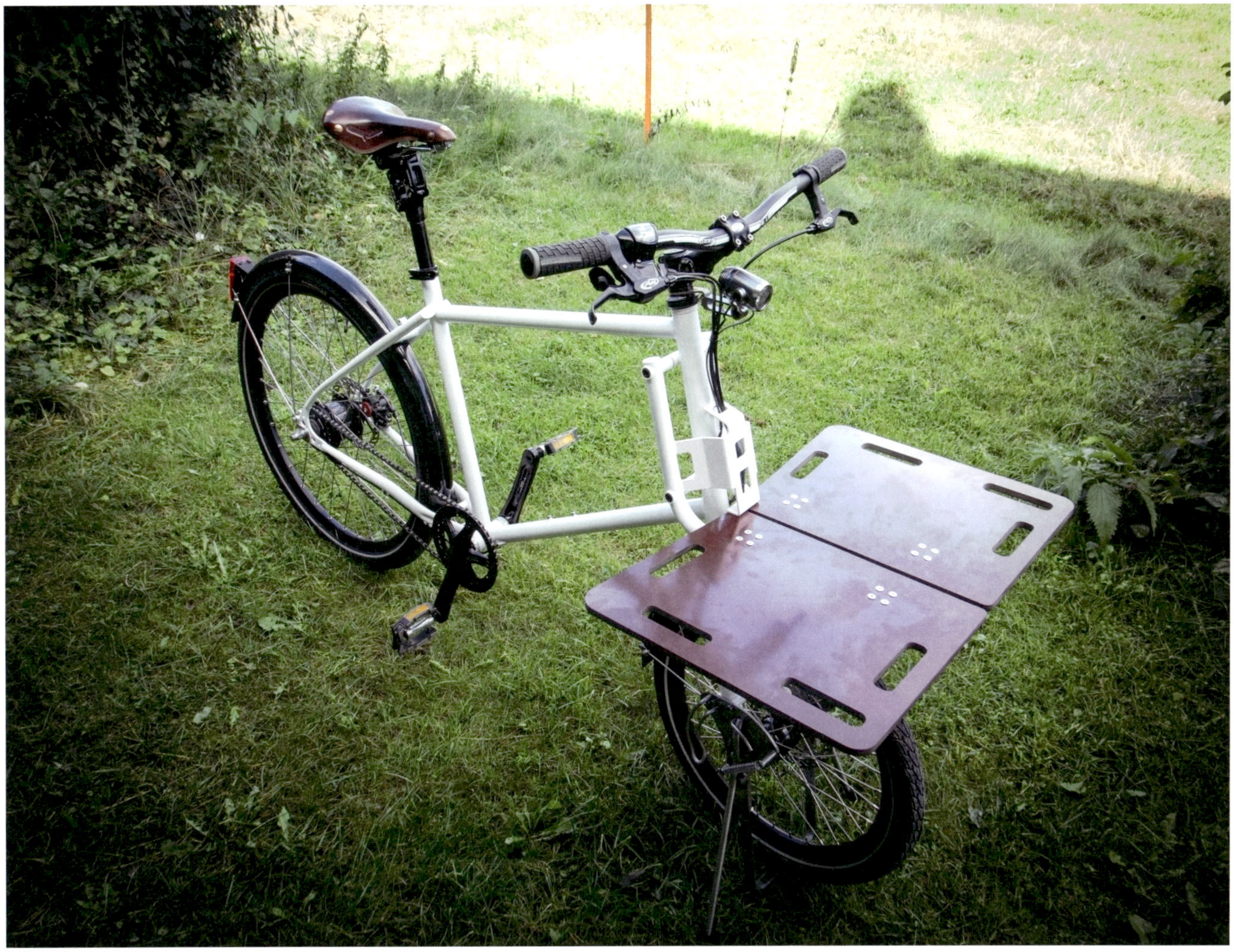

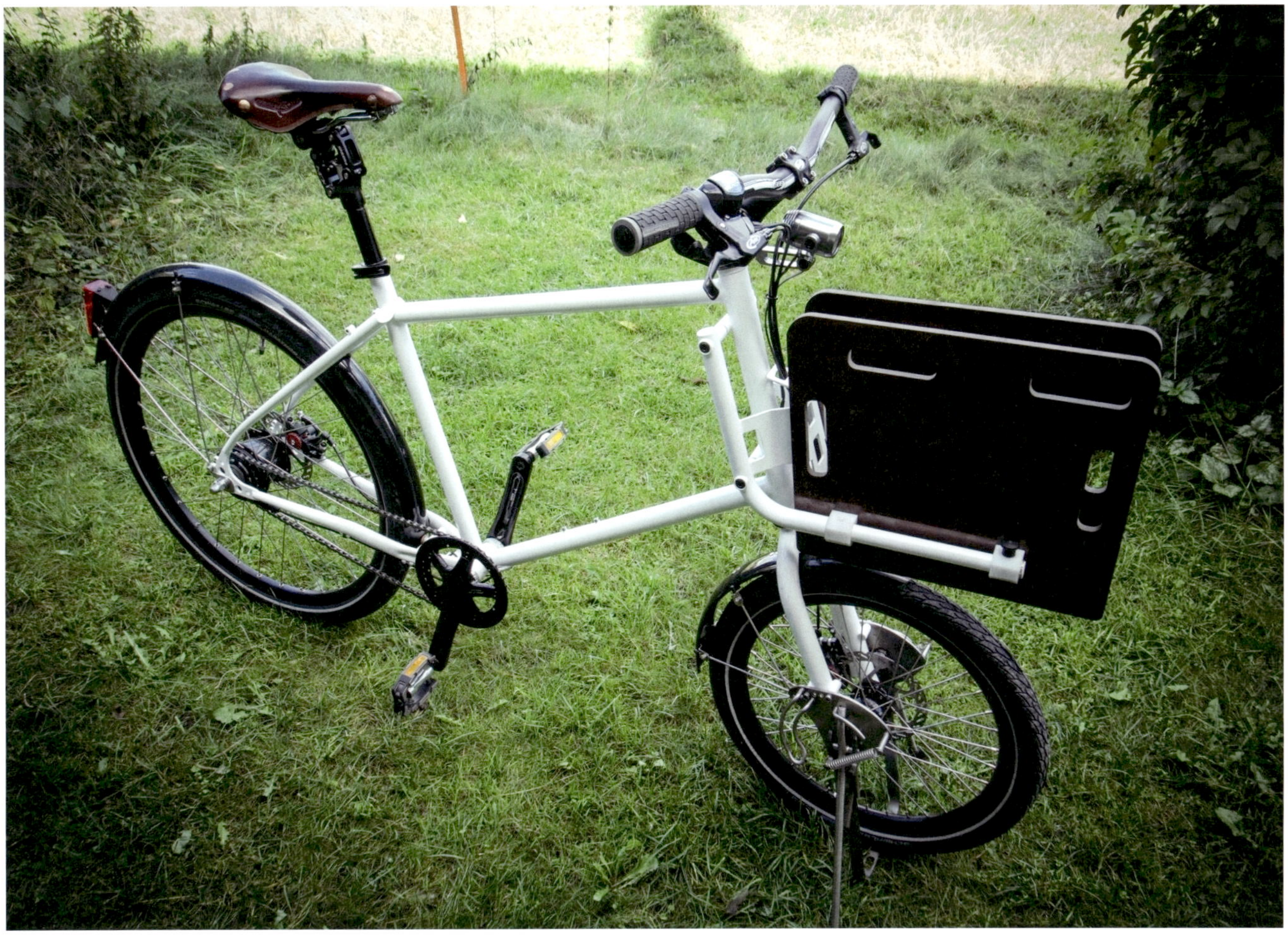

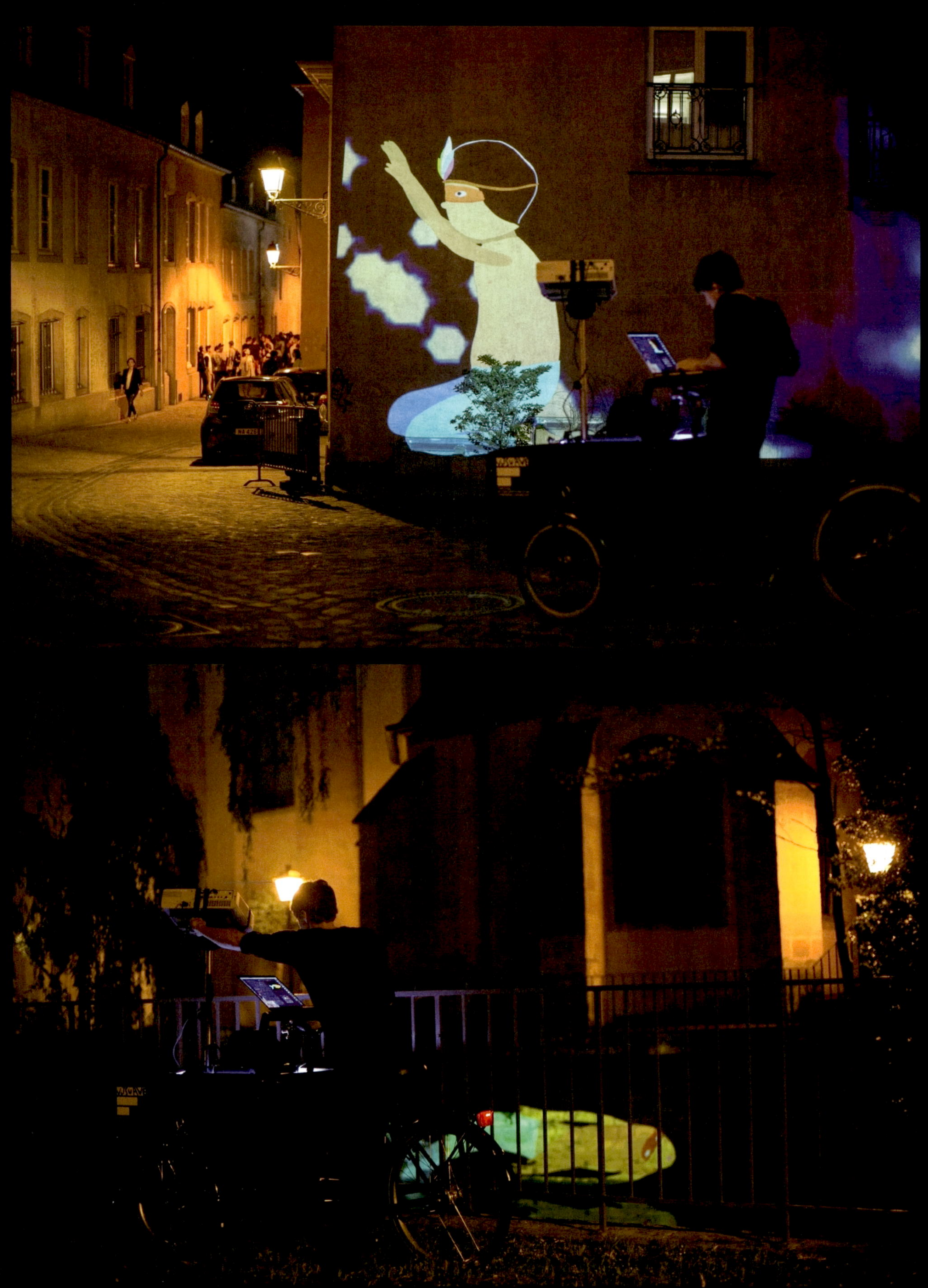

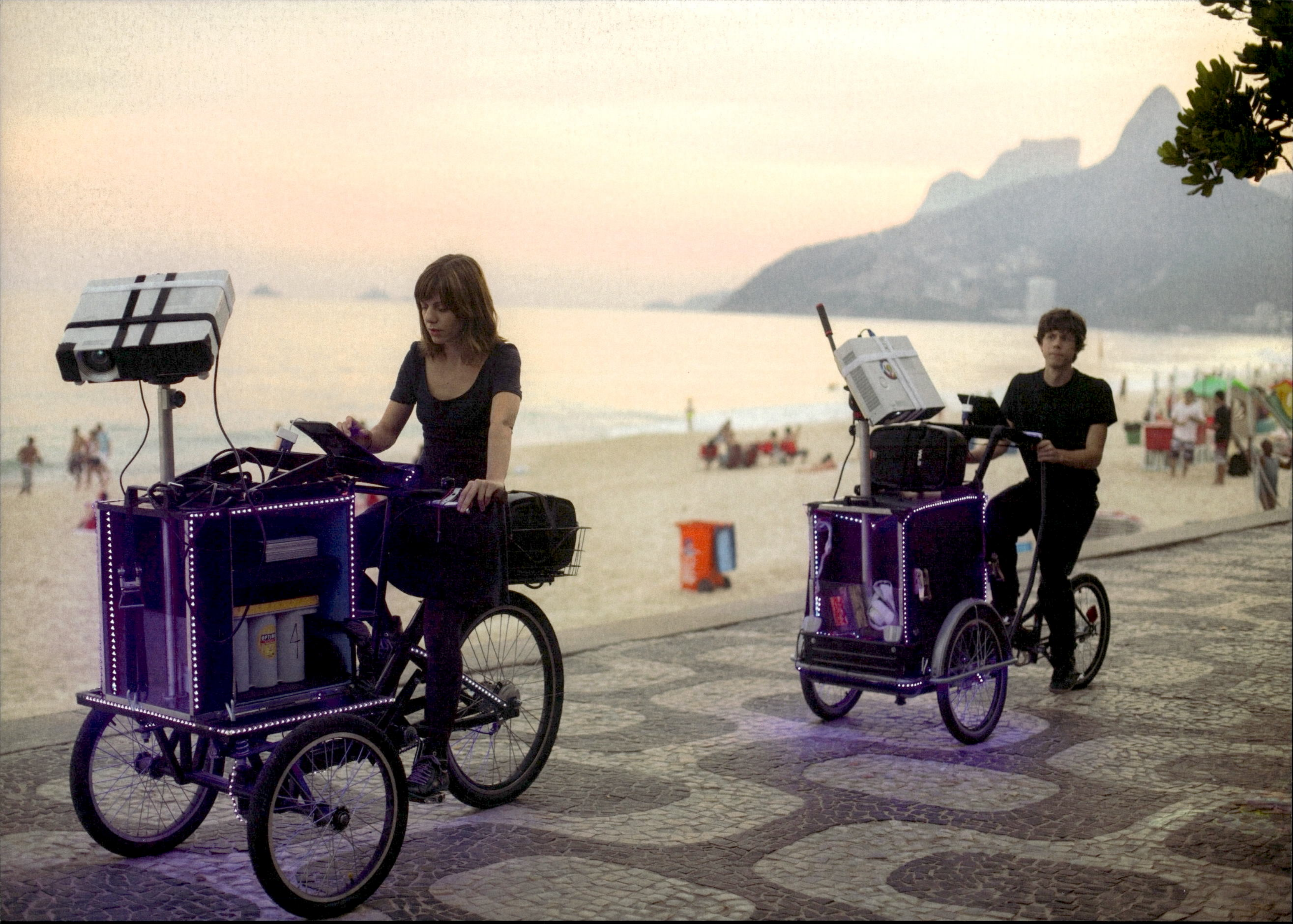

# Suaveciclo

**VJ SUAVE**

Cycling meets art in this project by the São Paulo-based new-media art duo VJ Suave, a.k.a Ygor Marotta and Ceci Soloaga. Using two audiovisual tricycles called Suaveciclos, each equipped with computers, projectors, speakers, and batteries, the pair projects traditional animation onto the city around them, creating videos manipulated in real time that run wild across the urban landscape. Their playful universe often deals with current issues, including four short urban projections entitled "Run," "Homeless," "La Cena," and "Trip," all of which have been presented in a variety of venues and media, including the Reina Sofia Museum, *Wired* magazine, the Japan Broadcasting Corporation, and MTV. The project has also been included in film and music festivals in Russia, Germany, Luxembourg, and Slovakia.

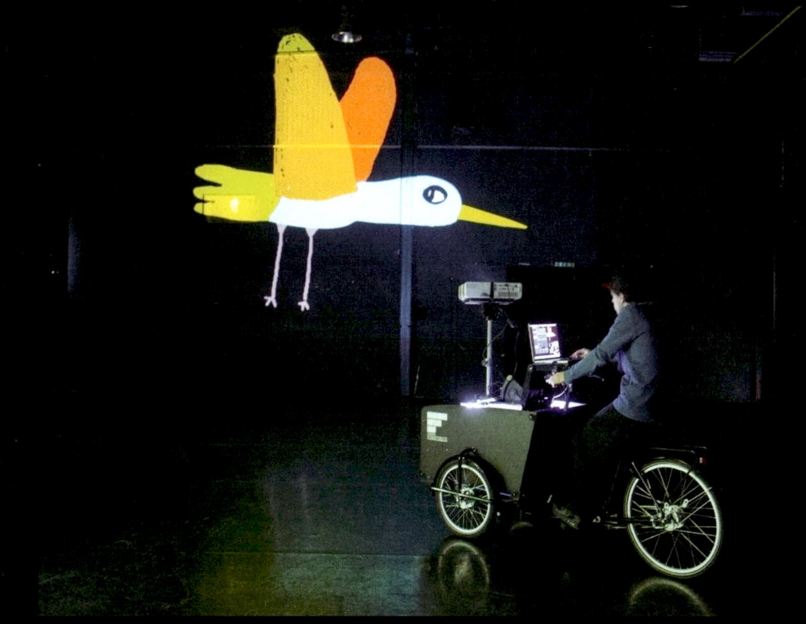

# Navigation

Remember biking with one hand on your phone to see where you were—or just guessing in strong sunlight or pouring rain? Navigation is ever more sophisticated, and with Bluetooth and phone-connected tools for getting around—often built into the bars and steering tubes—you can find out more than just where you are. Once upon a time, there was griptape. Today? There are smart grips.

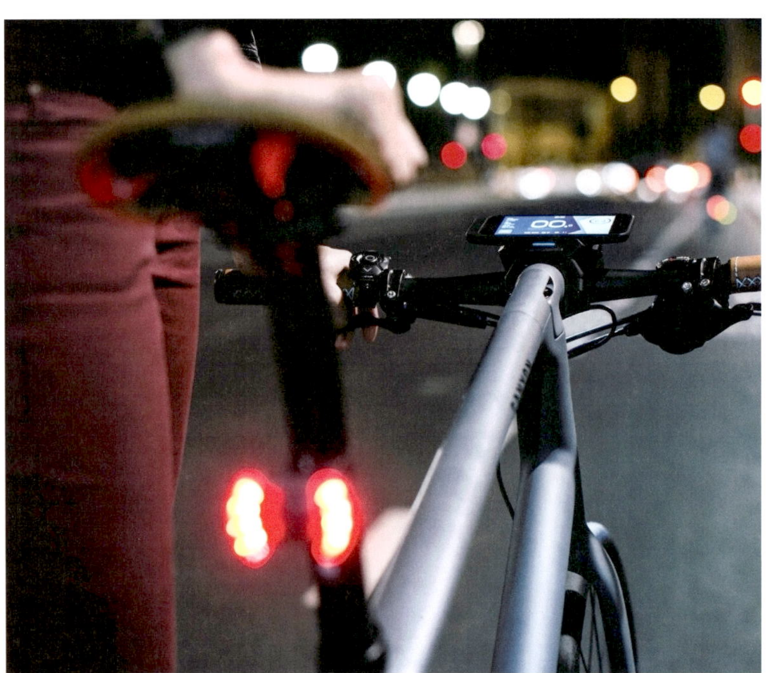

## COBI

Cobi is an acronym that stands for Connected Biking. This innovation is among the first integrated systems capable of intelligently linking a smartphone to a bicycle. The upshot: every bike, with or without an electric drive, can be transformed into a smart bike (even if the Cobi cannot actually raise a bicycle's IQ). The Cobi is a handlebar-mounted modular system that integrates six discrete accessories into a single compact design: dynamic front and rear lights, a navigation system, a smartphone holder with charging functionality, a bell, an alarm, and a bike computer. The technology, created by an in-house team directed by lead visual designer Paul Svoboda, can make riders smarter and bicycling safer and, because its six-part package forms the basis for more than 100 features, it may even change the biking experience for good.

## SmartHalo

### CYCLELABS

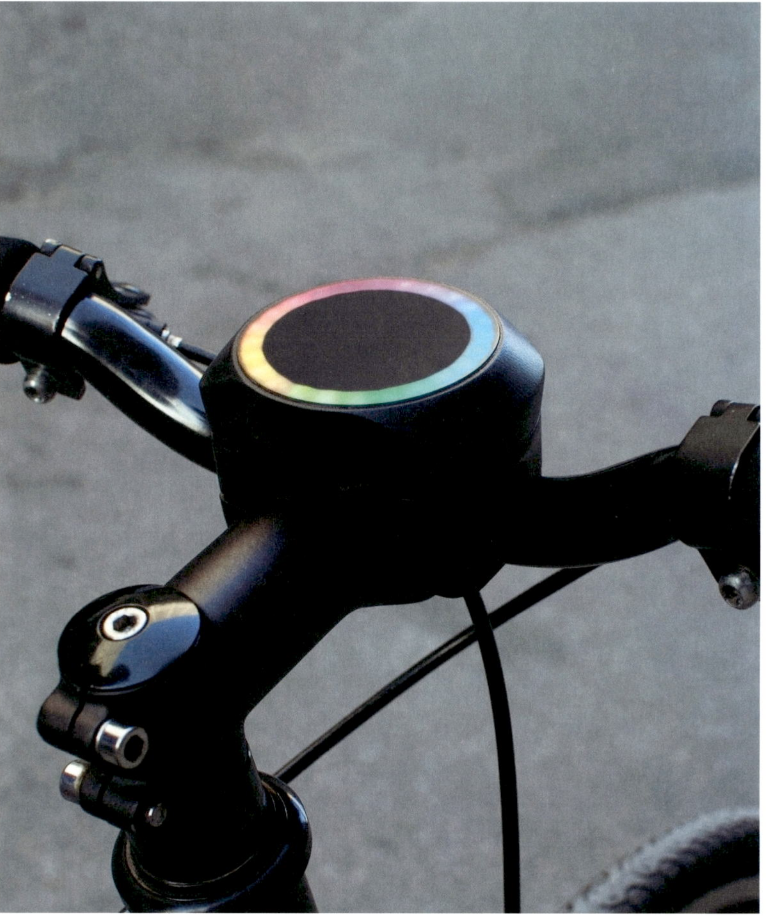

SmartHalo is a handsomely minimalist smart biking device with a pretty rainbow-lit dial designed for city cyclists who need to know where they are going and want to get there in one happy piece. Made by Montreal-based CycleLabs, its intuitive navigation system maps the quickest, safest routes to riders' destinations while saving their biking metrics with its automatic tracking capabilities. The device also features a powerful front light for illuminating night routes. When a rider's bike is parked, the SmartHalo ensures that it is safe from thieves: the system boasts a military-grade locking system that guarantees that it will stay mounted to the handlebar until its owner decides to take it off.

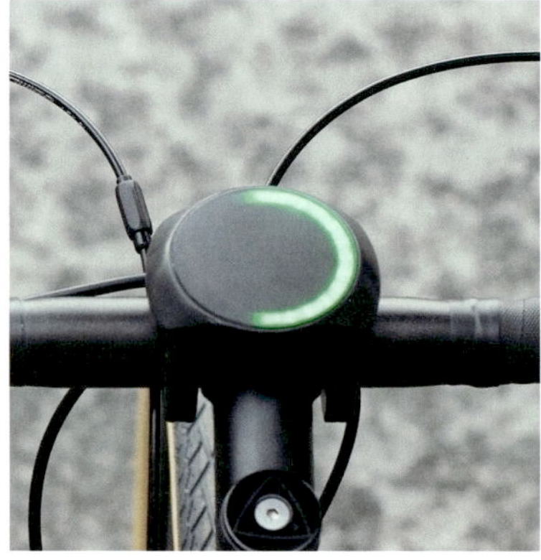

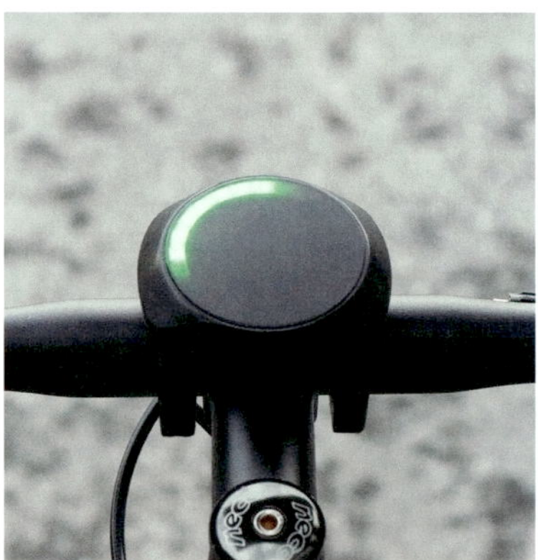

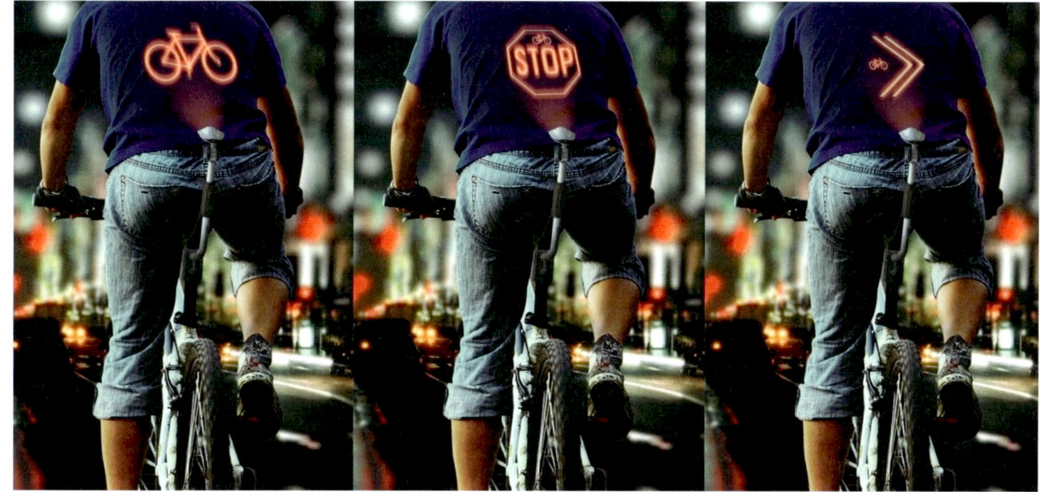


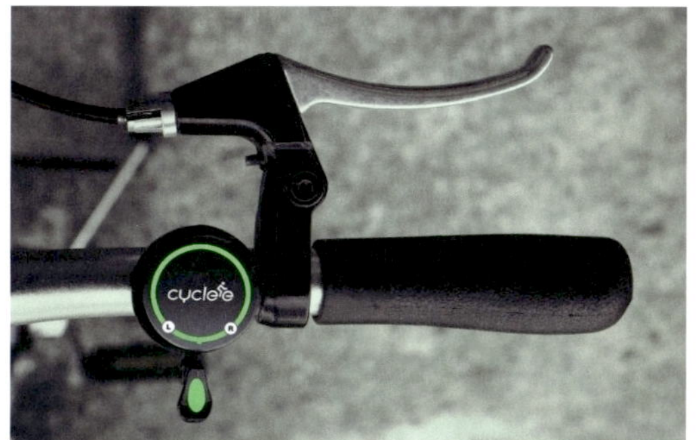


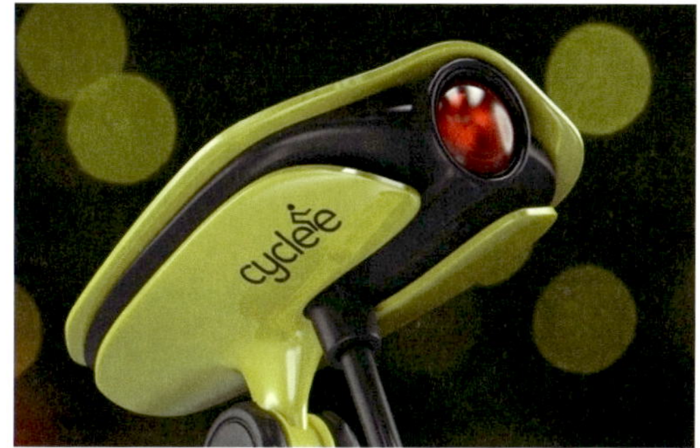


## Cyclee

ELNUR BABAYEV

The clever Cyclee system is a concept designed by Azerbaijani Elnur Babayev to project contextually relevant safety signage—STOP, a right-hand turn signal, and so forth—onto the backs of bicyclists who ride at night. Glowing soft and red like an ember, Cyclee's projections change depending on the rider's actions. Babayev's invention works with the help of a special chipset inserted into a proprietary device, making it possible to edit the entire program wirelessly and modify or even personalize the signage via a mobile application, the content of which is then uploaded to a bike-mounted device. Although the mounting component will vary depending on the bicycle being outfitted, Babayev plans to make it compatible with a variety of models.

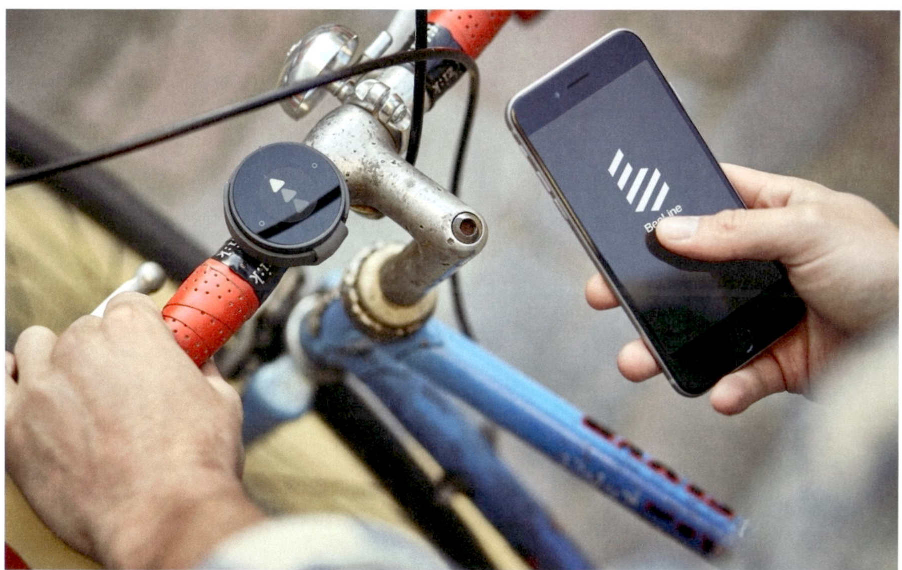


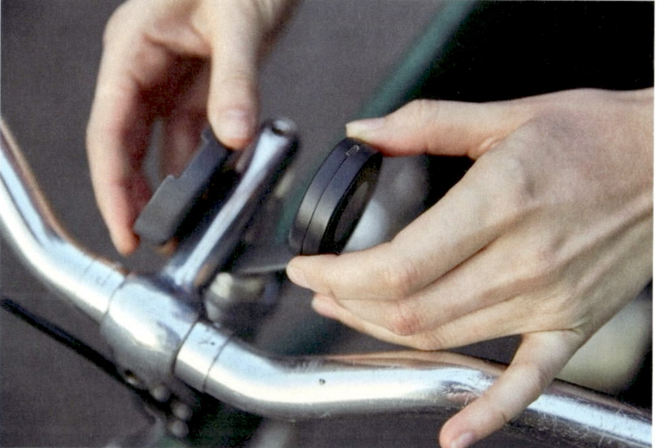

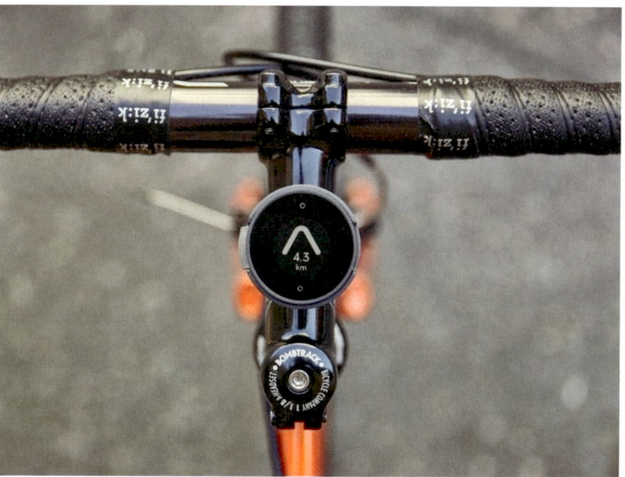


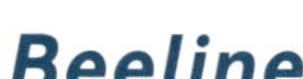

## Beeline

Founded in 2012, creative consultancy Map leads a multi-disciplinary team of industrial designers, strategists, and innovation experts who use designer-led analysis, observation, and research to produce compelling and beautiful products. Instead of a prescribed route, Beeline believes that a sense of direction is all that's required to keep a cyclist homing in on their destination. Their handlebar-mounted device strips navigation back to the bare basics, turning convention completely on its head and allowing natural instinct to take a front seat by pointing any cyclist in the right direction like a smart compass, allowing them to decide which turns to make. Controlled by smartphone, Beeline is simple to use, intuitive, and affordable.

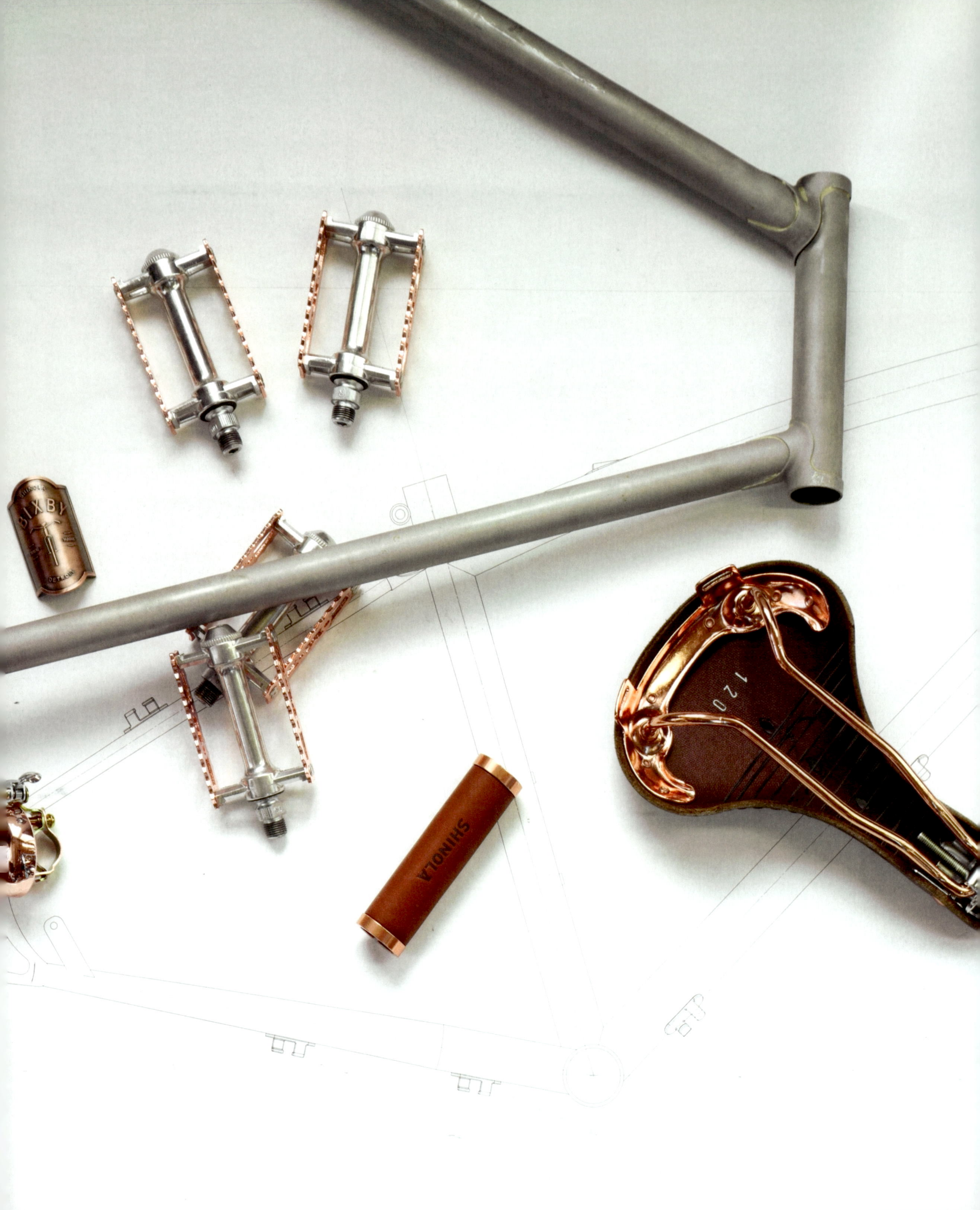
BIXBY
SHINOLA
120

# Shinola + Sky Yaeger

Detroit may no longer be the Motor City, but it still has wheels. The former automaking capital of America is now home to more than 170 miles of bike lanes—and to Shinola.

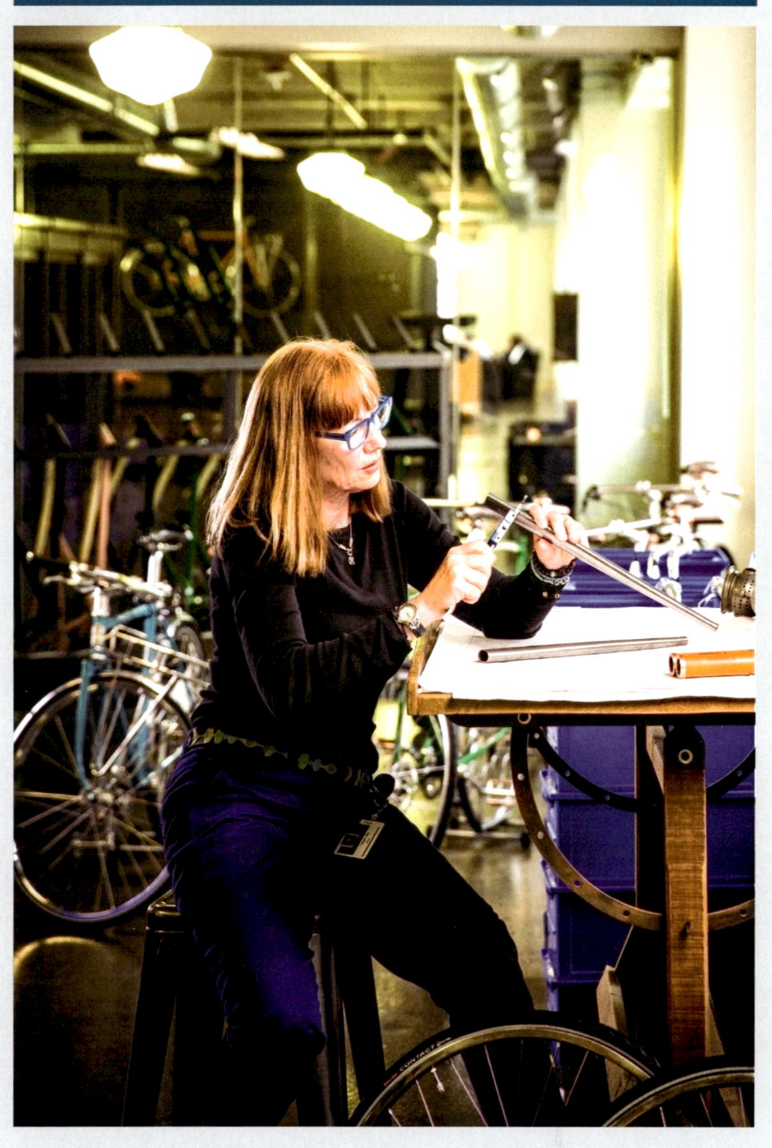

Shinola's bike designer Sky Yaeger, an innovative industry veteran

The four-year-old luxury brand, known for its fancy watches and its efforts to revive U. S. manufacturing, has moved to Detroit, and not just to make watches. The same craftsmanship and classic detailing that go into its timepieces are now being brought to bear on its bikes.

At a time when almost all American bicycle production had moved to China and Taiwan, Shinola made the decision to manufacture all of their products domestically in the USA. To lead the new bike team, the company tapped Sky Yaeger, whose past work included developing bikes for both Bianchi and Swobo.

Yaeger sometimes creates Shinola bikes designed in concert with Shinola watchmakers or partners with heritage brands like Wright Brothers and Filson to create special edition bike-and-wristwatch pairings, meaning that the detailing on the watches will match that of the bike components. "We've just sold out of a special Detroit Lions Limited Edition Arrow model," Yaeger says, "and we've made custom bikes for the Detroit Police Department, for patrolling Midtown, where our flagship store is located."

Shinola's greatest legacy may be its contribution to a new tradition of American artisanal frame-buildering. As a company, its commitment to building frames domestically directly stimulates job creation in America; wheels are manufactured in California, frames are crafted at Waterford Precision Cycles in Wisconsin, and final assembly takes place in Detroit.

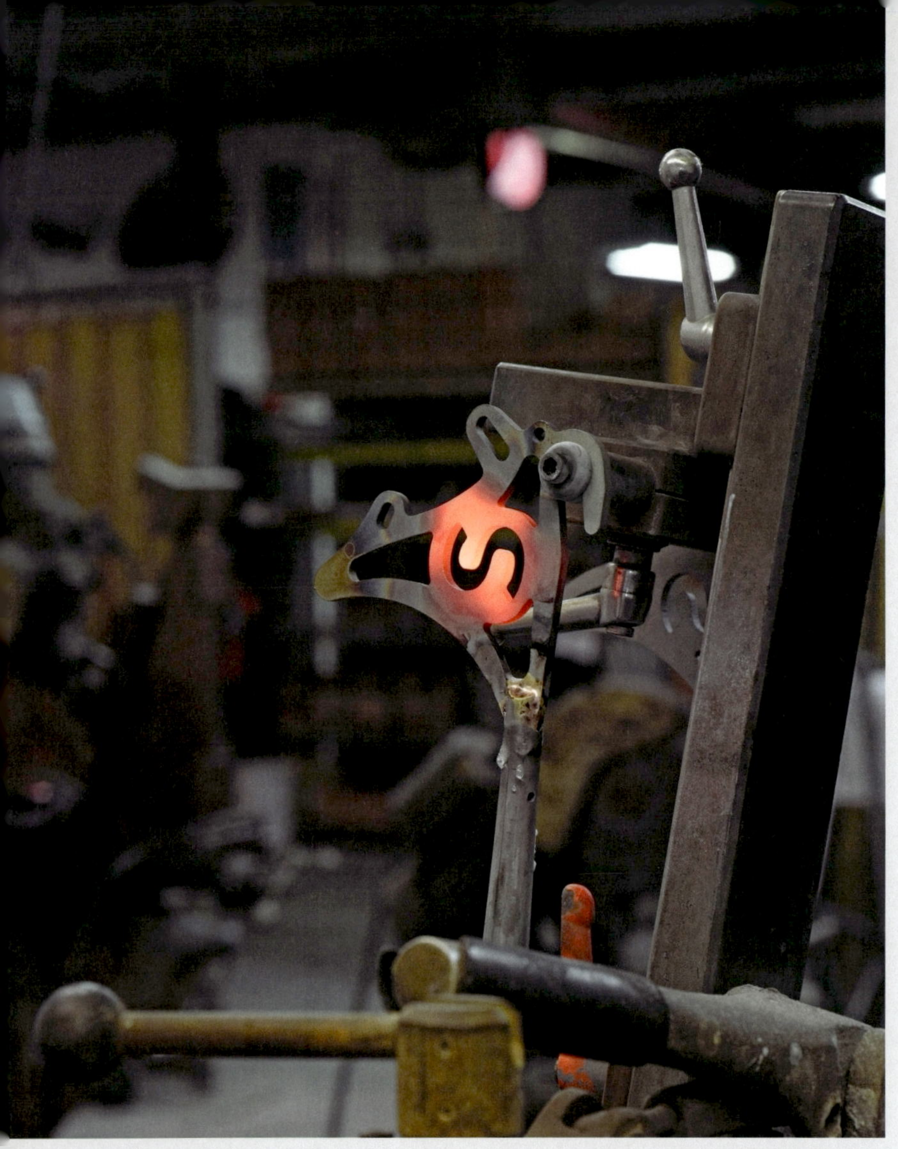

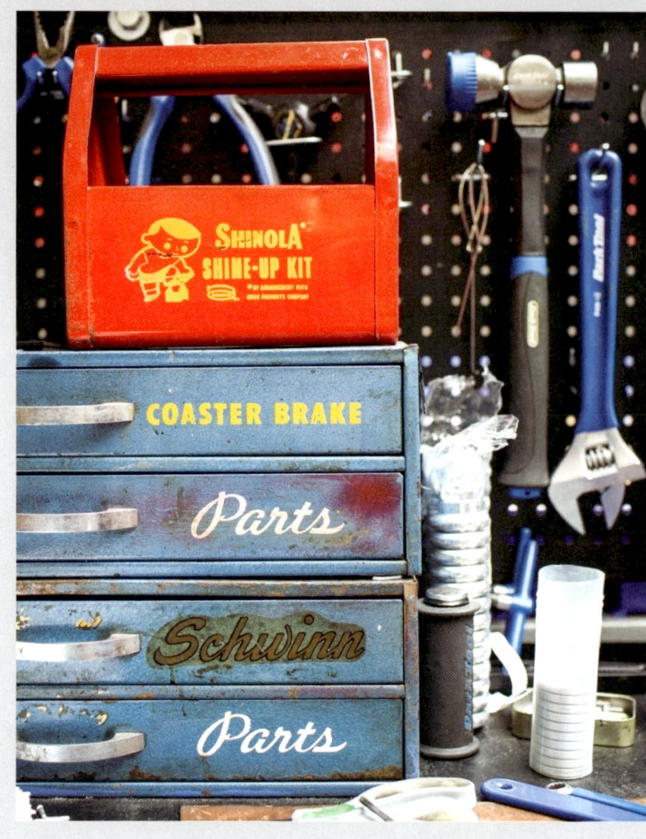


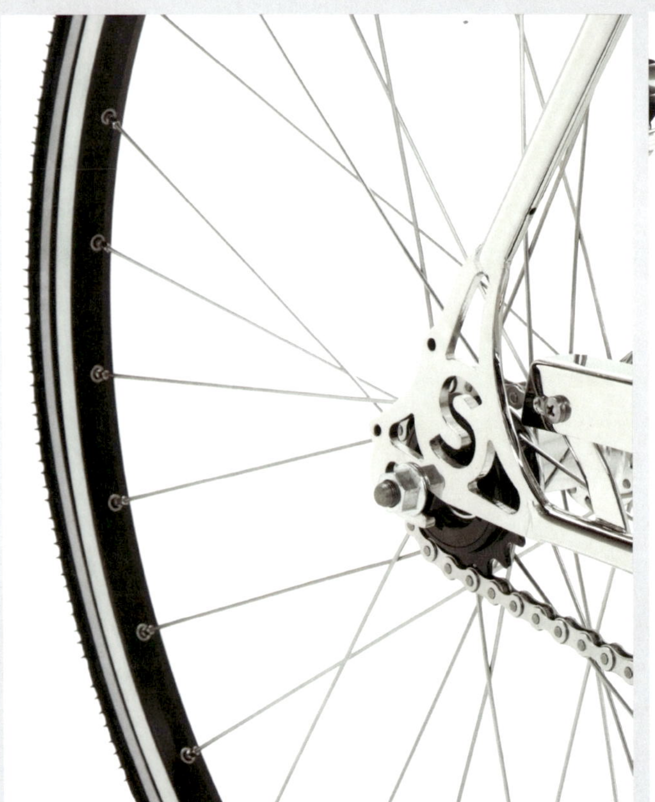

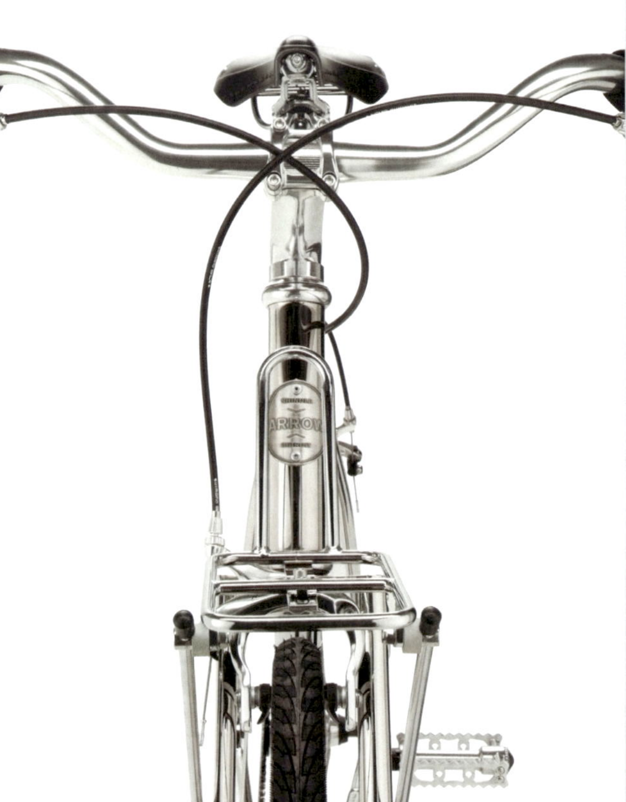

**top left:** Custom laser-cut rear dropouts feature the Shinola "S," which matches the same "S" detail cast in our proprietary fork crown.

**bottom right:** Experts individually handcraft frames and forks for the men's and women's bicycles.

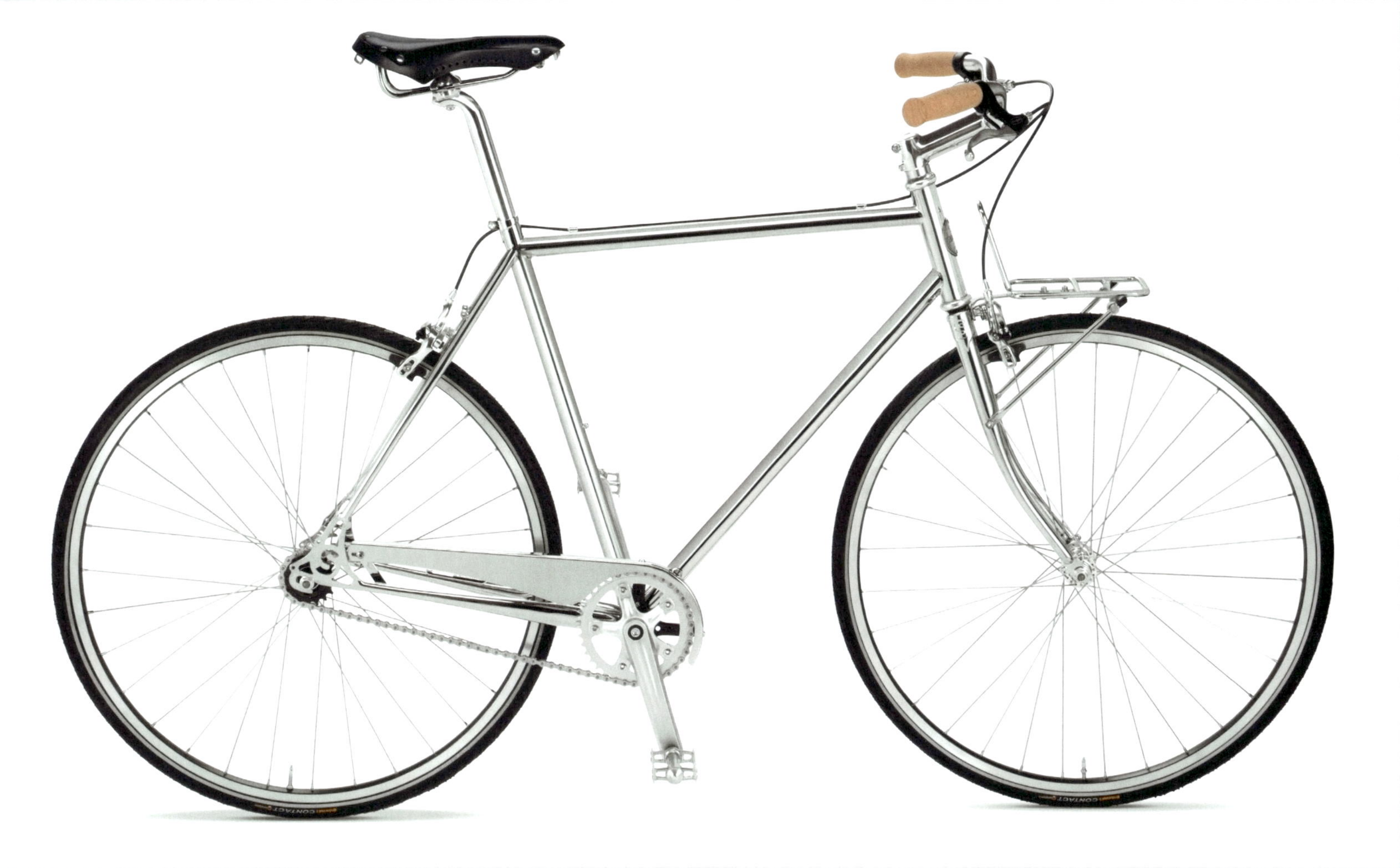

Assembling bikes by hand, particularly for small-scale production, requires an extremely skilled bike-building team. "Our assembly process starts with a bare frame and fork, in our Detroit store, out in the open for all to see," Yaeger explains. Her team cuts fork steerers, rivets on both the head badge and the chainstay badges, and then embarks on a meticulous assembly process that Yaeger describes as on par with a custom frame build. "We have a detailed assembly checklist that requires the assembler to sign off that each nut and bolt was torqued to the recommended spec," she says. "Each bike is built as if it was our own."

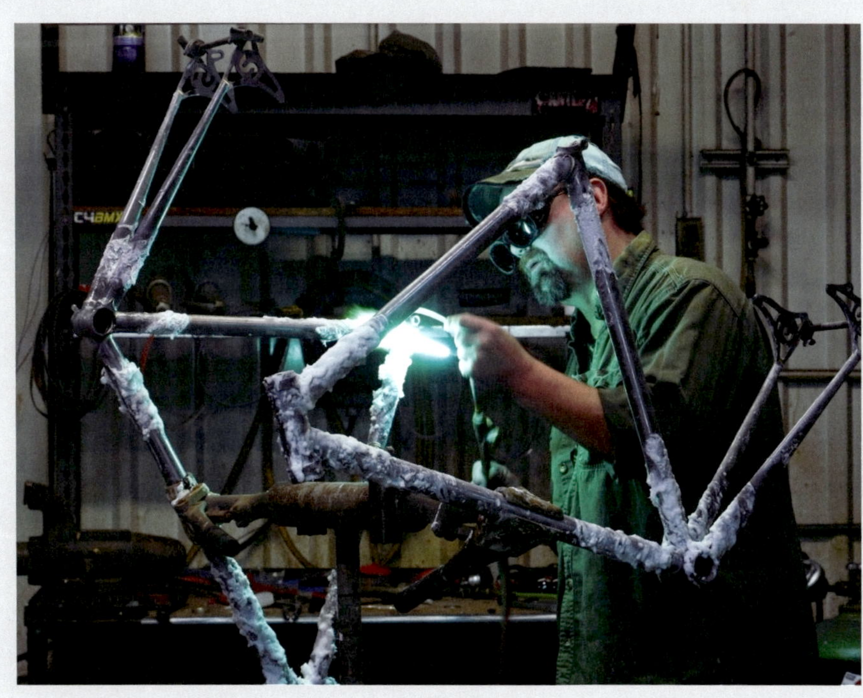

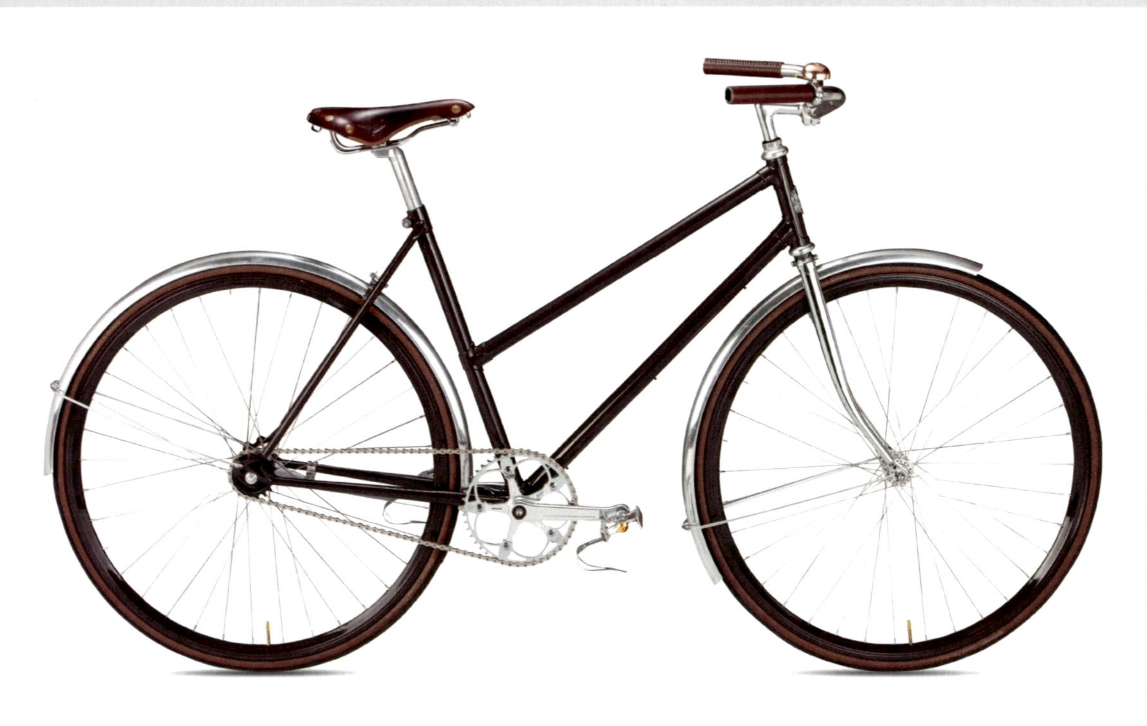

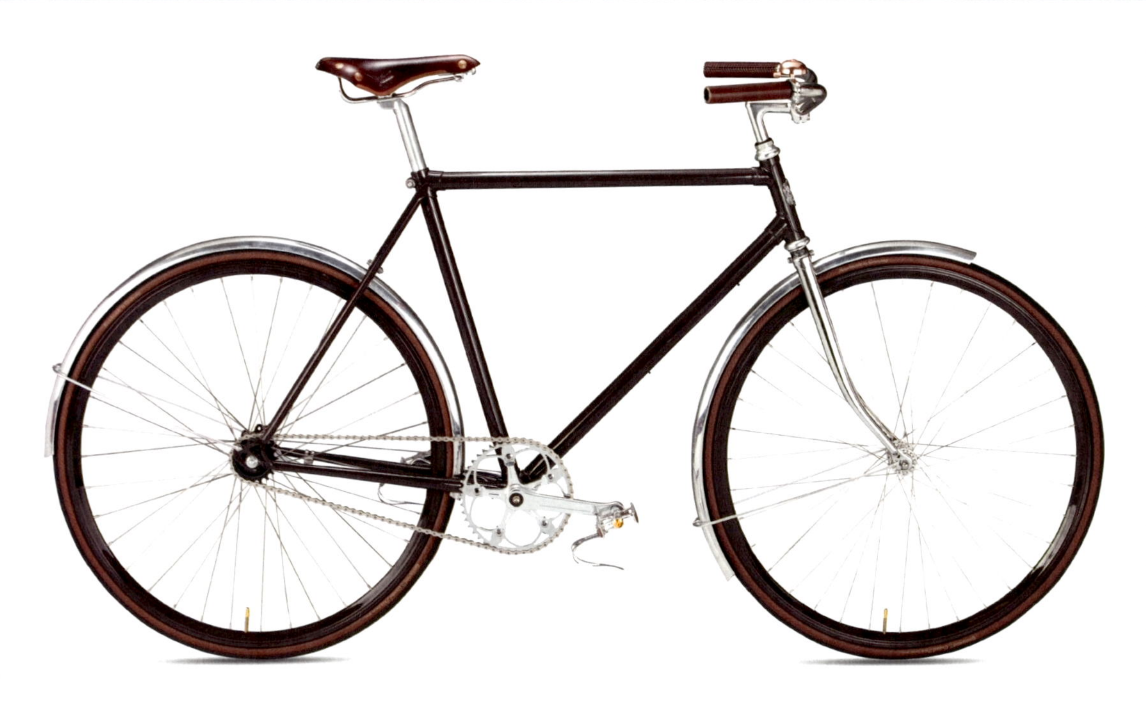

# *Velorbis*

How hard can it be to find a top-quality, classic urban bicycle with a stylish design aesthetic that reflects the elements of Danish design and Copenhagen's cycling culture? Turns out it's impossible—or was until the founders of Velorbis took matters into their own hands and built the bike they were searching for. In collaboration with Fritz Hansen, Velorbis designed the Arrow Seven 60, a modern city bike that celebrates the 60th anniversary of Arne Jacobsen's Series 7 chair. Made in Germany, it has a hand-built lugged-and-brazed frame with a Brooks leather saddle and Velorbis leather grips. The color of the frame and the wheels is bespoke Fritz Hansen brown. A final underscore to the exclusivity of the design: a range of unique features including a chromed fork, a leather nameplate, a copper bell, leather-bound toe clips, and high-gloss stainless-steel mudguards.

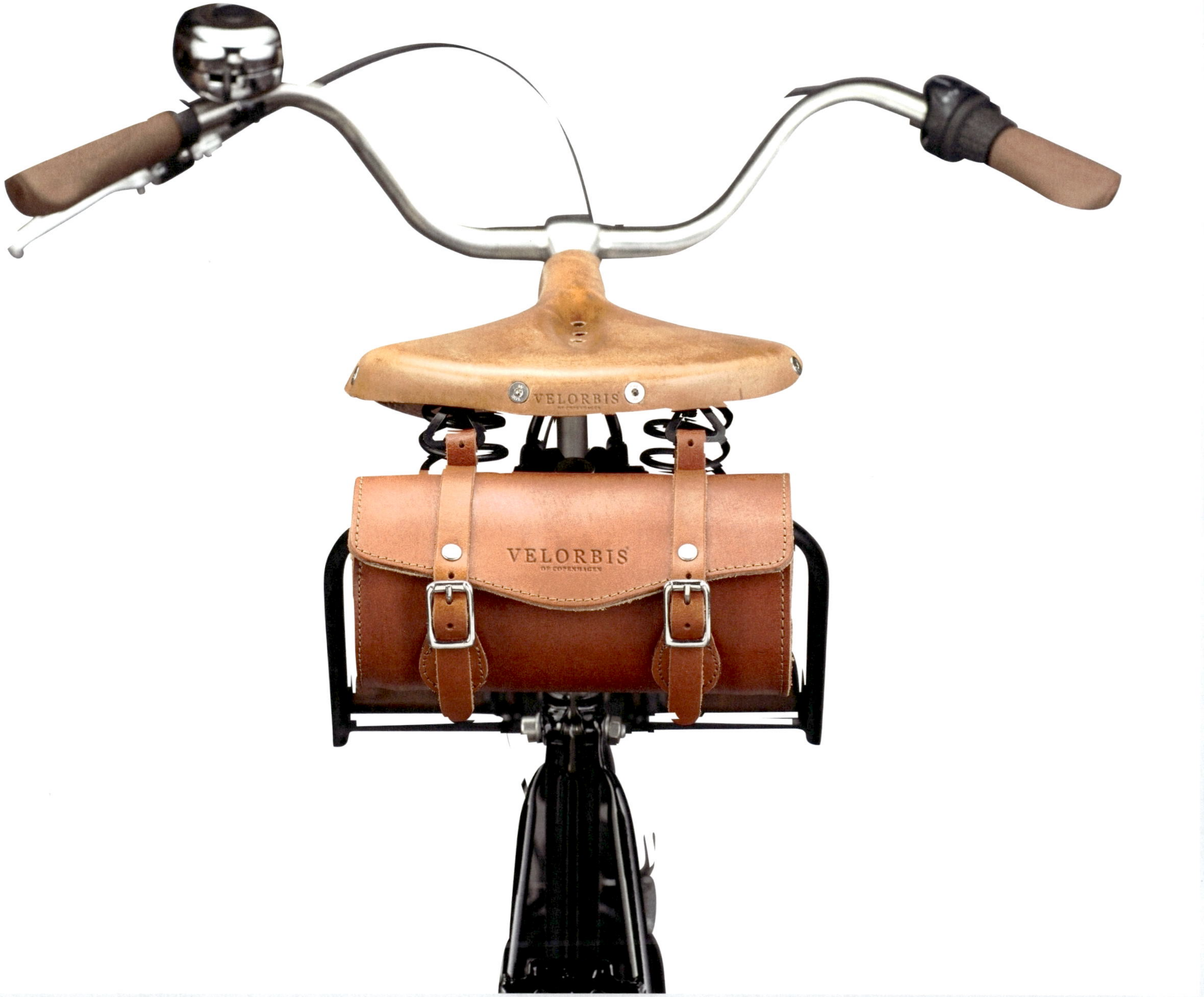

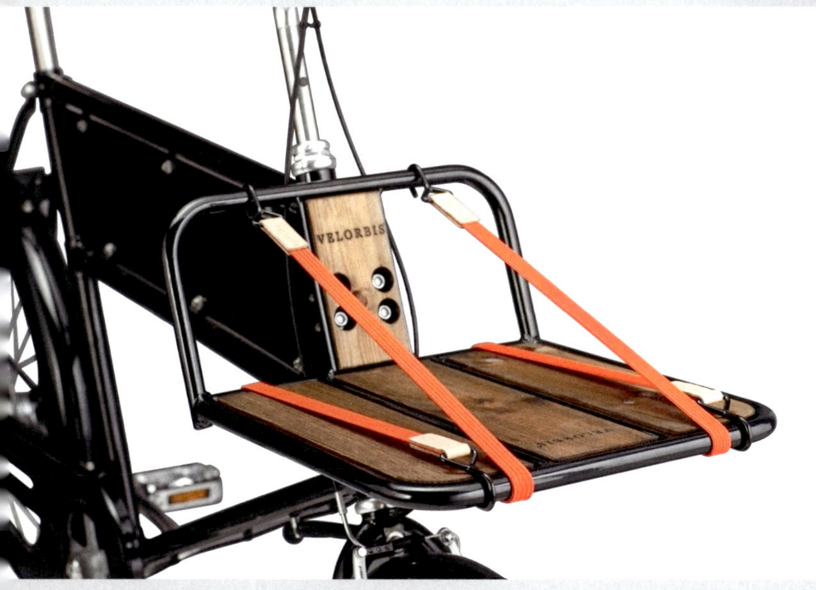
VELORBIS

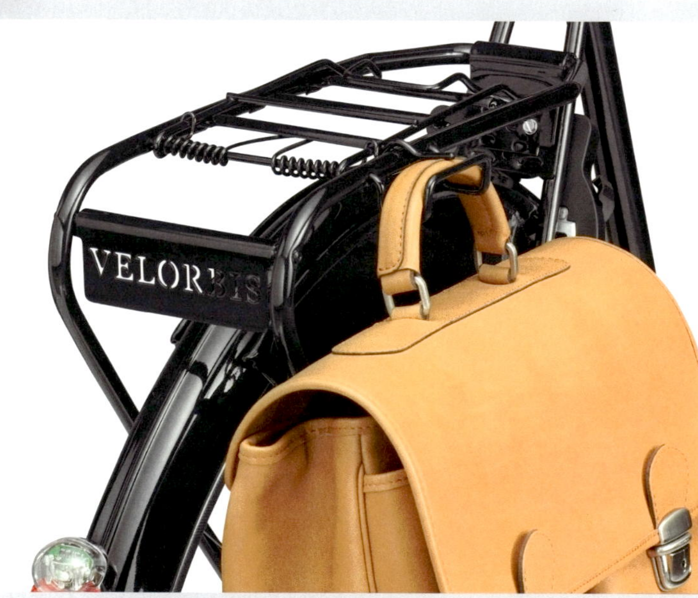
VELORBIS

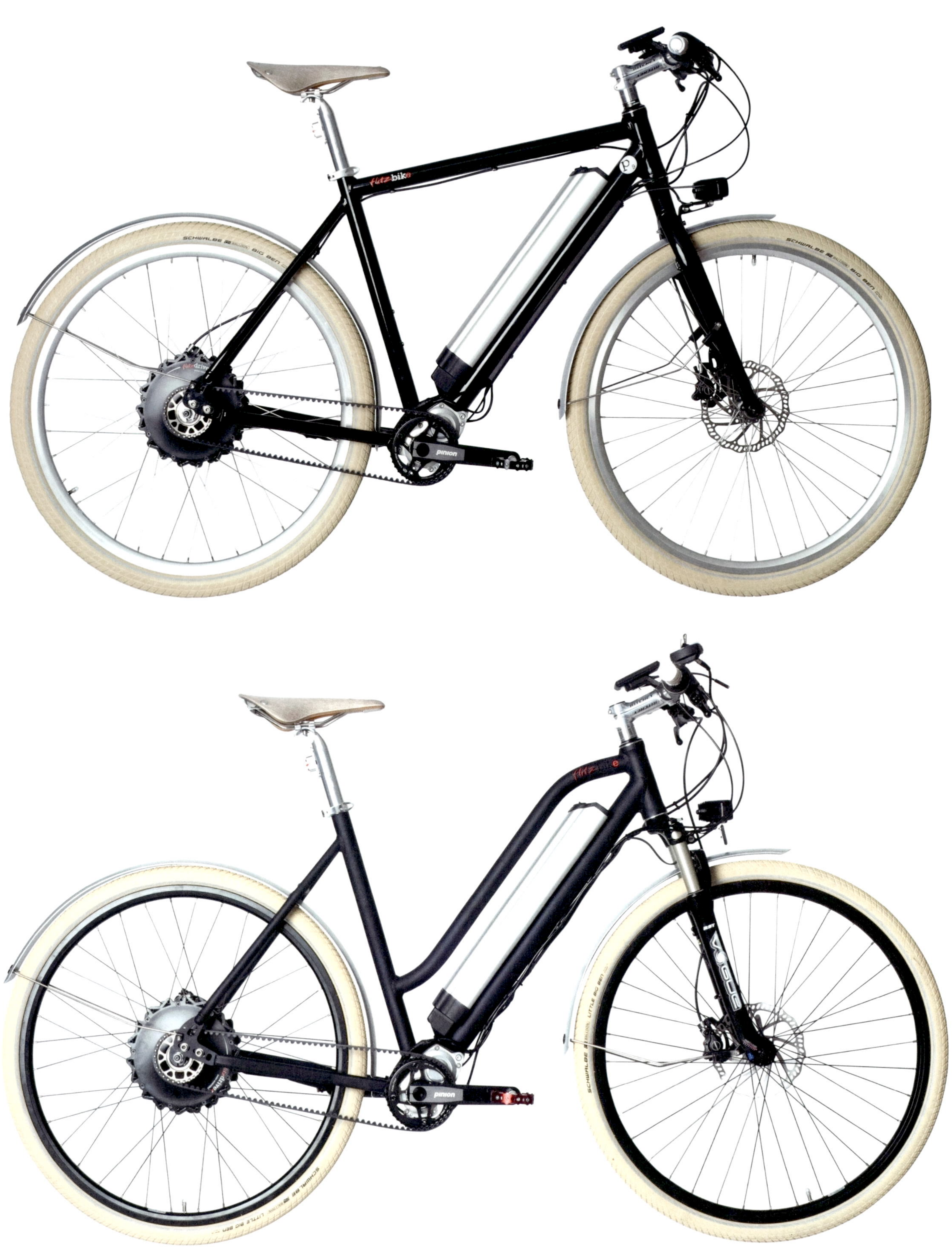
pinion
pinion

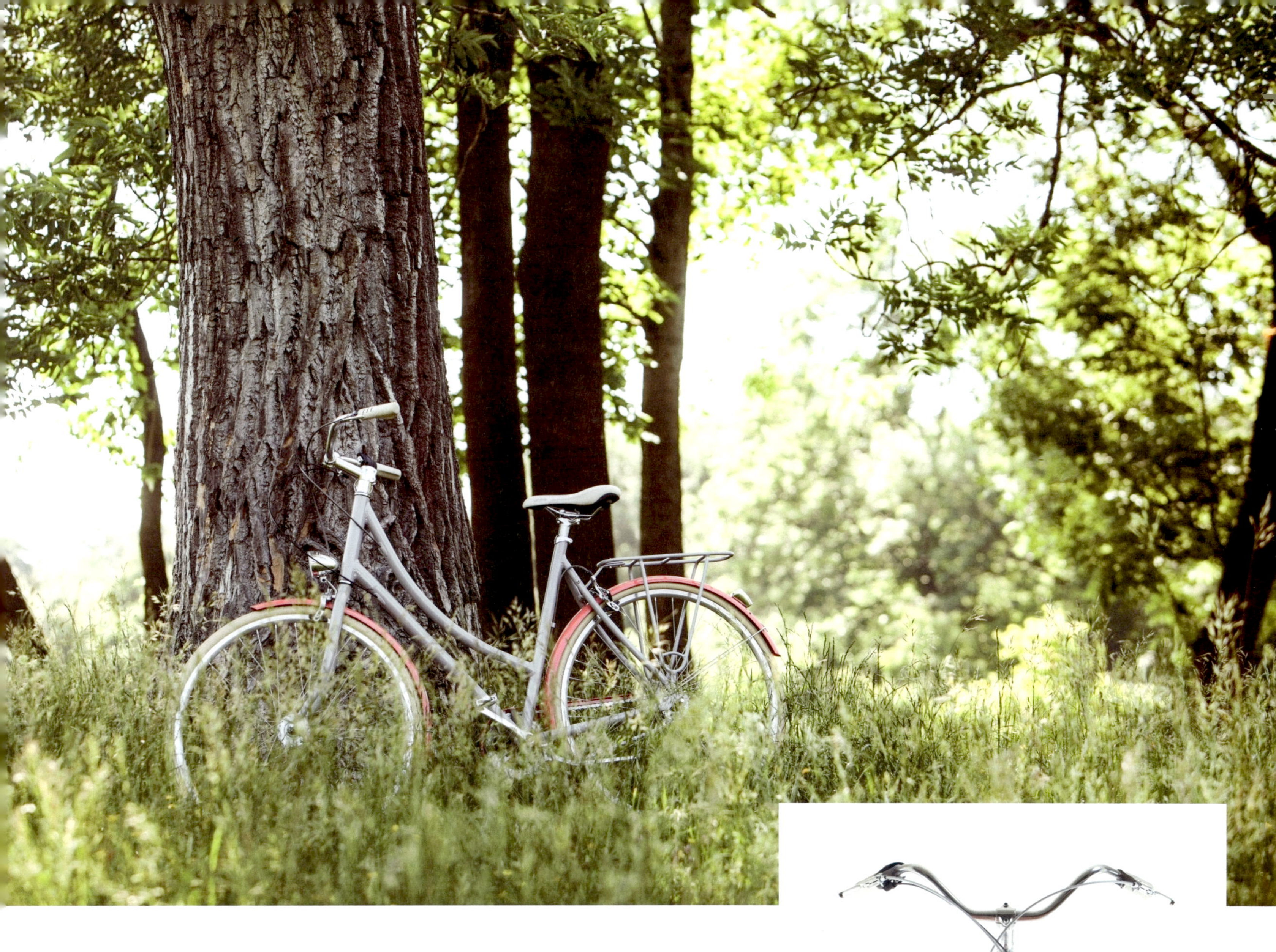

opposite page: ***P9 and the P9 COMFORT***

**FLITZ**

The days of the cumbersome electric bicycle are past. One of the points underscored by simply looking at a Flitz e-bike is that Flitz pedelec riders are not going to see their bike passing them at every turn like a Made-in-China brand: they are as uncommon (so far) as they are handsome. In fact, the P9 looks, apart from its motor, like a very sleek road bike (and, in fact, is available without a motor)—the point being that it makes little difference to the look and feel of your ride. P9s feature Pinion gearboxes, GO SwissDrive rear motors, 36-volt lithium-ion Varta Downtube batteries, barely-there mudguards, Brooks grips and seats, and blond Big Ben/Fat Frank wheels. The Comfort model also features a swoopingly graceful stepover frame.

this page: ***Porteur***

**URBIKE**

Inspired by the French paperboy bikes of the 1950s, the urbike Porteur is built to be a stable and practical commuter bike—but at only 15 kilograms, this aluminum remake is far from slow. Equipped with automatic dynamo hub lights, a reinforced luggage carrier, and a twin-point kickstand, this bike can take on the city in style. The bamboo basket inlays, genuine leather grips, and leatherette saddle give this city cruiser a touch of class. The Porteur's 700c racing-inspired tires let you sweep through the city with ease in a stylish city cruiser that is built to last.

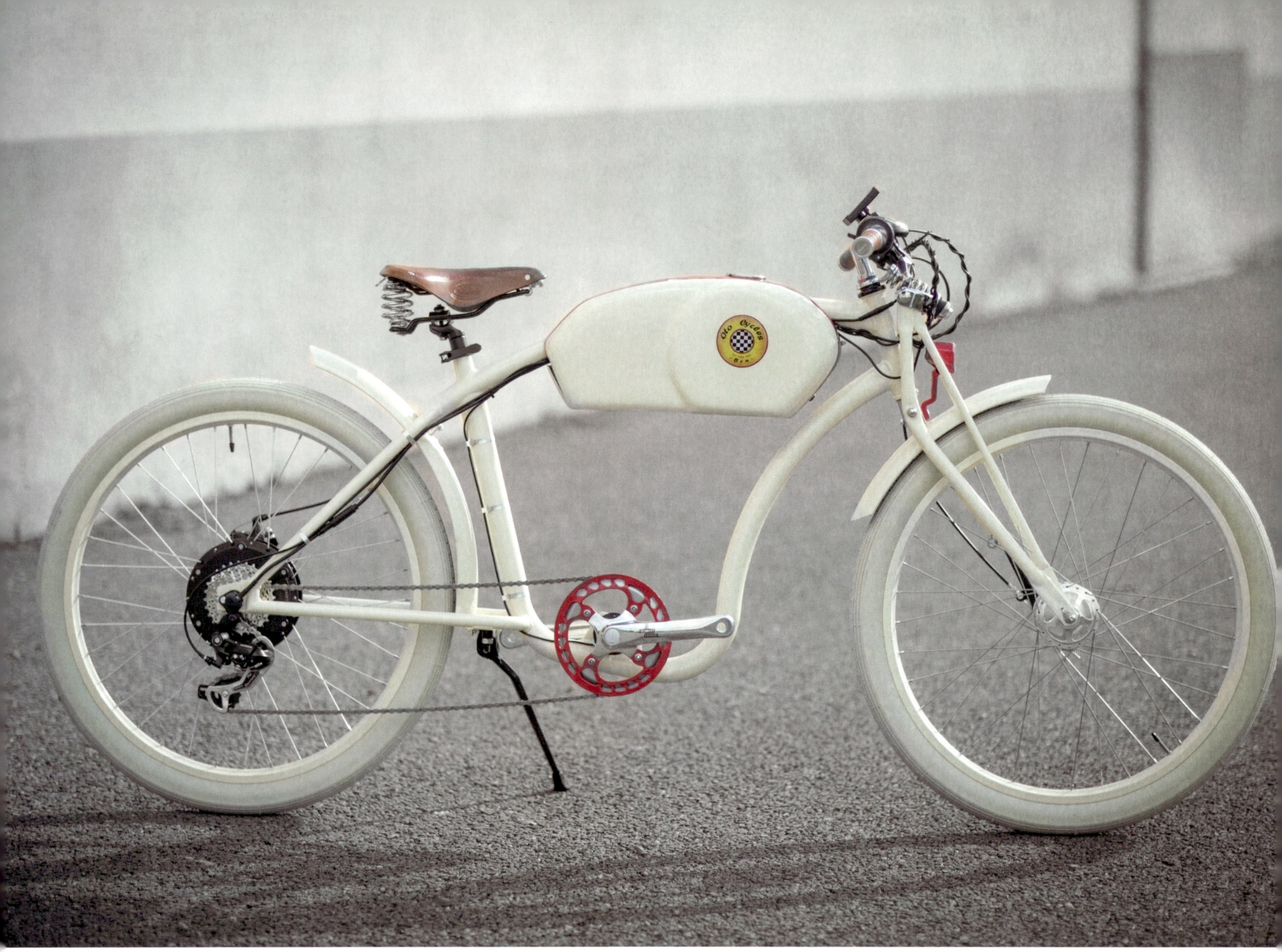

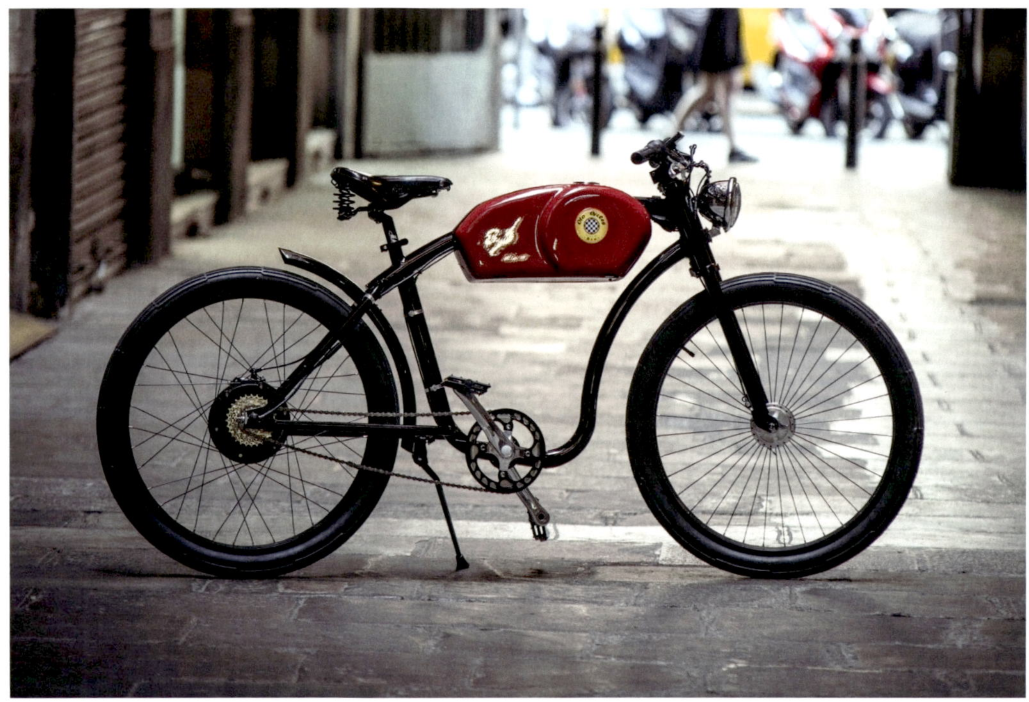

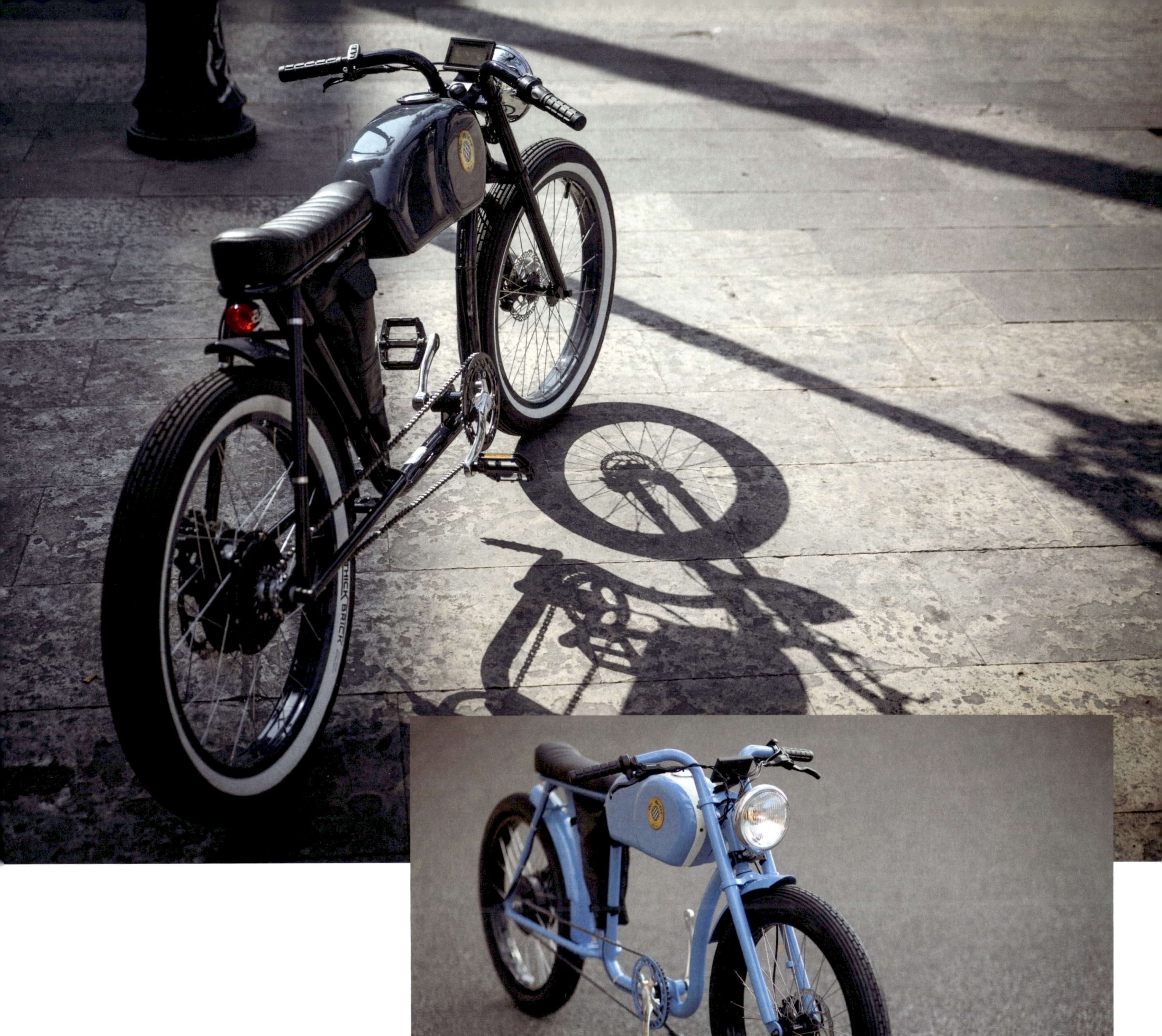

# *Oto Cycles*

Oto Cycles isn't messing around when they say no two of their bikes are identical; with 210 colors that can be customized in 44,100 combinations and the ability to personalize everything from the tires and saddles to the motor and battery, each is truly unique. Inspired by the designs of 1950s motorcycles, Oto Cycles was founded in Barcelona and now produces two motorized versions of its electric bike. Their bikes can reach speeds of 22 miles per hour (35 kilometers per hour) and cover distances of 30 to 44 miles (50 to 70 kilometers) thanks to Samsung NCM Cells batteries, which reach full charge in just four hours. Oto Cycles incorporates a PAS (Pedal Assistance Systems), a half-twist throttle, a five-level LCD display with cyclocomputer, a Shimano Revoshift 6V gear-shifting system, and even Start and Go technology that allows you to kick your bike into motion without having to pedal.

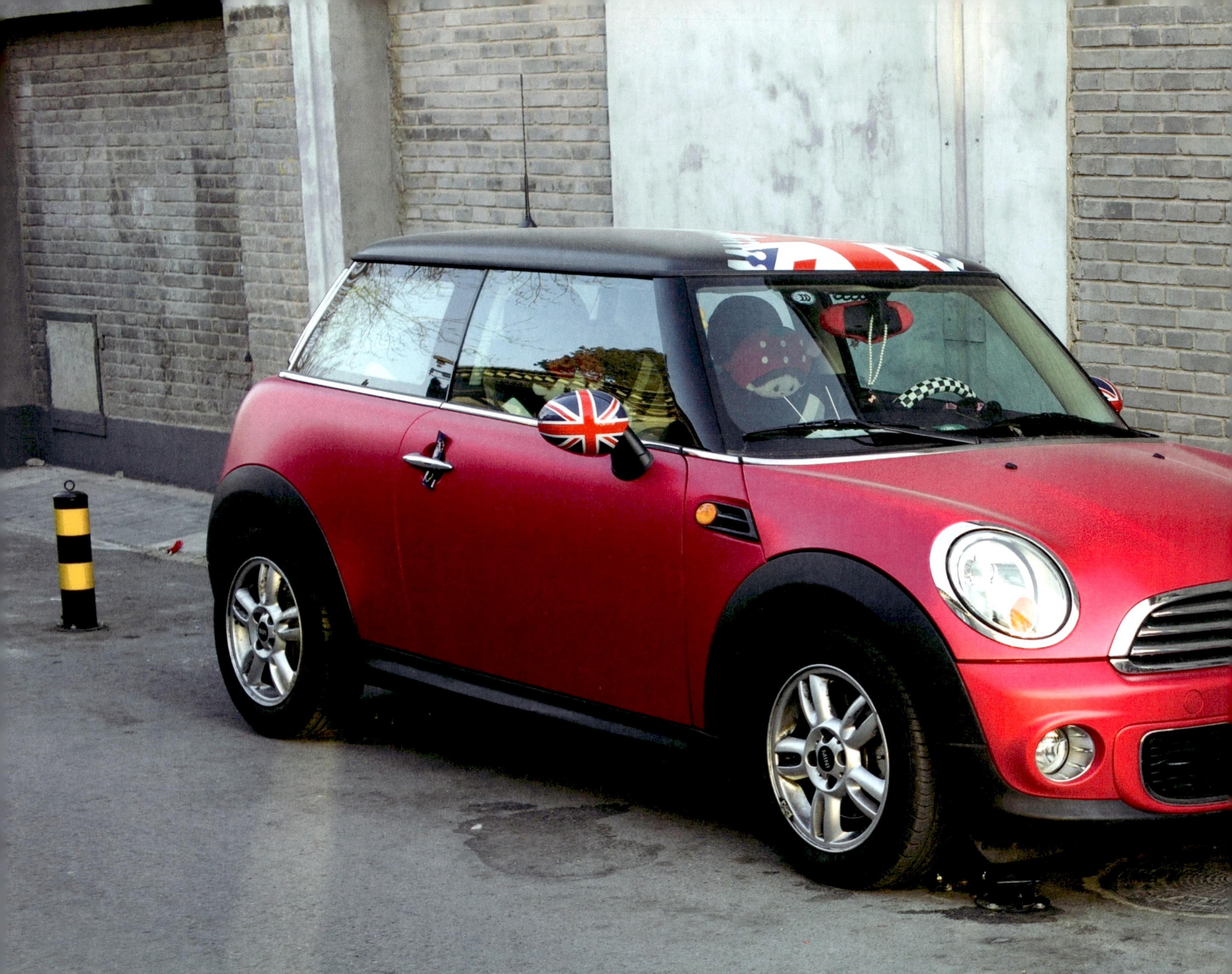

# Bicycles in Beijing, Now

XIAOMENG ZHAO

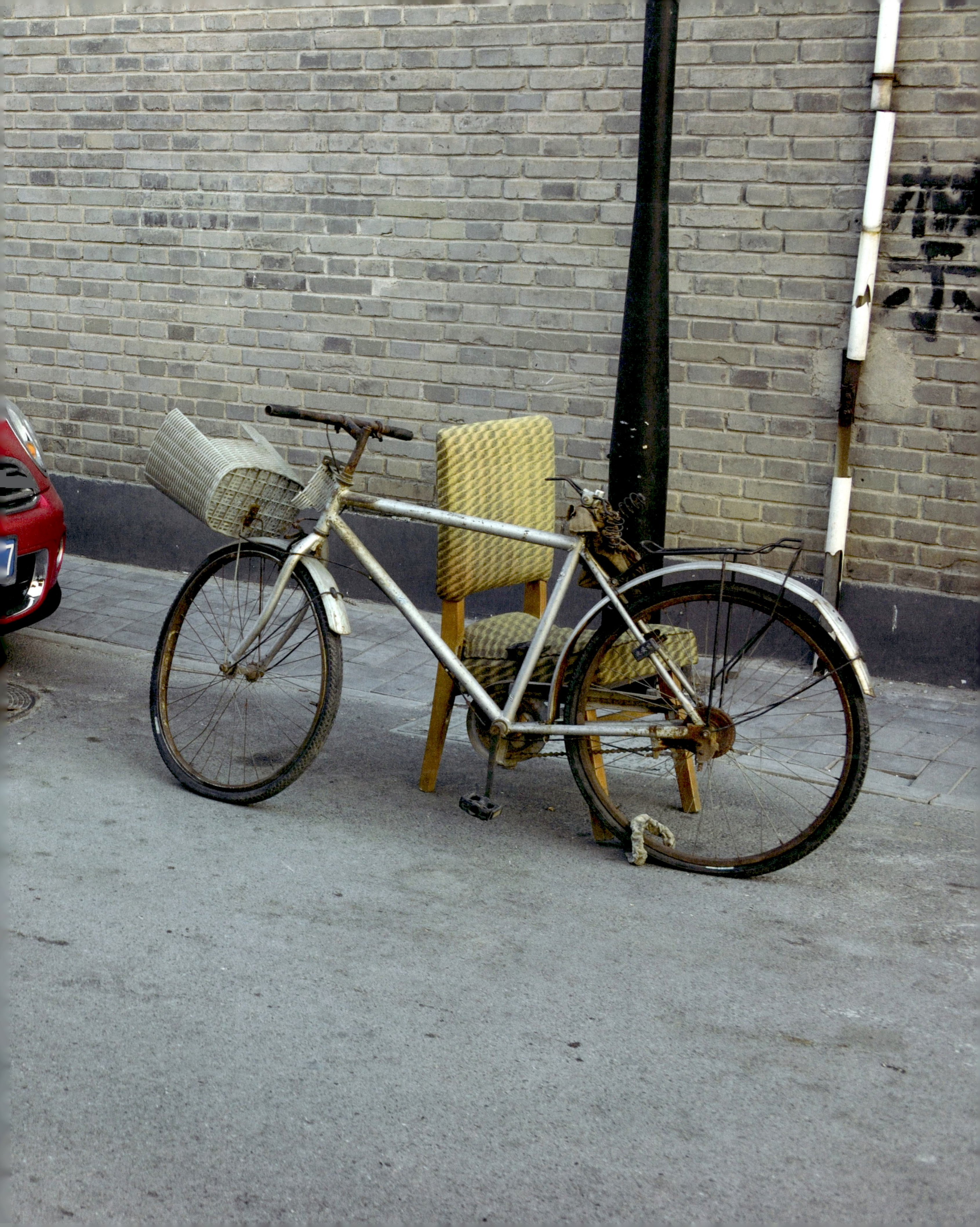

China was once known as the Kingdom of Bicycles; for decades, bicycles were the principal mode of transportation and an essential part of the Chinese lifestyle.

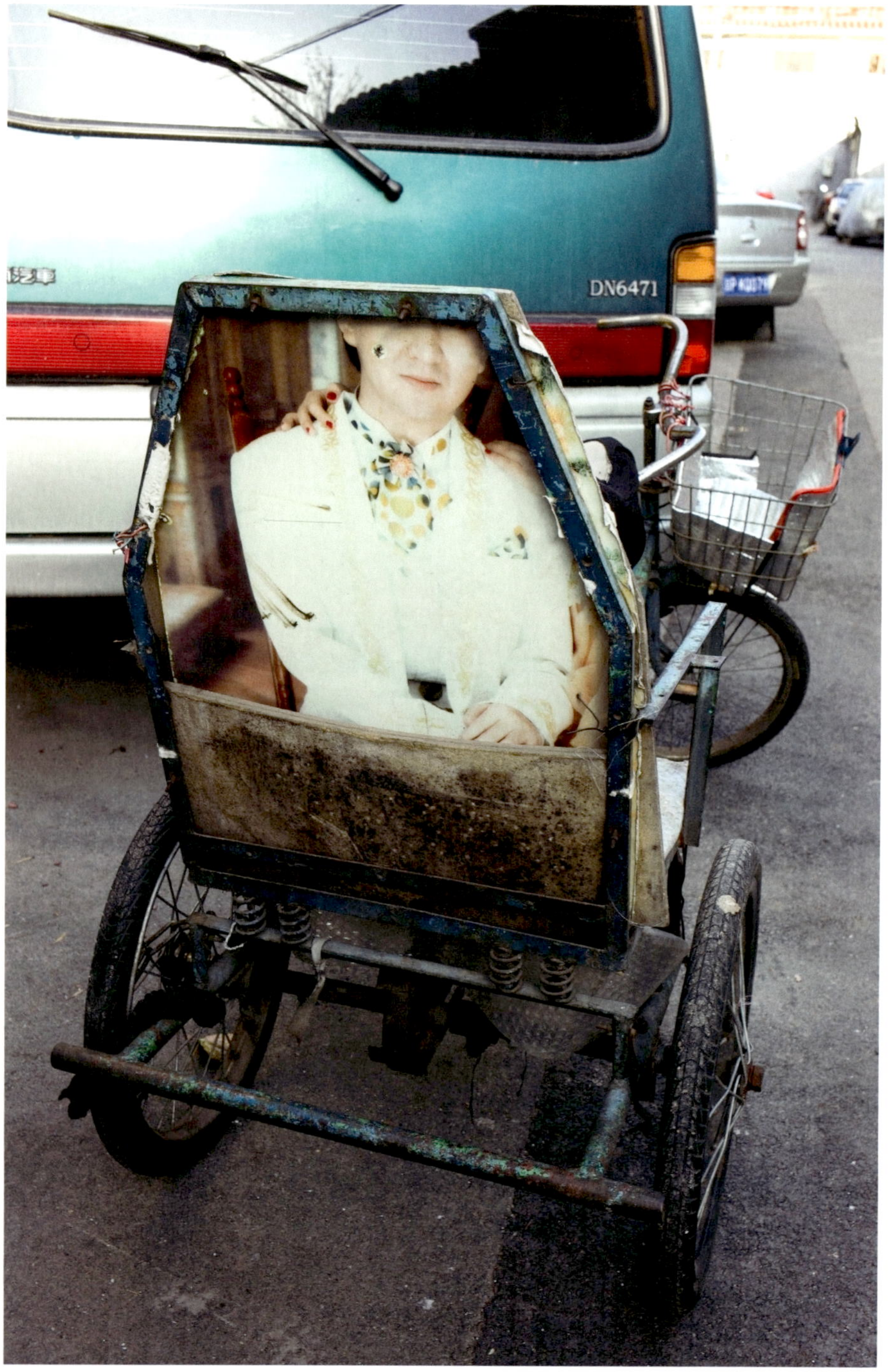

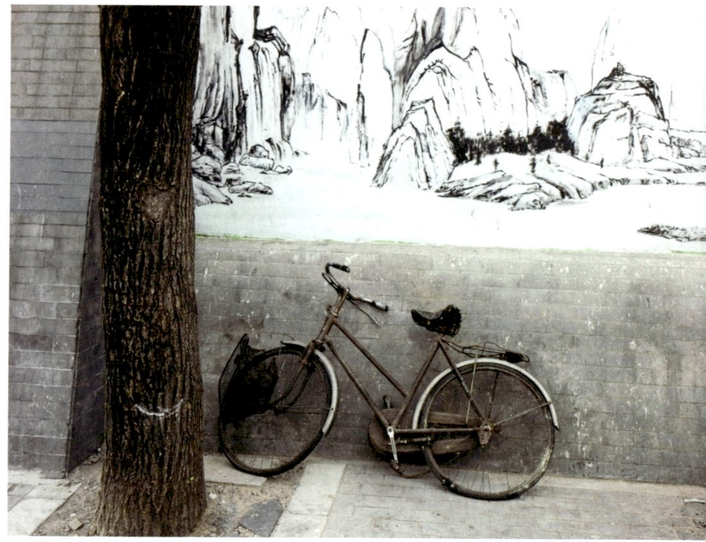

In time bicycles became a cultural symbol, a memory shared by generations.

Since the new millennium, car culture has taken hold of China, and the bicycle has been stigmatized as a symbol of poverty. Wondering where all the old bicycles went, Xiaomeng Zhao set off to find out, discovering them locked up, tucked away, repaired, reconstructed, and randomly parked by their owners. As witnesses to and victims of a major societal transition in China, bicycles are a reflection of how the Chinese are coping with seismic shifts in their everyday lives and culture.

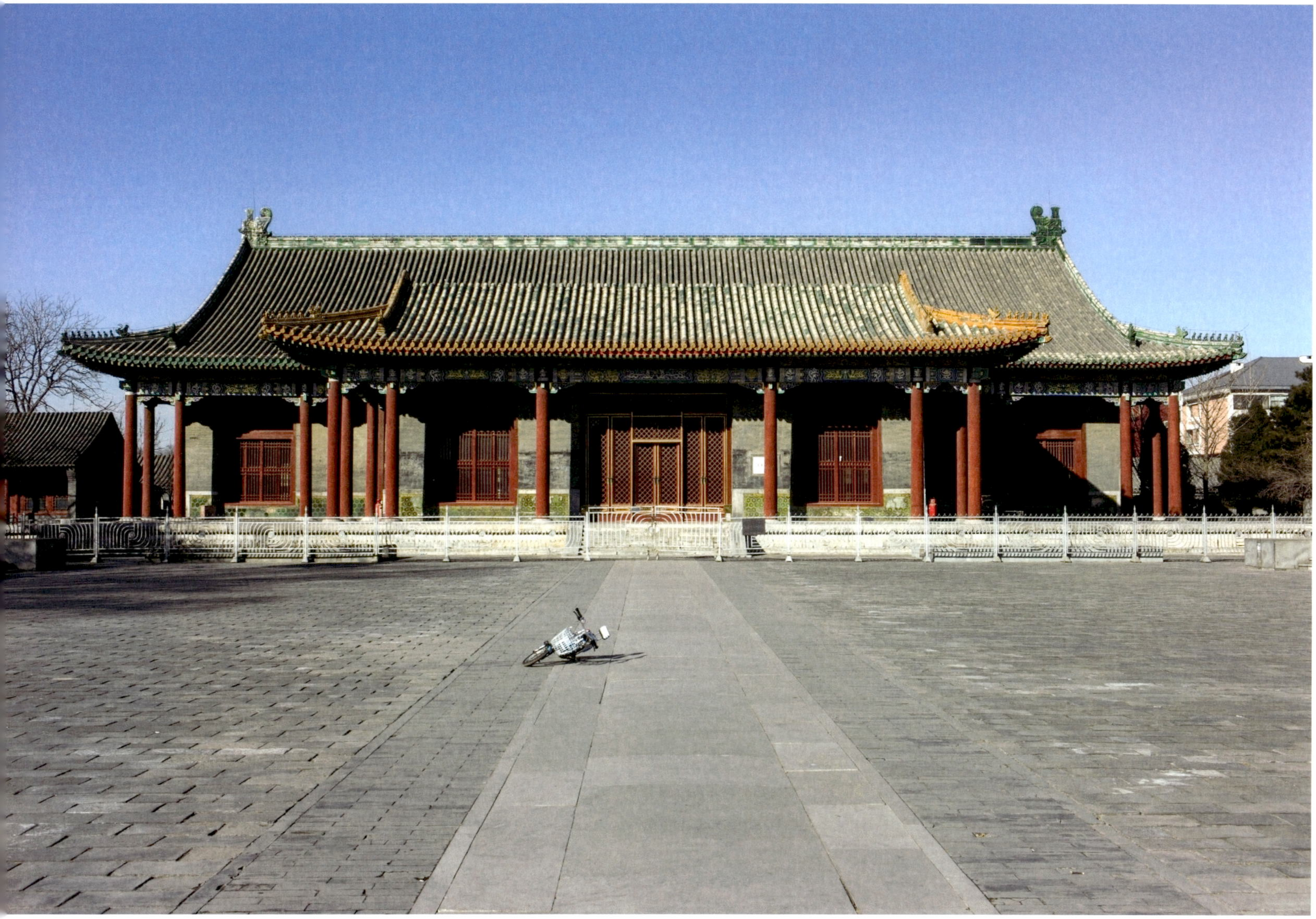

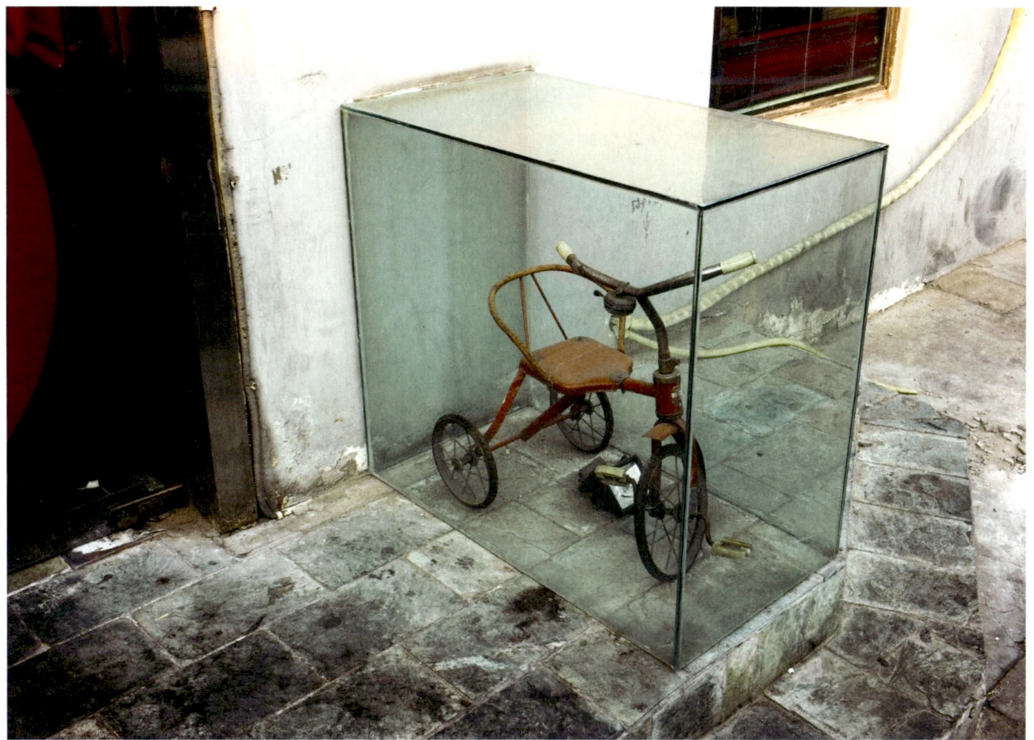

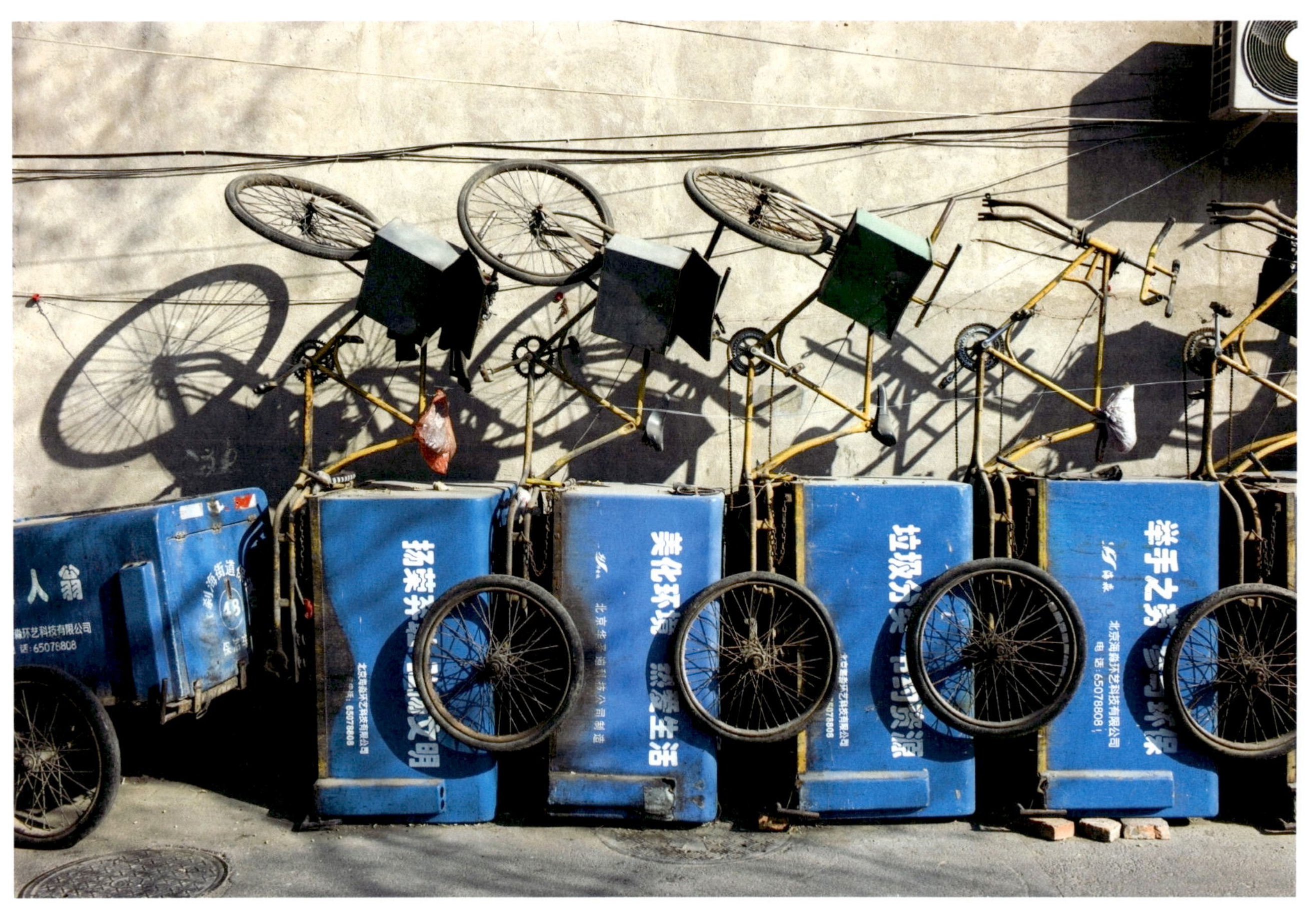

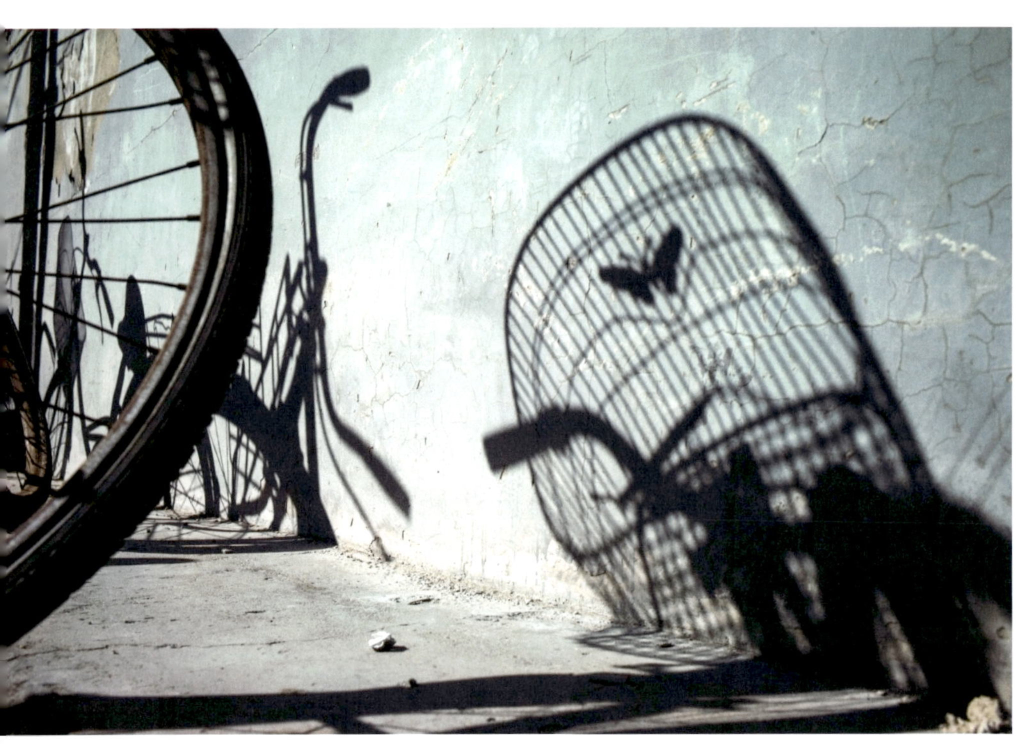

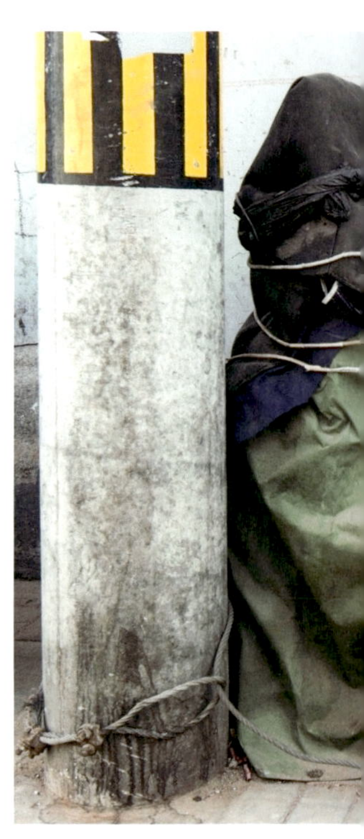

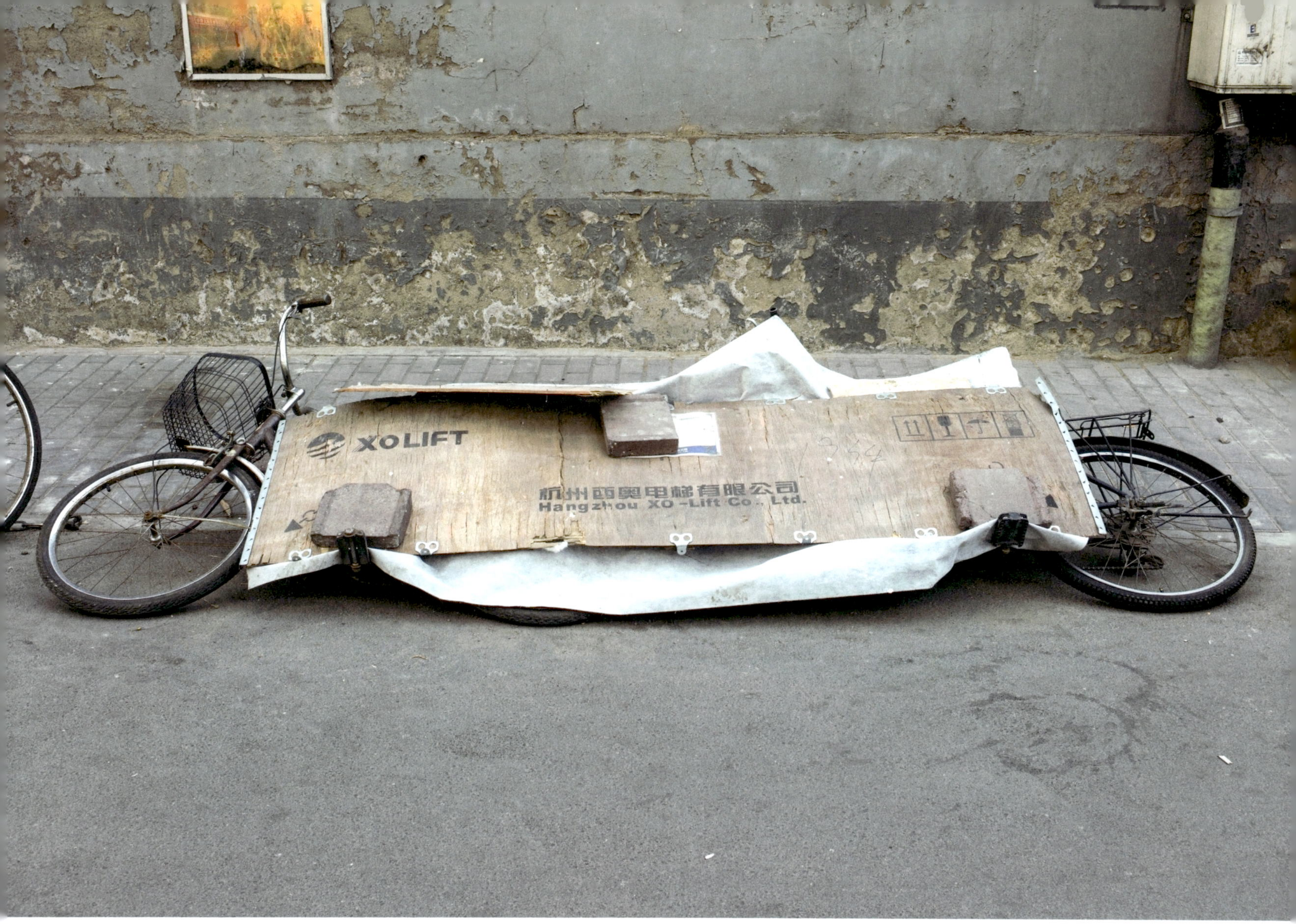

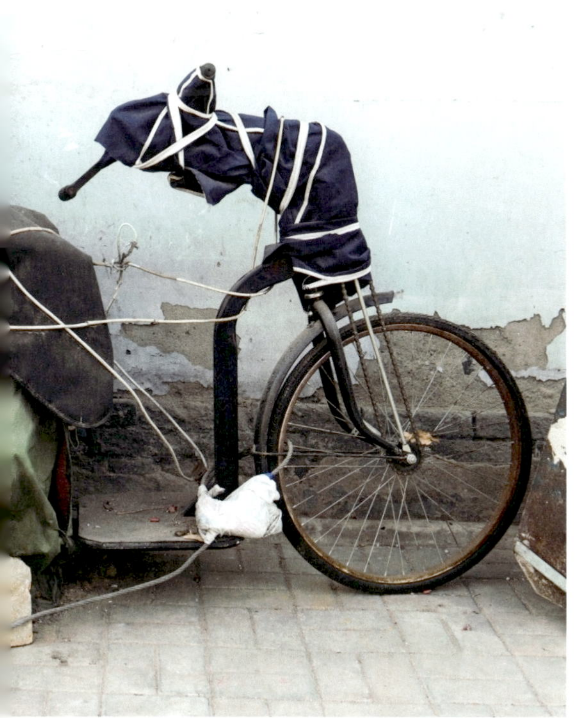

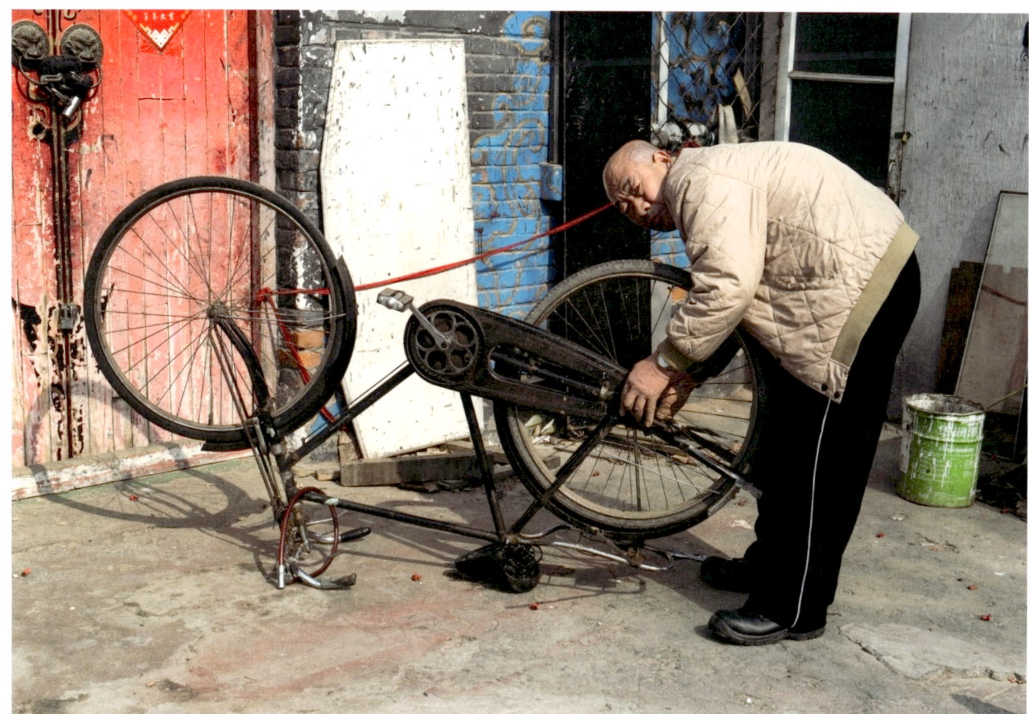

# Breakaways

**oppiste page:**
Festka (page 218)

Text: **SHONQUIS MORENO**

## *On racing bikes, sports, speed, velodrome drama, competition, and high-tech geometries*

Forget fifth gear, the race is fixed. There's pedaling, yeah, but then there's speed. We race the course, we race the guy in front of us, we race the clock. We like competition: Bring it on. There's getting around, but then there's geometry. There are the artisans and the artists, but in this tribe we like the engineers best. This is technique. This is technical. This is high tech. Mountain bikes devour mountains and road bikes get on the road, but our wheels toggle to meet any flavor of terrain. In the following pages, you'll find speed demons and derring-do. Look for the pros, the velodromers, the time-trialers, the streetcats, and the messengers. Yeah, there are miles of freshly painted bike lanes, but then there's drafting off the M4, in the middle lane going south on Seventh Avenue. Potholes? Potholes are opportunities. We ride short courses over hairpin turns and dream about setting land-speed records. The titanium in our knees sets off security at airports, and on weekends, we eat carbon and cobblestones for breakfast. We like to go fast—and whatever we do, we don't brake.

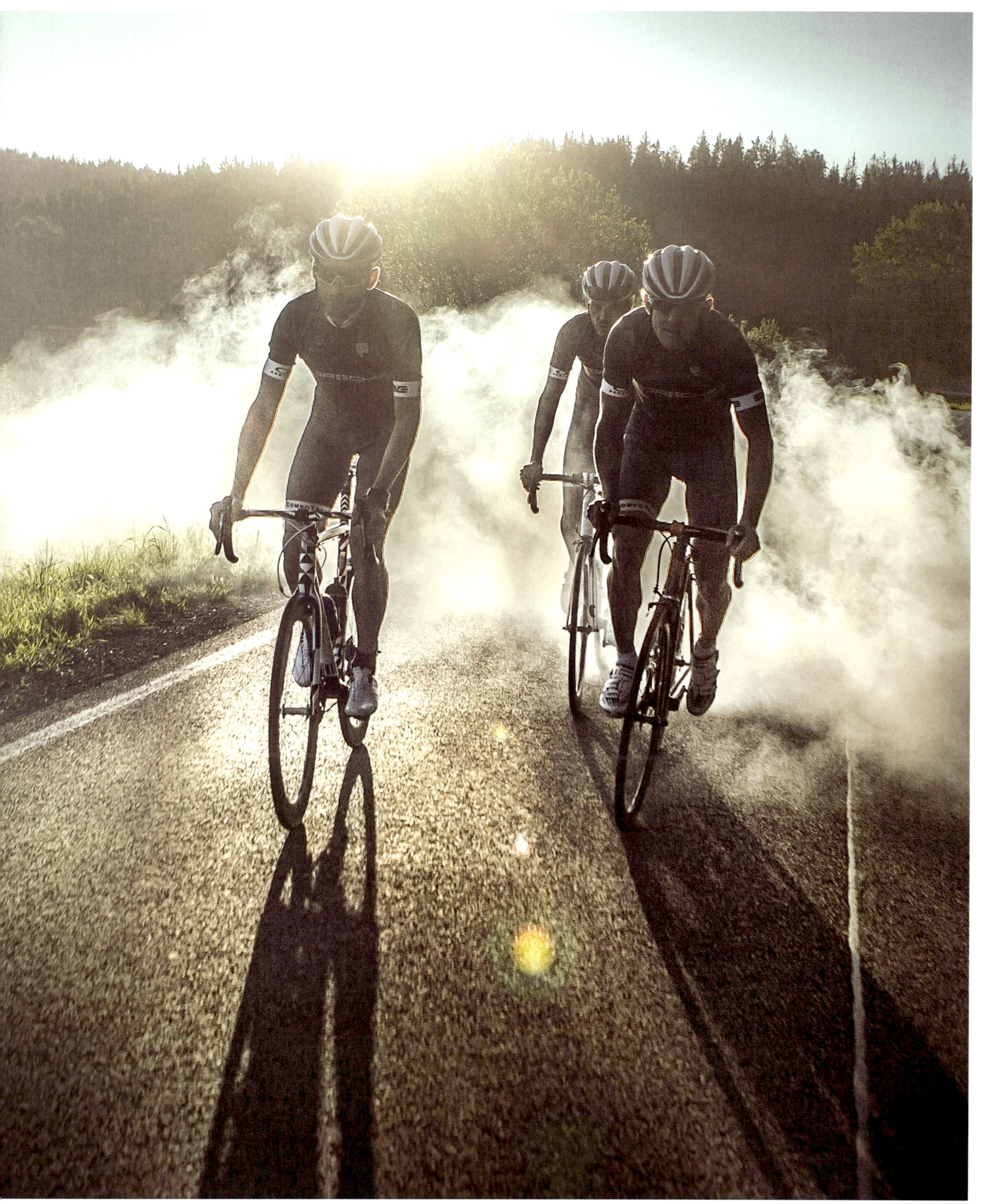

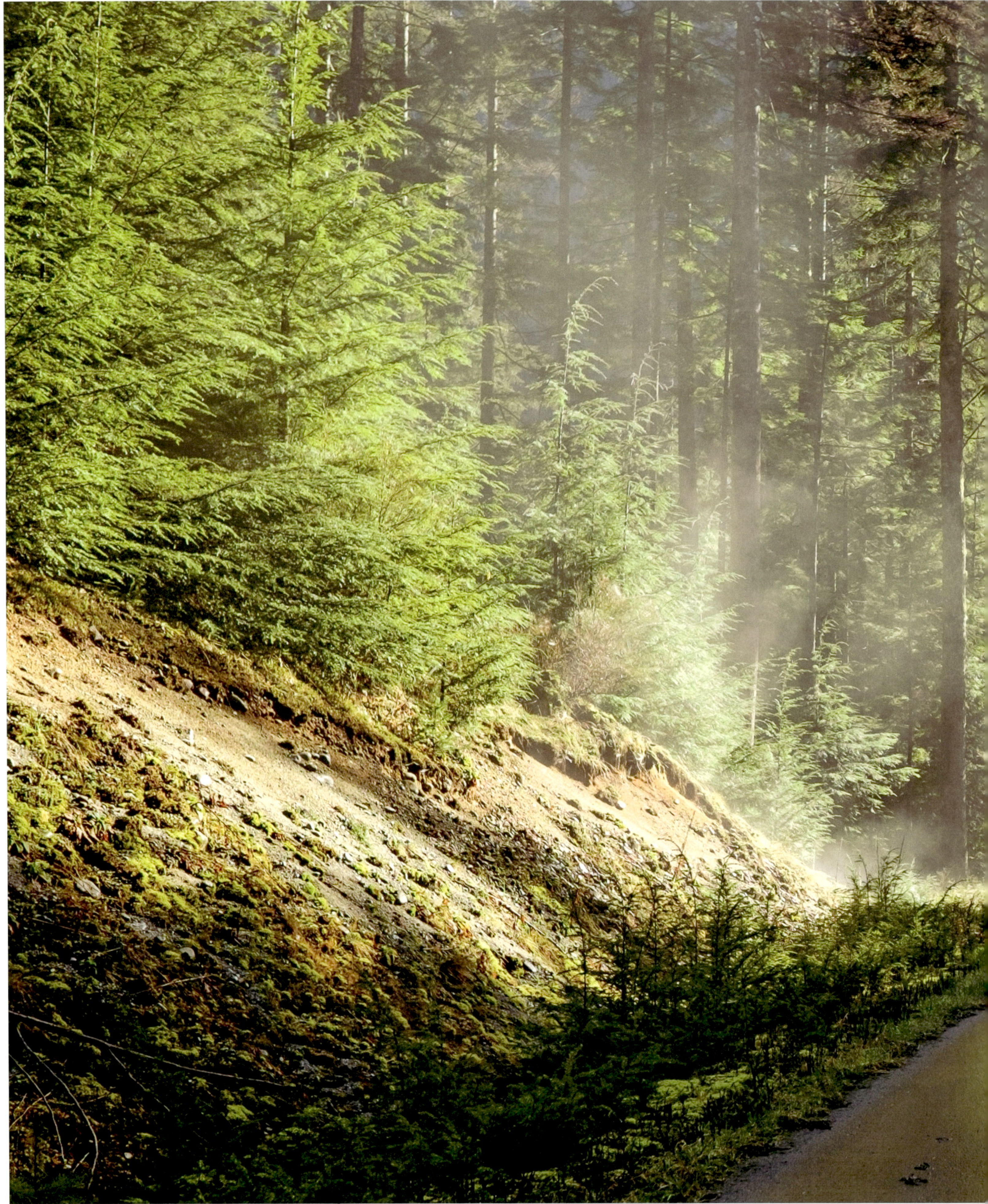

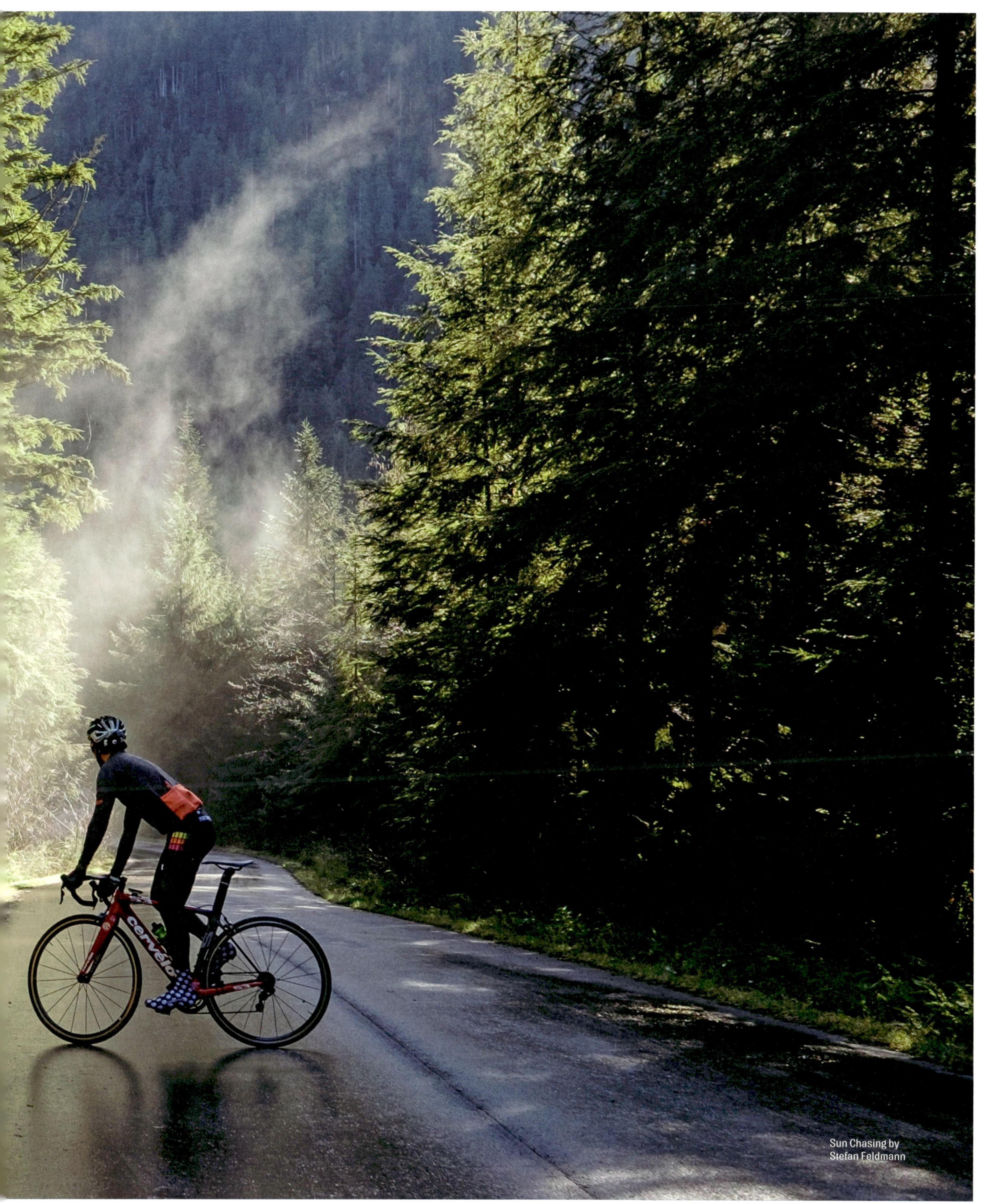

Sun Chasing by
Stefan Feldmann

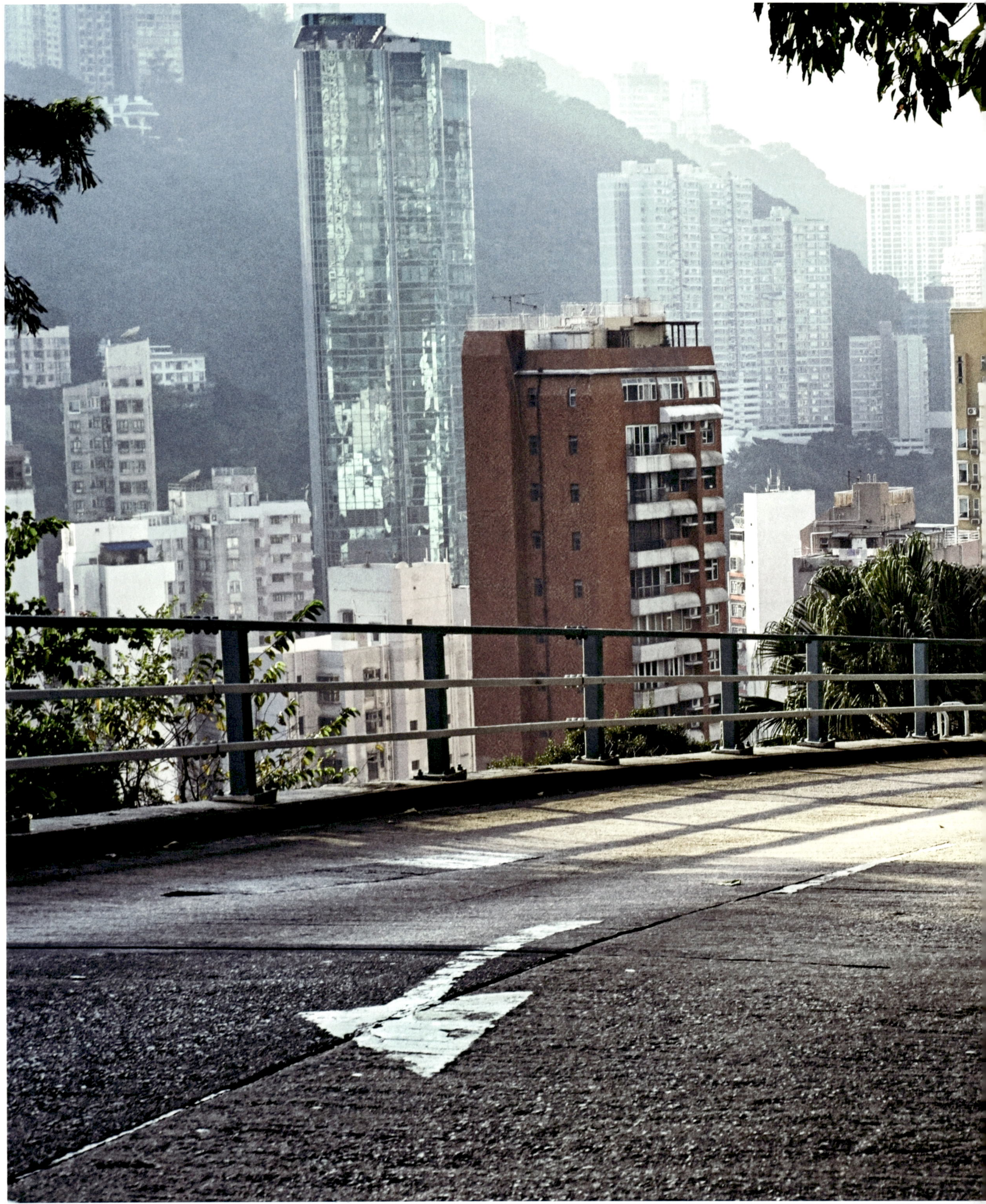

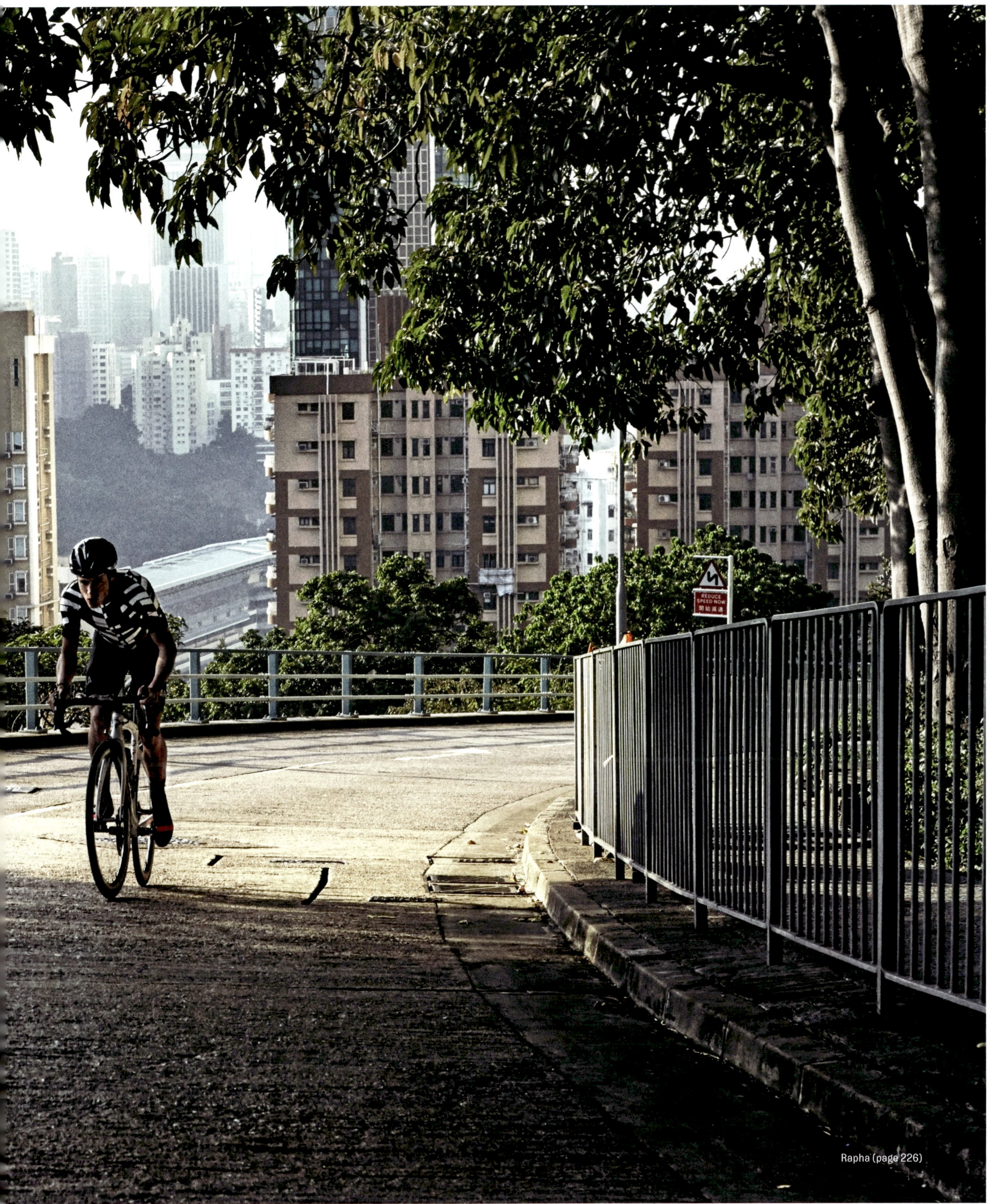


Rapha (page 226)

# Red Hook Criterium

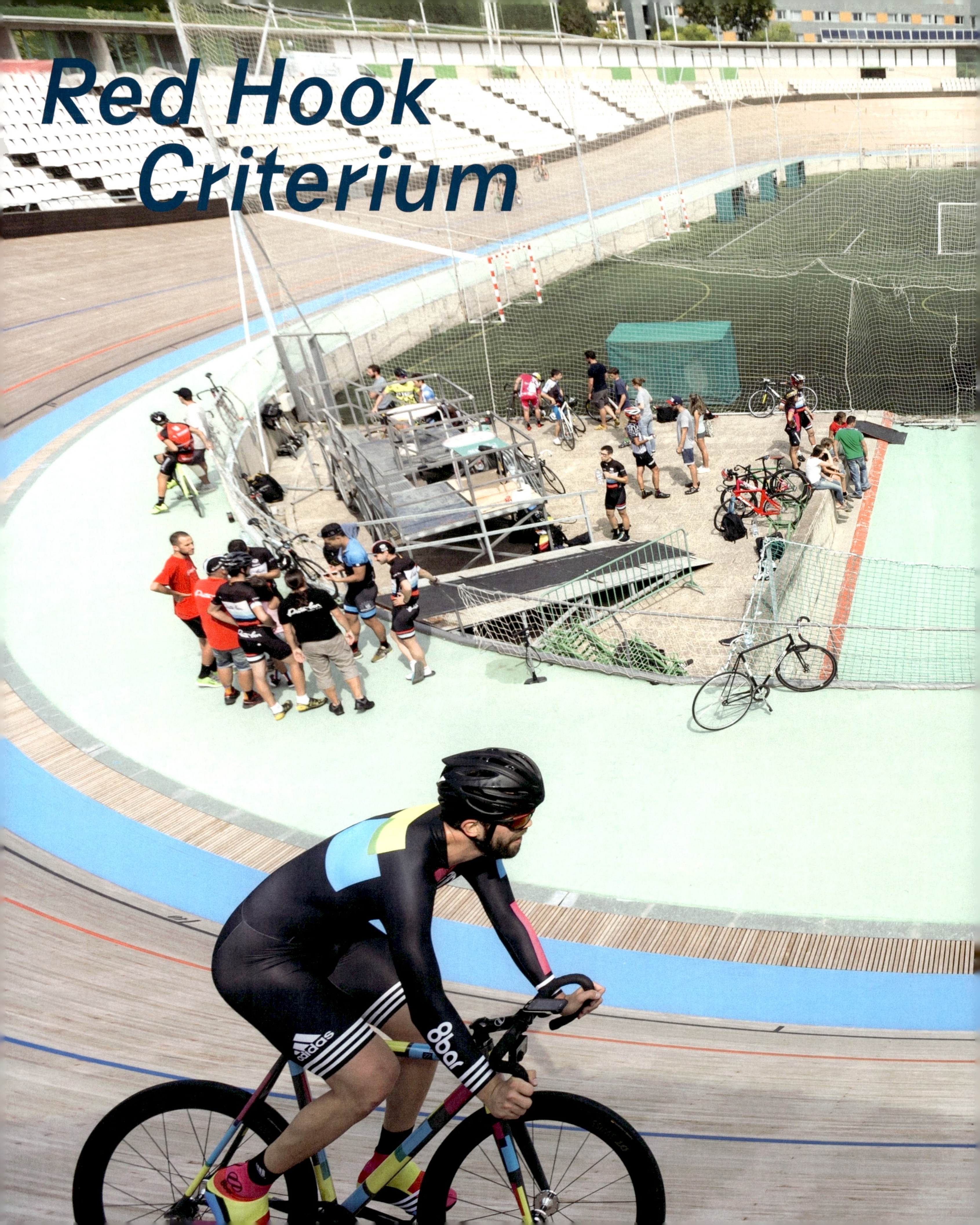

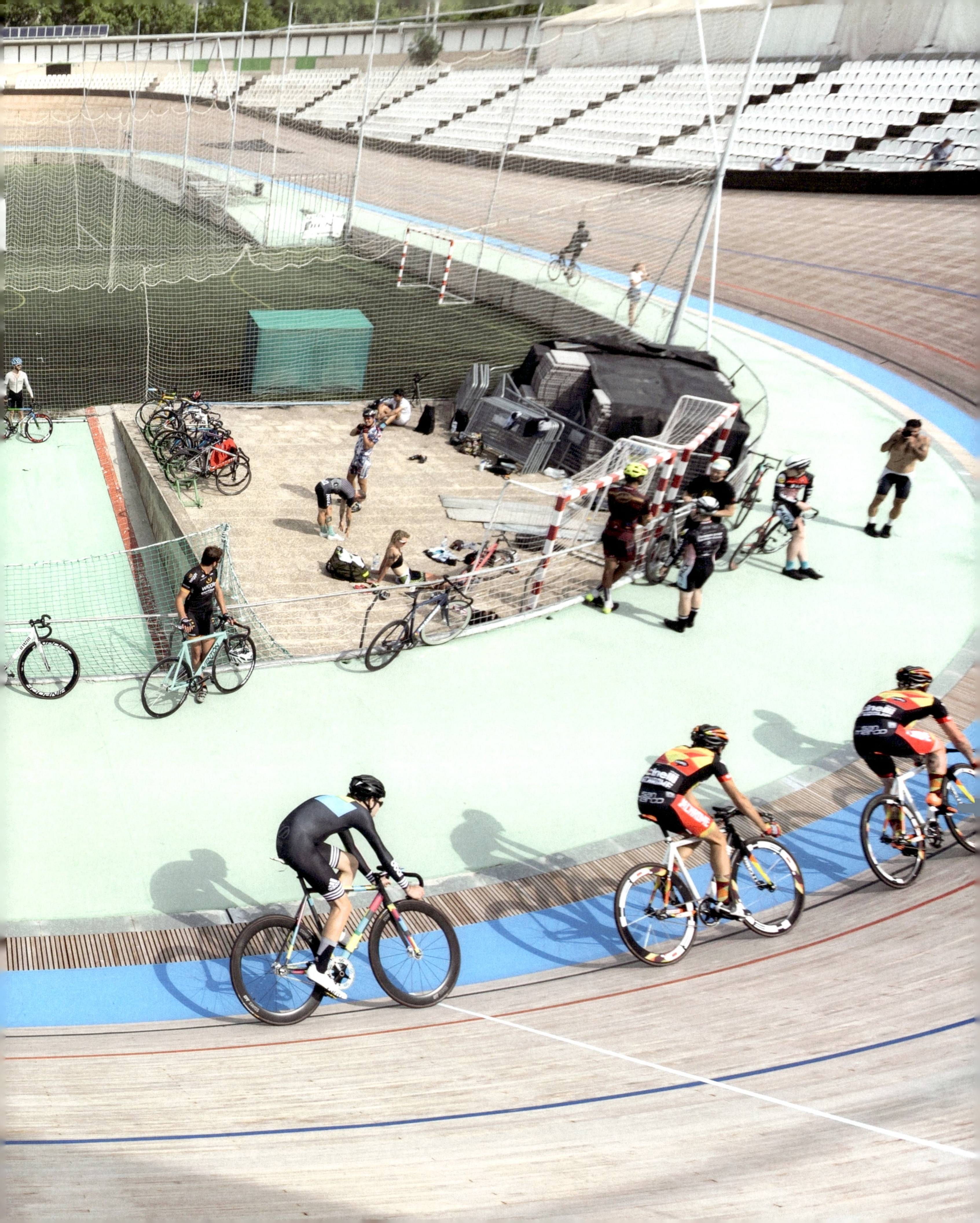

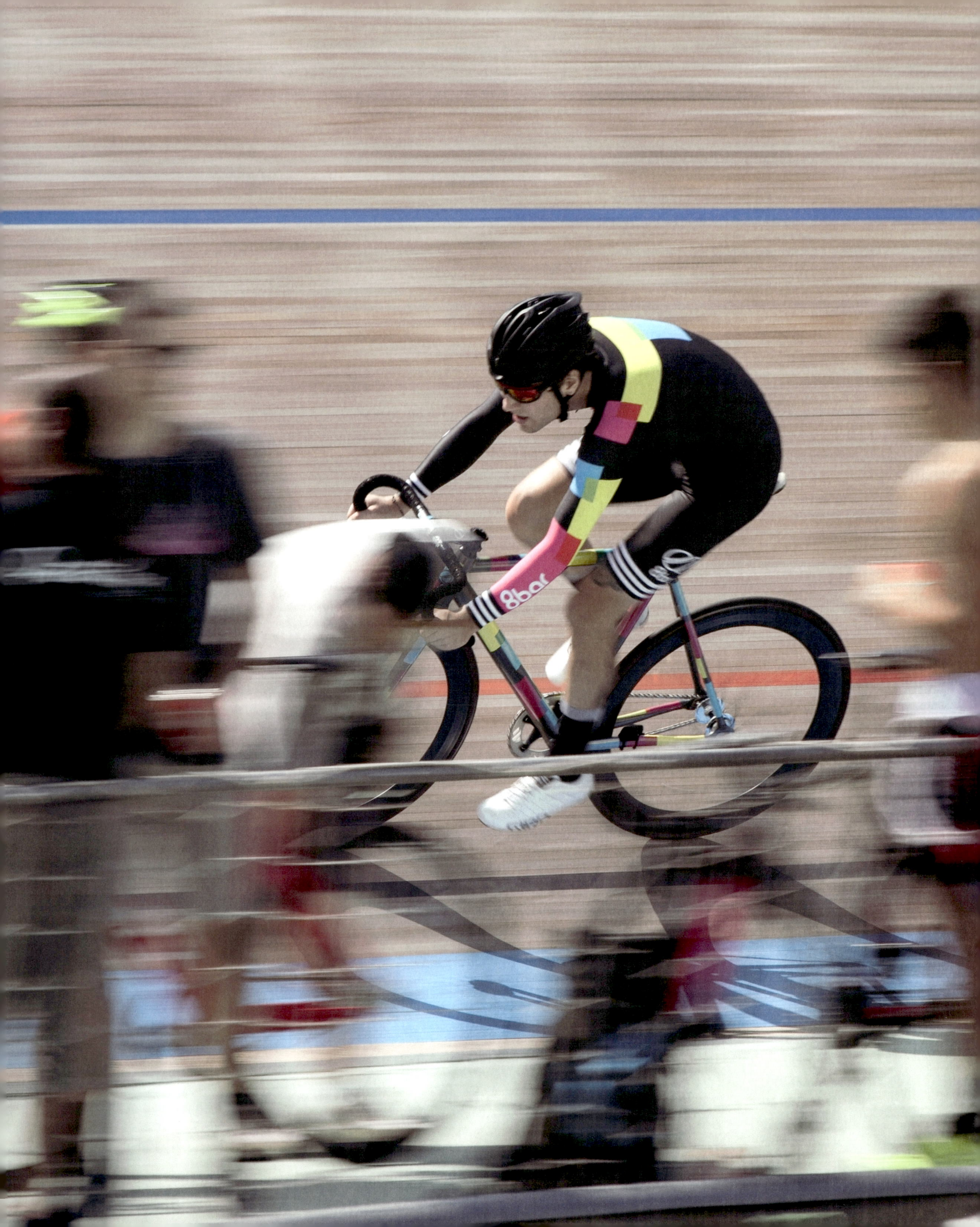
8bar

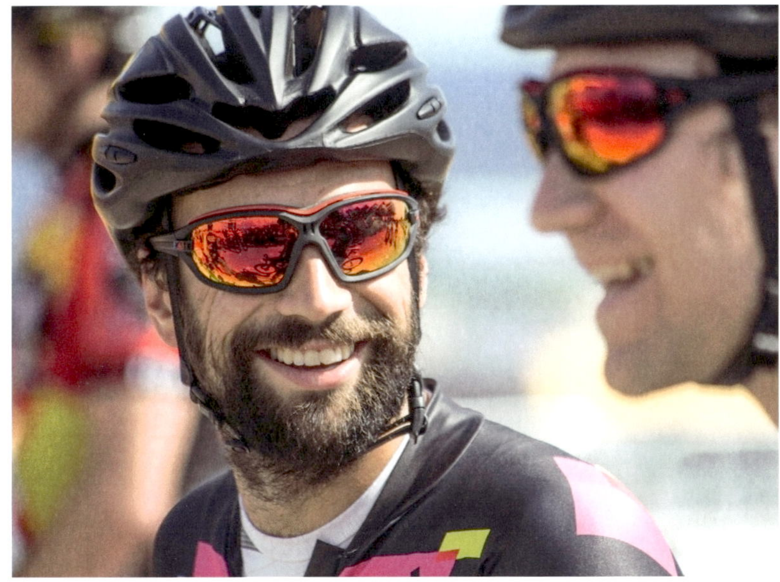

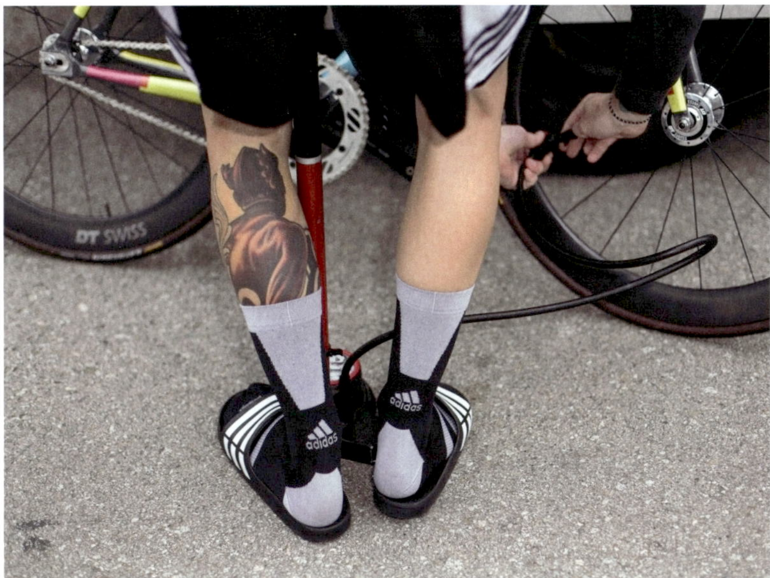


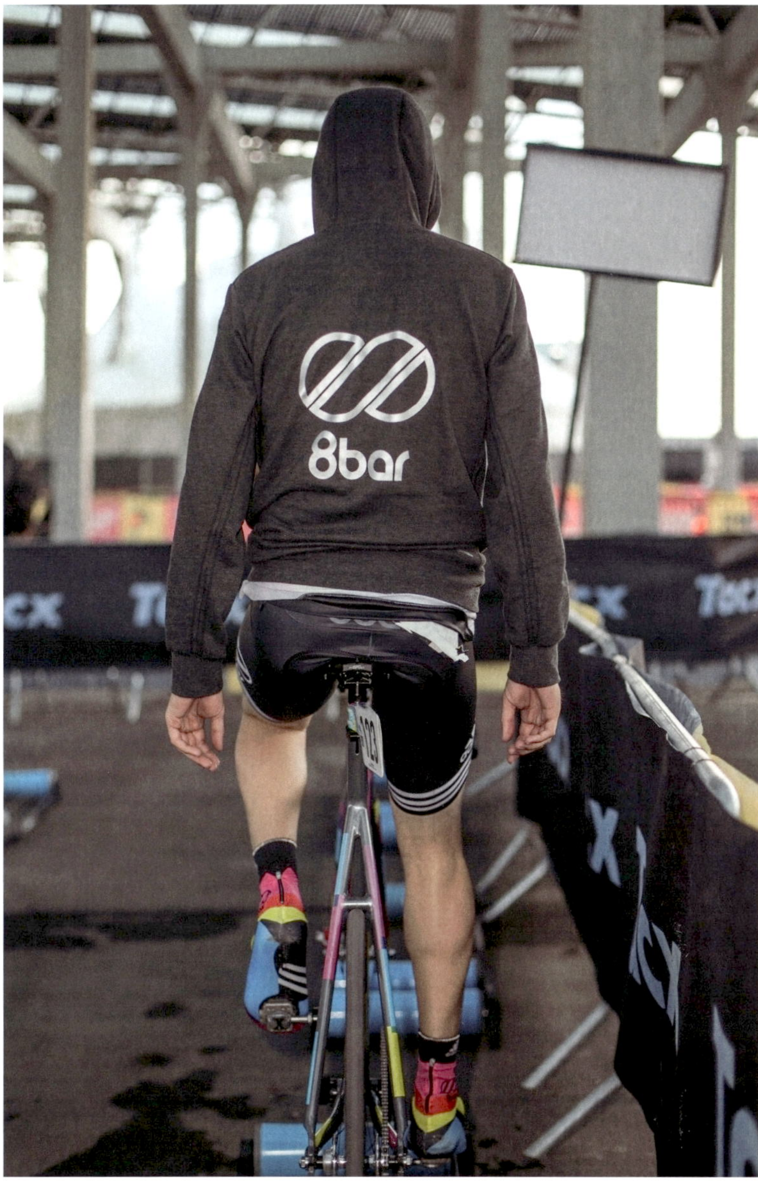


People of every color and stripe—wearing a plethora of colors and stripes—ride in the Red Hook Criterium, which bills itself as the world's premier track-bike race.

Crits are bike races held on abbreviated courses over multiple laps, emphasizing speed over endurance. Red Hook, Brooklyn, the race's eponymous original site, consists of a three-quarter-mile course threaded with tight technical turns over the neighborhood's historical cobbled streets, including a 180-degree hairpin and a high-speed chicane. Unsanctioned by any official cycling body, it has become an annual fixed-gear race hosted by (so far) Barcelona, London, and Milan. It draws from the super-fit ranks of professional road racers who are geared for physically intense riding, as well as attracting street-tuned wildcard bike messengers and urban cyclists. Competitors use fixed-gear bicycles that have no brakes. Instead, they decelerate—if they do decelerate—only by skidding skillfully.

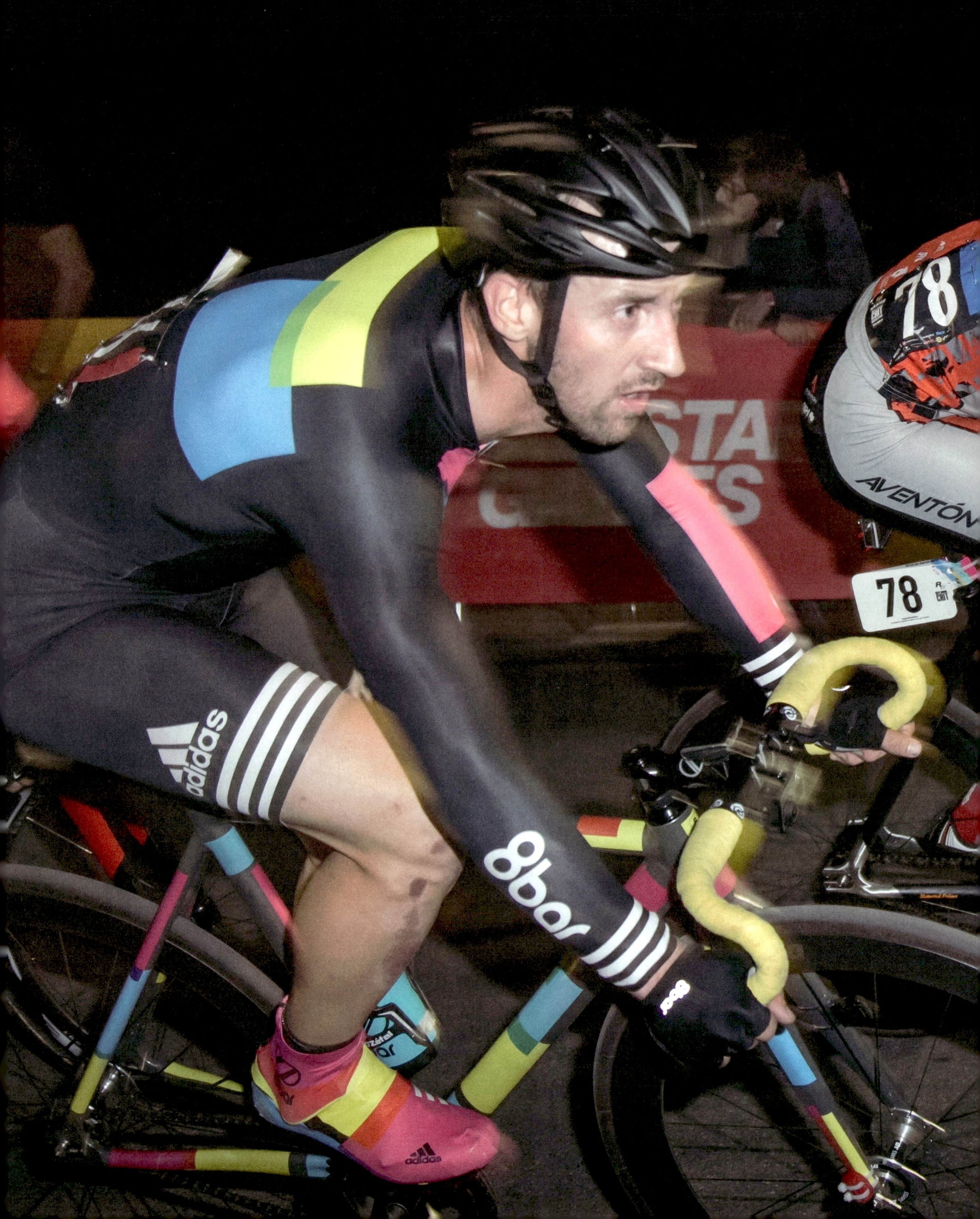
78
78
AVENTÓN
adidas
8bar
adidas

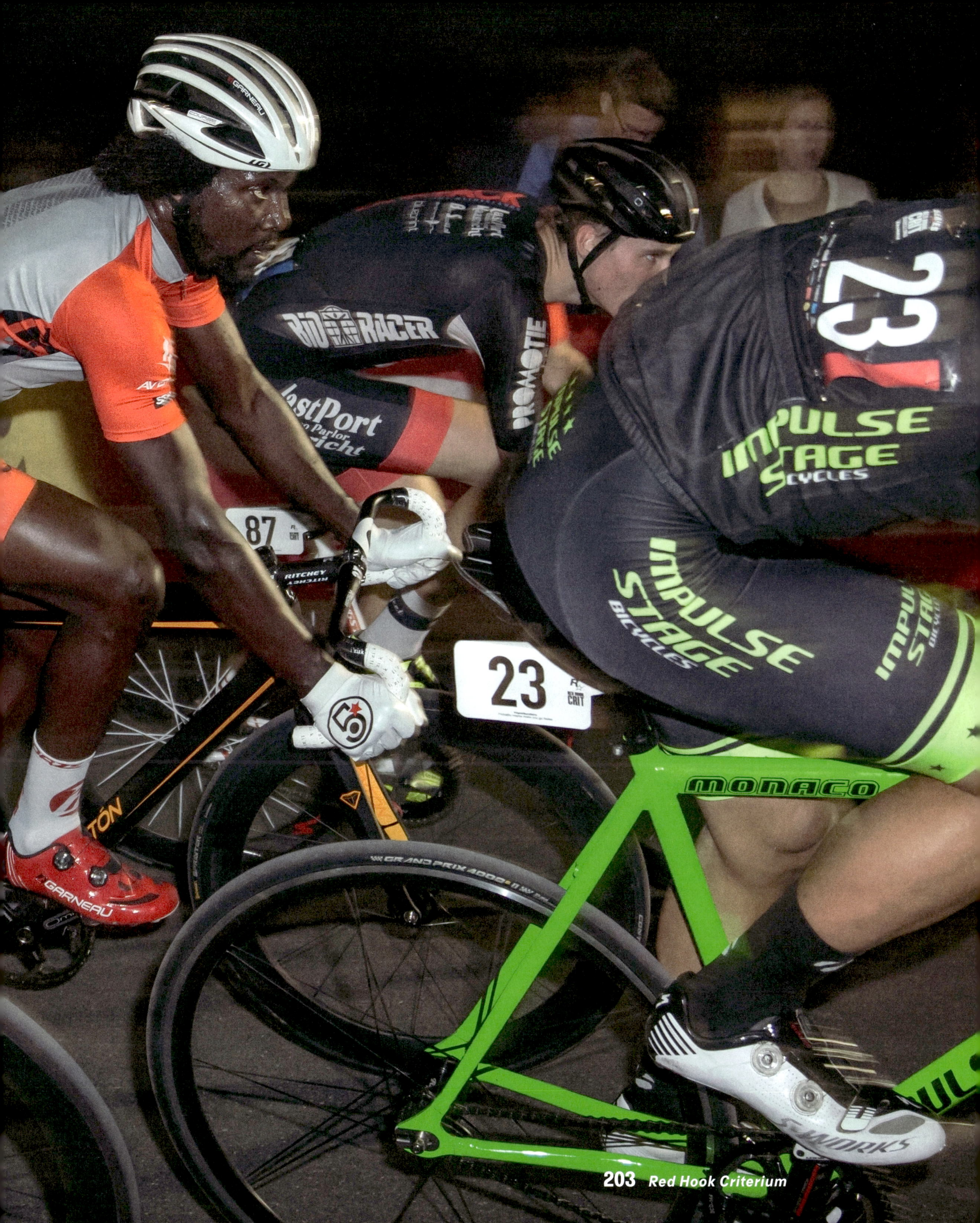

GARNEAU
RACER
PROMOTIE
87
RITCHEY
23
IMPULSE
STAGE
CYCLES
IMPULSE
STAGE
BICYCLES
MONACO
GRAND PRIX 4000
GARNEAU
S-WORKS

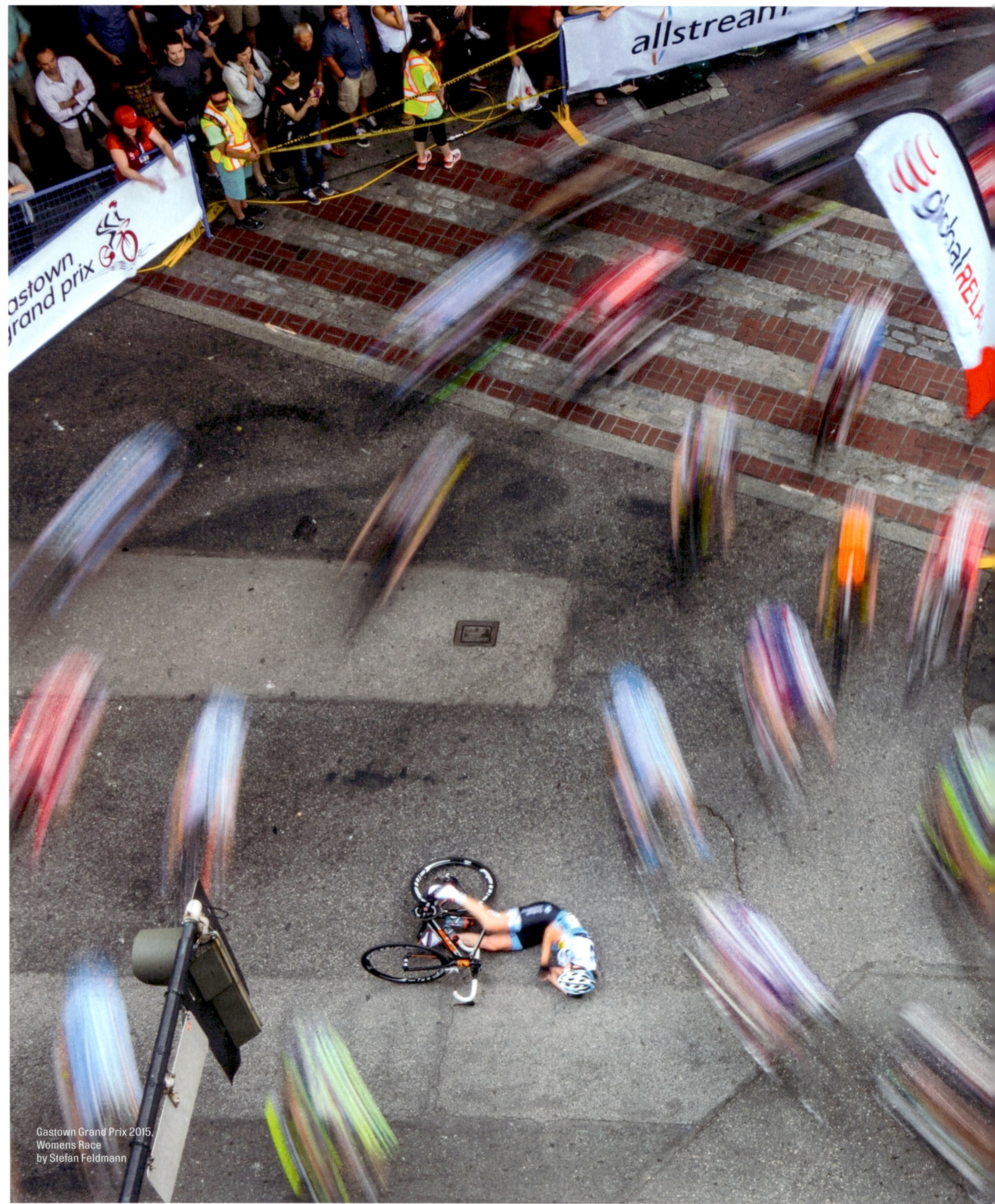


Gastown Grand Prix 2015,
Womens Race
by Stefan Feldmann

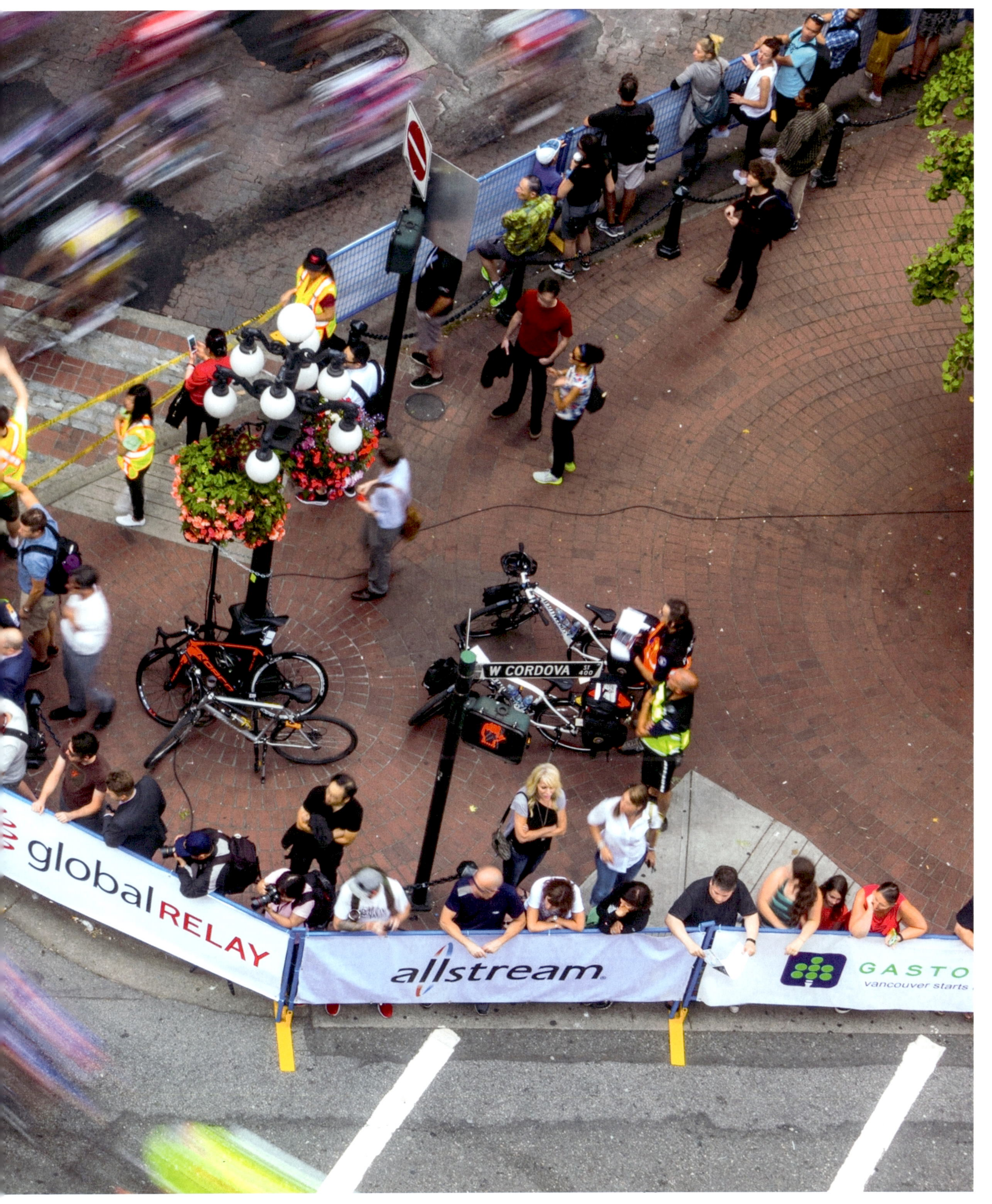

W CORDOVA
global RELAY
allstream

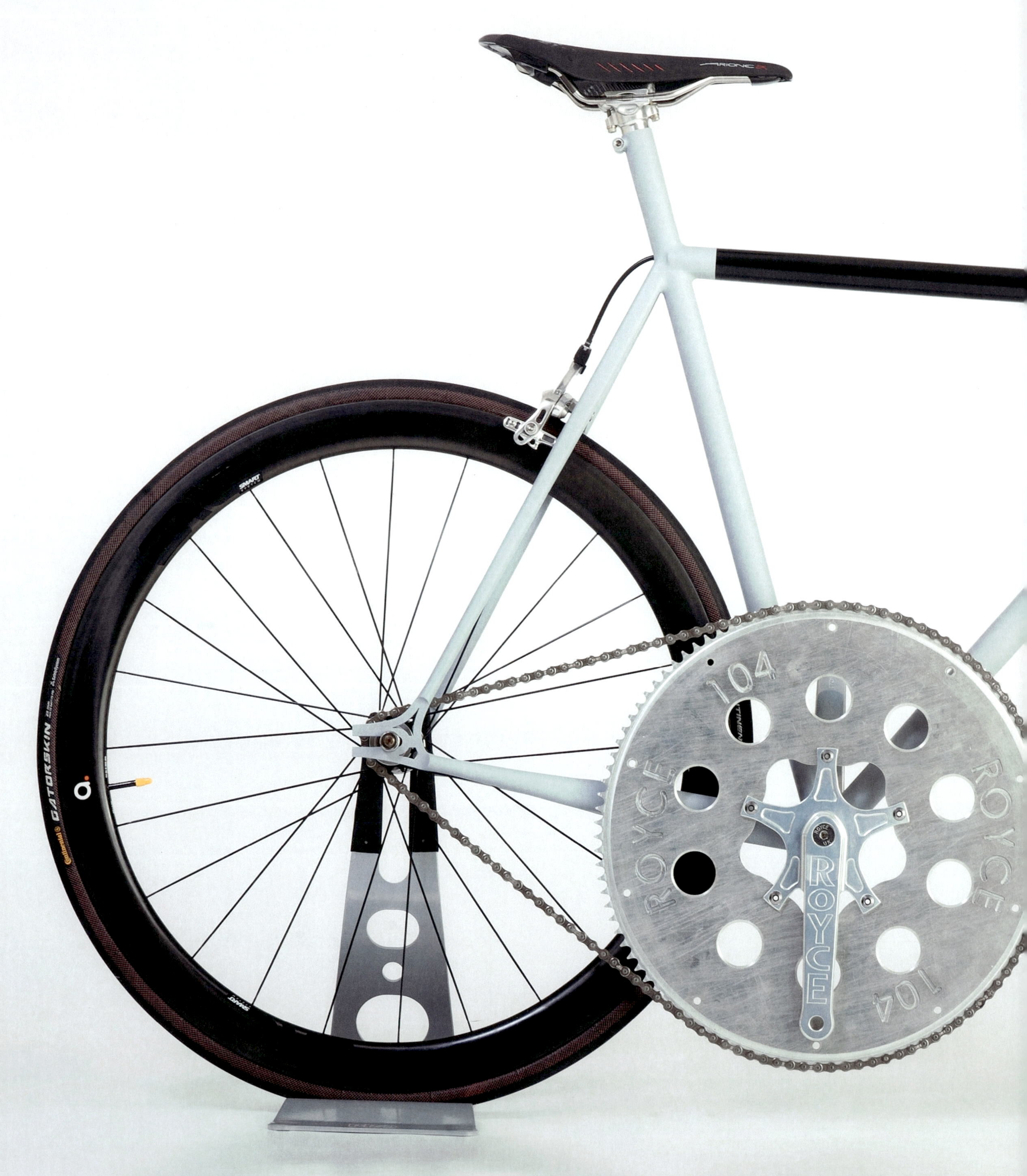

104
ROYCE
ROYCE
104
ROYCE
GATORSKIN

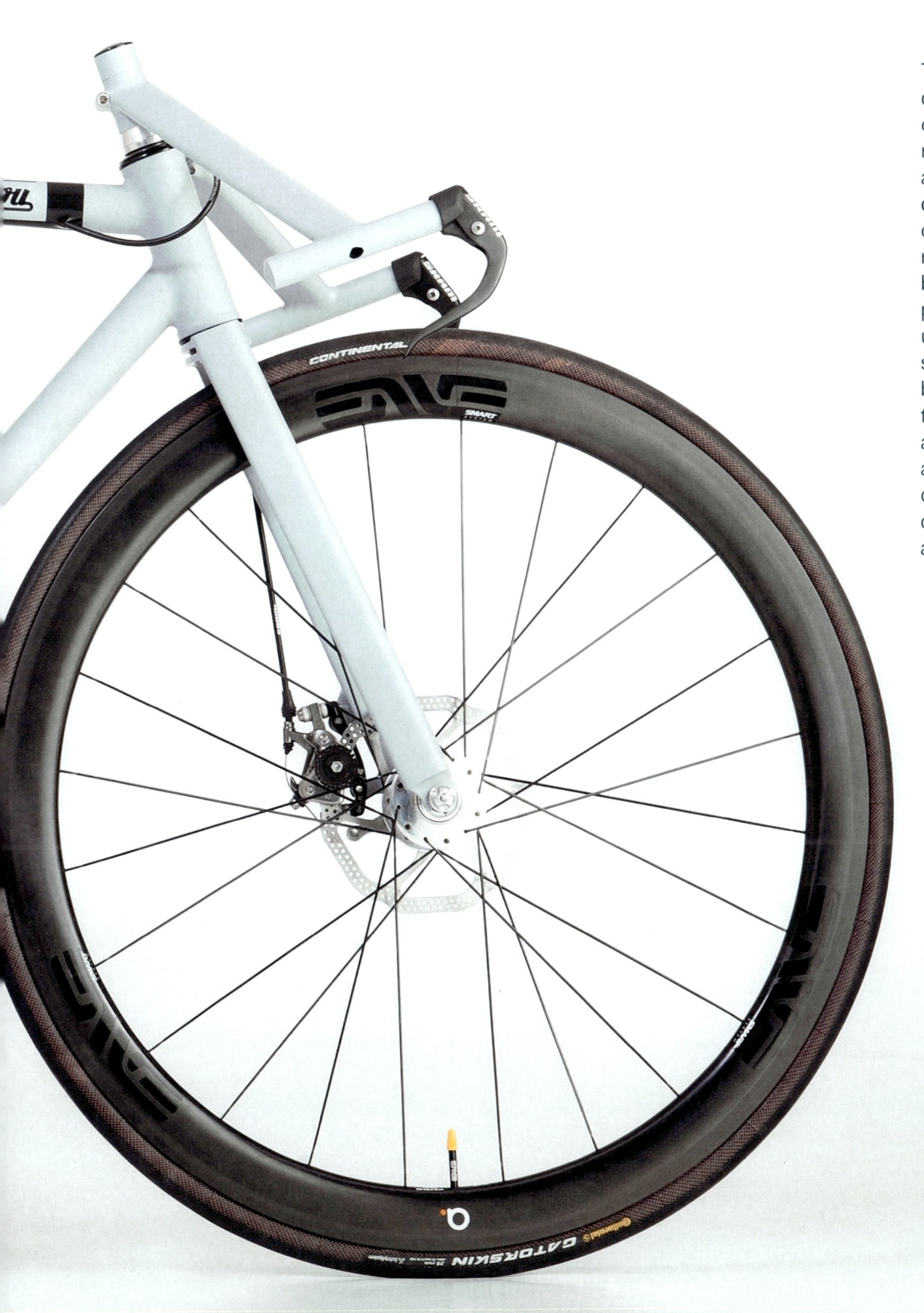


# *Land Speed Bike*

**DONHOU BICYCLES**

The "speed bike" or "100-mile-per-hour bike," despite its nicknames, its supersized carbon chain rings, and the precipitous drop of its minimal handlebars, is, says maker Thomas Donhou, "essentially a normal bike." It is designed to ride at speeds at which bicycle components are not tested to perform. To reduce speed wobbles and let him tuck in behind a draft vehicle and establish a super-low center of gravity for stability, he used opposed oval Columbus Max tubing for stiffness, custom bars, and a special bottom bracket. SRAM and AVID brake discs at the front bear the brunt of slowing down, while a caliper brake at the rear helps to slow pedal momentum. The "dog-legged" drive-side chain stay clears space for the 104-tooth chainring. "You wouldn't want to drop a chain at 70-plus miles per hour," he says.

# Bedovelo Track Hardcore

**BEDOVELO**

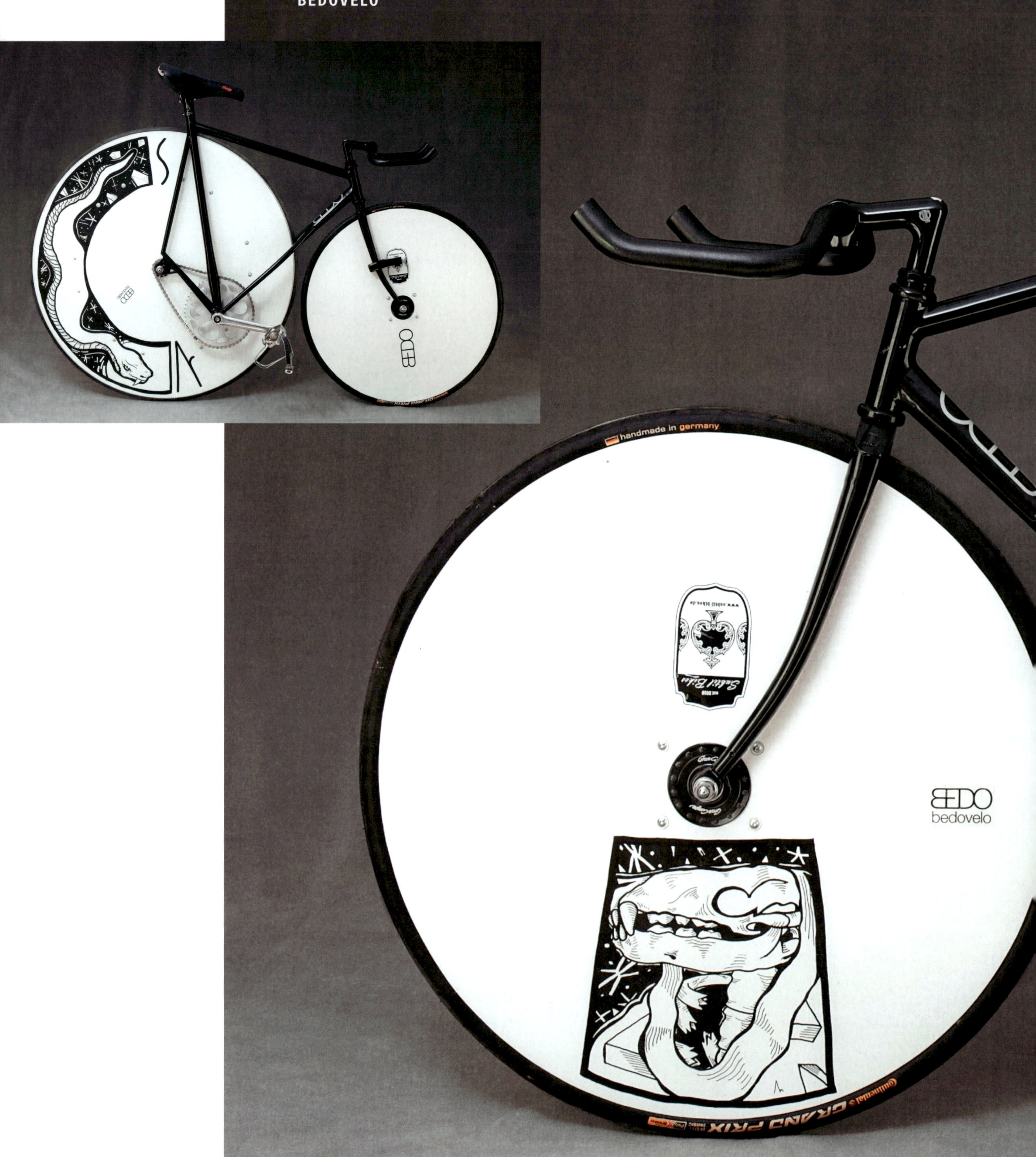

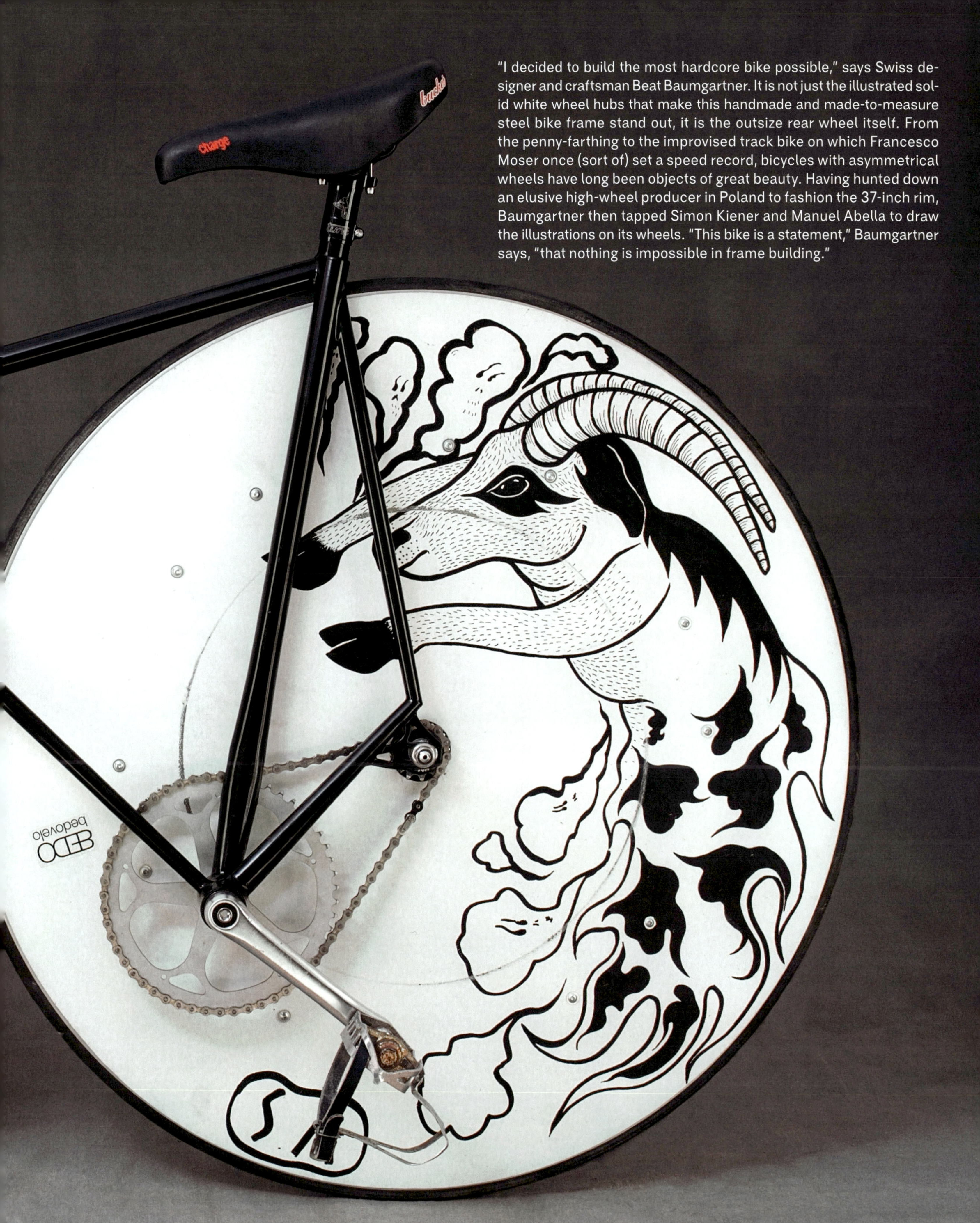


"I decided to build the most hardcore bike possible," says Swiss designer and craftsman Beat Baumgartner. It is not just the illustrated solid white wheel hubs that make this handmade and made-to-measure steel bike frame stand out, it is the outsize rear wheel itself. From the penny-farthing to the improvised track bike on which Francesco Moser once (sort of) set a speed record, bicycles with asymmetrical wheels have long been objects of great beauty. Having hunted down an elusive high-wheel producer in Poland to fashion the 37-inch rim, Baumgartner then tapped Simon Kiener and Manuel Abella to draw the illustrations on its wheels. "This bike is a statement," Baumgartner says, "that nothing is impossible in frame building."

# *Kuricin + Takhion MASS*

**TSUBASA**

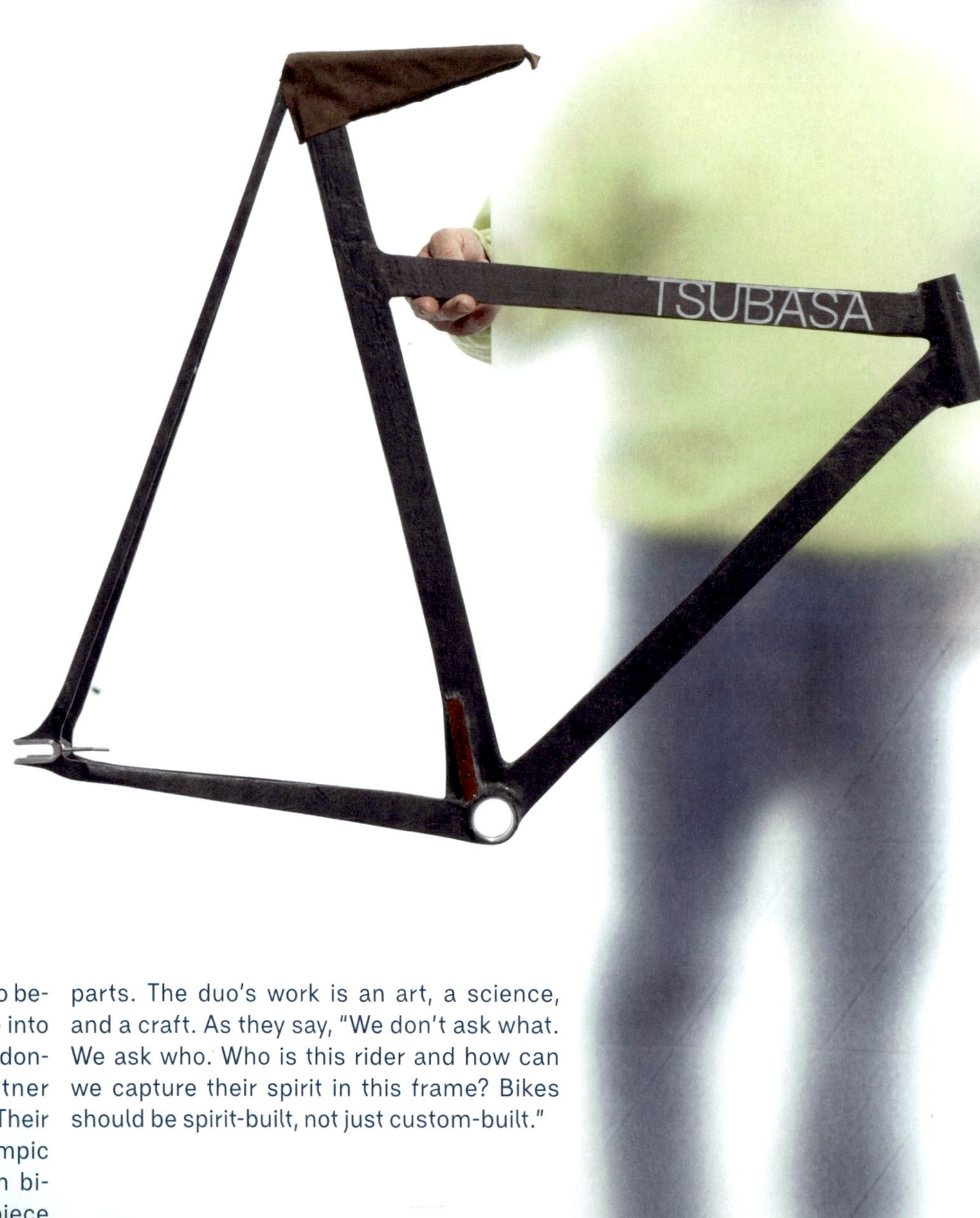


Inspired by ancient warriors who sought to become one with their horses as they rode into battle, Russia-born, Lithuania-raised, London-based Edvinas Vavilovas and his partner Reginald Vorontsov have high ambitions. Their mission is to reinvent the original Olympic gold-winning, record-breaking Takhion bicycle frame using proprietary single-piece technology. Their Tsubasa carbon-fiber frames are seamless, meaning they layer the material over and over to craft a single piece that threads carbon fibers continuously throughout the frame. This means their frames respond to the rider's motions as a single unit instead of from joint to joint. They also bridge the frame internally, increasing its rigidity and minimizing the diameter of the parts. The duo's work is an art, a science, and a craft. As they say, "We don't ask what. We ask who. Who is this rider and how can we capture their spirit in this frame? Bikes should be spirit-built, not just custom-built."

**this page:** Tsubasa Kuricin was designed for a track rider who required a light bike for explosive sprints.

**opposite page:** Recreate, re-design and make it even faster, once Olympic Gold winning, World One Hour Record braking frame—Takhion.

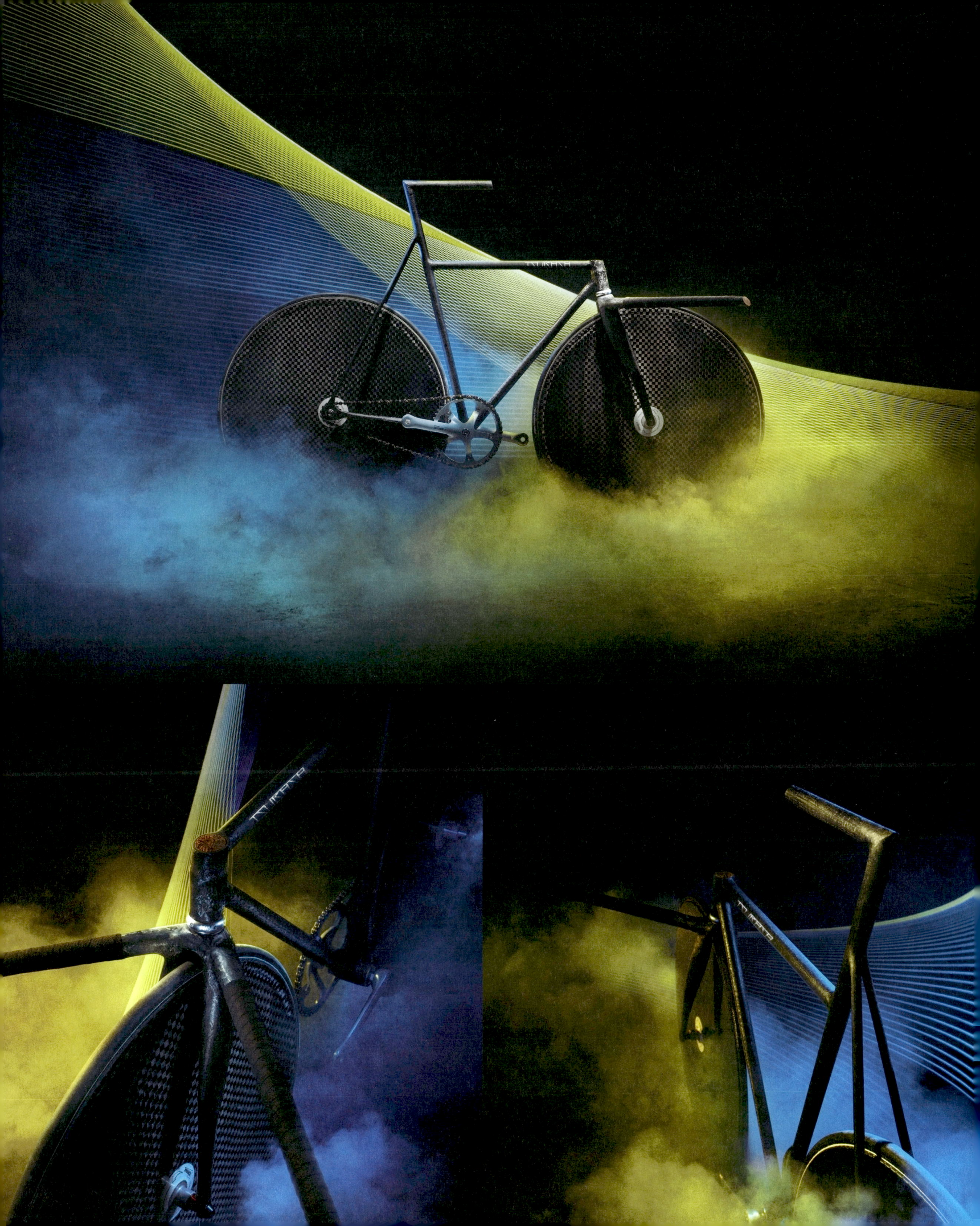

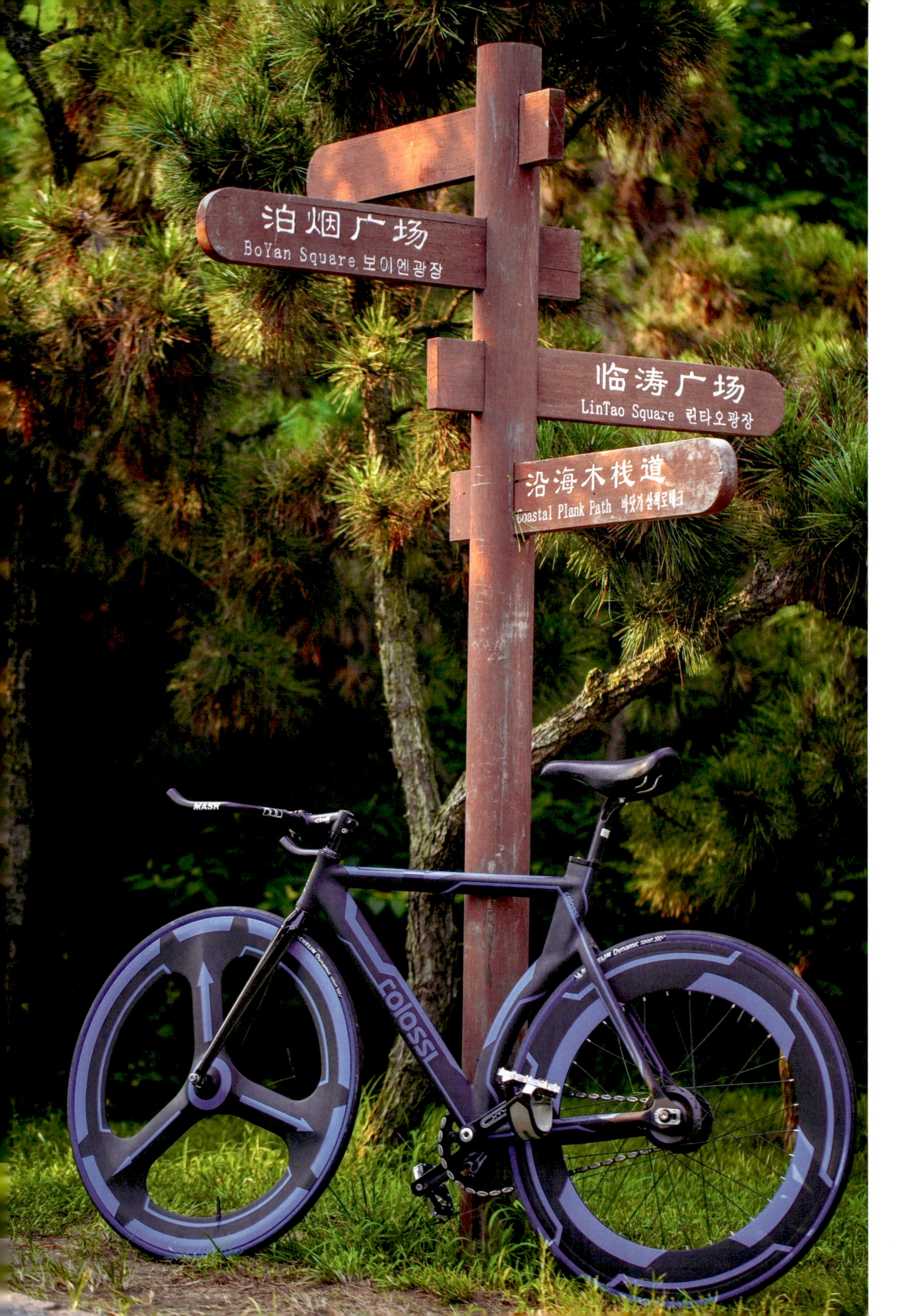

泊烟广场
BoYan Square 보이엔광장
临涛广场
LinTao Square 린타오광장
沿海木栈道
Coastal Plank Path 바닷가 산책로데크
colossi

this page: ***Experimental Time-Trial Bike***

**STURDY CYCLES**

Sturdy produced its experimental time-trial bicycle to study the effect of varying front-end geometry on handling when a rider assumes an aerodynamic tuck position. Bolts on the steel fillet-brazed frame are concealed so as not to impede airflow. The rider's position is fixed and a particular handlebar configuration is used to ensure that the body does not have to shift even when engaging the brake-lever elbow pads. This scheme channels the rider's efforts into the bicycle's geometry instead of frittering them away. The whittled-down front also allows the rider's shifts to be echoed in smooth transitions through the length of the frame. Overall, the effect is to make measurements of cause and effect during time trials much more precise.

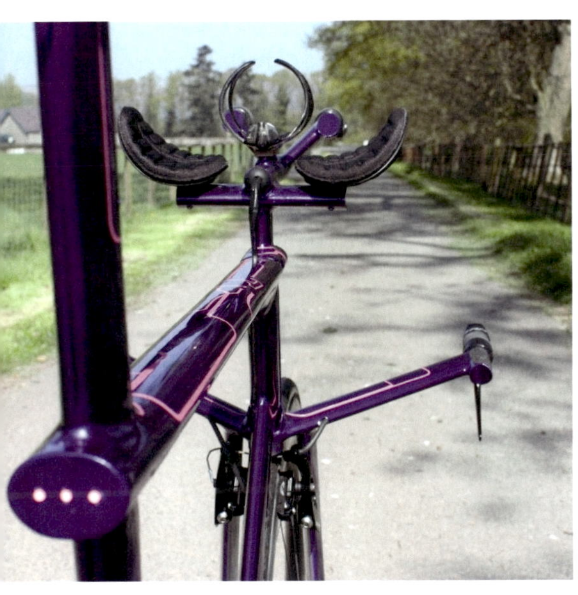

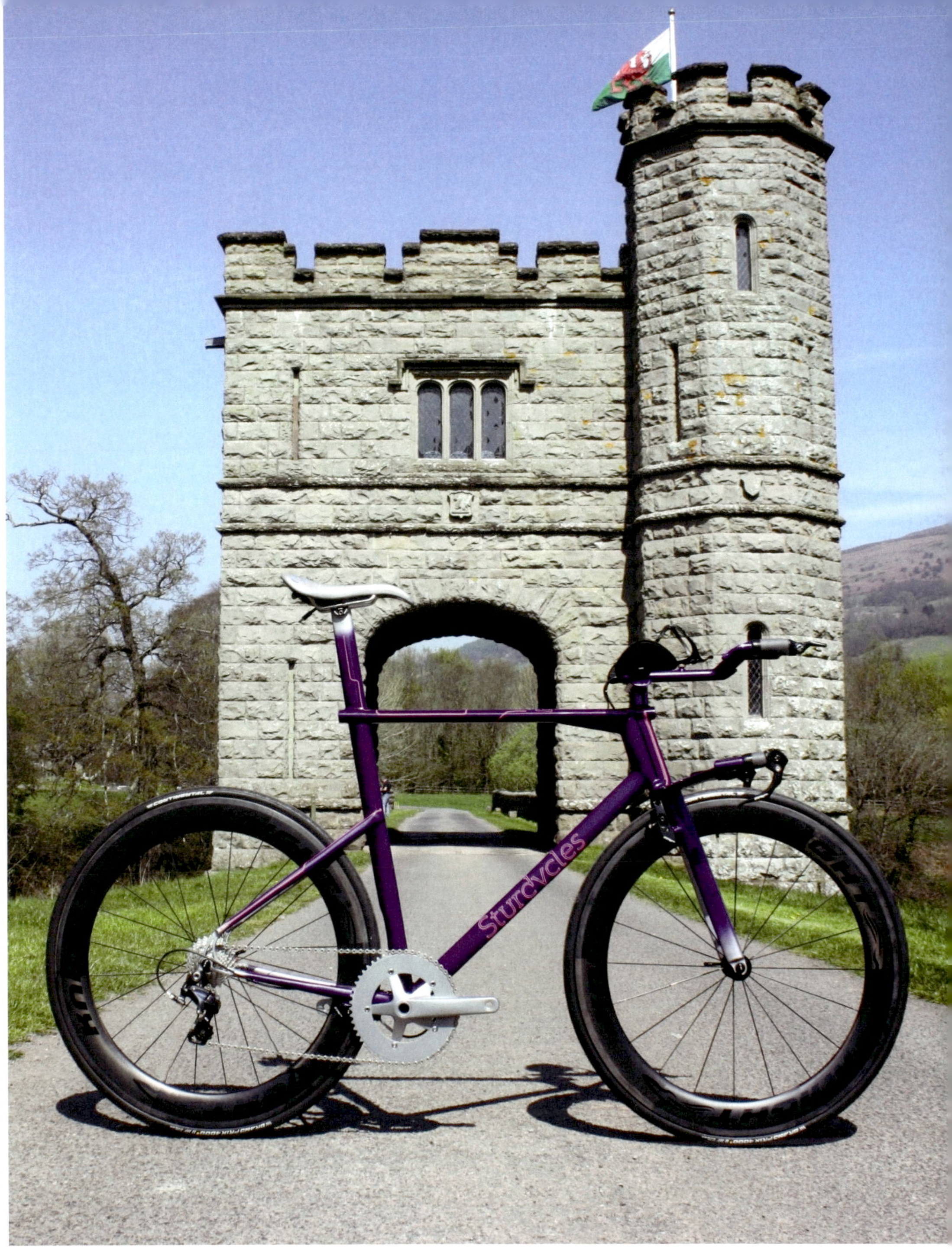

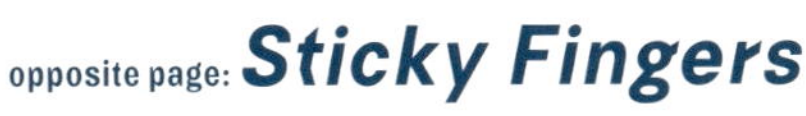

opposite page: ***Sticky Fingers***

**COLOSSI CYCLING**

Stiff, fast, and smooth, the wonderfully named Sticky Fingers sounds just a little obscene and looks sexy to boot. The Sticky is Jan Kole's interpretation of an all-around aero track frame that looks almost 2D, like a Tron cycle seen in the broad light of day. Kole's team designed its geometry to be ideal for riding both on the track and on the street. The builders smooth-welded its custom 6061 aluminum tubing and designed its clamp to suit any 27.2-millimeter seatpost, and then came the digital-display-like finish in a true electric blue.

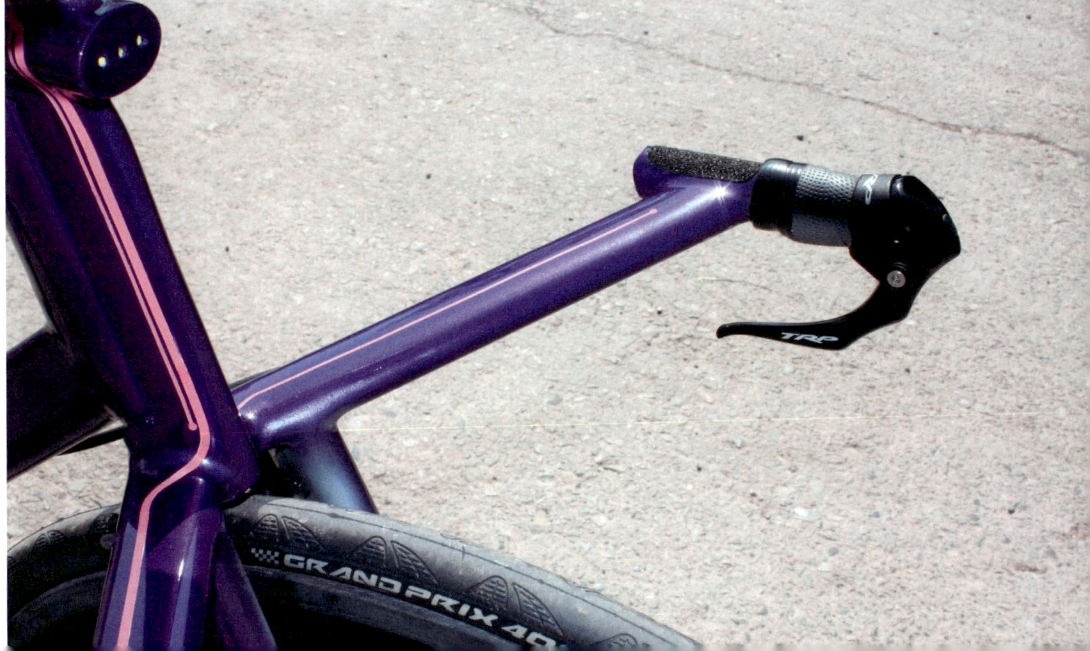

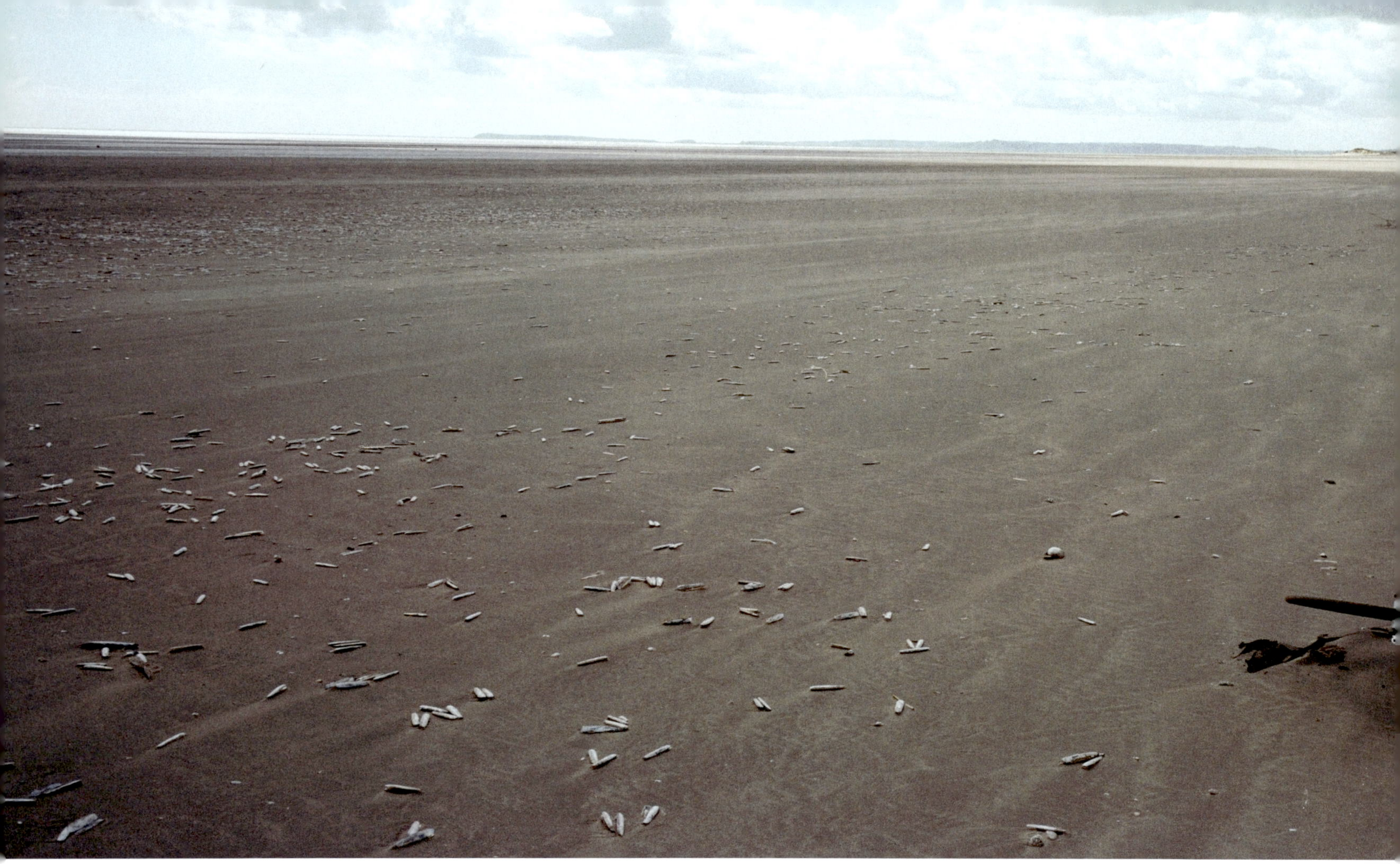

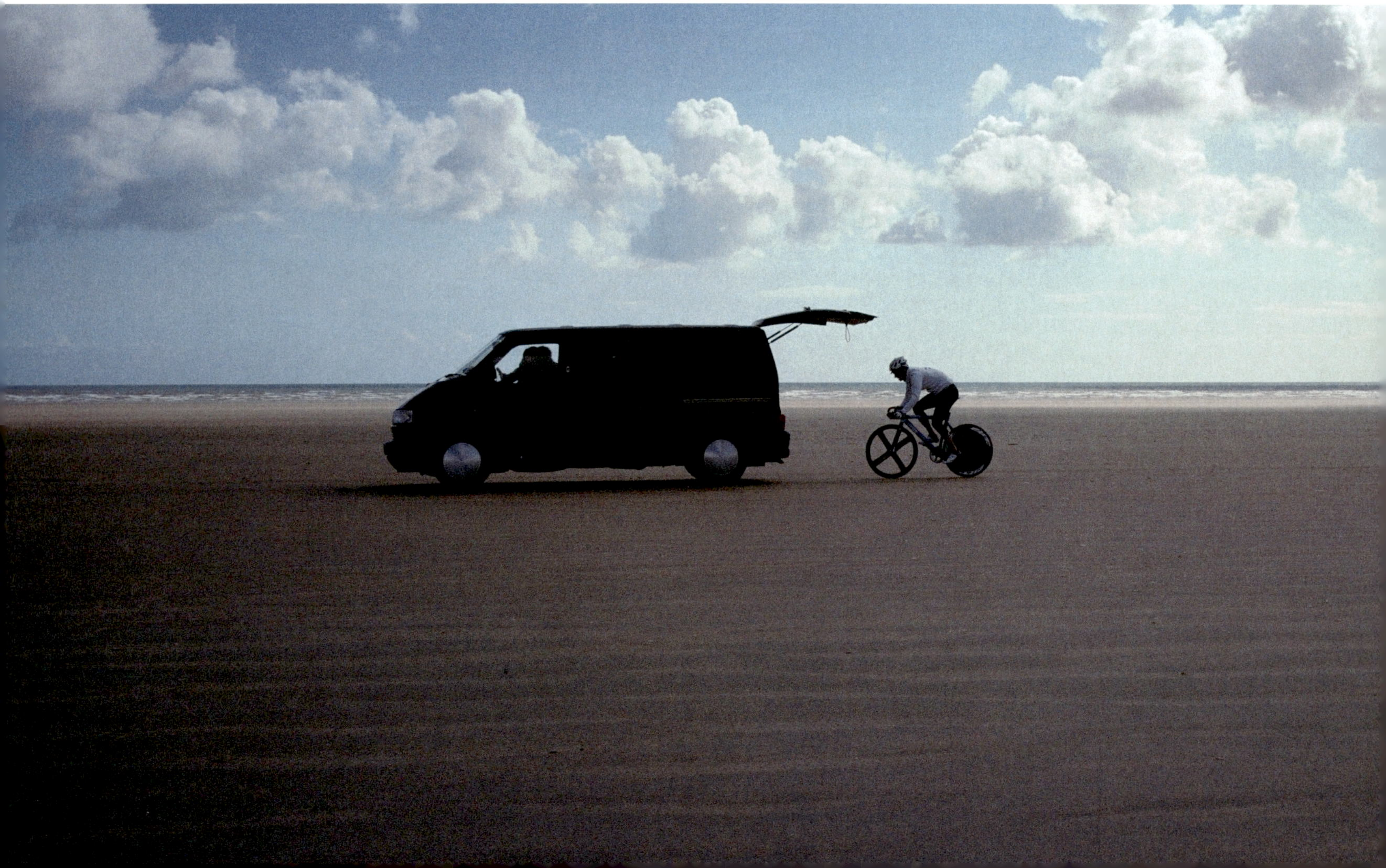

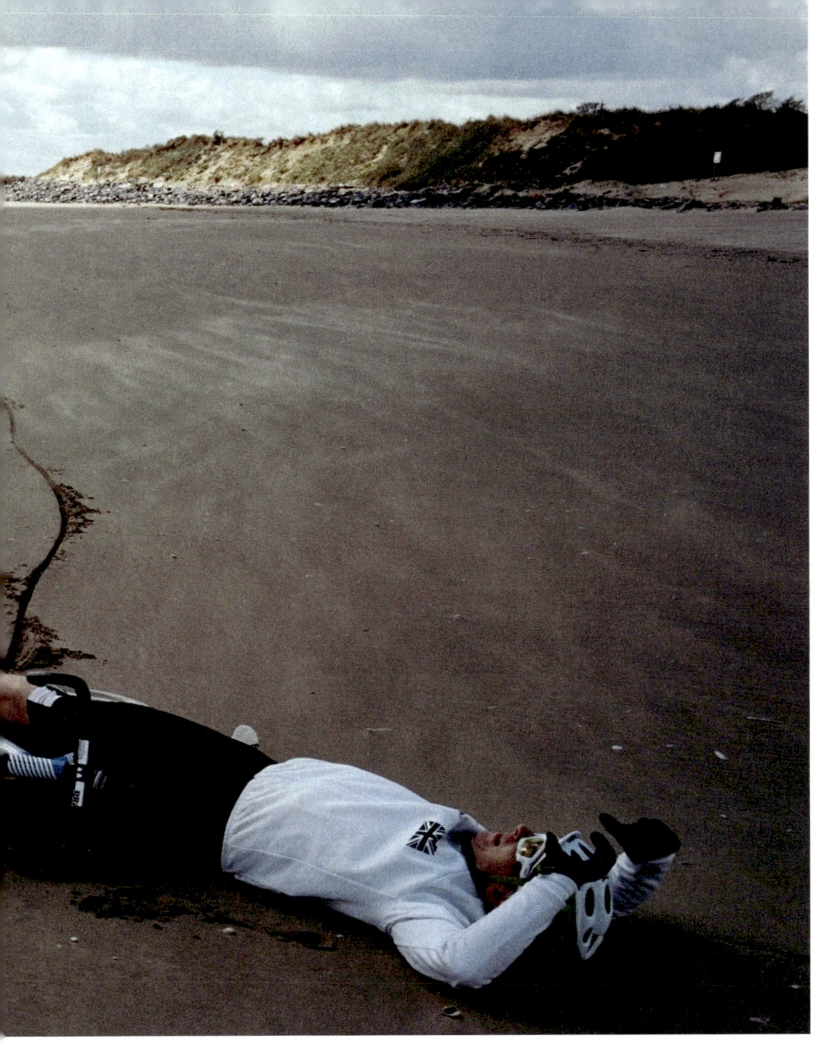

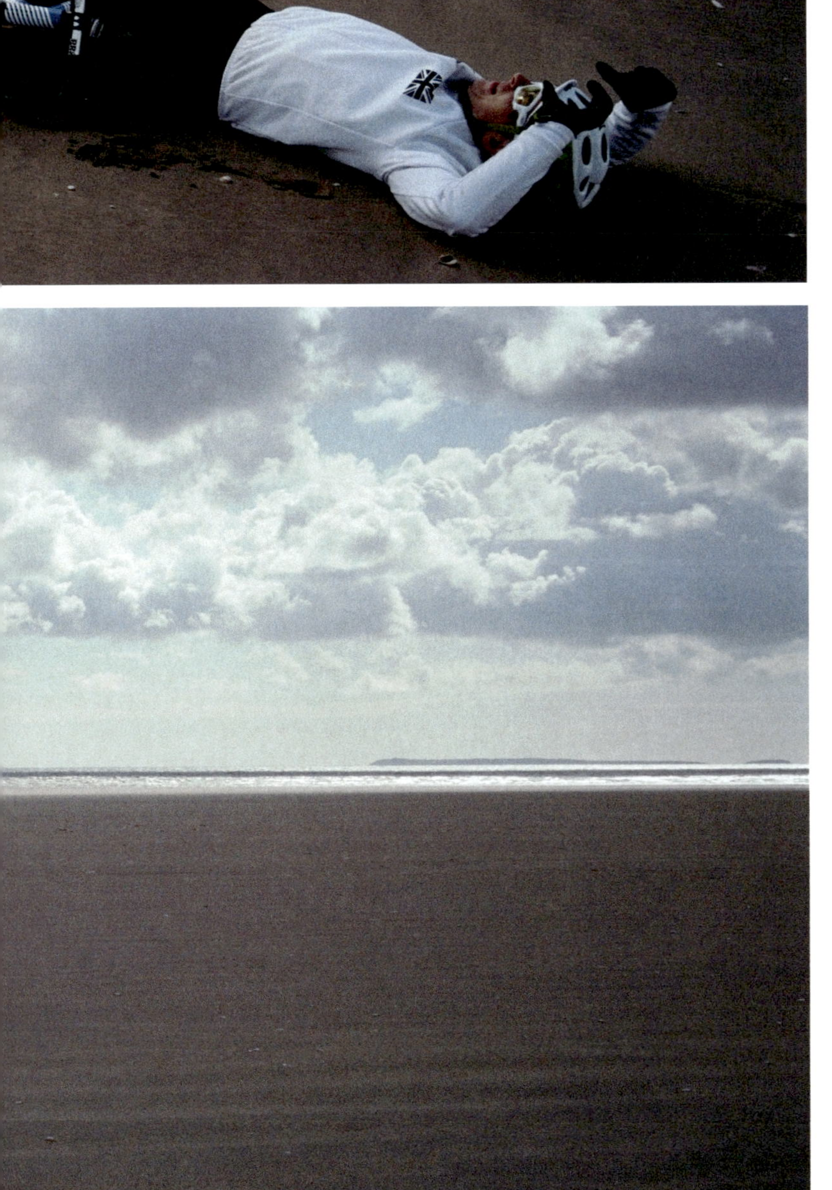

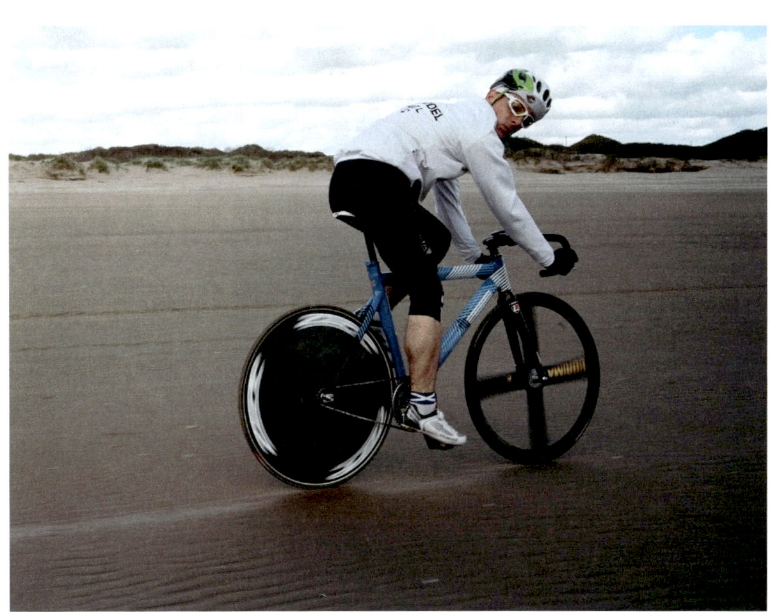

# 7 Mile Horizon

**DEATH SPRAY CUSTOM**

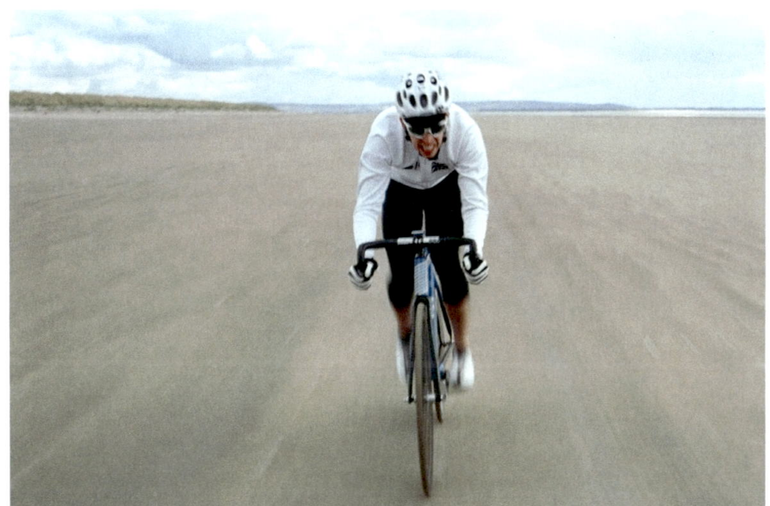

One-off, custom-painted carbon forks named for the seven deadly sins dot this artist collective's web shop. Its members are riders and gluttons for speed who mount installations of Hermes handsaws, Dior jacks, and Chanel wrench sets, sell rebel-yell-inflected components for both bicycles and motorcycles, and produce cheeky photo shoots of, say, a 1966 Triumph posed according to the British War Department's 1944 *Camouflage of Vehicles* field manual. For this project they rode a Bluebird track bike to Pendine Sands in Wales to pay homage to Sir Malcolm Campbell and his aero-engined Sunbeam Bluebird, on which he broke the land speed record in 1924. Powered by a bacon, egg, and sausage breakfast and geared at 51/15, they made their way over Campbell's track at a rather more sedate 16 miles per hour.

## *Big Bang*

DEATH
SPRAY
CUSTOM

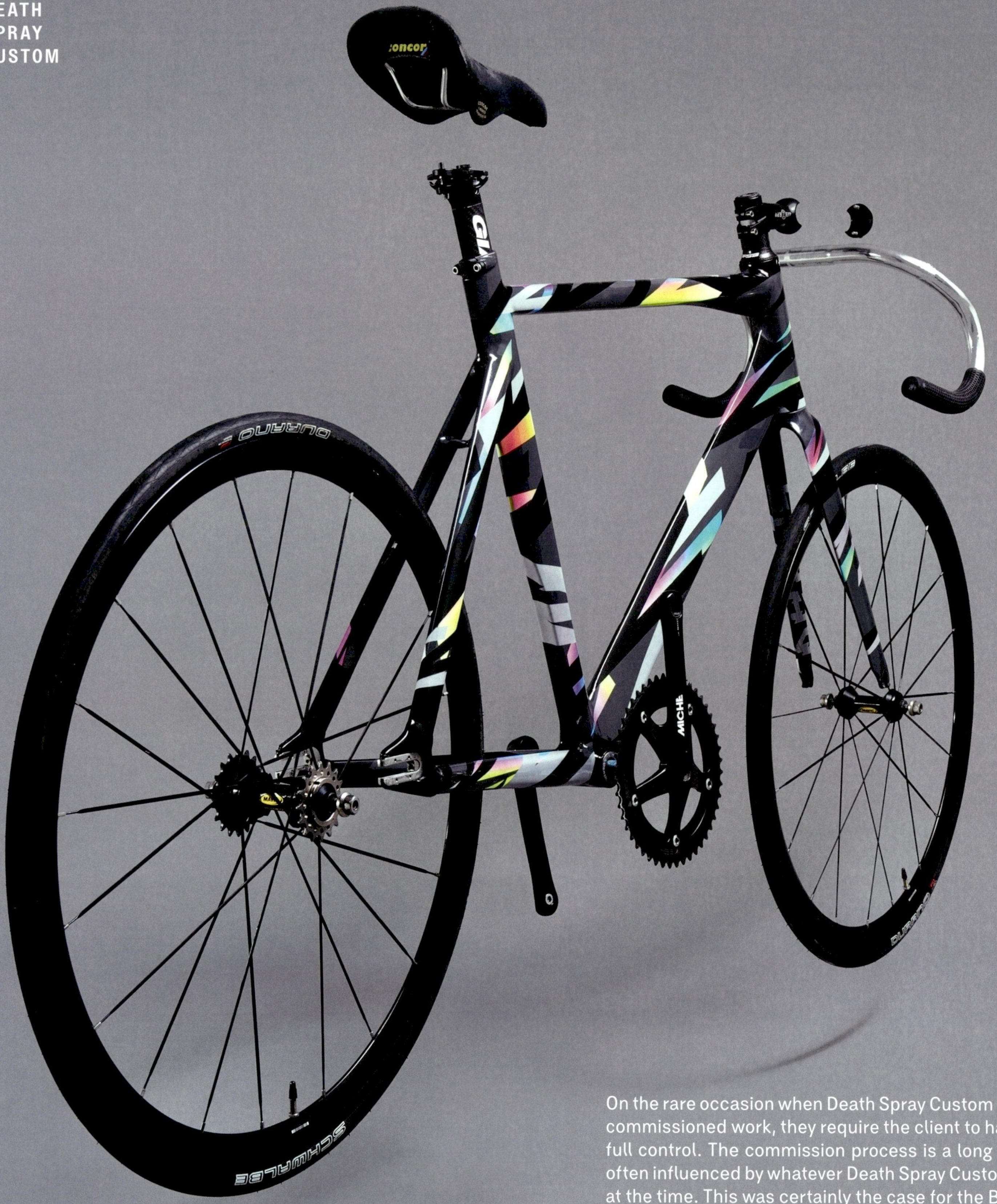

On the rare occasion when Death Spray Custom takes on commissioned work, they require the client to hand over full control. The commission process is a long one and often influenced by whatever Death Spray Custom is into at the time. This was certainly the case for the Big Bang, on which they used neon fades to create SL shapes representing the client's initials. The Big Bang name came from a discussion with the photographer, when somebody described the design as looking like an exploded diagram.

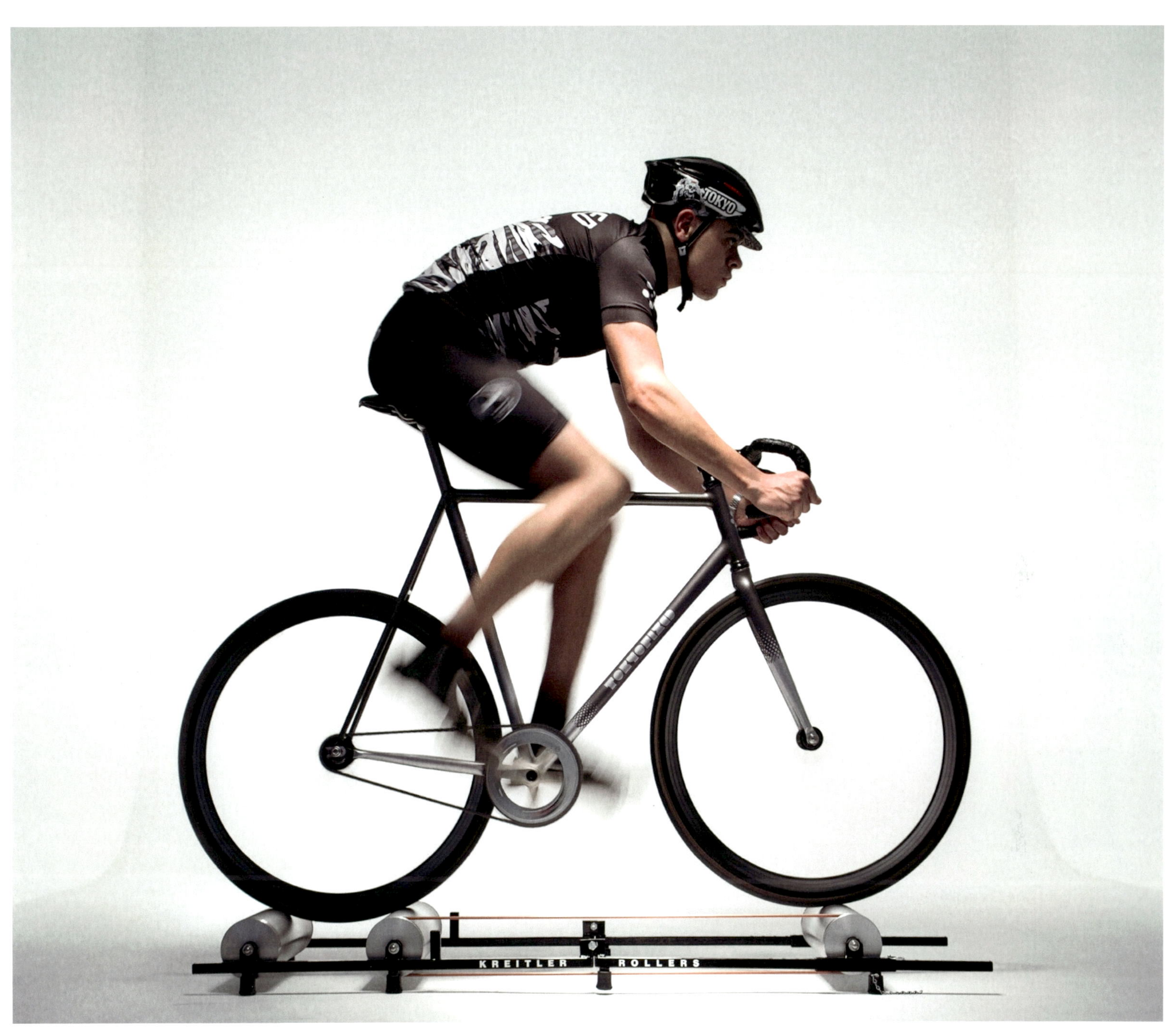


## *ONO*

**DEATH SPRAY CUSTOM**

When London-based cycle brand Tokyo Fixed asked if Death Spray Custom would like to do a limited-production bike, they decided on a lo-pro track bike with a fillet-brazed finish. The final piece was a painted prototype, which was then replicated in the factory.

# Festka's Michael Moureček

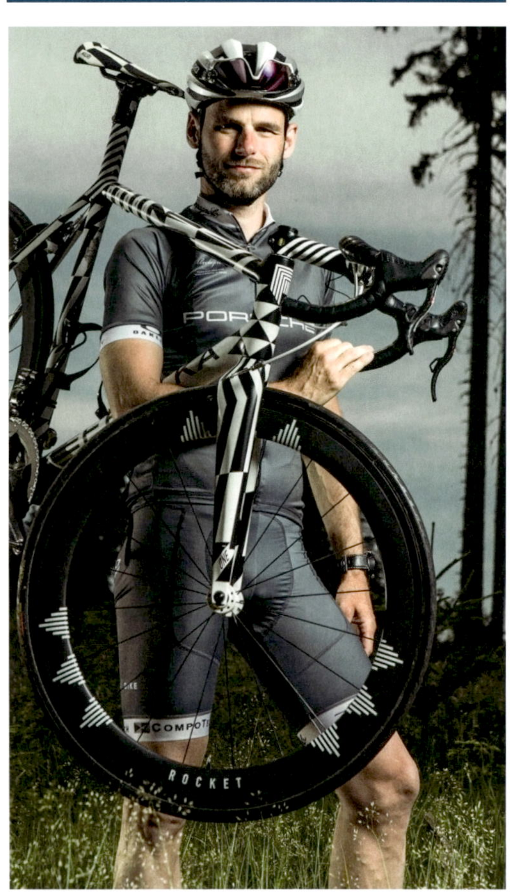


Ten-time road and track champion of the Czech Republic, Festka co-founder and product developer, Michael Moureček.

"We love what we do and in order to do what we love, we ride," say the guys at Czech frame-building workshop Festka.

Take, for example, the company's co-founder and product developer, Michael Moureček. Moureček retired from racing in 2006 as a ten-time road and track champion of the Czech Republic.

Moureček grew up on skis and wheels in a town tucked into alpine South Bohemia. He started racing at 16, and by 18 had earned a berth on the national team. Later, he raced professionally in Italy, then joined the Dukla Praha team. After retiring, he realized—for the first time in all those years of sponsorships, team colors, and conspicuously placed logos—that he wanted to choose the brand, the color, and the components of his ride: "I wanted a machine that would mirror me as a person and a cyclist." He failed to find one. So he and a friend founded Festka.

"Today, Festka is a brand for mature cyclists who are able to feel and distinguish the small details that differentiate us from mass production," Moureček says. But a quarter of their clients know nothing about biking—except that the people at Festka know everything about biking because they do a lot of it. Indeed, Moureček's team knows about reach and stack settings, the implications of the length and angle of head tubes. They are racer-engineer-makers whose hearts are stainless steel, titanium, or a Japanese carbon fiber typical in Formula 1 circles and the aviation industry. The workshop builds almost everything from scratch, making its logistics as complex as its bikes' geometry. Moureček has a different development team for each material, additional experts in charge of components, and a graphic designer and local artists he can tap if he needs the bike to be "an art piece."

Moureček also has a fitter who does the geometry, measuring clients on a bike and then drawing something akin to a made-to-measure fashion illustration. This geometer, Vojtěch Hačecký, is also a pro rider; he makes his drawings in hotel rooms after races and has many clients from the United States and Asia who have already been measured elsewhere, allowing him to make their geometries even more precise.

"Cycling is returning to its roots in recent years," Moureček says. "The 'social status' of cycling is booming. More and more people are aware of the bike that they choose to ride and the gear that they wear, not to mention the goal or philosophy that cycling presents for them." Festka clients can afford to be philosophers, daydreamers, and amateurs: Their frame builders are pros, and they've got the science covered.

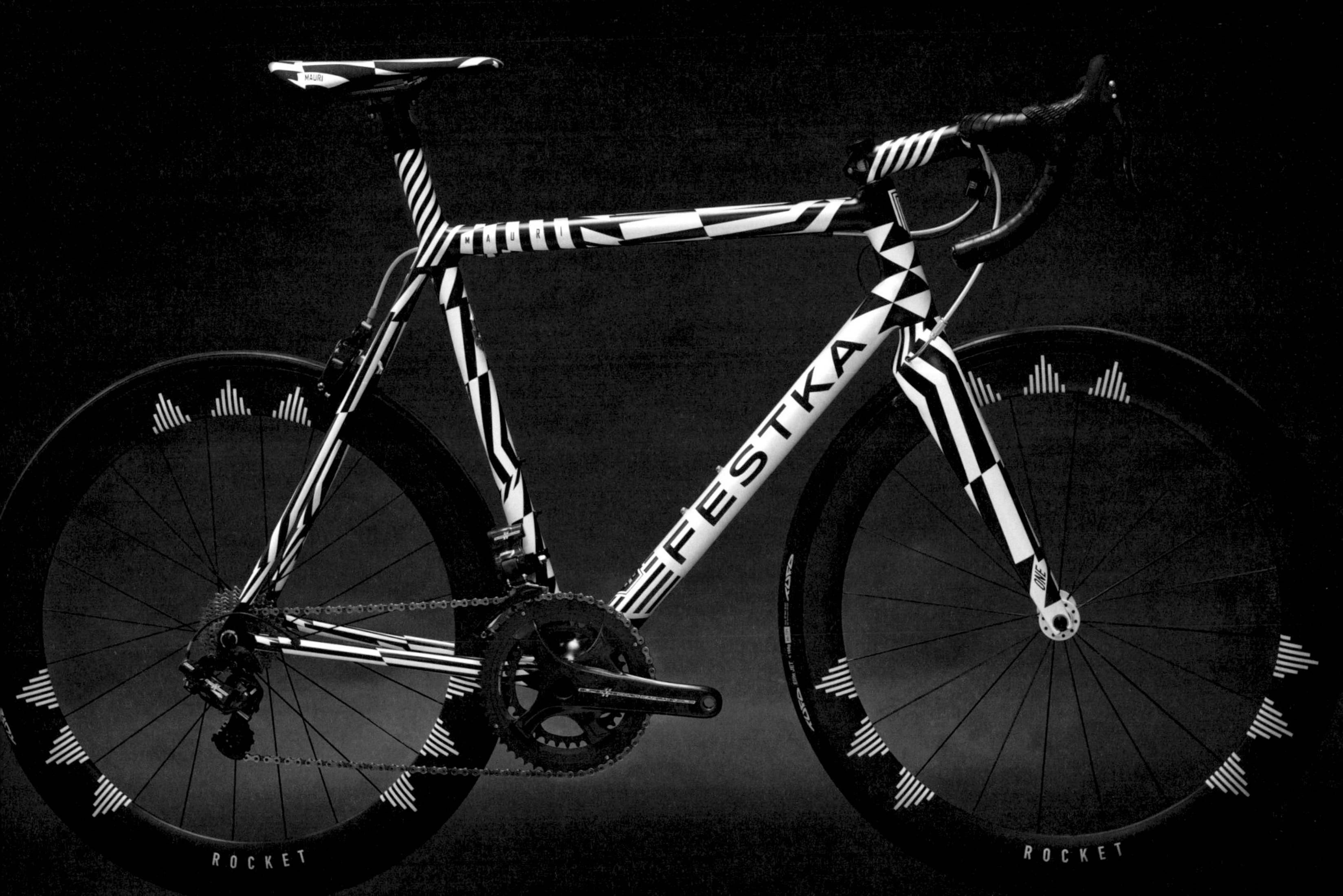


## *ONE LT Dazzle*

The ONE LT Dazzle had to be perfectly made and perfectly personalized: it was commissioned by one of Festka's founders for his personal use. To achieve that level of quality, the team approached the commission as they would have approached any other, constructing the bike "without compromise." To meet the needs of this most exacting rider, Festka's team constructed the ONE from the finest Japanese fibers and three tube layers, each of which performs a specific function. For this model, however, the designers reprogrammed "the robots" to craft a lighter tube that would nonetheless provide the proper stiffness. The finish, in black and white, took its cues from the dazzle camouflage used on auto prototypes and Second World War battleships to distort the perception of their speed and direction.

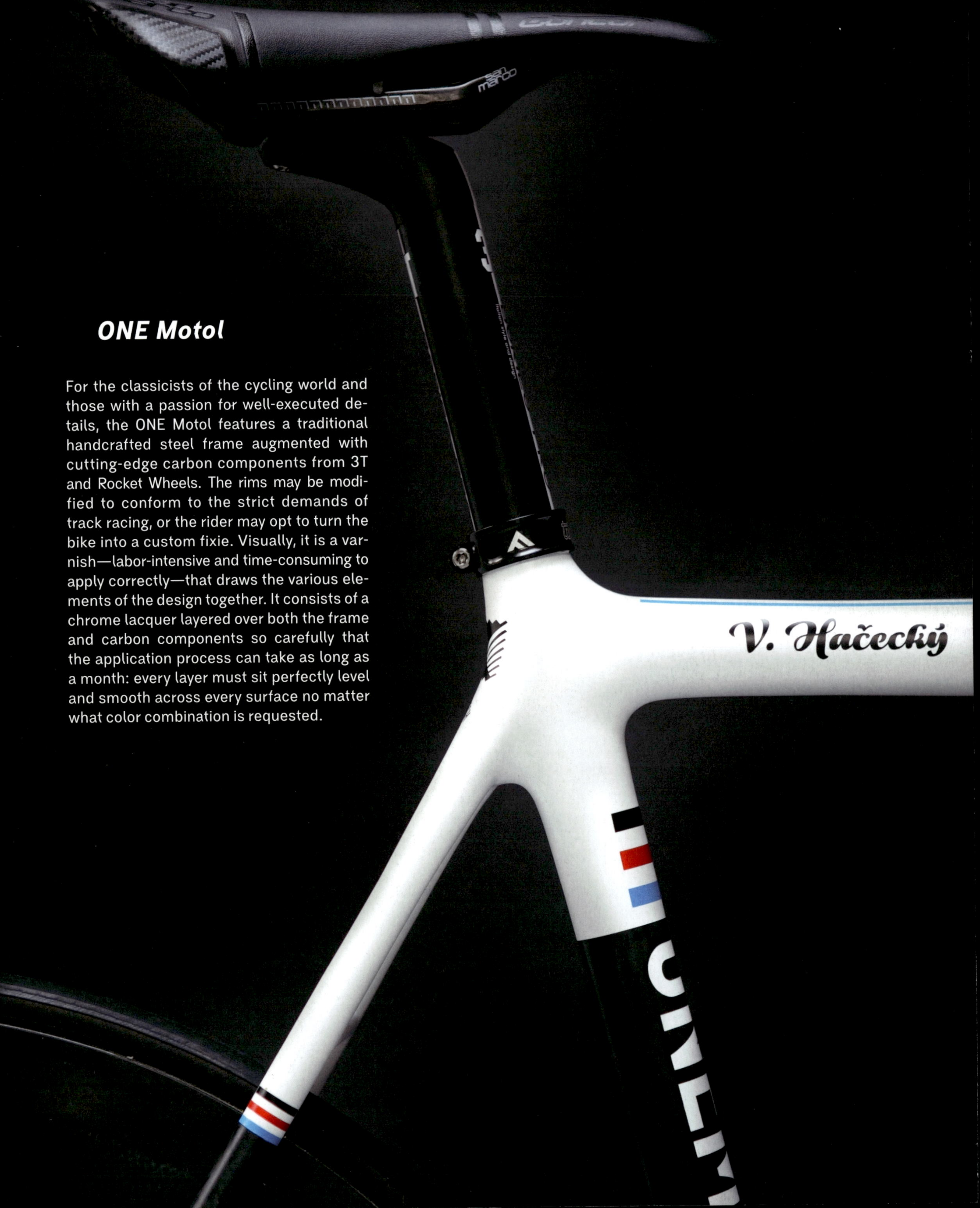


## *ONE Motol*

For the classicists of the cycling world and those with a passion for well-executed details, the ONE Motol features a traditional handcrafted steel frame augmented with cutting-edge carbon components from 3T and Rocket Wheels. The rims may be modified to conform to the strict demands of track racing, or the rider may opt to turn the bike into a custom fixie. Visually, it is a varnish—labor-intensive and time-consuming to apply correctly—that draws the various elements of the design together. It consists of a chrome lacquer layered over both the frame and carbon components so carefully that the application process can take as long as a month: every layer must sit perfectly level and smooth across every surface no matter what color combination is requested.

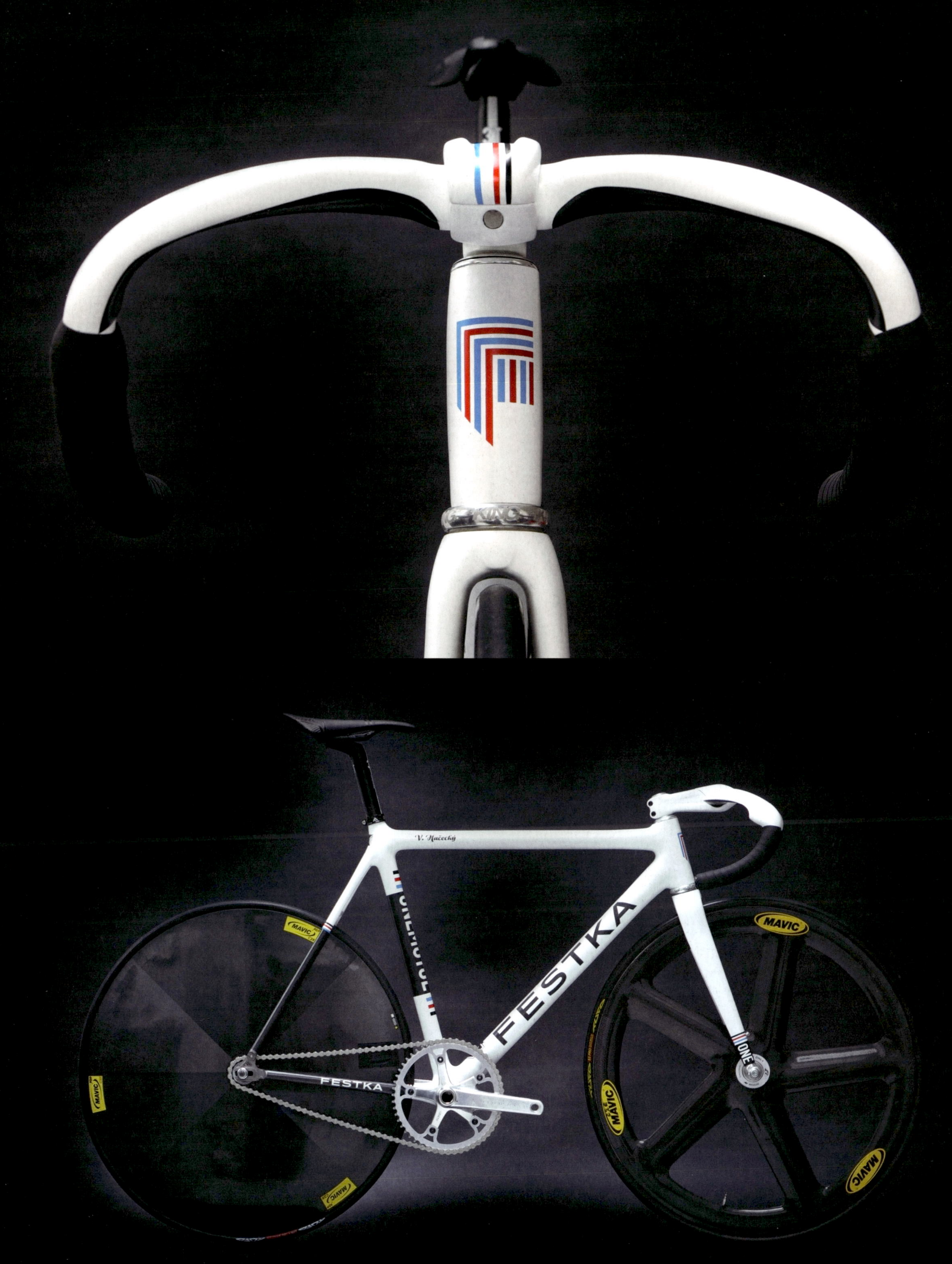
V. Hačecký
FESTKA
FESTKA
MAVIC
ONE

## Zona Track Art Edition No. 3

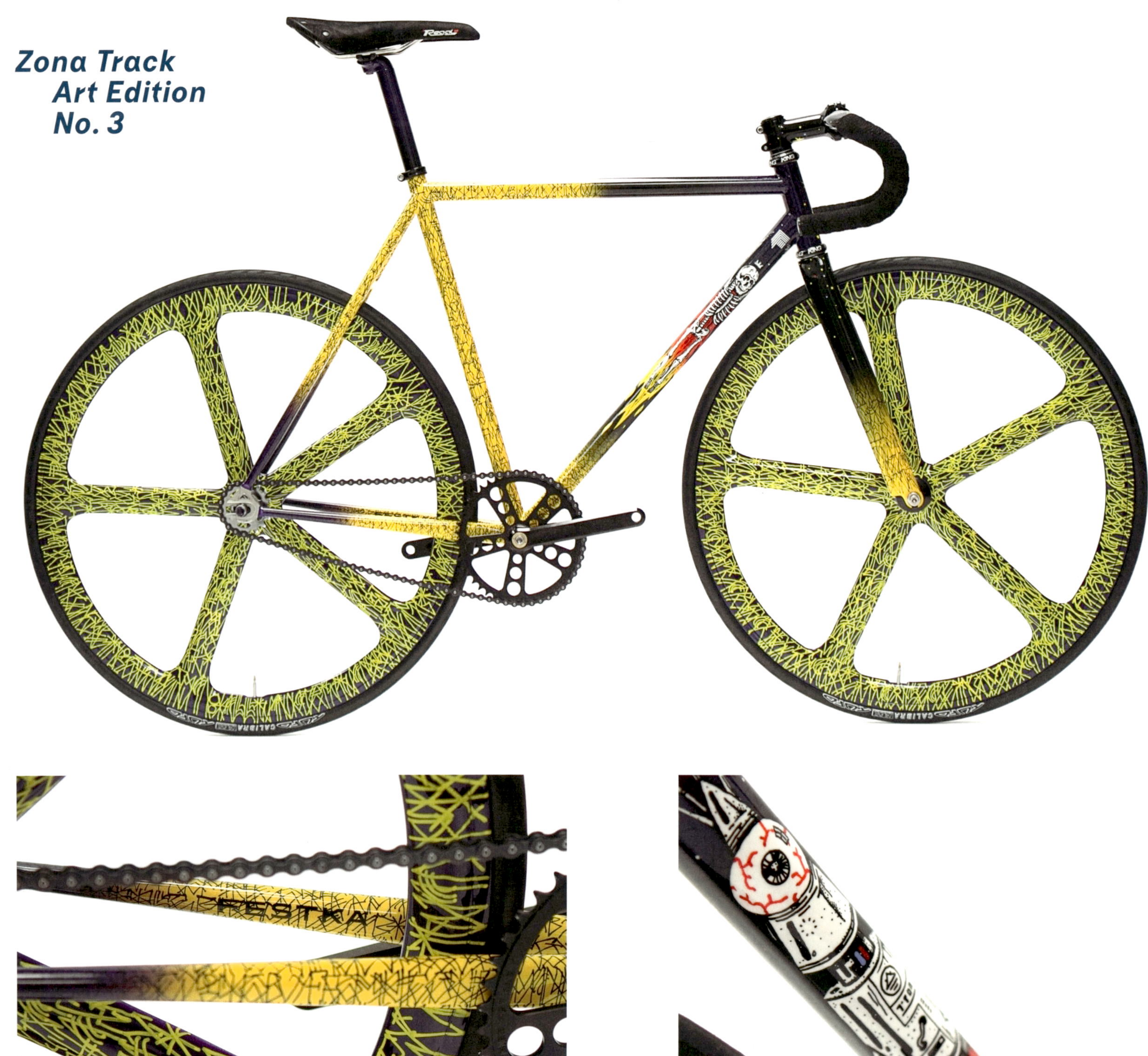

There are three frames in the Festka Art Collection. The Zona Track—which was launched in the cafe of Prague's National Gallery—is the third installment in the series. Czech artist Michal Škapa—a.k.a. Tron, the international graffiti writer—designed and hand-painted the frame, wheels, fork, and handlebars, which now bear disguised lyrics from songs by Queen and James Brown about bikes and riding. An urbane fixie with street-art-inflected good looks, it represents Škapa's development of a Brazilian graffiti script called Pixação. Škapa's scribbles, Roman characters, and rune-like lettering filigree the two Aerospoke wheels. Their application represents a synthesis of techniques and materials ranging from airbrushing to automobile paint and acrylic markers—and the work of three long days.

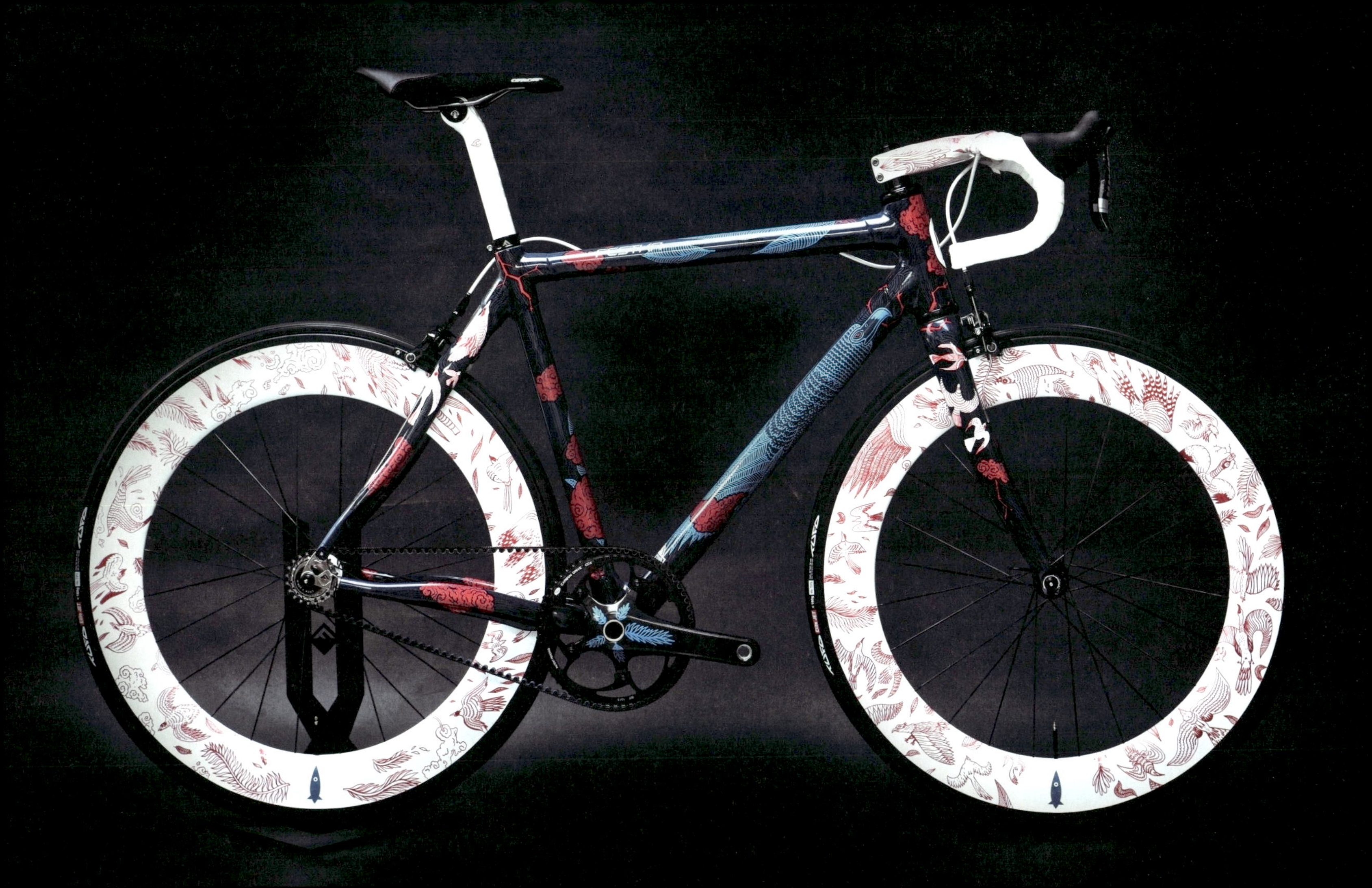

## *Zero Art Edition No. 1*

The artwork tattooing the Urban Zero, the first in the brand's Art Edition label, is not a bunch of stickers: the frame was hand-colored by two illustrators, Tomski & Polanski, using collaged elements from books and newspapers, Hollywood characters, and playing cards. Tomski & Polanski, whose work features in the Wes Anderson film *Grand Budapest Hotel*, are road cyclists themselves, and their work features a constant companion that all riders have greeted as friend or foe at one time or another: the wind. One of nature's elemental forces, it represents destruction, renewal, and peace. With a gear ratio of 60–22 and 50-millimeter Rocket Wheels, it can adapt to any terrain, just like the wind. And with a Gates Carbon Drive belt system, the wind is all that cyclists will hear as they speed along.

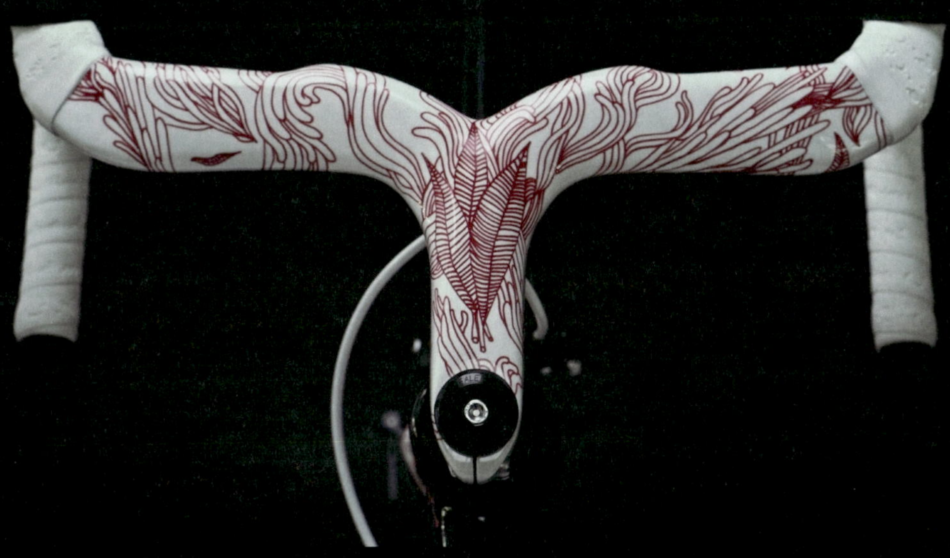

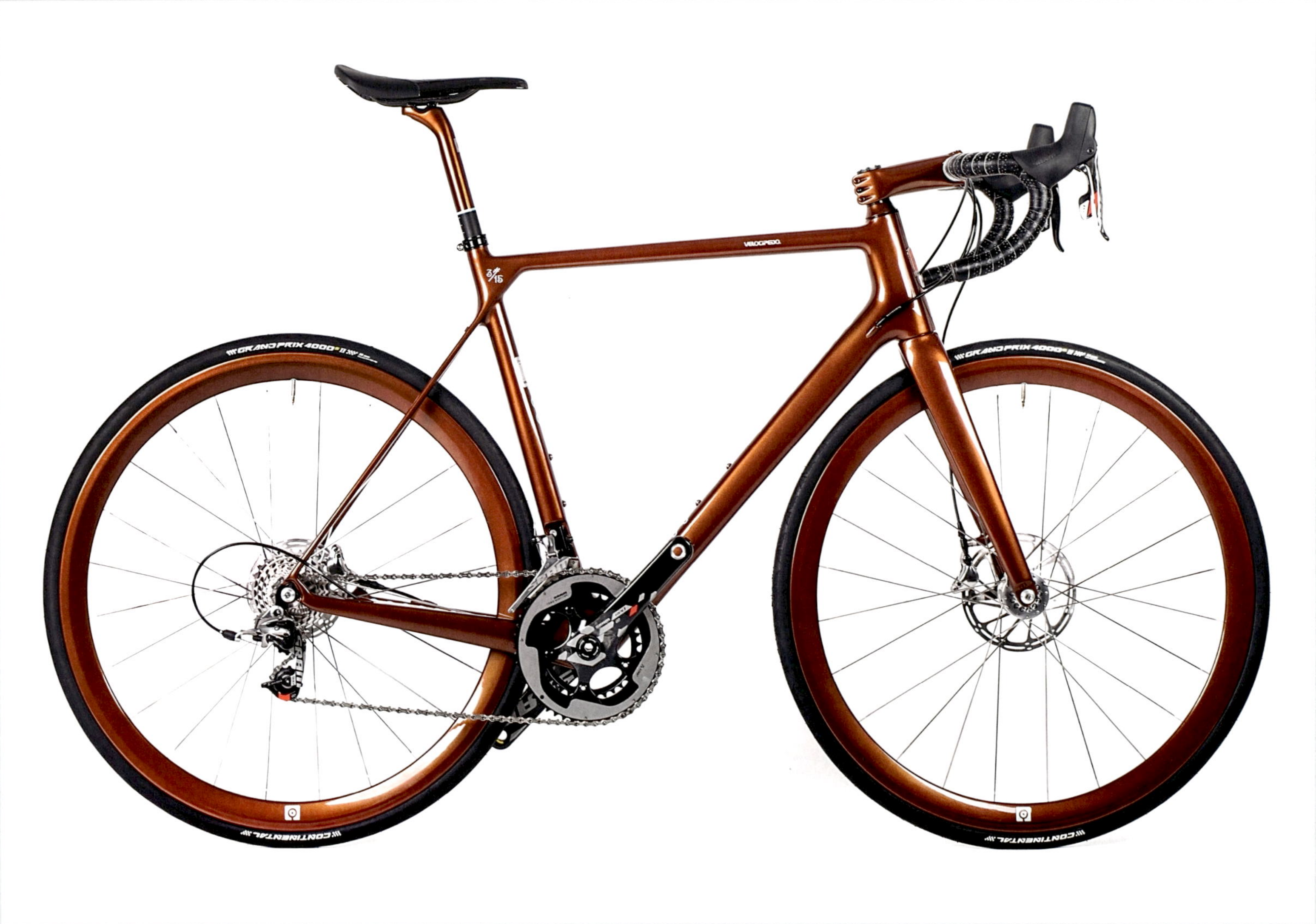

## *DisCourse*

**VELOCIPEDO.**

The DisCourse road bike—which comes in an edition of only 15—takes its name from the Latin word *discursus* ("to walk around"), referencing this lightweight bike's powerful disc brake, which does some robust slowing on fast downhills. But its painted titanium frame also alludes to "a dialogue with nature and different cultures." The pattern on the carbon-filament frame and fork—made with paint, not decals—evolves from an elegant theme wrought with Native American motifs into a complex Eastern pattern via repetition and compression, while its saturated colors also shift subtly from deep orange to deep red and brown.

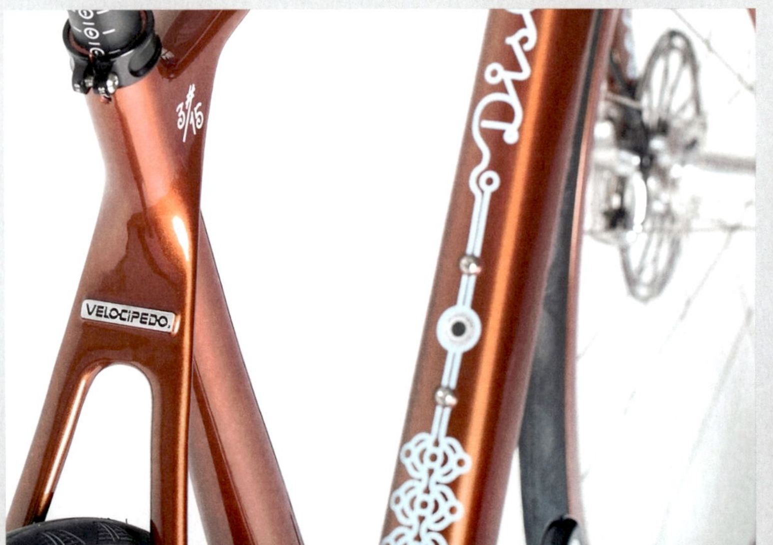


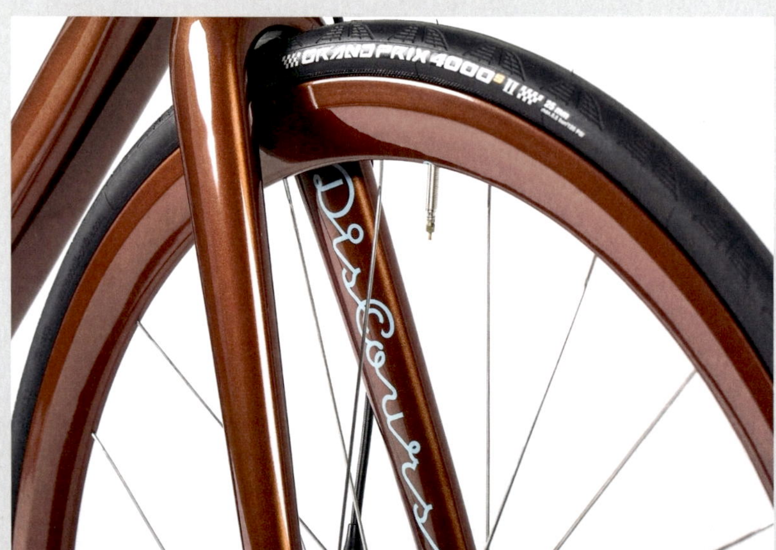

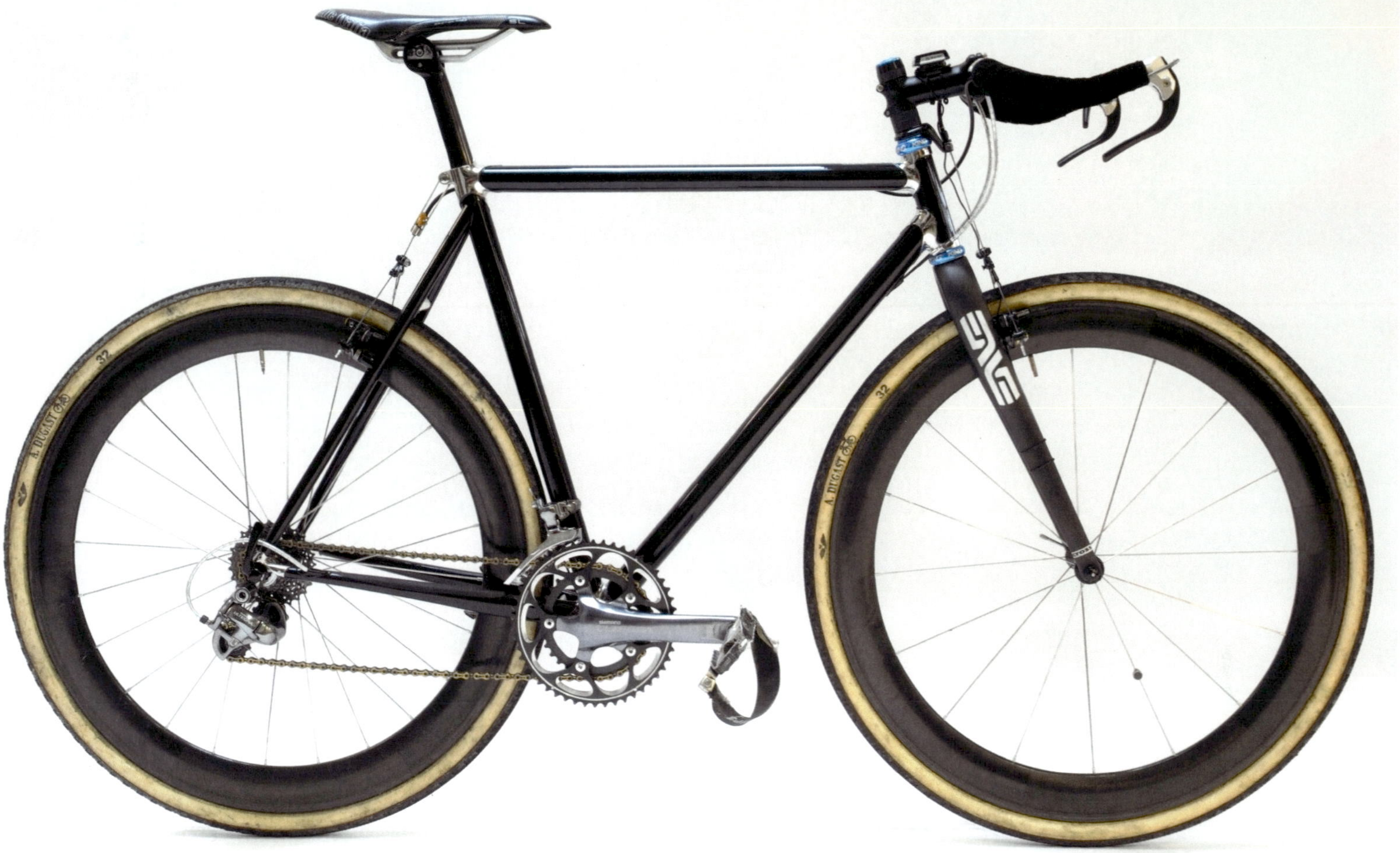

## *Bedovelo Crosser*

**BEDOVELO**

If you cannot find it, make it. Denizens of bicycle culture are nothing if not resourceful. Take Mario Scandella, fresh out of mechanics training, who built a cyclocross bike with bullhorn handlebars and made his shift and brake levers and his lugs himself. Using Columbus Spirit tubes, an ENVE fork, and Zipp carbon wheels, Scandella crafted what became one of Bedevelo's lightest builds ever after Baumgartner hired him to head up his repair shop. Purists may balk at playing Frankenstein with components, like flat mountain-bike pedals on track bikes, disc brakes on cross bikes, or precipitously rotated drop bars, but making one's own mix can also be a mark of creativity. Scandella's crosser demonstrates his knowledge of the market: bicycles have become as diverse as bicyclists themselves.

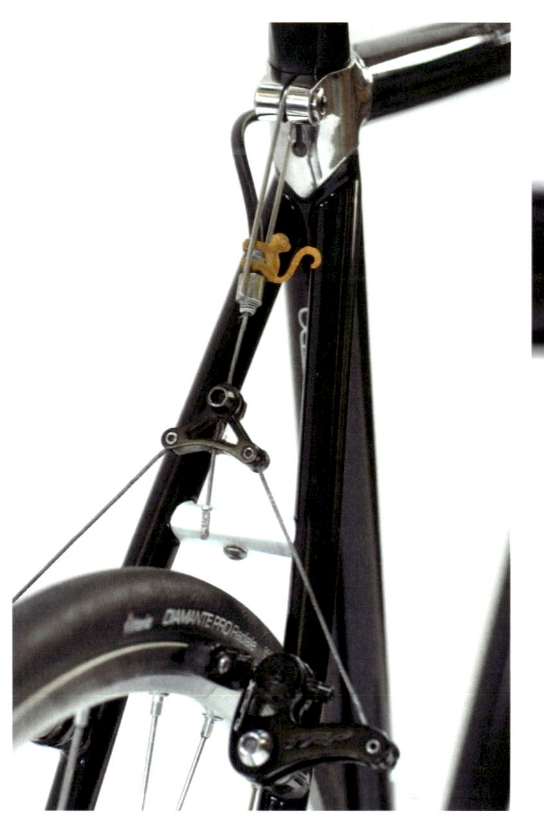


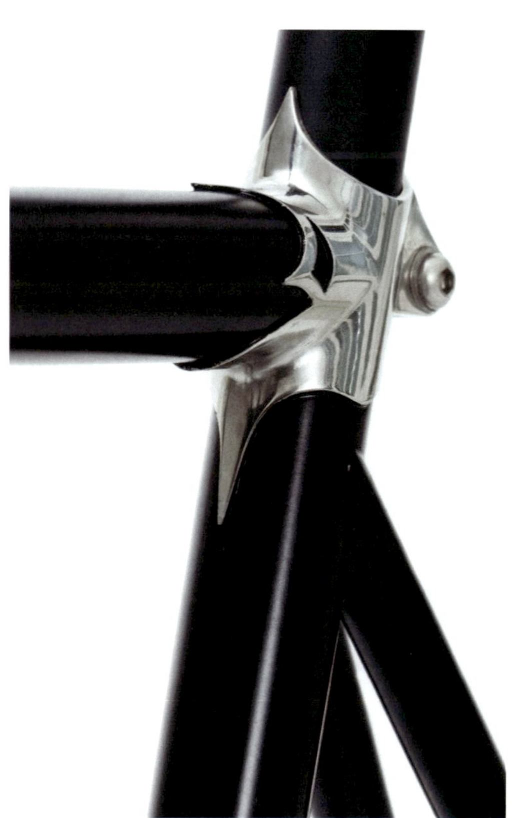

# Street race essentials

Technical no longer looks as technical does. With graphics based on individual time-trial data and complex geometries, not to mention the tony old-school jerseys that a few guys are still making, cyclists have choices today: New colors and patterns can turn a rider into an exquisite blur as she powers past everyone else on the track. Might even send a distracted competitor or two flying right off the Cote d'Azur.

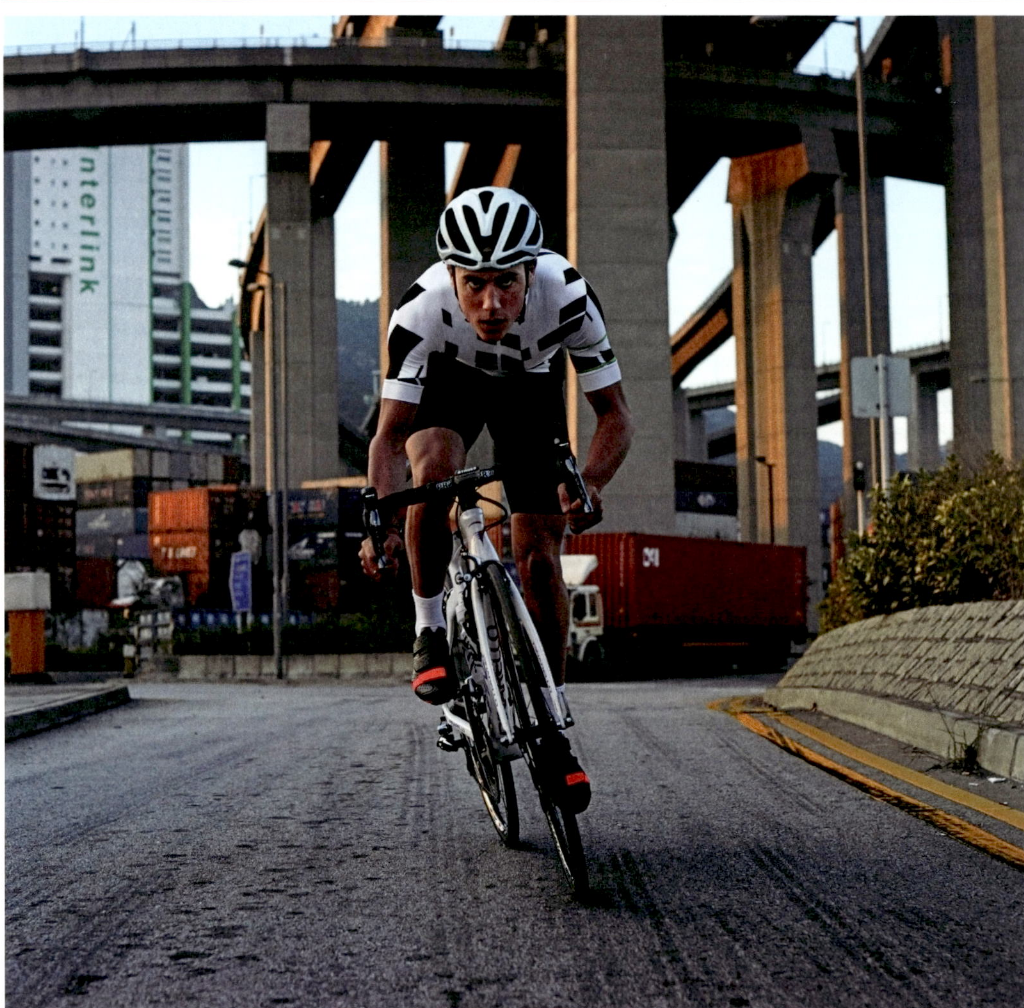


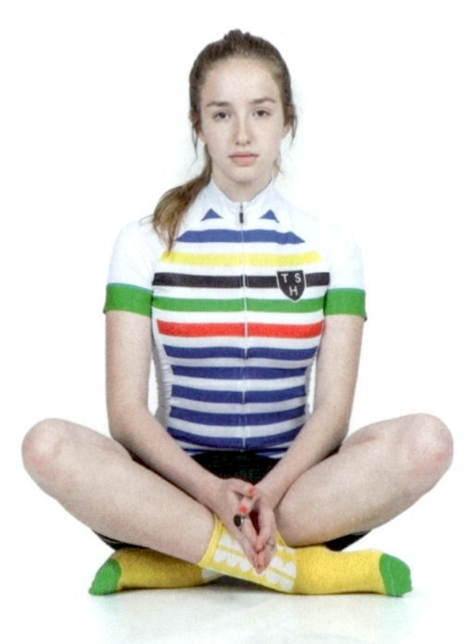

## Leave It On The Road + TSH Jersey

**TENSPEED HERO**

In October 2015, Tenspeed rode 800 miles in eight days with Michael Tabtabai, a friend and the organizer of cancer-fighting charity Leave It On The Road. The plan for 2015 was to bring friends together to fight cancer with bikes and cameras by raising a heap of money through the sale of cool gear and donations for City of Hope. And so it was. Their 2015 Resort Collection included the aptly named Leave It On The Road jersey for its cancer-fighting namesake.

## Pro Team Data Print Collection

**RAPHA**

Speed can be attained with comfort—and good looks. The Rapha Pro Team collection was born at the highest levels of competition. The refined road-racing apparel is tested and showcased by the riders of Team Sky in the professional peloton, where any minor flaw will be broadcast by the strains of their athleticism and the extremity of the conditions. Rapha collaborated with London-based design studio Accept & Proceed to create the textile graphics for its 2015 Pro Team Data Print collection. Accept & Proceed harvested ride data from the three weeks of a single Team Sky rider's grand tour to create the graphics for a line of high-performance jerseys, shorts, and hats. It plots the team member's performance levels for each stage in a pattern of precisely scaled chevrons that actually indicate the rider's distance, elevation gain, and Training Score Stress levels (TSS): a visual tribute to his effort and where it got him.

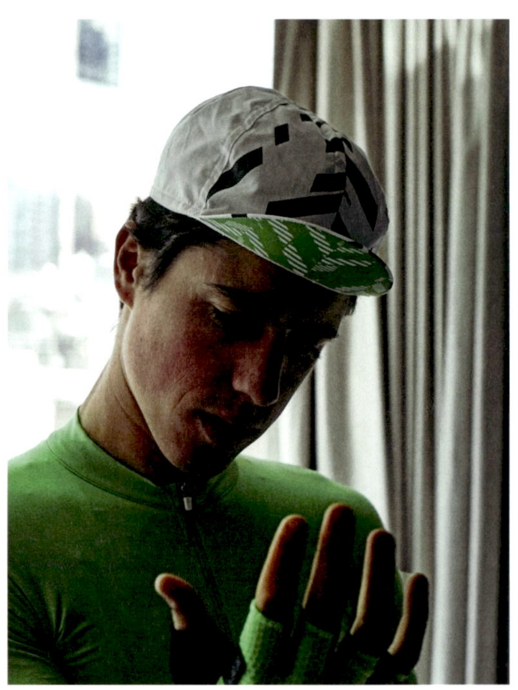

## *Huez**

When your namesake is one of cycling's most famous climbs, up the mountain of Alpe d'Huez, performance and style must be at the core of your brand. And so it is for cycling brand Huez*, which creates cycling clothing using the latest fabric technologies. Huez* has a vision of a world in which cycling is the main mode of transportation and where modern sportswear is so enriched with technology that people are healthier than ever before while also living in style. Their city range is designed to fit effortlessly into everyday life while still providing the ultimate in comfort when on the bike. The sports range capitalizes on the latest in fabric and garment construction to allow the rider to perform at his or her best.

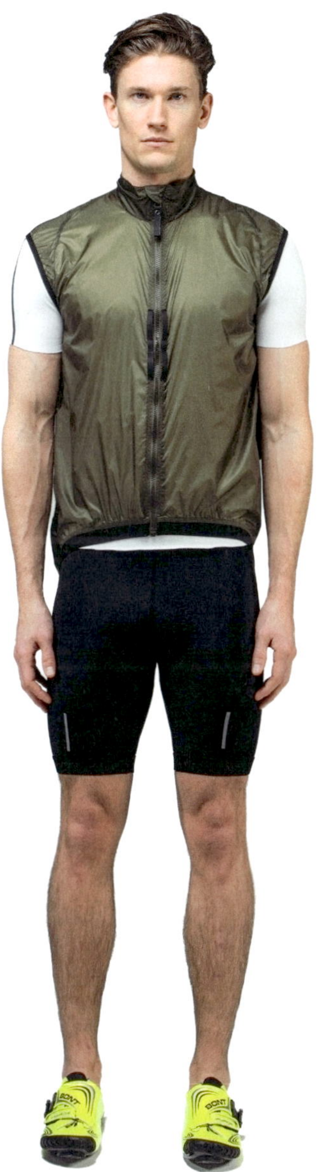

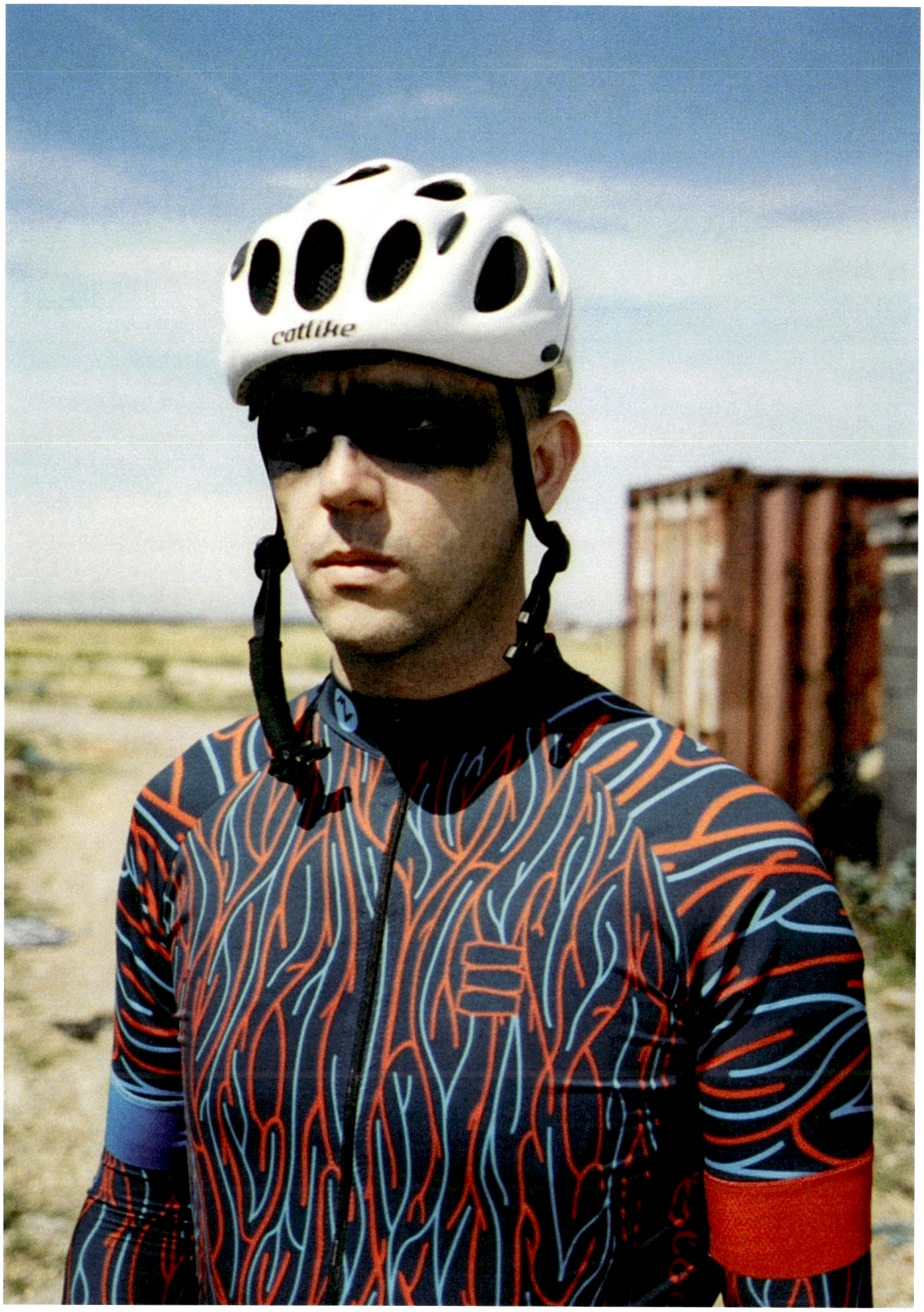

## *Blood Brothers*

**DEATH SPRAY CUSTOM**

Death Spray Custom is the multi-disciplinary practice of artist David Gwyther, whose love of the racetrack inspires his work, from a one-off livery for Nelson Piquet, Jr.'s NASCAR truck to Peter Sagan's Tour de France bike. Together with motorbike clothing brand Alpinestars, Death Spray Custom created their latest project, Blood Brothers, as a collaboration among some of the finest creators and brands in the world. Their mission: to create a sequel to the Anatomy Suit, one of the most talked-about pieces of motorcycle apparel in recent years. In this second collaboration with Morvélo, the Blood Brothers design, used on Cinelli bike frames and Alpinestars motorbike clothing, is applied to the Superlight jersey and sleeves, award winning bib shorts, and classic Italian cotton caps.

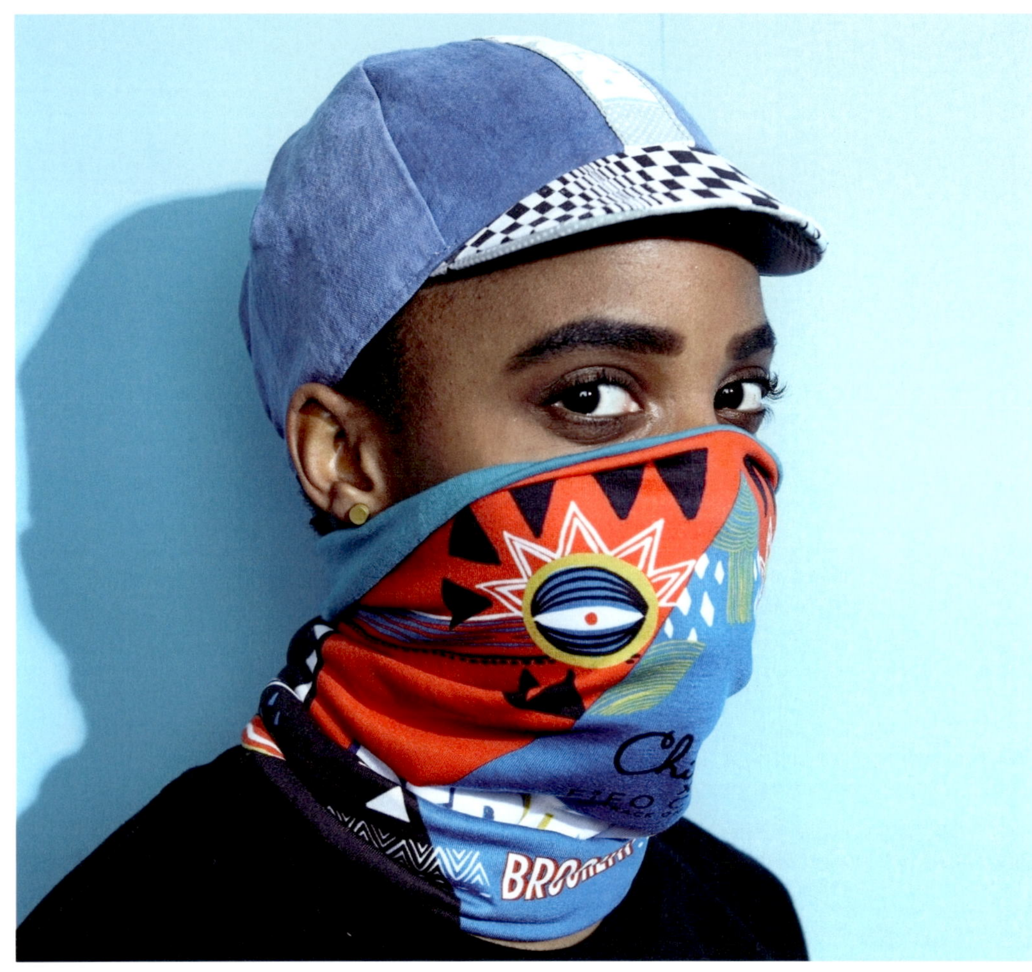


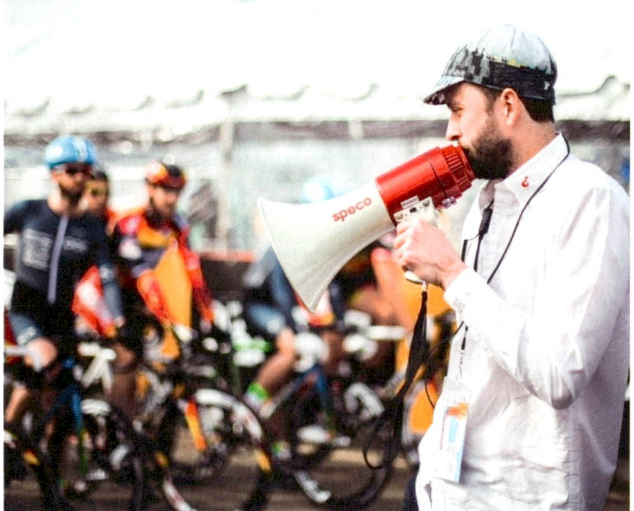


## FiFO Cycle

Travel and life on the road—these are the guiding design inspirations behind FiFO Cycle and their full range of caps and accessories for those who ride. By using only local materials for each piece they create, their partnerships support makers and small businesses from Brooklyn to Bogotá. Cycling teams, bike cafes, and museums have all commissioned small-batch designs from FiFO, including the Red Hook Crit, Cenelli, and the Brooklyn Museum. In 2015, FiFO Cycle kicked off a full line of essentials aimed at comfort on the road with Off Track and On the Road, a collection of travel necessities for trekking, hopping trains, touring, training, or just relaxing with friends.

## TSH Jersey

**TENSPEED HERO**

On weekends, you can find the heroes who run Chicago biking-apparel label Tenspeed Hero out riding, watching outdoor cinema in a city park, or looking for a sweet and bitter $5 IPA. Imagining their clients riding atop steep cliffs, over mirage-producing hot tarmac, down the tree-lined Oregon coastline, and along Northern California's foggy Highway 1, the designers at Tenspeed Hero create colorful, patterned products such as their women's Sherbet skinsuit and their men's blue-and-orange Razzle Dazzle jersey from kaleidoscopic high-performance Lycra and cyclocross fabrics.

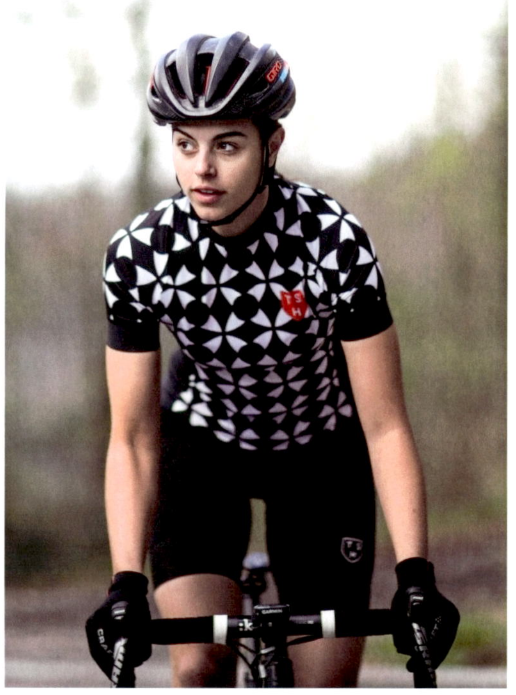

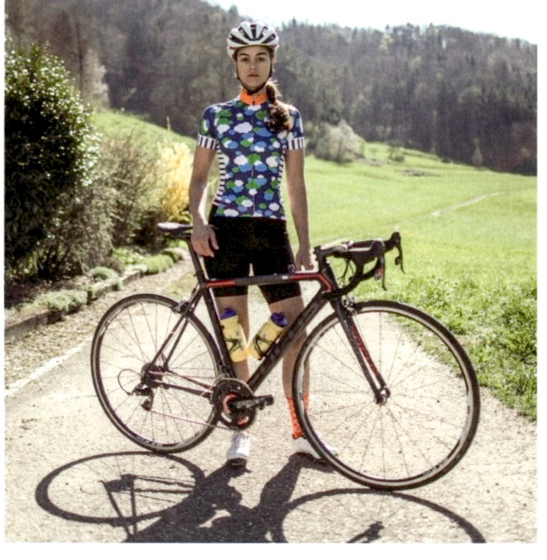

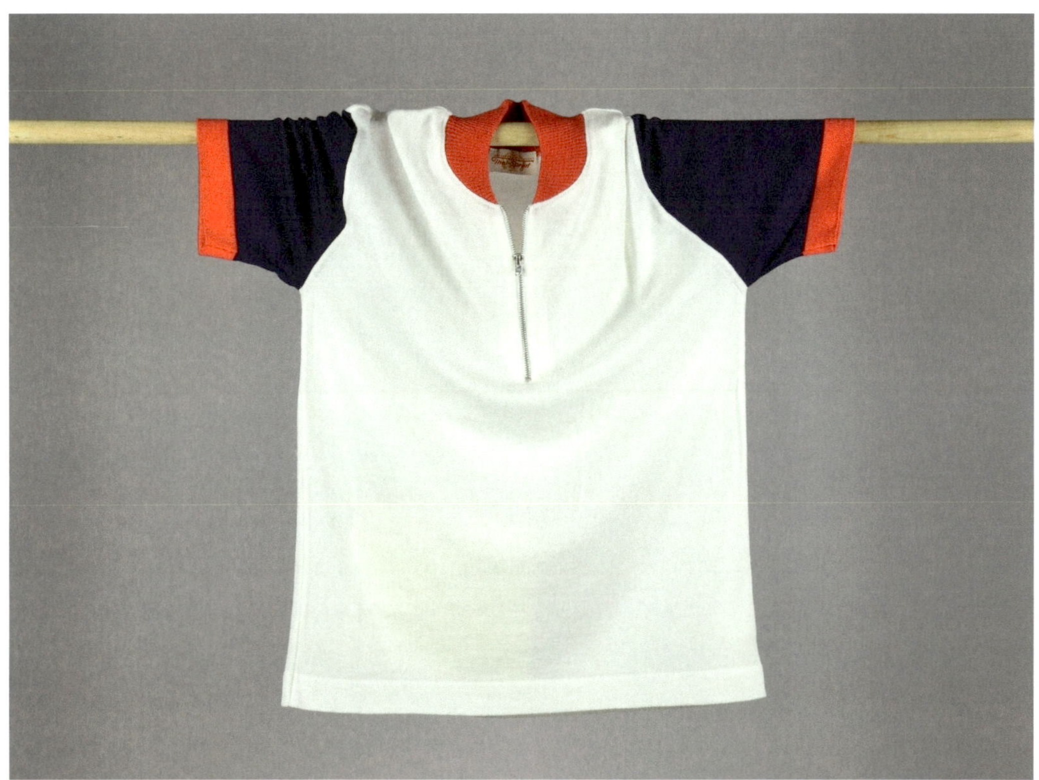

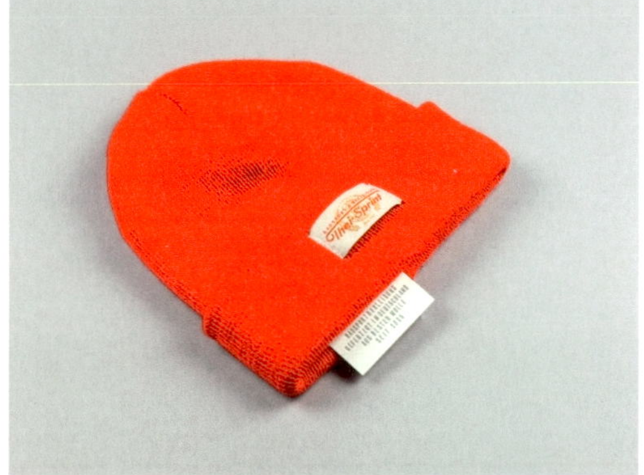

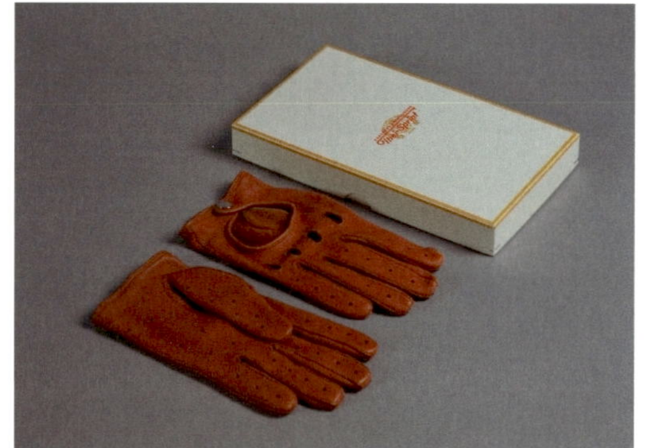

## Thei-Sprint

If you find yourself thinking "they just don't make it like that anymore," you may want to consider the bicycling apparel produced by this German manufacturer. Born in 1935, Heinz Theisen grew up to be a professional cyclist; after the Second World War, he began to craft his own equipment, jerseys, and gear. His red beanie and handmade jersey became famous after he won a 60-kilometer race to Cologne in October 1948 and went on to win more than 400 road and track races over the next 30 years. During this time, he and his wife also turned out jerseys and beanies for local riders by working on knitting machines in their basement. Today, the Thei-Sprint catalog includes the legendary TS-1 beanie, leather gloves, jerseys, and trousers that riders now associate with not just quality but authenticity, too.

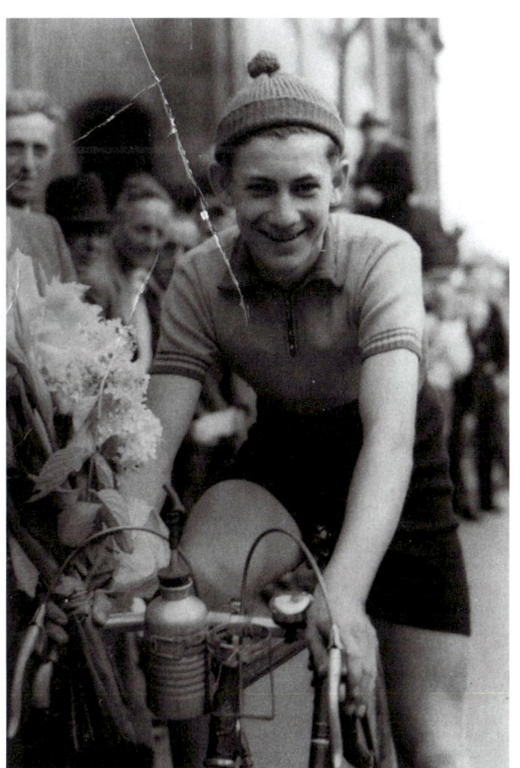

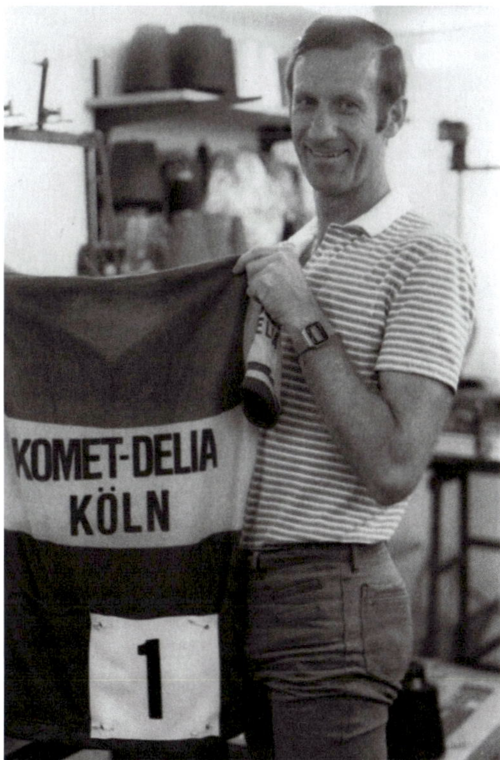


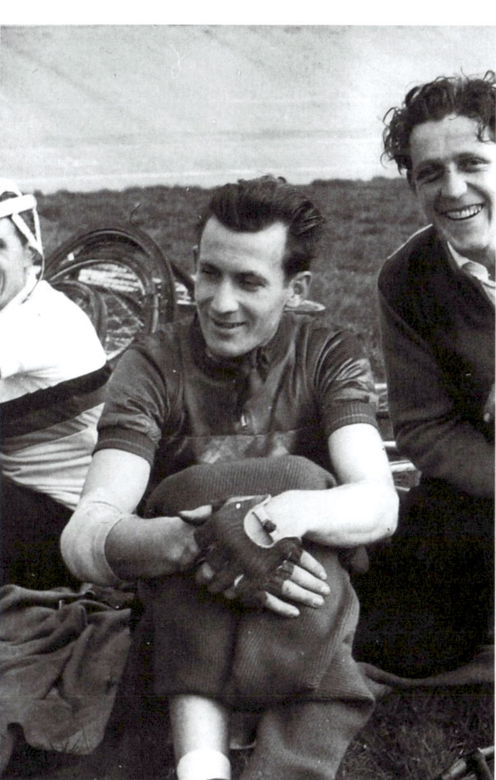

# Baum Doppio Tandem

**BAUM CYCLES**

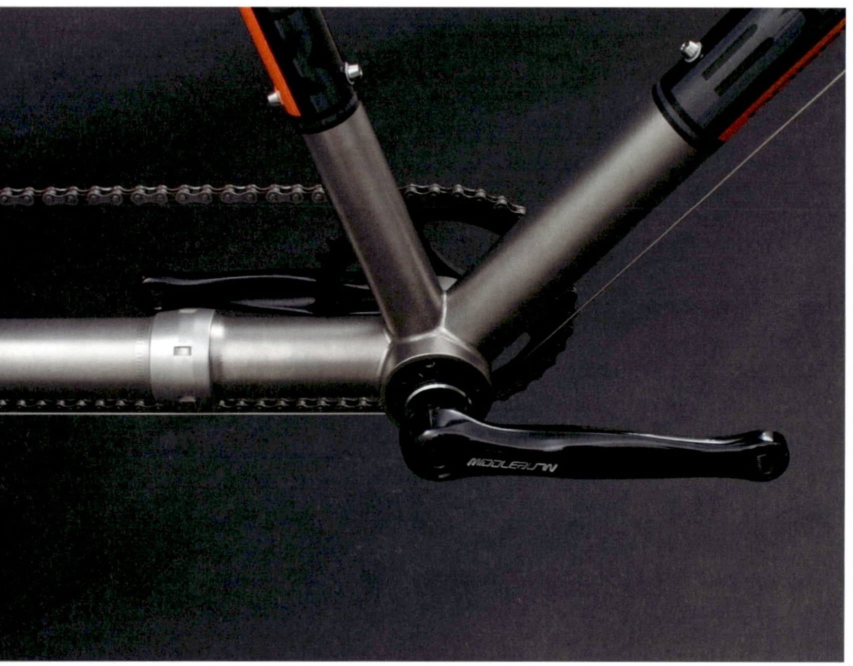


A frame builder who started out as an aircraft engineer and stainless-steel TIG welder is certain to build an interesting bike. Darren Baum began his cycling career as an A-grade rider; a car accident sparked an interest in how biomechanics and bike design can increase performance. Baum strives to build bikes that are not only light, fast, and comfortable, but that also become riders' favorites. That is why all stages of Baum manufacturing are completed in-house. They machine their own head tubes, bottom brackets, and dropouts to optimize the alignment, weight, and stiffness. Each frame is painted in Baum's own facility. The Doppio Tandem is a double shot of Baum's custom titanium road-cycling heritage, handcrafted to enable a team to travel, explore, and ride as one.

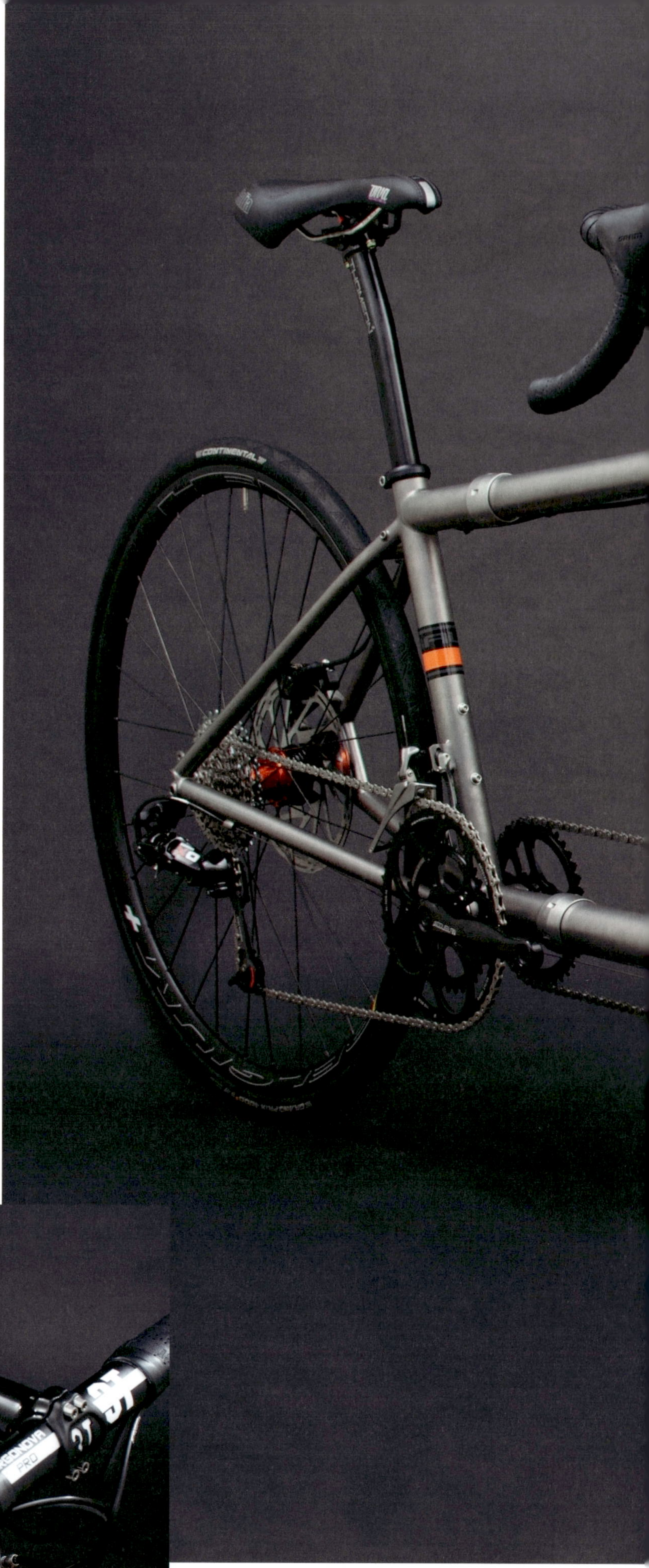

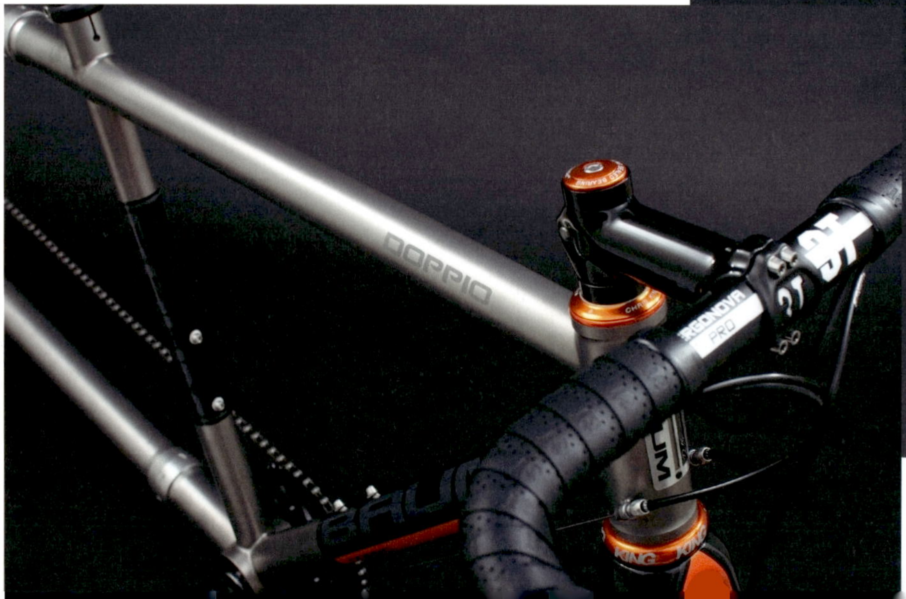

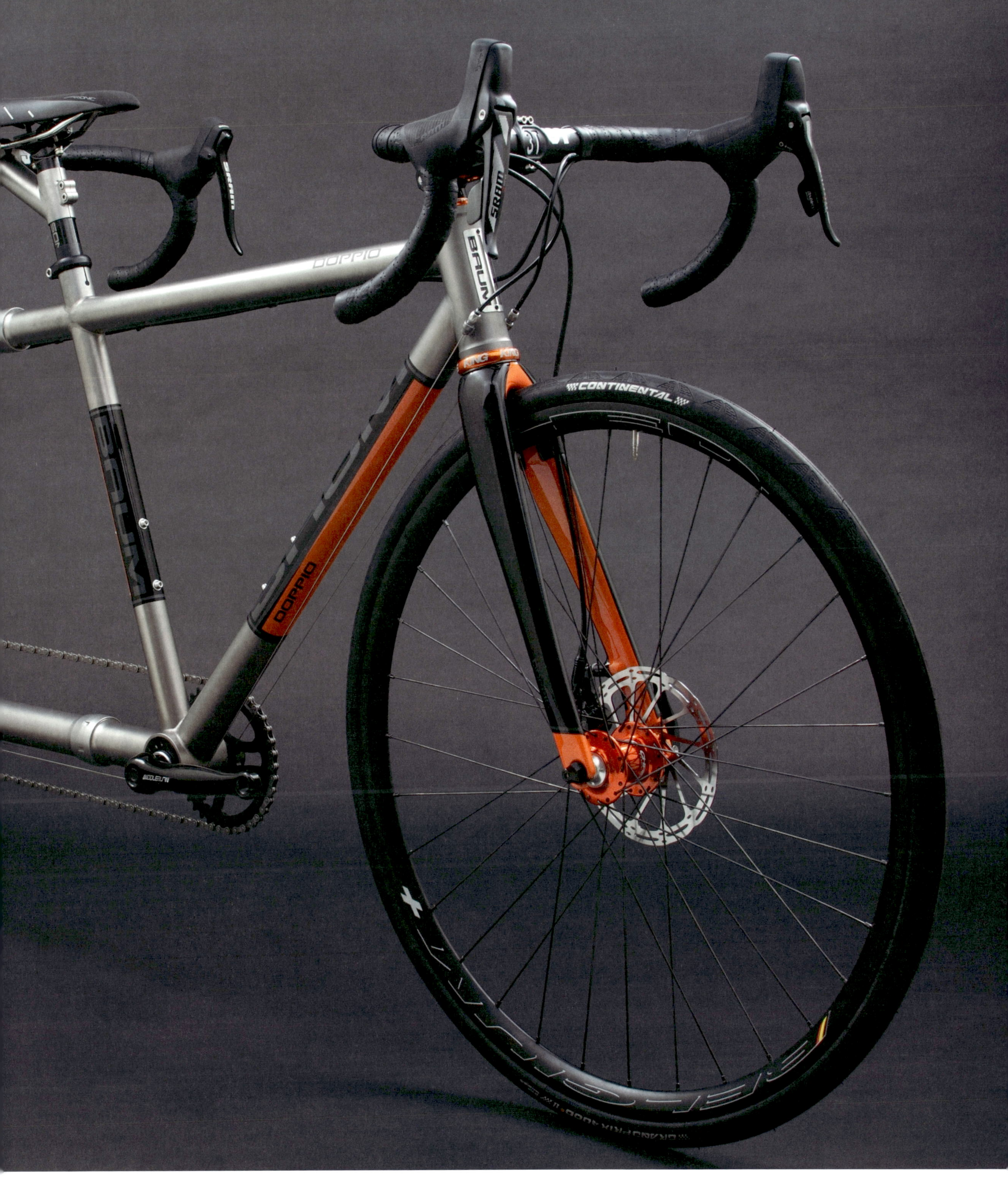
SRAM
BAUM
DOPPIO
KING
CONTINENTAL

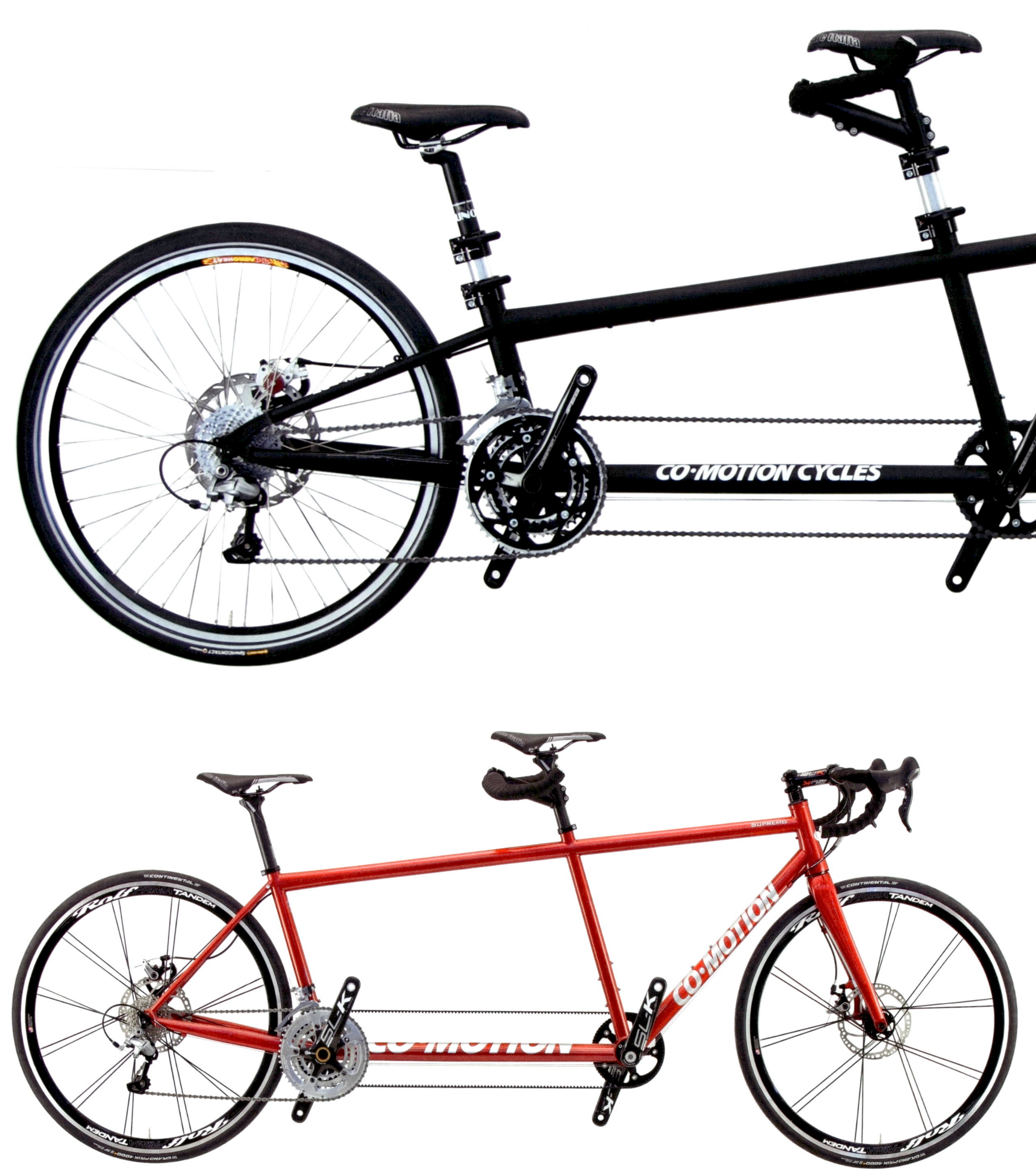

CO·MOTION CYCLES
CO-MOTION
SLK
TANDEM

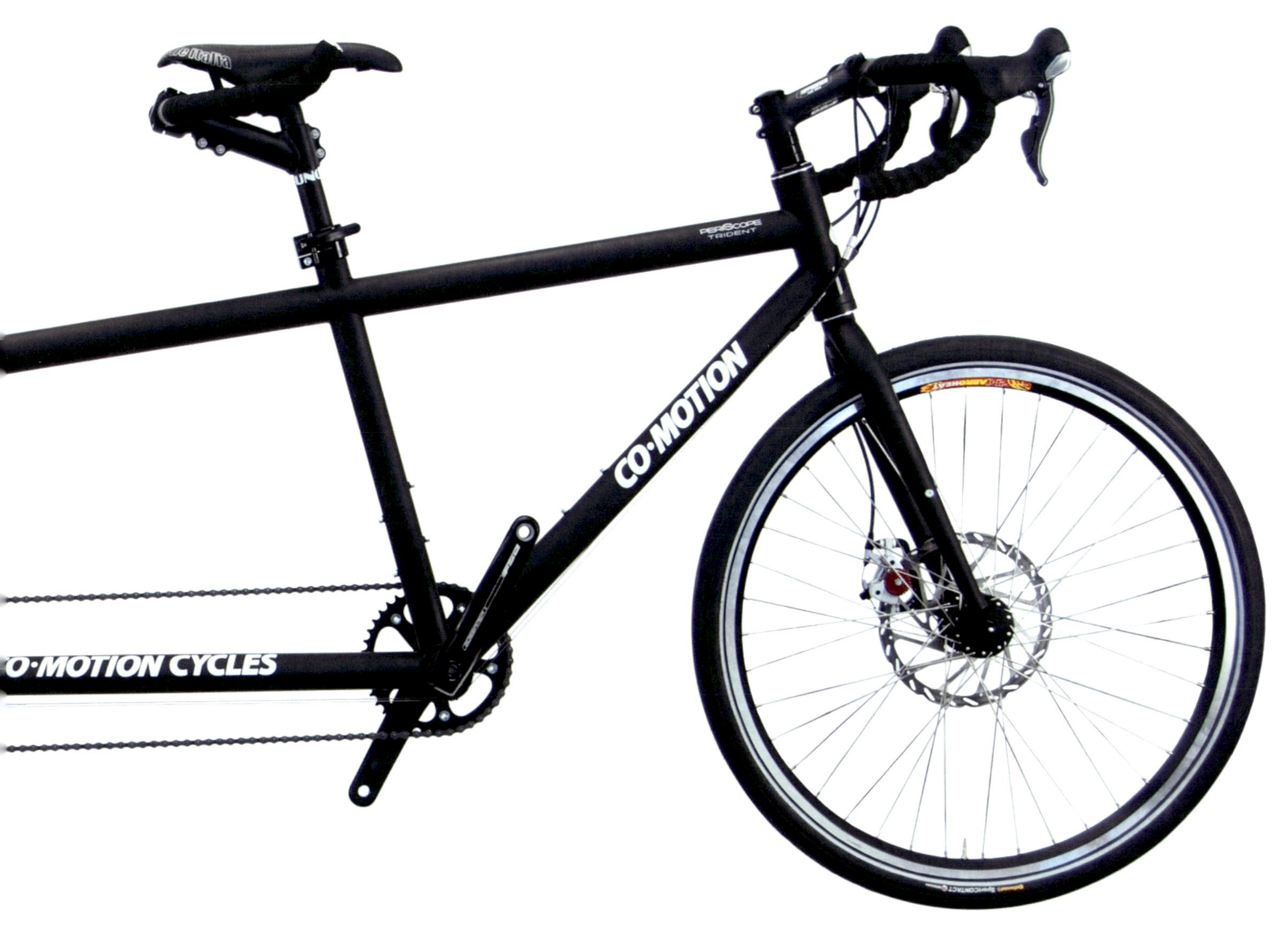


# PeriScope Trident & Supremo Tandem

**CO-MOTION**

Established in 1988 in Eugene, Oregon, Co-Motion Cycles is internationally known for making quality tandem bicycles like the PeriScope Trident, a three-person bicycle designed to allow growing families to ride together with children as young as four years old. With just a few adjustments, the PeriScope Trident converts to accommodate any number of child/adult rider configurations. The company's adventure and touring bicycles, including the Supremo tandem, which is feather-light and race-ready, have also begun to gain renown. Not to be confused with "retro" steel tandems, Co-Motion's bikes use exclusive Reynolds 631 air-hardened steel tubing and a Co-Motion designed carbon disc tandem fork, creating the perfect balance between a classic road-racing machine and unmatched ride quality.

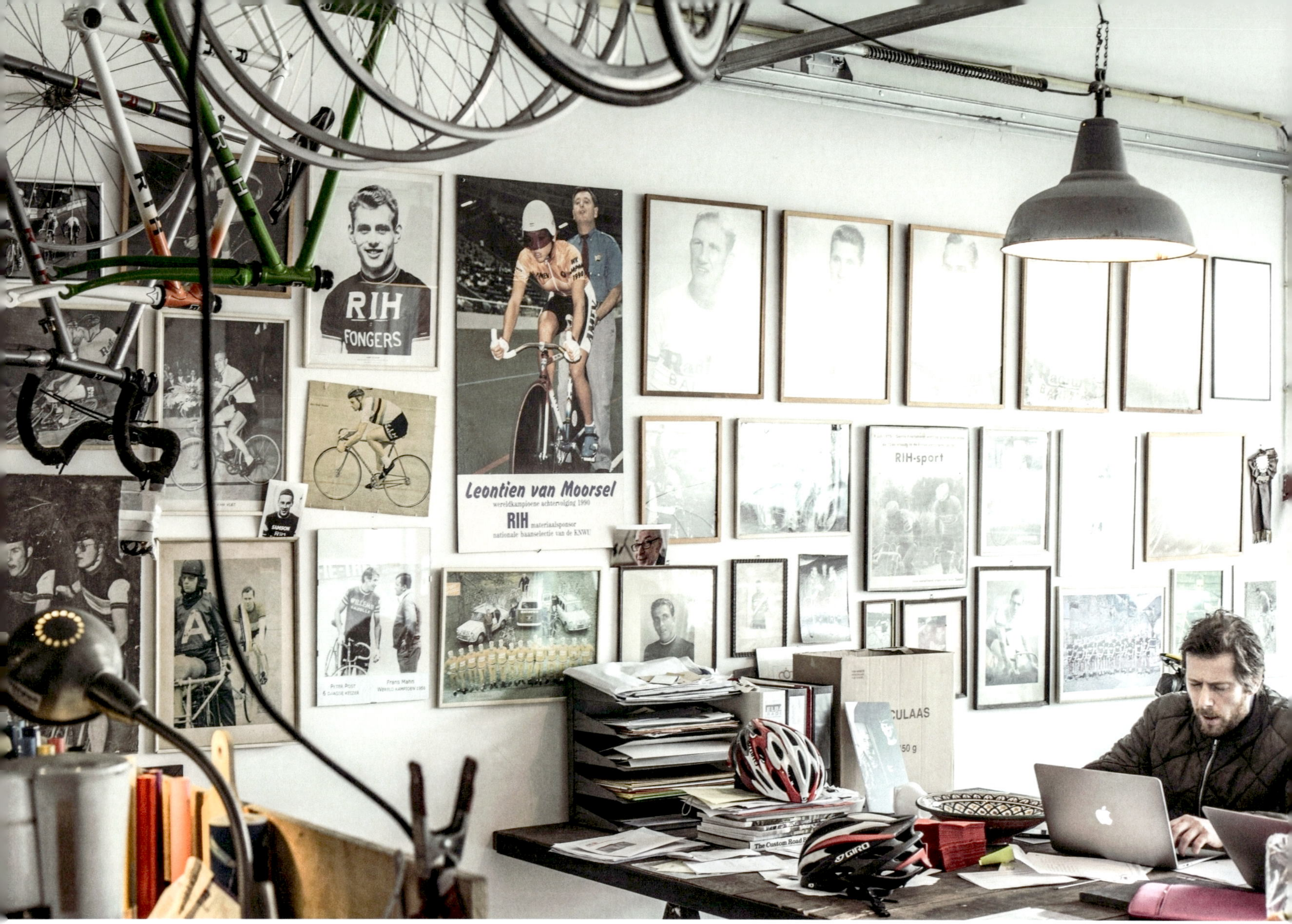

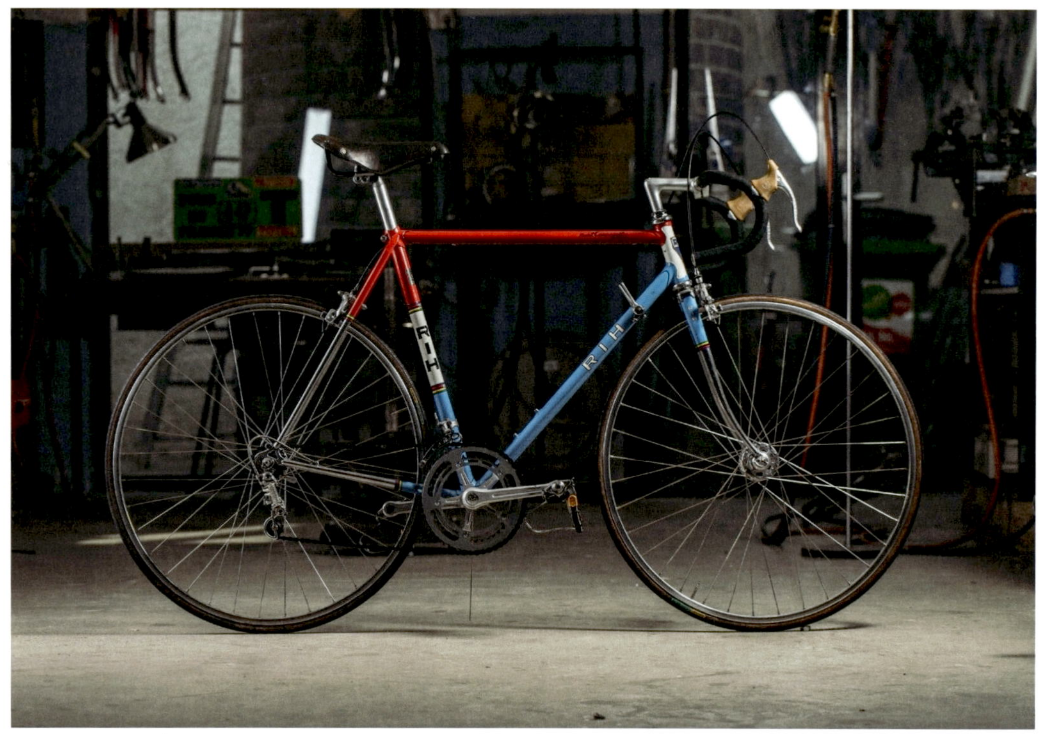
RIH

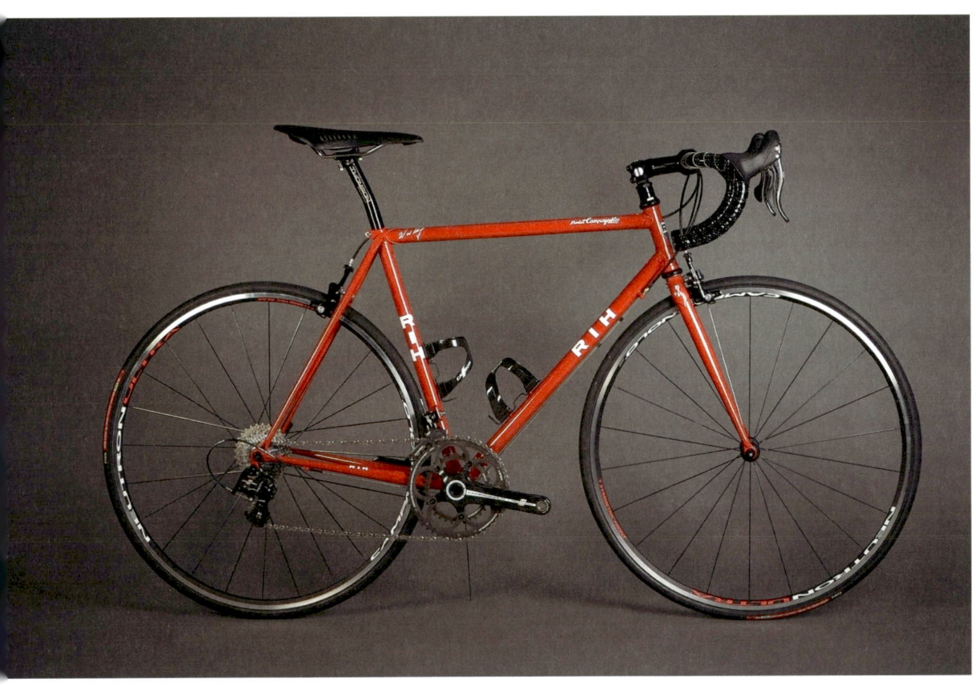

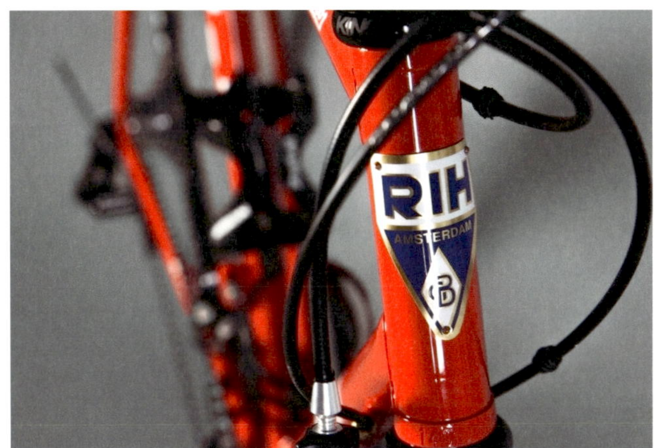


# RIH Sport Amsterdam

The legacy of RIH Sport Amsterdam is a long one: four generations of master bike builders stand behind their hand-built, high-performance racing bikes. Founded in 1921 by the brothers Bustraan, the company boasts over 90 years of experience, including 63 world and Olympic champions, and a history of building the highest-quality bikes for every client they work with. Based on a close collaboration between rider and master builder, the working philosophy of RIH Sport Amsterdam is aimed at discovering what each rider wants from his or her bike. In the end, the resulting bikes not only perfectly fit their riders' measurements and preferences—they are tailored to help them achieve their goals.

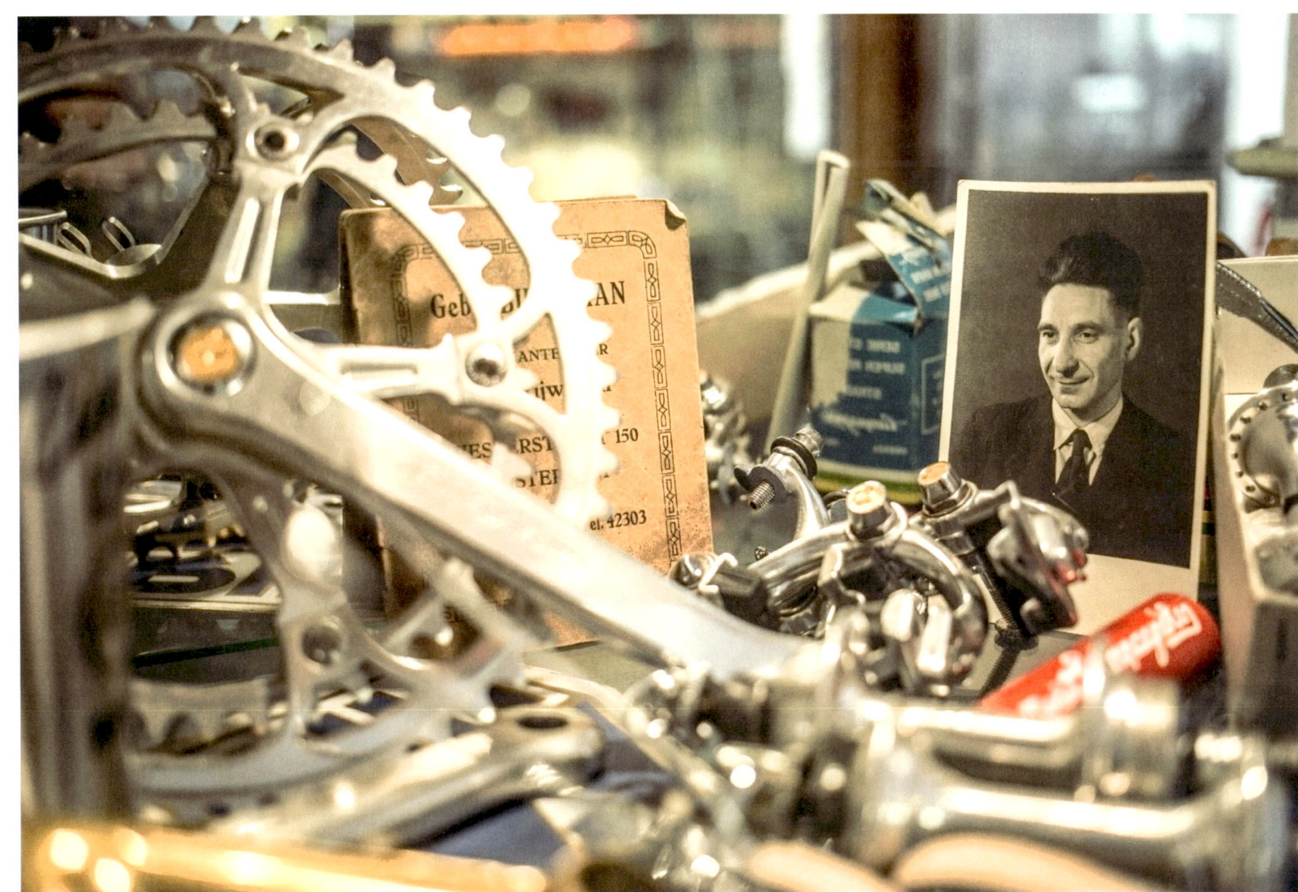

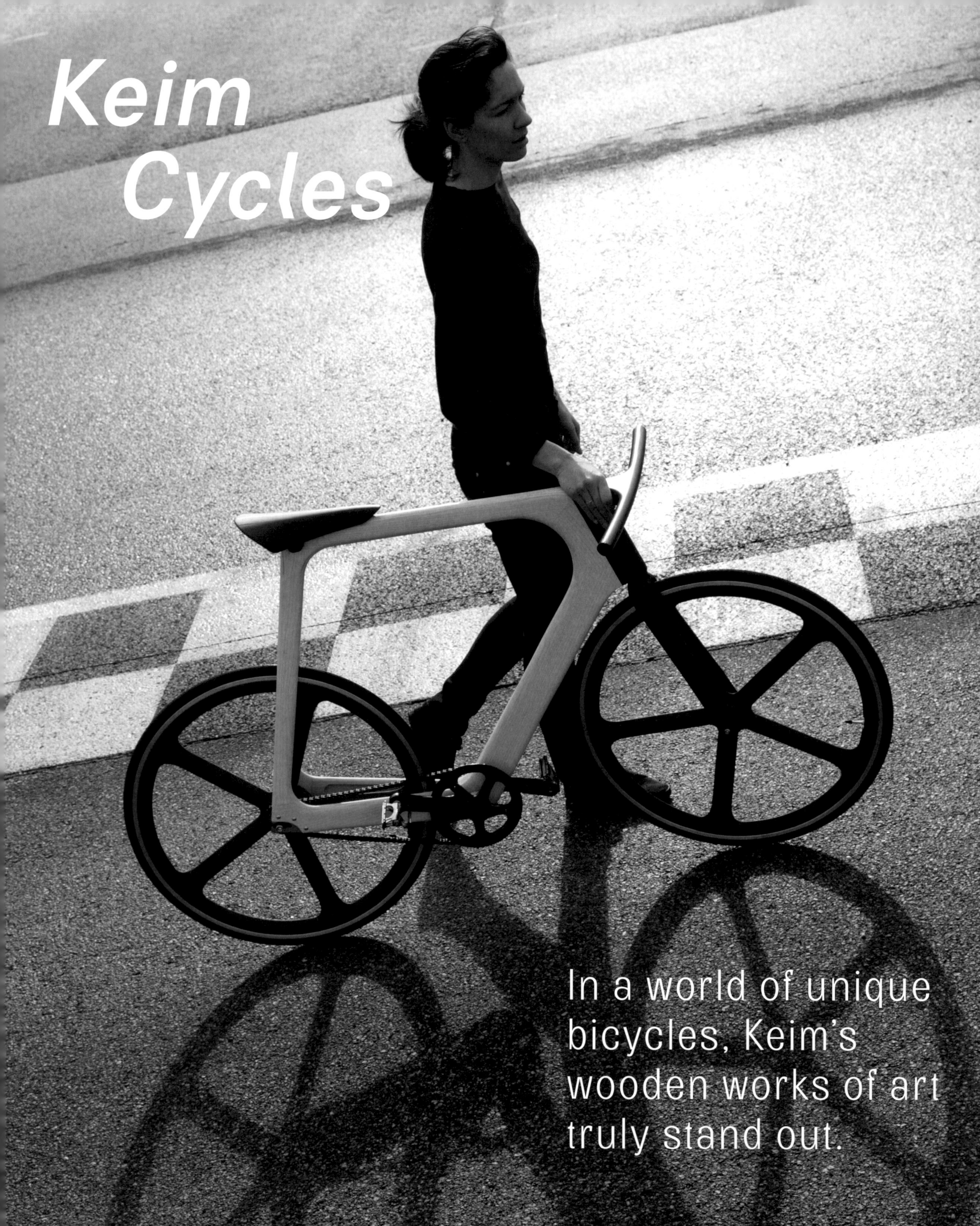

# Keim Cycles

In a world of unique bicycles, Keim's wooden works of art truly stand out.

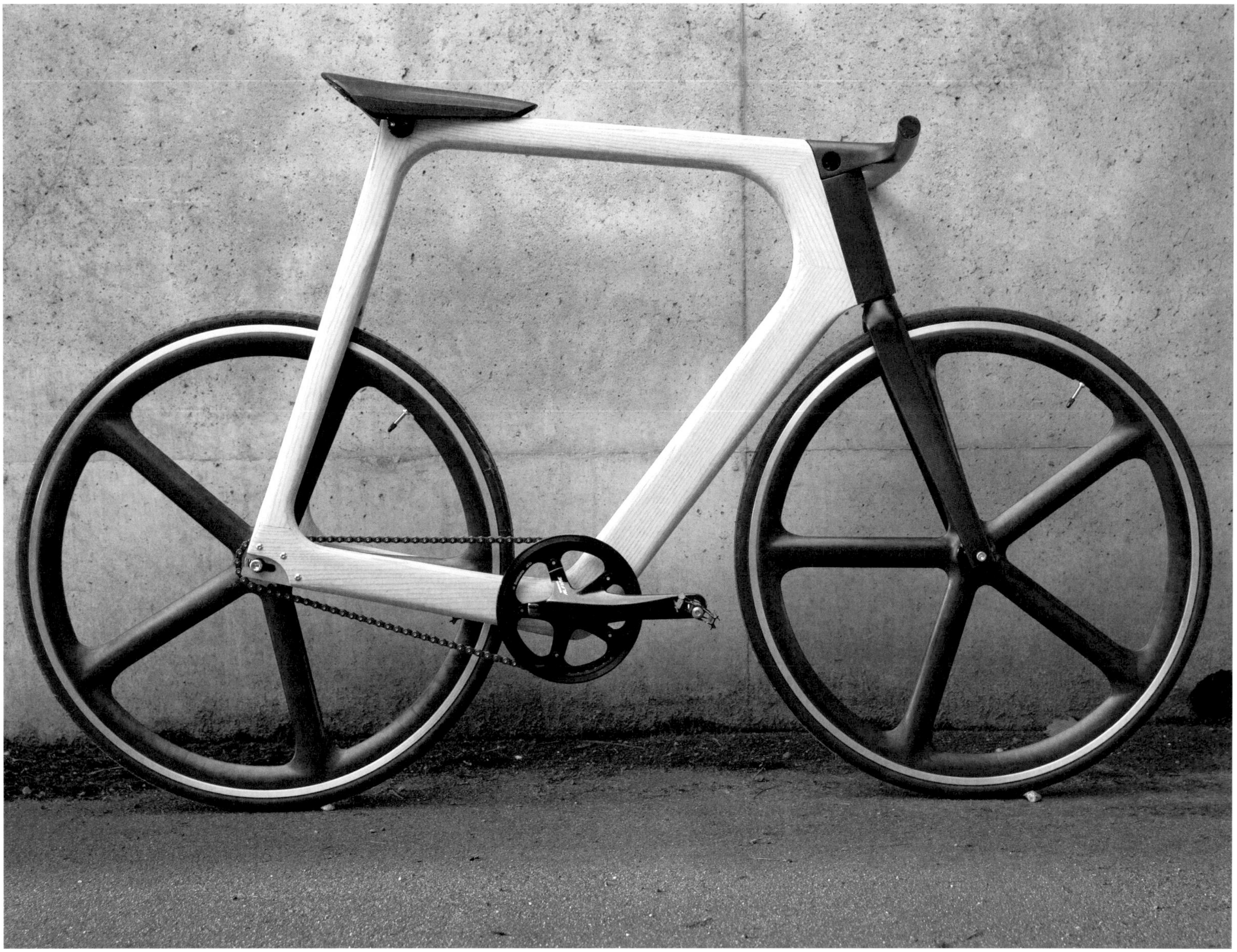

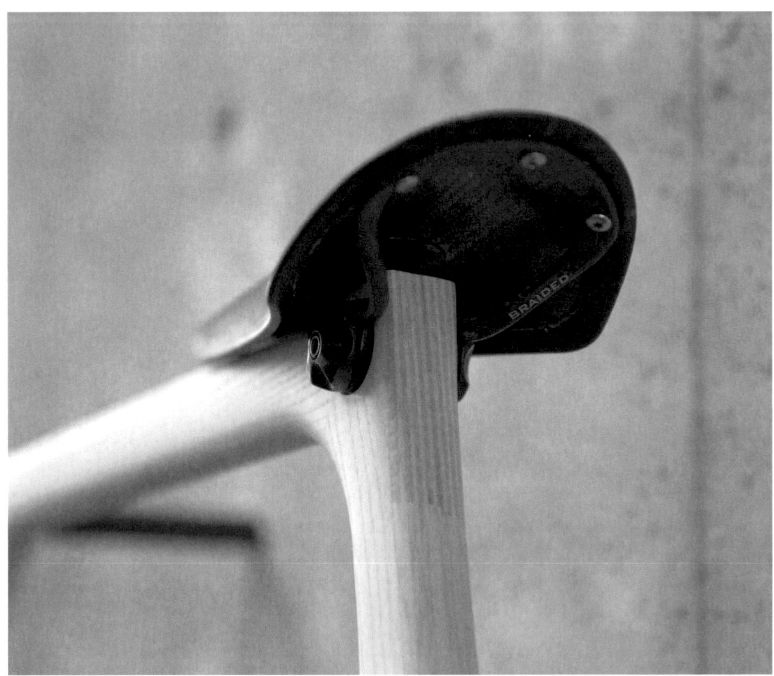
BRAIDED

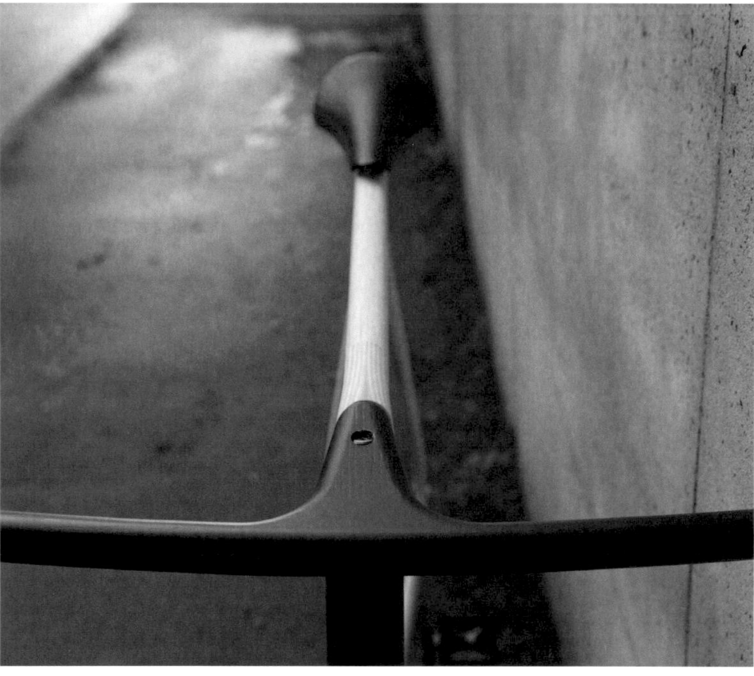

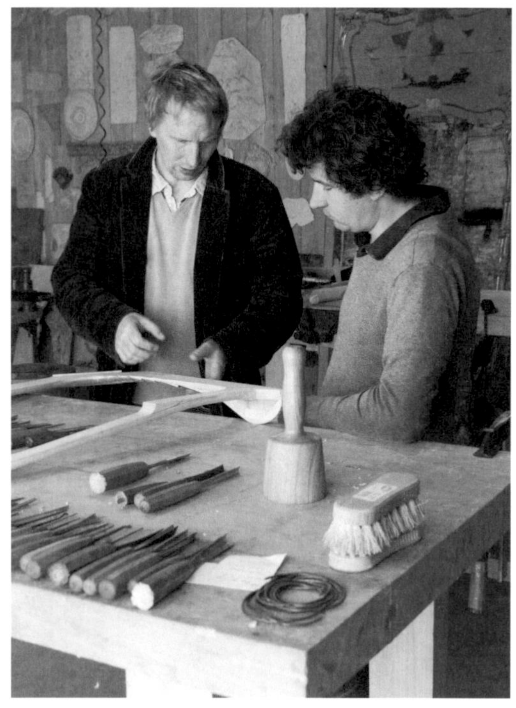

Based in the Loire Valley, central France's pedaling paradise, the manufacturer employs a radical formalism together with wood and composite technologies that place them firmly in the bike-making vanguard. Deep materials research, efficient manufacturing processes, and innovation in collaboration with the most accomplished artists and cyclists are Keim's signature. The brand's philosophy posits that a bicycle should become an extension of the human body, mediating a seamless transmutation of muscle energy into winged propulsion, so that the rider feels as if he or she is coasting with the wind. This means that the brand's bikes are consistently constructed to be featherweight, durable, and aerodynamic in a way that might have made Raymond Loewy, that master of streamlining, smile.

Keim works with CRITT Rochefort and Chatellerault for laboratory testing and structural simulation and—from veneers to varnishes—chooses and applies every material, component, and finish meticulously. The frame material comprises between 20 and 50 layers of vacuum-laminated white ash while the precise orientation of the wood grain exploits the robust mechanical properties of this species of wood.

In April 2014, Keim unveiled a model, the Arvak, that one might call sculptural if not for the extreme sleekness of its lines and curves. The Arvak frame is built from epoxy and composite wood and, with its barless, hollow, and homogenous monocoque wooden frame, is named for one of the mythological horses that pulled the chariot of the sun across the sky in Norse mythology. Its three makers designed it with a compact geometry, optimal stiffness, and minimal weight in order to make the ride silent and to ensure that it responds to the slightest cues from its rider.

A second model, the Alérion, features a carved frame that recalls Pegasus, the winged horse of Greek mythology, and the fabulous hippogriff, a creature with the body of a horse and the proud wings and head of an eagle. From its beginnings, Keim has always tapped artists and skilled craftsmen to bring poetry to its products. For the Alérion, the team called on woodcarver and sculptor Charles Boulnois to explore the formal potential of laminated wood and to synthesize alternative approaches to the material: one technical and radical, the other lyrical.

**top:** Alérion was born from a collaboration with Charles Boulnois, rewarded French sculptor.

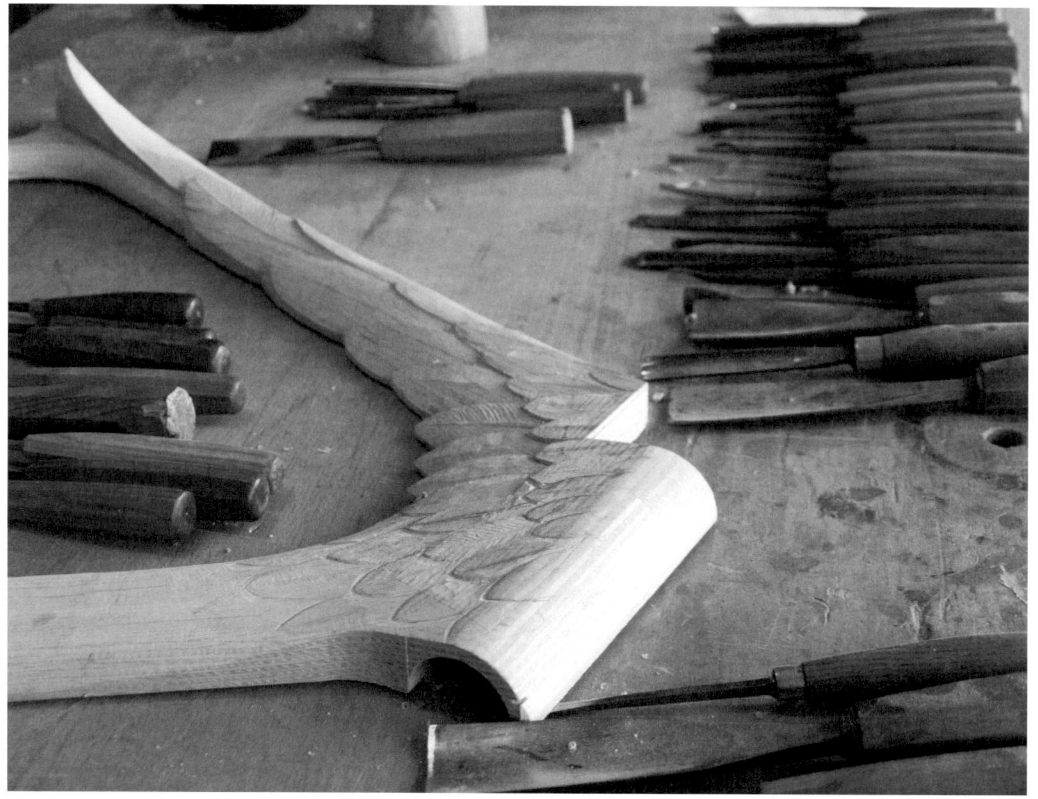

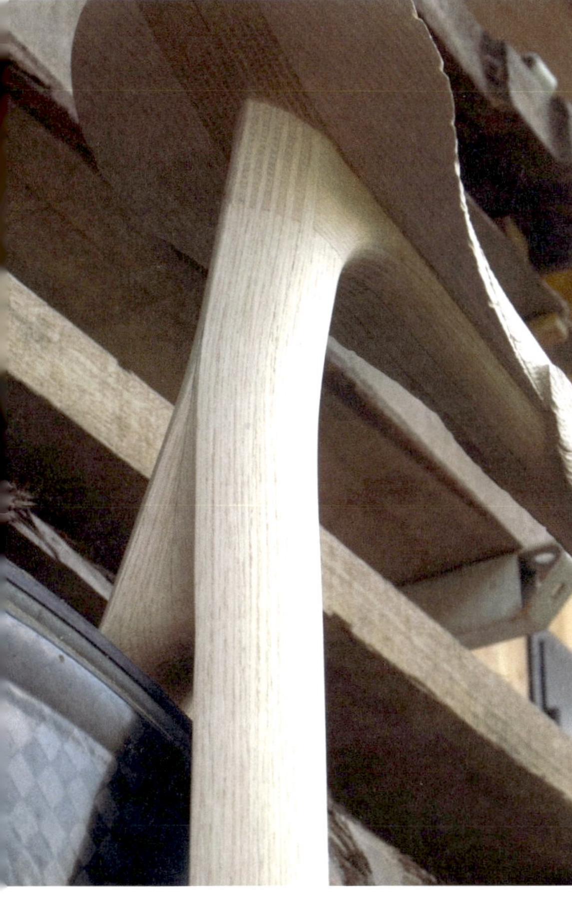

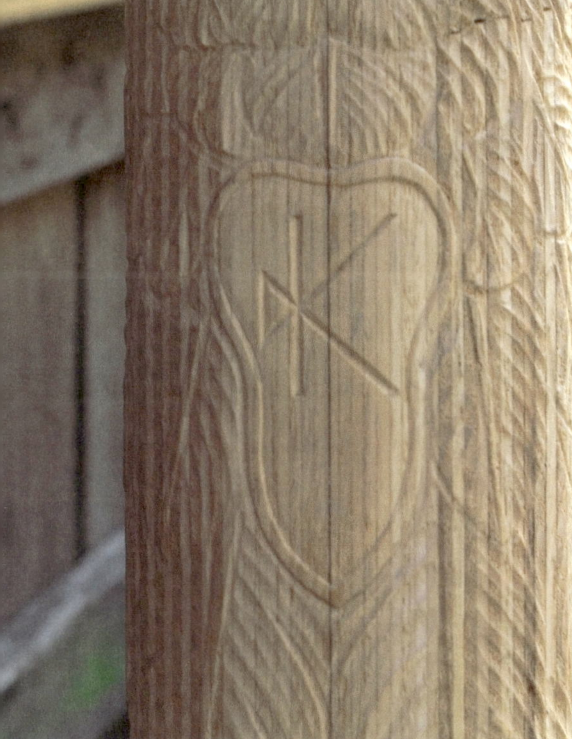

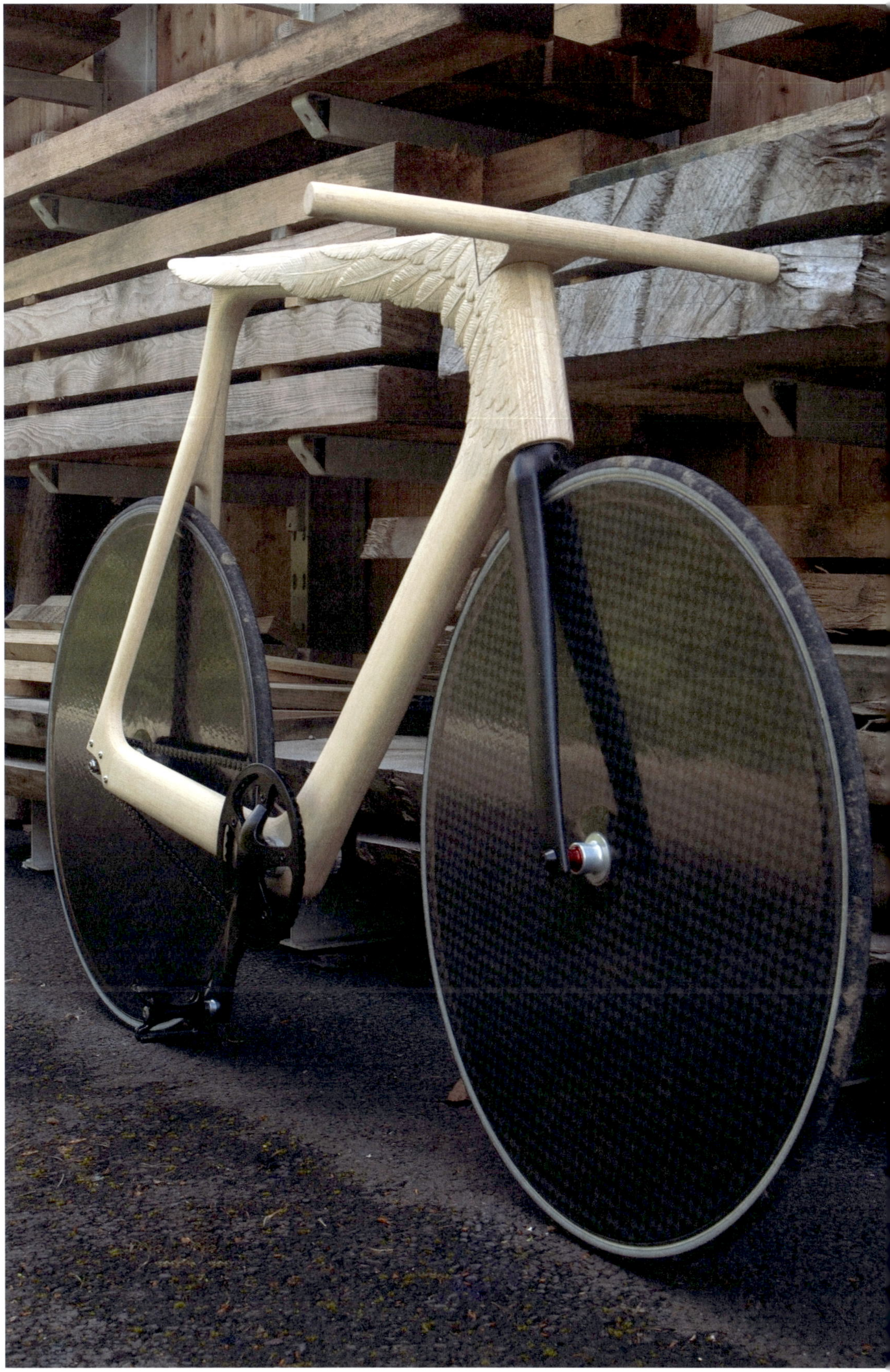

# Wooden Bike

**YOJIRO OSHIMA**

Yojiro Oshima's final project before he graduated from Tokyo's Musashino Art University takes the term "handcrafted bike" to a new level. His wooden bike is just that—the frame, wheels, handlebars, and saddle are all handcrafted entirely out of wood. As a graduate of the school's Craft & Industrial Design Department, Oshima set out to combine the benefits of a beam frame with the aesthetics of a standard frame. The result? A gorgeously sculpted wooden bike that delivers a comfortable ride. Its short, cantilevered seat beam reduces large impacts while the seat and chain stay remain fixed to maintain tension. The sculpted wooden handlebars feature integrated armrests, and "baton wheels" with arcs between the spoke and the rim cushion the ride.

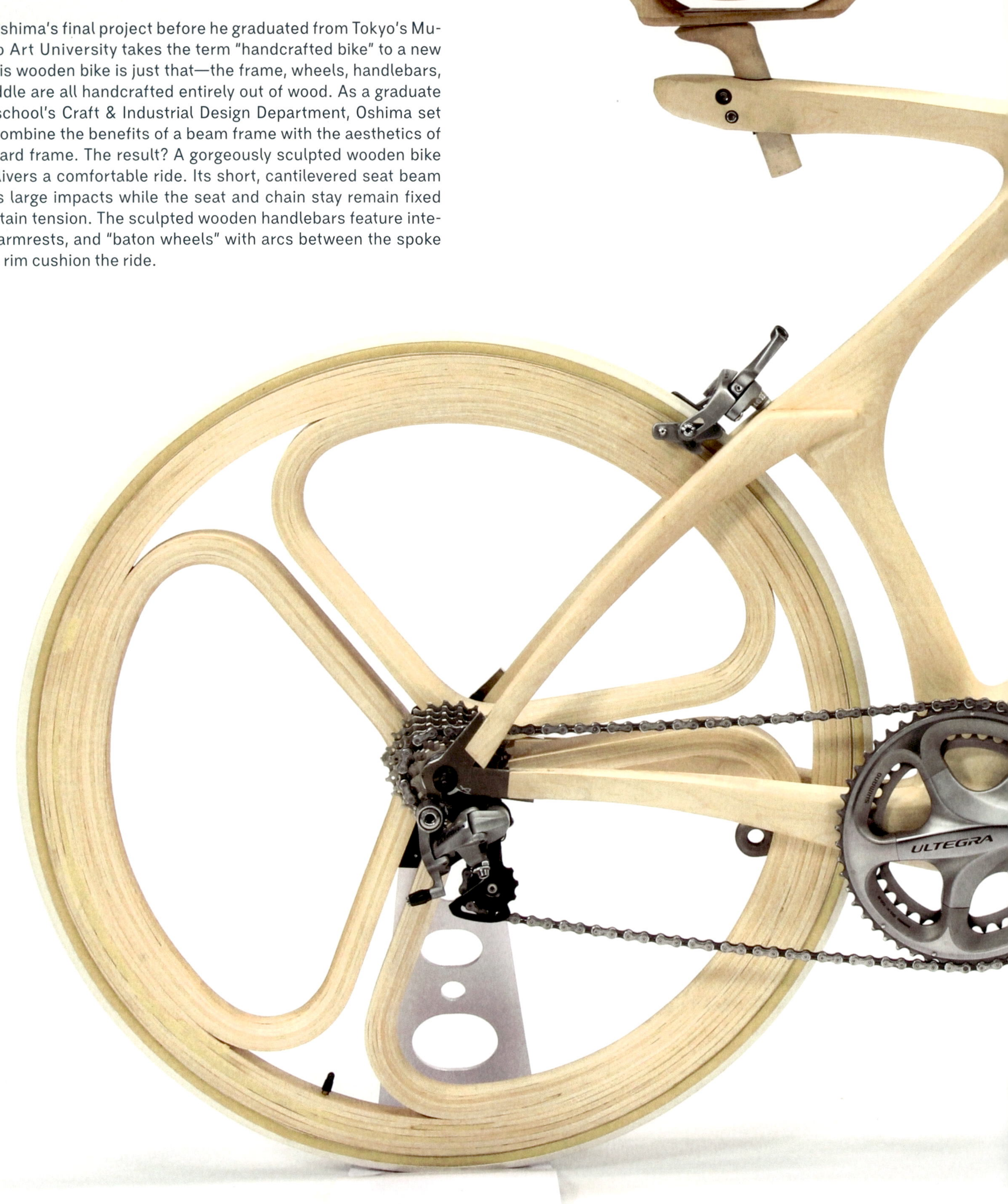

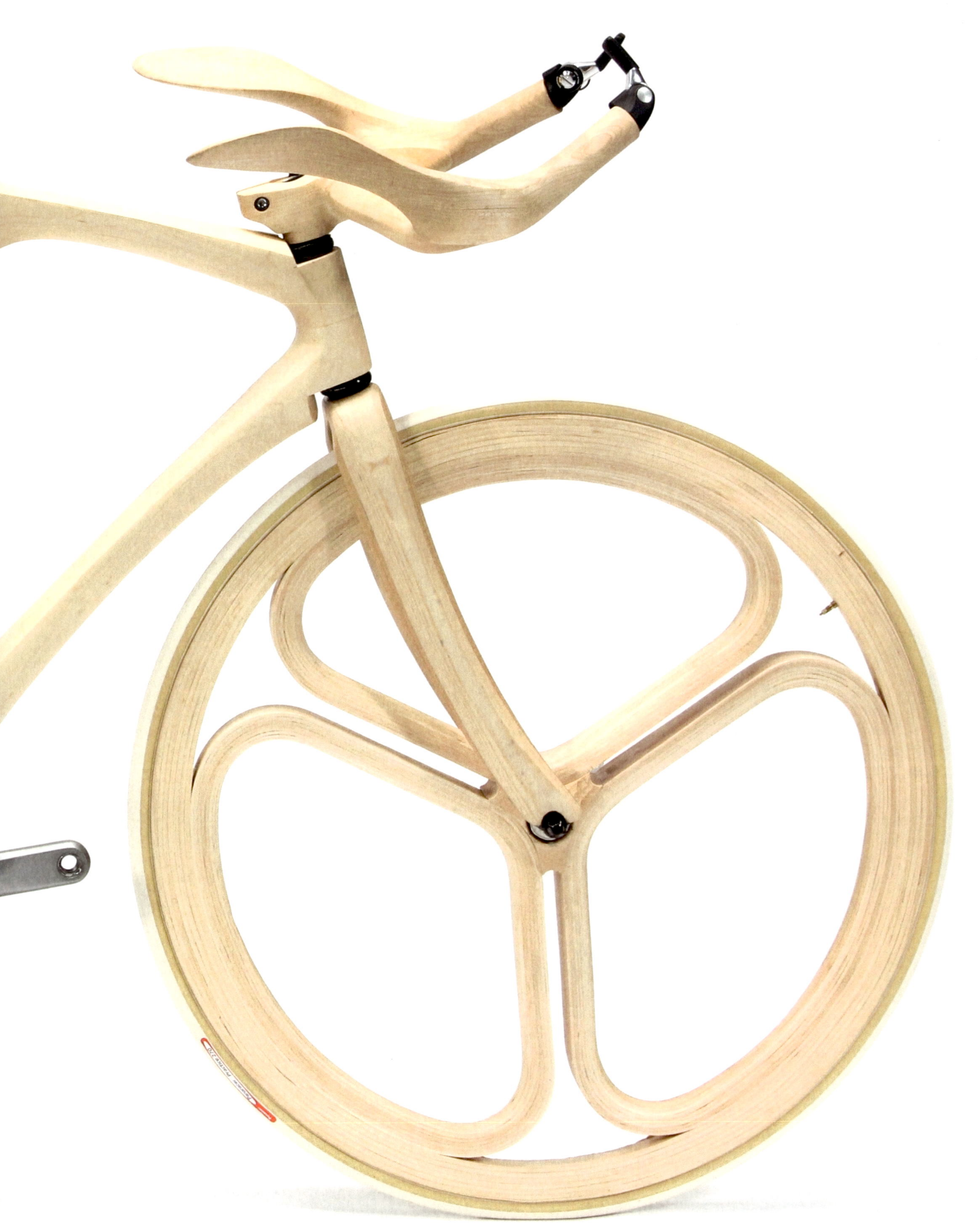

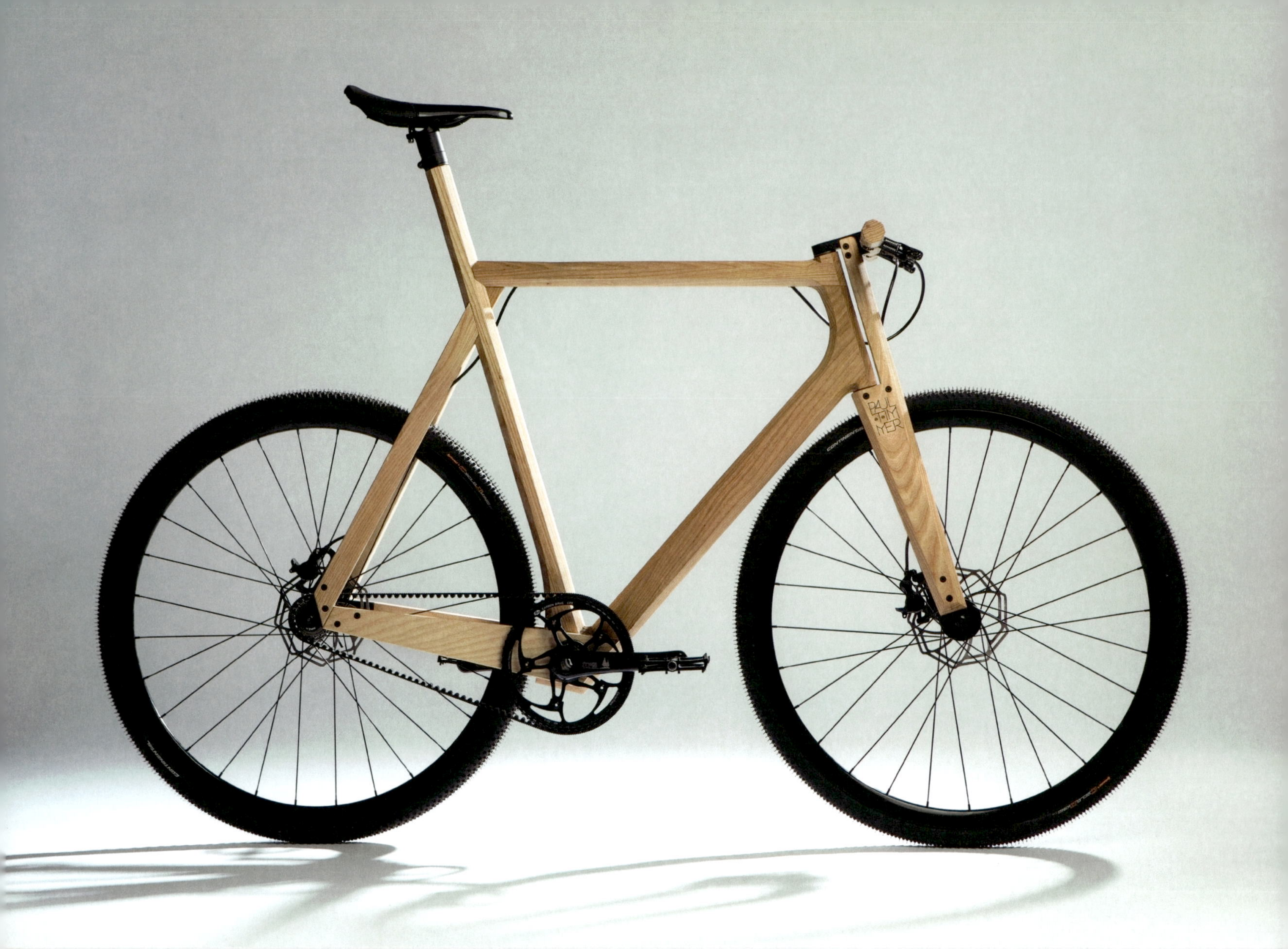

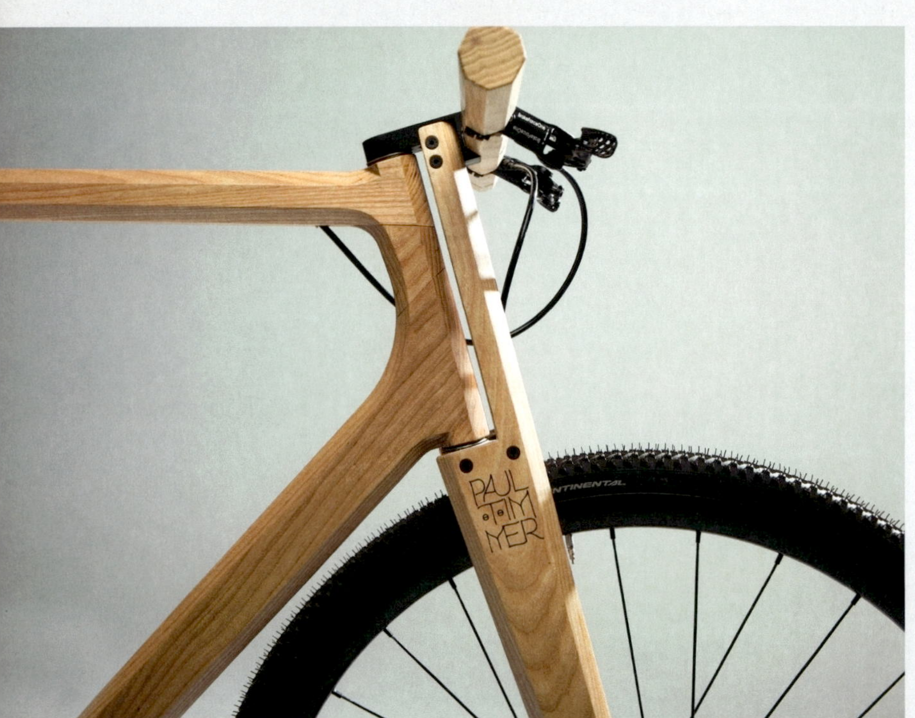


## *Wooden Bike*

**PAUL TIMMER**

A fanatic cyclist who has taken part in the Tour of Flanders and La Marmotte in the Alps, Amsterdam-based product designer and woodworker Paul Timmer is also adamant that wood is the best construction material available. To prove his point, he set out to design a premium wooden bike from the ground up. Its solid ash frame absorbs vibrations and bumps in the road—a quality that makes going back to a steel frame feel like a riding a tuning fork. The model also features an unusual fork construction that fixes the forks on bearings outside of the frame, a light, durable belt instead of a chain, and a custom-designed headset and dropouts printed on a 3D aluminum printer. Although Timmer's bike is currently a one-off product, plans are underway to produce and sell the bike to a larger market.

## Selva

As a production material, wood ticks all the right boxes: it is attractive, resilient, a renewable resource, and it provides a structural efficiency that makes it a favorite for building everything from houses to the world's finest musical instruments. Wooden frames are the trademark of Selva, a maker of exclusive bicycles created with a balance of cutting-edge technology and old-world artisanal skill. Selva has crafted these timeless objects since 2012 and clearly values what tradition can bring to modern cycling. Because each Selva bike is crafted from a different species of wood, every bike is unique and can be further customized upon request. Riders find riding the wooden bikes an amazing experience because they offer a solid, stiff frame that is also forgiving and comfortable.

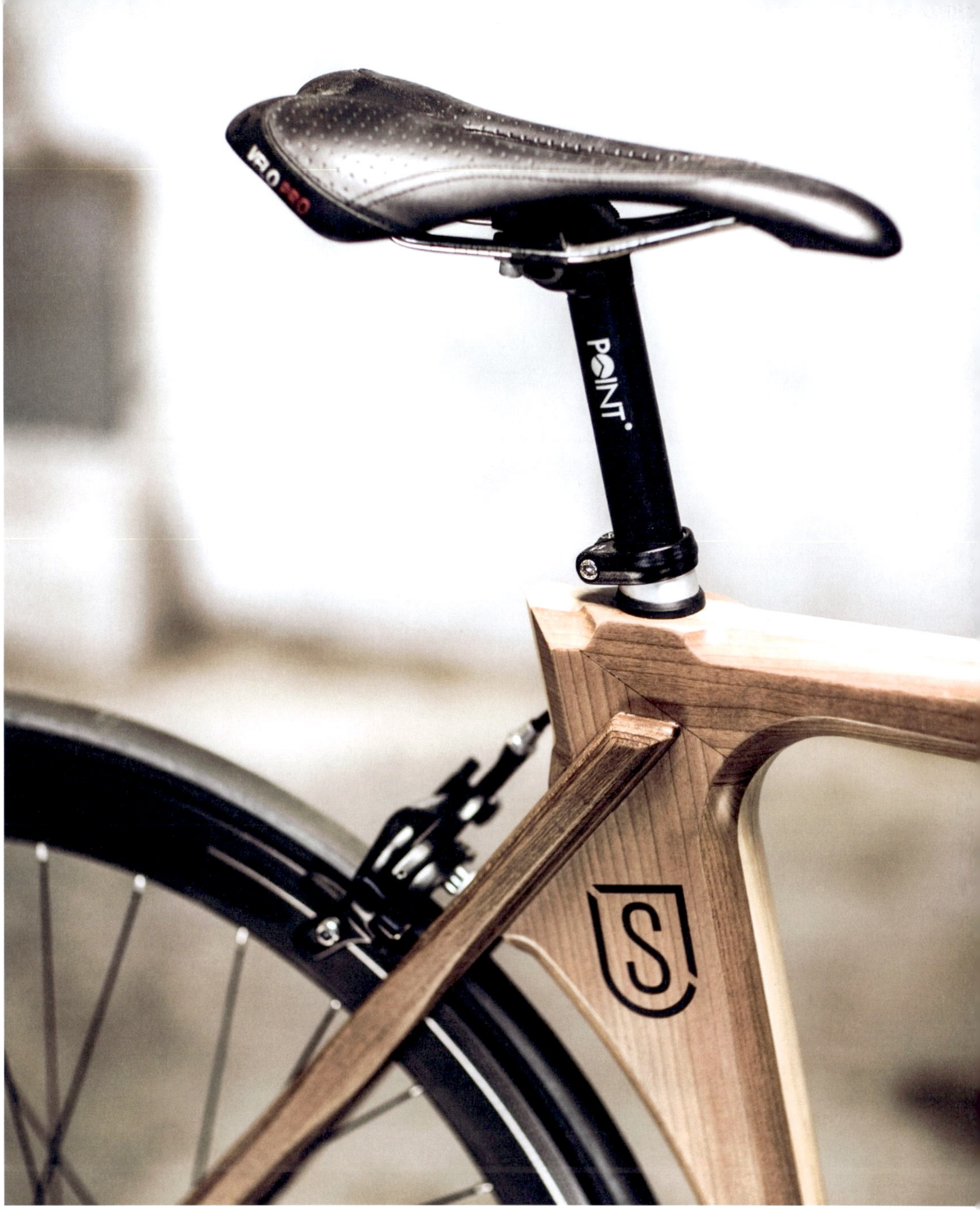

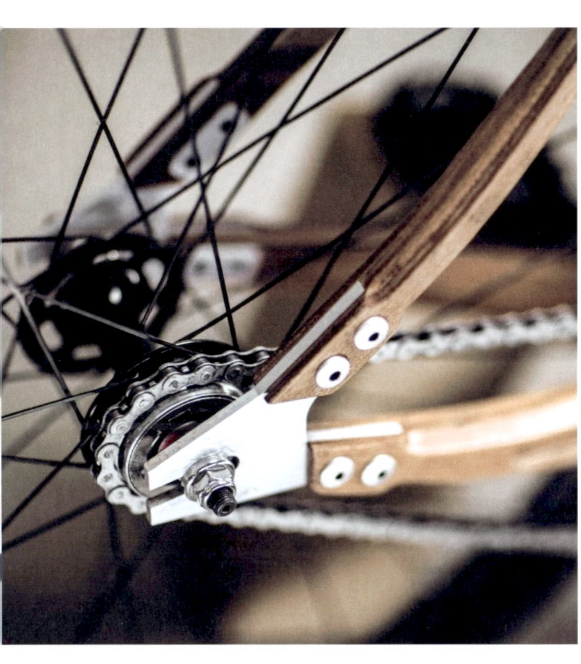

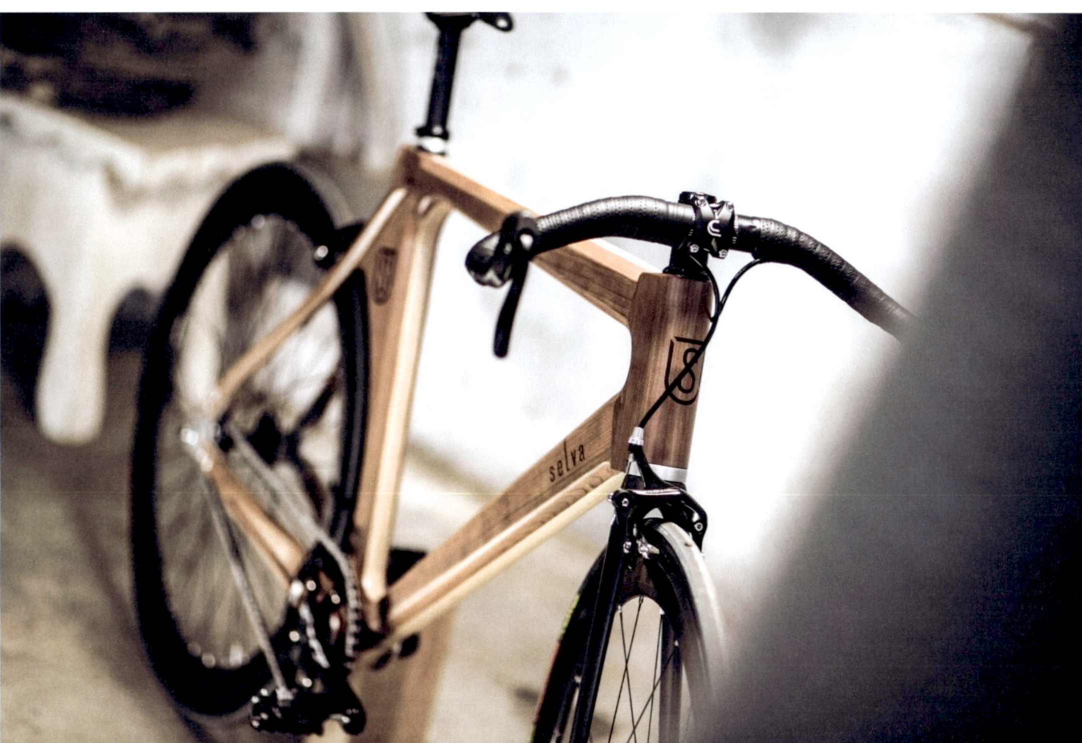

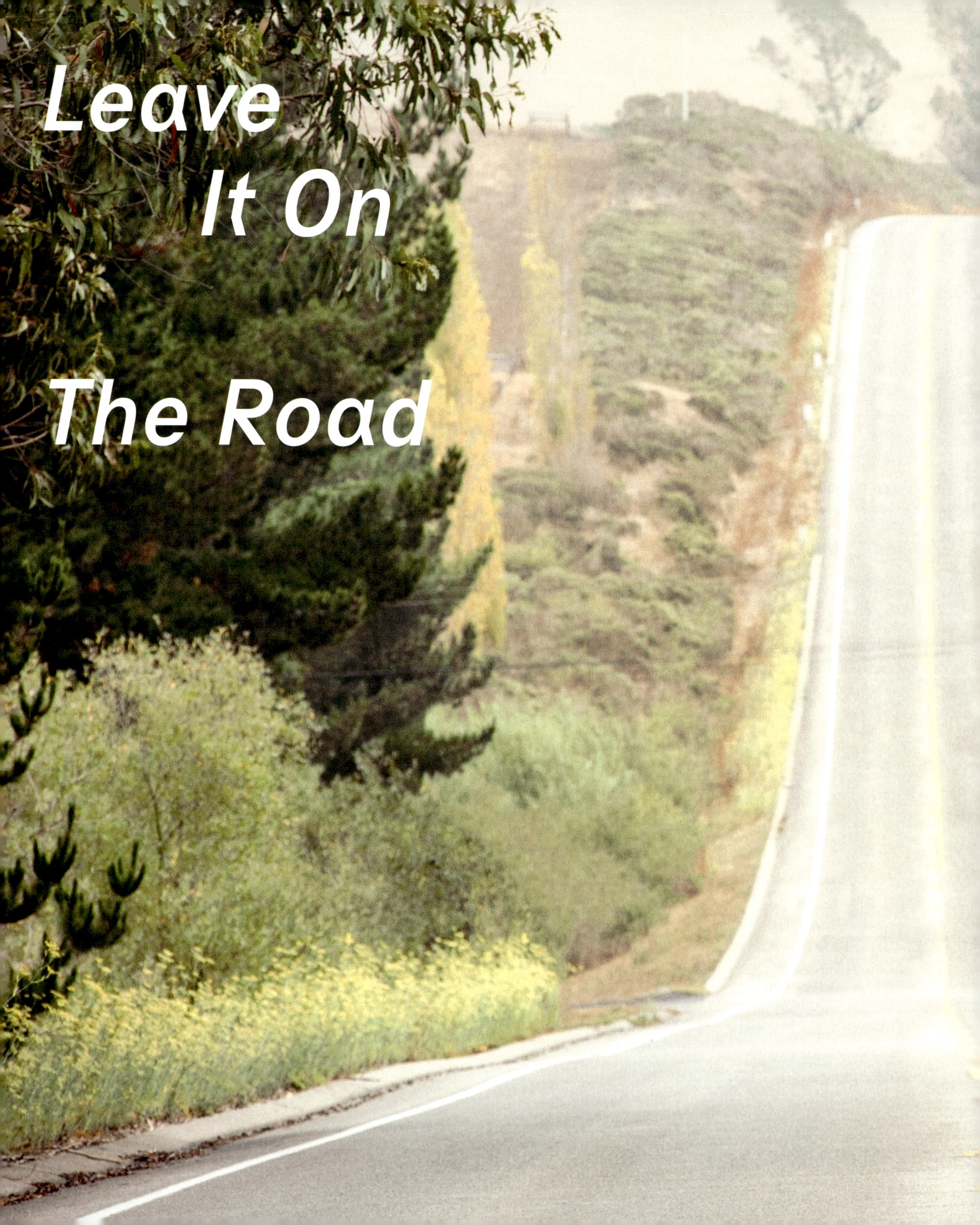
Leave
It On
The Road

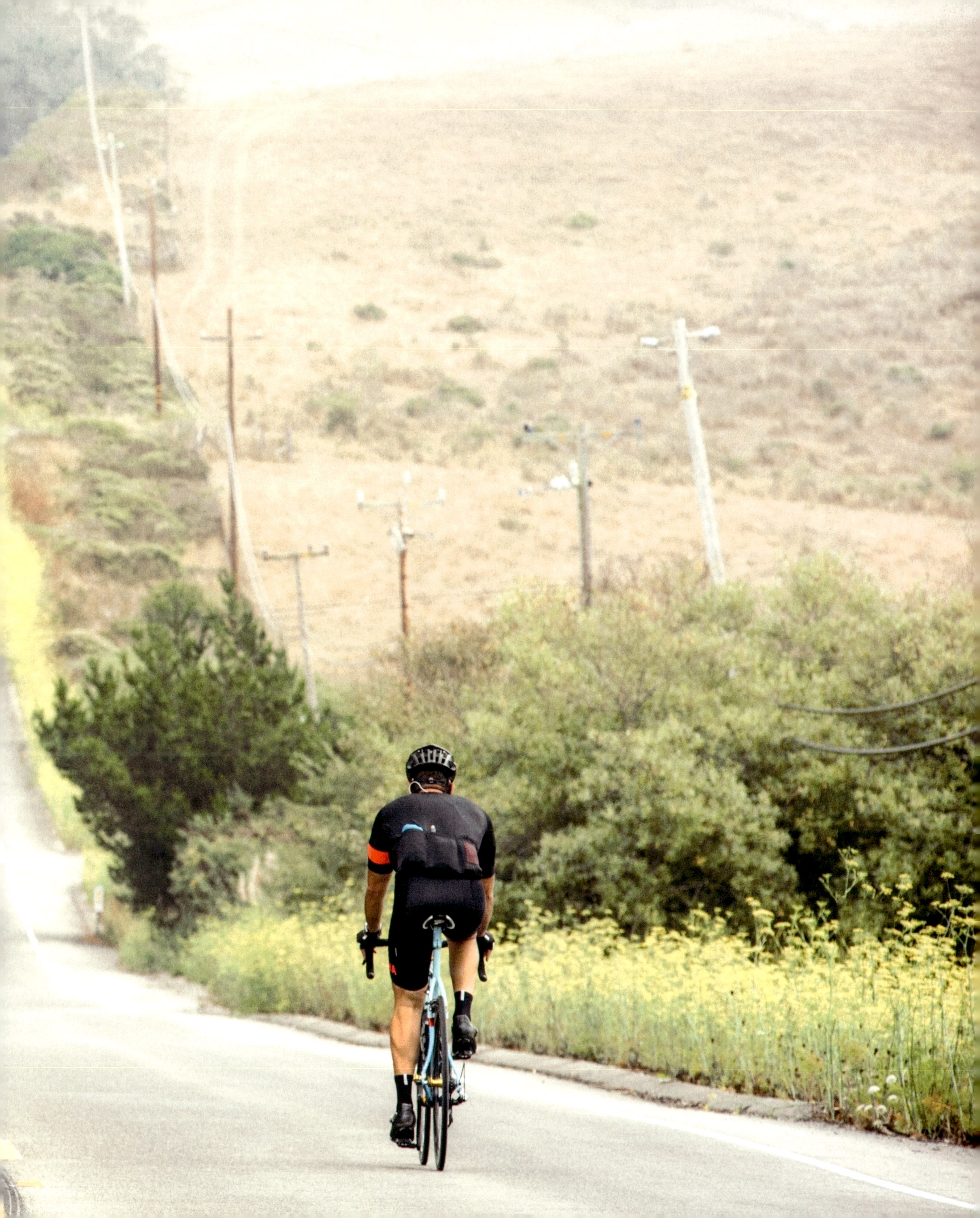

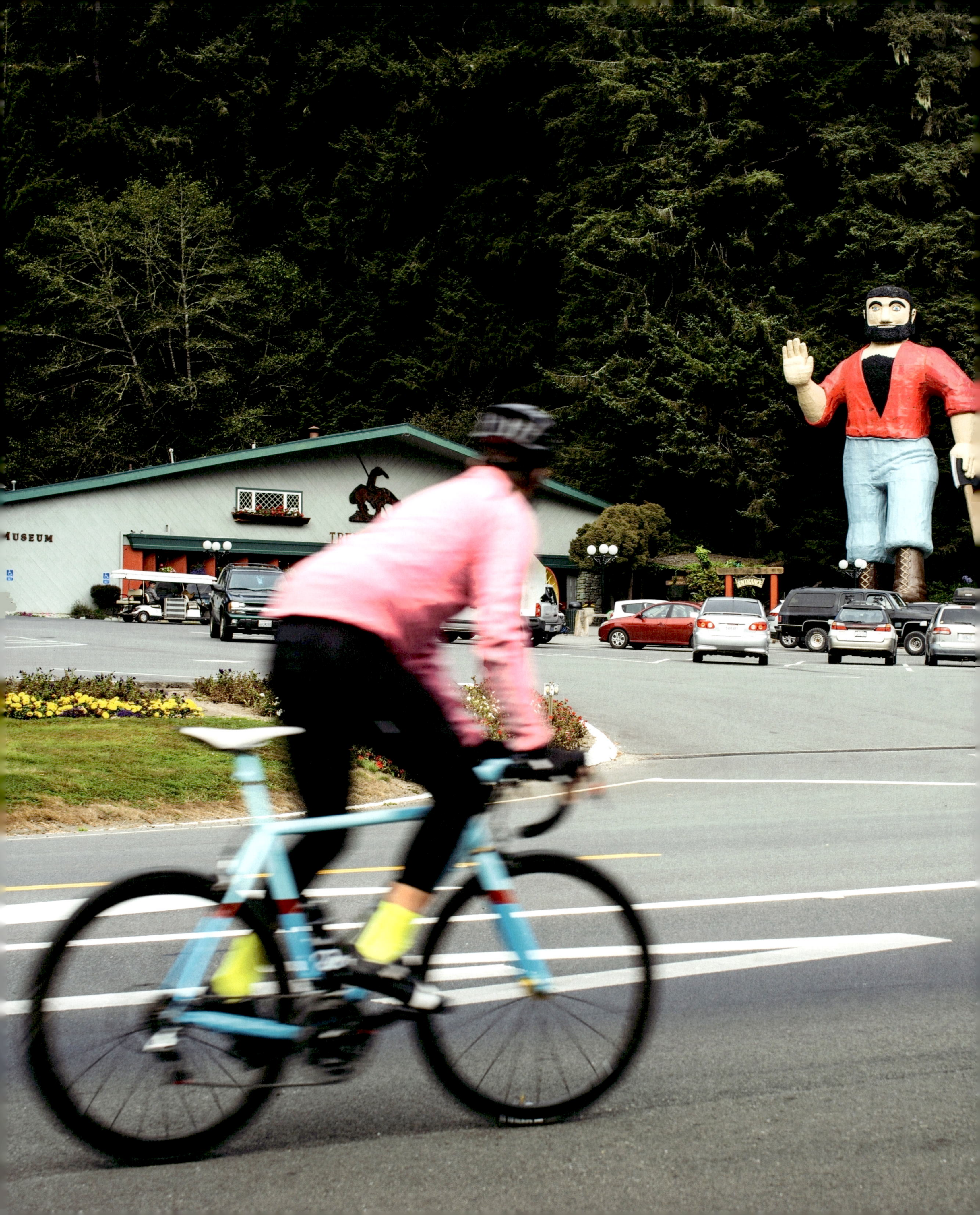
MUSEUM
ENTRANCE

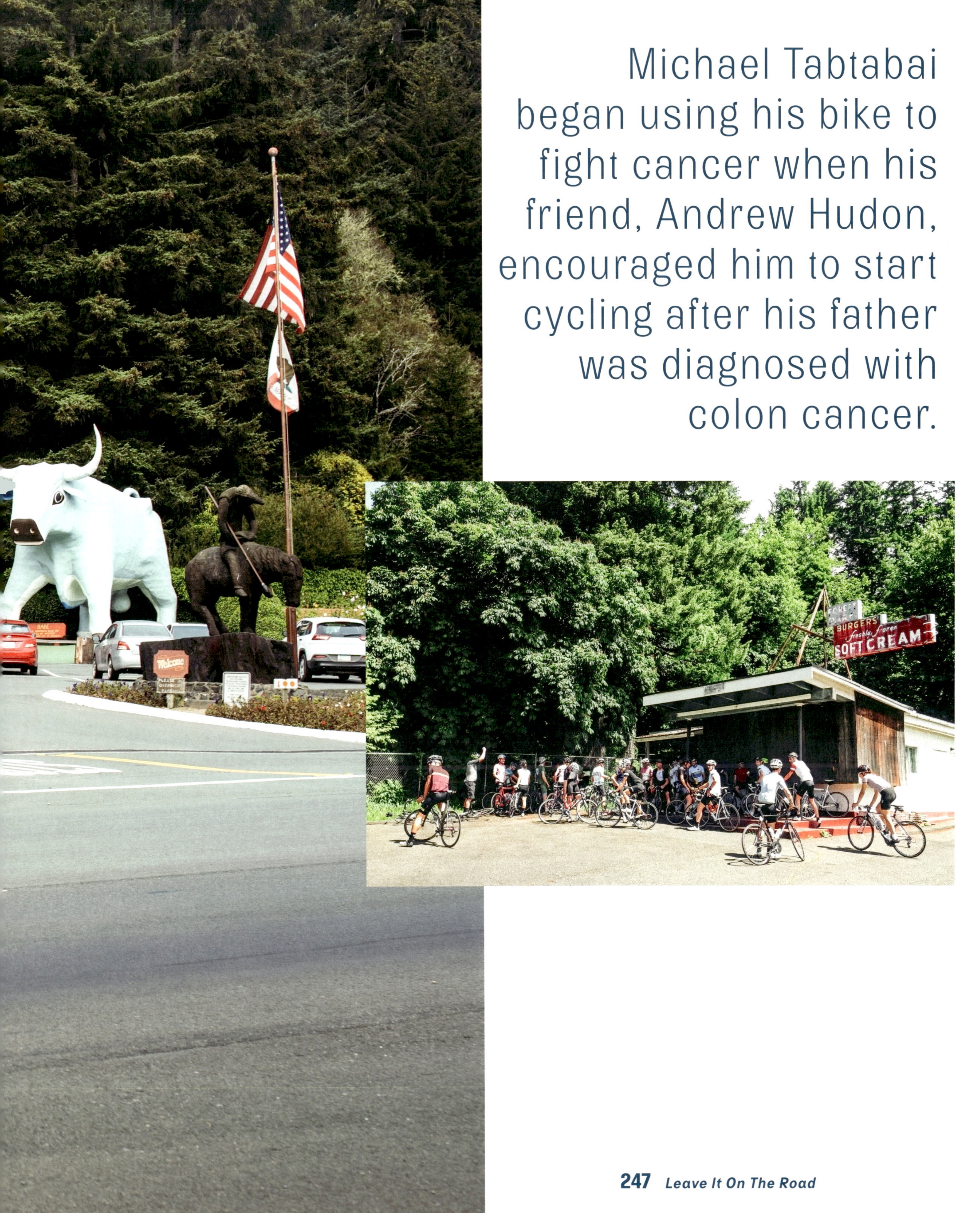


Michael Tabtabai began using his bike to fight cancer when his friend, Andrew Hudon, encouraged him to start cycling after his father was diagnosed with colon cancer.

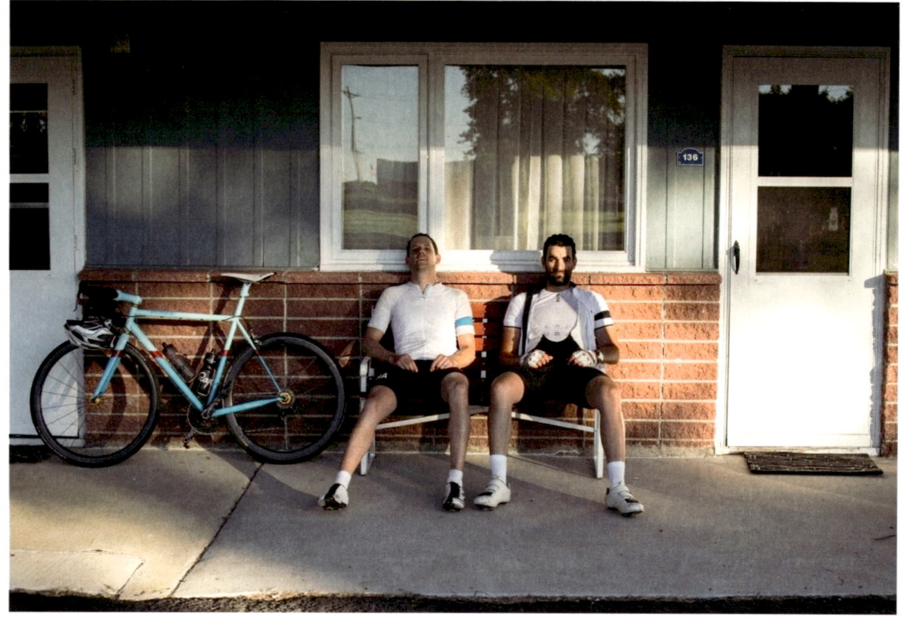

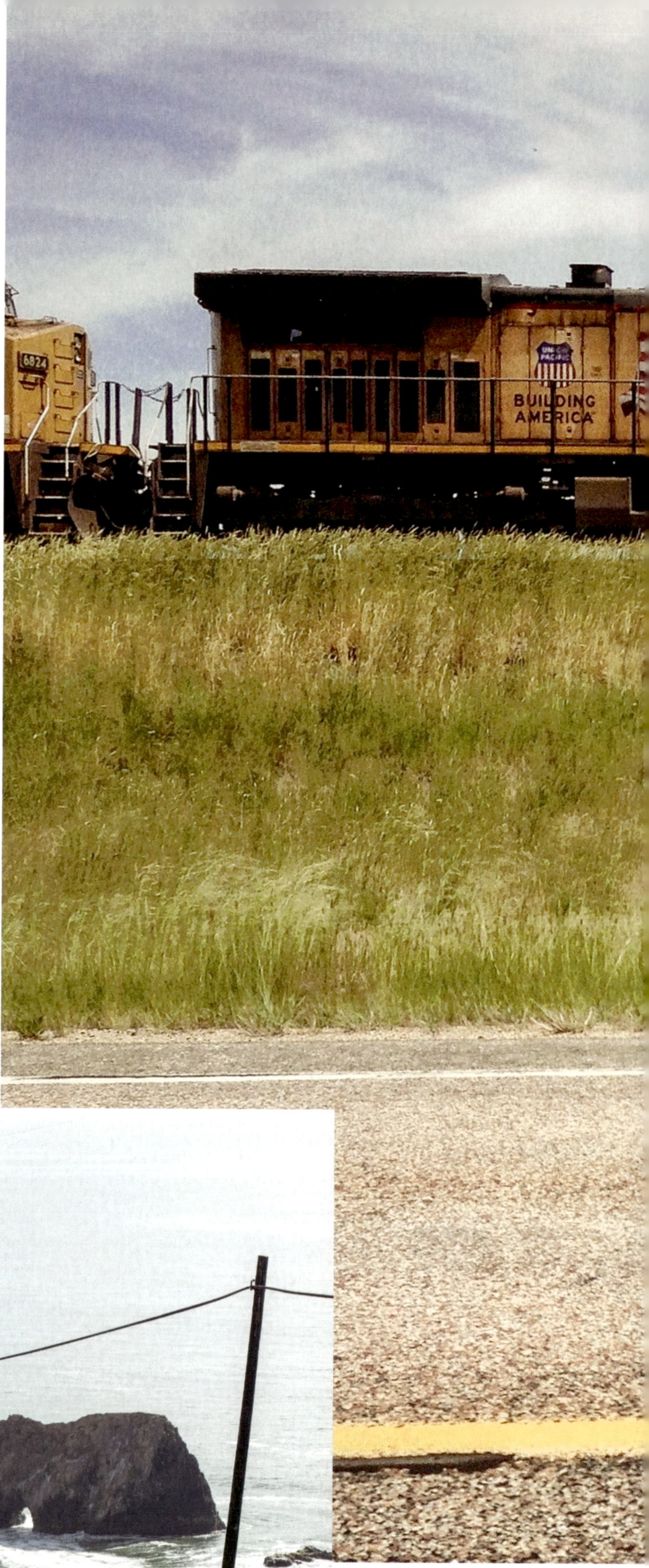

Beginning with a 100-mile ride to raise funds for the cancer center treating his father, Tabtabai and Hudon (who had previously organized his own fundraising rides for his mother's cancer), began organizing and leading rides together. An epic cross-country ride in honor of Tabtabai's father and Hudon's friend marked the establishment of Leave It On The Road in 2013. They rode 3,500 miles in 24 days while documenting their adventure on social media and raising $50,000 in donations for the Colon Cancer Alliance. The journey gained them thousands of supporters and continues to inspire others to get out and ride for cancer

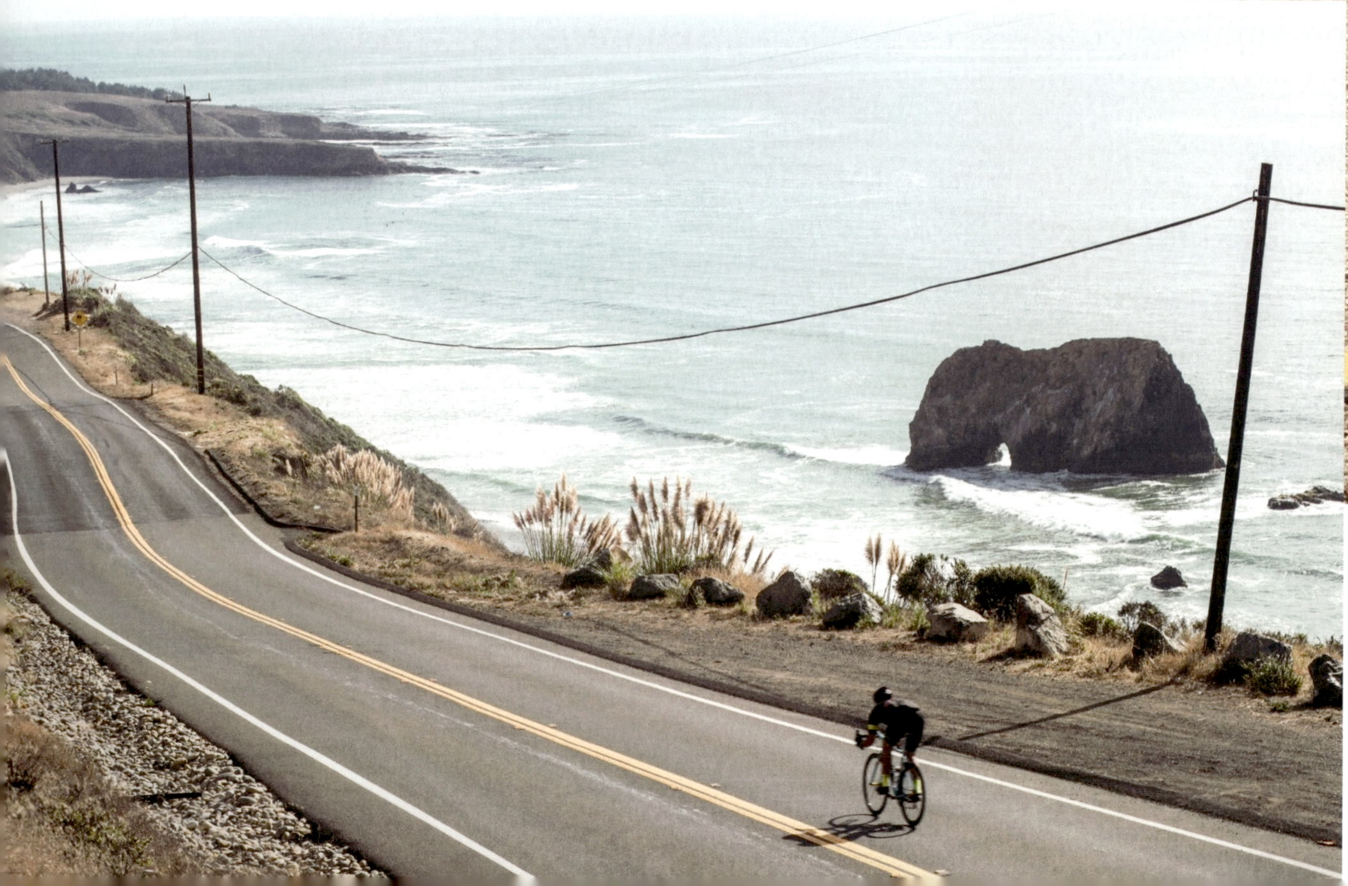

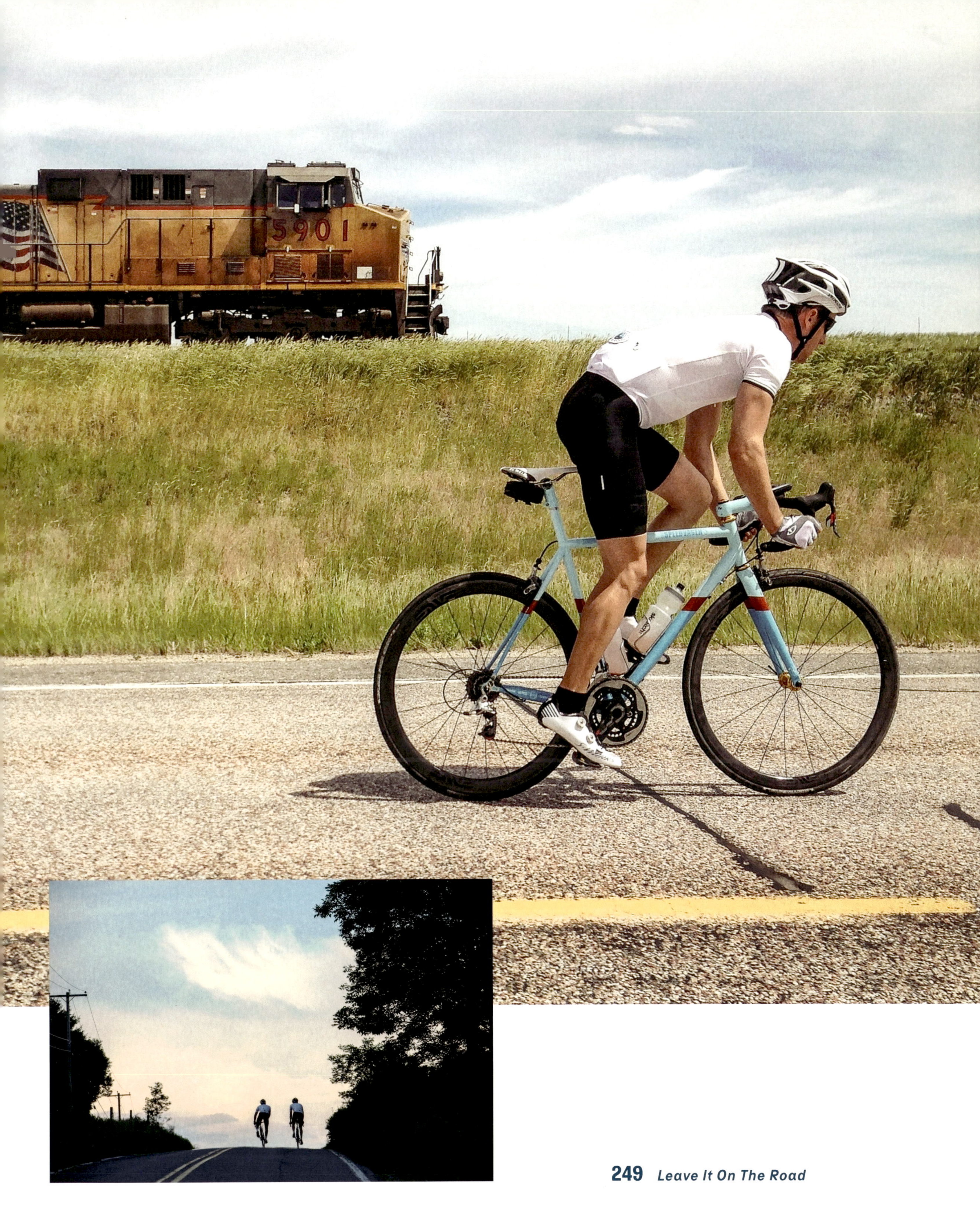
5901

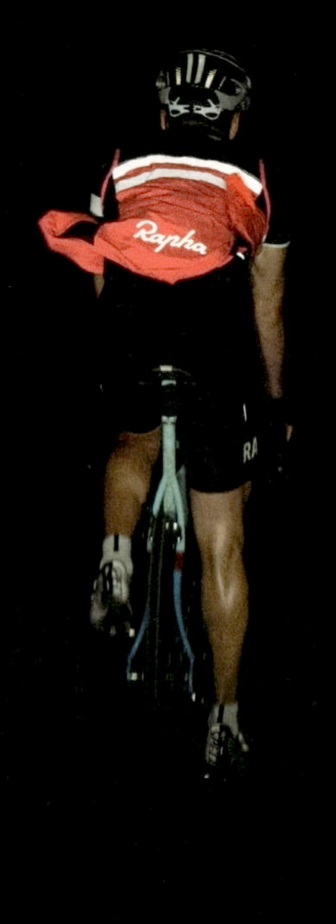


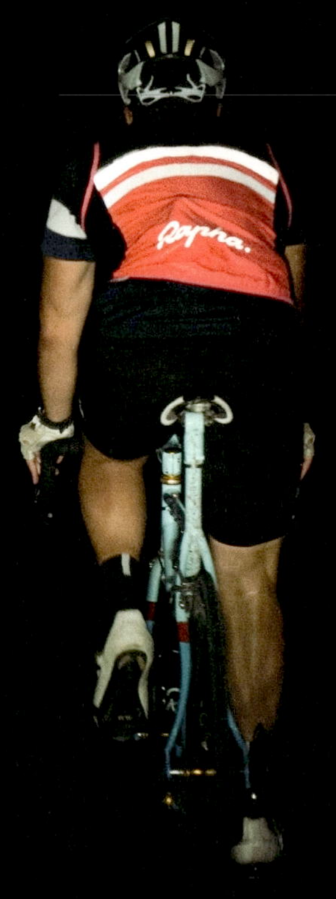


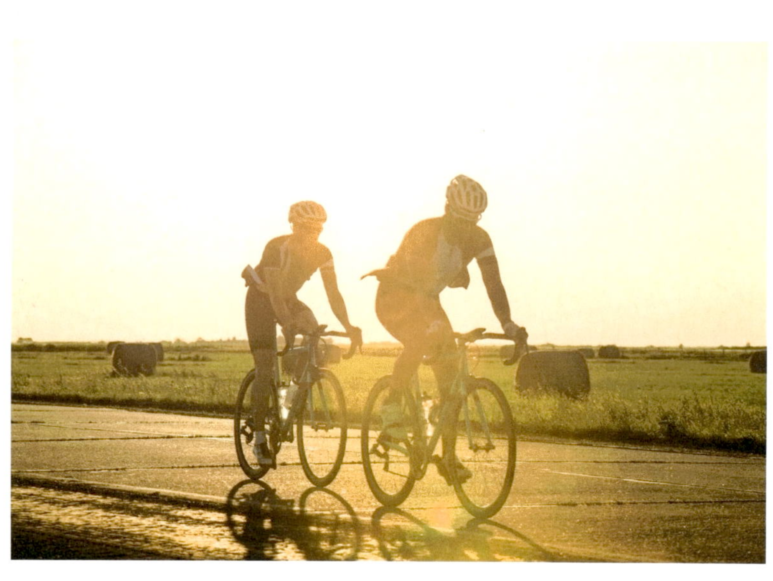

They rode 3,500 miles in 24 days and raised $ 50,000 in donations for the Colon Cancer Alliance.

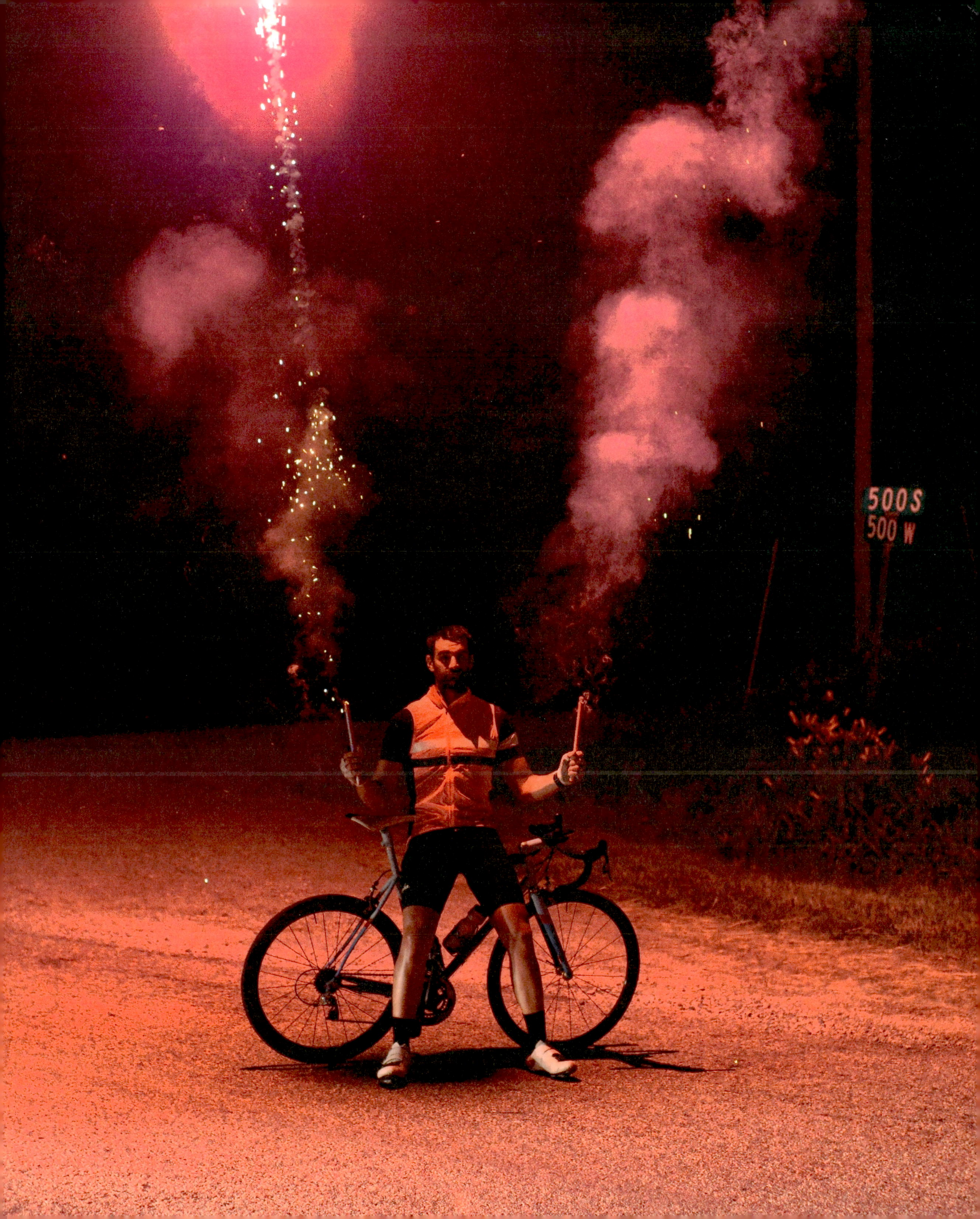
500 S
500 W

# Index

**opposite page:** Painting by Geoff McFetridge

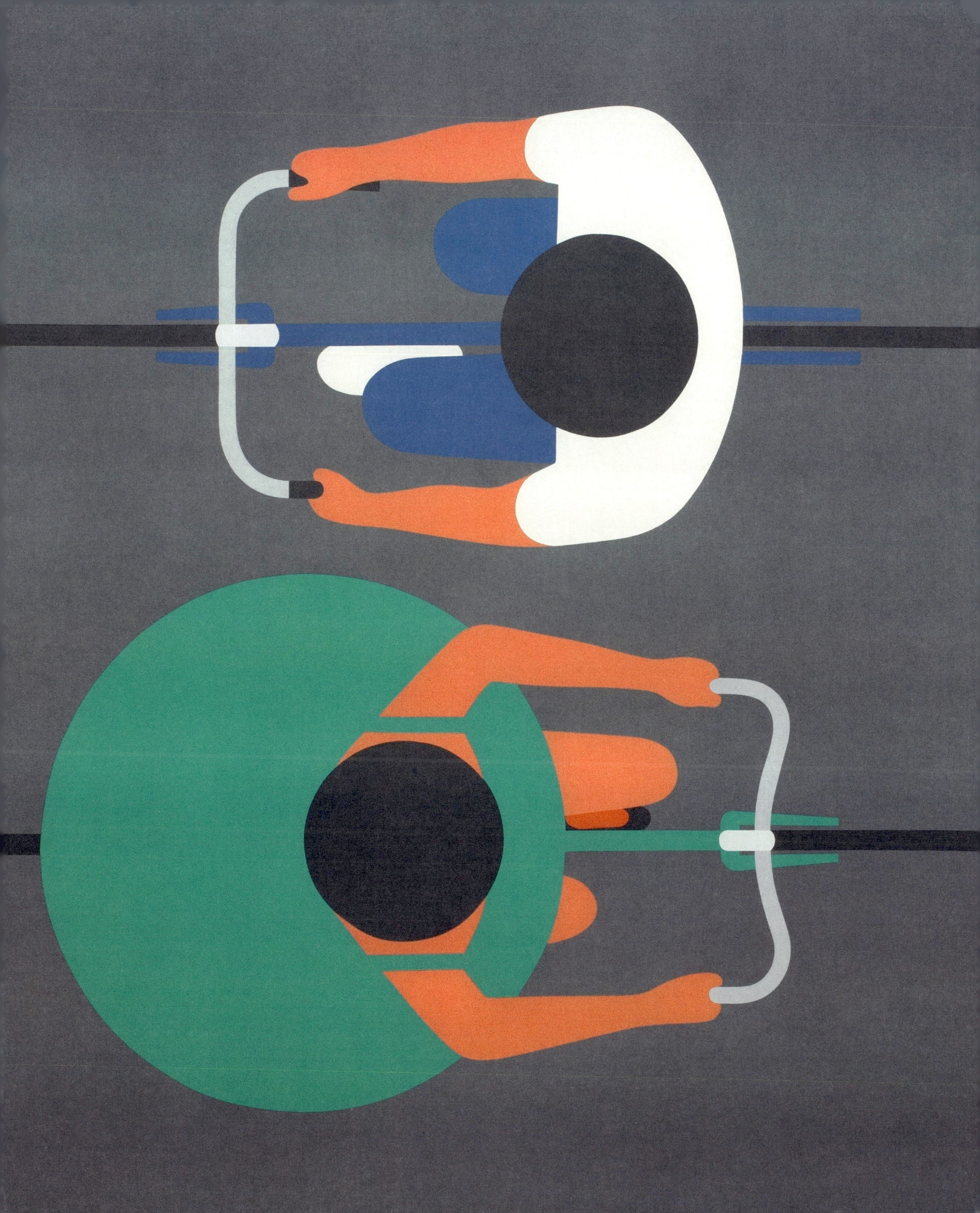

# Imprint

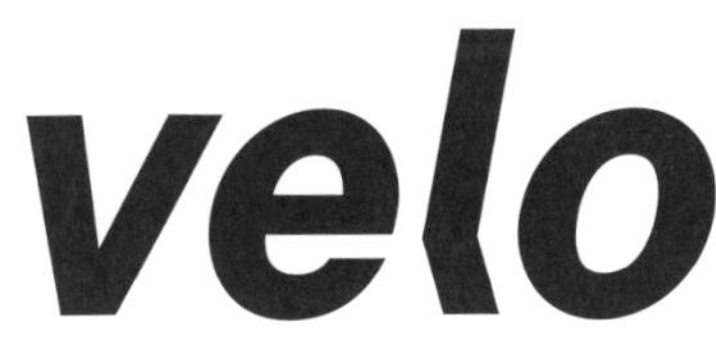

3rd Gear

*Bicycle Culture and Stories*

This book was conceived, edited, and designed by Gestalten.

Edited by Sven Ehmann and Robert Klanten
Preface and features by Shonquis Moreno
Texts by Rebecca Silus (pp. 8-15, 18-21, 30-33, 38-41, 48-50, 51 left, 52 bottom, 53 left, 66-71, 82-83, 87, 89-105, 108-111, 114-115, 117, 120-131, 140-141, 145-146, 150-155, 156 left, 157-159, 162-165, 170-173, 175 bottom, 180-181, 183-191, 216-217, 226 left, 227, 228 right, 230-235, 240-251)
and Shonquis Moreno (pp. 16-17, 28-29, 34-37, 42-45, 51 right, 52 top, 53 right, 64-65, 80-81, 84-86, 88, 106-107, 116, 118-119, 142-144, 147-149, 156 right, 160-161, 174, 175 top, 182, 198-203, 206-215, 219-225, 226 right, 228 left, 229)

Copy-editing by Kevin Brochet-Nguyen and Michael Eisenbrey
Proofreading by Michael Eisenbrey

Cover and layout by Jonas Herfurth
Cover photography by Julio Bustamente
Typefaces: BC Falster Grotesk
by Briefcase Type Foundry

Printed by Nino Druck GmbH,
Neustadt / Weinstr.
Made in Germany

Published by Gestalten, Berlin 2016
ISBN 978-3-89955-652-0



For more information, please visit www.gestalten.com.

Bibliographic information published by the Deutsche Nationalbibliothek. The Deutsche Nationalbibliothek lists this publication in the Deutsche Nationalbibliografie; detailed bibliographic data are available online at http://dnb.d-nb.de.

None of the content in this book was published in exchange for payment by commercial parties or designers; Gestalten selected all included work based solely on its artistic merit.

This book was printed on FSC® certified paper.

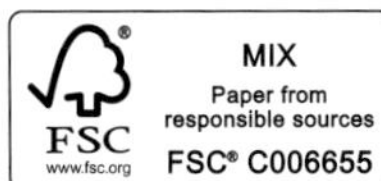

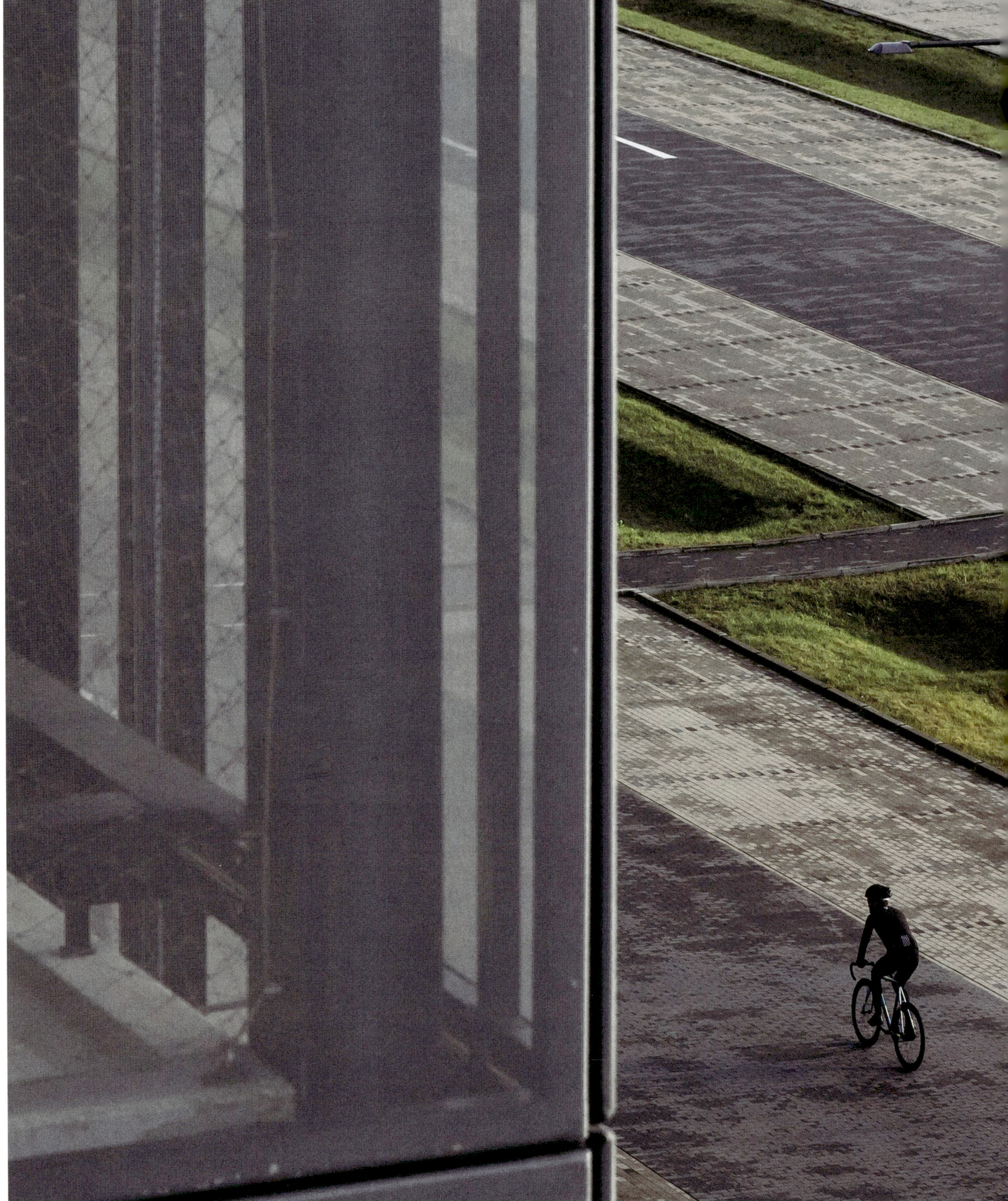